Language and Authority
in *De Lingua Latina*

Publication of this volume has been made possible, in part, through the generous support and enduring vision of Warren G. Moon.

Language and Authority
in *De Lingua Latina*

Varro's Guide to Being Roman

DIANA SPENCER

THE UNIVERSITY OF WISCONSIN PRESS

Publication of this book has been made possible, in part,
through support from the Anonymous Fund of the College of Letters and
Science at the University of Wisconsin–Madison.

The University of Wisconsin Press
1930 Monroe Street, 3rd Floor
Madison, Wisconsin 53711-2059
uwpress.wisc.edu

Gray's Inn House, 127 Clerkenwell Road
London EC1R 5DB, United Kingdom
eurospanbookstore.com

Copyright © 2019
The Board of Regents of the University of Wisconsin System
All rights reserved. Except in the case of brief quotations embedded in critical articles and reviews, no part of this publication may be reproduced, stored in a retrieval system, transmitted in any format or by any means—digital, electronic, mechanical, photocopying, recording, or otherwise—or conveyed via the Internet or a website without written permission of the University of Wisconsin Press. Rights inquiries should be directed to rights@uwpress.wisc.edu.

Printed in the United States of America

This book may be available in a digital edition.

Library of Congress Cataloging-in-Publication Data

Names: Spencer, Diana, 1969- author.
Title: Language and authority in De lingua Latina : Varro's guide to being Roman / Diana Spencer.
Other titles: Wisconsin studies in classics.
Description: Madison, Wisconsin : The University of Wisconsin Press, [2019] | Series: Wisconsin studies in classics | Includes bibliographical references and index.
Identifiers: LCCN 2018045765 | ISBN 9780299323202 (cloth : alk. paper)
Subjects: LCSH: Varro, Marcus Terentius. De lingua Latina. | Latin language—Grammar—Early works to 1800. | Linguistics—Rome—Early works to 1800.
Classification: LCC PA6792.A3 S64 2019 | DDC 878/.0109—dc23
LC record available at https://lccn.loc.gov/2018045765

ISBN 9780299323240 (paperback)

For being there at the beginning and sticking it out to the end:
JOHN HENDERSON AND GIDEON NISBET

Contents

	Acknowledgments	ix
	A Roadmap for a Ruinous Text	xi
	Introduction	3
1	Networking Varro	19
2	Romespeaking: Strategies for Citizens	42
3	Inspiring Latin	68
4	*Oratio* and the Read/Write Experience	96
5	As Old as the Hills	129
6	Powering Up the Community	160
7	A Family Affair	184
8	Varro's *Fasti*	214
	Conclusion: *Ending Up with Varro*	248
	Notes	261
	Bibliography	345
	Index	379

Acknowledgments

During a Roman holiday, one hot summer in the 1970s, I fell in love with the city; but without a month alone in Rome, in Colm Molloy's apartment, I might never have become a through-reader of *De Lingua Latina*. Since that unexpected adventure, many have helped along the way. Close to home, I have benefited from a year of research leave, generously granted by the University of Birmingham. Informal and work-in-progress group discussion with former and present colleagues (in our Department of Classics, Ancient History, and Archaeology), notably Gideon Nisbet—who has endured multiple versions—and Ken Dowden, has also produced many happy improvements to my argument.

David Larmour's ideas and suggestions have always made me think harder: a great collaborator is also an ideal critical friend. In Rome, where this book began and concluded, conversations over a bottle of wine and good food have given me ideas and even endnotes, and I have been especially fortunate in having had the chance to test my version of the "Varroverse" against challengingly enthusiastic requests to explain *more* from Agnes Crawford and Massimo Platini.

The invitation to present aspects of this work at a series of conferences has enormously enriched the kinds of audience and feedback I was able to access. Special thanks in this context go to Martin Bommas (*Cultural Memory and Identity in Ancient Societies*), Ida Östenberg, Simon Malmberg, and Jonas Bjørnebye (*The Moving City*), David Butterfield (*Varro Varius*), and William Fitzgerald and Efrossini Spentzou (*The Production of Space in Latin Literature*), whose hard work gave me opportunities to publish my ideas as they developed.

Early in this project, a week amid the manuscripts (Varro and other) at the Biblioteca Medicea Laurenziana (Florence) brought to life the challenges in the editorial and translation processes and helped define my approach to interpreting *De Lingua Latina*.

The academic community of Twitter has radically shaped my research practice in the past five or six years. The suggestions, exchanges of readings and ideas, moral support, and general interest expressed by (too many to mention individually) scholarly Twitter friends and acquaintances pervade this book. Twitter has created a whole other knowledge network, in the crackling heterogeneity of which has often emerged something greater than the sum of its parts—I like to think that Varro might have approved.

The finished book is thoroughly indebted to the editorial team at the University of Wisconsin Press, the confidence it showed in the project, and the outstanding work put in by the readers it commissioned. I have been fortunate to have had such excellent and constructive advice, and any errors or omissions are very much mine.

A Roadmap for a Ruinous Text

Once, there were **twenty-five books**; here is what survives, based on the primary manuscript tradition and using the accessible Loeb Classical Library edition produced by Roland G. Kent (1951), occasionally lightly edited to emphasize my interpretation.[1] This reading takes the *Codex Laurentianus* known as *F* as the primary manuscript, upon which (or upon the archetype of which) other variants draw (or to which they add detail).[2] I have also followed Kent's model for presenting the challenges in the Latin text; thus, anything conjecturally added to the text is set in < >, and letters or words that have been changed from the manuscript to produce better sense are set in italics.[3] In addition to Kent's apparatus, where particular words or phrases are significant for my discussion, or ought to be considered as part of a structural unit, I have used underlining and bold font (in the Latin), with corresponding emphases also utilized in the accompanying English translations.

- [lost] **Book 1**, likely programmatic.
- **Books 2–7** explore etymology and the application of words to things, *impositio* (see, e.g., *Ling.* 8.1).
  - [lost] Books 2–4 focused on the theory of etymology: was it a viable intellectual mode? Also: what it meant to work etymologically and the benefits of doing so (see, e.g., *Ling.* 5.1).
  - Books 5–7 lay down the meanings accruing from applied etymology and what happens when theory meets reality.
- **Books 8–13** grapple with *declinatio* (inflection): the family trees and social bonds that relate words one to another.
  - Books 8–10 echo books 2–4 structurally: this "theory" triad of Varro's second hexad presents steamroller arguments against and for the total dominance of *analogia* (Regularity) in Latin before producing a compromise, consensus position.

- [lost] Books 11–13 tackled morphology. If a model similar to previous triads shaped the study here, this was the pragmatically focused echo of books 5–7, probably articulating and implementing Varro's own balance between *ratio* and *consuetudo*.
- [lost] **Books 14–25** moved on to syntax (*coniunctio uerborum*)—speculatively, perhaps Varro's most developed articulation of (linguistic) social engineering.

Book 5

5.1	Restarting the project.
5.2–6	The task of the etymologist.
5.7–9	A philosophy of etymology and its archaeological quality.
5.10	A scheme for books 5–7.
5.11–12	The world is organized along fourfold lines.
5.13	Etymology as a rooty practice.
5.14–15	"Place" and spin-off associations.
5.16–20	Cosmic terminology.
5.21–23	*Terra* and territory, soil.
5.24–30	Wet things and water-courses.
5.31–32	Regions (world, Europe, Italy).
5.33–34	Auguries and (claiming) kinds of land.
5.35–40	Measuring, moving through, cultivating, civilizing, inhabiting land.
5.41–44	Rome and Sevenheights (Capitoline, Aventine, Velabrum).
5.45–54	The rest of Rome: defined by the Shrines of the Argei.
5.55–56	Place and political organization: Rome's tribes.
5.57	Starting again: what tends to be in places (first immortal, then mortal).
5.57–59	Deified Earth and Sky, and . . .
5.60–70	. . . how Earth and Sky and their characteristics and attributes create all else.
5.71–72	Watery deities (Neptune and nymphs).
5.73–74	Terrestrial deities.
5.75	Mortal creatures.
5.75–79	Creatures of the air and water and amphibians (including creatures whose etymological identity looks to Greece and Egypt).
5.80–101	Land creatures, divided three ways (humans and domesticated and wild animals):
	80–82 political and civic offices;
	83–86 priesthoods;

A Roadmap for a Ruinous Text xiii

	87–91	military offices (ending with army musicians);
	92	personal finances;
	93–94	trades and professions;
	95–96	wealth in cattle (with much overlap from Greece to Rome);
	97–99	goats, pigs, sheep, dogs;
	100–101	wild beasts (connecting this set from peninsular Italy to North Africa, Greece, and the Near East).
5.102–4		Inanimate life (emphasizing fruit, vegetables, cultivated flowers).
5.105–83		Manufactured things and associated objects and entities:
	105–12	food and cooking;
	113–14	cloth, weaving;
	115–17	military equipment and gadgets;
	118–20	food, container, dining technology;
	121–26	wine and drinking accessories and furniture;
	127	cookpots and cooking;
	128–29	furniture and beauty accessories;
	130–33	clothes;
	134–37	farming tools;
	138	grain processing;
	139–40	transporting produce;
	141–42	buildings, walls, fortifications;
	143–44	how to found a town;
	145–47	urban infrastructure, Rome as paradigm;
	148–50	Rome's Lacus Curtius;
	151	Arx and Carcer;
	152	Aventine sites;
	153–54	at the Circus;
	155–56	the Forum's political sites;
	156–57	between the Forum and the Tiber;
	158–59	Roman streets;
	159–62	domestic architecture;
	163–65	Rome's gates;
	166–68	beds, mattresses, coverlets;
	169–74	coinage and units of measurement;
	175–83	dowries, profit and loss, fines, payment, gifts, tribute, stipend, payments.
5.184		Ending the book(-scroll).

Book 6

6.1–2	Introduction. Times, verbs, and related terms.
6.3	What constitutes time terms?
6.4–7	Measuring the day.
6.8	Measuring the year.
6.9	Seasons.
6.10	The rationale for "month."
6.11	Epochs.
6.12–26	From natural taxonomy to civic (festal) days.
6.27–32	From days for the gods to days categorized for human interests.
6.33–34	Names of months.
6.35–36	Introducing temporality (verbs and derivations).
6.37	Primary verb forms (*primigenia*).
6.38	Prefixed verb forms.
6.39	The vast scale of the etymologist's task and the need to create paradigms.
6.40	Introducing time-words (verbs) whose roots are obscure.
6.41–42	From *ago* to identifying three modes of action.
6.43–50	Verbs and their spin-offs: considering, calling to mind, fearing, cultivating, wanting, fearing, remembering, grieving, being happy.
6.51–76	The second mode of "action": telling, speaking, conversing, talking, pronouncing, lying, naming, judging, dictating, teaching, discussing, neatening, conversing, fortune-telling, selecting, reading, harvesting, murmuring, roaring, shrieking, triumphing, vowing, hoping, guaranteeing, singing, making music, pleading and oratory, augural singing birds.
6.77–85	The third mode of "action" and the potential for confusion among "making," "acting," "conducting."
	. . .
6.86–88	Extracts from the Censors' Tables and Consular Commentaries concerning the Census and convocation of Assembly.
6.89–90	Discussion of calls to Assembly.
6.91–92	Quotation and discussion of evidence from historical documents relating to an indictment.
6.93–95	Discussion of prescribed forms of summoning the citizen-army.
6.96	Latin words that are thought to be configured from Greek.
6.97	"I shall stop there."

Book 7

7.1–5	Introducing the role of poetry (especially that about and situated in places, with regard to times and temporality), the complexities of archaism in verse, how meaning can hang on just one letter.
7.6–13	Temples (the Gaze, augury, viewing and boundaries, wilderness, guardianship, immediacy).
7.14–16	The sky, constellations, Moon, the Deliads.
7.17–18	*Umbilicus*; distinguishing field-land from territory.
7.19–20	Mysteries, Areopagites, and whether Olympus is a mountain or the heavens; leading to discussion of localization and the Muses.
7.21–23	Maritime confines, islands, ships, waters.
	<page missing>
7.24–25	Sacrificial victims, horns.
7.26–29	<with short lacuna> Latin Muses, archaisms in the Carmen Saliare, orthographic shifts, drawing in Oscan and Sabine.
7.30–31	Circumlocution and ambition.
7.32	Roots, signifieds, identity (for words).
7.32–33	Dogs, ships.
7.34–38	Contemplating *camilla*, piping, Fauns, plaiting verses, distinguishing garments, epic chefing.
7.39–40	Gleaming war elephants, Lucania, Libya.
7.41–42	The orator, some demonstrative pronouns.
7.43–45	Sacred banquets, shields, cakes, bakers, the annual Argei ceremony, priests deriving their distinctive names from now obscure deities.
7.46–47	Sabine acuity, puns on sauces, fish names originally Greek.
7.48	The sky is like Apollo's tripod cauldron.
7.49	Enemies and war.
7.50	Stars and constellations.
7.51	Superlatives/ends.
7.52	Sell-swords and robbers.
7.53	Tottering, tripping.
7.54–55	Processing wool, wickerwork.
7.56–58	Military roles.
7.59–62	Portents, annoyances, Greek one-pot meals, cross-routes.
7.63–69	Welts, slugs, two-bit whores, limping creatures, dominant wives, juicy thighs, abrasive cleaning, giant strides.
7.70–71	Praise-singing, leadership, the one-eyed.
7.72–79	Nocturnal time terms, with some asides.

7.80	Words relating to actions.
7.80–83	Elasticity, movement relation to positionality, speaking-names (and their trickiness in translation), the golden russet of dawn (cf. hair color).
7.84–85	Skin-on-skin action, some ritual prohibition of leather, the "nod" of power.
7.86	Eating Sicilian olive salad like crazy.
7.87–88	Lymphs (Latin nymphs), Liber, wine; the Graicism of "halcyon days" and "halcyon fashion."
7.89	Latin revelry comes from Greek merrymaking (and, some say, "comedy").
7.90	To take, to receive.
7.91–94	To make orderly; approximation, expressions of joy and woe, contention, lawsuits, justice, theft (including orthographic), more Greek connections.
7.95–97	Chewing things up, obscenity, words that sometimes get an "a" before an "e"; things better said and seen on stage, the sinister quality of good things; *omen* and mouths.
7.98–104	Deciding, being present, digging, nonsense sounds, averting, (people) cheeping, yelping, bleating, braying, neighing, howling, bellowing, roaring, shouting, chirruping, twittering, click-clacking.
7.105–6	Balancing, obligations, cash, orderliness, melting.
7.107–8	Acknowledgment that this has been a partial treatment.
7.109–10	Programmatic conclusion to triad. Scrolls shape books; separating the ears from the stalks; ending a six-book tranche on etymology.

Books 8–10

From etymology to grammatology, a polemical evaluation of the role of *analogia* (Regularity) in the development and structure of Latin.

Book 8

8.1–2	Programmatics: "speech" is tripartite. This book starts with declension and inflection. Nominatives or primary forms are like vertical "trunks" from which case/person forms make offshoots.
8.3	Inflection makes language practical: it builds relationships and supports unity of thought.
8.4–10	Inflection draws out the clannishness of language in use, yet some words have always been unfruitful (e.g., conjunctions, adverbs).
8.11–13	Parts of speech—starting with nouns because they have primacy.

A Roadmap for a Ruinous Text

xvii

8.14–16	Nouns vary to reflect their signifieds (e.g., gender) or to show relativity to other primary signifiers. Case forms systematize speech to the benefit of speakers.
8.17	*Cognomina.*
8.18	Terms deriving from living beings (e.g., Romulus-Rome-Roman).
8.19	Nouns formed for actions are too obviously different to need more explanation.
8.20	Verbs need "declined" forms to indicate time.
8.21–22	Voluntary (individually driven) and natural (consensus-based) derivation.
8.23–25	Another beginning: introducing "analogy" (a regularizing system) and "anomaly" (following the shifting irregularities of common parlance). Books 8–10 will be about the principles of derivations that the two models produce, and books 11–13 will explore their results. Book 8 will make the case against Regularity, book 9 the case against Irregularity; book 10 will focus on what unites them. Discourse will be the first focus.
8.26–28	Speech should be utilitarian; this needs to be clear and concise for speed and ease of intelligibility. If particular forms are habitual, functional, and thus understood, the constraints of Regularity are a distraction.
8.29–30	In clothing, architecture, food, difference makes sense as form follows function. Speech should be no different.
8.31–32	Utility can be joined by refinement as a guiding principle against Regularity.
8.33	Why impose a systematic Regularity over the Regularity that develops from habitual use? Only a crazy man would do that!
8.34–36	Why, when similar forms inflect similarly, do dissimilar forms not generate dissimilar forms by inflection? But not across the board?
8.37	When there is more "irregularity" than "regularity," surely the terms have become meaningless?
8.38	The appearance of Regularity in speech is too inconsistent and patchy to make for an overarching system. So it cannot therefore exist.
8.39–43	Those who believe in Regularity are ignorant of what "similarity" in grammar and syntax really means, bringing in irrelevancies such as the gender of the signified or whether it's a proper name and thereby confounding their own argument.

8.44–46	Parts of speech (naming, saying, supporting, joining); requirement for gender, number, case.
8.47–49	How can there be Regularity when, for example, some adjectives have only two gender forms? When some nouns are singular or plural only? When some case forms, for example, diverge from the nominative?
8.50–51	Pronouns complicate things further, and this material is so complex it will tax copyists to the breaking point.
8.52–56	Applying a name, inflecting a name, generating comparatives or diminutives (never mind the terminology of the farm, the sitting room, the shopping mall, nationality)—all are nests of Irregularity.
8.57–60	Agent nouns (e.g., "writer" from "writing") follow usage (*consuetudo*); participle generation, verbs across active and passive, show up Latin's Irregularity; ditto frequentatives.
8.61–62	The formation of composite words fails to follow normative paradigms.
8.63	Despite what Aristarchans say, not all words have case forms, and some have duplicate forms across a few cases.
8.64–65	Do "foreign" words simply not decline? No.
8.66	Many cases have duplicate forms that do duty unproblematically and without causing confusion.
8.67–69	Similar nominatives should generate similar case forms but don't, and Aristarchus' rebuff (to Crates' anti-Regularity position), that vocatives as well as nominatives have to be alike before the model works, doesn't actually address the question of nominative similarity.
8.70–74	Examples illustrating the problems generated by these assertions, across number and case forms.
8.75–78	Comparatives and superlatives in use fail to follow the artificial paradigms of Regularity and occasionally simply do not occur.
8.79	Some words exist in variants expressing diminution in size. But not all. Overall, use trumps grammatical imposition.
8.80–82	There is no Regularity in the derivation of proper nouns (e.g., why Roma from Romulus? Why is Perpenna not the daughter of Perpennus? Why is Athenaeus not from Athens?).
8.83	The naming of freedmen after the town that manumitted them opens up another area of complexity in practice.

. . .

Book 9

...

9.1–7	Programmatics.
9.1	Crates did not fully understand Chrysippus and Aristarchus.
9.2	The split between followers of *consuetudo* and followers of *ratio* is less severe than it might seem, since *consuetudo* and Regularity are less distinct from each other than those people believe.
9.3	Regularity derives from a certain mode of usage, but this model in turn delivers the variations of Irregularity. As for any human, body and soul together create the individual.
9.4	Distinguishing between "*natura*" and use of words—just because Regularities exist doesn't mean that they need to drive or define the whole system of language.
9.5	Some words reflect a people's usage, others an individual's or the use appropriate to a particular mode or employment of speech. Orators and poets have special license.
9.6	The *populus* is an autonomous self-fashioning engine; thus, the "people" ought to be a regulatory influence on the speech of individuals. Regularities are differently significant depending on one's place in the community and one's relationship to the people as a whole.
9.7	Next, refuting book 8, step by step, and filling in its gaps.
9.8–9	They are in error who assert that to speak well ("*bene loqui*"), following *consuetudo* rather than *ratio* is what counts. Instead, common use and theory are deeply entwined.
9.10–11	"Wrong forms" in language are like a clumsy boy who needs (perhaps forcible) retraining to inculcate the best habits.
9.12	In the visual and literary arts, usage can be recalibrated to suit the present without slavish attention to the past.
9.13	In war, as in other things, the wisest men are those who innovate, and innovation is part of the theoretical mindset.
9.14–15	The realities of punishment for real-world crimes versus the relative ease of punishment when grammatical correction is all that's involved.
9.16	Correcting speech is a process akin to weaning a baby.
9.17	New forms do not always receive a warm welcome in the Forum— this is where good poets and dramatists can spearhead the process.

9.18	There is a kind of Regularity in subscribing to usage where it is correct; sometimes we must also perforce follow along with usage where it is incorrect.
9.19–22	Usage (former and contemporary) and theory both need to feed into the process whereby language and discourse develop in collaboration.
9.23	The world (sky, sea, land) is suffused with Regularities, so how could there be one element (words) that did not partake in this model?
9.24–31	Examples of the pervasiveness of Regularity:
	24 the Tropics, Poles, solstices, and annual movement of constellations are echoing and repetitive forms;
	25 sun and moon similarly follow Regular paths across the sky and relative to north and south;
	26 the sea manages a fourfold system across twenty-four lunar hours, and the model persists across a monthly systematization (to find out more, read Varro *on Estuaries*);
	27 is this not all equally true of the agricultural cycle? are Asia and Europe not similarly furnished with rivers, lakes, mountains, plains?
	28 Birds have offspring that are like their parents, ditto fish and other animals, and this works too for hybrids such as mules;
	29 all human children are either boys or girls, with similar limbs and characteristics according to gender and similar relationships between soul and body;
	30 the human animating spirit (*anima*) is eightfold (five senses, thought, the procreative facility, speech);
	31 speech, for the Greeks, is four-part [recall 8.44, 45].
9.32	Verbs benefit from a tripartite system in tenses and persons, while similarities also govern forms for imperatives, wishes, and so on.
9.33	Taking a stand against Regularity means failing to perceive the nature of the world; taking a stand against Regularity means fighting the nature of existence and involves an argument based on deformed examples.
9.34	Distinguishing between natural and voluntary species of Regularity.
9.35	Voluntary and natural derivations embed an inconsistency in the system, but usage operates as a safety valve—allowing Regularity to be modeled anew.

9.36	Introducing a shift from general principles to specific examples.
9.37–39	Inflection observes four elements: a word's relationship to the signified; how it is in use; the nature of the signifier; and the signifier's relationship to like words.
9.40–42	Sound is important in defining similarity in words, but a type-based similarity can also operate (e.g., a group of names might be women's rather than men's, yet shoes, in practice, can be worn by either sex). Words that map onto "masculine" and "feminine" systems in inflection become gendered even when real-world gender is not at issue; skin color too may be a superficial distraction.
9.43–44	Declined forms can illuminate the darkness surrounding likeness in nominative forms, and word family relationships.
9.45	It is doubly foolish to deny Regularity on the basis that speech contains irregularity. A person wearing shoes has them on only a small part of his body, yet still he is shod.
9.46–49	If what humans crave is variety, then surely understanding and appreciating variety as an organizational principle requires some things to be similar and others dissimilar.
9.50–51	From Romulus to farm animals, what's crucial in mapping relationships and understanding how new words fit into existing word families is the inflected form.
9.52–54	Letter forms or monosyllables that do not decline inflect conceptually, when in use. With unique words, etymological backtracking can show deep associative patterns.
9.55–58	Not every signified has multiple gendered forms in use, and over time different behavior patterns led to shifts regarding which gender form was important and meaningful.
9.59	Neuter forms tend to dissimilarity among each other. Addressing the lack of case forms for names of gods and slaves, one should remember that case forms integrate the signifieds into a civic world of family and everyday experience.
9.60–61	First names are required to distinguish between clan members or between men and women.
9.62	Words that are voluntary in inflection across the genders participate in a greater Regularity by being separate in form, and complement those where natural inflection matches underlying Regularity.
9.63	Wholes that are essentially multipart entities need to reflect the overarching singularity of their nature.

9.64–69	Other examples relating to plural forms: from numbers to condiments, metals, comestibles, perfumes, baths, stairs, and hot springs.
9.70	Where not all cases are present . . .
9.71	Suffixes do not necessarily produce total Regularity between words, but there is typically a logic to any deviation.
9.72–74	Logically, going by sense, not all adjectives can have comparatives and superlatives or diminutives.
9.75–79	So, some words are not present across all case forms, but this is typically about usage and ease in speech; even extremely uncommon case forms nevertheless exist if they can be formed. But setting all that aside, a statue without its head remains itself, with its other Regularities intact, and can even be restored. Thus also language.
9.80–84	Aberrations in speech and morphology do not constitute a reasonable argument against Regularity overall.
9.85–88	Quantities, genitives, numbers.
9.89	Homonyms and the ways in which inflection defines and characterizes the significant differences.
9.90	Synonyms and the need to follow the nominative form when inflecting.
9.91–93	Examples of inflectional forms and other qualities that are false friends for Anomalists.
9.94	Pronouns can assist in distinguishing and characterizing Regularities.
9.95	Turning to verbs, Varro proposes to tackle objections to Regularity sequentially across tense, person, class, and divisions.
9.96–98	There's an internal consistency in verbs across tenses when selected for comparison from the same class and division.
9.99–100	Verbs in the complete and incomplete divisions similarly retain their Regularity if mapped within their division forms.
9.101	Not all of nature is identical, so why expect absolute granular similarities?
9.102	The real question should be whether any verb is deficient within its class. The crucial thing is to work from the primary form, the first-person speaker, in the present.
9.103	Inflected verb forms provide a way of unpicking the confusion where the primary forms provide insufficient clarity or distinctiveness.

9.104–5	Pronunciation and usage within grammatical voice typically support Regularity.
9.106–7	Quoting Plautus in support of the differences of agency between active and passive underpins the separateness as well as the contiguities between the systems; here, too, a reminder that departures from the forms found in Cato and Ennius make no dent in the overall Regularity of discourse (*sermo*).
9.108–10	Different conjugations make overall sense of differences in inflection across first-person-singular forms; within conjugations or (using gender as a schematic) across participles, Regularity is unproblematic.
9.111	Book 8 closed with the argument that Regularity cannot exist because its proponents cannot agree across the board or can agree only where their consensus goes again common use (*consuetudo*). This is wrong because applying this line to the arts in general (medicine, music, and more) will show that writers disagree, yet the arts themselves remain just as real even when writers fail to perceive them correctly.
9.112	When people use aberrant inflected forms, they do not destroy Regularity or the logic of the underpinning system (*ratio*); the science of speech (*scientia orationis*) is not undermined by an individual's exposure of his own ignorance.
9.113	Varro has done his best to refute the arguments of book 8, point by point, albeit briefly, in line with what we might think appropriate (*arbitraremur*). The world as a whole (various examples offered) is populated with things like and unlike, yet still order holds sway in the majority of cases. So too for Regularity in the Latin language;
9.114	since *consuetudo* for the most part enables Regularity, it should be followed except where it may prove offensive to impose an individual use on popular speech.
9.115	None of this is a surprise, since not all individuals can have equal rights, and poets have more leeway to follow Regularities than does the orator. Varro has done what he promised in this book. What more is there to say?

Book 10

10.1–2	Programmatic opening summing up on books 8–10, with book 10, uniquely, to tackle the "order" and "nature" underpinning both models. This means discussing what "likeness" and "unlikeness"

	are; what constitutes the scheme known as *logos*; ditto for the proportional scheme known as *analogia* [probably cited via Greek]; and what *consuetudo* (usage) is.
10.3–4	First, likeness and unlikeness. Every "like" (ditto "unlike") is at least bifold: the thing and its similar or dissimilar twin.
10.5	This scheme offers a different paradigm to that imposed by grammatical gender (masculine, feminine, neuter), that is, one set of things can be defined as similar or dissimilar, another set comprises things that are equally composed of the similar and the dissimilar (called by some "unlikeness").
10.6–8	The underlying dispute seems at heart to be terminological, and what's crucial is to scrutinize in what way the proposed "likeness" operates between two entities (i.e., one man may be said to be unlike another, even when in many of their parts they are alike; cf. "you sew" [*suis*], and "of a swine" [*suis*]; or *nemus* [grove] and *lepus* [hare]).
10.9–11	The ability to perceive the proportional relationship that underpins likeness is difficult, hence, no one has managed to do it satisfactorily before (cf. Dionysius of Sidon, Aristocles, Parmeniscus).
10.12–13	Likeness needs to be between primary forms (pre-inflection), and, within systems, between inflected forms, for Varro's defined Regularity, although since the two broad categories themselves have subcategories, he will return to basics to demonstrate that he is playing fair.
10.14	Some words simply are indeclinable (thus cannot participate in the outlined systematization of Regularity), whereas others have inflected forms. Trying to mix and match the two cannot deliver meaningful comparisons (e.g., *mox* and *nox*).
10.15	A second division of words participates in "voluntary" derivation (e.g., as Romulus gives a name to *Roma*), whereas others follow a regular system of natural derivation (e.g., the genitive of *Roma* is *Romae*); the former is rooted in *consuetudo*, the latter in *ratio* [accepting *orationem* over *rationem*, with Kent].
10.16	*Roma, Romanus, Capua, Capuanus*—no one can satisfactorily model a system that allows for all the derivations combining voluntary and natural schemes; when words are set to things by voluntary derivation, *consuetudo* inevitably ends up with chaos and confusion; Irregularity is inevitable in this scheme.

10.17	A third division involves naturally inflected words: those with case but no tense (e.g., nouns); words with tense but no case (finite verbs); words with both (participles); and words with neither (adverbs). Within this division, each subsection is only internally consistent.
10.18	Turning to the subsections: nouns and articles. Each is only Regular within its own group.
10.19	Regularity is barely a shadowy presence within the category of articles, and it is more present in the essential qualities involved than in the words themselves; in nouns, morphology and the words themselves (rather than the signifieds) are the primary location of Regularity.
10.20	Just as articles can be definite and indefinite, nouns can be common or proper (*oppidum, Roma*).
10.21–23	Varro develops a fourfold scheme for defining when comparisons can appropriately be made to determine whether Regularity exists in nouns and adjectives, which he conceptualizes as a checkerboard populated by mercenaries with the horizontal lines representing cases and the verticals, genders.
	. . .
10.24	Brief discussion of plurals and the single compound entity signified by a plural.
10.25–27	Examples such as sewing, running, teaching, and reading all show the significance of vowel length and spoken stress and recall to readers the need to pay attention to final letters.
10.28	Some words inflect directly from the nominative as a stem (*consul, praetor*), whereas others inflect from a stem observed only in the oblique cases (compare *socer, macer*), and this leads Varro to return to the matter of secondary derivations [words formed in support of the semantic field of a noun, see 8.14].
10.29	Comparisons (whether observational or relational) require context.
10.30	Varro concludes on nouns and turns to articles. Gender, number, case, and whether definite or indefinite are all relevant when classifying. But the tenuousness of Regularity here is too great to work through.
10.31	Words with tense and person but no case [cf. 10.17] inhabit six systems within which they inflect: tense, person, interrogative, declarative, subjunctive, imperative (with examples for each).

10.32	Four categories of these have tenses but not persons [impersonal forms].
10.33–34	Varro proposes to reserve the main discussion of more examples for his books [not extant] specifically focused on verb paradigms. Participles follow next.
	. . .
10.35–36	. . . we don't follow their lead when poets generate words incorrectly. *Ratio* systematizes working relationships for signifiers and inflected forms and in the forms that bridge the two.
10.37–39	How does a proportionate relational system function? This returns Varro to the Greek origins of *analogia* and its fourfold nature. Analog and analogy share an origin and are deeply interlinked. If one removes the ratio, analog and analogy fall apart.
10.40	A programmatic statement: Varro will not spell out every nuance for this proportional scheme; readers need to put their minds to work rather than awaiting his full explanation at some later point.
10.41	Numbers, families, times, all participate in this system.
10.42[4]	Poets use it in similes; geometers are attuned to it too; in speech, Aristarchus and his followers are especially sensitive to it.
10.43	Another, numerical, explanation: visualize a double ratio across a horizontal row (e.g., 1, 2, 4) and a tenfold along a vertical (1, 10, 100, and so on), with each presenting two analogs and a fourfold analogy.
10.44	A similar chart puts cases across the horizontal and genders on the vertical lines.
10.45	Regularity can be disjoined (1:2 as 10:20) or conjoined (1:2 as 2:4).
10.46	The fourfold quality also works with a musical analogy: a cithara has seven strings but two tetrachords; similarly, day four of the critical seven-day phase of an illness is watched especially carefully by doctors (days 1:4 predicts days 4:7).
10.47	Nouns manifest disjoined and fourfold Regularities; verbs, conjoined and threefold.
10.48	Verbs can denote incomplete and complete actions, and these two aspects need to be maintained as overarching systems when comparing forms. Those who do otherwise are not making a sound case against Regularity.
10.49–50	It may seem as if too few elements are sometimes available for Regularity to hold or, conversely, that there are too many, yet sets of two are always being compared with sets of one.[5]

10.51–52	Regularity has its foundations either in human will (how things are named) or in the nature of words (inflectional paradigms that are evident to the unlearned) or in both.
10.53	By combining "imposition" and "nature" in a scheme for Regularity, one must operate a flexible system relational to both strands. Imposition is for "us" to control, but we are controlled by nature.
10.54–55	It is crucial to recognize that inflectional schemes proceed from singular or plural case form, where only one or the other is at issue. If the word can signify singularity and plurality, then there must be two sets of paradigms, and a selection is required when investigating the primary form for mapping Regularity.
10.56–57	Three criteria are key when developing a model. One must begin from the clearest starting point, from what is least corrupted, and from natural order (rather than human arbitrariness). These three are less easy to find in singulars than in plurals; thus, one should start from plurals.
10.58–59	On encountering a rare corrupted form in the crucial nominative plural, one must correct it from one of the unambiguous oblique cases in order to ascertain what the nominative plural should have been and thus develop the paradigm correctly.
10.60–61	Foundational to all this is that the principles are grounded in nature because this is where the systematic relationships are most evident. Error falls mostly into impositions and thus nominative singulars, because humans are unskilled and disorderly and set names capriciously to things. Nature is mostly uncorrupted in itself, except where corruption has entered by way of ignorant usage.
10.62	If one must start from the singular, then the sixth case [ablative] is the place to start. This case is unique to Latin, and its endings provide a scheme for ascertaining the variations in play for the other cases: *terra, lance, leui,*[6] *caelo, uersu.*
10.63	Regularity brings three principles into play: what is within the things themselves, what is in the spoken forms, and what is in both. All three need to be kept in mind.
10.64	One can ignore the kinds of distinctions in the entities that are irrelevant to speech in the same way as craftsmen can tell which distinctions in the fashioning of buildings and statues and other artefacts are inconsequential.

10.65	Those that are relevant to speech [syntax and discourse] have a proportional relationship as words, but their underlying forms [*res*, hinting at signifieds] are divergent. Think of *Iuppiter* and *Marspiter*, alike in gender, number, case, and type [of signified].
10.66	The second principle is all about phonology (i.e., the proportionate relationship between the words as uttered rather than as grammatical elements). Examples are *biga*, *bigae* and *nuptia*, *nuptiae*, where there is no essential singularity or plurality at issue. Plurals derived from singulars are subordinate to the original singularity and thus have singular cardinal numbers to characterize them.
10.67	By contrast, the plural-only forms discussed earlier take plural forms of the numbers, acknowledging their lack of subordination to an imagined singular form.
10.68–69	The third principle to consider is twofold. The essence of the word *and* its spoken form have a proportionate similarity (e.g., *bonus*, *malus*). This is the perfect system, and it can be seen across home-grown vernacular, immigrant, and hybrid-stock words.
10.70	. . .[7] Many, not just poets, use the second kind—mostly from Greek, so the bastard forms too are mostly Greek-ish and thus too the Regularities.
10.71	We use all the available forms, but those who follow the middle way do best (by avoiding ostentatious Latinization and Graecism).
10.72	Regularity has its foundations in a particular likeness between essential qualities within words, between spoken word forms, and both taken together. Through comparison, the location and nature of the likeness can be tallied.[8] Neither the essential qualities of the word nor its utterance in use can alone allocate its place in the system because the likeness must be observable in both to function.
10.73	Three kinds of usage are evident: old-time (e.g., *cascus*, *surus*), "ours" now (e.g., *albus*, *caldus*), and a third that is neither (e.g., *scala*, *phalera*) and is what the poets use. If adding a fourth, it would be words that are not exclusively members of one category (e.g., *amicitia*, *inimicitia*).
10.74	The Regularity that is focused on the nature of words is not to be defined in the same way as that which is directed at the practicalities of spoken use. When the qualification "to a certain extent" is added, there is where poetic *analogia* is to be found. The people should adhere to the first and everyone within the

	community ought to adhere to the second, while poets should stick to the third.
10.75	Varro thinks these principles may have been outlined more carefully than clearly but at least not more obscurely than the attempts made on this topic by A–Z grammarians.
10.76	All will become clearer if each point is treated explicitly in order: what is meant by "word," "likeness of word," "inflection," "likeness of inflection," "the extent to which common use does not reject," "within certain limits."⁹
10.77	A "word" is the smallest indivisible part of spoken speech. Under natural inflection, "word" is "like" to "word" when there is morphological similarity in the signifieds and in the substance of the words, as well as in the inflected forms. "Inflection" is the pattern of change that takes place when words join relationally, in discourse, allowing the cognitive meaning to shift. "Likeness of inflection" is invoked when the process of transition between forms is the same for two words being compared.
10.78	Any objection (or not) relating to common usage is important because it reflects the fact that contemporary use allows some words to inflect against former norms or hardline, impractical rules.
10.79–81	With *analogia* explained, Varro turns to the forms where it should not exist yet is nevertheless hunted. Indeclinables are one set (e.g., "worthless," "soon," "scarcely").
10.82	A second set is words that have only one case in their spoken form (e.g., letter names)—*analogia* should not be the chase here. In a third set, too, *analogia* is not to be sought where the set of forms is unique to one word. Last, avoid chasing down *analogia* where the four words forming the grammatical comparison do not display an internally systematic relationship (e.g., *socer*, *socrus*, with the accusative plurals *soceros* and *socrus*).
10.83	True Regularity manifests across all these conditions: first, that the essential qualities exist; second, that they are in use; third, that they have names; fourth, that they participate in natural inflection [examples for the first two ensue, leading to 10.84].

Language and Authority
in *De Lingua Latina*

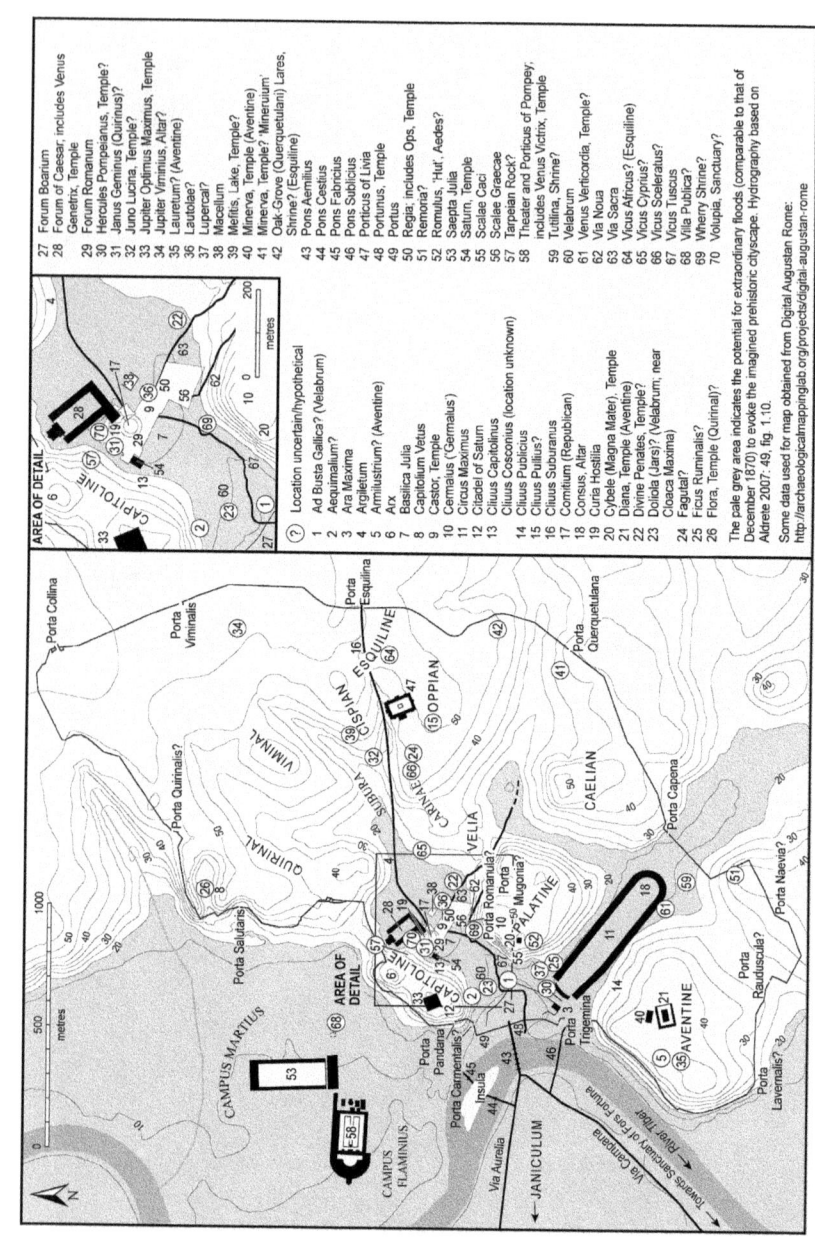

Rome (mid-first century BCE): The textual landscape of *De Lingua Latina*. Map drawn by Louise Buglass.

Introduction

... consigned to the attic of bibliographies.[1]

In Marcus Terentius Varro, the Latin language found a creative champion. A cautious catalog of Varro's literary production makes for seventy-four separate works, ranging from lit. crit. (including detailed word analysis of Plautus) to original verse composition (Menippean satires and other verse), theatrical history, epistles, and (auto-)biography; from political science, education and instruction, navigation, military protocol, and agriculture to philosophy, history, law, religion, linguistics and antiquarianism, and even (possibly) self-epitomization.[2] When scholarship brands Varro the "most important Roman polymath author," there is no exaggeration, but the weight of evidence is remarkably secondhand, given the (many lost) volumes that Varro produced.[3]

The opening "Roadmap," which guides readers through the extant text of *De Lingua Latina*, is an aid to keeping track of context for the examples and themes that I discuss, yet it also floodlights the holes in the extant text. Nonetheless, what remains is very much an authored work, as emphasized early in the first extant book (*Ling.* 5.1). Varro sets out a wide intellectual remit, a project crucial for every speaker's or writer's toolkit and central to citizenship: how it came about that "words" were put to ("*essent imposita*") "things" in Latin.[4] A set of first-person-singular statements vividly stakes out his role as protagonist, a figure who has achieved much already in books 2–4 (*institui, feci, misi*; tackling the disadvantages and advantages of etymology and explaining how it has been defined), and upon this foundation he can now deliver on his promises in what follows ("*in his ad te scribam*," in these, which I shall write for you). Books 2–4 were substantially rooted in theoretical concerns (*disciplina*); now, Varro directs his audience to understand the project anew. An unscientific "*opinor*," readers may note, rarely features in *De Lingua Latina*; *ratio* instead makes for a powerful guide.[5] This practical turn helps Varro develop and strengthen a case for what it is that etymology empowers the clued-in reader to do, as I discuss in "What Is *De Lingua Latina*?" later in this chapter.[6]

In disciplines such as Classics, unintentionally incomplete or compromised texts are commonplace. For *De Lingua Latina*, the impact has been to encourage an index-focused approach on detail and an avoidance of overview, literary readings. As we will see, however, Varro's antiquarian enthusiasm and etymological brio make this much more than a resolutely technical linguistic guide. A literary text is one that remains susceptible to analysis and that is not exhausted by one reading; this is why such works continue to excite interest long after their original contexts have melted away.[7] By these standards, Varro has produced a supremely literary work. In Language and Authority in "De Lingua Latina" I try out some of the many ways in which a through-reading of *De Lingua Latina* enriches, challenges, and transforms understanding of the late Roman Republic.

De Lingua Latina, elucidating and excavating the language for Latin speakers and especially for one particular addressee (Cicero), needs to be read against a back catalog within which Varro tackles just about every aspect of Roman culture. Varro's Latin is rich in quirks but also deeply intelligible as a language that could be proud of its polyphonous heritage. *De Lingua Latina* is not a straightforward linear catalog nor quite a miscellany;[8] nor does it promote an uncomplicatedly diachronic approach to language (despite the backward-looking thrust of the practice of etymology). Rather, I propose, this is more recognizable as an aspiring hypertext, a commonplace book with encyclopedic (as well as miscellaneous) qualities. My reading explores a structure at the borders of free association but operates in tandem with Varro's triadic architecture (etymology, books 5–7; grammar, 8–10). It is an approach nuanced by the cultural frictions of the era and by Varro's own literary sensibilities and his eye for the offbeat. The version of *De Lingua Latina* that emerges is a virtuoso performance that demonstrates how the study of Latin can itself be a virtuous invitation to emulation.[9]

My through-reading (a recurring term) found in Varro's text, in its etymological force and in its reverberations, a fascinating project defamiliarizing and refamiliarizing a language.[10] Cicero, writing around the same time that Varro was probably completing *De Lingua Latina*, has (Academic) Cotta snap back at (Stoic) Balbus' attempts at etymology: "in disentangling vocabulary you set about a wretched endeavor . . . a dangerous practice."[11] *De Lingua Latina* has convinced me otherwise: long-form etymological exploration can not only deliver a compelling narrative—and one of the subtlest forms of translation; it can be fun, too. Indeed, "etymology's great allure is its ability to trespass, to make the connections that ordinary parlance has forgotten, and to suggest an authority that a proper discipline like astronomy or religion cannot glimpse."[12]

Finding Varro?

Varro, like Aulus Gellius, is one of antiquity's best-known but unread authorities.[13] Gellius' own Varro is a companion-in-arms for the lively minded scholar and can be turned to for help in quashing bumptious boasters.[14] How, then, did the vigor and literary enthusiasm that made him so popular, at least with fellow intellectuals, end in footnotes and indices? If we turn back to 1954, Francesco della Corte characterized Varro as the third great "light" of Roman letters (along with Vergil and Cicero) but already a melancholy emblem of the chasm between classical antiquity and the present (so characterized by Petrarch, addressing an imagined Varro in 1350).[15] A remarkable feature of Varro's loss is how such a vast corpus could vanish so quickly. Varro developed no significant Renaissance posterity because inasmuch as he existed, he stood primarily as a trope for the ruin of time;[16] yet his interest in networks—intellectual, cultural, semiotic, and political—and, in particular, in scrutinizing their place at the heart of a holistically conceived *Populus Romanus* makes him a figure with deeply contemporary resonances.

Back in Varro's hometown (modern Rieti), in 1974, an international conference sponsored by the Centre for Varro Studies (on the bimillennium of his death) ranged widely, but in its catholicity (of which Varro might have approved) the proceedings lost the opportunity to set down a meaningful marker for Varro tout court—Project Varro, as one might term it, is absent. Nonetheless, there are significant highlights, for example Daniel Taylor's 1974 exploration of linguistic theory in *De Lingua Latina*—a significant landmark in recent attempts to understand the text—whose model Giorgio Piras (1998) has continued in many respects; both works remain indispensable in different ways for grappling with the linguistic theories deployed by Varro. In Thomas Baier (1997), Varro found a careful cheerleader but one whose interest in Varro's influence precludes a more wide-ranging and holistic investigation of his appeal; conversely, Burkhart Cardauns (2001) in a brief study has shown that Varro can emerge vividly from his surviving works, but on too small a scale to bring to life the imaginative worlds of *De Lingua Latina*.

Della Corte's exuberant biography is now hard to lay hands upon, but his enthusiasm finds an echo in Varro's remarkable presence in the index to Elizabeth Rawson's sober and magisterial 1985 study of late Republican intellectual culture (only Cicero is more ubiquitous).[17] For Elisa Romano (2003), Varro is an author who already understands the fragility of contemporaneity's grasp of the past and its significance. Making a satisfying and unifying genealogy is, for Romano's Varro, how one best understands oneself; so this is also a Varro who might recognize another "self" in Emmanuele Narducci's 2003 study of the echoes of Greece in Cicero's literary villas. To get to know Varro requires thinking about his sparring partner Cicero; their relationship provides much of the color for any "life" of Varro and for a meaningful understanding of his work.[18] Nevertheless, no study to date has managed to make sense of what Varro's persona, voice, and individual character brought to a treatise on Latin, addressing Cicero, during those difficult years in the mid-late 40s.[19]

Substantial analysis, especially the work of Daniel Taylor in championing Varro across five decades, has already elucidated the grammatical paradigms associated with *declinatio* (encompassing inflection and derivation) in Varro's thought and teased out the relationship between Varro's approach and those proposed in earlier and Hellenistic philology, a field with which he was deeply familiar.[20] Against this well-trodden terrain I am therefore in a position to break different ground.

"What I say is, hammer out life in reading and writing": Varro's words encourage a connection between author and reader.[21] Despite this and other promising hints ("I've smiled [possibly, "lived"] a lot, and been a bit of a player"), Varro is hard to make flesh and blood.[22] Chapter 1 sketches some scenes in imaginative biographic mode, benefiting in particular from Francesco Della Corte's groundwork (1954), but overall, my Varro emerges from *De Lingua Latina* as the sum of its enthusiasms, and sometimes this means making associative leaps in order to situate the text and its author within their most generously conceived imaginative and real-world contexts. This means that the cultural poetics of Varro's Latin sit at the heart of my study, which coins the word "Romespeak" (what it means to speak Latin; Latin order as Roman order; Latin as a world-forming toolkit) to illuminate the relationships between discourse, identity, grammatical declension, and political transformation that *De Lingua Latina* models. Individual chapters, focusing on selected sections but also tracking themes more widely, showcase how to read alongside Varro and how to explore his strategic technique of shaping and accumulating weighty arguments through spin-off and allusion.

This approach is indebted to Stephen Greenblatt's "self-fashioning" but glossed by John Dugan's incisive and eloquent application of the model to Cicero.[23] Greenblatt's innovation was to articulate the ways in which the individual self, composed of performative and fictive qualities, was simultaneously aligned with but also contested within specific sociopolitical conditions. Literature was crucial to this cultural creation of identity, and the personal order manifest in the concept of self that emerged made the production of literature a facet of the production of power. Greenblatt's model took shape within his study of Thomas More's expression of tensions between authentic and performative identities, but Varro's words suggest that he also conceived selfhood as the product of artistic endeavor. In Karl-J. Hölkeskamp's sense, this Latin-speaking self, empowered by command of discourse, etymology, and syntax, might draw on a stemma teeming with "symbolic capital."[24]

Chapters 1–8

Over the course of eight chapters I chart a thematically structured expedition through what remains of the text, while at the same time attempting to give a flavor of the through-reading experience. Having a text of *De Lingua Latina* to hand and a bookmark at the roadmap that precedes this introduction will be crucial; not every nugget gets quoted or dissected, and this is not an exhaustive guide. The roadmap should make evident that there still remain structural devices that give shape to the mostly surviving six books. Sometimes explicitly editorializing, *De Lingua Latina* inevitably interests itself in patterns and cumulatively develops narrative power through juxtapositions and patterns of exegesis. *De Lingua Latina*, brimming with literary allusion and cultural detail, is not a work composed to be "consigned to the attic of bibliographies."[25]

Chapter 1 takes Varro as its protagonist and explores what happens when his work is recontextualized within his real-world friendship group, men who were at the center of the last years of the Republic. Varro's relationships with Cicero, Atticus, Caesar, and other key players continue to wash over the readings in subsequent chapters.[26] Chapter 2 introduces what I term "Romespeak," the connecting device for examples of the kinds of close and associative reading strategies that underpin my analysis. This chapter is therefore a primer for adopting and applying my approach to *De Lingua Latina*. It takes a set of passages key to understanding Romespeak and examines how and why reading *with* Varro produces new and significant value and sharpens and enriches understanding of my key themes. Chapters 3 and 4 examine Varro's representation of the powerfully inspirational quality of literary poetics and eventually bring *oratio* into the frame as an expression of Latin expertise. Chapter 5 looks to Varro for two tours of Rome, finding a city of what Pierre Nora has termed *lieux de mémoire* that ensure a Roman future just as (according to Augustine) Varro once promised (every bit the new Metellus or Aeneas).[27] It is at this halfway-point restart in Varro's first hexad (books 2–7) that the deep significance of landscape as "ethnoscape" is made distinctively Roman.[28] Programmatically, the "placial" qualities of Varro's etymological speculation make it clear that Latin *langue* and *parole* are embedded in a conjunction of place and people, generating the new identity to be termed in Latin as Roman.[29]

In chapter 5 Romespeak takes on new significance, gaining an increased charge from location within exceptionally redolent sites and amid the late Republic's potent conjunction of new goals (and new dangers) attached to political and public speech.[30] Chapter 6 turns from the fabric of the city to its governance and to the terminology of civic and religious authority. This builds Romespeak into a mode acutely interested in the interrogation of order and shows just how committed Varro was to a project of requalification of political intelligence and recalibration of practical discourse in order to further a social-engineering project. Here, therefore, readers see various strands converge so that books 5–7 deliver a more coherent agenda for doing etymology well, with important and wide-ranging outcomes. Grammatology comes to the fore in book 8, but its principles, especially in Varro's determination to explore binary schemes forcing adherence to incompatibly hardline positions, are a powerful framework in Varro's scheme. In chapter 7 I focus on the role of case as a generative model before turning to other factors that contributed to the sustenance and growth of the Romespeaking community. Finally, chapter 8 takes a turn through Varro's year (time, the festal calendars, days, months). The language of time draws together Varro's etymological and grammatical explorations in order again to exemplify the underlying unity in *De Lingua Latina* and to provide a clear sense of the poetics of Varro's conceptualization of language as the seedbed of literary and political artistry.

What Is *De Lingua Latina*?

De Lingua Latina redefined the toolkit for the theory and practice of oratory (Cicero's expertise) and grammar (one of Caesar's ostentatiously nonmilitary pastimes) and probed the significance of every communicative act, however mundane.[31] A motivated reader might also find in the text a last-word cap to a long-running debate between two competitive intellectuals: Varro and Cicero, with Caesar (on *analogia*) making a third.

The politics of linguistics in the late Republic represents an important strand in this study, and where Caesar (*ratio* and Regularity as a point of political convergence) and Cicero (*mores* and usage underpinning res publica) represent a dyad acculturated by social and political dissonance, Varro was prepared to tackle the relationship governing who says what, and how, when, and why, in a nuanced fashion. As I argue, he was confident enough in his model of *auctoritas uerborum* to stand up and advocate for a middle way (*Ling.* 10), even when the political success of that model, the Augustan Principate, was still an unimagined prospect. Sometimes *anomalia* (or Irregularity) is a marker for *rightness*. Thus, Varro's emphatic opening of the third triad with an argument against Regularity as a baseline proposition for language in theory and practice (*Ling.* 8) is a warning not to assume that an eventual rapprochement with Caesar diminished his ability to define his own position.[32] That this consensus position is a key issue for *De Lingua Latina* rather than an isolated grammatical crux is evident from early in book 5, where Varro negotiates a relationship between the extremes of "past" and "future":

> Vetustas pauca non deprauat, multa tollit. Quem puerum uidisti formosum, hunc uides deformem in senecta. Tertium seculum non uidet eum hominem quem uidit primum. Quare illa quae iam maioribus nostris ademit obliuio, fugitiua secuta sedulitas Muci et Bruti retrahere nequit. Non, si non potuero indagare, eo ero tardior, sed uelocior ideo, si quiuero. Non mediocres enim tenebrae in silua ubi haec captanda neque eo quo peruenire uolumus semitae tritae, neque non in tramitibus quaedam obiecta quae euntem retinere possent. (Varro, *Ling.* 5.5)[33]

There are few things that the passage of time does not distort, and many that it eliminates. The one you once saw as a beautiful boy, you now see twisted by old age. The third generation does not see a person in the same way that the first saw him. Therefore those things that oblivion has taken even from our ancestors, these escapees not even the assiduous pursuit mounted by Mucius and Brutus could recover.[34] Even if I myself am not able to hunt down this quarry, I shall not on this account be the slower; indeed, I'll even be swifter if I'm able. For there is no trifling darkness in the wood where these are to be captured, and they leave no well-trodden paths to take us to where we want to go. Nor indeed do the tracks lack obstacles that can delay the hunter.

It is a truism that time passing changes everything, yet Varro's metaphor breathes vitality into what could have been a banal sentiment.[35] Following the signs of language takes one through a landscape shaped by the ideation and intentions of the author, the literal and semantic shifts in use of words, and the changing position and cultural affiliation of the reader, all metamorphosing over time (the trope returns at *Ling.* 7.2). This is a position not unfamiliar from the speech allotted to Atticus in Cicero's *Brutus*.[36] It may be unexceptionable (or rather clever) as a position for an historical linguist, but Varro's delivery of the message emphasizes how language (and therefore a people) changes because it is alive—a position drifting out of alignment with that represented by Cicero's Atticus and hinting at the messy consensus position (not Cicero's *or* Caesar's; neither autocratic nor oligarchic *analogia*) that he schools his audience to reach (books 8–10).

What makes *De Lingua Latina* especially complex is that it gives no single straightforward account of itself that encompasses all of its multifarious enthusiasms, anecdotes, arguments, and agendas. Neither a miscellany nor an encyclopedia, nevertheless it exhibits aspects of both. To get the most from its subtle but powerfully influential structure requires a second (and third and maybe fourth) reading, that is, an active-anthologizing approach to handling the text.[37] Despite, and perhaps a factor in, its fragmentary survival, *De Lingua Latina* deals in subtly connected bite-size morsels, and it is this, rather than an interrogation or recuperation of its losses, that fascinates me. For the purposes of my analysis, I have avoided any attempt to integrate the free-floating fragments and concentrated instead on the united material as organized in the primary manuscript tradition.[38]

Reading *De Lingua Latina* as an encyclopedia makes it, in Umberto Eco's terms, "the regulative hypothesis that allows . . . speakers to figure out the 'local' dictionary they need in order to ensure the good standing of their communicative interaction."[39] Back in the world of Classical scholarship, discussing that devoted Varronian Isidore of Seville, John Henderson writes of the danger of getting bogged down in etymologizing: it has "*throughout* played second fiddle to a project in cultural mnemonics according to which Isidore's reader is installed in the obviously godgiven position of destination for the entire thrust of geopolitical history."[40] Alongside explorations of Isidore, studies of Aulus Gellius (another fan of Varro) and Pliny the Elder have begun to investigate the structural and holistic narrative imperatives of texts previously favored in data-driven footnotes.[41]

The contexts for these authors are rather different, but in their various ways they reflect an approach to narrative that is in sympathy with my reading of Varro. Taken as a group, and setting aside for a moment the issue of didacticism as a mode and the exigencies of composing an indexable (or easily searchable) work, these authors are most aptly characterized as miscellanists. Miscellanists are difficult to get a fix on, yet find form and shape within rather than despite a certain fragmentary or episodic quality.[42] The ideal miscellany invites random dipping in and rewards nonlinear reading patterns with unexpected nuggets;

yet the miscellany also delivers an ethos, an insight into the thought processes of an author's persona, and it tests the limits of what an audience can be asked to understand, to process, and to derive meaning from. *De Lingua Latina* delivers on all counts.

There is more to Varro than miscellany or encyclopedia, and his lifetime output returns again and again to the history and ethnography of the Roman people. In doing so, it makes a substantial case for assuming that the production of a deep and rich understanding of what constituted Rome coursed through his lengthy list of "publications."[43] Moreover, in revisiting this cluster of historical interests from different angles, Varro accustoms his audiences to know him as the keeper and producer of their historical selves. *De Lingua Latina* thus represents one instance in a lifetime's study of etymology in the broadest sense: how the production and explication of the backstory of words and semantic structures (or people, or rituals, or technologies) communicate and refresh citizenship and identity for individuals and collective. Etymology, in this way, becomes a peculiarly potent and totalizing mode. Varro signposts his discriminatory authority as the master etymologist subtly throughout but also explicitly when, for instance, he uses the formula *nisi . . . potius*. This formula crops up nine times across the intact work.[44] Sometimes, as at *Ling.* 5.25, it helps enrich the word games, in this example with a pun on the potentiality of puteal sites (they should be potable—if they're putrid, and so on, well, it's the pits).[45] More seriously, when producing an unexpected set of etymologies for consul (*Ling.* 5.80; see chapter 6), it underscores the role's susceptibility to revision and, importantly, to reconfiguration.

Varro's own ethnographic and antiquarian studies of Rome are not substantially available for detailed comparison, but we can see that, unlike, for example, later works such as Pliny's *Natural History* or Aulus Gellius' *Attic Nights*, both of which interest themselves in Roman lore and epistemology, Varro's choice of subject allows him to examine what unites Latin speakers (Romespeak) and how, without the right kind of intellectual equipment and understanding of the *longue durée*, an overly fixed position on what makes for tradition, or *analogia*, or *anomalia*, can also destroy unity. He can do this by creating and occasionally interrogating a porous collection of etymologies, calling upon a gamut of authorities from the expected (typically grammarians and philosophers) to the more surprising (poets). In the process, the language that emerges proposes a reformed body of tradition and family values with its roots in what we might call discourse analysis—using "discourse" in the sense employed by poststructuralism to mean language (written, spoken, or visual) or a system of ideas in use within a specific set of contexts (historical, social, and ideological).

Although Varro is not always ostentatiously in "antiquarian" mode in *De Lingua Latina*, nevertheless he is an antiquarian by inclination and expertise, one well versed in tackling earlier "antiquarianism" head-on. Writing on Aulus Gellius, Erik Gunderson asks: "What does it mean to read the antiquarians? What does it mean to write on them? Where do the world of the book and the book of the world meet? And is this paratopological intersection something indexed, or is it instead experienced directly? Does one comment on the antiquarians or merely with them?"[46]

Similar questions inform my study: what does it mean to "teach" a language to native speakers? Where do the world of Latin and the book of Latin meet? Does the former frame the latter? Or are the two equal partners? By delivering an etymological and linguistic salvo *ne plus ultra*, Varro ensured that his propositions, explanations, and even inventions would root themselves deeply, and the loss of so much of the work speaks to its successful consumption within a changing zeitgeist.[47] Nonetheless, his elliptical, narrative-heavy, and meagerly signposted study is—by design—hard going for anyone intent on mining it solely for definitive grammatical rules or paradigms.

Varro's is not a formally indexed work (contrast Pliny's *Natural History*), though traces of a descriptive scheme are apparent; it has therefore fallen to later editors to generate indices. Editors, and their ideal, imagined audiences, have thereby defined the possible search-strings to which "Varro" will be able to respond. This approach works against the structure of books 8–10 in particular. It also obscures Varro's lively use of speech and quotation in the first person. This is especially clear in the dialogic unity of books 8–10, structured in the form of a debate. By presenting two mirror arguments, arguments against and then for the existence of *analogia* (books 8–9), he nods to the elephant in the room (Plato's *Cratylus*), demonstrates skills as a forensic orator and protagonist, and also grasps the opportunity to tackle the ramifications of each position with a formal gloss of objectivity. The rhetorical quality of these books offers Varro an opportunity to show off his skills in a manner different from the more straightforward persona (the etymologist) of the previous triad. In choosing a form with Socratic overtones but also deeply embedded in Roman rhetorical education (*controuersiae*), Varro delivers a master class for the through-reader.

As often as not, Varro's explanation of a word's root meaning startles, confounds, or challenges common sense. One of my key claims is that this is not merely pedantry or obscurantism. Instead, the seeming irregularity of attention devoted by Varro to his exempla and etymologies reflects challenges to cultural norms that characterized the late Republic. It represents a provocation to the orderly mind (and human nature tends to assume a design—some sort of system or hierarchy); it encourages questioning of those "ready-made syntheses, those groupings that we normally accept before any examination, those links whose validity is recognized from the outset";[48] it nods to the artificiality of the project he has undertaken; and it defamiliarizes even the most apparently banal assertion of etymological self-evidence in ways that provoke questions along lines still recognizable in late-1960s intellectual radicalism.

Stepping back from *De Lingua Latina* to consult "Varro" becomes an interrogation of a genre-devouring body of work spanning a crucial period in Rome's history. As the corpus was consumed and regurgitated, the factoids, sound bites, paradigms, and so on remained, and they continue to form the go-to basis for scholarly footnotes, for dictionary entries, for *answers*.[49] That the man posing the questions, however implicitly, has for the most part disappeared has proved unproblematic for scholarly generations eager to access and mine the data source. Losing Varro in many respects adds gravitas and a patina of objectivity to every citation. Everyone in the game *knows* (the indexes of) *De Lingua Latina*, but no one *reads* (the Varro in) *De Lingua Latina*.

Introducing Books 8–10: More than Technicalities

To appreciate the subtle unity of Varro's vision, one needs to read all the way through, yet the dynamism and cultural immediacy of books 5–7, full of etymological panache, might seem to be abandoned with the complex technicalities of books 8–10 (arguing the cons and pros of *analogia*, and a consensus position). My study emphasizes reading strategies wherein Varro's interest in linguistics and syntax is significant even in the midst of his more ostensibly narrative, etymological material, and vice versa. For this reason, although in my chapters 3–8 etymology and grammar are treated thematically and respecting the narrative flow, the thought processes and concerns of books 8–10 are proleptically influential across books 5–7.

Across books 8–10 Varro argues three different positions with respect to the role of *analogia* (a system of proportional relationships whereby what is right is achieved by close adherence to *ratio*; I tend to translate this as Regularity, but it might also be rendered Consistency) and *anomalia* (a model that downgrades the force of systematization, instead prioritizing the importance of usage, *consuetudo*) in linguistics. Varro makes these terms central to his vision of linguistic systematization and a striking feature of his self-fashioning as an expert on Latin—and they are also redolent with political symbolism. As context, Caesar had dedicated *De Analogia* to Cicero, presumably in the wake of

Cicero's *De Oratore*. These intellectual connections enrich *De Lingua Latina*'s political power and shed light on the complex relationship between intellectual performance and pragmatic action in this era.[50]

Book 8 opens with an overview, including an outline of case forms (Hercules, from nominative through to genitive).[51] Names (*cognomina*) lead to the memes of linguistic family history (*Ling.* 8.16–17); thus, family (*genus*) is crucial from the outset: some names ("such as Prudent, Candid, Prompt") allow distinction by incremental difference (one might read this as "suffix," from a family perspective) to allow a "family" to deliver comparative members (example, "*a candido, candidius, candidissimum,*" and so on, *Ling.* 8.17). The argument by juxtaposition emphasizes genealogical inconcinnity. Not all those in the same family or branch will have the same qualities or share them to the same extent, yet relational systematization (Hercules; grammar; acculturated family trees) will tie the disparate character(istic)s together.[52] It is only after this substantial introduction to the book and the two upcoming book triads (*Ling.* 8.1–24) that Varro opens the case against Regularity as the foundation of language.

One purpose of book 8 (*Ling.* 8.25 on) is to persuade that dissimilarity cannot itself become evidence of a *regular* discriminatory system. Only the crazy will persist in conserving paradigms that have fallen out of practice.[53] Not only is it the case that "*ab dissimilibus dissimilia ut Priamus Paris, Priamo Pari*" (from unlike forms come unlike outcomes, *Ling.* 8.34), but, as all Latin speakers will know, the similarity between wolf (*lupus*) and hare (*lepus*) is only word-skin deep; moreover, dissimilar nominatives can of course gain congruity in inflection. Even in absolutely identical words there can be treachery in signification: Alba, for example, might be Rome's mother city (Alba Longa) *or* Alba Fucens, depending on which people one is construing (Albani versus Albenses, and so on, *Ling.* 8.35). If *analogia* is not a total system of unwavering similarity, then it can exist only as a point of academic interest: "because there is 'unlikeness' in more words [than there is 'likeness'], Regularity ought not to be followed in conversational speech."[54] This is an all-or-nothing opening salvo, and it is interesting that an attack on the tenets of *Analogia* is the first argument out of the box.

When revisited from book 9's contrary perspective, the story is inevitably different.[55] The homely lentil (*lens*), with its associate *lupinus* (the funny-money lupine, or the wolfish adjective), stands as an exemplar of natural Regularity ("*ut sit in motibus caeli*").[56] But Regularity is an elastic concept, and in its voluntary mode, "*quod ea homines ad suam quisque uoluntatem fingat*" (since humankind fashions [words] each according to his will, *Ling.* 9.34), it still underpins the relationship between unique ethnicities and the languages they produce. Greeks, Syrians, Latins—all have separate vocabularies attuned to their requirements without disturbing the principle of Regularity. Regularity, that is, order on a grandly humane and epistemological scale, can accommodate this. Closer to home, it is exemplified when readers understand that just as Romulus delivers "Roma" by act of will (and Tibur, the Tiburtes), the declined forms follow naturally, so that what "I say" (present) is parent to what "I was saying" and "had said" (imperfect and pluperfect).[57]

Book 8 begins to define *analogia* obliquely when Varro broaches the topic of "voluntary" and "natural" modes of applying words to entities and deriving layers of meaning; he starts with what one might term the "voluntary" slaves of grammar:

Sic tres cum emerunt Ephesi singulos seruos, nonnunquam alius declinat nomen ab eo qui uendit Artemidorus, atque Artemam appellat, alius a regione quod ibi emit, ab Ion<i>a Iona, alius quod Ephesi Ephesium, sic alius ab alia aliqua re, ut uisum est. (Varro, *Ling.* 8.21)

In this way, when three men have each bought a slave at Ephesus, perhaps one derives the slave's name from the vendor, Artemidorus, and calls him Artemas; another, drawing on the region Ionia, because Ionia was the region where he bought him, chooses the name Ion; the last, because it was in [the city of] Ephesus, picks Ephesius. Thus each, despite similar conditions, finds a different name to fit the bill.

It is important to recognize that these individually flavored and personally motivated "namings" are in tune with the etymological mode Varro has developed in books 5–7. In part, they derive from the inclinations and interests of the slaves' new owners, and they factor in the contextual aspects of the transaction that suit each individual case. By contrast, all three men, once they have fixed on appropriate names for their new acquisitions, inflect the names according to their Latinate declension. In this way utterances and names are modulated into something that renders each personal linguistic intervention intelligible within a semiotic community. One's neighbor, friend, or banker may not know or have any familiarity with Artemidorus the slave merchant or understand, for example, what mnemonic baggage the nickname Artemas might carry for the slave's new owner, but he knows what its genitive will be. When correctly declined and slotted into Latin sentences, all the new-minted slaves are reborn as intelligible Roman signs. This last Varro terms "natural" derivation, a model that shares features with the "natural" position as expressed by Plato's Cratylus (and Socrates) and with the "conventional" position of Plato's Hermogenes.⁵⁸

Varro gets more specific:

> quod utraque declinatione alia fiunt similia, alia dissimilia, de eo Graeci Latinique libros fecerunt multos, partim cum alii putarent in loquendo ea uerba sequi oportere, quae ab similibus similiter essent declinata, quas appellarunt ἀναλογίας, alii cum id neglegendum putarent ac potius sequendam <dis>similutidinem, quae in consuetudine est, quam uocaru*nt* ἀ<ν>ωμαλίαν, cum, ut ego arbitror, utrumque sit nobis sequendum, quod <in> declinatione uoluntaria sit anomalia, in naturali magis analogia.⁵⁹ (Varro, *Ling.* 8.23)

Because, in both modes of derivation, some instances will move toward similarity, others toward dissimilarity, Greeks and Latins have fashioned many books on the subject. In some of these, there are those who think that in speaking, it is necessary to follow those words that have been derived from similar referents in similar fashion—which they called *analogia*—others held that this should be disregarded and, instead, that irregularity should be followed, as in common usage—which they termed *anomalia*. But in my opinion, we should follow both, because in "voluntary" derivation there is Irregularity, and in "natural," even more evidently, there is Regularity.

Hence, to impose a specious logic based on similarity (an academic thesis or systematic, paradigm-based approach to linguistics) and to police language on its account (*analogia*) is as unhelpful as to allow a free-for-all based on an essential relationship between the perception and essence of an object (*anomalia*).⁶⁰ Caesar's most powerful extant use of language, in his *Commentaries*, exemplifies the overwhelming impetus of mass communication. Everyday speech must be both the speech of the individual *and* the discourse of a community, and it can deliver surprising results. Nevertheless, as Varro's story about the slaves shows, even the most apparently unsystematic and "inclination"-based semiotic set can still be argued to follow, "naturally," the appropriate normative pattern of inflection, delivering something explicable and meaningful on a deep level.⁶¹ Without *anomalia* the language community will not develop productively and become more complex, but without *analogia* only nonsense and fragmentation can ensue.⁶² This story illuminates Varro's vision, reached in book 10, of what productive compromise might offer. It also delivers an irresistible joke, if the timing is right: Artemidorus the Ephesian slave merchant? Rather, Artemidorus the Ephesian geographer.⁶³

Early in book 5, Varro characterizes Latin as a semiotic system driven by movement:

> unius cuiusque uerbi naturae sint duae, a qua re et in qua re uocabulum sit impositum. (*Ling.* 5.2)

> each and every word exists as a duality, comprising what it comes from and what it is applied to as a term.

Central to this strand is a powerful impetus that Varro is perhaps formalizing but not inventing: when he introduces book 8 (and opens a new triad), he emphasizes the motility of language: words are at their core inflections plugged into a dynamic semiotic system. They "move" back to entities or concepts (the "real" or the "signified"), against which they are understood, and model their points of reference at the point of application in discourse (*parole*, as Ferdinand de Saussure would call it).⁶⁴ For this reading, both extant triads (books 5–7, 8–10) open up different approaches to the proposition that all words exist simultaneously in past and present senses (what they are applied to "now" depends upon where they are coming from, etymologically), while also performing an endless cycle of transmission. Looked at in these terms, one goal of the etymologist is to illuminate and categorize what really persists beneath the ebb and flow of language and its acculturated qualities. Varro teaches the mastery of reality through meaning, and deep knowledge of the array of truths in language offers glimpses of the ideal.

In his book *Latin Language and Latin Culture*, Joseph Farrell succinctly summed up how Cicero played with a connection between territorial and linguistic wealth or poverty,⁶⁵ but Lucretius' well-known comment that "the poverty of our ancestral discourse" (*patrii sermonis egestas*) drags him away or perhaps diverts him (*abstraho*) from the task of setting out how the universe is inherently a work in progress is also relevant.⁶⁶ His shortage of appropriately acculturated and flexible language threatens to compromise access to a real understanding of how the world works—without an ability to anchor discourse with points of reference that retain meaning for past and present and across genres, disorientation might ensue. Varro's Latin rebuts this possible anxiety by offering mastery of "the empire of a sign."⁶⁷ Programmatically, with the terminology *fons* and *riuus* (*Ling.* 8.5) Varro shows a dynamic language able to keep up with scientific progress (*riuus*) exactly because it has a close eye kept on its origins (*fons*) by well-equipped semioticians and cultural historians. Apprehending existence means mapping and claiming the experienced world semiotically (language builds empire) and, thereby, epistemologically (knowledge builds empire). As speakers (and readers) renegotiate their world through the filter of Varro's Latin signs, they also confront a described world that semantically is always contingent and in progress (*riuus*) and that responds to retroactive as well as expansive intellectual forces (*fons*).[68]

Readers might well wonder what *De Lingua Latina*, supporting such a spectrum of responses, could achieve. Varro's presentation of the work to Cicero (and their correspondence) is an ever-present counterpoint to the work's content and to Varro's textual persona. Throughout my study I emphasize, through frequent contextual bumps, how urgently utilitarian, right across the political spectrum, command of Latin had become. As Ronald Syme once summed up: "Civil war, tearing aside *words*, forms and institutions, gave rein to individual passions and revealed the innermost workings of human nature."[69] Varro's book about language could as easily attract an unreflective ancient audience looking for straight answers or *bons mots* to spice up convivial conversation as it could delight a logophile.[70]

Words are manipulable.[71] Inevitably, there is more than one "book" available in Varro's handbook, and different concerns break cover at different points; this is the point of literariness.[72] One of this study's most keenly hoped-for goals is to see other readings taking center stage in years to come. My translations are inevitably influenced by published predecessors, and the explanations in commentaries too have had a formative role in how I have put English to the Latin. There is room for argument over what exactly Varro was saying, but it was clearly something complex.

chapter 1

Networking Varro

Immortales mortales si foret fas flere,
flerent diuae Camenae Naeuium poetam.
Itaque postquam est Orchi traditus thesauro
obliti sunt Romae loquier lingua latina.[1]

Immortals to lament mortals? If that were the orthodoxy,
then the divine Camenae would lament Naevius the poet.
And this is why—after he was consigned to Orchus' vault,
they forgot at Rome to speak the Latin language.

A Survivor's View

Imagine Varro in the early 20s BCE, a spry but elderly gentleman, enjoying the warm glow of an autumn afternoon and contemplating his survival and the terrible losses that entailed. The dappled sun and atmospheric shade of a portico, a cup of wine, and the splashing of a fountain encourage thoughtful reflection on a long life and difficult decisions in turbulent times. Sabines, proverbially, had a "mystical" streak: "*Sabini quod uolunt, somniant*" (Sabine desires take shape in dreams).[2] On such a pensive afternoon, Varro, perhaps reclining on a cushioned couch or under a rustling tree, might well have been transported back to a time before Actium and Triumvirs, before his on-off friend Cicero's gruesome death, before proscriptions, back-stabbings, and the vicious bloodshed of civil war, to his early years in Sabine Reate—where he was born, in the late second century.[3] Reate at the time was a prosperous town with a fertile hinterland, enjoying the benefits of a century and a half or so of full Roman citizenship.

Sketching a quiet shared moment with Varro may seem whimsical, but his vast, almost entirely lost literary productivity makes him very hard to get to know as an author, despite the range of third-party testimonia.[4] I am encouraged by W. Martin Bloomer's study of the role of imagination in Roman schooling to think that this approach nonetheless has form.[5] It is also the case that a cautious return to some of the tropes of biographical criticism has begun to flavor literary studies in the past couple of decades, in particular as scholarship has become more dissatisfied with a rigid approach to textuality. Shane Butler's exploration of what made Cicero eventually fall victim to Marc Antony demonstrates how productive imaginative biography can be as an analytical device.[6] This is a thought experiment, moreover, that returns us to the creative ethos of biography as a form of self-fashioning with deep origins in antiquity.

Why is Reate significant? Varro's childhood predated the full enfranchisement of Italy, and his early career must be set against a backdrop of the tensions between local and Roman identities to which his sparring partner Cicero trenchantly alluded.[7] From Varro, years later, we get a sense of Reate's significance when he makes it the home of a girl who made good on an inexplicable baby in the time-honored way: blaming a fervent encounter with the god Enyalius, aka Quirinus, for her pregnancy and a son, Modius Fabidius. As a good son, Fabidius then dutifully founded a city, Cures, in his father's honor.[8] Other, less cheeky stories about the Sabines must also have flickered in and out of Varro's Roman identity, for instance, characterizations of the Sabines as luxury-loving "Etruscans" and as a decadent and self-serving people.[9] Or, by contrast, Cato's wish-fulfillment story of a hard-living, severe, "Spartan" Sabine ethnicity.[10]

For Rome, Sparta benchmarked a long-vanished experiment in a radical commonwealth; Spartans' toughness and legendary pragmatism existed in a bubble whose glistening relationship to reality was all the more tenuous because significant for nostalgic self-fashioning in the competitive world of late Republican politics.[11] If Cato's *Origines*, as Gary Farney persuasively argues, gives the role of eponymous founder to a Spartan, Sabus, then it becomes a short step to see how Sabine myth-making would reinvigorate Rome's legendary exilic origins and heterogeneity.[12] "It is almost as if the Romans, having used the Sabines as their mirror, as a means of differentiating themselves from their enemies, at some point allow them through the looking-glass to become the Romans."[13] As Andrew Wallace-Hadrill suggests, the complex and synchronic relationship in this part of Italy that linked Greeks, Italians of different flavors, and new Romans would continue as "a perpetually renewable dialogue."[14] A significant role for an antiquarian and ethnologist in exploring how this melee fed into language must have been not just inevitable but exciting.[15]

This was a society within which claiming the right flavor of ethnicity and a potent genealogy—as famously evidenced by Julius Caesar's rebooting of the Trojan franchise—was creating a new brand of celebrity politics. Being just "Spartan" enough might successfully characterize Sabine ethnicity as a distinctive improvement on Athenian and Hellenistic Greek models: Spartan Sabines, in this version, were a crucial support for reinventing Romulus' ragtag band as military and moral empire builders. In the process, Sabine families such as the Claudii and Valerii and, perhaps by implication, the Terentii gained distinction and a place in the increasingly cosmopolitan power structures at Rome.[16] As Cicero neatly put it (writing to Gaius Trebonius in 46), Sabine birth glossed a man for success; casting an eye back from extreme old age, Varro might have agreed.[17]

Young Varro, equipped with a self-made consular in his family tree and embarking on his own career in Rome, could already have imagined himself to be the complete package.[18] Burnished with a Roman education, he may even have considered himself the very type of "the incorporated outsider who embodies Rome's morally upright past."[19] With the clarity of hindsight, and by the early 20s, Varro might well have regarded his younger self rather more sardonically; yet that ambitious, clever, industrious, and well-connected young man achieved what many of his contemporaries did not: he survived and, if we believe the assertions of *De Re Rustica*, remained productive. The years that followed his studies (with the philologist and scholar L. Aelius Stilo and the reforming Platonist Antiochus of Ascalon) made him witness to an era defined by a struggle for control over the meaning of Rome, between warring factions and violently competitive clans, all claiming genealogical, historical, and moral authority.[20] That struggle played to his evident inclinations as an intellectual and a scholar, as well as to his political enthusiasm and energy—and frequently returned, like my imagined, pensive Varro, to the question of origins.

Varro shared his philosophical studies under Antiochus with Cicero and with Cicero's brother Quintus.[21] This connection with the *Cicerones* was to last Marcus Cicero's lifetime, and it colors this study in particular because book 5 of *De Lingua Latina* signals the relationship.[22] Leah Kronenberg has persuasively argued that Varro's only fully surviving work, *De Re Rustica*, is autobiographical at least in that it offers a dialogic riposte to Cicero's *De Republica*.[23] This reading sits well with Varro's playful use of "speaking names" to marry farm management to the operation of the res publica, and in that context *De Lingua Latina* re-emerges as an early phase in this literary joust, an exploration of the performative responsibilities of the individual citizen-speaker within the commonwealth.[24]

Where Cicero's *De Officiis* highlights what a young Roman citizen should aspire to offer to the State, Varro's *De Lingua Latina* eloquently and pragmatically shows such a citizen how it is done, using the citizen's most personal skill set (verbal performance) to relate different flavors of Latinity to Rome.[25] In the process, Varro positions himself as a standard-bearer for the power of Latin as a deeply historical and culturally alert successor to the problems and paradigms of Plato's *Cratylus*.[26]

Much of Varro's literary work probably postdated the frenetic early years of his career-building, and it seems likely that the time after Philippi saw a burst of literary activity. Nevertheless, throughout his life Varro must have been writing. Varro dedicated what may have been his earliest formal work, *De Antiquitate Litterarum*, to the tragedian and grammarian L. Accius at some point before 86, showing an already developed interest in the history of literature and its antiquarian idioms.[27] By this point he was well embarked on his public career, having held the post of *triumuir capitalis* in 90 and a quaestorship in 86.[28] According to Appian, the next stage in Varro's move up the *cursus honorum* was a praetorship in 68, but the years since 86 had been busy ones: legate under C. Cosconius in the Illyrian war (78/77), then proquaestor to Pompey in the Sertorian war (77–72).[29] At some point during the late 70s Varro may have been inspired to compose a handbook of statecraft (Εἰσαγωγικός) for Pompey, newly consul-elect in 71 and ten years younger than himself.[30] Then, echoing Pompey's power in a minor key, Varro seems likely to have held the post of tribune of the plebs in 71/70.[31]

This successful hookup with Pompey continued. Retrospectively at least, Varro's effective handling of Pompey and play-off of allegiances between Pompey and Caesar demonstrated what must have been an acute political nose and a strong dollop of savvy.[32] Cicero's long-standing cultivation of Pompey and his subsequent transfer of support to Caesar was far less successful, and the fallout may ultimately have woven its way into events of the mid-40s; that some of the tensions of the relationship came back to haunt Cicero is evident from his later rebuttal (in the *Philippics*) of accusations of sarcasm and inopportune criticism at Dyrrachium, six or so years earlier.[33]

Returning to Varro: shortly after his people's tribuneship (in 67), Varro gained a successful naval command under Pompey in what was to become one of the stand-out campaigns of the era: the war against the pirates. The significance of this appointment in Varro's self-fashioning is evident—he uses it as the mise-en-scène for the second book of his handbook *De Re Rustica*.[34] Although one needs to be wary of taking narratorial assertions at face value when dating texts, it is likely that *De Re Rustica* was a product of Varro's later years. Hence, my notion that youthful success, and in particular his maneuvering between Pompey and Caesar, might have occupied his mind on a warm evening in the garden is not just an attractive thought experiment; it has some textual support.

De Lingua Latina presents itself as a creation of Varro's late middle age, the year(s) immediately before Cicero's death. Given the complexities of production context for determining final publication in antiquity in general and the impossibility of pinning down any immediate evidence for reception that might chronologically fix one or more editions of the work, it would be hard to argue conclusively that a process of ongoing revision or re-editing did not occupy some of Varro's old age.[35]

Other politico-military appointments seem to have followed for Varro—perhaps a legateship (in the Third Mithridatic War) and a propraetorship (in Asia, in 66).[36] What is evident is that Varro managed his visibility effectively, making his Τρικάρανος (*The Three-header*), perhaps in the form of an op-ed political pamphlet responding to the so-called First Triumvirate, mark a high-profile intervention in a developing crisis.[37] Varro's Menippean verses give him form as a satirist, and the title for his "threesome" makes satirical political commentary an attractive proposition. Perhaps it was the impossible monstrosity of "three-headed" autocracy—factionalism and discord already built in, two against one—rather than extraordinary power itself or its current or past holders that caught Varro's imagination? Readers might also recall that Varro's satire *Marcopolis: On Political Power*, which, although too fragmentary to be meaningful as it stands (in isolation), was likely to have been echoed in sentiment in later comments such as "*tanta porro inuasit cupiditas honorum plerisque, ut uel caelum ruere, dummodo magistratum adipiscantur, exoptent*" (anyway, greed for honors has infected the majority to the extent that they'd even opt for the heavens to fall, if that was the price for getting a magistracy).[38]

Could it be funny to make a joke about this? This is literally (three heads make for three faces—two might make one Janus, but three?) and metaphorically (one's face is oneself) about (losing) "face" (defacement, disgrace).[39] If so, Caesar got it (and getting the joke, signaling one's wit and urbanity, was wallpaper for ambitious politicians), or didn't care, or just hoped to co-opt an influential critic.[40] Read this way, it could become part of a relationship that also featured Varro's appointment by Caesar to the Board of Twenty on the Agrarian Commission (in 59), a role that was also offered to Cicero but rejected.[41] Even this potentially poisoned chalice (putting Varro in the position of supporting Caesar and Pompey specifically and jointly but in different ways) appears to have assisted rather than hindered his public position and his influence with Pompey: looking a decade forward, he was on Pompey's military staff in Spain at least in 50–49, where he confronted the overwhelming superiority of Caesarian forces (and chose to surrender the one legion of two remaining to him).[42]

Our main account of Varro's politicking in the run-up to this surrender comes from Caesar himself, and his surprisingly close focus on Varro's position and self-fashioning is intriguing:

> Marcus Varro, in Further Spain when things first came to a head (and on learning of the state of affairs in Italy), was in doubt about the Pompeian cause and used to speak in extremely friendly terms about Caesar. He took the line that, although his post as legate formally gave Gnaeus Pompey first call on his loyalty, nevertheless there was little to choose in differentiating it from his esteem for Caesar. <u>He was not unaware of what constituted the duty of a legate</u>—one who held a position of trust—nor of his own resources, nor of the inclination of the whole province in Caesar's favor. These concerns featured heavily in his conversation, and he made no decisive move for either party [*Haec omnibus ferebat sermonibus neque se in ullam partem mouebat*]. But afterward, when he learned that Caesar was detained before Massilia and that the forces of Petreius had brought the army of Afranius to battle, that significant reinforcements had come to their assistance, that both hope and expectation were great, and that the whole province of Nearer Spain had banded together; on learning of these, taken with what straits befell Caesar after Ilerda when provisions were in short supply, plus Afranius' extensive and inflated communique, <u>he began to match his moves to those of fortune</u> [*se quoque ad motus fortunae mouere coepit*]. (Caes. *BCiv.* 2.17)

Caesar's dry and often sardonic stop-press account suggests that by the early 40s, Varro's attention to both men was judiciously and minutely balanced ("three heads" become "two") and that he both recognized the rapidity of political shifts and the mutability of roles and took steps to keep himself a little ahead of the game where possible.[43] To find a different perspective and add context, we can turn back a decade to Cicero's correspondence. Varro appears to have been tasked by Atticus (in 59) with operating on Cicero's behalf to influence Pompey, or at least Cicero presents it that way. Yet Varro's tactics gradually led Cicero to more and more open epistolary criticism as the months progressed; eventually he described him, in stingingly allusive Euripidean terms, as "'ἑλικτὰ καὶ οὐδέν'" (crooked, and nothing) but also seemed to offer a waspish, albeit rueful, justification for Atticus' unpredictable friend: "'τὰς τῶν κρατούντων'" (the follies of the powerful).[44] It is easy to see why Cicero might have felt that Varro was self-serving and duplicitous and perhaps even politically naive (especially if one knows the first of the Euripidean tags). Yet if the Τρικάρανος appeared at the time when the reality of the "First" Triumvirate began to bite and Cicero supposed Varro to be willing to act as a conduit or cypher, giving him another opportunity to influence Pompey ("*Multa per Varronem nostrum agi possunt*,"[45] much can be achieved through our man Varro), it must initially have seemed as if Varro were offering a useful tool for additional fine-tuning of Cicero's own political authority.

Tempori Seruiendum Est
(Cicero to Varro, "Go with the Flow," *Fam.* 9.7.2)

As 59 dragged on, Cicero's continuing self-assessment with regard to Varro and Pompey is illuminating:

> Varro is making things right for us; Pompey is fond of me, and holds me dear. "Do you believe that?" you ask. I believe it all right, he totally persuades me, but that's because I want to believe. Pragmatists, in every work of history, maxim, and even poem, advise caution and warn against trust. I follow the former (in that I am cautious), but the other, not to trust, I just can't do that [*facere non possum*]. (Cic. *Att.* 2.20.1)

Cicero seems to propose here that Varro's good offices were by this time about as credible as Pompey's affection. Cicero positions himself as appropriately cautious but—if he has a fault—still a believer in an essential bond of trust between good men. Yet his comments make it clear that trust is increasingly contingent. Pompey was very much not, by this time, Cicero's true friend (if the subsequent unfolding of events is our guide), and if we read this against Caesar's comments quoted earlier (*BCiv.* 2.17), then Varro had perhaps also seen that Cicero's underlying political inflexibility ("*facere non possum*") might bring him down.

Cicero and Caesar both, in different ways, identified Varro as someone who ran with the hare and hunted with the hounds (Cicero, with a melancholy bitterness). As Caesar's closing comment suggests, he may also have seen something of his own opportunism in Varro's tactics: the ability to follow fortune's lead (or, more poetically, to seduce Fortuna to one's cause) was also part of Caesar's bag of tricks.[46] Varro, in the meantime, was off the grid politically for much of the 50s but must have continued to maneuver between both sides. Cicero's exile (58–57) sheds further light on the friendship. In September 58 Cicero referred to Varro as a kind of proxy correspondent via Atticus,[47] but he clearly also maintained hope of more concrete support: commenting in understandably self-pitying terms to Atticus, he observed that "Varro's talk [*sermo*] builds my hopes of Caesar; on which note, it would be helpful if Varro himself put his back into the cause! Which *of course* he'll do of his own accord [*profecto cum sua sponte*], not just at your instigation."⁴⁸ Nonetheless Varro clearly maintained relations of some sort (however sentimental or nostalgia driven) with Pompey, whom he rejoined from Hispania at Dyrrachium late in 49, along with Cicero.

Cicero was bitterly funny, perhaps unintentionally so, on the atmosphere in the Pompeian camp at Dyrrachium at this stage. He observed in a letter from 46 that he and Varro were considered by many of the more bellicose to be fellow travelers at best, a judgment based on Varro's "inclinations" and Cicero's "speeches."⁴⁹ After the final defeat at Pharsalus (in 48), Varro returned to Italy. We can turn to Cicero's treatise on divination for clues as to how regretful Varro might subsequently have felt about the general mood in the last days and about his necessary but unenviable position on the wrong side. Presenting his thoughts as part of a conversation with his brother Quintus, set on his lovely Tusculan estate, Cicero "recalls" how Gaius Cosconius brought a disturbing prophecy to the Pompeians at Dyrrachium; this Rhodian oarsman's bloodthirsty vision of destruction, flight, and conflagration caused only concern to brother Quintus but put "those learned men," Varro and Cato, into a state of utter terror ("*doctos homines, uehementer esse perterritos*").⁵⁰

Many former Pompeians benefited from Caesar's famous clemency in the aftermath of Pharsalus, and although Cicero identified Caesar's *clementia* as evidence of a kind of cunning, a populist gesture rather than the mark of a truly humanitarian spirit, he himself was perfectly capable of grandstanding to Caesar on the theme when it suited.⁵¹ One might imagine a tinge of schadenfreude in Varro's reminiscence, two decades on, of the tangled and intense loyalties of these years and the twists and turns in his own fortune and that of Cicero, subsequent to that storied and prophetic night, far from home.

Without any way of accessing something like Varro's own version, any understanding of his self-fashioning during the years of Caesar's growing autocracy is highly speculative. Nevertheless, since the first year of his return to Rome after Pompey's defeat saw the dedication of a major work—*Antiquitates Rerum Diuinarum*—to Caesar as Pontifex Maximus, we can assume that he was heavily engaged in research and writing during the 50s.⁵² Since Caesar had held the position of Pontifex Maximus since 63—when he ran a lavish election campaign—it seems more than likely that the dedication from Varro was part of a long-term strategy. In tandem, around this time Varro may have produced a posthumous tribute of sorts to Pompey, in three books, *De Pompeio*; such a project, at that historical moment, might well have increased his attraction (for Caesar) as a man who "can't be bought."⁵³ As Varro gazed back over the balancing act he performed during this era, he might have allowed himself a certain self-satisfaction. Despite maintaining the right to a political and military public presence (unlike Atticus) and serving loyalties that seem occasionally at least not to have aligned with his inclinations, he had succeeded in sculpting a persona that would, in the end, guarantee his survival: Varro the polymath. Crafting this identity clearly played to his scholarly and intellectual inclinations, but it also demonstrates his mastery of the gamesmanship the era required.

That theirs was a deadly game, played out in every aspect of Roman existence, can be seen in Cicero's comment to Varro (sitting things out in Tusculum) in April 46: "we need to avoid men's eyes, even if we're unable to avoid their tongues: those who flaunt their victory also need players for the role of vanquished, while those who are most vexed about the vanquished lament our survival."⁵⁴ Cicero's emphasis on the physicality of speech and its potency (*lingua*, the tongue, licks speech into place as it muscles men into roles) connects it directly to the display and performance culture of elite Roman society.

With this as his context he set out their next, shared challenge: managing their visibility and concomitant susceptibility to attack because of their status as figureheads and survivors.⁵⁵

> Cicero to Varro, Rome, c. 22 April 46:
> Just let us hold firm on one thing: to live united in our studies [*una uiuere in studiis nostris*]. In former times we sought them out for pleasure, now they prove our salvation. We won't refuse, if anyone should wish to call us in (whether as architects or even as laborers) to work on the Republican construction site [*non modo ut architectos uerum etiam ut fabros, ad aedificandam rem publicam*]—in fact we'll happily make the running. If our efforts are useful to no one, still our task is to read and write "Republics" [*tamen et scribere et legere πολιτείας*]. If the Curia and the Forum are unavailable, well, we'll remake them in our writing and through our books, like the old school polymaths [*ut doctissimi ueteres*], and we'll serve the commonwealth [*gnauare rem publicam*] by means of our research into custom and law [*de moribus ac legibus quaerere*]. (Cic. *Fam.* 9.2.5)⁵⁶

Much has been written in recent years about the ancient "Art of Memory" and its concretizing and topographic qualities.⁵⁷ It is impossible that Varro's retrospective stroll through the vaults and porticoes of his memory would not have been densely textured by busts of Cicero and snippets from his extensive repertoire; this was, after all, the man who described Varro as Rome's ultimate *cicerone*.⁵⁸ As Cicero observed, an enthusiasm for research is what characteristically united the two men, but *quaero* is not simply "seeking," it is also "questing": this is the public intellectual as action hero, searching for something lost, something that has been missed, a pursuit at once intellectually charged and contemplative.⁵⁹

Cicero's "*ut*" connects Cicero and his addressee to men who were by then alive only in memory and tradition ("*una uiuere*," a heroic comradeship). *Facio* makes real the Republican construction project that Cicero specifies for the two men and nudges readers to make a connection with mnemotechnics (making spaces into an aide-mémoire and designating them as sites encouraging recall and reinvention), but we have already been sent in this direction ("*ut architectos . . . ut fabros, ad aedificandam rem publicam*").⁶⁰ (A little ironic, given Cicero's wry response to Atticus' request for a speaking role for Varro in *De Republica*.)⁶¹ Whether sitting in the halls of Pollio's library, in his own study, or in whatever shady spot he chose for contemplative relaxation, Varro must have let his mind too wander back to the quirky and occasionally uncomfortable relationship between the two men.

Varro, unlike Cicero, seems to have found a way to reconcile his desire to be of service to the res publica with a remarkable skill in avoiding contentious factionalism when tackling themes of public interest.⁶² According to Suetonius, Caesar soon reciprocated the scholarly dedication of the *Antiquitates* (and confirmed Varro's status as a public intellectual): he commissioned Varro to create a public library for Rome.⁶³ Caesar's assassination brought that plan to a halt; the reversal in Varro's fortunes was completed when he found himself on Antony's proscription list, losing significant properties but ultimately keeping his life.⁶⁴ An interesting contemporary tell on Varro's relationship with Caesar is that the man who then interceded with Antony on his behalf, Q. Fufius Calenus, was not just a friend of Antony (and opponent of Cicero) but also a long-term, staunch Caesarian.⁶⁵

Although we can assume that Varro kept his head down for the following decade, he clearly maintained significant connections and a sufficiently lustrous scholarly persona that he was honored with a portrait bust in the public library project for Rome when it was revived under the auspices of C. Asinius Pollio (another partisan of Caesar); Pollio returned from military success in Parthia with the money and resources to make a lavish foundation as part of the restoration of the Atrium Libertatis, sometime in the early 30s.⁶⁶ The distinction of being the only living Roman to have a portrait bust on display in the new library must have been a sweet one, particularly in the political and social turmoil of the breakdown of the Second Triumvirate and the years of renewed civil war. I like to imagine Varro settling into his years of political retirement at work in the reading room of Pollio's library, enjoying the glory of his immortalized marble (or perhaps bronze) self gazing serenely and instructively on librarians and scholars alike.

Just as the details of where Varro spent his time after his brush with Antony are unknown, setting dates to items in Varro's catalog of works is also for the most part impossible. The 30s, still turbulent, still violent, must nonetheless have been a fertile time for Varro's writing and research (somewhere out of sight), but even during his most active political and military years Varro had clearly managed to continue to maintain his scholarly interests and his sense of self as an author. As he scrutinized his achievements with the hindsight of extreme old age, even if many of his companions as well as his estates were lost to him, the extraordinarily diverse and fertile imagination and curiosity that characterizes his vast body of work must have seemed guaranteed to provide textual immortality.

Cicero's Dedication to Varro

The theme of reciprocity to which Cicero alluded when writing to Atticus in June 45 (*Att.* 13.12.3) recurs in the (not much) later *De Officiis*. Cicero hints that scholarly reciprocity may be a less straightforwardly benevolent exchange than the notional model would suggest: "what do we do," he asks, "when the favor [*beneficio*] is provocative?"[67] Despite Cicero's ongoing fossicking for a book of Varro's to call his own, the (re)dedication of *De Lingua Latina* to Cicero (what survives is the opening of book 5, so this is not the headliner) is hardly vivid; indeed, Cicero's name does not feature in it.[68] One might wonder how Cicero could see the work as adding widespread luster to his reputation or being promoted by him;[69] a more extensive dedication may well have headed the work, assuming it was received by Cicero in his lifetime, but at best it dropped out of the text in transmission.

Thus, Cicero's comments to Atticus concerning the dedication of his *Academica* and how to include Varro suggest that Cicero never fully managed to conquer his unease concerning Varro's attitude toward their friendship: after two years of "running hard without advancing a length," Varro seemed no nearer to completing the promised dedication of a "doubtless magnificent and weighty" work to Cicero.[70] When Cicero calls Varro a "Kallippides" in his working habits, in this context, there may also be proverbiality in play. Later, the emperor Tiberius was (Suetonius recounts) jokily known as that well-known

Greek Kallippides by all and sundry because he kept promising to tour the empire, only to remain at home.[71] An emperor (or a person) going nowhere fast.[72]

To get a flavor of what Cicero might have hoped for from such a dedication (in its ideal form), we can turn to his eventual letter of dedication to Varro (of the *Academica*), in July 45, which I present in full:

> To lobby for largesse [*munus flagitare*], albeit promised—even the masses don't make a habit of that, unless incited. Still, your promise has whetted my anticipation [*ego exspectatione promissi tui moueor*], moving me to offer a gentle reminder (not to lobby you) [*ut admoneam te, non ut flagitem*]. But in that vein I send you four unbashful monitors. You're well aware of the "front" of the juvenile Academy: what I'm sending you is straight from the hub. <u>They</u>, I fear, may lobby you, even though their mandate is only to request.
>
> Indeed, I've been on tenterhooks for some time and restraining myself from composing something for you first, before I'd received yours; that way I could repay you with a gift of similar value [*possem te remunerari quam simillimo munere*]. But since you are making rather slow (that is, as I make sense of it, <u>careful</u>) progress [*tardius . . . ut ego interpretor, diligentius*] I just couldn't hold back from publicizing the bond of enthusiasm and affection that we share, by means of a literary work of the kind that suits my capabilities. I have therefore staged a conversation between us at Cumae, together with Pomponius [Atticus]. To you I have assigned the parts concerning Antiochus (I reckoned myself to be right in assuming your approval); what concerns Philo, I've taken for myself. I think that on reading you will be surprised that we've been in discussion about something which we have <u>never</u> discussed, but you know how Dialogues go. In future (late in the day, perhaps), my dear Varro, such conversations will flourish, if it suits and for our own benefit; let the Fortune of the republic take responsibility for past events, the present is in our charge.
>
> How I wish that we could pursue our interests in peaceful times and, even if not <u>quite</u> constituted right, in a settled community! Yet in that case, other affairs would intrude on us, bringing honorable responsibilities and tasks; for now, what would existence be without the life of the mind? Even with my studies I scarcely cherish life; take them away and that small existential pleasure is gone. But much more on this when we're together.
>
> I wish you happiness in your change of address and your purchase and think you're doing the sensible thing.
>
> Take care, and keep well.[73] (Cic. *Fam.* 9.8)

Here, Cicero makes explicit how much he has to gain by the promised but delayed gift exchange.[74] The language plays with a hard-nosed vocabulary of political obligation and trade. This address revels in the nuances that the rhetoric of dedication and its faux-contractual nature can evoke. The opening gambit is especially juicy: Cicero, mock-*déclassé*, lumps himself in with the worst of the rabble at a time when the life-or-death aftershocks of street violence and mass political bribery were still fresh. The conjunction of *exspectatio* (an object of desire, as some thirteen years earlier Varro's good word had already been for Cicero)[75] and *promitto* (to promise, but with an potential sense of presage, prophesy or forebode) suggests uncertainty.[76] *Munus* hints at a municipal function or duty, and for citizens enjoying the benefits of a *municipium* its mutuality encourages the social bonds that gift exchange enhances. In their shared (and necessary) expenditure on municipal upkeep, citizens de facto create and maintain the town by gifting it to themselves physically and ethically. This, of course, is Varro on *munus*.[77] By linking *munus* to *flagito*, Cicero has decoupled its positive associations and contaminated the productive reciprocity that one might have expected in this dedication.[78] Within a couple of years, Varro would turn the tables in the promised work, *De Lingua Latina*, and recall Cicero to the publicly productive, civic meaning of the term.

Cicero acknowledges the intellectual and psychological complexity of this letter and its context in a letter, written shortly after, to Atticus:

> But why is it that you shake in your shoes [*perrhorrescas*] when I let you know that it's at your risk [*tuo periculo*] that the books are to be given to Varro? Even at this stage, if you have any doubts, speak up. I think the books are spot on. I want Varro to have them, especially since he is keen, but you know him: "a man to be feared; quick to blame even the blameless."[79] So there often comes to mind his face, grumbling perhaps that "my" case in the books is more lavishly argued than "his." . . . But anyway I do not despair of Varro's approval [*ego non despero probatum iri Varroni*], and, given our expenditure on the oversize paper, I'm happy to stick to the plan. . . . But please tell me, didn't you rather like my letter to Varro [*ualdene tibi placuit*]? Curse me if I ever again take such pains over something [*Male mi sit umquam quicquam tam enitar*]! (Cic. Att. 13.25.3)

In an elegantly understated discussion of the previous year's correspondence between Cicero, Varro, and Paetus, Eleanor Leach observes that this was Cicero's most ebullient period of epistolarity, with about a quarter of the *Ad Familiares* (as they stand) dating to this era.[80] As she goes on to remark, the sequences that link Cicero to Varro and to Paetus have "a self-conscious artistry" that "appears most significant when viewed from an interpretive perspective focused upon Cicero's anxieties of personal identity experienced amidst the disorienting circumstances of Caesar's dictatorship."[81] Indeed colored differently, this works equally well for the letters I have been considering. When Cicero makes himself (by Homeric quotation) Patroclus to Varro's Achilles, Cicero's spin on what might be behind the rivalrous tension that these letters illuminate breaks cover.[82]

Cicero both did and did not acknowledge Varro's scholarly ascendency, but, by claiming him as a character (in the letters but also of course in the *Academica*), Cicero achieved a measure of control over Varro's image and in particular over his posterity. Cicero's letters and treatises survive, by design, and in doing so they eclipse Varro's lost back catalog and overwhelm (for the most part) Varro's authorial self-fashioning. Cicero's Varro, like his other characters, is designed to offer a rich vein of contrast and dialogism within which Cicero can situate himself to suit the moment. For that to work, Cicero's Varro needs to be both significant (he must seem to be a trophy) and also less perspicacious than his author (outside the scholarly realm, at least). This makes Varro Cicero's clever and well-regarded but ultimately plain best friend.

Cicero's tone over the long course of the correspondence with and *about* Varro, worrying away at their political and intellectual points of convergence, is suggestive. It implies a recognition of the intimate connection between the two men and a concern with understanding how and why their paths diverged and crossed, despite the ostensible parallelism that would seem at first glance to have been inevitable. Writing to Varro in June 46, Cicero tried to cut a long story short, acknowledging that his control of discourse had failed him ("*longius quam uolui fluxit oratio*") and that what he *really* wanted to highlight was his vision of Varro as a Great Man (with all the Pompeian grief that might also imply), rich in the skills of intellectual husbandry, a great survivor:

> For I have always made you for a Great man [*te semper magnum hominem duxi*], and continue to: in this stormy weather you are almost unique in reaching the harbor. You gather to yourself [*percipis*] the greatest [*maximi*] fruits of learning [*fructusque doctrinae*], so that in the objects of your contemplation and your manner of conduct [*ea consideres eaque tractes*] you find habitual fruition and delight [*usus et delectation*] that far outstrip the exploits and "pleasures" [*actis et uoluptatibus*] of the indiscriminate masses [*omnibus istorum*]. (Cic. *Fam.* 9.6.4)

The perfect form "*duxi*" seems to play on *dux* (commander), as *magnus* hints at Pompey the Great;[83] the pun, along with a nod to the commonplace of the ship of state, intensifies the political nuances of this passage.

Back in April 46 (*Fam.* 9.2.5), we saw Cicero fashioning a relationship with Varro in which the two were united in a life of scholarship ("*una uiuere*"), and this is the paradigm that foregrounded the *Academica* when he recast it for Varro: Varro is tied to Atticus and Cicero alike through their shared studies and their long-standing friendship.[84] Ultimately this will be wherein greatness lies—a "triumvirate" of the mind, designed for a new era.[85] This reading finds support in Cicero's letter dedicating the *Academica* to Varro (*Fam.* 9.8, presented earlier), where his tendency to push the responsibility of influencing Varro onto Atticus in their correspondence becomes a vision of the trio as complementary equals. Nevertheless, Cicero's seemingly tentative assertion of his ability to judge what Varro might approve of ("*quas a te probari intellexisse mihi uidebar,*" *Fam.* 9.8) hints at the fiction and undermines the vision of a shared agenda uniting like minds. The fictional quality of these dialogues is part of their shtick, and Cicero acknowledges as much; this is the version "for public consumption."[86]

Working this out, we have the sequence of letters from June through August in which Cicero continued to look to Atticus for approval of the project and a gloss on Varro's response to and appreciation of the dedication.[87] Choice among Cicero's comments are his request that Atticus explain his intelligence that Varro was eager for a "Cicero" to call his own (*Att.* 13.18) and his remark on how Atticus is wrong in assuming that Cicero has bagged Varro as a speaking character in order to bask in the glory of the trophy, especially since his rendition of Antiochus on behalf of Varro is both intellectually acute and, apparently, more stylish than the original (*Att.* 13.19.3, 5). Nevertheless, Cicero continued to doubt the whole enterprise as the summer months drift by, and then in August silence descended on the project. We have no further letters from Cicero to Varro after the dedicatory letter of July 45 (*Fam.* 9.8), and parsing this abrupt excision of the matter from the published correspondence (no mention of the dedication, either, in subsequent letters to friends) is tricky.[88]

Atticus, the man who in many respects acted as a kind of publisher (it may be better to think in terms of agent) for Cicero, was also the editor (or, perhaps, the curator) of their personal correspondence.[89] It seems likely therefore that Atticus actively chose to preserve the sequence of querulous letters from Cicero concerning Varro and the *Academica* with an eye to their wider impact; there is, however, no certainty that subsequent letters on the topic (or an eventual dedication from Varro) did not exist, and if they did, we have no way of knowing how they might have transformed the canonical *Ad Atticum*.⁹⁰

A Citizen Inscribed

O wretched roof... Marcus Varro meant this for a place of study, not a voluptuary's lair [*libidinum deuersorium*]. In former days, imagine what conversations [*dicebantur*], what deep thought [*cogitabantur*], what literary endeavors [*litteris*] that villa used to host! The laws of the Roman people, memorials of our ancestors, a systematization of all knowledge and of all learning [*iura populi Romani, monumenta maiorum, omnis sapientiae ratio omnisque doctrinae*]. (Cic. *Phil.* 2.104, 105)⁹¹

In all of this, Varro's political identity has remained curiously intangible, but in Cicero's comments on Varro's *fortunae* in his second *Philippic*, the quoted passage's reverberation between worldly goods (plural) and "good fortune" not only belatedly recalls Caesar's comments on Varro's ability to nose out Fortune's drift;⁹² it also offers a telling juxtaposition for Varro—the two complimentary trios characterizing Varro's tenure as *dominus* of the Villa at Casinum.⁹³ Read straight, this passage is a noteworthy reinscription of Varro as a guru through whose vital good offices the *populus* (Rome at large) could still, in 44, best access and express its (ideal) real nature. It is through Varro's example that Cicero pairs speech with the laws of the people, matches considered thought with the instantiation of ancestral worthies, and links written composition with the sum of all knowledge.

Cicero (and others) found themselves in an impossible position regarding "popularity" in this era.⁹⁴ Back in the 60s, one might have agreed that "the relationship between conflict and consensus [was essentially] complementary rather than contradictory,"⁹⁵ but times had already changed. In the mid-40s, Cicero's Varro, "*sanctissimi atque integerrimi*" (Cic. *Phil.* 2.103), a figure wholly self-sufficient in his identity as scholar-citizen despite attacks on his property, might hint at an optimistic *modus vivendi*.⁹⁶ Yet the lingering impression from this passage is of the untouched and self-sufficient citizen whose withdrawal embraces alternative and less positive nuances from the superlatives *sanctissimus* and *integerimus*: mortality or old age, disengagement, and indecision.⁹⁷

Cicero's surviving textual corpus at least gives many instances of *populus* in context across his authorial career. What can be said about Varro's position on the role of the *populus*? Inasmuch as we can tell, it seems closely entwined with his tribal and ancestral self-fashioning. Peter Wiseman's working hypothesis that Dionysius of Halicarnassus' *Antiquitates Romanae* represents an annotated version of Varro's *Antiquitates Rerum Humanarum et Diuinarum* offers an intriguing prospect for fleshing this out.[98] Wiseman's detailed argument makes its case cumulatively rather than conclusively, but it offers an attractive framework.

In the first place, Wiseman nudges readers to think again about who Varro was and where he was from—the matter of local loyalties among Rome's political class. Varro led us to believe that he belonged to the Quirina tribe and traced his roots to the Reatine territory.[99] By tribal name, then, and through the complex semiotics of what constituted the different aspects of Roman tribal identity, Varro more than Cicero was familially and semantically embedded in an authentic world of pre-Roman settlement. This also flavored his deployment of the *langue* and the *parole* of the power structures that cannibalized the early stories to generate a type of autochthony (the metamorphosis of Quirinus into Romulus).[100]

An example of Varro's thinking on the relationship between private citizens and magistrates displays an astonished disappointment that, by his own time, magistrates were so protected from the people that legally and physically they were virtually untouchable; indeed, surrounded by their entourages, they actually disrupted popular ownership of civic space.[101] The tone and sense may represent a Varronian formulation of the commonwealth: a positive emphasis on the role of the *populus*.[102] We see that the same positive emphasis continued to be evident in *De Lingua Latina* and in *De Re Rustica*. By contrast, after his speeches against Verres, Cicero's published rhetoric made little positive capital out of the role of the "people" as a valuable partner for the senate.[103]

This could reflect Cicero's increasingly jaundiced perspective on popular politics and a growing disbelief in the potential for a popular reclamation of the conservative center ground. Back in 70, in the wake of Sulla's empowerment of a greedy aristocracy and removal of the traditionally negotiated balance between senate and the people, Pompey's reinstitution of the key civic posts of censor and tribune by popular demand must have heralded (for Cicero) a new era of mature collaboration in which a valid role was owed to the people, writ large. Within a decade, the détente was at an end. Letters from the late 60s and into the 50s vividly signal Cicero's bitterness at the "popular" betrayal of Roman ethos and mores when the price was right.[104]

By contrast, the figure of the Varronian scholar, politically astute, in command of the tiniest nuances of language, could stand as a leader of the *populus* as an entirety: SPQR. This was a figure whose ability to make sense of the competing claims of discourse and usage and to distinguish between the false friends of grammatology and poetic authority in exploring the innate, naturally powerful qualities of Latinity, really could effect change.[105]

While it may be that "in the years that saw the assassination of Julius Caesar and Marcus Tullius Cicero, no inevitable logic compelled an author to stuff twenty-five books with etymologies and obsolete words,"[106] nonetheless *De Lingua Latina* made perfect sense in just this fractious political context—not just as a retreat from dangerous engagement but as a timely intervention in the discourse of civics. Thus, what *De Lingua Latina* says about *populus* merits a closer look. In books 8–10 the lively debate between Regularity and Irregularity (to which I return in chapter 4) illuminates a different quality of frustration with the citizen body to that displayed by Cicero and offers glimpses of the inevitability of a unifying position.[107]

In book 8 readers find inflected forms to be emblematic of a human disinclination for hard work (the other class of nouns, those sui generis, have to be learned). More positively, they are also indicative of the heuristic flair that characterizes cognition. As soon as words enter the *langue*, popular command of *parole* (that is, *consuetudo* or usage) means that by definition the whole people without hesitation is immediately speaking the declined forms ("*sine dubitatione eorum declinatus statim omnis dicit populus*," *Ling.* 8.6). This representation of the *populus* as by nature authoritative agents of embedded linguistic vitality is lightly compromised by the subsequent comment: new slaves, entering a large household, can do the trick, too. But, rather than being a blunt comment on popular speech, this instance is indicative of the difference between slave and citizen speech: slaves quickly learn grammatically to manipulate the names of a defined subset of entities (fellow slaves), whereas the *populus* is working with an infinite verbal palette, by nature theirs.[108]

Near the beginning of book 9, Varro plunges deep into the issues surrounding Regularity and Irregularity. *Parole*, Varro observes, drives both word families to flourish.[109] He proceeds to state that some words are locked into popular discourse, whereas others belong to individuals; but this is not simply a blunt comment on popular speech. Instead, this is about how rules (*ius*) apply differently to the linguistic usage of an orator and that of a poet.[110] Bloomer suggests that the poets "offend" Varro (*Ling.* 9.5) but eventually moves toward a formulation closer to my point: the poets are a special category of the *populus* and function (if appropriately handled/controlled) as a vital linguistic force (and new blood).[111] Taken together, Varro's choice of *copula* to characterize what binds and distinguishes words (a community of the unwilling) and how interpersonal relationships become instantiated in spoken language hints at a humane and flexible interpretation of how speech and culture intersect.[112]

A people ("*populus uniuersus*"), Varro implies, needs a systematized language in which shared meaning allows individuals to unite as a communicating entity. As a collective, the *populus* self-corrects when Regularity is endangered, drawing new norms out of anomaly. Thus, the people are the architects as well as the exponents and guardians of the paradigms that make sense of language and maintain its vitality. Varro develops this by way of the figures of the orator and the poet. For the individual orator, relentless imposition of Regularity is vexatious (*offensio*), helping neither himself nor (if an advocate) his clients— the orator needs to be securely plugged into the standard idiom of the people but also must be able to demonstrate a distinctively colored and idiomatically lively command of language (Irregularity). The poet, the extreme example, "*transilire lineas impune possit*" (can transgress all boundaries with impunity), commanding core common parlance (Regularity) and mainlining spoken or rhetorical idioms in ways that may or may not sit securely or straightforwardly intelligibly with standard parlance (Irregularity). This all works if the relationship between *populus, ratio,* and good governance is solid and ranks the *populus* above individuals:

> Ego populi consuetudinis non sum ut dominus, at ille meae est. Ut rationi optemperare debet gubernator, gubernatori unus quisque in naui, sic populus rationi, nos singuli populo.[113] (Varro, *Ling.* 9.6)

> I do not stand, in relation to the people's usage, as a master; instead it masters mine. As a helmsman ought to obey reason, as everyone on a ship should obey the helmsman, that's how the people ought to obey reason and individuals to obey the people.

Rome needs a new toolkit in order to capitalize on individual genius and inspired poetry. In acknowledging his relative rather than absolute authority, Varro also makes a subtle point about his expertise, in particular the significance of his critical and analytical faculties. This discussion moves back into focus when Varro turns to the dynamics of linguistic change, characterizing types of threat in terms that sound suspiciously rooted in current affairs:

> Quare qui ad consuetudinem nos uocant si ad rectam, sequemur . . . si ad eam inuitant quae est deprauata, nihilo magis sequemur, nisi cum erit necesse . . . nam ea quoque, cum aliqua uis urget, inuiti sequemur. (Varro, *Ling.* 9.18)

> Therefore those who call us toward common usage, if it is correct usage, we shall follow . . . if they entice us toward corruption we shall not follow,

except by necessity ... for by necessity we follow, unwilling, where force drives us.

The *populus*, Varro continues, has a duty to identify and foster exemplary and historic forms and modes (which will enhance language) and to suppress defective models. Individuals too have a (subordinate) part to play in this husbandry of *langue* through their deployment of universalizing and individuating exempla of their Roman speech.[114] Sometimes this means drawing in and assimilating new words because for Romans in this era it is possible and productive.

My final example for Varro's *populus* circles around a passage from book 10. Reaching book 10 (*Ling.* 10.15–16), Varro notes that his prime example of elective derivation is Romulus' imposition (*impono*) of the unexpected form "Roma" as a name. By not questioning this nomenclature, Romespeakers normalize something that is in fact unique. That Latin predates Rome is an issue that the extant text does not confront.[115]

Varro twice raises "Romulus" as a problem source of "Roma" when working through types of derivation in book 8.[116] Proper nouns (*nomina*, 8.80), Varro tells readers there, are distinguished by the specificity of their signifieds. These words embody unique singularities, but, more interesting, some proper nouns themselves derive from other proper nouns, creating word families that map onto real life. What Varro is alluding to on a personal level is how family names inflect and are gendered and how irregular yet time-honored this syntactical prosopography is. When talking territorially, we can see the cultural significance of this kind of exploration in the strong role given to the Trojan cycle in the proposed sample set: Paris and Helen but also Ilium from Ilus and Ilia from Ilium. Some people get their names from common nouns (for example, Albius from *album*). But in particular, here, exemplifying such lack of Regularity, we have the derivation from Romulus of Roma, and this is not comme il faut.[117] When Varro returns to this, he makes a strawman argument, one that will be relevant to my final example (from book 10):

Qui dicunt quod sit ab Romulo Roma et non Romula neque ut ab oue ouil*ia* sic a boue bouil*ia*,[118] <non> esse analogias, errant. (Varro, *Ling.* 9.50)

Those who say that since from Romulus comes Roma and not Romula, and since we don't get "oxfold" from "ox" in the way we get "sheepfold" from sheep, therefore there is no Regularity: they are misled.

For a start, the specter of autocratic foundation and its core semiotic anomaly is raised and connected to another proposition to expose the flaws in a hackneyed ("*Qui dicunt*") axiom.[119] Sheepfolds had cropped up in their more political guise early in book 8 (following discussion of the appurtenances of the *equites*. and succeeded by words marking up urban experience). The book 8 payoff was that the mini-catalog was end-stopped by a statement of the tangled relationship between city, citizen, and individual:[120]

> Quae in eas res quae extrinsecus declinantur, sunt ab equo equile, ab ouibus ouile, sic alia; haec contraria illis quae supra dicta, ut a pecunia pecuniosus, ab urbe urbanus, ab atro atratus. Ut nonnunquam ab homine locus, ab eo loco homo, ut ab Romulo Roma, ab Roma Romanus. (Varro, *Ling.* 8.18)

> Those things that in declension relate to external circumstances are: from horse, horse stable; from sheep, sheepfold; and thus others. These are the opposite to those that were mentioned above, such as: from money, moneyman; from city, city slicker; from black, in mourning. Thus sometimes from a man a place spins off and from that place, a man: so from Romulus, Rome, and from Rome, Roman.

The Ovile (or Ovilia), connected to the Villa Publica on the Campus Martius, herded citizens, like latter-day Arcadians, to vote in the Comitia Centuriata and Tributa. By the time Varro was writing, Caesar's planned redevelopment of this traditional and definitive political space was gaining dimensionality—the new Saepta Julia.[121] Varro's *bouilla* (*Ling.* 9.50; the near homophone still sparks if it stands even if reading *bouilia*) makes available a barbed paronomasia, echoing a punning "sheepfold" joke familiar to Cicero because he had used it himself.[122]

So, where's the humor? The town of Bovillae lay on the Via Appia, not far from Rome. Thought to have been an Alban colony, Bovillae was the location of the Julian family's ambitious claims to Alba Longa (and Venus) in the late second century.[123] It is not clear how vividly this fed into Roman political chatter, but it must have been useful and memorable enough to be revitalized as part of the ceremonies attending Augustus' death.[124] Bovillae can thus make this partly a story about Caesar, the Julii, and the ways in which language and power collaborate. For Cicero, however, another Bovillae story might more immediately spring to mind: the death of Clodius near a local shrine of Bona

Dea (what Cicero memorably called "the battle of Bovillae") and the ensuing turmoil, which found echoes in the aftermath of Caesar's assassination.[125]

To sum up on this: a Roman, self-identifying as *Romanus*, systematically aligns himself with an autocratic founder. This, despite speaking Latin, the name of a different potential foundational figure (Latinus), one recalling an older civilization.[126] The frisson between the two persists in Varro's emphatic characterization of Romulus' naming of Rome as an act of will (*imperite*), enshrined as Regularity by popular usage. "I call it nature [*natura*]," Varro observes, "when a name is universally accepted, yet without questioning the person who imposed it as to how he wants it to be inflected, we 'the people' inflect it as follows: *Romae, Romam, Roma*."[127]

Varro's Regularity thus also signals the possibility of a coalition of the willing that embraces and draws strength from a foundational anomaly (Romulus names Rome), acknowledges autocracy, yet also depends on popular waywardness and unexpected meetings of minds.[128] The result for popular *parole* and thus, in effect, for the collective *ciuitas* is that, because named entities are accepted as being irregularly labeled, no subsequent model of discourse normalization can ever fully harmonize a system. *Turbulenta necesse est dicere*" (speech *by necessity* became factious, *Ling.* 10.16). Elective derivation, exemplified by Romulus/Roma/Romanus, is at the root of this turmoil.[129] Language changes through consensus, it perforce produces cohesion, and the messiness at its heart is intrinsic to its functionality.

The Habits of Interesting Times

When Varro chose *erro* to express how some people lose sight of the truth (*Ling.* 9.50), he drew upon a verb closely and famously associated with himself (by Cicero, awaiting the much-delayed dedication of *De Lingua Latina*):

> [Cicero:] tum ego, "sunt," inquam, "ista Varro. Nam <u>nos in nostra urbe peregrinantis errantisque tamquam hospites</u> tui libri quasi domum deduxerunt, ut possemus aliquando qui et ubi essemus agnoscere." (Cic. *Acad.* 1.9)

> Then I commented: "Yes, that's the case, Varro. For when <u>we were in our very own city yet still wandering and straying as if strangers</u>, it was your books, so to speak, that led us home, so that we were at last able to recognize who and where we were."

The Rome conjured up by Cicero here is one in which every citizen is at once guest, stranger, and even tourist (*hospes*), characters trapped in a *nostos* that

Varro's guidance can draw to a conclusion. Varro's fractured survival as a three-dimensional author is a subject to which this book returns frequently; knowing where to mark the gaps that divide the flesh-and-blood author, the author spelled out via the word-after-word process of reading a text, and even the author-as-character is a vanishingly productive project. Even if Varro's "influence, not always at first-hand, was all pervasive," it remains a melancholy "tribute to his achievement" that "he has perished by absorption."[130] Nevertheless, an author such as Varro challenges readers to face up to the dilemmas of biographical criticism in ways that apparently better-known characters such as Cicero and Caesar do not.[131]

My introductory chapter proposed some of the ways in which a fragmentary corpus enriches contemporary understanding of Classics, itself a lacunose and highly personal discipline, in which texts and passages have survived and flourished at the whim of a relatively small and unrepresentative group of enthusiasts and scholars. The twenty-first-century culture of the *physical* book, in general, tends to force authors such as Varro well back in any line for a revival; delivering an economically viable and broadly attractive (that is, marketable) study of a text that is mostly blank space might seem an impossible challenge. Yet, as Nicholas Horsfall (quoted in the previous paragraph) observed, it is exactly because we have "lost" Varro that his former significance fluoresces; in a world of new technologies of reading and writing, of archiving, commenting, and editing, Varro becomes a powerful instrument for exploring textual networks and the power of the word at a granular level.

By commencing with the conceit of an aged intellectual and "retired" statesman, this chapter sought to inject additional color and life, however fanciful, into a surprisingly shadowy figure whose work echoes cavernously through the destructive and creative enthusiasms of his era. An exhaustive and minutely detailed autopsy is elusive and tends to drift often into territory controlled posthumously by Cicero, yet it is also in the relationship between these two men and its literary outcomes that we may find new ways of marking up the different public roles available to a literary-minded and politically engaged citizen in the late Republic. In *Language and Authority in "De Lingua Latina"* I tackle Varro expansively but also, by homing in on the literary and ideological qualities of narrative, structure, and reading experience in *De Lingua Latina*, maintain a close focus on what has been termed the *animus* of the work.[132] Through a sequence of close readings to illuminate the grain and texture of this version of Romespeak, subsequent chapters explore what made Varro not just required reading but the media intellectual of his day: the uniquely humane, allusive, witty, and weighty mode he adopted.

chapter 2

Romespeaking

Strategies for Citizens

[Cicero] "It is not such a distinction [*praeclarus*] to know [*scire*] Latin well as it is a disgrace not to know it, and it seems to me that it is less the characteristic of a good [*bonus*] orator than it is of all true Romans."[1]

THE THESIS OF THIS BOOK is that *De Lingua Latina* led Varro's audience on a journey of discourse enrichment, at the end of which all successful Romespeakers could contribute actively and consciously to a consensual civic ideal. This ideal, responsive to the era's politics of polarization and failing consensus, showed Varro's audience how to embrace a new kind of authority within which habit and practice (*consuetudo*), in the hands of his empowered readers, need not always be right (*anomalia*) to be good. Manuals often operate simultaneously as DIY guides, as signals that a topic is complex (because it requires explication), and as indicators of shared cultural aspiration to master or redefine new areas, in effect replacing technical complexity with simplicity and speaking to an "educated reading audience through which dedicated texts are circulated."[2] In this chapter, six sections work through a series of exemplary readings that shed light on Varro's Romespeak and prefigure the themes and narrative elements expanded upon in subsequent chapters.[3] Romespeak itself is the focus of the first section, followed by a section on memory and etymology. The next two sections explore the significance of narrative and discourse enrichment for Romespeak, while the final two sections bring action and eloquence into the mix.

Romespeak

It is never uncomplicated to try to read meaning into narrative; indeed, "language cannot produce [absolute] truth as a correspondence of the word-world relationship." It is, instead, "a tool used to achieve our aims and cope with the world," wherein words become meaningful when understood in use.[4] Varro's study of Latin offers a way of thinking about how and why certain groups of people organize their shared narratives and forms of expression distinctively (in my coinage, Romespeak) but also in a complex fashion. By the time Varro reaches his developed "consensus" position on grammar (*Ling.* 10), he has already shown the force of storytelling to create meaning through anomaly, adjacency, and syllogism (etymology). His grammatological family histories and omnivorous habits of quotation and citation show that what is satisfying and what creates a sense of authenticity is not always what is logically correct (*analogia*). The Varro of Cicero's *Academica* (1.9) enabled Romans at last "to recognize who and where we were"; yet, to become true authorities, readers of *De Lingua Latina* must understand not just what Varro says but also why *he* says it, in particular ways, and how context and focus make a difference to the meaning produced from each act of apprehension:

> Non reprehendendum igitur in illis qui in scrutando uerbo litteram adiciunt aut demunt, quo facilius quid <u>sub ea uoce subsit</u> uider*i* possit: *ut* enim facilius obscuram operam <M>yrmecid*is* ex ebore oculi uideant, <u>extrinsecus</u> admouent nigras setas. (Varro, *Ling.* 7.1)

> There should be no rebuking those who, in examining a word, add in or subtract a letter in order that <u>what underlies each phrase</u> can be more easily discerned: it is comparable to the way in which the eyes can more easily see Myrmecides' nearly invisible works in ivory when they are <u>set off</u> against black bristles.

This is the power of Varro's Romespeak: sometimes anomaly is necessary in order to achieve what is good for everyone, and to identify that hard-to-find sense there must be citizens trained in creative and skillful irregularity. This passage's simile, comparing the work of the linguist to the process of aiding the display of a work of art too fine to be immediately accessible, highlights the materiality of words and their real-life substance.[5] It also asserts the potential for artifice in words (like Myrmecides' ivories), their susceptibility to context, and the curatorial and occasionally transformative effort required to draw out or highlight their fullest array of meaning for the Roman public.[6]

Varro's handbook primes Romespeakers for participation in the thrills of the chase ("*haec captanda*," *Ling.* 5.5), with Latin a prize well worth taking ("*eo quo peruenire uolumus*," *Ling.* 5.5). To spot novelty that can become good practice is possible, through Varro, because Varro has illuminated not only the forest but the trees and the tracks ("*semitae*"), too (*Ling.* 5.5–6).[7] In this way Varro challenges Cicero, who, describing M. Antonius' oratory, makes clear that knowledge produces good practice that defines true citizens. Varro's Romespeak, in a remarkably generous way, enables the reverse. I suggest that Varro allows and endorses what Quintilian would later call "*auctoritas uerborum*" (Quint. *Inst.* 1.4), a pragmatic authority of words in use that is distinctive to and derives meaning from individual authors.[8] This is directly in competition not just with the ideas of Cicero—demonstrably less successful at playing long-game politics and also interested in etymology—but also with the thinking of Posidonius, the benchmark against which a specifically *Roman* project along Varro's lines must have been measured.[9] This Varro is a supporter of consensus (shared meaning) but also of the need to acknowledge and capitalize on productive novelty where it emerges with authority.[10]

I argued in chapter 1 that Varro's "*Roma*" has didactic force and informs his position on what *populus* signifies. Now we should consider how Varro discusses and contextualizes the terminology of speech. "*Dico originem habet Graecam quod Graeci* δεικνύω. *Hinc Ennius: 'dico qui hunc dicare'*": the originally Greek act of producing spoken words (*dicere*; despite textual wobbles, Varro must have had something like Kent's δεικνύω as the Greek source word) is linked to *dicare* (to show), a pairing authorized by Ennius—and, as a great, early, translator, he should know.[11] Varro reaches this assertion after a discussion of "elements" of speech and the discourse of naming (*Ling.* 6.51–60), before introducing a sequence of increasingly politicized actions and concepts that make plain what becomes possible when one has gained deep knowledge of semiotics, and he is also able to put that expertise into practice (ending up with the Roman triumph, at *Ling.* 6.68). This nexus attunes readers to what lies behind a series of key civic functions and institutions, to which Varro then turns.

Romespeak brokers power, and Roman order depends on Latin speech, uttered by those in command of their language. First, meet the judiciary: the *iudex*, judge, is the one who mediates a verdict ("*iudicare . . . ius dicatur; hinc iudex*," 6.61)—the pronouncement gains force by being spoken aloud and authoritatively in the appropriate context.[12] Similarly, the conduit to the power to dedicate ("*dedicatur*") a temple is a formula repeated after the pontiff by the magistrate ("*a magistrate . . . dicendo*"). In both instances the ability to control a pattern of words and deliver them at the right moment is instrumental in the generation of civic structure and cosmic order. From "information" ("*indicium*," another branch of "speech"), the public act of proclamation ("*indico*") follows.[13] *Dicere* operates here as the source of both, and the sequencing emphasizes a close generic relationship between communicative knowledge and the ability to act effectively and informedly. Despite uncertainties in the text at this point, *indico*'s association with the declaration of war, public disclosure, and formal evaluation effects this semantic twist.[14] The cognitive bundle is important, and I treat it extensively in chapter 6, but it is also narratologically significant for this introduction to Romespeak:

> ... indixit funus, prodixit diem, addixit iudicium; hinc appellatum dictum in mimo, ac dictiosus; hinc in manipulis castrensibus <dicta ab> ducibus; hinc dictata in ludo; hinc dictator magister populi, quod is a consule debet dici; hinc antiqua illa <ad>dici numo et dicis causa et addictus. (Varro, *Ling.* 6.61)

> [from "speaking" comes] ... : "he spread the word" about a funeral, "he appointed" [or perhaps, "deferred"] the day, "he passed judgment" on the case; from this was named the "catchphrase" in mime, and "witty." Hence, to the troops in camp: diktats from the generals; hence too the "dictates" of the game, and the dictator, master of the people, because he needs "to be declared" by the consul. From this come those old tags "'bought' for a pittance" and "for the sake of the 'lawsuit,'" and one "bound over" [for debt].

There is a lot going on here. Varro's episteme uses the dissemination of authority through different discursive modes as a bridging device and leads to a distinctive vision of the relationship between power, knowledge, and memory in Rome.[15] Funerals (*indixit funus*) were by this time affairs of chronic significance and life-and-death implications way beyond the obvious.[16] Publicizing a funeral could suggest a more than familial and reverential agenda and foregrounded the mnemonic power of a family's *maiores*. When Varro explicitly brings funerals into the discourse web of speech and leadership, he plays on etymology as what Mary Carruthers has characterized as an "inventional" technique "both for remembering and for further inventing"; as she goes on to sum up, this kind of etymologizing makes for "elaborately punning riffs of memory, that do to a word what jazz does to a written musical phrase."[17]

The formal and legal phrases that Varro turns to next (*"prodixit ... addixit"*) lead readers associatively to another performative context, the popular stage (*"dictum in mimo"*). This topos might recall the matter of wit and indeed control of laughter as political tools (*dictiosus*).[18] Varro's anaphoric *hinc* emphasizes and encourages a synoptic reading. An elite male funeral delivered "theater" (complete with masks) and speeches, and the kind of funeral that might become a major public event also connoted military power. In this context, to revisit *dictator* as a product of a mature and stable oligarchy has optimistic overtones. For this figure, authorization by the "consul" is matched by a necessary acceptance by "the people."[19] The closural tags about debt servitude, legal procedurals, and dodgy dealings underpin a sense that contemporary Roman mores are under scrutiny, but nothing here seems likely to topple the status quo.

Dico, Varro goes on to say, underpins "teaching" and "leading" (*doceo, duceo*); the generosity of speaking knowledge to another embodies its educative aspect, which in turn shows how teaching is also an exercise in leadership. With just the change of a few letters ("*litteris commutatis paucis*"), *ducere* gives rise to *docere* and, extending the principle, *disciplina* and *documenta*, that is to say (Varro states), "teaching-*exempla*."[20] Next Varro works through clarity and lucidity in *disputationes* and *sermones* (*Ling.* 6.63–64) from two perspectives. First (*Ling.* 6.63), he traces a connection from *putare* to *disputatio* and *computatio*, because long ago *putum* meant *purum* (clean). When words are arranged clearly and orderly (*pure*) so that there is no confusion and meaning is transparent, discourse (*sermo*) becomes discussion (*disputare*, "to discuss"). By contextual analogy, this is also a little bit like landscape gardening-cum-accounting (the *putator* tidies up trees; an account is reckoned up, *puto*, when "net," *pura*).

Varro's second bite at this takes readers to *dissero*, a word that has a metaphorical ("*translaticio*") as well as an "agricultural" dimension (*Ling.* 6.64).[21] The key point follows: an interrogation of *dissero*, in which Varro skillfully blends the homonymous forms to deliver a nexus of agriculture, kitchen gardening (how to succeed in speech: master organization by type and plot), and skilled speech (make the same moves as the gardener). Then, shifting the line of derivation laterally, "sequence" (*series*) spawns "discourse" (*sermo*), "garlands" (*serta*), productive diversity (one man alone cannot make a conversation), hand-to-hand combat, and how to set someone legally free. *Sermo* and speech reverberate throughout this discussion, and Varro emphasizes the significance of this material with a first-person introductory interjection ("*opinor*"); his readers could not get this story from just any source, only from Varro.

Shortly after concluding his discussion of the serial quality of *sermo*, Varro returns to *lego* (*Ling.* 6.66).[22] Unsurprisingly, *legere* matters and has a wide semiotic range; "choice" (and, by implication, election and voting) is crucial to any significant public expression of persona. This is the aspect with clear relevance for Romespeak and this chapter's discussion. As context, Varro eschews a glaringly obvious segue he might have made from *sortilegus*—a by-product of the Chancy business governing collegiality and (common) property—which he leaves almost as a throwaway in the previous section.[23] Instead, Varro's explanation of *legere* literally embodies choice as a species of selective understanding and definition; the eyes conceptualize, but with a real-world, corporeal dimension bringing together selection and reading/comprehension.[24]

Legere dictum, quod leguntur ab oculis litterae. (Varro, *Ling.* 6.66)

To choose/comprehend, because letters are chosen/comprehended by the eyes.

At least some of Varro's audience, familiar with Greek, surely expected allusion to λέγω, but Varro provocatively bypasses the homophone, significant especially after his insistence on the (to the eye) less obvious derivation of *dico* (*Ling.* 6.61).[25] *Lego* is marked up, in this way, as a verb of gathering and unifying but also one of perceiving, sorting and selecting, and even harvesting. All these senses feed into "reading" and the primacy of the eyes.

This route into the semiotic field of "reading" makes it a core citizen act, drawing together productivity, canniness, and a sense of collective identity. The subtle politics of this set of explanations comes through in the very next proposition: "*ideo etiam legati, quod <ut> publice mittantur leguntur.*"[26] This state-sponsored harvesting of the pick of the citizen crop for public service (pulling *legare* into the remit of *legere*) is echoed in the more literal grape and olive harvest that follows: here, the public-servant "legates" are echoed by the agricultural laborers, *leguli* (pickers).[27]

Item ab legendo leguli, qui oleam aut qui uuas legunt; hinc legumina in frugibus uariis; etiam leges, quae lectae et ad populum latae quas obseruet. (Varro, *Ling.* 6.66)

In the same way, from "picking" comes "pickers": those who "collect up" olives and grapes; hence, "pulses" in all their varieties. Likewise "laws," which "having been determined" are proposed to the people so that they might observe them.

With this set of derivations Varro encourages readers to contemplate the nitty-gritty qualities of hard work in tandem with the need to understand the impact of certain choices. He also neatly parallels the world of the agricultural laborer with that of the successful politician. A barbed dig at Cicero might have been evident, to Cicero at least, by way of Varro's Menippean comment "*sed uti serrate / haec legumina arte parua pauca, cicer, eruiliam*" (But one sows these *pulses* with scant skill: chickpea, vetch, *Sat. Men.* 244.2). The significance of this semantic field for *legumen* is evident when it reappears in Varro's late work *De Re Rustica*.[28] The intratextual momentum ending up with *De Re Rustica*—in addition to the name pun on "*cicero*" that only not-quite appears at *Ling.* 6.66— implies dialogue with Cicero, especially with his work on the nature of the gods (in progress in mid-45 and therefore very much on Varro's horizon):[29]

> [Q. Licinius Balbus]: "And so we have the earth [*terra*], flourishing with grain [*frugibus*] and all manner of pulses [*leguminum*], which she pours forth as the greatest largesse: would it seem that she produces all this to benefit wild beasts [*ferarum*], or mankind [*hominum*]? What shall I say about the vines and olives, whose copious and delightful fruits make no impact on animals [*bestias*] at all? For the herd [*pecudum*] has no knowledge [*scientia*] of sowing and cultivating, nor of the timely reaping and gathering of produce, nor of storing up and preserving; and so all these products are both enjoyed and tended by mankind." (Cic. *Nat. D.* 2.156)

Varro's politically organized and hardworking "gleaners" ("*leguli*"), sensible of a wide array of natural and civic propositions for survival as a collective, respond to Cicero's display of a Stoic ensemble of insensible wild beasts, dumb farm animals, and landsmen. Varro's Academic worldview, unlike that of Cicero's Balbus, finds in Romespeakers the primary organizational and generative force. This reading is underlined when Varro continues by directionally linking the foraging for firewood to the buildings that house a hearth and, finally (*Ling.* 6.66), the industrious ("*diligens*") organization that is the Roman legion, leading eventually (*Ling.* 6.68) to the Triumph.

To sum up: when discussing Rome's Latin speech terms (at *Ling.* 6.55–58 and 6.61–62), Varro is proposing a nexus that associates the terminology closely with publicly significant actions (*loqui, pronuntiare, dicere,* and others) but glossed by the kinds of activities that his landowning contemporaries might find most likely to be accomplished out of town. *Sermo* (conversation), *dissertus* (skillful in speaking), *serta* (garlands), and the cultivator who *disserit* (disseminates) filter in as the excursus progresses (*Ling.* 6.63–64), and together these words form a conceptually dense set of ideas. Collectively, they make up intentionally valuable elements in a heuristic scheme.[30] They invoke the kind of philosophical stroll through a conversational, cultivated landscape of *otium* familiar from Cicero's dialogic villa settings and a scenography that would eventually be developed extensively in *De Re Rustica*.

Romespeak and Etymology

Education and therefore processes of recall are the heart of Romespeak. Varro's model orients readers within Romespeak's domain by way of an agreed, shared systematization of memories and discursive prompts. Etymologies are crucial to the replication and renewal of this consensus. Carruthers has argued that they are not so much definitive explanations of meaning as they are beginnings of stories: generators of associative "markers that can help to orient and join up the ways that the story is 'ruminated' in people's minds," linking past to present meaningfully.[31] Early in book 7, discussing the historic-linguistic significance of Latin poetry, Varro shows how poems in themselves typically fail to record the nuances and life course of words and derivations; their readers need to work hard if they are to burrow down to the roots of words in a meaningful way.[32] By contrast, Varro's own etymologies make good on the family history of Latin, telling those stories that the poets failed to articulate (*Ling.* 7.3). In her study of ancient etymological thinking, Ineke Sluiter emphasizes just such a genealogical impetus in certain discursive practices, one that is focused on seamlessly bridging the gap between the present and the moment of a community's foundation.[33] Varro's approach is intelligible in these terms, especially when he continues the line of thought using an acutely Catonian metaphor:[34]

> si non norim radices arboris, non posse me dicere pirum esse ex ramo, ramum ex arbore, eam ex radicibus quas non uideo ... tamen hic docet plura et satisfacit grato, quem imitari possimusne ipse liber erit indicio. (Varro, *Ling.* 7.4)

> [it can't be stated that] if I don't know the roots of a tree, I am incapable of saying that a pear is from a branch, the branch is from a tree, which in turn is from roots which I do not have sight of ... such a person [giving it a go] still has much to teach and satisfies an appreciative audience. Whether we can make a similar contribution, this book will bear witness.

This in turn branches off from an earlier and equally vivid discussion of roots in language:

> Sed qua cognatio eius erit uerbi quae radices egerit extra fines suas, persequemur. Saepe enim ad limitem arboris radices sub uicini prodierunt segetem. (Varro, *Ling.* 5.13)

[concerning the primal classes of words] But wherever the family of the word we're interested in should be, even if it has forced its roots out beyond its natural territory, we'll still follow it. For often the roots of a tree by the property line will have advanced out under a neighbor's cornfield.[35]

Telling any story means tracing the path from root to branch and hooking events together in a meaningful and (this is crucial) memorable way. For this reason, it makes sense to introduce two "memory" passages (in book 6) as context before moving on to the "narrative" in the section "*Narro*: Telling Tales and Making Speech" in this chapter. The first passage (*Ling.* 6.43–44) addresses a family history built around *cogitare* and *cogitatio*; the second (*Ling.* 6.49) shows how, through *mens*, this clan relates to *meminisse, memoria,* and *monimenta*.[36] The plot is tangled but suggests an "ethical mediation" (Carruthers's phrase).[37]

Cogitare a cogendo dictum: mens plura in unum cogit, unde eligere possit. . . . A cogitatione concilium, inde consilium; quod ut uestimentum apud fullonem cum cogitur, conciliari dictum. Sic reminisci, cum ea quae tenuit mens ac memoria, cogitando repetuntur. Hinc etiam comminisci dictum, a con et mente, cum finguntur in mente quae non sunt; et ab hoc illud quod dicitur eminisci, cum commentum pronuntiatur. Ab eadem mente meminisse dictum et amens, qui a mente sua discedit. (Varro, *Ling.* 6.43–44)

Cogitare [to consider] is said to come from *cogendus* [continuity; to gather together; convene; harvest; compress; give form]: the mind gathers together several things in one place, from which it can make a selection [or "elect"]. . . . From *cogitatio* [consideration] comes *concilium* [council], and thence *consilium* [counsel]. Hence, when a garment is pressed at the laundry it's said to be put into proper shape. Thus *reminisci* [to call to mind] denotes those things that are held in the mind and memory and brought out of storage by deliberation. From this also comes the designation "to fabricate" [or invent a story; *comminisci*]: deriving from *con* [together] and *mens* [mind]. This is when things that have no existential reality are devised in the mind; and from here we reach what is termed *eminisci* [to think up; imagine], when the *commentum* [pretense] is spoken aloud. From this same *mens* [mind] we have the terms *meminisse* [to remember a fact, speech, or experience] and *amens*, used of someone who has taken leave of his senses.

The elucidation of *cogitare* in the context of memory exemplifies and sums up many of the etymological issues this section is interested in. It sits near the beginning of a phase in the text where Varro has signaled the need for his audience's renewed attention ("*admonui*," *Ling.* 6.40).[38] To advise (or warn), which is to show forethought and take part in public affairs, also marks a return to the storehouse of memory to draw allusions from the most apt comparisons, "*is qui monet, proinde sit ac memoria*" (*Ling.* 6.49)—he who reminds or advises is undertaking an act comparable to "remembering." In mnemotechnics, the "rememberer" is the key figure, central to the creation and articulation of narrativized memory. Varro condenses this by focusing on how the act of reminding (or warning) is akin to the creation of *memoria*, a role in which he has adroitly cast himself. How this frame of reference influences readers' informed command of speech is the focus of Varro's next narrative arc.[39]

Narro: Telling Tales and Making Speech

Varro arrives abruptly at *narro* (*Ling.* 6.51) and then moves briskly through *narus* (up to speed on, acquainted with, knowledgeable about) to generate the narrative that makes things happen: "*narratio, per quam cognoscimus rem gesta<m>*."[40] From here he turns to "that man speaks" ("*fatur is*," *Ling.* 6.52) and eventually to the *Fatuae*, the "loquacious" nymphs associated with Faunus/Fatuus (*Ling.* 6.55).[41] Speaking refers to the production of intelligible words in meaningful combinations or contexts, and this is what constitutes a grown-up, a Romespeaker capable of partaking in public life.[42]

> Fatur is qui primum homo significabilem ore mittit uocem. Ab eo, ante quam ita faciant, pueri dicuntur infantes; cum id faciunt, iam fari. (Varro, *Ling.* 6.52.)

> That person "speaks" who first produces from his mouth a meaningful utterance. From this, before they are able to do so, children are called "nonspeakers"; once they are able to do so, they are said "to speak."

Speech signifies agency, but the agency is not always vested in the one physically making the utterances; hence not all speech is Romespeak. This is illustrated by prophecy terms ("*fatuus*"), which have a narrative quality by virtue of their association with the activities of the Parcae (by speaking, *fando*, the Fates set a span for each individual life). From this Varro reaches *fatum*. Storytelling ("*narro*") is thereby intimately connected to the life-and-death moments of citizen experience: birth, first meaningful discourse, a life's destined trajectory, and extinction. But prophetic speakers and augurs are unusually complex because of the distinction between relaying prophecy and "speaking" truths. We see this tension as Varro considers eloquent speakers ("*facundi*").[43] Here, "fateful matters" ("*res fatales*") are part of a genealogy that leads to those who have a facility for speaking (ordinary speech, with a "c" from *facile*, becomes a kind of eloquence) in any of several distinct categories of speech act. Varro rams the point home with a showy display of alliteration—grabbing a stem from *uates* and hooking it up (by presenting an ipso facto morphological drift from "u" to "f") with *for, fari*:[44]

> qui fa<u>c</u>ile fantur fa<u>c</u>undi dicti, et qui futura praediuinando soleant <u>fari</u> fatidici; dicti idem <u>uati</u>cinari, quod <u>ue</u>sana mente faciunt. (Varro, *Ling.* 6.52)

> those who speak easily are called eloquent, and those who make a habit of speaking the future through foreknowledge are fate-sayers; they are also said to "prophesy," because they do this with frenzied mind.

Narrative design emphasizes the direct link between speech and the experience of citizenship. Legal and legitimate speech occupies "*fasti dies*" (*Ling.* 6.53), and the positive, appropriate utterance of magistrates in that context links *dies fasti* to their progeny: *dies nefasti*.[45] The nuancing of legitimate speech, surely an enormous concern in this era, leads Varro to augury, returning us to a vocabulary set that, readers will remember, Varro has already highlighted in his discussion of *ago*.[46] Through branches of speech, augurs set the celestial and (ex-urban) terrestrial limits for augury; thus, *templa* (to which I return in chapters 3 and 5) and *fines* proceed from augural speech acts.[47] In each case the augurs as speakers are themselves the generating force (or "authors") for this systematization of existence.

Hot on the heels of *templa* and *fines* comes Varro's elucidation of *fana* (sanctuaries). They are named in similar fashion because the pontiffs, in consecrating them, have also spoken (*fati*) their boundary. A full treatment of *fines* itself is missing (if it existed), but, by "speaking" the bounds of the key sacred civic topography into existence, Varro has selected a word that will crop up a couple of decades later when Vergil's Jupiter promises "'*imperium sine fine*,'" a formulation that Ovid would deploy in his own complex literary study of the legitimization of speech over time.[48]

After some comments on technicalities of sacrifice, Varro abruptly halts any perceived drift when he redirects attention back to *fari* and the wider world of communicative discourse (*Ling.* 6.55). *Fari*, the characteristic humane activity, is the very word that produces drama (*fabulae*) and, in turn, its subsets tragedy and comedy, expositions in different ways of human nature.⁴⁹ *Fari* introduces terminology of confession, response, questioning, while *fassi*, *professi*, and *confessi* are behind *fama* and *famosi*. Careless and imprecise or, alternatively, vicious and harmful speech thus joins with notoriety. This volatile combination leads to "deception" (the passive form *falli*).⁵⁰

"*Quod fando quem decipit ac contra quam dixit facit*"—just by speaking, Varro seems to suggest, one at the very least runs the risk of encountering chaos: a disjunction between speech, sense, and intent.⁵¹ Even nonverbal deception connotes language and the perversion of a semiotic system. Varro's analogy in wrapping up this complex is rather quaint: the "foot" is at once human and a part of a made object (bed) and also of a homely root vegetable (the beet). The range of associative interpretations for this cluster, immediately recognized or not, starts to form a community of meaning. *Pes* is potentially deceptive *because* it is so basically useful to even the most rudimentary community (foot, bed, beet). Participating in this community means always being alert for deception within the system but also recognizing that in deception lies a sign that shared meaning exists. If *res* did not tell stories, they could not tell lies.

Later, Varro comes at the question of how speech connects to cosmic forces from another angle. After concluding his discussion of *cerno* (including its role in defining how one wears one's hair, how one portions out one's estate, how one makes the life-or-death choices in battle), Varro moves on to *spectare*, presented as a descendant of a hoary old ("*antiquus*") word, *specere* (*Ling*. 6.82). The venerability is glossed with a quick-fire citation of Ennius (wherein one of Rome's enemies of the second century, Epulo of Istria, spectates, "*spexit*"),⁵² clearing the way for Varro to bring auspices back into the frame, recalling readers to a subtle potential for contingency within the stresses of contemporary politics.

> Et quod in auspiciis distributum est qui habent <u>spectionem</u>, qui non habeant, et quod in auguriis etiam nunc augures dicunt auem <u>specere</u>. (Varro, *Ling*. 6.82)

> And [we also have the term *spectare*] because in the taking of auspices there is a division: those who are on <u>observation</u> duty, and those who are not; in addition, because in the taking of auguries even now, the augurs say "<u>to observe</u>" a bird.

In the context of Varro's guarded warnings about seeing what you expect (whether with hope or fear), we hear now that, within the auspicial process, some but not all will have the right to partake in the formal "watch" ("*habent spectionem*," *Ling.* 6.82); more bluntly, at a given moment, some will have the power of observation and "right" (however constituted) perception and mediation of the vision, whereas others will not.[53] This is played out across a couple of other examples: scouts are the ones we send ahead, specifically to scope out what we want;[54] anyone can "see" the stars, but many, perhaps most, will misinterpret or wrongly translate what they see. The skill to know what one sees and to be able to express it is key, and, building specifically on the model of authorized Observation falling upon specific magistrates in the practice of augury, we see exactly how close the relationship is between civic ritual vision (enshrined in the practice-specific verb *specere*), speech (defining and producing the augural event), and, eventually, the resulting augury-sanctioned action.

Romespeak is the language of those who are comfortable with the power of words and discourse to affect reality, the most material literary manifestation of which is usually the inked scroll or the wax tablet. Varro locates the verb *scribo* among the primordial or origin words ("*primigenia dicuntur uerba ut lego, scribo, sto, sedeo et cetera,*" *Ling.* 6.37). Creating, processing, articulating, and inhabiting are all in play.[55] When "a man writes," what follows is that adjectives and adverbs spin off so that, by design, "a learned man writes learnedly." Thus, the primary encoded behavior in Varro's chosen *primigenia* makes the act of writing foundational. Words have metaphorical value as empowering tools of the trade, but they are also appropriate objects of study, the means to articulate that study, and the bridge between long-ago reality and the contemporary world (recall *Ling.* 5.5); words are also, therefore, community builders, shoring up a consensus on what constitutes civilization, shared truths, and values.

Glossing and Enriching

Romespeak means having control over the recounting of history (one new thing after another, given exemplary meaning through reflection and narrativization). When readers reach book 7, they find that command of Romespeak also embraces the poetic role of *uates* (telling the future as well as making sense of the past).[56] There (*Ling.* 7.36), Varro juxtaposes Latin Fauns (etymologized as *fari-fandus-Faunus*), woodland prophets that communicate in Saturnian verse, with the term *uates*—the "old" name for poets, applied to reflect their plaiting together (*uieo*) of verses.[57] *Vieo* will have been encountered earlier (*Ling.* 5.62), where a sequence of allusions ties life, sex, Venus, poetry, and conquest together, entwining the *uates* and the poet with the triumphant Venus (Pompey's patron; Caesar's ancestress, Rome's foremother).[58]

To arrive at Fauns, Varro begins (from *Ling.* 7.34) an arc starting from *camilla* (handmaid or female attendant), exemplified by a quote from Pacuvius' *Medus*; next, he moves to Samothracian mysteries, then to Callimachus, on to Ennius, and eventually to Etruscan pipers before arriving at Fauns. This is an excellent example of how Varro's cumulative and associative discourse enrichment functions, but what can this context tell us?

In Varro's book, *camilla* is a tricky term to gloss.[59] His use of *glossema* indicates that what we are engaged in is not just a mechanical process of translation ("*qui . . . interpretati*"); it concerns the scholarly unpacking of meaning, itself powered by antiquarian knowledge. The Greek γλώσσημα has a pedigree instantiated (now) only in the Aeschylean fragmentary tradition, so Varro might be hinting at a comparably dense interpretative tangle for Pacuvius' term.[60] Varro does not often use the term *interpretor* or the other forms related to *interpres*, and, given the ostensibly practical nature of his handbook, this in itself might seem surprising. Perhaps this setup indicates Varro's interest in encouraging his audience to think about which code-switching and translation activities they valorize and why, and to reflect on how these activities change their communicative perspectives.[61]

Within thirty years, *camilla* would become synonymous with the Volscian war hero whose death Vergil plays out poignantly in his *Aeneid*. The "purity" of the Volscian Camilla gives her some of the qualities of an acolyte—tying in neatly with the phrasing in Pacuvius ("*Caelitum camilla, expectata aduenis*," *camilla* of the gods, much anticipated, you arrive).[62] As Varro goes on to observe, the female form *camilla* has a matching opposite, the *camillus*, the attendant at wedding rites who guards the mysteries.[63] A Hellenophile reader, interested in esoteric religions, might have made a near-homophone leap to καδμῖλος by this stage, perhaps even expecting the sounds-alike Κάδμος to make a guest appearance. Neither is interjected by Varro, but this is not just about quotation intensified by learned Callimachean allusion or the polishing and resetting of a resistant dramatic nugget from Pacuvius.[64]

Instead, immediately after the quote from Pacuvius' *Medus* (7.34), Varro glosses it as one that plugs into Roman linguistic expertise ("*interpretati*"). He then delivers his own literary critical salvo, "*addi oportet, in his quae occultiora: itaque dicitur nuptiis camillus qui . . .*" (it's logical to make the connection to affairs of a more secret nature, where he is named *camillus*, who . . .). Varro might have simply used *adde* (moreover; add to this the fact that . . .) to open the clause, but instead his formulation ("*addi oportet*") suggests that any reasonable person would see how the first explanation founders in isolation.

A few decades later, Vergil's Camilla, the virgin warrior, devotee and favorite of Diana, is fatally distracted from battle by the priest Chloreus—does she want his gold for herself or as a temple dedication?[65] Vergil offers both explanations (his Camilla is a complexly nuanced "outsider"), but, whichever one chooses, "Camilla" is hooked at death into the materiality of religious practice. His Camilla is emphatically a *uirgo*—it is never part of her (*Aeneid*) story arc to participate in a marriage ceremony directly (just like Varro's *camilla* and in contrast to his *camillus*).[66] Vergil may well have conjured up this specific Camilla, but the likelihood of a connection is strengthened when we recall that Servius (commenting on *Aeneid* 11.543; also picked up in Macrobius) "notices" a link from Vergil's generational etiology to the nexus identified by Varro.[67] Varro's discussion suggests that Vergil's nuances, drawing on the term *camilla* (and with *camillus* in attendance), were part of a pattern book available to dip into for cultured conversation.[68]

Coloring in Varro's likely frame of reference and the approximate homonyms of καδμῖλος, Κάδμος is also part of a thoughtscape that, when explored by Ovid in the *Metamorphoses*, finds in him an apposite alternative Aeneas, an archetype for understanding how a great family's clan history reverberates through its city-state, from exile to foundation to exile.[69] Thus, Cadmus and Aeneas, Troy, and Eastern origins, explicitly converge not long after Varro's etymological study. Varro's not talking about Cadmus (with his legendary credentials as inventor of letters)[70] in this textual context, in a book about language and communication, could represent another loud silence, especially since Cadmus, in myth, visited Samothrace before founding Thebes and metamorphosing into a snake. Samothrace is where Varro opens the door for my reading.

What could it mean, to read Phoenician Cadmus into the text's associative world? Legendarily, at the beginning of writing itself, he left home in order to track down the kidnapped Europa and found himself reinvented as the founder of Thebes.[71] A by-product of this civilizing process was dragon-slaying and dragons' teeth-sowing, which made for a new race, the Spartoi; Francis Vian traces a genealogical link from Cadmus' dragon-men to the Aegeidae and thus to Sparta, locating Cadmus at the beginning of the story of Sabine significance in shaping Roman Italy.[72] Cadmus, of course, would go on to marry the Samothracian Harmonia, along with whom, as Ovid vividly tells it, he was eventually transformed into a serpent.[73]

To sum up: like Vergil's Camilla (and Ovid's Cadmus, complete with snaky family history), Varro's masculine *camilla* leads to something "other": first to the mysteries of Roman religious marriage rites, then, in a more radical rift, to Samothracian mysteries and one termed "Casmilus," a mysterious deity ("*dius quidam*") who attends upon the Great Gods.[74] In short, this is one of those delightful tangles that Varro might be expected to unpick incisively (especially on the basis of his opening gambit). Instead, the topic is abruptly abandoned, concluding with the comment that instantiates Varro as one *doctus poeta*—allusive rather than explicit—in conversation with another: "*Verbum esse Graecum arbitror, quod apud Callimachum in poematibus eius inueni*" (I reckon this to be a Greek word, because it was in Callimachus, in his poems, that I discovered it) (Varro, *Ling.* 7.34). Callimachus, the ultimate learned name-drop, has the final word, guaranteeing Varro's *arbitror* (I consider this to be . . . ; I am eye-witness to . . .) but also emphasizing an educated, evidence-based evaluative process at the heart of this analytical close-out.[75]

With this in mind, let's step back briefly and think about the impact of this glimpse into Varro's working practice and critical program. *Arbitror* is a formula favored also by Cicero—his forensic and political speeches (especially the *Philippics*) and also his rhetorical and philosophical works are peppered with this way of presenting an "opinion" conclusively.[76] What is more, given that this is Varro's long-awaited work dedicated to Cicero, a finely tuned reciprocal compliment might seem to be on offer, since *arbitror* is also the term that Cicero's imagined Varro uses when scene-setting for *De Lingua Latina* itself, in response to (Cicero's) Atticus' request for an update:

> [Atticus]: "Varro's Muses have been maintaining their silence for much longer than usual, but I don't suppose that fellow's production has ground to a halt! Rather, I suspect that he's keeping a lid on what he's writing." "Far from it," [Varro] replied, "indeed I consider it to be recklessness to write down something that one wants to keep under wraps. That said, I do have a major, long-term project in hand: something for this fellow here"—referring to me—"is what I've begun work on, a really substantial undertaking, and the object of much honing and polishing on my part." (Cic. *Acad.* 1.2)

Varro's riposte to Atticus, as scripted by Cicero, sounds intuitively about right. This is the obvious reply that a statesman with an eye to long-term gains via political flexibility should make, and even more so in the twenty-first-century world of online "oversharing" of disasters and the perils of instant "reply-all" feedback. *Arbitror* (*Ling.* 7.34; first person, present, Varro "speaking" directly) features eleven times in the extant *De Lingua Latina* and typically flags up a noteworthy example where Varro's evaluation should make a difference.[77] Alongside its Ciceronian flavor, *arbitror* also evokes the travails of characters in comedy as they negotiate the psychodramas and plot twists of "everyday" life on stage in Plautus (and less frequently but still significantly in Terence).[78]

What conclusions might we draw? With *arbitror* Varro has here tagged Callimachus as an authority, setting the go-to Greek etiologist firmly within his range and proposing an off-the-cuff evaluation of a complex factoid (a nationality for *casmillus*). His Callimachean gloss on an obscure, hard-to-elucidate etymology, one that connects the Latin *camilla* to an attendant serving the Samothracian Great Gods, makes Varro's *arbitror* signal literary and intellectual authority. Varro has also hinted at the availability of secret knowledge to which he is in some way a party (picking up on the mystique of linguistics, heralded at *Ling.* 5.8). If we draw in Cicero's dialogue, we see how the power to control the time and context for concealing and revealing has moment for "Varro": indeed, it is represented as a feature of his thinking and his work. The role of things that are *occultior* in Varro's exegesis indicates that his audience needs to know how and where to look harder—one needs a *camillus* to manage the mysterious processes that join one to another (*nuptiae*). Such a person has lively but not totalizing authority (a Hermes/*casmillus*), and while Callimachus delivers a Greek gloss, Varro's tweak presents something slightly more complex—the initiation rites on Samothrace, the Great Gods, *and* Rome's foundations.

The Samothracian Great Gods, also known as the Cabiri, invoke the world of Magna Mater, a significant figure in the island's cult practice. In this way, connections to the Trojan Cybele, or Idaean Mother, break cover. For Varro's through-readers, there is a piquancy in recalling his earlier discussion of the relationship linking Earth, Sky, and the Great Gods of Samothrace as cosmic forces present at the beginning of the world.[79] In addition, if Servius reports accurately on Varro in his commentary on *Aeneid* 1.378, we get another tantalizing assertion: Varro explicitly made Samothrace part of the Phrygian world, that is to say, a feature of the original home of the civic Penates who accompanied Aeneas (back) to Italy.[80] Dardanus was known as the one who brought the Palladion from Samothrace to Troy; for Vergil's Latinus, time's oblivion has dimmed this as a traditional association, but Dardanus was Etruscan before his travels to Phrygia and Samothrace.[81]

Back at *Ling.* 5.58, Varro had already tied this material to the authority of a reference work known as the *augurum libri* (*Books of the Augurs*).[82] On one hand, Varro is asserting a tangible point of reference very different from the dimly remembered *fama* of Vergil's Latinus; on the other, he is also implying a personal quality to the inferences and evaluations on display. Auguries, like foundation stories, have a paranormal quality that requires careful exegesis by trained "readers."

The density of this allusive network demands concentrated thought and some leaps of the imagination—yet this very complexity is ideal material to fulfill a Callimachaean brief familiar to Rome's *literati*. Reatine Varro's interest in a Sabine filter for understanding Rome, taken alongside his career-spanning interest in literary experimentation and his expertise in rooting out the histories of Rome's peoples, practices, and language, makes it less of a stretch to follow this thread.

From Callimachus to Ennius is, in Varro, hardly a leap.[83]

Apud En<n>i<u>m:
  Subulo quondam marinas propter astabat *pl*agas.
Subulo dictus, quod ita dicunt tibicines Tusci: quocirca radices eius in Etr<ur>ia, non Latio qu*a*erundae. (Varro, *Ling.* 7.35)

In Ennius:
  A "*subulo*" once was standing, right by the expanses of the sea.
"*Subulo*" is the term because this is how the Tuscans term "flutists." For this reason its roots must in Etruria, not in Latium, be searched out.

Even without the emendation providing Ennius' authority, the quotation delivers a satisfying enrichment for the Spartan/Sabine nexus proposed earlier: standing by the shore in the verses, the quirky *subulo* looks out to sea (Italy's migrant past) and toward an Etruscan, not Latin, worldview.

Varro thus draws readers explicitly back into a world of diasporic Latin roots and alternative genealogical traces—a world that the brief etymology for *subulo* nevertheless embeds in Rome's language—while highlighting the potential alterity of these complex family trees. This is a family with fractures in its collective memory, leading to forgotten "branches" and unexpected offshoots. *Subulo* is by no means a common word in everyday (literary) use (after all, that's why *tibicen* is the normative term in play). *Subulo* is perhaps *more* familiar as a cognomen—Cicero makes capital out of the praetor of that name, a man involved in the Gracchan crisis.[84] To make sense of this, through-readers should recall Varro on *cano*, which (along with *oro*) I discuss in detail in chapter 3. Back at *Ling.* 6.75, Varro explained "to sing," whereby *cano* became the original action term for music making of all kinds, including *tibicen*. Flute playing is thus already deeply embedded in the beginnings of song and speech (to which Varro immediately turns, *Ling.* 6.76). Varro returns to *tibicen* at *Ling.* 8.61, emphasizing how closely the two activities (flute playing and singing) are entwined (*tibiae* plus *cano* delivers *tibicines*). So when readers reach and eventually also look back to Ennius' *subulo*, the experience is already sensitized to make the leap to what follows: another (but unattributed) quote from Ennius. In other words, if one recognizes that this next is from Ennius, one has another clue to the developing textual connectivity: "With which verses once the fauns and far-seeing poets (*uates*) used to sing."[85] Who are they?

> Fauni dei Latinorum, ita ut et Faunus et Fauna sit; hos uersibus quos uocant Saturnios in siluestribus locis traditum est solitos fari <futura, a> quo fando Faunos dictos. Antiqui poetas uates appellabant a uersibus uiendis, ut <de> poematis cum scribam ostendam. (Varro, *Ling.* 7.36.)

> Fauns are deities of the Latins and can be male and female, *Faunus* and *Fauna*. In the verses called "Saturnian," tradition has it that in woodland places they used to "speak" [the future,] from which "speaking" they were termed Fauns. Long ago they used to call poets "far-seeing versifier" [*uates*], from their entwining of verses. I will demonstrate this when I write about poems.[86]

This is definitely Latium, a sylvan, mysterious, and god-haunted environment of the sort that later authors, in particular poets, were to delight in sketching for Rome's prehistory. What this "tells" us is that for Varro, speaking is a deeply autochthonous act for Rome, one that distinctively enriches the ontological relationship between Rome's Saturnian and Romulean foundations.[87] Even before language was fully caught up with speech acts, nature deities were singing Latium, and therefore Latin, into being. Their generative discourse was prophetic (*uersus* is the linguistic connector for the bifold etiology), productive of a historicized speech mode marking up Latin (vatic verse: *antiquus* locates the developing etiology within a kind of literary-cultural continuum), and embedded in the legendary reign of Saturn, whose verbal authority persisted within authentic Roman metrical composition (*Saturnius uersus*).

Being a *uates*, this passage suggests, is thus about design, controlled flexibility, skill, and a tangible fluency with language, bringing a conclusion to the issues raised by Varro's earlier deployment of *uieo* in book 5.[88] There, weaving verses was akin to divine cosmography, with the caveat that not fully understanding the kinks in the linguistic framework could make for uncomfortable conclusions (we saw Venus' role as a complicating factor in the discussion earlier in this section). Here, with focus narrowed, the complex texture of verse foresees and reifies a newly Saturnian and Latin Rome.

Action

Before Varro introduces "memory" (discussed in the section "Romespeak and Etymology" in this chapter), he tackles "action."[89]

> <u>Incipiam</u> hinc primu*m* quod dicitur <u>ago</u>. <u>Actio</u> ab <u>agitatu</u> facta. Hinc dicimus "<u>agit</u> gestum tragoedus," et "<u>agitantur</u> quadrigae"; hinc "<u>agitur</u> pecus pastum." Qua uix <u>agi</u> potest, hinc <u>angiportum</u>; qua nil potest <u>agi</u>, hinc <u>angulus</u>, <uel> quod in eo locus <u>angustissimus</u>, cuius loci is <u>angulus</u>. (Varro, *Ling.* 6.41)

<u>I shall start</u> first with what's termed "I [en]<u>act</u>" [or drive forward/perform/plead/achieve/do/produce]. <u>Action</u> is made out of <u>motion</u>. Hence [using the same word] we say "the tragic actor <u>performs</u> [enacts] a gesture," and "the four-in-hand chariot <u>is driven</u>"; from this, then, "the flock <u>is driven</u> to pasture." The term <u>alley</u> comes from the kind of space where this class of [action-performance] <u>movement</u> is scarcely possible; from where this <u>movement</u> is not possible at all, comes the term <u>corner</u> [perhaps here: bolt-hole; retreat, turning-point or point of reversal], or alternatively, it is because it's in a place of the <u>utmost confinement</u> [or perhaps restriction] that the "<u>corner</u>" belongs.

Readers such as Cicero, at ease in code-switching, would be likely to trace the Greek homophone ἄγω through Latin's *ago*.[90] Indeed, I have argued that this passage should be read in light of Cicero's use of *actio* in his *De Officiis*.[91] There, *actio* bridges private and public tropes for appropriate and meaningful citizen behavior.[92] Varro, however, homes in on the sense "stage performance." From tragedy to triumph to pastoral, there is a highly literary, Greek-flavored, and performative subtext to this sequence, one that sits comfortably with the performative quality of etymology already evident in Socrates' role in Plato's *Cratylus*.[93] The strong connotations of Varro's four-horse team make sense in this context, and for through-readers (recalling *Ling.* 5.145) the otherwise jarring "alley" ("*angiportum*") becomes sequentially meaningful.[94] The *angiportum* restricts action and provides a check to the kinds of genre and behavior that previous examples highlighted: it evokes the semantic fields of farmed land, city, and military and intellectual landscapes of empire.[95] These restrictions are amplified in *angulus*, a kind of negative space that Varro draws out from *angiportum*. An *angulus* diverts those who enter unless they choose to grind to a halt and can be surprisingly polyvalent; use by Horace and Propertius suggests a symbolic metaliterary value on the cusp of developing.⁹⁶ The semireversal encoded by *angulus* returns readers to the fruitful world of *actio*, deploying phraseology that recalls the saying *dictum (ac) factum*, meaning "no sooner said than done" or "to speak is to act":

> Actionum trium primus agitatus mentis, quod primum ea quae sumus acturi cogitare debemus, deinde tum dicere et facere. (Varro, *Ling.* 6.42)

> Of the three kinds of action, the first is mental activity, because in the first place we are obliged to think through the things we are going to do, and only then to move on to speaking and doing.

Varro characterizes mental activity here as the crucial precursor for the two identified outward-facing actions (speaking and doing). What follows shows the wide-ranging significance of this material:

> De his tribus minime putat **uolgus** esse actionem cogitationem; tertium, in quo quid <u>facimus</u>, id maximum. Sed et cum <u>c</u>ogitamus quid et eam rem *a*gitamus in mente, <u>agimus</u>, et cum <u>pronuntiamus</u>, <u>agimus</u>. Itaque ab eo orator <u>agere</u> dicitur causam et augures augurium <u>agere</u> dicuntur, quom in eo plura dicant quam faciant. (Varro, *Ling.* 6.42)

> Of these three, **the masses** are least likely to think that intellectual consideration is an action, whereas the third—in which <u>we do</u> something—they rate highest. Yet it is the case that when <u>we consider</u> something [*res*] and <u>we turn it over</u> in the mind, <u>we are acting</u>, and when <u>we make a speech</u> [/perform/narrate/utter], <u>we are acting</u>. Therefore from this the orator is said <u>"to plead"</u> a case, and augurs are said <u>"to conduct"</u> an augury, even when there's more saying than doing involved.

Sociological categorization is in play: "we" are not the masses (*uolgus*).⁹⁷ "Our" crucial acts are behaviors characteristic of an educated elite, but the juxtaposition of oratory and augury is noteworthy.⁹⁸ There is a proverbial or formulaic quality to the association of *dicere* and *facere*, which suggests that "politics and portents were complementary factors in a dialectic relationship."⁹⁹ Varro's discussion highlights the potential for uncertainty, at least among those without appropriate guidance, when evaluating how politics might have compromised genuine augural divination.¹⁰⁰

Varro's wider project (encompassing human and divine affairs to create a suite of resources for the best kind of citizen and the highest excellence in public service) is enhanced by this etymologization of augural language, suggesting the potential for the revival of a deeply authentic communicative power that bridges truth and reality.[101] If readers feel the need to reflect on the gap between performative speech and augural conduct in this context, Varro has key terminology to hand: "to consider" ("*cogitare*") is from "gathering together" ("*cogendum*"); thus the mind ("*mens*") "gathers together" several things in one place ("*plura in unum*"), from which it is able "to (s)elect" (*Ling.* 6.43).[102] This selective, active intellect looks set to open a weighty discussion, but Varro confounds expectations by juxtaposing a seemingly throwaway etymology for cheese-making—from pressing concerns to pressing curds.[103]

Eventually, Varro returns to the third phase of "action" (*Ling.* 6.77), specifically, when people make something ("*faciunt*"). *Facio* is an action that the unwary may think has a likeness ("*similitudo*") to *agere* (to act) and *gerere* (to undertake/carry out); herein lies a wrong turn ("*error*"). This is very much not, Varro emphasizes, all one concept. It allows him to point out some broad lessons:

> Contra imperator quod dicitur res <u>gerere</u>, in eo neque <u>facit</u> neque <u>agit</u>, sed <u>gerit</u>, id est <u>sustinet</u>, tralatum ab his qui onera <u>gerunt</u>, quod hi <u>sustinent</u>. (Varro, *Ling.* 6.77)

> Against this [the example of the poet] the commander, because he is said <u>to carry out</u> matters, in this way he neither "<u>makes</u>" nor "<u>acts</u>," but "<u>carries out</u>" that is to say "<u>sustains</u>," a sense transferred from those who "<u>carry</u>" burdens, because <u>they sustain</u> them.

Hence, one can conduct affairs (for example, as a commander—*imperator*) without being the generator of the conflict or the one whose physical actions constitute the battle itself. *Gero* can thus gather *sustineo* into its semiotic range, since by a species of translation (*transfero*) the *imperator* of the example is both bearing (*gero*) a burden and also sustaining it (*sustineo*).

In book 7, action terminology takes on a different and peculiarly political cast. At *Ling.* 7.66 we are served up unionized (*acsitiosae*) women in Plautus.[104] What might readers make of this? One might imagine the often vividly political women of Old Comedy translated into babbling female "activists" ("*actiosae*," Varro says). This could work if *axitiosae* (with a cs/x slippage) is broadly political—Varro derives *axitiosae* (feminine) from a masculine source term (*agendo*, doing). Varro shores this up by attribution to the grammarian Servius Claudius: "*Claudius scribit axitiosas demonstrari consupplicatrices. Ab agendo axitiosas: ut ab una faciendo factiosae, sic ab una agendo <axitiosae, ut> actosae, dictae.*"[105] The comedic context (quotes from Plautus) makes this focus on troublesome women unsurprising, but a more immediate politicization emerges from Varro's illustrative parallel derivation: *actiosae* (and/or *axitiosae*) is like, he says, making *factiosae* from *faciendo* (partisan, or faction-forming). In this way factionalists are paralleled with politicized women, and, in the process, factionalism gains a feminine (and perhaps ridiculous) quality.[106]

In this context, to read *partes* (*Ling.* 6.57) as "factions" makes sense. It introduces a lengthy sequence exploring the relationship between the public qualities of pronouncement and self-expression within which individual autonomy is a crucial, complementary part of consensus and stability.[107] *Pronuntiare* (*Ling.* 6.58) picks up this polysemic train of thought. Here, the political, religious, and performative intertwine in an encouraging vision of the discursive body politic that refreshes the verb *nuntio* (*Ling.* 5.87) and delivers on *nuntius* (*Ling.* 6.58). There will be a positive cosmic echo of this bundle later (*Ling.* 6.86) in a quotation from the Censors' Tables (where a celestial *nuntium* responds to the censor's taking of auspices to close a successful census).

Pro-, prefixing *pronuntio*, has (Varro tells us) the same force as *ante*. The spatial and qualitative senses of *pro-* combined with *nuntiare* keep the idea of placiality in mind even as the narrative, moving on to *proludo* (*Ling.* 6.58), reaches toward "playing out" or "rehearsal" (in front or in advance of an audience).[108] Performance and oratory hint at Greek and dramatic territory, but the homophonous Greek πρό and ἀντί are further unexpected absences,[109] and Varro's etymological drift encourages a new (perhaps newly Roman) way of conceptualizing what actors do. Actors are said "to make publicly known" ("*pronuntiare*") because they take to the stage (*proscaenium*, recalling the similar locational specificity for the Sabine scenario developing *loquor*, using prefixes, at 6.57,[110] but also alluding to the technical vocabulary of Greek stagecraft). The stage is where actors *enuntiant* (make known, mediate) the workings of the poetic mind. Actors are not *quite* messengers ("*nuntii*"), but they are from the same semiotic pool—a *nuntius* says "new things" ("*nouae res*"), which looks likely to be a Graecism.[111] Why? Varro's turn to Campania for illumination offers a long-ago, vowel-shifting ancestry: Greeks made Neapolis, but way-back-when Romans came up with the hybrid form Nouapolis, a "new" kind of political order, apposite for a new kind of speech (Latin).

That this is all in some way circling the nature of Romespeak and its wormhole back to foundational first principles becomes more apparent when we read on and find that what comes next is "novelty" (*Ling.* 6.59). Speaking *in propria persona*, Varro identifies the slippage in language that has led the masses ("*uolgus*") to swap in *nouissimum* (newest, hot off the press, trend-setting) for *extremum* (last, last word). "In my memory" ("*mea memoria*"), Varro comments, old men, and even his and Cicero's mentor, Aelius, found this too hard to take: this was the era when the ultra-new (the word; the connotation) was becoming the norm. If Varro seems to be wandering here, he immediately brings us back in line with a trio: "*nouitas* [newness, novelty] *et nouicius* [novice, neologism] *et noualis* [fallow or, by contrast, only just first ploughed land]." The polysyndeton (*et*) bolsters a catalog-like quality but also hammers home the connectivity. The first two elements help gloss the problematic quality of newness that confronts those whose roots are in Rome's times past (old men recognizing the extreme circumstances that switch *nouissimum* on), but the third is intriguing. The sequence explaining *noualis* runs:

Sic ab eadem origine <u>nouitas</u> et <u>nouicius</u> et <u>noualis</u> in agro et sub <u>Nouis</u> dicta pars in Foro aedificiorum, quod uocabulum ei peruetus*tum*, ut <u>Nouae</u> Viae, quae uia iam diu uetus. (Varro, *Ling.* 6.59)

So from the same origin: "<u>novelty</u>," and "<u>neologism</u>," and "<u>first-ploughed</u>" (of a field); and by "the <u>News</u>" is how a section of buildings in the Forum is termed, even though the name itself is by now antique, just like "<u>New</u>" Street, a street that has long been old.

Varro brings two central and deeply historical areas of the city into the frame here, encompassing by reference the Forum and alluding to commerce (the buildings in question are the Tabernae Novae, newer than the opposite Tabernae Veteres) and a very specific infrastructure (emphasis by repetition of *uia* and its association with long-ago construction projects).

The End Result: Speaking Well

Loqui (*Ling.* 6.56) should recall through-readers briefly to *locus* (place), from which we learn *loqui* derives.[112] Someone who is said to be speaking ("*dico*") for the first time ("*quod qui primo dicitur*") is uttering terms ("*uocabula*") and other words ("*reliqua uerba*") before he is able to articulate each one in its correct place ("*locus*")—first speech, therefore, is redefined as a kind of alphabet soup, meaningful only by chance rather than by design. Communicative speech (talking, not simply uttering sounds) depends on an intelligible and meaningful positionality (*locus*). Varro follows up (still at §56) with a further explanation from the Stoic philosopher Chrysippus[113] and shifts verbs (leaving *dico* and rejoining *loquor*): such a person (the imaginary first-speaker) is not talking but only making the likeness of talking, in the same way that the *imago* of a man is not actually a man. It is the same, he argues, for ravens and crows (the mimic-birds) and for children at first commencement of speech. Well before Ovid's magpies (*Met.* 5.294–99) crystallize the uselessness of merely imitative loquacity, Varro makes plain that words are simply babble when their place in the civic world of properly plotted discourse is not meaningfully aligned. Varro's position is thus subtly but importantly different from the Ciceronian model proposed by Thomas Habinek—yes, *dico* signals that a statement of authority is at issue, but for Varro individual authority is not necessarily or always the primary marker of validity; collaborative discussion and conversation (*loquor*) make powerful instances of consensus building.[114]

Getting speech right is important. Without positionality (context, syntax), words risk being just noises and talking becomes squawking. Authentic speech is the preserve of one who, in talking, puts each word knowingly in its own place and in this way can place himself and others appropriately in the community. Such a man can then be said to have "spoken out" (*prolocutus*) when he has effectively communicated what is in his mind by talking (*loquendo*), that is, putting the right words in the right places in the right order.[115] Speaking one's mind or expressing one's existential beliefs ("*in animo quod habuit*," Ling. 6.56) leads to a brief discussion of formalized ritual Sabine speech practices, an apt way into thinking about the ethnic qualities of Romespeak.

From the act of speaking out (*proloquor*, with its embedded sense of place) comes *eloquor* (to speak intelligibly and stylishly) and *reloquor* (to reply or respond in speech). Textually, these terms are situated by association deep in Sabine "territory": they are defined very specifically in relation to particular instances of speech-and-answer divine communications within the *cellae* of Sabine sanctuaries.[116]

Treated next, two adjectival derivations, *loquax* (one who speaks too much) and *eloquens* (one who speaks abundantly), point up the delicacy of the boundary that divides full expression of ideas and rich discourse from ceaseless chatter. This duplex model continues with *colloquium* (a coherent, discursive event). Its flip side (*adlocutum*) is what women do when they approach someone with exhortatory intent.[117] Another unusual formulation, *loquela*, ensues; this, according to some ("*dixerunt*"), is a very specific way of characterizing a word when uttered within discourse ("*in loquendo efferimus*"). To speak in an orderly, elegant fashion ("*concinne loqui*") brings Varro to the end of this phase in the discussion. Polished, apt formulation in discourse is pleasing and harmonizes the parts or divisions of speech effectively. This kind of speech is what characterizes a good community: it implies conversation where the "parts" collaborate to produce joined-up society.[118]

This chapter has taken Romespeak as its focus and has introduced examples of Varro's material relating to aspects of identity, perception, textuality, speech, and action to showcase the richly narrative qualities of *De Lingua Latina*. These worked-through samples set the scene for subsequent chapters, and they model the kinds of wider significance that reading Varro contextually can deliver. Thus, when in book 8 readers encounter Varro expanding upon his own authority as part of the setup for the new hexad, it will make sense that he does so by introducing a literary metaphor for word-clans: the first is like a spring (*fons*), the second, a stream (*riuus*).[119] People, it seems, find difficulty in learning (that is, memorizing and recalling) and in using those words whose backstories are closest to pure inspiration; they prefer those whose family trees make mnemonics (and tracing a genealogy) most straightforward. *Fons*-type words require a whole work of history ("*historia opus est*") if they are to retain their place in Latin.[120] It is tempting to see this, when framed as part of an authorial intervention, as an allusion to the secluded spring made famous by Callimachus as his literary source.[121] Callimachus is of course playing on a motif already present in Hesiod, and such an intertextual nod embeds literariness in Varro's authorial self-fashioning.[122] Varro's stance here in book 8 (beginning his first grammatical hexad) is didactic in the mold of Hesiod and Callimachus just as much as it is in books 5–7; like Horace, his *opus* has monumental qualities.[123] Romespeak represents a uniquely authoritative skill set, and Varro continues to refine what his role as author might mean, as I discuss in subsequent chapters.

chapter 3

Inspiring Latin

Varro's etymologies and linguistic rationales are vivid and memorable. Although often seemingly ordinary and by no means elegantly styled in a conventional sense, Varro's explicatory stratagems soon begin to worm their way into a reader's mental processes. In chapter 2 we started to explore Romespeak's distinctive potential for telling on Rome: knowing Varro's poetry-powered Latin equips the reader to take meaningful action and recount it powerfully, rather than simply (as Quintilian would put it) enabling the ears to luxuriate in a respite from the rigors of forensic oratory.[1] This chapter works broadly with Varro's allusive literarity to show how exploring the byways of Latinity delivers a creative inspirational agenda, one that would contribute to his loss-by-assimilation as preceptor for the world of Imperial rhetoric. The text is amusing, astonishing, and thought-provoking—it takes through-readers on a journey into an urbane world of eccentric gatherings and eclectic conjunctions and, in the process, conjures up the messy vitality and radical innovation characteristic of late Republican Rome.

Pragmatically, a manual professing to command Latin will brush up against the requirements for developing Roman *eloquentia*. When choosing to write in didactic mode, an author promises to make new practice available to the successful reader, who gains command of his expertise. A linguistic handbook might be imagined to prime its audience to perform with authority, transforming inky lines of text into their own newly empowered and technically informed rhetoric. Straightforwardly, *De Lingua Latina* should inspire its readers to speak with a fresh understanding of the historical qualities of their language. Yet inspiration takes various forms, and this chapter is also interested in how the structures, forms, and sounds of Latin as a literary language produce a kind of systematic inspiration. Varro, a poet himself and therefore etymologically a "maker," finds inspiration and authority in verse authors; books 5–7 of *De Lingua*

Latina are this chapter's touchstones for examining how poetic quotation and allusion enrich the work's overall significance and get things done.[2]

I begin with the potential power of the poet, artful speech, and the significance of verse quotation. This leads us, in the next section, to Varro on "song" and, after that, to the narrative dimension that inspired Varro's "meanders." Finally, the last two sections explore literarity as a process of modeling behavior through beginnings and endings. By the end of this chapter, what emerges is the sinewy quality of Varro's poetics and the granular nature of the text's ability to urge readers into original and expansive ways of understanding new and old issues.

Poets, Artfulness, and Textuality

When Varro conjoins poets, actors, and commanders (*Ling.* 6.77), he is simultaneously asserting the difference between the poet "making" (*facere*), the actor "acting" (*agere*), and the *imperator* "carrying out" (*gerere*), and ensuring that the three are indelibly linked. Artfulness is connected to res gestae, and in Varro's next character, the *fictor* (a sculptor or fashioner of three-dimensional objects), the significance of this kind of etymological networking is methodologically apparent:[3]

> Ut fictor cum **dicit** fingo, figuram **imponit**, quom **dicit** formo, formam, sic cum **dicit** facio, faciem **imponit**; a qua facie discernitur. (Varro, *Ling.* 6.78)
>
> Just as the "sculptor," when **he says** "I shape" [invent], **puts a** shape to something; when **he says** "I form," [he gives it] "form." Thus when **he says** "I make" [bring something into existence], **he puts a** façade [external, characterizing, individuating appearance] on it. From this façade it becomes possible **to determine** type.

Varro's *fictor* is a powerful agent of discrimination, a key behavior for community formation and stratification. This sequence shows the *fictor* sculpting how things are and also shaping the inhabited world in a way that strengthens heuristic practice. At a very basic level, the *fictor* makes it possible to define (*dico*) items as clothing or as dishes and so on. *Fictores* are creating the products that characterize the basis of civilized life, but they are also, through the semiotics of first-person-singular forms, asserting an array of trades, showing how their characteristic words bring the stuff of day-to-day life into existence. *Fingo* in this context hints at meta-literary layers. Readers might hear an echo of Lucretius' characterization of the poet as a "framer" of words (Lucr. 5.3) and recall Varro's earlier description of the artful coinage (*ficta*) of Juno Lucina from "*iuuando et luce*" (*Ling.* 5.69).⁴

Delicate distinctions continue to develop when Varro concludes on *facere* (connecting up *agere*) to explain the action of the verb *amministro*.

> ab <u>agitatu</u>, ut dixi, magis <u>agere</u> quam <u>facere</u> putatur; sed quod his magis promiscue quam diligenter consuetudo est usa, translaticiis utimur uerbis: nam et qui <u>dicit</u>, <u>facere</u> uerba <u>dicimus</u>, et qui aliquid <u>agit</u>, non esse <u>inficientem</u>. (Varro, *Ling.* 6.78)

> [the executor/doer/manager], from his <u>action</u> (as I have said),⁵ is considered rather "<u>to act</u>" than "<u>to make</u>" [/do]; but because the verbs tend to be used indiscriminately rather than carefully, we transpose them in use. E.g., someone who "<u>says</u>" something, <u>we say</u> "<u>makes</u>" words, and someone who "<u>acts</u>," that he is not "<u>doing nothing</u>."

Someone who takes an executive role ("*amministrat*"), delivering an intellectual or perhaps organizational rather than a concrete output, should partake in the connotations of *ago*. This model maintains him as an <u>agent</u> rather than a <u>fac</u>tor, yet the power of *parole* has transformed "our" usage (*utimur, dicimus*) of all this terminology (*facio, dico, ago*). Varro's careful exegesis of the whole complex of terms suggests that one who "speaks" is now become one who "makes words," while one who "acts" is recast as one who is "not unproductive" (*inficiens*).

Does this suggest that Varro foresees a popular downgrading of speech (to an artisanal subset of *facio*, a kind of philosophical τέχνη), or would this even represent a downgrade? The text becomes particularly subject to emendation at this point, and drawing firm conclusions is difficult. Varro appears to move on and discusses the act of shining light into the darkness ("*adluceo*," *Ling.* 6.79), then the notion of the "quest" ("*quae res*"—the thing sought and brought back) and the "investigator,"⁶ and eventually the overwhelming power of the eyes and the primacy of sight among the physical senses ("*sensuum maximus in oculis*"). The sequence works effectively as a structural turn, taking readers back to the realm of appearance versus reality and alluding implicitly to the materiality of the text as a work of art. It also introduces Varro's connection of speech acts, performance, and the related themes of artfulness and intertextuality.

Authored texts are artful constructions and thus connote a personal quality. In chapter 2 I proposed preliminary approaches to Varro on Romespeak as a mode of literary authority. Here, I build on those model readings through analysis of a series of passages that discuss literariness and its historically inflected connection to versification.[7] These sample passages highlight the programmatic significance of the trained author—a figure who must combine creativity with technical skills and hard work—for understanding how the text primes doing more in Latin.[8] This outcome is crucial for understanding how quickly the reach of Varro's project moved from experimental vision to mainstream thinking—as Quintilian's appropriative version exemplifies.

Early in book 7, Varro comments in some detail on versifying and sheds further light on his interest in *fingo*. The passage (*Ling.* 7.2–8) repays careful attention:

Cum haec amminicula addas ad eruendum uoluntatem impositoris, tamen latent multa. Quod si poetice <quae> in carminibus serva*u*it multa prisca quae essent, sic etiam cur essent posuisset *f*ecundius poemata ferrent fructum . . . neque multa ab eo, quem non erunt in lucubratione litterae prosecutae, multum licet legeret. (Varro, *Ling.* 7.2)

Even with your employment of these tools to root out the intention of the nomenclator, much remains hidden. But if poetry, which has in verses preserved many antique words, had in like manner set down the "why" of them, poems would bear fruit more abundantly . . . and there are many [words] that are untraceable by anyone whose night-work is not favored by scholarship, no matter how much he might read.

Varro sketches a vivid if hackneyed scene: the unlucky would-be scholar, struggling fruitlessly with intractable "root" words and arid verses through the hours of darkness. All that remains is for the notoriously impossible Salian Hymn to be thrown into the mix for the scene to be complete; and that cliché is indeed what follows.[9] Varro then tells his readers that Aelius—a man at top of the game in Latin scholarship—worried away very profitably at the *Carmina Saliorum*, expedited by attending to one meager letter ("*exili littera*").[10] Even allowing one telling letter in a word to slip by, Varro suggests, means that all may be interpretatively lost. What follows suggests that his tongue is firmly in cheek. "*Nec mirum*" (no wonder) there are disasters attendant on such inattentiveness! After all, Varro continues vividly and anecdotally, Epimenides (Greece's Rip Van Winkle) was a stranger after a fifty-year snooze; more worryingly, he observes, Livius Andronicus' Teucer was forgotten within a blink of fifteen years (*Ling.* 7.3).

Taken together, these propositions connect poetic discourse to a genealogical impetus in language and a process of forgetting and remembering (how to put words to) ancestral values and modes. This push-pull dynamic is especially important when the authenticity of a community is entangled with its ability to talk about, share, and reinterpret a common history. The Salian Hymn bubbles up from the source (*fons*), all the way back in the reign of Numa Pompilius *if not earlier*. This means that the earliest verse forms, if studied and understood, allow access to the beginnings of Roman identity for those who can trace their linguistic family tree. What remains to be seen is what one can do with the results of this erudition and how potent the source inspiration can remain at such a laborious and scholarly remove.

To draw these strands together and sum up, we see that Varro's exegesis (*Ling.* 7.2–3) sketches a verse-heavy "horizon of expectations."[11] His illustration offers readers an (otherwise) unattested play by Livius featuring Teucer, rather than (for example) Pacuvius' *Teucer* (cited by Cicero and apparently the proverbial version).[12] He compounds this obscurism by matching it to another complicatedly "Greek" (Cretan) legendary figure, Epimenides, who is curiously unpopular as a Latin exemplum.[13] Epimenides is significant because he draws a major Athenian culture hero, Solon, into the frame.[14] Any reader who spots this will find in it a Greek parallel for Varro's inclusion of Numa, another "educator" figure. In the meantime, Teucer is famous for articulating the notion that home is something one embodies, a function of the self—an idea under scrutiny in an array of Latin literature during this era and in subsequent decades.[15]

It was in the time of Numa, Varro goes on to assert, that Latin first became poetic ("*quo Romanorum prima uerba poetica dicunt Latina,*" *Ling.* 7.3). Varro's point is that an *interuallum* (pause, space between two things) may separate "us" from the "*prima uerba poetica*" of our *Roman* ancestors, but by definition "*prima*" asserts that a community of shared poetic and therefore authentic understanding connecting then to now can still be discerned and subscribed to, even if individual ancestral features are no longer easily intelligible. This is a very different model from the prioritization of elegant inspiration that underpins Horace's characterization of poetry (*carmen*) in *Epistles* 2.1, rather more like a reinvigoration of Ennius' Roman *poemata* as a distinctive "verbal performance type" and a renewal of the significance of artistry and endeavor.[16]

Book 7 declares itself as Varro's compendium of poetic words ("*Dicam in hoc libro de uerbis quae a poetis sunt posita,*" *Ling.* 7.5), but through-readers will know that poetic vocabulary has been significant for Varro's Latin from the beginning (as we have it, *Ling.* 5.1).[17] Nonetheless, do not blame a hardworking scholar for gaps in some hero's genealogy, Varro says (calling readers to order) when *you* can't remember all of your own family tree (*Ling.* 7.4). Instead, as discussed in chapter 2, he says that one should consider terming someone a "good man" who has made many apt comments on the origins of words—that is, someone who has put his Romespeak to practical use and to the benefit of the community—and avoid censuring someone who has contributed nothing practical. Not everyone can be a *bonus*, after all, and not all words have an evident *causa*; nevertheless, as a pear comes from a branch and the branch from a tree, the tree still comes from roots even when they cannot be seen. That Varro chooses to emphasize poetry programmatically at the opening of the first and last in this triad (5.1, 7.1) encourages all readers to look for the poetic angle as a route to greater understanding and to recognize its significance in strengthening the living language. Varro's poetic universe makes honorable space for hard graft.

When one hopes ("*sperat*"), Varro suggests ("*potest esse*," *Ling.* 6.73), one is indulging in wishful thinking ("*spes a sponte*") and imagining that what one desires is about to happen. Fear thus represents the opposite of hope—it occurs when dark inclinations seem about to be fulfilled. To illustrate (*itaque*), Varro proposes a snippet of Plautus' *Astraba*. Although the text is subject to restoration, for this discussion the sense is secure enough to give: "I long to pursue my hope [*spes*]," and "gladly I pursue my hoped-for girl [*Sperata*]." In these, Varro gives us a conflation of grammatically feminine Hope and the kind of impossible beloved so popular in comedy. He glosses the quotes by saying that the boyish speaker ("*adulescens*") is "*sine sponte*" (almost Hope-less) in every sense because there is no reality in his "hope" or in the inclination or in the chase ("*neque ill <quae> sperata est*").[18] The performance act within which comedic verse gives life to the improbable and allows audiences safely and entertainingly to examine and consume its logics is as significant a factor as scholarship and authority for the aspiring Romespeaker—a good man whose hopeful practice brings a knowledgeable, pragmatic, and progressive community into being.

Varro on Song

Varro's interest in how, when, and why verse might be performed is evident in his treatment of the verb "to sing" ("*cano*," *Ling.* 6.75) and its connection to oratory (*oro* and its word family, to which he turns next, *Ling.* 6.76). In this juxtaposition, Varro articulates an important relationship, one characterized by Habinek as both oppositional and central to "the Roman system of verbal artistry."[19] To begin with singing:

> Canere, accanit et succanit ut canto et cantatio ex Camena permutato pro M N. Ab eo quod semel, canit, si saepius, cantat. Hinc cantitat, item alia. (Varro, *Ling.* 6.75)

"To sing" [/"play music"], "he sings to," and "he sings a harmony," just as "I sing" and "song," come from Camena with the M changed to N. Whence the one-off term "he sings," but the more habitual "he songifies." Hence "he often sings," and so on.

"To sing," in this model, implies a lively community of song—singers, musicians, audience. The third-personification of the examples, "*accanit*" and "*succanit*," suggests a world in which it is almost commonplace to break into occasional song. This is both a vision of song entwined with speech "made special . . . in effect, speech that has been ritualized," as Habinek puts it, and a world within which song offers its own particular genealogies of authority.[20] Unpacking the domain of song gives an activity that has spun off a frequentative mode, hence a separate action term: "*saepius, cantat*"—he's just gotta sing, but by implication a performance of someone else's composition, or perhaps on command. *Canto* gets this peculiar force through derivation from the Camenae, a dynamic highlighted by Habinek for Vergil but already evident here.[21] A whole cataloged orchestra of instruments and musicians then concludes the musical entertainment (*Ling.* 6.75), but the stagey atmosphere and the interplay between authority and the power of utterance continues when Varro turns next to *oro*: performance straight from the lips (*Ling.* 6.76).

The juxtaposition carries over (from *Ling.* 6.75) a whiff of pantomime, the kind of variety show beloved of the *populus*.[22] This quirky vibe persists as the etymology draws in augural practices before returning to musical production by an unexpected route:

> Oro ab ore et perorat et exorat et oratio et orator et osculum dictum. Indidem omen, ornamentum; alterum quod ex ore primum elatum est, osmen dictum; alterum nunc cum propositione dicitur uulgo ornamentum, quod sicut olim ornamenta sc*a*enici plerique dicunt. Hinc oscines dicuntur apud augures, quae ore faciunt auspicium. (Varro, *Ling.* 6.76)

"I speak" [/"argue"] is so called from "mouth"; so too, "he concludes" ["persuades"/"speaks at length"], "he prevails upon," "speech," "speaker," and "kiss." From the same, "omen" and "embellishment": the former, because it was first expressed from the mouth, was termed *osmen*; the latter is now commonly deployed in the singular form (*ornamentum*), but, just as in days gone by, most of the dramatic poets use the plural form (*ornamenta*). From here, "singing" birds are spoken of among the augurs, because they make their presages by mouth.

From "mouth" comes the act of pleading, whether in court, on political business, or more straightforwardly for show. All these are part of one's public "frontage" (the face/mouth) and sealed in sequence with a kiss. The vividly physical qualities of the kiss tinge the productions of the mouth—speech in all its polished forms—with a diminutive after-shot (*os-culum*).[23] Kissy-kissy oratory, the sequence seems to suggest, leads to something less than substantial or at least emphasizes a quality of self-fashioning at odds with authentic authority. The first two sections of chapter 4 return to the specifics of Varro on speech and oratory; omens are an important element in understanding the relationship between inspiration, performance, authority, and Romespeak. Omens are another discourse mode requiring exegesis, joining song and verse, and depending on an interplay between speaker, context, formula, and meaning. Like oratory, they come from the mouth, but, as we have already seen (recall *Ling.* 6.42) in chapter 2, Varro's "augur" is not a straightforward role. Here, augural pronouncements are complicated by association with *ornamentum* and verse composition, with onstage poetry and popular idiom (*uulgus*) in the mix. The complexity is emphasized by narrative context: to reach these augurs and their "singing birds" means recognizing the associative link with the work of orators and the dramatic poets (whether for display or persuasion) and considering the nature and derivation of the authority to pronounce.

Comments made by Cicero, Varro's "model reader," could add further nuance. Writing to Aulus Caecina in 46, Cicero observed:

> If you had a system, based on certain Etruscan teachings that you received from your father—a noble and excellent man—and it did not prove deceptive, nor shall I myself be deceived by my prophetic skill. It derives from the advice and precepts of men of the utmost wisdom and (as you know) extensive study of theory, and also from long experience of leadership in public affairs and the great vicissitudes that have attended on our times. I place all the more trust in this divinatory skill because it has deceived me on nothing throughout these dark and disturbed days. I would tell you some of the predictions I have uttered if I were not afraid to seem to have fabricated them with hindsight. . . .
>
> Moving on, since, as augurs and astrologers are accustomed to do, I have as a public augur established with you the authority of my auguries and divinations on the basis of my track record, this prediction should hold weight. I do not hazard [*auguror*] this from the flight of one kind of bird of omen [*oscinis*], or from the sinister song [*cantu sinistro*] of another, as our method has it . . . but I have other signs that I keep an eye

on [*obseruem*]. They may be no more certain, but there is less scope in them for confusion and error [*obscuritatis uel erroris*]. For the purposes of this act of divination, two kinds of signs are observed: one kind I draw from Caesar himself, the other, from the tenor and development of public affairs. (Cic. *Fam.* 6.6.3–4, 7–8)

This letter addresses a man experiencing something all too familiar to Cicero: exile—in Caecina's case, the result of an incautious pamphlet denouncing Caesar.[24] What makes this interesting as context for Varro's comments is the explicit parallel drawn between the public augural system and that devised by Cicero, a system based on his ability to judge character, on his understanding of the era, and on his skills in reading the signs in public affairs. The "Cicero method," he asserts, is guaranteed by a back catalog of successes. Perhaps the joust with Clodius counted in Cicero's favor at the time of writing, given the apparent security of his position—and the demise of Clodius; although taking that unexpected death as part of his "I couldn't have made it up!" shtick also works.[25] Overall, the version of Caesar that Cicero offers in this epistle is a kind of popular Svengali, clever ("*acutus*"), farsighted ("*prouidens*"), and sensible of the power of the Etruscan "mafia."[26]

Cicero's letter intimates that systems are contingent: they flex in tune with the cultural contexts that flavor them (civic, Roman, Etruscan, personal), and they also present scope for getting the response one expects. None of this is unique, but, as a sequence of proposals concerning the relationship between quality and contingency when reading the signs and the inexorable logic of transforming Caesar himself into the object of augural scrutiny, the letter offers a remarkable snapshot of a distinctively contemporary epistemological crux. Where, Cicero almost asks, does acuity as a public augur end and the role (perhaps enforced or ventriloquized) of the "parrot" (playing on *oscen*) begin? Moreover, readers might wonder where Cicero would have drawn the line between this direction of reasoning and the wider metaphorical implications of Varro's emphatic consensus position on grammar, a position characterized as a solution to a vividly oppositional conflict between traditional authority and shared usage as systems for meaningful expression (*Ling.* 10).

Read against the quoted passage from Varro (*Ling.* 6.76), the prophetic song of the omen-birds is also the end of a story arc: the second phase of Varro's exploration of "action" (contemplation and cogitation). Varro's continuation ushers in the last and most popularly valued kind of "action": "doing" (*facio*).[27] Varro will next recall the poetic mode when he explores sensory terminology (*Ling.* 6.80–85), quoting Ennius (*Ling.* 6.83) to make his point that hearing (*audio*, I hear; *ausculto*, I listen) seems to derive from ears (*aures*). The conclusion to the sentence, a follow-on etymology for *aures* ("*aures ab aueo*," 6.83), is the result of emendation but offers a reading that works elegantly in context. Ears are crucial for a city of speakers; hooking in one's hearers as avid fans—*aueo* (I am eager)—who learn as they listen feels right in narrative terms.[28] Further, *auscultare* (to heed) derives from *audire* (to hear, learn, understand), because to heed means to attend upon what one has heard. This derivation effectively enables the learning process associated with what I have termed Romespeak, especially its community-forming qualities and its ability to connect study with action (making the ears a "tool for thinking" in Sluiter's sense or perhaps, in this context, a "tool for interpreting").[29]

For Varro, Ennius' *Alexander* supports this enthusiastically active listening mode: "'Long indeed have my mind and my ears been avid [*aures auent*], / avidly [*auide*] awaiting news from the games.' It's because of the greediness of the ears that theaters are packed out."[30] As Varro tells it, in the act of making Ennius seem (*uidetur*) to put on a show (*ostendo*) starring the noun ("ears") as a root word, he produces a deeply corporeal way of showing the inextricability of the connection between the theater and (Greco-)Roman life: it is this avidity on the ears' part that keeps the theaters (*theatra*) filled, which in the wider context of Varro's argument shows how Romans are by nature eager to engage their discriminative faculties and consume embodied discourse. To put it another way, theatrical shows in the broadest sense (taking in Ennius' *ludi*) perform to a primed audience (if they have read their Varro), whose physiology is part of their role; anyone equipped with ears is already an audience member and Romespeaker in waiting.[31]

One more sequence is important for this section: how Varro draws the Latin Muses into the frame.[32] After a blank (in *F*), the manuscript picks up with *Camenae*. The text pulls together a fragmentary, unascribed quote from Ennius,[33] commentary on early spellings, and the assertion that the (uniquely Varronian) form *Carmenae* is part of the family ("*ab eadem origine sunt declinatae*," *Ling.* 7.26). The spoken S of antiquity, Varro remarks, frequently morphs into a contemporary R (a point illustrated by a relatively lengthy quote from the *Carmen Saliare*). By knowing this, Varro foreshadows a semiotic link between *carmen* and *Camena*, one that becomes explicit when he has cataloged the kinds of words associated with this slippage from S to R.[34]

At the beginning of *Ling.* 7.27 sits what seems to be an illustrative list for the same point: an orthographic shift between S and R. For instance, Varro offers treaties (*foedesum/foederum*, emended from *faed-*), comparative value judgments (*plusima/plurima*; *meliosem/meliorem*), the sand in the arena (*asenam/*

arenam), and a doorkeeper (*ianitos/ianitor*). But this is only a brief interruption before returning to the matter in hand:

> Quare e <u>Casmena</u> <u>Carmena</u>, <e> <u>Carmena</u> R extrito <u>Camena</u> factum. Ab eadem uoce <u>canite</u>, pro quo in Saliari uersu scriptum est <u>cante</u>. (Varro, *Ling.* 7.27)

> Therefore from <u>Casmena</u>, <u>Carmena</u>, <and> from <u>Carmena</u>, with R extracted, comes <u>Camena</u>. From the same word: "<u>sing</u>!" [*canite*], in place of which in Salian verse is written *cante*.

One might wonder at this point whether the gendering of inspired "song" as female (*Carmena, ae*), might nod to *Carment-is* and her alternative ending in *-a* (in addition to the obvious, inspirational *Camenae*). For through-readers who eventually reach *Ling.* 7.34, this material might also encourage further attention to Varro's subsequent Callimachaean quarrying of *camilla*.[35] Retrospectively at least, §27 reverberates in the transition from *camilla* to *casmillus* at §34, but whereas the story of *camilla*, as it develops to *Casmillus*, helps fashion a Latin prehistory for a Greek term, Varro makes no allusion to any "interim" form in *carmill-*. A link joining *Camena*, *Carmena*, *carmina*, and *camilla* is left to the attentive reader, already attuned to the need to read more into Varro's silences.[36]

The lack of other evidence for a form *Carmena* suggests that Varro's audience might already have needed to work hard on swallowing this mash-up, but it also emphasizes the need for ingenuity and lateral thinking when following Varro's lead. Latin song and inspiration are tied together here as having inherent, complex connectivity, but at the heart of this story lies the idea that despite an allusively interconnected (Hellenic) Mediterranean culture, Latin poetic inspiration (the familiar Camenae) has a quality of separateness from Greek (the Muses). This makes for distinctive (even quirky) genealogical word tangles and a distinctive historicity for the development of Romespeak as authoritative (with its power transmitted directly from the Camenae) and in need of Varro's expert mediation.

What might readers think, if *Carment-a/-is*, prophetic nymph and mother of Evander, springs to mind?[37] She could certainly add value here (particularly with Varro's *Carmena* in our sights), rather as she would later for Vergil. Vergil editorializes the significance succinctly when elaborating on the Porta Carmentalis: "*nymphae priscum Carmentis honorem, / uatis fatidicae, cecinit quae prima futuros / Aeneadas magnos et nobile Pallanteum*" (an ancient honor for the nymph Carmentis, prophetic poet who first <u>sang out</u> the great future for Aeneas' line and renowned Pallanteum).[38] Following where Varro goes next suggests that Vergil was dipping into the same pool (*Casmena/Carmena/Camena*): from that *spoken* word (*ab eadem uoce*) comes "sing!" (plural imperative, *canite*).[39] Utterance with a tonal quality (*uox*) combines with inspired song in Latin to make a new formulation exhorting Romans to "sing!" The form's novelty and interest are embedded in its difference from the model "*cante*" (evidenced by the *Carmen Saliare*).

This interplay between old and new, flagged by the looming presence of the proverbially ancient *Carmen Saliare*, delivers an unexpected twist. The term *Casmenae* is associated by Varro with the adjective *cascus*, the Roman name Casca, and the town Casinum, building in quotes from something called the *Carmen Priami*, and from Ennius; from what seems to be a proverbial couplet from a "Manilius," and from an epigram by "Papinius."[40]

The first of these ("Song of Priam") juxtaposes the three key terms directly ("*ueteres Casmenas cascam rem*," *Ling.* 7.28). In the beginning, therefore, *cascus* is part of the semiotic field of "old" (*significat uetus*). Next, its origins, Sabine, ultimately give it Oscan roots. Varro speaks directly here, without a mediating singsong authority.[41] What is especially inspirational for this chapter's concerns is Varro's management of a rapid shift in tone from the *Carmen Saliare* and "Song of Priam," through antiquarian aside, to Ennius' portentous characterization of "what the archaic Latins, the long-ago [*casci*] people, produced [*genuere*]."[42] The tonal shift is delivered by Varro's editorializing transition—Manilius, not Ennius, put it better ("*Eo magis Manilius quod ait*")—showing how wide-ranging knowledge makes comparative study and creative insight possible. With Ennius abandoned, we plunge from those patriotic epic origins into the authority world of social comedy and barbed humor. "No wonder that Oldie [*cascus*] married Biddy [*casca*], / Since he fixed up a wedding with a high price tag." Papinius' nasty punchlines on a young Casca hammer this home ("*item ostendit*"): an aging mistress turns the relationship into a joke every time she murmurs "my Casca" to her boy toy: "you're just a stripling, your girlfriend's pensionable!" the epigram ends.[43]

Varro takes the example of Casinum (*Ling.* 7.29)—where he had a fine property, including the aviary later made famous in *De Re Rustica* (3.4–5)—to demonstrate the real-world truth of his connection of *casmen, carmen, cascus, cano*, and the Sabine *terroir* as a sequence of authoritative intersections. It was part of Samnite territory, Varro states, but in what looks like another convergence of orthography, etymology, and history, the Samnites had Sabine origins ("*hoc enim ab Sabinis orti Samnites tenuerunt*," *Ling.* 7.29). This reminds readers of the ongoing underlying Sabine foundations for Varro's Romespeak, especially as he immediately continues "our people even now call it Old Forum."[44] Samnites become Romans by filiation, and the ends are tied up on recalling Varro's earlier assertion (*Ling*. 7.28) that Sabine is a descendant of Oscan. Thus, several Atellan farces associate *cascus* with the "old man" (*Pappus*) character, because the Oscans, Varro says, call a *senex casnar*.[45] The action term for both sets of denotative speakers ("us," "the Oscans") is "*appellant*." *Cascus*, therefore, is properly Sabine and associatively, as Varro insists via the three-letter match, Oscan. This claims Atellan farce as *echt* Roman in the best sense—because it is comedically lodged in the ur-form of Sabine.[46] This sequence shows that sometimes Ennius is not the ultimate authority; such a colorful word game with a sexy/dirty political undertone is of course so much pithier than anything Ennius might have dreamt up (Varro's juxtaposition suggests).

The energy underlying the etymologies of *Ling*. 7.26–29 pushes readers to engage with the literary and metapoetic quality of Varro's organization, so in narrative terms it is unsurprising that by way of ("what the Greeks call") a proverb ("dog isn't meat for dog," *Ling*. 7.31, repeated at 7.32) he turns to talking "around" something as a modus operandi:

> Profecto a uerbo ambe, quod inest in ambitu et ambitioso. . . . Adagio est littera commutata a<m>bagio,[47] dicta ab eo quod ambit orationem, neque in aliqua una re constitit sola. (Varro, *Ling*. 7.30, 31)

> Actually, *ambages* [circumlocution] is from the word *ambe* [round about], which is inherent in *ambitus* [encircling; canvassing; showing off; corruption], and in *ambitiosus* [entrapping; smothering; showy/superficial; fawning; ambitious]. . . . "Adage" is only a swapped letter away from "digression," which is said for when one goes in circles in discourse and does not settle firmly on one thing alone.

"Yet," Varro continues, "there are three connected things that need to be taken into consideration in the origins of words: what caused the word to be applied and to what, and what it actually is" (*Ling*. 7.32). Varro's example suggests that items one and three are equally problematic and identifies a gender/form mutability around "dog" (as against dog/bitch: separate words) as his prime example. Ennius, quoted using "bitch" ("*canes*"), is joined by Lucilius (for the singular usage), but Varro excuses this ("*neque reprehendus*") because Ennius should not be blamed in that he is following precedent, traditional usage, and popular sense.[48] What sets this sequence apart is its clear assertion of the significance of worthwhile novelty (it's also okay not to follow Ennius et al.! *Canis* singular is acceptable, as the proverb shows, *Ling.* 7.32) at least inasmuch as it marks up a lively tradition.

If we revisit Varro's "three things" in this context we can see that they also recall fluent readers to his handbook's program (*Ling.* 7.32). First, to deploy the power of speech demands understanding the originary temporality and chronological weight of words, and this requires knowledge of the past (what "thing" a word came from, before the word itself was needed), the future perfect (where its application will ultimately have taken it), and the present (what it is in itself). Next, there are wider reverberations when Varro says that it is in the past ("*a quo sit impositum*") and the present ("*quid*") that the greatest uncertainty occurs. Ennius and Lucilius get it both wrong *and* right.

Although it is not immediately evident as one reads, Varro's dogg-erel (Ennius, Lucilius, proverb) helps shore up a satisfying conclusion and to realign this material with his earlier investigation of song. When dogs bark they "sing out" the signals ("*signa canunt*"), and it is in this very specific trait that their name (*canes* from the polysemic *cano*) derives. Dogs are "the singing ones," "the celebrators," or perhaps even "the publicists." And in all this they give shape to those nighttime secrets that otherwise go unspoken: "*et quod ea uoce indicant noctu quae latent, latratus appellatus*" (*Ling.* 7.32), perhaps recalling the scholarly night-work with which Varro opened book 7 ("*in lucubratione*," *Ling.* 7.2). Back at *Ling.* 7.2, Varro observed of etymology that much remains hidden ("*tamen latent multa*"); returning to 7.32, we can now see the wider significance of how thoroughly the semiotic dogs, as a collective, "sing" what is hidden into existence and consolidate the book's programmatic argument, while at the same time making clear that their "natural" expression lacks the reflective dialogic quality and intellectual endeavor associated with Romespeak.[49] This substantially refines Varro's perspective on "song," making clear the more than aesthetic qualities in the production of communicative sounds even in a language whose system appears to be primarily formulaic. From *cano*, dogs are daily performers of the obscure yet still powerful connections between superficial and deep understanding, between natural or instinctive engagement with the cosmos and learned behavior through which civilization develops.

With this, therefore, we also see Varro's model of consensus (a coalition of the "willing") sharpen further. Shared poetic rhythms, forms, and songs need not be intelligible to transmit powerful messages, and a shared set of practices and norms, transmitted through the structures of discourse, brings the community to life and ensures its protection. The shape of that community and its values are the business of everyone, but also, especially, the responsibility of the scholar and public intellectual whose work delivers what is arcane into meaningful intelligibility and who makes manifest the right kind of *auctoritas uerborum* as an inspiration to the citizen body.

As book 7 progresses, Varro appears to be leaving the deep etymological ancestry of derivations ("*quae latent*") more and more to his audience to figure out. This meandering drift meshes neatly with his early comments in the book, repeating (to some extent) a notional program of moving away from etymology as set out in book 5.[50] Quotations and the stories they drag into the picture are, I suggest, being leaned on heavily to enable this increasing workload for readers. With that in mind, Varro's literary exploration of the terminology of walking impediments (that is, impediments to movement) presents an ideal case study to show the power of quotation to highlight the consensus-forming power of exclusionary politics.[51]

Varro begins with a quote from a lost Plautus: "*Scratiae, s<c>rup<i>pedae, s<t>rittabillae, tantulae.*"[52] Starting with *scratiae* (perhaps, desiccated old women), Varro derives this from *ex(s)creo* (to cough up), indicating (following a sensible emendation) that they are "dried up" (*siccus*, in every sense).[53] Next for scrutiny is the unusual *scrup<i>peda* (hobbling). Rather than starting with a vivid exegesis involving feet on sharp stones (*scrupus/scrupeus* and *pes*), what Varro offers first is a pathological etymology that runs counter to obvious approaches: this is a physiological condition (*scaurus*, swollen ankles, plus *pes*), and he cites Aurelius as his authority.[54] So the first appropriate pattern of derivation for the context (comically repellent old women) is not to make them pathetic (by giving their movement external cause—sharp stones) but to represent them etymologically as impeded by their own swelling extremities.

Varro keeps prodding at this: apparently, Iuventius the (little-attested) comic poet used to say that *scrup<i>peda* came from a type of hairy caterpillar ("*Iuuentius comicus dicebat a uermiculo piloso*") that tends to be found among foliage ("*frons*") and has many feet ("*cum multis pedibus*"; the metrical witticism seems obvious). By tagging Iuventius explicitly as a "comedian" in this etymological context, Varro makes it hard not to find a complex, crisply nuanced joke. For a start, *uermiculus* is itself uncommon in (extant) late Republican Latin but has artful, satirical associations in deponent verb form in Lucilian use. It makes sense to read this in because it is Varro's friend Cicero who gives the citation (*uermiculatus*, something knotty and complexly patterned, especially perhaps mosaic work, designed to resemble the tracks made by worms).[55]

In *De Oratore*, Cicero alerts readers to Lucilius' lines as a ventriloution of Mucius Scaevola, showcasing the political heft of words arranged sinuously, aptly, and wittily. This metatextual "vermiculation" cues up a connection between comedy (Iuventius, Plautus) and (Lucilian) satire. It emphasizes a taste for the fantastic in performance (toying with the idea of many-footed, hairy, bug-women), and, in factoring in Cicero's allusion, it highlights the problem of reconciling public performance and political gravitas with authorship as a Roman identity package. To unpick this notion of pliability and contextual sensitivity further might beg the question of whether the (satirical) "caterpillar," nicely set up amid leafy boughs ("*frons*"), is equally at home on the stage ("*frons*").[56]

The bug's "shaggy" ("*pilosus*") qualities hint at untamed, primitive nature, yet the stagey quality of intertextual materials suggests that each *pes* (foot) needs to embrace its polyphonous (*multi*) metrical-verse connotations. Explanations and attestations continue to encourage quotation. Going back to etymological basics, one Valerius takes *scrup<i>peda* as a combined derivation from "foot" and "ruggedness." With the uncommon *scrupea*, a literary-poetic combination is in the wings. Valerius' etymology opens the door to Ennius and to Pacuvius,[57] before Varro finally offers a particular formulation from Accius' *Melanippus*: "you cast off your belief system [*religio*]? Then you're taking on a difficult burden [*scrupea*]."[58] This last formulation adds an ethical dimension, perhaps suggesting wider systemic implications. Accius conjures up someone who shifts one "burden" only to take on one much more ontologically onerous (the combined physical and moral qualities in *scrupea/scrupeus*).

One final gambit rounds off Varro's collection of quirky words concerning halting and fluid movement. Slap-bang after the line of Accius, readers find themselves at the word *strittabillae*. This (Varro asserts baldly) comes via *strettillare* from *strittare*. *Strittare* means someone who barely can stand ("*eo qui sistit aegre*"). With this, readers find the logic gaps between the transitions in this discussion closing. *Strittare* pulls together the hobbling, swollen-ankled women of the first phase and the morally impaired character in Accius—leaving the reader comprehensively wrong-footed. And with that, Varro moves on.

Poetry and the Divine

"*Incipiam hinc*" (*Ling.* 7.6): *De Lingua Latina* systematizes and acculturates the world-forming and cosmic qualities of discourse, as we have already seen in Varro's interest in augury and omens. Varro's assertion commences the book proper and introduces readers to its overarching structural theme: place-words used by poets.[59] To draw these issues into focus, this section analyses Varro's excursus on the creation of *templa* (*Ling.* 7.6) in verse context, which begins a sequence stretching to §13.[60]

"I shall begin here," Varro observes, starting with *templa*:

>   Unus erit quem tu tolles in c*ae*rula caeli
>   Templa.
> Templum tribus modis dicitur: ab natura, ab auspic*ando*, a similitudine;
> <ab> natura in caelo, ab auspiciis in terra, a similitudine sub terra. In
> caelo te<m>plum dicitur, ut in *H*ecuba:
>   O magna templa caelitum, commixta stellis splendidis.
> In terra, ut in Periboea:
>   Scrupea saxea Ba<c>chi
>   Templa prope aggreditur.
> Sub terra, ut in Andromacha:
>   Acherusia templa alta Orci, saluete, infera.
> (Varro, *Ling.* 7.6)

> There will be one whom you shall elevate to the azure temples
> Of the sky.

"Temple" has three meanings, drawing from nature, from formal auspices, and from similarity: with regard to nature, in the sky; from taking formal auspices, on earth; from similarity, subterranean. In the sky, "temple" is used as in [Ennius'] *Hecuba*:

> O great temples of the heaven-dwellers, commingled with the
>   shining stars.
> On earth, as in [Pacuvius'] *Periboea*:
>   Over sharp stones, hard by the temples
>   Of Bacchus it approaches.
> Below the earth, as in [Ennius'] *Andromacha*:
>   By the Acherusian flow, lofty temples of Orcus, be greeted in the
>   underworld.

Varro's three examples focus attention on the marvelous, otherworldly, and unknowable qualities of *templa*, emphasizing their separateness from the everyday world of humankind, their ability to translate mortals into the world of the gods. Varro's quotes emphasize the sensational qualities of these varied temples, and a vividness develops by way of the verb *tueor* (*Ling.* 7.7–9), a particularly complex and reifying form of observation ("the object of the gaze was originally called a *templum* from *tueri* [to gaze], therefore the sky, at which we gaze [*attuimur*], was called *templum*," *Ling.* 7.7).[61] The human gaze is inexorably drawn skyward; hence "temple" became a term for "sky." To help us understand this universalizing proposition—one that roots human experience within a deep chronological prospect—Varro brings in quotes from Ennius and Naevius.[62] Only in this kind of richly understood cultural landscape can such an extraordinary duration of humanity's shared values and evaluative skills become real.

When Varro's opening quote takes celestial *templa* as the prime word for this category, he also challenges his audience to pick up on the literary allusion—a popular but unascribed tagline from Ennius' *Annales*, foretelling the apotheosis of Romulus. The quotation offers a sense of familiarity—"*Unus erit*"—but also might bring readers up short.[63] The elevation of Romulus is not the focus here, nor the melodrama of the verse context; instead, Varro's focus is in illustration of *templa*.[64] At the very least, the quote neatly lays bare the complexity of how history speaks to myth through verse, since Varro has chosen to quote the allusion to Romulus' deification that comes *after* Ilia's prophetic dream. By contrast, in *De Diuinatione* Cicero picks out the melodramatic possibilities offered by the speech and sadness of the young vestal, a passage that would have gifted to Varro the high-octane emotion of Ilia throwing up her hands "*ad caeli caerula templa*" when abandoned by her nocturnal vision.[65]

Varro's readers must first recognize that the lines are Ennius.' They may then note that Varro is choosing to avoid an obvious and contextually relevant narrative catalyst (the dream). Finally, they can see that these choices point up the meshing of private concerns (Ilia), family complexities (Ilia, Romulus and Remus), and the public qualities of the cosmos as a stage for their playing out (Romulus and Remus and then Romulus alone)—and that the nuances of poetry make it especially well adapted to explore how meaning draws together micro- and macrocosms.

Varro's actual focus here is the *templum*, a delimited space where the gods are in some sense "at home" to mortals. As in the case of Romulus' apotheosis but in more structured form, this is a site where mortals and immortals can exchange addresses. *Templa* can, readers learn, be celestial, earth-bound, or subterranean, and for each "precinct" or "domain" Varro includes a dramatic verse quotation. This means gathering together Ennius' *Hecuba* ("O great precincts of the heaven-born, united with the sparkling stars"), Pacuvius' *Periboea* ("To jagged rocks, the precincts of Bacchus, s/he draws near"),[66] and Ennius' *Andromache* ("Salutations, mighty infernal precincts of Orcus, by the Acheron"). As Jerzy Linderski hints, Varro is showcasing the gappiness between poetic and public, civic discourse, but there is more to Varro's trio of examples than a cavalier attitude to temple definition. Verse illustration is what *enables* this special kind of communication to happen, and it requires an engagement with issues of poetic license and irregularity, albeit framed within an intelligible system, that will become crucial for understanding Varro's consensus position on grammar and, I argue, on life, as he presents it in book 10.

Poets, and in particular perhaps dramatic poets, are required to deliver a more than pragmatic and quotidian interface with the cosmos and its esoteric qualities; yet they must also absolutely serve up scenes and encounters that offer distinctive meaning and immediate signification to their earthbound audiences.[67] In deciding *not* to select the more dramatic example of Ennius' annalistic *templa*, Varro strips bare the editorial processes of authorship when fashioning new works from a familiar canon. In selecting three illustrative examples of dramatic poets sketching *templa* as immortal locales, encompassing the heavens, the earth, and the world below, Varro is offering an important insight into how context generates meaning. This is not just about the poets quoted or a technical explanation for *templum*. Instead, this dryly procedural context is undercut by the metaphorical loading that the four quotations make available.

Just as ears made hearing—and auspicious authority—anywhere realized by the eyes (*tueor*) becomes a *templum*; hence, for example, the sky (as subject of the gaze) is a *templum*.[68] Interjecting Ennius—"trembled the mighty precinct of high-thundering Jupiter"—adds a dizzying synesthesia to the power of this executive gaze.[69] Gazing purposefully at the sky is what defines it, transforming it into a god-haunted place. Hearing and seeing the results of this etymology (and sensing the trembling, the thundering) reifies the esoteric qualities in play when deciding between awe-inspiring climactic conditions to which humanity is subject and the (metaphoric) potential of thundering Jupiter, a human construct.

In the Beginning, Starting from Scratch, or Ending Up?

Beginnings and endings in books 5–7—or, what makes one start and finish anything—are the focus for this chapter's two concluding sections, and to understand their nuances we must range back to Cato's *Origines*. This is where practicalities meet inspiration and the creative urge.

De Lingua Latina (as it stands) offers no origin for "origin" (*origo*), and Latin etymology remains silent on the subject. We might speculate about a likely sense overlap with the Greek κτίσις (originary foundation) and ἀρχή (beginning; first site of power),[70] but the sound-alike ὄρνυμι (in the sense "to call forth" or " to awaken") must be at least distantly present for Varro and his circle.[71] Toward the end of book 6 (the penultimate book of his etymological hexad) Varro acknowledges that he has put together many words on just a small array of topics, so he will correspondingly prune what remains; this will be discussion of the words where "they [/some] think" that Latin (proverbially? ill-informedly?) finds its origins in Greek ("*quae in Graeca lingua putant Latina*").[72]

The beginning of the end of book 6 is marked by an extended excursus on the relationship between *inlicium* (summoning, inducement) and *inlicio* (to summon, or entice), drawing together significant quotations from an otherwise unknown commentary on a capital indictment.[73] These relatively long and undigested quotes are presented without much reference to any linguistic issues—their inclusion seems instead to be as legal markup for a sequence of core citizen practices and behaviors. A brief discussion of legal terminology then leads Varro to comment on prolixity, to promise immediate conciseness, and to present a raw catalog of Greek origin words (*Ling.* 6.96). With that he concludes:

Quod ad origines uerborum huius libri pertinet, satis multas arbitror positas huius generis; desistam, et quoniam de hisce rebus tri<s> libros ad te mittere institui, de oratione soluta duo, poetica unum, et ex soluta oratione ad te misi duo, priorem de locis et quae in locis sunt, hunc de temporibus et quae cum his sunt coniuncta, deinceps in proximo de poeticis uerborum originibus scribere in<cipiam>. (Varro, *Ling.* 6.97)

Concerning the origins of the words that this book has as its remit, sufficiently numerous of this kind have, in my judgment, been set down. I shall stop. And since I have contracted to send you three books on this subject matter, two fulfilling the promise for oratory, one for poetry, and I have sent two to you to clear the debt on speech (the first concerning places and what things are in places, this one concerning temporalities and the things linked to them), what follows in the next book is that I shall begin to write about the origins of words in poetry.

This salvo is full of themes relevant to being a Cicero and emphasizing *origines*. Varro's choice of *pertineo* as the action term for these "origins" (and the generalizing subject *quod*) draws together implications of pervasiveness, implacable agency, and ownership (connected in part but not wholly to Varro himself by the first-person *arbitror* of the next clause). It also marks Varro's book as something more than just a textbook. *Origines* transforms this interim closing statement into a subtle evocation of the pristine credentials of a Cato, but it also hints at a contiguity between their two projects.[74] In chapter 2 I noted that Cato and Cicero's Cato (*De Senectute*) shimmer behind some of Varro's etymologies. With *origines* and in this programmatic context, readers might see signs of a comparison between Varro's intellectual mission and what might have constituted Cato's.

Cato features frequently *in propria persona* in Varro's late work on the countryside, but he is very much on the radar in De Lingua Latina.[75] *Origines* mark the beginning and the end of book 6, and although the fragmentary nature of Cato's game-changing *Origines* makes in-depth comparison challenging, nevertheless certain big themes emerge in ways that seem to mesh with Varro's interests. When Varro comments that the baggage attending on verbal *origins* has been set in place (*pono*) quite enough already, a jibe at Cato is not impossible. Cato's *Origines* was at least susceptible to being read as *historiae* by Nepos' time (*Cato* 3.2–4), but this is by far the least interesting or productive way of characterizing Cato's achievement.[76] We might think instead of doing *Origins* as producing a seminal monument: one that would instantiate Cato as a success story (in his own terms) and as a voice of and for Rome (contextualized by increasing interest in the perspective offered by philhellenism).

As far as the arrangement of the fragments allows us to judge, the publication of Cato's *Origines* must have delivered something uniquely interesting for a generation increasingly accustomed to transformation and perhaps hungry for a narrative of cohesion and foundation. In *Origines*, Romans gained a collection knitting together origins for Rome itself and also for the array of city-states that made up the peninsula—the first meaningful and coherent realization of brand "*tota Italia.*"[77]

In a passage on the origins of the Latin people (cited in Servius), Cato offers a way of understanding what might constitute a historical people, Roman and Italian, through a shared discourse of individual civic and territorial "etymologies."[78] Enrica Sciarrino sees in Cato's model a kind of practice of "cultural dispossession" attendant on the Roman appropriative historical gaze.[79] A "catalog" quality evident in the first three books of Cato's *Origines* may be one way in which that work signaled itself as part of a performance culture eager to appropriate and cannibalize not just Greek literature and drama but also the valuable diaspora of Hellenism embodied in the myths and city-states of Italy. In this model, Cato's *Origines* becomes "an admissible resource meant to sustain a preexisting elite lore," freezing out the "mediating function of poetry and poets in intra-elite exchanges and in the mechanisms that regulated the reproduction of the elite," and thus unsympathetic to Varro's position.[80]

Cato's new and unique Latin discourse, mediated for the few—a kind of elite harmonics—would become a vehicle for training ambitious individuals in a hi-spec package of rhetorical tactics and tropes. Unforeseen by Cato, educated, politically talented Romans, armed with these very tools and hungry to grab power in the *res publica*, were also thus equipped to challenge the elite's hold on what constituted *mos maiorum*.[81] If Cato was interested in marking out the elite as a distinctive group within a nonetheless harmonious Roman society, armed with its own newly glossed cultural practices by way of his handbook, through dramatization of its rootedness in "tradition," and by participation in a revived sense of purpose, Varro's pragmatic and associative approach was rather different.[82] In this reading of new beginnings, Varro's project suggests a pragmatic acceptance that this divided body politic has been pushed to the point of coming undone; he seizes a vanguard role to unite *langue* and *parole* positively as exemplars of sociopolitical forces and offers new collaborative tools with which to explore and understand a discourse-world evolving poetically through consent—not imposed by prose authority.

In the context of *origines*, Varro's riff on *umbilicus* in book 7 takes on additional meaning. "This is what the Greeks call ὀμφαλός; what they say is the tomb of Python. From this our 'interpreters' have termed ὀμφαλός *umbilicus*" (*Ling*. 7.17). Varro's allusion to *interpretes* evokes a wider literary-cultural debate about how best or most intellectually credibly to characterize the process of cultural translation from Greek to Latin.[83] He says that the first, popular, Roman solution is wrong, but in an interesting way. It errs by taking a literal approach to a Greek assertion of what looks like sympathetic physiology (for Rome and for Romans, this explanation suggests, the *umbilicus* is the thing in the middle). It all stems from the Greek ὀμφαλός, introduced by Varro toward the end of the account. The problem arises, it seems, when people unquestioningly assume that cultural translation works neatly and unquestioningly embrace a Latinized version of a Greek meme that is in itself incorrect: Delphi is *not* at the center of the world, nor is the Treasury at the center of Delphi, so Romespeakers need to know how to return to generative first principles to derive meaning securely.[84] In fact, one also needs to have the facility to feed in natural science (Pythagoras-style) in order to follow Varro's logic that "as is the case for the beginnings of human life, similarly for the world; for there, everything is born of the middle, since the earth is the center of the world."[85] If one is equipped appropriately, then creative generation of shared meaning and of community becomes possible.

This reading of Varro requires Caesar's presence as both an advocate of (grammatical) "regularity" and an icon of (political) anomaly and also as a man for whom language was a crucially important weapon. He needed *parole* to be operating effectively to deliver his constituency and also to secure his iconic role for the *populares*. Nevertheless, to control the outcomes of this brand of politics, he required the power formally to interject radical and intelligible (but palatable) change.[86] That is to say, Caesar also needed skillful control in order to manipulate *langue* in a *timely* way—he needed to be a master of καιρός. The linguistic model that Varro will roll out in books 8–10 offers metaphorical insight on political meltdown. These books will chart how *analogia* is under threat from *anomalia*, yet also demonstrate that if one analyzes the faceoff between the two, one finds that what appears to be a traumatic fracture within the Republic (or, discourse) will, albeit slowly, heal itself. Perhaps in this way even Caesar will be normalized if the traditional political and linguistic semiotics can be guarded and maintained by people who recognize the power and value of a contrapuntally balanced system.[87] For everything that appears, Varro will argue, something naturally disappears; yet novelties too become naturalized in popular use. Although Varro does not always quite make this workable in detail, in it lodges the power of his message.

When Varro concludes book 6, he observes of the two books (5–6) already sent to Cicero that this pair has tackled speech and focused on place and time. The closing book of the triad (book 7) will move on to elucidate something quite different. The emendation "*in<cipiam>*" is plausible and makes for a stylish end to the book by juxtaposing "origins" with "beginning," embracing the limitless infinitive "to write," and echoing in reverse the momentum of the earlier "*desistam*."[88] This interim valediction delivers another juicy morsel—it outlines the delivery of the text to Cicero. "I have sent" ("*misi*") two books; one must be this very book, which Cicero as dedicatee may be imagined to be unrolling.

On the basis of this comment, books 5 and 6 seem to have constituted a distinct phase in the project's "publication." This packaging of a two-plus-one ("*de oratione soluta duo, poetica unum*," *Ling.* 6.97) dedication tells Varro's audience that the distinction between prose (oratory) and poetry is deeply embedded. The supposed bundling of "all" relevant examples for poetic words in one book suggests that poetry operates conceptually in a very different way from prose. In this model, *oratio* makes logical a place/time split (one book each, *Ling.* 6.97); verse, which Varro has selected to draw the etymological hexad to a conclusion, can be treated holistically. Prose speech is at once more massive (two books of Varro) and divisive (first in the sequence but requiring two different approaches). Varro's readers must join him in rethinking what constitutes mastery of Latin prose before turning to what makes Latin verse tick, and, in the process of working through Varro's system, they learn to consolidate Rome-speak as a diachronic and synchronic mode.

The conclusion to book 6, read in this way, offers a different angle from that presented when Varro closed book 5, the first in the triad. Ending book 5, Varro was already (compare 6.97) deploying *pertineo*:

Ad uocabula quae pertinere sumus rati ea quae loca et ea quae in locis sunt satis ut arbitror dicta, quod neque parum multa sunt aperta neque, si amplius uelimus, uolumen patietur. Quare in proximo, ut in primo libro dixi, quod sequitur de temporibus dicam. (Varro, *Ling.* 5.184)

What we counted to be in the domain of place terms, and of terms concerning what pertains to places, has been articulated in sufficient detail: it's not the case that not enough examples have been laid bare, and even if we wished to lay out more, the scroll will not allow. Therefore in the next book, as I stated in the first, I shall speak about what follows on, concerning temporality.

The programmatic nature of the introductory and concluding sections for these books is highlighted if through-readers recognize the repetition of *pertineo*, especially considering additional echoes in *satis* and *arbitror*. Here, however, Varro emphasizes what has been spoken ("*dico*") rather than what has been physically marked down ("*pono*," in book 6), suggesting a sense of transition from spoken to written language and from the instinctive and natural, to the more conceptually complex.[89]

There are humor and charm in Varro's articulation of a kind of authorial impotence in the passage just quoted (*Ling.* 5.184). The humor bubbles through the alliteration and assonance of the "if" clause as he marks the implacable constraints (a double negative) of the book scroll's limits. This playoff between the physical limits imposed on the writer by the book scroll ("*uolumen*") and the temporal exigencies of vocabulary enriches Varro's closural address. In the process, Varro pokes at an issue in which Michel Foucault would interest himself and that this section picks up from the first section in this chapter, "Poets, Artfulness, and Textuality": "is not the material unity of the volume a weak, accessory unity in relation to the discursive unity of which it is the support?"[90] In the physical reality of book scrolls, material disunity in a multivolume work is part of its identity. What remains under Varro's control (at least when he addresses a through-reader) is how discursive unity is experienced: book 5 characterizes itself here as having been about *terminology* ("*uocabulum*" or "*langue*"); the introduction to book 6 (*Ling.* 6.1) then pairs (the *origines* of) *uerba* with *uocabula* and counterpoints them vividly with the acts of writing (regarding book 5) and speaking (book 6) before book 6 ends with a return to *words* ("*uerba*," or "*parole*").

Origines uerborum qua<e> sunt locorum et ea quae in his in priore libro scripsi. In hoc dicam de uocabulis temporum et earum rerum quae in agendo fiunt aut dicuntur cum tempore aliquo ut sedetur, ambulatur, loquontur; atque si quia erunt ex diuerso genere adiuncta, potius cognationi uerborum quam auditori calumnianti *geremus morem.* (Varro, *Ling.* 6.1)

The origins of the words that are place terms and relate to things in places, I have written about in the previous book. In this, I shall speak about time words and about those things that are actualized through performance or are articulated with some inbuilt temporality, such as "sat," "walked," "spoken." And if there should be other words, even of a different type, attached to these, I shall prioritize family ties over the vexatious plaints of the audience.

Varro's first-person plural at the close of this introductory statement unfolds a vigorous program. Kinship in discourse and relational patterns in semiotics are what count, and to decode the acts ("*in agendo*") of everyday life in Latin one requires a textual expertise that goes way beyond ordinary dialogue or routine oratory, however tedious this may seem to his audience. Indeed, the phrase "*geremus morem*" obliquely confronts the notion of res gestae by articulating a communicative mode that draws on a sense of shared performed practice (*mos gesti*).[91] The vividness of the metaphor with which Varro closes this introduction underscores the point: linguistic expertise is a performative skill whose nuances stretch out into family connections and webs of affinity—popular subject matter par excellence for stage shows and the forensic stage alike.

Book 7 opens the last book of the etymological hexad and makes a new beginning. This is where Varro explicitly sets himself the task of reclaiming poetic expression from what might be termed the ruin of time ("*ruina*," *Ling.* 7.1), but it will not just be about cataloging poetry for cannibalistic citation by the elite (as we saw with *Ling.* 7.31–32). Popular parlance, even if that means hybridization by way of Greek loan words (*Ling.* 7.31), keeps a language alive— those who add or subtract letters to make poetic sense clearer are not to be found fault with (*Ling.* 7.1).[92] This opening to book 7 shows Varro's understanding of the problem of poetic fossils to be subtly different from that which Cicero proposes (with regard to Cato) in his *Tusculan Disputations*.[93] Varro's comments in introducing book 7 (*Ling.* 7.1–4) articulate a concern that the technical authority of the *poetae* risks losing contemporary force because it is becoming too embedded in historical shibboleths, but, taking a line from Cicero's *Orator* (*doceo* conceived in opposition to *probo*, *Or.* 142), Varro may also be alluding to a problematic cultural perception of pedagogy with respect to language (do native speakers need to be taught their birthright?). In Varro's book, authentic Latin verse traditions need to move out of the scholarly domain and reclaim popular meaning in Latin *parole*, mediating between past and present as best they can and reclaiming the role of the poets (*"poetae"*) in transmitting and actualizing the practical achievements of civilization.[94]

The concluding phase of Varro's introduction to book 7 was a focus for the first section of this chapter, "Poets, Artfulness, and Textuality," but we are now better equipped to do more with it. The first sentence looks like another nudge toward a wordplay on Cato's *Origines*:

> Igitur de originibus uerborum qui multa dixerunt commode, potius boni consulendum, quam qui aliquid nequierit reprehendendum, praesertim quom dicat etymologice non omnum uerborum posse dici causa<m>. (Varro, *Ling.* 7.4)

Therefore, with regard to the origins of words, it is better to count as being one of the right sort the man who has neatly articulated many such, rather than criticizing someone who finds the task impossible. This is the case especially because etymology [a transliteration from the Greek] states that not all words are susceptible to explanation.

It is easy, in Varro's scheme, to appraise someone who displays great etymological dexterity: he is a "good man," a *bonus* (glossed by *consul-endum*, the juxtaposition works in a political angle); perhaps a "Cato" or a "Cicero," definitely a "Varro." When faced with the need to appraise someone who cannot see his way to verbal origins, Varro argues, best to say nothing rather than launch into criticism. If one can lay bare the steps that link from "cavalry" (*"equitatus"*) back to "horse" (*"equus"*) but go no further (he continues), these are still valuable lessons that will make someone happy (*"tamen hic docet plura et satisfacit grato," Ling.* 7.4)—book 7 (*"ipse liber"*) will be the proof (*"erit indicio"*) of whether Varro himself can achieve as much as an educator.[95]

Where Varro goes next (still part of his introduction to book 7) allows us to revisit the conclusions I drew on *Ling.* 7.5 (in the first section, "Poets, Artfulness, and Textuality") in light of the rest of this chapter's readings. A revised conclusion on this material finds a manifesto for how poetry can jump the gap from minority geekdom to accessible toolkit and inspirational force: "*Dicam in hoc libro de uerbis quae a poetis sunt posita*" (I shall speak in this book about words that have been set in place by poets).[96] The slight tension between *dico* and *pono* as discourse-forming action terms gains texture when read in terms of Cato, Cicero, and the bigger cultural battle to reclaim control of written form and literary genre from canonical Greek gatekeeper texts.[97] The pragmatic, material quality in Varro's *langue* gives a newly poetic voice to the prosaic building blocks of Latin (*dico, uerba*) and encourages readers to see that "we" Romespeakers are doing it already; the know-how to understand what results from drawing past (what the poets most tellingly made) and present (this book about words) into a new mode ("I shall speak") is all that needs to be retrofitted. Varro's choice of words wrests poetry from the marginal status occasionally evident in Cicero's vision[98] and reinvents it as having all along been raw material (*pono*) naturally embedded in what already makes for Latin speech (*dico*), just waiting for the right explicator. Poetry is too important to be left to poets; it still makes a difference in Varro's manifesto.

Telling When It's Over

Of course, even Varro cannot make space for everything in wrapping up book 7, as he warned his audience earlier. In his conclusion to book 7 he makes clear that there remains much left out that might have been discussed but that still lies buried in verse context ("*multa apud poetas reliqua*," *Ling.* 7.107). Varro underlines the complex editorializing process behind this throwaway comment when he straightaway commences an almost comically whistle-stop list of otherwise unelucidated names, titles, and words used in poetry. The sequence (*Ling.* 7.107–8) has a scatty logic, but the imagery of illumination and of doors unbarred to stand wide open ("*fores panduntur*," *Ling.* 7.108) suggests a metaphorical summation of Varro's work—unlocking a new and enlightened world of opportunity for readers.[99]

Book 7 finally ends with a return to the materiality of the text and, specifically, the impact that multiscroll technology has on the work's intellectual unity (*Ling.* 7.109–10). "The book is not simply the object one holds in one's hands," as Foucault puts it; even for an audience accustomed to the pauses that multiscroll works embed, Varro's interrogation of a lengthy text's integrity across numerous scrolls acknowledges that "it loses its self-evidence; it indicates itself, constructs itself, only on the basis of a complex field of discourse."[100] "I'm afraid [*uereor*]," Varro says, "that there'll be more who will blame me for writing too much on this subject than who will accuse me of leaving items out."[101] One might take this as simple smugness—who could plausibly accuse Varro of leaving out anything pertinent?—but the follow-up suggests instead that Varro is emphasizing the delicacy of his cultural palette and his crucial ability to suit himself to circumstances. In the process, he gains the ability to create his own order:

ideo potius iam reprimendum quam procudendum puto esse uolumen: nemo reprensus qui e segete ad spicilegium reliquit stipulam. . . . Quocirca quoniam omnis operis de Lingua Latina tris feci partis . . . ut secondam ordiri possim, huic libro faciam finem. (Varro, *Ling.* 7.109–10)

Therefore I now think that limits rather than extrusion is what this book scroll needs: no one is called to account who leaves the stubble in the cornfield for gleaning. . . . For this reason, since I have made three parts of the whole work *On the Latin Language* . . . [and] so that I can make a clear beginning to part two, I shall make an end to this book.

Varro's signoff for book 7 has some glitches as the text quoted here stands (including an oddly repetitive summary of the work so far and the anomalous quality of *omnis*), but where it delivers real value is in its closural intervention in the developing narrative. Varro revisits the artisanal qualities of the project, and he also reminds his audience of the material restraints to which every intellectual product is subject, the physical limits of a scroll. Making the most of this thinking space is *not* about scholarly *minutiae* or encyclopedism (and the gallop through barely commented-upon terms to which he has only just treated readers makes this vividly clear). It is about recognizing that in a corpus of omnivorous scholarship (as in real life) everything connects to (and mediates) everything else, that inspiration can trigger unexpected outcomes, and that what is extraneous for one project may be central to another.

chapter 4

Oratio and the Read/Write Experience

A word has a meaning only in the context of a sentence.[1]

POPULAR POLITICS AND ORATORY go together, hand in glove. In a democratic oligarchy rooted in competitive political mechanisms, some systematization of rhetorical practice and didactics is inevitable. This pattern finds its origins in the beginnings of democracy in Greece, where the successful practice of persuasion spawned an all-but publishing industry on theory and praxis.[2] Rome built on this experience, and this chapter explores the nature of how individual speech relates to language—spoken, read, and written—in Varro's scheme.

By the mid-first century, aspiring public figures in Rome had a wealth of Greek handbooks elaborating the theory of rhetoric and its schools of thought to draw on for inspiration. These were works conceived and developed in the great courts of the Hellenistic world and were increasingly attuned to intellectual, philosophical pyrotechnics rather than to oratory in the wild. Yet a thread continued to connect Hellenistic rhetorical discourse to the popular politics and democracy of an earlier age, and in this one can see the hook that drew Rome into the mix.[3] The extent to which Cicero and his fellow rhetoricians managed (or even wanted) to integrate Roman practice seamlessly into Greek theory is a huge question and not one that this book tackles.[4] Instead, my focus is on how Varro's exploration of the roots and nuances of words produces a book that reboots Latin at a much more basic level than Cicero's *De Oratore*. With Varro, therefore, this chapter goes under the hood to the verbal mechanics of oratory.

Much has been written on Roman rhetoric and on Cicero's role in its development.[5] To paraphrase Cicero in Saussure's terms, *langue* and *parole* needed to be understood as inextricably linked; indeed, writing on oratory, Cicero noted that setting oneself apart from the popular mode of discourse and from the habitual practice of commonsense use is the greatest fault in speech.[6] Spoken

Latin (*parole*) is also a key ingredient in Varro's balanced system, hence its place in this chapter; taking the titular *lingua* (tongue, recalling the ears and eyes of chapter 3) at face value, his is a book about how utterances (*loquor, dico*) build into dialogic sense (*sermo*), one interested in the mechanics of understanding and composing discourse within a historical and political frame.

This means that Varro is primarily interested in language as communication charged with reciprocity. Varro's scrutiny of language leads to consensus because, as framed by Ludwig Wittgenstein, "it is not only agreement in definitions, but also (odd as it may sound) agreement in judgements that is required for communication by means of language."[7] This kind of deep-level analysis and agreement (see *Ling* 9.92) underpinning *sermo* signifies much more than a simple concurrence on rules for Latin grammar and syntax or on the most persuasive tactics of oratory.

As Varro later puts it, in book 10, if one takes the trouble to work on semiotics (something for which poets and grammarians are known; Varro is silent on orators here), one finds a deep logos delivering complex systems of word association available to the experienced tracker.[8] The "rules" are only the luggage tags; without (opening) the baggage itself, they fail to deliver the goods. To understand how Varro is equipping his readers, in the first section I tackle speech in a very practical sense: what it means to name and utter (within) a language. Exploration of the foundational material underpinning set piece rhetoric sets up a discussion in the second section of Varro's *oratio*: speech as a system shared within a like-minded community, increasingly re-presented for an audience in the know to peruse at leisure and to admire outside the circus of public life. *Oratio* leads on to "conversation," the focus of the third section, drawing out the semiotics of discourse and analyzing how exchanging words builds community. Finally, in the fourth section I tie together a range of strands to do with comprehending and producing language and replicating: how to read, what saying "I read" means, and the implications of reading for Varro's development of Latin.

I Speak (Latin), Therefore I Am (Roman)

This section tackles how the development of syntax and a shared ownership of modes and characteristics of expression enable individuals and communities to self-identify. We can begin to explore this community by examining Varro on two significant names (Latin, Romulus) and on the process of naming. Names, we will see, make "saying" possible and eventually enable individuals and groups to make choices and exhibit discrimination in how they "call" and discriminate between things.

Writing *De Lingua Latina* begs the question, why *Latin*? Did Romulus' language have a name? Was it "Latin" background chatter that framed the quarrel between Romulus and Remus? These are questions already rumbling at the beginning of book 5. There, Varro announces that he has been and will continue to be looking at the distinctive qualities of discourse formation in the *lingua Latina*, while also flagging up Greek intellectual practice as the ongoing interlocutor and paradigm.[9] As Rome's nation-defining language, the name "Latin" is a paradox.[10] *Latin-a* invokes a complex, often conflict-driven etiology for Rome's existence within an already inhabited and civilized region (akin to asking whether *Ameri*cans should speak *Columb*ian, or claim an indigenous name). It also flags up the ways in which dominant ideologies interact with *parole*.

> [Scipio] "I agree; so, are you saying that Romulus was a king of barbarians?"
> [Laelius] "If, as the Greeks say, everyone is either a Greek or a barbarian, I'm afraid that he was a king of barbarians; but if the term is applied to <u>customs</u> [*moribus*] and not to <u>language</u> [*linguis*], the Greeks were no less barbarians than the Romans, in my book." (Cic. *Rep.* 1.58)

The Greeks (eventually) had a word for speaking in Latin, fixed on Rome: Ῥωμαΐζω.[11] Using *Roma* to indicate *Latina* seems to have been an anomaly in Varro's era, except for *Romanus*, which can characterize a quality of behavior that embraces aspects of discourse (frank, lucid).[12] *Romanus* as plain-speaking has additional ideological value as an indicator of forthright and practical action, not technical speech or rhetorical fireworks. It also hints that not all "talking Latin" is as no-nonsense and valuable as "talking Roman."

Varro's primary audience is Rome's best (and perhaps brightest, and male) inhabitants, meaning that he is writing for a group that has signed up for a skill set that includes at least a Greek gloss to their education. Genuine bilingualism is unlikely to be core to Varro's constituency, but Varro's Latin makes a virtue of its early hybridity: his is a language that exploits its legendary origins to make a case for pan-Mediterranean authority.[13] Nevertheless, Reatine Varro is not exactly proposing that his audience imagine itself or its founding fathers as polyglot or as speaking a naturally hybrid language divorced from very specific historical triggers and sociopolitical circumstances. Recognizing where Latin has cannibalized, "re"-claimed, or built in and on Greek (and other) forms is key to understanding just how ostentatiously, even gratuitously implausible and provocative Varro's propositions sometimes are, especially in their silence on where and how such code switching and cross-cultural development might affect an educated Roman Latin speaker, native or "learned."[14]

Varro reaches the verb "to say" ("*dico*," *Ling.* 6.61) through a sequence of discussions of Greco-Roman–flavored nouns and verbs (*Ling.* 6.51–60) for which *lieux de mémoire* are significant.[15] This context is worth recapping because of the friction between *Roma* and *Latina*. How one expresses oneself intelligibly in speech reveals one's identity on a fundamental level, and one particular group of passages shows how a Greco-Italic gloss makes a substantial difference to Varro's overall vision.

We need to keep in mind that novelty and naming are close kin in Varro's scheme and draw together explicit performance context and the implicitly performative modes of announcing and publicizing:[16]

Nuntius enim est a <n>ouis rebus nominatus, quod a uerbo Graeco potest declinatum; ab eo itaque Neapolis illorum Nouapolis ab antiquis uocitata nostris. (Varro, *Ling.* 6.58)

For a messenger was named from new things, which could be derived from a Greek word; whence in this way their NeoCity [*Nea-polis*] was called NewCity [*Noua-polis*] by our long-ago folk.

Varro explains here that a *nuntius* draws his identity from "news," itself possibly descended from a Greek term. This lineage makes sense of Varro's subsequent proposal—that there was a diachronic connection early in Rome's history between the language of Campania and that of Latium. It also implies that the notion of change and novelty as "news" is productive of new Latin sense. The connection of *nouus* and νέος encourages reflection on the hybridity of language, while the archaic neologism *Nouapolis* might push for an underlying communion between the non-Roman peoples of Italy and the world of Greece, mediated by the mytho-historically supercharged coast around Naples. There is also here a hint that the civilization that emerges from the point of convergence between different flavors of "foreign" was from the beginning highly flexible and resilient. *Nouapolis* is at once a translation from and cousin to a once current Greek reality.

As Varro approaches *dico*, therefore, through-readers might recall the *Italian* politics of naming rivers (*Ling.* 5.29–30) as they reflect on new-old juxtapositions and semiotic shifts from the Greek "novelty" city Neapolis to the old-time Latin ancestral coinage *Nouapolis* (*Ling.* 6.58)—and in the process recognize that they have observed the genesis of a new, hybrid form, part Latin, part Greek transliteration—before arrival at Rome with *sub Nouis* and *Noua Via* (by Varro's day, two ancient sites in the Forum area: "*iam diu uetus,*" *Ling.* 6.59).[17] This sequence leads into a detailed discussion of the semiotics of "new"—temporal, descriptive, and topographic—which brings Varro back to the wider semantic process of calling by (a) name:

> Ab eo quoque potest dictum <u>nominare</u>, quod res <u>nouae</u> in usum quom additae erant, quibus ea<s> <u>nouissent</u>, <u>nomina</u> ponebant. Ab eo <u>nuncu</u>-<u>pare</u>, quod tunc <pro> ciuitate uota <u>noua</u> suscipiuntur. <u>Nuncupare nomi</u>-<u>nare</u> ualere apparet in legibus, ubi "<u>nun</u>cupatae pecuniae" sunt scriptae; item in Choro quo est:
>
>   Aenea!—Quis <is> est qui meum <u>nomen</u> <u>nun</u>cupat? (Varro, *Ling.* 6.60)

From that [i.e., new] it is also possible to say that something is "<u>named</u>," because when <u>new</u> things were brought into use, in order that people <u>might know</u> them, they set <u>names</u> to them. From this, "to pro<u>nounce</u> in public," because this is when new vows are undertaken for the state. That "to pro<u>nounce</u> in public" has the same import as "to <u>nominate</u>" is apparent in the laws, where "<u>nominated</u> monies" are recorded; likewise in the Chorus, as here:

    Aeneas!—Who is it who <u>calls upon</u> [nominates] my <u>name</u>?

Here, naming is intrinsically bound up in knowledge and connected heuristically to experience. Naming has prospective force for the state, and in its insertion of novelty ("*res nouae in usum*") it indicates conclusively that progress means change. This passage gathers religion, law, and finance as branches of newness and knowledge; the (author unknown) dramatic quotation, implicating Aeneas, hints at the novelty of what Aeneas' flight from Troy would produce: new Latin names for the framework of a new Roman state. If communities did not keep having to grapple with new things, nothing would be called anything; civilization exists because language is needed to help communities engage with what has not already always been there. In sum, it is only by (once) being <u>new</u> that anything can be <u>named</u> and <u>known</u>.

From "naming," Varro then reaches "saying." This marks a return to "*dico originem habet Graecam, quod Graeci* δεικνύω" ("I say" has a Greek origin: that which for the Greeks is "I show," *Ling.* 6.61).[18] The significance of *dico* was foregrounded earlier in book 6 when Varro bundled it with the other action-generating and speech-related terms as part of his explanation of what is forbidden on *dies nefasti* (*Ling.* 6.30). On such days, the praetor may not utter (*for*) the verbs *do*, *dico*, and *addico*. Banishing these verbs means that action (in the politico-legal sense) is impossible ("*itaque non potest agi*"). The slipperiness of this prohibition on praetors is evident in the existence of a contingency plan. There needs to be a way to wipe the slate for a magistrate who utters one of the weighty speech terms thoughtlessly (*imprudens*).[19]

Despite the difficulty of fixing the text here, some facet of *dicare* needs to inform Varro's *dicere*, and he continues by proposing that *iudicare* (to judge) derives thus from "*ius dicatur*" (justice is spoken *and* "seen to be done," *Ling.* 6.61).[20] The public performance of Roman justice, the notion of an ethical system demonstrably underpinning the State, is in this way prefigured by the story of *dico* and its Greek relations. Individual and community speech acts are part of a complex unifying ontological system within which saying, calling something by name in Latin, makes Rome real as a dynamic social construct. It is this assertive but also iterative quality of *dico* that Habinek describes as "the power generated by language's ritualization into song without, through its very presence, necessarily invoking a ritual context."[21]

This set of associations is therefore already in place for through-readers when they begin the second hexad. By trying out pro- and anti-Regularity poses in book 9, Varro delicately structures a gradual symbiosis between total Regularity and the "mixed," consensual position that he eventually proposes in book 10, but for the most part his book 9 persona speaks wholeheartedly in favor of *analogia*.[22] At *Ling.* 9.34, Varro explores the proposition ("*dicunt*," some say) that there are two kinds of Regularity: "natural" (or real) *analogia* and "voluntary" (which does not map onto true *analogia*). What comes next is important for this chapter's argument about identity and hybridity as the powerhouse of *Latin* discourse:

> Ego declinatus uerborum et uoluntarios et naturalis esse puto, uoluntarios quibus homines uocabula imposuerint rebus quaedam, ut ab Romulo Roma, ab T*i*b*u*re T*i*burtes, naturales ut ab impositis uocabulis quae inclinantur in tempo*r*a aut in casus, ut *ab Romulo* <u>Romuli</u> <u>Romulum</u> et ab <u>dico</u> <u>dicebam</u> <u>dixeram</u>. (Varro, *Ling.* 9.34)

> I myself think that inflections of words can be both "voluntary" and "natural": voluntary, for the things on which humankind has imposed certain names, such as from Romulus, Rome, and from Tibur, Tiburtes; natural, as when from the imposed names there is inflection in respect of time or case, such as *from Romulus* the genitive *Romuli* and accusative *Romulum* and from "<u>I say</u>" the imperfect *dicebam* and the pluperfect *dixeram*.

"Romulus" exemplifies how names intersect with people and so give rise to complex systems; this appearance builds on his presence in book 8 (along with Remus) as the key example of what constitutes a proper noun.[23] At *Ling.* 8.18, the proposition that a toponym can derive from a person and then produce a designation term is exemplified: "Thus, sometimes, from a man, a place; from that place, a man—as from Romulus, Rome; and from Rome, Roman."[24] In this way Varro invokes a direct personal link and (in the context of *dico*) agency for place, person, name, and speech act. Moreover, "saying" something is contextually Greek-flavored (recalling *Ling.* 6.61 and δεικνύω). This terse etymology, Varro's readers might suspect, makes Rome's foundation story (from Romulus, to Rome, to Romans) one of ethnic and linguistic rapprochement.[25] This ideological drift also reflects the narrative progress as Varro works his way toward recommending consensus, in book 10.

As a complex of associations, these sections illuminate Varro's concept of a hybrid identity for Latin and Rome, strengthened and enriched by knowing the points of linguistic congruence. It also reminds readers of the ebb and flow between languages in use. The ongoing dialogue among Greek, Latin, and other Italic languages (not to forget the sudden incursion of Syrian; see *Ling.* 9.34[26]) keeps all of them in collaboration on the bigger project of meaningful communication in a polyglot community. The matter of who (the Greeks or the Romans) speaks more authoritatively on the relationship between their languages is already at stake in the discussion of synchronicity and diachronicity in language development that helps introduce book 7, but it remains an unresolved strand in Varro's study (see *Ling.* 8.23).[27]

When Varro proposes a resolution (in book 10) to the friction that he talks up between *analogia* and *anomalia* in books 8 and 9, it is contextualized by readers' memory of these issues. Book 10 develops Varro as a consensus former within a pluralistic system, in the process implicitly advertises his political utility, and returns explicitly to the notions of provenance and cultural identity in vocabulary and syntax.[28] I quote the key passage in full:

> Sed prius de perfecta, in qua et res et uoces quadam similitudine continentur, cuius genera sunt tria: unum uernaculum ac domi natum, alterum aduenticium, tertium nothum ex peregrino hic natum. Vernaculum est ut sutor et pistor, sutori pistori; aduenticium est ut Hectores Nestores, Hectoras Nestoras; tertium ilium nothum ut Achilles et Peles.
>
> De <his primo> genere multi utuntur non modo poetae, sed etiam plerique omnes qui soluta oratione loquuntur. Haec primo dicebant ut quaestorem praetorem, sic Hectorem Nestorem; itaque Ennius ait:

Hectoris natum de muro *i*actari<er>.
Accius haec in tragoediis largius a prisca consuetudine mouere c*o*epit et ad formas Graecas uerborum magis reuocare, a quo Valerius ait:
Accius He<c>torem nollet facere, Hectora mallet.
Quod aduenticia pleraque habemus Graeca, secutum ut de nothis Graecanicos quoque nominat*us* plurimos haberemus. Itaque ut hic alia Graeca, alia Gr*a*ecanica, sic analogiae.

E quis quae hic not*h*ae fiunt declinationes, de his aliae sunt priscae, ut Ba<c>chides et Chr*y*sides aliae *iu*niores, ut Chr*y*sides et Ba<c>chides aliae recentes, ut Chr*y*sidas et Ba<c>chidas; cum his omnibus tribus utantur nostri, maxime qui sequontur media in loquendo offendunt minimum, quod prima parum similia uidentur esse Gr*a*ecis, unde sint tralata, tertia parum similia nostris.

Omnis analogiae fundamentum similitudo quaedam, ea, ut dixi, quae solet esse in rebus et in uocibus et in utroque; in qua<m> harum parte<m> *quod*que sit inferend*u*<m> et cuius modi, uidendum. Nam, ut dixi, neque rerum neque uocis similitudo ad has duplicis qua*s* in loquendo qu*a*erimus analogias uerborum exprimendas separatim satis est, quod utraque parte opus est simili. Quas ad loquendum ut perducas accedere debet usus: alia enim ratio qua facias uestimentum, alia quemadmodum utare uestimento.

Usui<s> species uidentur esse tres: una consuetudinis ueteris, altera consuetudinis huius, tertia neutra<e>. Vetera, ut cascus casci, *s*urus *s*uri; huius consuetudinis, ut albus caldus, albo caldo; neutrae, ut scala scalam, *p*halera *p*haleram. Ad quas accedere potest quarta mixta, ut amicitia inimicitia, amicitiam inimicitiam. Prima est qua usi antiqui et nos reliquimus, secunda qua nunc utimur, tertia qua utuntur poetae. (Varro, *Ling.* 10.69–73)

But first, concerning perfected Regularity, in which both the entities and their spoken terms are bound together by a certain similarity of which there are three kinds. One is the vernacular and home-born; the next is an immigrant; the third hybrid, born here from foreign stock. The vernacular type is such as cobbler and baker [dative forms in *-i*]; the immigrant type, such as Hector and Nestor [accusative forms in *-as*]; the hybrid, such as Achilles and Peles.

This first type is used by many, not just poets, but even by the majority of those who talk in casual speech. Initially, as with *quaestorem* and *praetorem*, there used to be said *Hectorem* and *Nestorem*. Thus Ennius says:

Hector's son from the wall be thrown.

Accius in his tragedies began extensively to shift these [words] from their early usage and to recall them instead to their Greek word forms; hence, Valerius says:

Accius did not wish to use *Hectorem*, he prefered *Hectora*.

Because most of the immigrant words we have are Greek, it follows that as far as hybrid nouns go, what we have are mostly Greek-ish. Therefore, just as in these types, some words are Greek, others are Greek-ish, thus also in the systematization of Regularity.

And concerning the hybrid declined forms that have come about in this country, some of these are early (such as *Bacchides* and *Chrysides*), others are younger (such as *Chrysides* and *Bacchides* [short e]), and others yet are recent (such as *Chrysidas* and *Bacchidas*). Of these, we use all three, but those who make a habit of following the middle forms, in speaking, give the least offense. This is because the first forms seem to bear too little resemblance to the Greek, whence they are transposed, and the third group bear too little resemblance to our own forms.

The foundation of all Regularity is a certain similarity. That, as I have said, which is usually in things, and in spoken words, and in both. It should then be seen in which of these divisions each [word] should be entered and of what kind it is. For, as I have said, neither the similarity of the "things" nor of the spoken words is separately sufficient to express the double Regularities of words that we seek in speaking, because there needs to be a similarity in both divisions.²⁹ In order for you to introduce them effectively into everyday speech, there's a need for actual use. After all, there's one method by which you make a garment, another altogether by which you wear it.

There seem to be three categories of use: one, which was habitual in days gone by, the second, that of our own day, a third that is specific to neither. Veteran words are those such as *casc-us, -i* [old], *sur-us, -i* [stake]; in contemporary use are such as *alb-us* [white], *cald-us* [hot], with datives in *-i*; specific to neither, *scal-a, -am*, [stair], *phaler-a, -am* [ornamentation]. To these can be added a fourth mixed group, such as *amiciti-a* [friendship], *inimiciti-a* [enmity], with accusatives in *-am*. So: the first division is those words used in antiquity, and that we have abandoned; the second, those which we use now; the third, that class used by the poets.

This passage offers a conspectus on the relationship linking time, discourse, and acculturation. It speaks to a broad communicative horizon, across whose landscape the careful can continue to identify and make sense of traces of abandoned and unusual linguistic forms, and, in its interest in the relationship between foreign (primarily Greek) and native (how "we" have it) words, it embeds the factors of time and heredity in the building blocks of language.

We can see something comparable in play in Cicero's work on the nature of the gods (dating to 45). Here, he has Lucilius Balbus (expounding on cosmic order) say:

"[Air] is itself a Greek word, but it has yet, by now, been taken over [*perceptum*] in use by us; it's even commonplace as real Latin. This [air] in turn the immeasurable *aether* embraces, which consists of the loftiest flames—this term [*aether*] we may also borrow, and so *aether* may be spoken in Latin just as *aer* is, although Pacuvius presents a crib:
This which I speak of is 'heaven' to us, but the Greeks name it
aether—
Just as if it were not a Greek who was saying this. 'But isn't he speaking in Latin?' Indeed, if we were not hearing him as if he were speaking Greek! The same fellow gives in another passage:
When born Greek [*Graiugena*], speech [*oratio*] itself makes that evident."
(Cic. *Nat. D.* 2.91)

In a shared system of discourse, this passage suggests, there is an essential quality connecting authentic experience of reality with speculative natural science and setting them against the frictions between geopolitical and cultural identities. This is the case, it seems, however much one might try to disguise it through code switching or in-language translation. Thus Cicero and Varro, in various ways, found these points of convergence between language and the expression of knowledge worth attempting to identify and articulate. In the same year, Varro's take on this is mapped by Cicero as follows:

[Varro:] "But tackling what results from both [force and matter], this they named 'body,' as if it was qualitatively of a certain nature—for surely, since unusual things are under consideration [*ut in rebus inusitatis*], you will allow us occasionally to use unheard-of words [*utamur uerbis interdum inauditis*], as the Greeks themselves do, who have now been handling these matters for some time."

"We will indeed," said Atticus; "you will even be allowed to choose Greek words if Latin should happen to fail you [*si te Latina forte deficient*]."

[Varro:] "That's generous of you; but I will make a big effort to speak Latin, except in the case of such words, so that I will call things 'philosophy,' or 'rhetoric,' or 'natural science,' or 'dialectic,' which (just as many others) custom has inscribed as Latin [*quibus ut aliis multis consuetudo iam utitur pro Latinis*]. Therefore I have termed 'qualities' what the Greeks call ποιότητας, which itself among the Greeks is not a common word [*non est uulgi uerbum*], belonging rather to the philosophers; as is the case for many such terms. Indeed, the terminology of dialecticians is not that of the people [*publica*]—they use their own words; this holds true in general for most of the arts. Either there need to be new names coined for new things or existing names need to be repurposed [*ex aliis transferenda*]. Because the Greeks, who have been handling these matters for centuries, operate in this way, how much more apt that it should be allowed to us, who are now for the first time trying to investigate [*tractare*] these matters!" "Quite so," [Cicero] said, "Varro, it seems to me that you will in fact have served your fellow citizens [*tuis ciuibus*] well if you add to their store not only of facts [*copia rerum*], as you have done, but also of words." (Cic. *Acad.* 1.6–7)

Cicero's Varro is characterized as a wordsmith as well as a good steward, but the overarching point is a shared interest in understanding and exploring the nature of the slippage between the two languages and its creative effect on Latin speakers. Varronian speech, in this context, becomes something not just acculturated and dialogic (with his fellow citizens, with his friends, with Greek) but also actively creative and individual to himself. That it is Varro who is augmenting Latin in the opening phase of this dialogue allows Cicero tacitly to add weightiness to the reciprocal linguistic project (his literary "gift" from Varro) that he has designed the *Academica* to prefigure. Making words becomes the new way in which Varro crafts the friends' increasing currency of choice and necessity—dialectic.

Oratio Itself

This section takes us from assigning and assimilating names in discourse to producing the formally patterned speech that can be characterized as *oratio*. *Oratio* is a crucial point of intersection between the ideas of spoken or conversational Latin and the written language.[30] Sounds, articulated into meaningful words and connected as discourse (*lingua*), are formed physically from the mouth (*os*). To speak is at once to make and to act, an oratorical performance rooted in the physically hidden, wet, devouring, private recesses of the mouth;

and the mouth (as denoted by the term *os*) in turn shares its form with "bone"—the body's frame and the rigid corporeal icon that marks a body's last service to the family and final burial (*os*).[31] The Roman body gives structure to Latin language.

To begin with Varro's programmatic opening salvo on *oratio* in book 8:

Quom oratio natura tripertita esset, ut superioribus libris ostendi, cuius prima pars, quem admodum uocabula rebus essent imposita, secunda, quo pacto de his declinata in discrimina ier*i*nt, tertia, ut ea inter se ratione coniuncta sententiam efferant. (Varro. *Ling.* 8.1)

That formalized speech is naturally tripartite, I have shown in preceding books; of which the first part is how terms were set to things, the second, by what model declined forms have become distinct, the third, how, when united rationally with each other, words express purposeful ideas.

When vocabulary forms *oratio* it gains strategic and logical form, and Varro's deployment of the unifying term *pactum* and the connective participle *coniunctus* delivers a message of order and community. What is more, this passage proposes a "natural" organizational relationship between formal discourse and text, both of which depend structurally upon a beginning, middle, and end. If we read for the widest context, Varro's "*oratio natura tripertita*" might begin to sound rather like Caesar's now famous three-part division of Gaul, which he had glossed in the first place as a site of alterity ("they" do not define themselves in "our" terms) and next as a more general function of speaking different languages.[32] *Lingua, instituta,* and *leges*—parsing Caesar's trio as language, practice, and precept.

The remainder of this section focuses on a set of examples showcasing how Varro models controlled, designed speech as a self-fashioning device for a community and how this might begin to break down into something less than ideal for practitioners.[33] We should start with the point where speech defines a very specific and politically charged persona:

Apud Ennium: "Orator sine pace <u>redit regique refert rem</u>." Orator dictus ab oratione: qui enim uerba haberet publice aduersus eum quo leg*a*batur, ab oratione orator dictus. (Varro, *Ling.* 7.41)

In Ennius: "The orator <u>returns</u> without peace, and hands <u>back</u> the <u>affair</u> to the <u>king</u>." An orator is here so-called from "oration": he is the one who puts words together in public before the person to whom he is an envoy, from which "oration" he is called "orator."

The etymology has a relentless, repetitive quality and unexpectedly prioritizes the orator's role as ambassador and go-between rather than as autonomous protagonist.[34] Cicero, or those familiar with his thinking, would be likely to recall the debate that he had memorably dramatized a decade or so earlier (*De Oratore*) and revisited a few years before Varro's handbook in a dialogue on the merits of particular orators, dedicated to Brutus.[35] In the later work, "Cicero" states:

> For I wish it to be evident that in such a great and ancient commonwealth [*in tanta et tam uetere re publica*], with the greatest rewards proposed for eloquence [*eloquentiae*] and though all have desired to speak [*cupisse dicere*], not many have dared, and few have been able [*non plurumos ausos esse, potuisse paucos*] . . . but the quality of the orator shall, from that which his speech achieves [*efficiet*], be judged [*intellegi*]. . . . And so there has never been disagreement between learned men and the people as a whole concerning what makes for a <u>good</u> [the right sort of] or a bad [the wrong sort of] orator [*de bono oratore aut non bono*]. (Cic. *Brut.* 182, 184, 185)

Cicero's orator is characteristically a significant, daring executive who stands or falls by the results of his speech rather than because of its stylistic merits per se (although of course only the successful marriage of style *and* substance effects change). Unsurprisingly (for Cicero), effective rhetoric leads to political progression and stands in for *aristeia*. The individual authority and agency of Varro's orator in the previously quoted passage (*Ling.* 7.41) has, by contrast, been sublimated by the role in which Varro's etymology casts him. This orator has command over words but acts as someone who has been sent out to fulfill a persuasive or communicative mission specified by a higher authority.

Varro's etymology at *Ling.* 7.41 subtly undermines the amount of individual kudos available to his orator and might also represent a redefinition against Cicero's introduction to *De Oratore*. There, knowledge, autonomy, and fluency were central to what he termed "*uis oratoris*" (1.20–21)—the orator's own forceful agency. In this context, we should compare the characterization of the orator delivered by "Crassus":

> "Neque uero mihi quidquam," inquit, "praestabilius uidetur, quam posse **dicendo** tenere hominum coetus, **mentes allicere, uoluntates impellere quo uelit; unde autem uelit, deducere.** . . . Quid enim est . . . aut tam

potens, tamque **magnificum**, quam populi motus, iudicium religiones, Senatus grauitatem, **unius oratione conuerti**? Quid tam porro **regium**, tam **liberale**, tam **munificium**, quam opem ferre supplicibus, excitare afflictos, dare salutem, liberare periculis, retinere homines in ciuitate? . . . Ut uero iam ad illa summa ueniamus; **quae uis alia** potuit aut disperos homines unum in locum congregare, aut a fera agrestique uita ad hunc humanum cultum ciuilimque deducere, aut, iam constitutis ciuitatibus, leges, iudicia, iura describere?" (Cic. *De or.* 1.30, 31–32, 33)

"And there is nothing, it seems to me," he said, "more outstanding than to be able, **by speaking**, to get a hold of assemblies of men, **to captivate their minds, to drive their partialities, in whatever direction one should wish; or indeed to divert them from whatever one should wish**. . . . For what is there . . . that is equally **powerful** and as **magnificent** as that popular tumult, the morality of judges, the dignity of the Senate, should **all hang on the speech of one man**? Moreover, what is so **kingly**, so indicative of **freedom**, so **munificent**, as to bring aid to the suppliant, to enliven those who are wretched, to give safety, to set free from danger, to retain men in a state of citizenship? . . . So, we come at last to the pinnacle: **what other force** could have gathered disparate people together in one place or led them from a feral and primitive life to this one, where our cultivation is humane and civilized, or, after the establishment of communities of citizens, to give shape to laws, courts, and justice?"

Interrupted by a spirited rebuttal from "Scaevola," "Crassus" comes back with a totalizing argument for the orator as the ideal, educated citizen, authoritatively at home in political and legal wrangling alike.[36] Contextualized by *Ling.* 7.41 (as quoted earlier), Varro's emphatic positioning of the verse from Ennius makes *rex* dominate the proposed derivation: when a speech is required—historically contextualized in this etymology as a function of autocracy—it gives rise to a speaker (not vice versa). Readers familiar with Cicero's work might find in this a subtle reflection of the times. Measured speech was increasingly jostling for supremacy with the kinds of contingent, occasional, and context-driven rhetoric that depended heavily on street politics as well as the more formal *contiones*. Nevertheless, forensic oratory continued to be a vivid locus of display and power.

It is significant that the first main phase of argument in *De Lingua Latina* 8 (making a case against the existence of Regularity in language) returns to oratory:

Omnis oratio cum debeat dirigi ad utilitatem, ad quam tum denique peruenit, si est aperta et breuis, quae petimus. (Varro, *Ling.* 8.26)

All speech ought to be aimed at utility, which it can finally attain only if it is clear and brief, which is what we seek.

Varro goes on to observe that an obscure and longwinded speaker is hated, that clarity is what delivers intelligibility, and that brevity makes for speedy understanding.[37] In practice, people who tend to consistency and have enough self-restraint to be concise have no need for a more complex systematization of discourse.[38] If the right sort of speech can deliver this, then what sort of layabout has the leisure to figure out a system of explanation: either it works or it doesn't.[39] In everyday life, utility is what one looks for, not whether something matches in a scheme; indeed, this argument goes, if there is no possibility for variation (and if systems must operate rigidly), then our pleasure in each encounter and individual use is diminished.[40]

Varro does show how the position developed by Cicero needs scrutiny, but he nonetheless needs to demonstrate the added value of technical expertise if readers are not to throw their scrolls incautiously aside. Thus, at *Ling.* 8.44 Varro sets out the practical utility of his intellectual expertise. Equipped with his four-part grammatical model—nouns, verbs, indeclinables, and forms such as participles (which are a bit of each of the first two)—attentive readers can hack the discourse world.[41] Terms that Varro proposes as relevant for these parts of speech ("*has uocant*") are "naming," "speaking," "supporting," and "joining" ("*appellandi*," "*dicendi*," "*adminiculandi*," "*iungendi*").

Oratio in this context (8.44) makes sense of the pragmatic, such as "human" (*homo*), and of the mythic or literary universe, such as "Nestor," and generates the kind of speech act (verb) that is "I write" and "I read" ("*ut scribo et lego*"). This includes complex unities, "writing" and "reading" (terms that join case and time, or adjectival and verbal aspects), and finally produces catalyst terms such as "learnedly" and "appropriately."[42] Spotting the odd one out seems easy—Nestor, surely? But his role as a counselor in the *Iliad* makes him an intriguing point of reference for a "handbook."[43] As Hanna Roisman has pointed out, Homer's Nestor may not always be exactly right and his advice is not always acted upon, but having a Nestor around is reassuring and helps the (language) community to get on with things.[44] No wonder Varro found him suitable as a recurring character in *De Lingua Latina*—he crops up again as a devil's-advocate example (with Hector) of how syllabic pattern stresses might seem to disprove the existence of regularity (*Ling.* 8.72) before shedding his anti-Regularity implications in the final (extant) book to feature, as we saw in the previous section, as an instance of Roman confidence—words really can in fact be returned (retuned) to their "original" Greek enunciation without endangering Latinity (*Ling.* 10.69, 70).

Nouns (what one calls a thing, thus a part of speech) are "named," and in Varro's exegesis of this terminology readers find further evidence of Varro's interest in the cultural politics of *oratio* as theory and practice. On his return to the defense of Regularity, early in book 9, Varro produces a metaphorical example for well-ordered speech: a dinner-party faux pas. His anxious host shifts the furniture obsessively to ensure that his guests understand their relative positions:

> Nam ut, qui triclinium constrarunt, si quem lectum de tribus unum imparem posuerunt aut de paribus nimium aut parum proferunt, una corrigimus et ad consuetudinem co<m>unem et ad aliorum tricliniorum analogias, sic si quis in oratione in pronuntiando ita declinat uerba ut dicat disparia quod peccat redigere debemus ad ceterorum similium uerborum rationem. (Varro, *Ling.* 9.9)

So it is that where those who have set the dining room, should they have placed an unmatching one among the three couches or (if in a matching set) should they have pushed one too much or too little forward, we join together as one to make the correction and refer to common usage and the analogies of other dining rooms. In the same way, if someone in speech, in his delivery, should so inflect his words as to speak irregularities, we should correct what he mistakes in accordance with the scheme of other similar words.

The dining room becomes a stage for social performance—a common enough proposition—and at the same time stands in for a balancing act that compares (*et . . . et*) reason and popular currency. How does one decide, when adjusting the couches, just how far is "enough"? What are the implications in trusting too far to what everyone thinks "the rule" is and insufficiently recognizing the value of other instances one has enjoyed? Should one's guests (or "audience") become part of any process of realignment?[45] How forcefully should tradition be imposed? Varro's use of "*una*," together with a sequence of first-person plurals, hints at a collective re-education of the errant host/speaker. It also hints at the inevitable inequality embedded in *consuetudo communis*; what kinds of people are the go-to resource for those who want to speak well ("*qui bene loqui uelit,*" *Ling.* 9.8)? The kinds of people who own houses with *triclinia* and host dinner parties of the sort where minute shifts in position and accommodation matter enough to demand painstaking effort from the host.

The dinner party as a metaphor for *oratio* works on several levels; dinner parties (within certain parameters) are spaces of convivial equality, where different ranks mingle and where women may have a participatory role otherwise denied to them. The stratification encoded in a formal seating plan and the minute attention to the arrangement of the three-couch model manifest some of these tensions: a display of ostensible equality, but encoded with the expectation of respect for gradations of status. The dining room is an interesting metaphor for another reason, too. A formal dinner party in a triclinium models a discursive space in which conversation is facilitated by means of social engineering; but it also evokes the "Greek" convivial space within which big ideas might, if one gets the ingredients right, be tested—or that denotes decadence, corruption, and excess if not—and reclining to eat was, of course, a Greek practice before it was reinvented as a traditional "Roman" one.[46]

The dining room thus stages, generates, and stands in for discourse, while at the same time operating as a site where transgressions against correct *Roman* behavior are likely to cluster. The dining room can become, in effect, laboratory space for identity fashioning and helps to ease the potential friction between Varro's less and more positive representations of *oratio*. This reading is enhanced by Varro's next metaphor—the body too needs to be shaped rigorously into appropriate citizen posture for self-projection in every sense.[47] Getting it right (or wrong) can become a project with real-time social implications for getting through the day and for maintaining face, but, as Varro goes on to note, in a sequence of sarcastic propositions, there is no actual guarantee that what one has finally defined as *consuetudo* (the presumed commonsense consensus whereby guests tacitly agree not to mess with their host's arrangement of couches) actually delivers the appropriate experience all the time.[48] Getting *consuetudo* right can be effortful. Hence, as chapter 1 began to think through:

> Quas nouas uerbi declinationes ratione introductas respuet forum, his boni poetae, maxime *scaenici*, consuetudine subigere aures populi debent, quod poetae multum possunt in hoc. ... Consuetudo loquendi est in motu. ...
>
> Quare qui ad consuetudinem nos uocant, si ad rectam, sequemur: in eo quoque enim est analogia ... sic populus facere debet, etiam singuli, sine offensione quod fiat populi ...
>
> Verbum quod nouum et ratione introductum quo minus recipamus, uitare non debemus. Nam ad usum inuestimentis aedificiis supellectili

nouitati non impedit uetus consuetudo: quem enim amor assuetudinis potius in pannis possessorem retinet, quem ad noua uestimenta traducit? (Varro, *Ling.* 9.17, 18, 20)

Such new inflected forms of words, introduced in accordance with reason, the Forum [marketplace] reviles; these the worthy poets and, in particular, the dramatists should force—through habitual use—upon the ears of the people, because poets have great power in this sphere.... Common usage in speech exists in flux....

Therefore, those who call us toward common usage, if it is correct usage, we shall follow: for in this too can be found Regularity... [although force majeure sometimes imposes bad models, skills rather than defects are what should be propagated:] thus should the people do, even at an individual level, where it can be done without offense against the People as a whole....

Where a word is new and has been introduced in a rational way, we should therefore adopt it; we should not shun it. For where it's a matter of usage, in clothes, buildings, and household goods, ancient custom does not prevent novelty: for what habitué would love of ingrained habit keep in rags, when style leads him to new garb?

This is from the pro-Regularity book 9, so Varro's argument emphasizes that making the right decisions for how one speaks *and* how one evaluates and adapts to changing patterns of use becomes a totalizing endeavor. Varro continues the discussion through the metaphor of imported Greek fashions in pottery and cups, arguing the insanity:

Et tantum inter duos sensus interesse uolunt, ut oculis semper aliquas figuras supellectilis nouas conquirant, contra auris expertis uelint esse? (Varro, *Ling.* 9.21)

And would they have it that there is such a gulf between the two senses that for their eyes they are constantly seeking out some new models of furniture, but they wish their ears to have no part in this?

And finally:

Quare qui negant esse rationem[49] analogiae, non uide<n>t naturam non solum orationis, sed etiam mundi; qui autem uident et sequi negant oportere, pugnant contra naturam, non contra analogian, et pugnant uolsillis, non gladio. (Varro, *Ling.* 9.33)

Therefore those who deny that there is an organized system of Regularity fail to see the nature not only of speech but also of the world. Those who see it and deny that it should be adhered to, they are fighting against nature, not against Regularity, and they are fighting with tweezers, not with a sword.

Regularity, here in book 9, can represent a cosmic organizing principle, one with intimate implications for the most mundane of tasks and one that can survive attack because, on a deep level, no serious destruction of Regularity is admitted to be possible. This is what the consensus position developed in book 10 makes plain.

There is a complex tonality to Varro's style, and, although *De Lingua Latina* can be extremely frustrating, it is rarely dull. To illustrate in the context of this chapter's concerns, this section concludes by reading a little further on from the passage quoted earlier.

Varro returns, at *Ling.* 9.47, to the notion of the dinner party and recalls the convivial atmosphere that (by furnishing readers with skills in discourse) the text also enables. The context (*Ling.* 9.46) for this new dinner party is more amusing than that offered for the equivalent phase in book 8, which it echoes structurally. There, when dress was scrutinized in the lead-in, it was primarily the respectable outer garments of citizens (with perhaps a whiff of naughtiness present in the idea of a *pallium*-wearing woman, *Ling.* 8.28–32). By contrast, in book 9, we have a mildly saucy treat:

> itaque in uestitu in supellectile delectari uarietate, non paribus subucilis uxoris, respondeo, si uarietas iucunditas, magis uarium esse in quo alia sunt similia, alia non sunt: itaque sicut abacum argento ornari, ut alia <paria sint, alia> disparia, sic orationem. (Varro, *Ling.* 9.46)

> [As for what they say regarding dissimilarity—it is that] just as in clothing and in furniture we delight in variety; there's no delight in having wifely lingerie all the same.[50] My response to this is that if variety is pleasure, there is greater variation in the way in which some things are similar and others are not. So, as a sideboard is decorated with silver so that some <are similar, others> are dissimilar, the same holds for [formal] discourse.

As the passage quoted here shows, Varro cheerfully satirizes the proponents of irregularity by conjuring up a vision of female underwear, only to undercut it with the argument by association that to titivate, one has first to recognize that a slip is a slip. That the dining-room analogy illustrates contrasting arguments concerning Regularity in each book demonstrates its power as a discursive space and identifies it as a site of productive friction. What kinds of things are, in fact, suitable for dinner-party conversation, and how closely do they reflect what host and guests are really thinking? Are all the guests mentally undressing their fellow diners, a background process while the food, wine, entertainment, and conversation flow? And how much does it matter, if guests (or, broadening the context, an audience) are running this and other similar evaluative processes as the event (or speech, or text) proceeds?

In Conversation

This section moves from performative discourse (*oratio*) to the more tidal qualities of reciprocal speech or conversation (*sermo*). *Sermo* should be an important word for Varro, but its relatively few appearances suggest both that this might not have been an angle Varro wished to pursue exhaustively—and that where it does feature, it may be productive to pay attention.[51]

Sermo first comes into focus in book 6, as part of Varro's treatment of *disputatio* and *computatio* (introduced in chapter 2), which develops an analogy tying speech to kitchen gardening (*Ling.* 6.63–64). Here, I emphasize its delivery of a key definition, one that also underpins the process of reading (discussed in the next two sections):

> Sermo, **opinor**, est a serie, unde serta; etiam in uestimento sartum, quod comprehensum: sermo enim non potest in uno homine esse solo, sed ubi <o>ratio cum altero coniuncta. (Varro, *Ling.* 6.64)

> "Conversation" [or informal discourse], **I think**, derives from "series," whence "garlands"; like in the case of a "mended" garment, because it's something put together. For "conversation" is not possible where one man is on his own but operates where speech is connected with speech.[52]

Individuals are capable of uttering (a) "speech," yet, without a point of intersection or human context, such unique utterances fail to be sequenced as conversational, reciprocal discourse. They exist outside the collective, excluded from the community created through a consensual, tested, and commonly used mode of expression. By introducing this topos as his own opinion (and juxtaposed directly with *sermo*), Varro produces what one might term a conversational moment. Conversation, the production of collaborative discourse, is something that demands reflection and commands his attention. The double analogy he produces affiliates "conversation" with the idea of logical sequence and has another effect, too: it colors the notion by making it cousin to the garlands that characterize pleasure and celebration in civic and private forms and, especially for the latter, at parties.

Garlands are fashioned by design, but not necessarily for tightly organized occasions. Garlands can also evoke diversity—lots of different flowers woven in. Varro's readers would certainly be aware of the figurative use of ἀνθο-λογια (flower gathering) for literary "garlands." The other element in the explanation offers greater nuance. An item of clothing requires stitching, handwork, and physical organization (the work of one or more individuals), and, unlike the garland, it is a necessity in the life of an individual and demonstrates an individual's standing in a community.

A garland, like a conversation, first suggests exclusivity (one must be in on the context to make sense of it or receive an "invitation" to participate); a garment, qualified by *comprehendo*, adds substance to the explanation. *Comprehendo* gathers together a range of concrete qualities associated with grasping or apprehending, containing, combining, and describing something; it makes for a potent mix of intellectual and physical control over an entity's singular qualities.[53] An isolated individual cannot partake in *sermo*, and Varro's second choice "joining" word (*coniungo*) sharpens the analogy. Conversation is not just about "speech" or even about speaking turn and turn-about; it is about reciprocity and about participating in a shared project that unites through ties of relationship. *Coniungo* also implies contiguity, making *sermo* about interactions between people who share a physical rather than just an intellectual space, however elastically conceived. Hence, when we rejoin *sermo* at the beginning of book 8, we have some substantial backstory in place:

Declinatio inducta in sermones non solum Latinos, sed omnium hominum utili et necessaria de causa. (Varro, *Ling*. 8.3)

Inflection has been established in discourse—not only in Latin but in that of all people—because of its utility and indispensability.

This further gloss on *sermo* gives the added sense of communality of discourse that makes *homines* part of a family. *Necessarius* (the adjective) builds on the connotations of kinship and societal bonding that we have already encountered in *coniungo* and adds another layer of naturalness to the bonds—a sense that this is one of the most basic prerequisites of life. That *homines* is Varro's chosen term to signify "humanity" delivers a sense of the universality of the proposition but also subtly encourages his readers to consider what is most or least noble in the shared human identity that the term denotes. *Homo* can signify "man," "person," "dependent," "mortal," or even "fallible."[54]

Human mortality as a characteristic gloss for inflection implies a teleology that is embedded in processes of regular grammatical structure, as the introductory material to book 8 draws out:

> Quod huiusce libri est dicere contra eos qui similitudinem sequuntur, quae est ut in aetate puer ad senem, <puella> ad anum, in uerbis ut est scribo scribam. (Varro, *Ling.* 8.25)

> Since it is for this book to speak against those who follow similarity—which is, as in the course of life, from boy to old man, <girl> to old woman; in verbs, as "I write" is to "I shall write."

The paradigms that govern Regularity are like the (natural) relationships that connect childhood to old age or link what Varro is writing now (book 8) to what comes after. Undermining this natural force will be a tricky task.

Sermo is up first (*Ling.* 8.25), but it is not until *Ling.* 8.30 that Varro comes to grips with the term, making the anti-*analogia* argument (book 8's premise) that like-for-like Regularity is not the primary feature of *sermo*. *Sermo*, like garlands (*serta*), admits variety on a linguistic level, and irregularity ought therefore to be accepted since the goal of discourse is utility; indeed, (we might imagine Varro's persona here continuing), discourse still basically works. Later, at the final appearance of *sermo* in book 8, we see something similar tried out: the fact that there are many more individually irregular words than there are paradigms of regularity means that conversation (or discourse) does not require *analogia* (*Ling.* 8.37).

Yet even though this might seem emotionally satisfying (unique, individual speech patterns and idioms ought to be a man's defining characteristic), Varro's argument had earlier asserted that a schematization of inflected forms was a crucial aid for delivering community among those who speak, driving Romans (*nos*) and Greeks alike to decline nouns so as to fashion socially nuanced bonds (*Ling.* 8.16). Thus, one approaches the notion of speech as emblematic of variety but also as overshadowed by a series of major prior position statements that undercut the force of the argument as it develops.

When *sermo* next appears (*Ling.* 9.1), it is in the context of Chrysippus, the Stoic philosopher and logician, and Varro is making the opening moves in his argument for the existence of Regularity. Chrysippus, a sharp operator ("*homine acutissimo*"), nevertheless seems (Varro proposes) to have missed the deep logic of what underpins *analogia*.⁵⁵ Chrysippus' deployment is interesting because while in this phase of the narrative Varro positions him as an anti-Regularian and as the author of a pro-*anomalia* study of irregularity, when he is reintroduced in book 10 (Varro's book of compromise) it transpires that he could also be represented as in favor of using the principles of Regularity to correct parts of speech in accordance with grammatical paradigm.

This is a position that is underpinned by Varro's earlier allusion to Chrysippus in support of his own declared intention to follow kinship patterns in verbal analysis (*Ling.* 6.2) and his subsequent approving citation of Chrysippus (*Ling.* 6.56, introduced in chapter 2): without the ability to organize words into their appropriate places and thereby give meaning to utterances, one finds that "*negat loqui, sed ut loqui*" (one doesn't talk, one merely seems to talk).⁵⁶ What this suggests is that Varro's Chrysippus is capable, despite an ostensible endorsement of *anomalia*, of perceiving the need for adaptation and flexibility within the paradigm and the broader concept of a linguistic episteme. He signed up for a worldview in which irregularity might appear to triumph, but he was still eager to address the infelicities and problems that hard-line Irregularism might determine to ignore.

At *Ling.* 9.19, discourse is embellished with a variation on one of Varro's favored metaphors—the linguist as hunter. He has proposed that "*consuetudo loquendi est in motu*" (speech in use is always in flux, *Ling.* 9.17); paradigms shift and are interpreted varyingly as a consequence of the vagaries of conversational discourse. This makes it imperative to examine each new word or form on its own merits and in the light of reason and elegance. There is a danger, the text allows, in the kind of inflexible antiquarianism that leads to pedantry, yet by mining the past for vanished idioms one may also reclaim something "new" and valuable. Indeed, as the argument later develops (*Ling.* 9.107), sometimes usage develops differently nuanced forms that can coexist happily, even enriching discourse—in book 9, this takes us to the question of passive (drawing in reflexive meaning) and active moods in verbs.

An exemplary pair of conundrums (*Ling.* 9.106) are produced: first, the active and passive forms of *lauo* conjure up two vivid contexts: a nurse bathes a child, who in turn can be described using the passive "is bathed"; we go to the bath house, where we reflexively bathe ourselves and are passively bathed; "active" suggests an object, while the self-conscious nuances can imply that one is performing self-care—as Varro puts it, *lauor* delivers "I bathe myself").⁵⁷

Varro's bathing dyad—first, the practical, perhaps pragmatic cleansing of a child by a carer; next, the adult trip to the bathhouse, with myriad social and performative triggers in play—delivers readers to a second example: a grammatical disjunction (*Ling.* 9.107). Cato and Ennius give a perfect form *solui* (deriving from *soleo*), but this is not how common parlance (the *uolgus*) would have it. This might seem to present a conversational fracture between ancestral culture heroes and everyday *parole*, but in Varro's scheme here it is not a problem; it can slot into the position he set out earlier.[58]

De Lingua Latina brings its readers to see that the difference between *langue* and *parole* or between different flavors of *parole* is part of what gives texture to discourse and makes conversational sense. The "bathing" example and its follow-up show how language's communicative functions operate synchronically even when a diachronic impetus seems to be to the fore. What delivers communicative meaning is the context of utterance and the shared understanding between speakers and listeners. In effect, Varro is again offering what Wittgenstein would later term a "language game" in which the sense (what is it that "to bathe" conveys?) and/or the form (how a tense is conjugated) can combine to create a complex and meaningfully shared "content."

Reading and Discrimination

If a word is to make sense, its users need to know how to disambiguate its relationship between potential points of reference and its own verbal identity.[59] This is an involved task. As Varro's anti-*analogia* persona puts it:

> Qu*a*ero enim, uerbum utrum dicant uocem quae ex syllabis est ficta, eam quam audimus, an quod ea significat, quam intellegimus, an utrumque. (Varro, *Ling.* 8.40)

> What I want to know is whether, when they [the *analogists*] say "word," it is the spoken word made up of syllables (the word that we hear), or the thing that the word signifies (what we understand), or both.

Words are elements in a semiotic system that is somewhere between oral performance and dialogic reciprocity and that cycles through modes and patterns connecting words on the page and in the eye, mouth, and ear. The vocal quality of reading, in Varro, is a good place to start because issues of reading and selection, converging in *lego*, underpin the notion of discourse as a civic act.

Back in book 6, *lego* (to read, organize, pick out, elect, gather up, wander, observe) introduces a significant cluster of words (*Ling.* 6.35). Varro chooses "read" (*legisti*, "you have read"), "running" (*cursus*, something having been run), and "playing" (*ludens*, a present participle) as prime examples for discussing how temporality is evident in vocabulary. As a trio, the verbs represent in microcosm the community of Romespeakers. Who performs these actions? First, "you" are the (s)electors and readers—educated citizens, playing a part in politics and other weighty business; next a group who that might consist of slaves (who "owns" the field of running in the city?) or those politicos hurrying up the *cursus honorum* (where a "race" to the finish is respectable); finally, the players, the devotees of amusement, mockery, dalliance, with *ludo* hinting at the power trips of sponsored games.[60]

That Varro proceeds to use *lego* as the prime example to explain conjugations (*Ling.* 6.36, "*ut ab lego leges, lege,*" so from "I read" comes "you read" and "'read'") suggests at the very least that he finds it linguistically interesting and capable of delivering grammatical value for his purposes. But the semiotic range of *lego* and its Greek homophone offers further enrichment.

The patterns of inflection for which *lego* represents the broad paradigm are, first, forms that deliver temporality but no declined case: "you will 'read,'" "'you: read!'"[61] Next, Varro introduces the kind of inflection where case exists independent of time, as in "a selection" (or "a reading [out]"; readers might recall the real-world combination *lectio senatus*)[62] and "reader." Third in the set is that which encompasses time and case, exemplified in "reading" (*legens*, present participle) and "being about to read" (future participle). Finally, in fourth place comes the model for forms that have neither time nor case, presented as the adverb *lecte* (select/ive/ly) and superlative (*lectissime*). It is noteworthy that these two forms are extremely rare.[63] Thus, in selecting *lego* as a model, Varro has made it necessary to deploy a suite of forms that are unlikely to seem straightforwardly idiomatic, at least in a literary context.

Rather than assuming that Varro has chosen eccentrically or thoughtlessly, through-readers might instead deduce that *lego* is meaningful for Varro. Vocabulary with a temporal quality comprises a vast (but in some heuristic sense accountable) set, as Varro has noted (*Ling.* 6.36). He acknowledges and emphasizes this again when he continues by saying, deadpan, that if we start from Cosconius' proposition that the prime forms ("*primigenia*") of such words number a thousand (a manageable figure), then once we begin to trace their inflectional families we logically reach the figure of 500,000.[64] Every origin form, in this scheme, delivers something in the region of five hundred spinoffs, however implausible this precision might seem.

Rationally, readers must recognize that such a precise cataloging proposition conceals something messier and more illimitable, especially when the "countlessness," and "immensity" ("*immanis*") of the set are announced.[65] Indeed, in his conclusion to the first phase of this argument, Varro actually encourages his audience to read these "atomic" word forms in the cosmic terms of Democritus and Epicurus (and all those who postulate a limitless number of primary "elements") and thus, we might imagine, equally suitable for axiomatic statements.[66] If the paradigms can be rationally reverse derived, then being able to deliver individual explanations for each and every form's genesis stops being the defining feature of the etymologist.

Varro's spotlight positioning of the processes of selection and reading (visual and aural construction and recognition skills; word-for-word decisions on meaning) at the beginning of this section strengthens the argument that *lego* emblematizes the whole project of mapping inflection. Choosing a polyphonous word such as *lego* emphasizes how the existence of many meanings, at an elemental moment in Latin, is central to the diversity of the mature language. If *lego* can deliver a key paradigmatic set and if we find ourselves reading it as a "telling" word with thematic resonance, then we will expect there to be some meaningful connection with whatever comes next in the text.

What follows (*Ling.* 6.37) is a set of four named words that Varro presents as equally radical ("*primigenia*"). The direct connection with the previous proposition is made by the re-presentation of *lego* as word one. The other three are *scribo* (I write), *sto* (I stand), and *sedeo* (I sit). The rest (*cetera*) are left to the imagination. Putting *lego* first encourages a narrative reading. That "writing" follows on from "reading" hints that action should follow mastery of the nuances of a textualized corpus of some sort; in a word: education. Cognitive and motor skills are at issue. Reading or "selecting" (however defined) has distinctive somatic qualities: one is engaging the senses (sight, perhaps touch, and, on some level, hearing) and intellectual faculties and interpreting and forming an opinion on a body of material (however constituted—text, propositions, citizens). Writing too is a multisensory act, with the physical production taking in a range of acts, from inking letters to the actualization of a version of reality through description.[67]

The nuances of *sto* deliver the straightforward positionality of a physical stance, but, depending on the context, this can signify a certain immovability or endurance (statues, too, can "stand") or a species of hanging around.[68] Likewise, *sedeo* sits well with this reading since, as with *lego* and *sto*, there are sociopolitical as well as personal implications—"to sit" is the activity one undertakes when performing judicial duties, for example, at the Rostra or in the context of a tribunal.[69] But "sitting" is also an activity that characterizes idleness, at the opposite end of the spectrum of engaged citizenship.[70]

Approaching the words to which these prime forms give rise reminds readers to keep *lego* in mind as more than simply a random example. Words that spring ("*oriuntur*") from the prime set are exemplified via "you read," "he reads," and "I shall read."[71] The origins of these prime words are, perhaps, impossible to elucidate, but the words themselves remain a small, definable set: a kind of natural language within whose confines the most primitive Latin speakers could be imagined to be at home. Varro then moves on to the generation of words through prefixing by working through forms ending in -*cedo* (positionality is the semantic link here with the words we encountered just before).[72]

Finally, as indicated earlier, Varro returns to the issue of what constitutes the primordial word pool, using Democritus and Epicurus as stalking horses (*Ling.* 6.39). Here, rather than simply asserting that there *just are* a thousand prime words, we are encouraged to think about the matter in parallel with an atomic philosophical position that allows for the postulation of elemental qualities, delivering an unlimited number of elements for which a description and a place in the world can be described but for which no "origin" story is forthcoming. The etymologist is similarly able to postulate, but, rather than declaring the set unlimited, Varro repeats Cosconius' figure (a set of one thousand elemental word forms).[73] This repetition and its context (first introduced as Cosconius' model, then contextualized in terms of unlimited elements) suggest an unlikeliness to the neatness of the round figure, but, as Varro continues (*Ling.* 6.40), the point develops that he was making a presentation on the *range* of what exists and in the context of what is meaningful.

Reading through the Text

My analysis of the examples clustering around *lego* in book 6 and, in particular, my conclusions on his programmatic positioning of *lego* show that Varro's key words for etymology and grammar have rich semantic and semiotic fields that encompass much more than paradigms and linguistic encyclopedism. In this reading, if you have an expert navigator piloting you across the limitless sea of language then the chaos-logic of illimitability is no barrier to *auctoritas uerborum*, and language becomes a gateway to power sourced from any useful historical moment. Here, everything is open to recuperation, and semiotic systems (including syntax, grammar, and meaning) are always of the moment and of their own authentic moments. Thus, Varro's decision to highlight *lego* begins a proposition that delivers its payoff when through-readers eventually realize just how significant the process of selection can be.

There are three other places where *lego* features significantly and supports this interpretation. First, *Ling.* 6.66. Readers have worked through the primacy of *lego* (when considering the radical qualities of verbs); next comes a sequence of "speaking" terms (*Ling.* 6.51–65). Varro moves from *narro* (I tell), to *for* (I say) and its multifarious family, then on to *loquor* (I talk), *pronuntio* (I pronounce), *nomino* (I name), *dico* (I speak), plus various spinoff explanations, such as *puto* (I reckon, arrange), *dissero* (I sow, engage in discourse), and finally on to *sors* (lot, destiny, chance).[74] This sequence is significant context for the re-emergence of *lego* because it leads readers through a set of approaches to the production of communicative meaning and ends in a direct connection between "conversation" ("*sermo*") as a species of "joining"[75] and the kinds of military, legal, and religious practices and conventions that underpin the Roman community.[76] Collaboration is crucial to both.

Lego (*Ling.* 6.66) in this narrative context is part of a sequence that emphasizes the physical links bridging the gap between communication and community. I introduced this passage in chapter 2, so the point here is to remind us of its implications within the wider narrative arc of *lego*: it can come to be all about how one physical sense (sight) takes responsibility for the selection process ("*quod leguntur ab oculis litterae*"), even though there is no actual root element or etymological link to sight or ocular terms. Selection with the eyes delivers *lego* as a "reading" verb in which the body operates on the physical text to produce something meaningful.[77]

Lego continues to recur at strategic moments. In my next example, early in book 8 (*Ling.* 8.3) and still in Varro's prefatory material (before the development of the anti-Regularity argument), *lego* is the exemplary verb for inflection. As quoted in the third section of this chapter, "In Conversation," *Ling.* 8.3 outlines the position that inflection is a characteristic of all human speech because it is what makes speech fit for purpose. Here Varro develops something akin to the infinity of vocabulary familiar from his earlier allusion to Democritus and Epicurus when considering the task of scoping the pool of existing words: "*infinitae enim sunt naturae in quas ea declinantur*" (for their possibilities, once inflected, are infinite). Without the paradigms of inflection, he continues, even the kind of vocabulary set that might be learned would be a feeble stand-in since a consensual and complex meaning would no longer play a full part in the semiotic system.[78]

"What it is that we see [*uidemus*] is that there is a likeness where something is an offshoot [*propagatum*]" (*Ling.* 8.3). When one takes a cutting, one expects the new plant to bear a familial relationship to its parent, and Varro's illustrative example is the bond between *legi* (perfect) and *lego* (present): even though each takes place at a different time, there is a qualitative connection in the action that each denotes. Varro's counterfactual proof revolves around a comparison with the relationship between (the words) "Priam" and "Hecuba," a pairing introduced to show what happens when one has no paradigm. The marital relationship between these two, in myth, is accessible only if one recognizes the names as invoking these specific characters. Without the knowledge to map the names to individuals within a story, the words "Priam" and "Hecuba" have no obvious affinity. This contrasts with our exemplary forms of *lego* and, as Varro reminds us, with the declined forms of the nouns, whose *unitas* is apparent if one takes as examples *Priamus* and *Priamo*. To understand the complex network that underpins reality on a deep level, we might infer, requires more than the basic vocabulary and more than a command of general knowledge.

Moving into the main argument in book 8 (*Ling.* 8.44), we revisit writing and reading in the context of individual parts of speech (as we saw featured earlier in this chapter). For the purpose of recognizing *lego* within Varro's read/write continuum, recall that *scribo* and *lego* are the examples chosen to represent verb forms, and this is followed up a few sections later when we encounter types for nouns with their roots in verbs: a *scriptor* gains his identity through the act of writing and, similarly, a *lector*, from reading.[79] The contiguity between the acts denoted by these two verbs makes them an ideal and obvious pair, but it also encourages a semiotic overlap between reading, editing, participating in public affairs, and composing.[80]

Soon (*Ling.* 8.58), *lego* reappears yet again, but with a very different juxtaposition. Here the broad context is the exposition of active and passive. Varro picks up on the appearance of *amo* (from the preceding section, 8.57) and decouples *lego* from *scribo* to pair it instead with "I love." This allows him to model how participles develop and leads to an elegant confluence for a book on language but with a strong interest in literariness, especially poetry (we find ourselves at a meeting of loving and being loved, reading and being read). In their inconsistency of development, the argument runs, these disprove the existence of Regularity—one might be tempted to wonder whether the new configuration (read/love) is also proposing a reflection on the relationship between reading about love and love bound up in what one reads.[81] In an Irregular worldview, loving is readerly, and reading is a sensual passion. Varro has, after all, stressed the bodily, sensory basis of *lego*, and the erotic agency of the eyes would be familiar to readers of Lucretius book 4.

It is not until *Ling* 9.32 that *lego* enters the lists again. Here, in the book arguing in favor of Regularity, Varro is on a roll with an address to his audience:

> Quis enim potest non una animaduertisse in omni oratione esse ut legebam lego legam si<c> lego legis legit, cum haec eadem dicantur alias ut singula, alias ut plura significentur? (Varro, *Ling.* 9.32)

For who can fail to be of like mind in noticing that in all speech, there are [temporal] forms as follows: "I was 'reading,'" "I 'read,'" "I shall 'read,'" and likewise [personal] forms in "I," "you," "he, she, or it," although these same forms may be said in such a way that sometimes the singular and sometimes the plural is signified?

In other forms, too, such as imperatives, forms expressing a wish ("*in optando*"), and interrogatives, there is an ongoing need for disambiguation on the part of the speaker and his (or her) audience. Speaking and listening and participating in Latin discourse demand cognitive processes that (Varro's decision to compose this handbook suggests) are significantly enhanced by an understanding of their rules and rationales. Simply following paradigms because they appear to be the bedrock of Latin discourse means ignoring the tacit cosmopolitanism of the system. Varro's argument continues to stir things up by suggesting (in the character of the pro-Regularity speaker) that, by denying the existence of *analogia*, one is defining oneself as someone incapable of seeing the real meaning not just of speech but of what constitutes the world (*Ling.* 9.33; my concluding chapter returns in detail to the significance of this model).

When book 9 subsequently makes a lengthy return visit to the matter of systematizing verb forms (*Ling.* 9.96–110), readers should be unsurprised to find that intratextuality, particularly between the first two books of this triad, puts *lego* up first (*Ling.* 9.96, in parallel with *disco*), even though here we are deep in the pro-Regularity argument (that is, in parallel but also in contrast to the narrative position allotted to *lego* in book 8). The symmetry with the earlier *lego–scribo* connection delivers a slightly different thematic take on how the sense and the forms of these verbs enforce rather than diminish Regularity across the tenses. It also makes *lego–amo* a third "natural" pairing.

We see this when Varro amplifies the echo of *lego* from book 8 to explain the next phase in the argument, that within each verb's family there is a rational consistency, and so it is deeply flawed to argue that (for example) the existence of three passive forms for *amo*, one with two parts—*amor* (I am loved), *amabor* (I shall be loved), and *amatus sum* (I have been loved)—means that rationality breaks down for the whole paradigm (*Ling.* 9.97).[82] This is how *lego* and *amo* have again ended up as a "couple." Here, rather than exemplifying the inconsistency of participles, the two verbs are indicative of the kinds of intimately relational paradigms that deliver Regularity even when superficially or in microcosm *anomalia* appears to be present.

Lego is again Varro's first example when he introduces a further phase in the argument (*Ling.* 9.101), this one concerning imperatives and subjunctives (mood)—nature is surely not to be censured for not shaping all living entities exactly the same. Why indeed, he continues, would we expect (for example) the imperative mood to have the regular set of tenses when no one is likely to be giving commands relating to the past? Varro illustrates using *lego*. Three forms (three, alluding numerically to the trio of tenses) relating necessarily to incomplete action comprise the imperative and subjunctive. These are, however, in themselves complete and in line with Regularity and are not to be imagined as in any way lacking. With *scribo* introduced as a secondary example, Varro looks to ascertain a pattern—we always should return to the person of the speaker, acting in the present tense: "*sic hic in forma est persona eius qui loquitur et tempus praesens, ut scribo lego*" (*Ling.* 9.102).[83]

Book 10 is, of course, the book of reconciliation between the opposing poles in the notional pro- and anti-*analogia* argument. Varro's introduction to book 8 is long, embedding a significant delay before the book gets going on the negative argument. This undermines the anti-Regularity position before one reaches it. Thus, when one arrives at Varro's exposition of the pro-Regularity case (in book 9) and then moves to book 10, momentum and trajectory suggest that one is approaching something at once conclusive and personally satisfying for the author. At *Ling.* 10.47–48, the final appearance of *lego* in the extant text, we find that the context is set up by the presentation of two nouns that offer a paradigm for what Varro terms disjointed Regularity (explained as being like stating that the ratio 1:2 is equal to the ratio 10:20). The nouns *rex* and *lex* (like the examples) behave in equivalent ways when declined (hence, a pattern of Regularity), but, when considered without the context of patterns of inflection in and of themselves, they are separate and operate independently. *Lex* is not, of course, semantically part of the family of *lego*, yet as declined it delivers forms that add value to the contiguity; and juxtaposing "king" with "law" is semiotically eloquent.[84]

"King" and "law" also make provocative associates when read against what follows, Varro's mathematical explanation of conjoined Regularity: it works just as if the ratio 1:2 is considered equal to the ratio 2:4 because two takes a role in each proposition.[85] This is exemplified by verbs when examined across three tenses: "*ut legebam, lego, legam*" (I was reading, I read, I shall read), since past:present has present:future as its equivalent. Moreover, Varro argues, present tense forms (whatever their number) relate to an incomplete action, whereas the perfect relates to completed action. So the paradigmatic *lego* (present, incomplete) cannot pair relationally with *legi* (perfect, complete). This exclusion of the perfect thus makes sense of why verbs are not part of a naturally fourfold model of Regularity (as set out at *Ling.* 10.46). Present (incomplete) *lego* does not make common cause with past (complete) *legi*.[86]

In support of this model as exemplified using *lego*, Varro offers some potentially troubling connotations by way of *tundo* (I strike), *pungo* (I puncture), and, introducing the passive to the mix, *neco* (I kill) and *uerbero* (I beat). It is with *amo*, "I love," that his design becomes apparent—this was not simply a disconnected tour through verbs relating to violence because it recalls readers to thoughtful consideration by reintroducing *lego* as a companion to *amo*. Reading and loving, brought together, offer some contiguity and bind the set of vigorous action terms into something contained by the known pair. This is different from the model in book 9. *Ling.* 9.96–97 presents *lego*, then *amo*, before moving on to "violence" terminology, including *pungo* and *tundo* (*Ling.* 9.98–99).

Conclusion

Varro's profession of Latin, articulated in his introduction to book 10, is more than just a trope.[87] By setting himself up as the authority on Latin coding, Varro is also spotlighting the changing values and registers of Latin that reflect and in turn shape the new world order for every speaker.[88] Decoding Latin, for Latin speakers and readers, elegantly and relentlessly points up how far from a straightforward vernacular Latin can be. To put it bluntly, although "Latin," not "Roman," wins the name game and defines the language of empire, of the city, and of the peninsula, Varro's audience still needs to understand how to mediate between the competing internal and external constituencies and their variant and potentially eccentric forms of *parole*. This requires a nuanced understanding of what words-in-use (Varro's *sermo*, *dico*, *loquor*) signify.

Varro's was an elite culture of letter writing, and the "philosophical" tract too could borrow much of the apparatus of the epistolary conversation, even as it might also evoke the securely textual isonomy of the scripted dialogue.[89] Learning Varro's Latin lessons successfully makes fluent, intuitive speech work hard for the speaker; for the *orator* it might promise an effortless flow of eloquent, apt Latin (ripe for textualization). Yet, unlike Cicero, Varro, in writing on Latin, avoids any overarching dialogic narrative structure. Varro's educated audience, Roman luminaries, Cicero, and others, fail to get speaking parts. Instead, quotations (that is, edited highlights, selected by Varro) rather than interlocutors make up the dramatis personae. This tactic gives Varro leeway in terms of how he fashions the *memoria* of his work for posterity ("the entry into the textual community"),[90] but it also points up a second-fiddle quality for "live," Ciceronian *oratio* (part of the domain of *sermo*, *Ling.* 6.64).[91]

Unlike *sermo*, the textbook and performative qualities of Varro's *oratio* risk taking it out of the cut-and-thrust of conversational engagement. In *De Lingua*

Latina, although intertextuality and, thereby, textual community are intensely significant, Varro's analyses prioritize the cognitive and conceptual payoffs of engaging in discourse (*sermo*), whereby the individual speaker requires ex tempore compositional and argumentative skills (effectively primed by Varro's bite-size etymologies and enjoyment of memorable factoids) rather different from those qualities of planned and potentially monologic performance that seem to characterize *oratio*. As this chapter has argued, however, *oratio* appropriately conceptualized can also strengthen Varro's developing consensus model. For this to work, orators need an ability to manipulate not just words but also the semiotic web within which Latin meaning operates (from "family" to "family jewels," as Mark Forsyth almost puts it).[92] How language generates meaningful, communicative discourse must be through a process of implicit (or explicit) appeals to basic and more complex conventions (shown off in *oratio*) understood to be shared by key participants and exercised in conversation.

Chapters 2 and 3 developed examples leading to a reading whereby alertness to the nuances of Varro's selected words begins to illuminate his and his audience's wider frame of reference. In this chapter's fourth and fifth sections I tracked one thematically significant term (*lego*) through the text to get a better understanding of the potential of such cross-over terms connecting discernment, interpretation, and discourse to switch on the politics of Latin. *Lego* is an obvious example to pick. This is not just because of its associations with "literariness" in the broadest sense but also because it signals the most basic act of politics—the act of *choosing* what comes next. Reading Latin is what actualizes Varro's study. Without some notionally practical impact on one or more readers, the "handbook" as a text fails. Varro's text needs, as well as needs to create, its own ideally skilled readers. There is in this way a genuine feedback loop, reciprocal self-fashioning between the text and its ideal audience.

Simmering away in this chapter has been the role of comparison with Greek models and how Latin operates within a linguistic family context. When Latin's place in the Mediterranean language pool is at issue, it is unsurprising that the role of place in generating and developing a language and a people-with-a-language bubbles up. My next chapter tackles Italic and Greek echoes in Varro's Roman sites. The Latinate city of the fifth book of *De Lingua Latina* is colored by words and derivations that might encourage a *flâneur*, meandering through the city as through Varro's miscellany and enriched by an understanding of how language makes spaces into places, to pause to consider how language as discourse also articulates citizenship as a brand of localism.

chapter 5

As Old as the Hills

The swish and crackle of paper is the underlying sound of the metropolis.... What is visible and real in this world is only what has been transferred to paper.[1]

THIS CHAPTER STARTS FROM Varro's grand vision of world building, before turning to Rome, the eponymous imperial capital. Here, it selects elements of Varro's two itineraries that redefine the city as a zone of anomalies that become canonical, spaces that become places, and foreigners who turn out to be central to the res publica collective.[2] Varro's stories are certainly rich with historical, antiquarian, and civic interest—their tributaries, meanders, and intersections would soon be flowing through the poems of Vergil, Propertius, and Ovid, in poetic distillations of the arcane, learned, funny, and folksy paths that weave through his Rome. In particular, book 5's tales of the city introduce readers to what Steven H. Rutledge terms Rome's inbuilt biographical quality: "the birth, life, and death of the founder that left its mark on the city" but not, as Varro has emphasized, on the name of its language.[3]

The dialogue between time, language, and community through which a group develops its cultural memory is never uncomplicated. The sociologist and urban theorist Lewis Mumford once proposed that "in the city, time becomes visible."[4] Urban time, Mumford continued, is characterized by "the diversity of its time-structures," and it is in the complexity of their layering that a sense of unique historicity or antiquarian interest collects around certain key sites.[5] As quickly becomes clear, Varro's Rome is not straightforwardly accessed as a logical itinerary that works easily in line with the constraints of real-world time and space.[6]

Varro's identification and examination of Rome's sites of meaning illustrate how knowing *more* shapes a community's physical world; this is the "analogical city" exemplified in M. Christine Boyer's encouragement toward "a deep-structural reading of secret insights into a city's topography, a downward voyage into their archaic underworld."[7] Varro's itineraries illuminate what is interesting, pleasurable, and memorable (Boyer's terms) to demonstrate how reading *about*

Latin shapes a city of symbolic and emblematic sites, a city whose hilly terrain and heterogeneous first families were believed to have combined uniquely to unite landscape and people. Varro's choices draw attention to sites that impressionistically highlight Rome's mosaic qualities and that, in their excavation, demonstrate a productive friction between familiar and strange that is peculiar to urban wayfinding. Varro's project of familiarization does not, however, alienate his Romespeakers—it brings them home, knowing as never before that (and how, and why) there is no place *like* home. To be fully Roman, citizens need to keep learning to recognize Rome anew—just as Cicero (nearly) said.[8]

Unsurprisingly, Varro's Rome represents a rich repository for developing the ancient Art of Memory.[9] The "real" Rome, in Baudrillard's sense, signifies a lost shared ideal of the commonwealth, making the competing signs of the res publica important sites for the negotiation of values.[10] Reading Rome's ancient sites right had genuine historical consequence exactly because these "heritagescapes" continued to be refashioned, restored, and recontextualized in tune with changing interpretations of the past.[11] Parts of the urban fabric may, at any moment, be in plain view but culturally invisible, unnoticed (or imaginatively occluded) insofar as their stories fail to gel with the memories and needs of an author or audience. Conversely, some sites may even be invisible, lost, or unavailable to specific viewpoints, yet still feature in the mind's eye.

Varro makes *locus* (place) his first springboard for exploring how the world is divided up (*Ling.* 5.13), a subject that occupies the first section of this chapter.[12] *Locus* leads into the famous metaphor whereby word trees have roots that perform radical spatial destabilization by ignoring property lines (*Ling.* 5.13).[13] To transgress a boundary typically requires awareness of what it represents and how it works. Varro's metaphor plays on a nexus of vision and interpretation to produce what the social geographer Edward Soja terms "realandimagined" sites, places that have both material and conceptual realities.[14] These are sites that respond actively to viewing, and in Varro's book they operate rather like rocks in a stream around which those walking in the city, swerving to follow the flow of "realandimagined" meanders, themselves cause ripples, facilitating what Walter Benjamin terms "the awakening of a not-yet-conscious knowledge of what has been."[15]

It is in this context that this chapter's second section draws together two key sites uniting book 5's first and second Roman itineraries: a hill and what lies buried beneath the land it rises from.[16] The third section introduces Varro's Argei shrines as a system of topographic organization, and the fourth works through some examples where these Argei shrines function as nodes of movement through the scripted city. In the fifth section I explore a series of case studies related to the shrines, urban zoning, and the *regiones*, while the sixth and seventh analyze agenda-setting infrastructure: from routes to boundaries and ways in and out. The final section returns to Varro's *templum* to interrogate its spatial dynamics as a site for encountering the divine and to draw together this chapter's cosmic and world-building strands.

A Whole World, in Brief

Even before Varro's totalizing family tree of grammar (in books 8–10), one whose *ratio* can be understood by way of scientific genealogy to deliver intense symbolic capital, his etymological program has shown what is possible if skillful command of apt data is in place. Epistemological control over the cosmos, the widest possible context for Varro's community of Romespeakers, produces the richest array of information and examples. Varro sets out the cosmic frame early on:

> Pythagoras Samius ait omnium rerum initia esse bina ut finitum et infinitum, bonum et malum, uitam et mortem, diem et noctem.... quod stat aut agitatur, corpus, ubi agitatur, locus, dum agitatur, tempus, quod est in agitatu, actio. Quadripertitio magis sic apparebit: corpus est ut cursor, locus stadium qua currit, tempus hora qua currit, actio cursio. (Varro, *Ling.* 5.11)

> Pythagoras the Samian says that in all matter, the beginnings are binary, such as finite and infinite, good and bad, life and death, day and night.... whatever occupies a position or is in motion, is body; where it is in motion is place; while it is in motion, makes for time; what is inherent within the motion, is action. The quadripartite division will be more apparent from this: the body is like a runner, place is the stadium in which he runs, time is the duration in which he runs, action is the running.

From here, the text rushes readers from the lofty first principles of heaven and earth through to a geopolitically alert assessment of the different points of reference that territorial nomenclature can evoke: Asia can be "Asia, not Europe," of which Syria is a subset, or "Asia" in which one finds Ionia and that is "*prouincia nostra*."[17] This scheme provides a substantial treatment of the heavens, taking Varro from his initial allusion to Pythagoras (as quoted) back to Hesiod. Was it *caelum* from *caelatum* (the sky as high-relief sculpture, a natural ecphrasis in the making), as his old mentor Aelius has it? Or a function of opposites, perhaps from *celatum* (hidden—in plain sight)? While the first explanation is satisfying and elegant, the second has the merit of keeping Varro's opening binarism (heaven/earth) in play.[18]

What follows (*Ling.* 5.19–20) is, textually, particularly difficult. A summary of the basic sense suggests that Varro returns readers to the primal moments of world formation when chaos produced the first forms and a hollowed mass became the encircling sky. Varro's eagerness here to connect *cauum* to *caelum* is perhaps rooted in a determination to give a Hesiodic gloss to the developing ur-landscape, complete with a stellar vault of heaven. In the process (by way of a quote from Ennius' *Agamemnon*) he also ecphrastically evokes Aelius' explanation: heaven, chased like a legendary shield, encloses and decorates (or, drawing on the connotations of the shield, defends) a corrugated landscape of caves, caverns, and deep valleys. Here, the deep places of the earth seem to be exposing their genealogical debt to chaos, and the elegant, literary heavens make for a sophisticated progeny in which human concerns are writ large.[19] The payoff, as ever, is in the detail.

Looking closely, we find Varro connecting chaos to *caelum* by way of *cauum*, *cauea*, *caullae* (*cauile*), *conuallis*, and *cauernae*. It is in these beginnings, products of chaos, that Hesiod situates the origins of the cosmos, but these words prove to be more acculturated than their primal wilderness meanings suggest. *Cauum* as a substantive evokes *cauaedium*, described by Vitruvius (*De arch.* 6.3) as an inner courtyard feature of the prosperous Roman domestic setup, whilst the *cauea* corrals domestic animals and provides a roost for theatergoers;[20] *caullae* is a significant cosmological term in Lucretius, signifying some sort of opening, an entrance or exit point. This leaves only *conuallis* and *cauernae* as reasonably authentic and straightforward natural features for the Hesiodic nod concluding the section: "*sic ortum, unde omnia apud Hesiodum, a chao cauo caelum.*"[21]

The human, Roman quality to these primordial terraforming moments comes into focus when Varro returns to earth ("*terra*," *Ling.* 5.21). He accompanies readers from Hesiod and the primal panorama (hollow heavens and an earth within which humans are both spectators and consumers, under surveillance) to the humane, well-trodden earth, subject to human dominance (recalling Aelius as an authority). *Terra* connects *teritur* (the etymological origin, according to Aelius) and an old spelling for "earth," *tera*. By plugging this morphological point into the discourse of augury (specifically, the *books* of the Augurs, *Ling.* 5.21) and making it about orthographic change highlighting a Roman authenticity, Varro shows how the grinding qualities of daily use affect the semiotic and ontological sphere. *Tero* is a technological, manufactory verb, which neatly emphasizes the qualitative and semiotic difference between the earth (fashioned in collaboration with humankind) and the heavens (grandchild of chaos).

The earth is also thereby connected directly to animate life, in motion. The community-forming implications of this division become clear when Varro unpacks *territorium*. It is the Common Space (*locus communis*)—the land left in common to the tillers of the land ("*coloni*")—and thus most "trodden."[22]

Sevenheights: Ups and Downs

Hills—or *montes*, that is, heights, mounts—are what first define Varro's Rome, not walls,[23] and readers who join this first extended visit to Rome (*Ling.* 5.41–56) find themselves amid the famous *seven hills*.[24] This is the first expression in Latin of the Eternal City's most enduring meme. Varro's track record is at least hepta-curious, and *seven* hills promise a specificity that can remain tantalizingly undetermined (in *De Lingua Latina*). In their superfluity these hills make Rome's nook in the Tiber's embrace into an almost ridiculously inevitable site for city foundation.[25] Multiple heights, Varro's *montes*, continue to punctuate the city, equipping Varro's readers to find their way right back to the mothership and their earliest Roman selves by mapping the development of language in relation to occupied space.[26]

If Remo Gelsomino's determination to credit Varro as the inventor of the "city of seven hills" is on target, proof remains elusive.[27] Varro may or may not have been the inventor of or the only agent for the long-running seven-hills franchise—and who knows whether Cicero's usage is his own or a reverb from Varro's fascination with sevens?[28] Nevertheless, that Propertius could produce an erotic send-up, juxtaposing Rome, "lofty city of seven heights, which oversees the whole world," with the jumped-up threat from Cleopatra shows how iconic and clichéd the image had become within a few years of Varro's death.[29] It is with the novelty of the emphasis on "seven" in Varro's time in mind that, rather than leaning on the enduringly hackneyed Seven Hills, I translate Varro's usage as Sevenheights.

Varro makes the iconicity of his scenography clear for through-readers:[30]

<u>Ubi</u> **nunc** <u>est Roma</u>, Sept*i*montium **nominatum ab** <u>tot montibus</u> quos **postea** <u>urbs</u> muris <u>comprehendit</u>. (Varro, *Ling.* 5.41)

<u>Where</u> **now** <u>is Rome</u> **was called** Sevenheights, **after** so many heights which the <u>city</u> **later** <u>encompassed</u> with walls.

Dies Septimontium **nominatus ab** <u>his septem montibus</u>, in quis **sita** <u>Urbs</u> **est**; feriae non populi, sed <u>montanorum</u> modo, ut Paganalibus, qui sunt <u>alicuius</u> <u>pagi</u>. (Varro, *Ling.* 6.24)

> Sevenheights Day **was called after** these seven heights, on which the city is sited; it's a holiday not for the whole people but only for the lofty ones, as with the Paganalia, which is only for suburbanites ["people of the *pagi*"].

Varro's strong denotative emphasis and active verbs are nuanced by the two temporal adverbs (now; later), and the spatiotemporal qualities of *ab* (from; after). *Ab* creates a fleeting sense of chronology that is highlighted by *postea* and the present/perfect slippage of *comprehendit*. Rome becomes, in this way, a diachronic and synchronic entity, one that in dialogue with its archaic name (the apparently descriptive Sevenheights) has always been part of the oh-so hilly (*tot*) landscape as it morphs from Rome, on through the deceptively retroactive Sevenheights, to the generic all-encompassing form, the *urbs*.[31]

Caroline Vout argues that Varro's Septimontium represents Rome's first flowering, with the real-world hills of the late Republican city representing equivalents to the prehistoric heights, not a transhistorical topographic system.[32] Looking at the first of the two passages, one can take that a step further. Having many heights is distinctive; having sufficient to enable the selection of seven (from an even larger array of possibilities) makes proto-Rome especially satisfying as a place to imagine the planning of a new and defensible city. Seven makes for a substantial number to demonstrate that Rome's foundation and youth were not just auspicious but majestic and that—perhaps uniquely and for the first time—the city's creation engendered and represented a connection between topographic and cultural significance. Seven, already an organizational principle for Varro, delivers, with hills to spare.[33]

This is important when Varro returns to the festival in book 6, the second passage quoted earlier. Here, invitations to Varro's Sevenheights club are reserved for elevated inhabitants, but since he does not name his intended hills, any Roman hill dweller within the walls is embraced. Everyone else becomes one of those *paganici*, which in this model, at this point in *De Lingua Latina*, appears to apply only to those down in the low-lying (flat) areas—low-lifers, part of the crowd.[34] Readers find this sketched by inference when Varro discusses the *pagus Succusanus* as a preferred alternative wordplay for *sub-urb*an *Subura*'s origin—more on this in the third section of this chapter. Varro's articulation of topography as both a complement to and an indicator of structural organization shows how Rome's geopolitics have an inherently "leveling" quality; hills and valleys connect the elevated and the lees but also expose Rome as a city of inherent and symbolic divisions. That Caesar was a man of the Subura salts the association.[35]

To sum up, the coinage Sevenheights, even if not first or uniquely Varro's, is an intriguing descriptor. It gives Rome an inevitability in terms of magnificence, symbolic heft, and dimensions (the number seven), uniquely determinative topography (the specified heights and depths that create a hilly landscape), and strength through community (seven hills collapse many identities into one site). Sevenheights even makes capital from Varro's enthusiasm for hybridization in language: the resulting whole visibly and vividly retains its individuating parts and surpasses their sum. Whatever its origins, the term finds its first extant Latin expression here, and Varro's explication at least hints that it is not a standard toponym; lack of contemporary examples shores up the notion that Varro is going out on a limb. His demonstrative statement makes a play for revisiting the whole idea of unity from diversity and how anomalies (hills), if appropriately encompassed and schematized, become part of a wider but defined and paradigmatic texture.[36]

Varro's built Rome will therefore give monumental form to what nature had already laid out. Rome's walls will frame and define the hills (in Soja's terms, "iconic emplacements") as signs of a unique environment and a distinctive place.[37] Readers arriving at Varro's textualized Rome first meet this hilly landscape and quickly find in it a rich and long-standing sense of connectivity between humans and environment. This history of engagement is buried but recoverable: Varro shows us how to dig it out of the names under our feet.

> E quis Capitolinum dictum, quod hic, cum fundamenta foderentur aedis Iouis, caput humanum **dicitur inuentum**. Hic mons ante Tarpeius dictus a uirgine Vestale Tarpeia, quae ibi ab Sabinis necata armis et sepulta: cuius nominis monimentum relictum, quod etiam nunc eius rupes Tarpeium appellatur saxum. (Varro, *Ling.* 5.41)

> Of these [heights], the Capitoline is so-called because here, when the foundations of the temple of Jupiter were being excavated, a human "head" **was said to have been discovered**. This mount was formerly called the Tarpeian, because of the Vestal Virgin Tarpeia who there was killed by the Sabines with their shields and buried. A memorial remains of her name: even now the cliff is called the Tarpeian Rock.

Varro quickly sketches in the significance of vision when he presents the first hilly etymology: the future-perfecting gaze of a disembodied head, an economical way for Varro to situate readerly perspectives, making the head into what

Jacques Lacan terms a "*point de capiton*," a site of stabilization of meaning (or "quilting") but one that is in this case illusory.[38] This buried, excavated head might also be read in terms of what Lacan terms *objet petit a* (the focus point for and the object of desire), which can exert a pull only on those whose perspective or position as viewers is compromised in some way.[39] Here, Varro's readers are compromised by their lack of knowledge (a lack that Varro is gradually remedying), by their dependence for information on where Varro takes them and what etymologies he presents, and on how slickly they are able (or allowed) imaginatively to take control of the newly glossed empires of knowledge that he opens up.[40] Yet the silent, lost-and-found head exists only in the historical imagination and the telling ("*dicitur inuentum*"), and its power persists only in metonymy.[41] It is for citizens to dig in (or down)—"*cum fundamenta foderentur*"—in order then to raise the hill artificially, modeling Rome's commanding and expansive imperial significance and reinventing the naturally iconic elevation on the skyline by means of their new temple's vast bulk.[42] Tarquinius Superbus' major works on the Capitoline temple included the creation of a platform for the construction and, in the process, were said to have involved the destruction of ancient Sabine shrines marking up the hill as part of the (resolved) conflict zone between Romulus and Titus Tatius.[43]

The "realandimagined" discovery of the head thus emphasizes the inherently habitable qualities of what Freud called (referring to Rome) this "psychical entity."[44] The buried-head motif also foreshadows the next burial alluded to, that of Tarpeia, whose appearance reminds readers that there is always more than one way to spin ("*appellatur*") a story or a site. Varro apportions no blame in this allusion to Tarpeia's fate and also makes no allusion to the motifs of renewal connected to the Parilia—Rome's birthday and a pastoral festival (21 April), which the reference to Tarpeia as Vestal Virgin would (at least later) associatively trigger.[45]

To wrap up, this reading introduced Varro's Capitoline etymology, the first landmark in this city tour, as a presage to the combination of change and continuity that enabled the growth of empire and guaranteed the foundation of the Republic. With Tarpeia, Varro's Capitoline Hill tacitly recalls the struggle for supremacy between Romulus and Titus Tatius and the definitive integration of the two peoples (one of them Varro's Sabines) in its wake. With the anomalous qualities of the *caput* given Roman meaning at the heart of the political trauma that would generate the new Republican order, the phrase "*fundamenta foderentur*" (the foundations were being excavated) emphasizes his message that pursuing the roots of meaning can require invasive tactics. *Fundamentum* delivers "foundation" or "basis" but also hints at "beginnings" and, figuratively, at something fundamental to existence. *Fodio*, on the other hand, is not simply about digging: it connotes aggression (stabbing, piercing), burial, and undermining, in addition to working over the soil and digging plants in.[46] Varro's disturbing Head of State prefigures a resilient body politic for the future *caput mundi*.

The diachronic fluidity of this exemplary site as a *point de capiton* is evident when Varro's next move rescripts the Capitoline in terms that underline its metonymic significance: "*Hunc antea montem Saturnium appellatum prodiderunt*" (this hill was formerly called the Saturnian, as some related, *Ling.* 5.42), with Ennius, as Varro observes, calling Latium the "Saturnian Land."[47] The Capitoline headland is therefore not just Rome but also Latium, a totalizing isovist, and an example of the illusory quality of the depth of stable meaning it appears to manifest.[48] *Prodiderunt* emphasizes the polyphony, and Ennius' name adds gravitas to the three scenes that Varro offers in illustration of the intellectual heavy lifting that he needs to perform on readers' behalf, if illusions of stability and permanence are effectively to be scrutinized.

> Eius <u>uestigia etiam nunc manent</u> tria, quod Saturni fanum in faucibus, quod Saturnia Porta quam Iunius <u>scribit</u> ibi, quam <u>nunc uocant</u> Pandanam, quod post aedem Saturni in aedificiorum legibus priuatis parietes postici "muri <Saturnii>" sunt <u>scripti</u>. (Varro, *Ling.* 5.42)

> Of this there <u>remain even now</u> three <u>vestiges</u>: that there is a sanctuary of Saturn by the access route; that there is a Saturnian gate of which Junius <u>writes</u>, there, <u>now</u> generally <u>called</u> Pandana; that behind the temple of Saturn, in the laws relating to private buildings, the rear walls are <u>recorded</u> as "Saturnian."

The underlined text emphasizes the interplay that Varro "quilts" between experiential reality and oral and written traditions. First, a temple of Saturn *still* marks the pass. Next, adding complexity, an account of a former gate known as "Saturnian" is ascribed to "Junius" (likely the jurist M. Junius Brutus, who held a praetorship in 142), a site now recognizable as the Pandana Gate.[49] Finally, private houses behind the temple of Saturn are legally designated as having "Saturnian" rear walls.

The Pandana Gate, which does not feature in Varro's later circuit of Rome's walls and gates, repays further attention in this context.[50] Festus (a couple of centuries or so later) explains that it was called the Open Gate "because it was always open" ("*quod semper pateret*") following a clause in an agreement Rome signed with either the Sabines (as Festus records) or the Gauls (according to

Polyaenus' collection of military exploits).⁵¹ Festus' etymological effort is likely to be working with a tradition already doing the rounds in his main source, Verrius Flaccus, in the Augustan era; this pushes the reading back at least to the late first century and makes likely the availability of an etymology using *pateo*, or *pando*. Varro might also have opted to feed in the deep trauma of a treaty requiring a *Capitoline* gate to be kept open: nonstop access for Sabines (such as himself) *or* Gauls (once, Rome's destroyers; more recently, Caesar's conquered). Instead, Varro concludes blandly with a "Saturnian" feature in legislation concerning private houses, thus shifting emphasis from communal defense to the legislative systems that modulate an individual home's place in the urban fabric.

From the polyvalent patriotism of the Capitoline Hill Varro takes readers to the more ambivalently situated Aventine, where things become even more complicated. "*Auentinum aliquot de causis dicunt*" (*Ling.* 5.43): "Aventine" has an array of recorded explanations well beyond the "*appellatum prodiderunt*" of the former Saturnian mount. Varro will (need to) propose one favored *causa*, but to get to that point involves options.

The first explanation locates us in the world of Naevius and at the beginnings of a distinctively Latin literature. By name a place of confluence, Naevius' avian etymology ("from 'birds,' because birds would make their way there from the Tiber") conjures up an image of flocks winging their way from the river, across the famously watery reaches of the primitive city, to roost on the liminal Aventine (rather as one still sees parakeets flocking to and fro in the early morning and evening).⁵² Setting aside Naevius, others ("*alii*") have an alternative explanation: the Alban king, Aventinus (the legendary great-grandfather of Romulus and Remus), was buried there. This etymology is structurally significant because it echoes the sepulchral quality of the Capitoline etymology and prefigures another set of burial sites (*Ling.* 5.157), discussed later in this section. It also (if readers have not made the mental leap) ensures that Rome's regal period is in focus: now two out of the two visited hills draw on that era for their etymologies.

One final Aventine etymology is offered before Varro's "*ego maxime puto*" locks things down: others (*alii*) propose that the word might be a corruption of A<d>*uentinum* from *aduentus*. This flows as follows: from (Varro's first, Naevian) flights of birds (hinting at the Aventine as an augural site with a natural centripetal aspect), to a royal Alban name (connected to Romulus and Remus), to a group of name-generating Adventurers ("*ab aduentu hominum*"). As Varro observes, the adventurers' arrival (and settlement) is still in evidence topographically via the landmark Aventine temple of Diana, the HQ for Latin rights.⁵³

All these explanations are attractive, but what Varro says he *really* thinks will make the Aventine more integral to Rome's enthusiastic success in terraforming and taming the environment than these explanations imply: it must derive from *aduectus* (transport by horse, carriage, ship, water). Varro then clarifies with a story about the specific kind of transport that makes for an Aventine:

> nam olim paludibus <u>mons erat ab reliquis disclusus</u>. Itaque eo ex urbe <u>aduehebantur</u> ratibus, cuius uestigia, quod ea qua tum <aduectum> dicitur <u>Velabrum</u>, et unde escendebant ad <in>fimam Nouam Viam locus sacellum <Ve>labrum. (Varro, *Ling.* 5.43)

> Back in the old days the mount <u>was cut off from the remainder</u> by swampy pools. For this reason <u>they were skiffed</u> there from the city on rafts, of which there are traces in the naming of the <u>Velabrum</u> itself [Wherry], and of the place where they used to land, at the bottom of New Street—the "<u>Wherry</u>" shrine.[54]

This transitory, fluid space evoked by etymological know-how emphasizes the foundational significance of water for Rome. In connecting the two hills, it also chimes with the Tiber's more wide-ranging infrastructural import. By Varro's day Rome's access to (and control of) water had become iconic. The watery substrata led to Roman hydraulic innovation, and technocracy would enable the translation of water into land and of fluid space to acculturated place (in this instance, from mosquito-plagued lagoon to Forum Boarium, Circus Maximus, and environs).[55] Varro's transactional and transitional Velabrum ("Even now 'wherrying' [*uelatura*] is the term for when this is done for payment," *Ling.* 5.44) makes it a point of intersection for urbanization, engineering and invention, and nature but also a site highlighting the different ways in which center and periphery can be construed. As "*reliquis*" (underlined in the quotation) hints, Varro's Aventine has a claim to represent the heart of Rome—it may be "cut off," but, reversing that logic, everything else is the leftovers. This comes into focus when we reach *Ling.* 5.45: "*Reliqua urbis loca olim discreta*" (the city's remaining [/leftover] locales were long ago separated out), at which point Varro turns to the Argei shrines and a different organizing principle for Rome.

Varro returns to the historical density of the Velabrum and its environs in itinerary two, as he talks readers along a route from the Forum, through the Velabrum (with the Velabrum Minor presented as a runoff from Lautolae: "*ab his . . .*"), to the Aequimaelium (*Ling.* 5.157) and a mysterious site near the foot of the Capitol.[56] Etymologically, Varro's Aequimaelium results from the razing of Spurius Maelius' house by common consent in the wake of his attempt to reinstitute and claim the monarchy.[57] This toponym helps maintain a sense of structure by evoking one of Varro's etymologies for the Macellum (its iconic emplacement of Macellus, a warning against thievery, *Ling.* 5.147), but without lingering, Varro moves on abruptly and without signposting from Maelius' crime to reach the site known as "at the Gaulish Tombs" ("*ad Busta Gallica*").

> Locus ad Busta Gallica, quod Roma recuperata Gallorum ossa qui possederunt urbem ibi coaceruata ac consepta. Locus qui uocatur Doliola ad Cluacam Maxumam, ubi non licet despuere, a doliolis sub terra. Eorum duae traditae historiae, quod alii inesse aiunt ossa cadauerum, alii Numae Pompilii religiosa quaedam post mortem eius infossa. (Varro, *Ling.* 5.157)

> The place "at the Gaulish Tombs" derives from when Rome, reclaimed, had piled up and fenced in at that spot the bones of the Gauls who had held the city. The place called "the Jars," near the Cloaca Maxima and where it's not permitted to spit, gets its name from underground jars. Two stories are transmitted about them: some say that the bones of corpses were in them; others, that some sacred items of Numa Pompilius were, after his death, buried in them.

As far as external evidence goes, this segue keeps the focus on the same sort of area as the Aequimaelium and by implication ("*ad Cluacam Maxumam*") locates the Jars somewhere associable with the Cloaca Maxima and still in the fluid Velabrum zone.[58] These tombs form part of a monumental memory landscape, and they mark the spot where, when the city was reclaimed from the conquering Gauls, the enemy bones were piled together and fenced in. Varro's connection of the place "at the Gaulish Tombs" with the Jars and the Cloaca Maxima presents a trio of subterranean sites whose existence manifests a positive relationship between Rome and its buried roots. As a zone embodying and exemplifying contestations of meaning, ownership, and orientation (up/down; in/out; wet/dry), it also guarantees Rome's safety. We can see the optimism in Varro's treatment if we compare Livy's version (22.57), a story of a more recent and brutal burial, the propitiatory live inhumation of two Gauls and two Greeks in the Forum Boarium in 215, ordered by the Books of Fate.[59] This comparatively positive return to the Velabrum builds on Varro's first visit and emphasizes the power of curated knowledge in expertly defining and giving meaning to citizen experience and the dense and polyvalent properties of Rome's hidden voices and identities.

Introducing the Argei

On leaving the Velabrum for the first time, Varro next recounts how the twenty-seven shrines of the Argei were dispersed across a four-part urban scheme with discrete topographic referents (Suburan, Esquiline, Colline, and Palatine *regiones*).[60]

"*Argeos dictos putant a principibus, qui cum Hercule Argiuo uenerunt Romam et in Saturnia subsederunt.*"[61] By reading Varro, his audience acknowledges its need for a Varro to consult on matters such as this, and it accommodates the idea of deep complexity within what he unscrolls. The mysterious (in their Roman incarnation) Argei and their persisting arcana arrive with Hercules at Rome, fresh from the world of myth and epic, and continue to shape and give meaning to citizen experience. So even though the annual drowning of the dolls is left unmentioned until book 7, its implicit presence will eventually make further sense of Varro's trajectory from Saturn's Capitoline hill to the Aventine and on to Argive urban (re)zoning of Saturnia. The intensely physical nuances of *subsido* (consult *OLD*, all senses) make vivid the image of these wandering *principes* at last giving way (to exhaustion?), staying put, subsiding to the ground, and establishing themselves territorially.

Varro's transition from primitive punters and a swamp-girded Aventine to the deeply archaic and sacral topography of the Argei is signposted intratextually ("*reliqua urbis*" begins *Ling.* 5.45, echoing "*ab reliquis,*" *Ling* 5.43).[62] In reality, the transition implicitly highlights how the annual Ides of May procession associated with the Argei could bring readers full circle at the Velabrum, a procession whose discussion Varro reserves to *Ling.* 7.44.[63] This procession moved through the physical city in apparently erratic ways (because of the distribution of the Argei shrines) but culminated at the regal-era Pons Sublicius, the Tiber crossing nearest the Aventine itself. When through-readers reach *Ling.* 7.44 their perseverance is rewarded and encourages rethinking the treatment of the Argei in book 5.[64] In Varro's book 7 account, the rush doll Argei, one per shrine, eventually end up as annual and titular Argive sacrificial victims: drowned in the Tiber to ensure the safety of the commonwealth and sacrificed from that historically and religiously significant bridge that connects the city to the Tiber's left bank and ultimately to the Janiculum, at a point probably slightly north of the Aventine (around the northwest end of the Circus Maximus).[65]

Despite Varro's earlier rejection of the adventuring Adventine etymology (*Ling.* 5.43), once the Pons Sublicius enters the picture (*Ling.* 7.44) Ancus Marcius (legendarily, the bridge's builder) is present by inference. Ancus Marcius supposedly settled the Aventine with Latins—that is, he translated Latins into

Romans, moved an embodiment of Latium to Rome, and in doing so culturally re-engineered what the Aventine name sounded like and identified. He was perhaps also believed to have brought the hill within Rome's walls—moving the wall means moving the hill from one kind of space to another, from without to within.[66]

It would be surprising if Cicero and his intellectual coterie were not also primed by the zeitgeist to recall the backstories rippling around the Pons Sublicius. After the bridge's supposed construction by Ancus Marcius, the Pontifices were responsible for maintaining it against the ravages of Tiber floods; this was, after all, the site of Horatius' legendary heroic stand against Lars Porsena and the Etruscans.[67] Horatius bought time for the bridge to be destroyed, cutting off the invading forces, but more recent and memorably bloody history also stained it: in 121, this bridge was C. Gracchus' route as he fled mob violence (probably responding to and associated with the Senatus Consultum Ultimum to suppress the threat posed by Gracchan politicking) after a rally of his supporters who were at that time occupying the Aventine temple of Diana—another famous site with regal associations, this time Servius Tullius.[68] From there, a tragic theatricality shades accounts of Gracchus' final trajectory and futile Tiber crossing. The currency of the flight as a motif suggests that it too was likely in the mix for Varro's audience—perhaps particularly poignantly for Cicero.[69] The story's associative connection of Aventine, bridge, and Tiber is what makes an implicit allusion especially likely.

Joining the Argei Dots

From the Aventine, standing thus in the presence of Hercules (*Ling.* 5.45) and recalling the end point of the Argive procession at the Pons Sublicius, readers might well have in mind another and very local Herculean site, the Ara Maxima, and also the (at least one) temple to Hercules in the region of the Forum Boarium at the west end of the Circus Maximus.[70] This real-world topographic cluster helps further shore up the locational organization for anyone in a position to follow Varro's script. What follows sees Varro's gaze flow wide-rangingly out into the city, tracing the notional distribution of Argei shrines (although Varro notes only fourteen of the twenty-seven and pauses the tour at only twelve) and the relationship between the four archaic regions.

The Suburan is the first of the four to be explored (*Ling.* 5.46). It offers Varro an unmissable opportunity to investigate what makes for civilization, Rome-style, and as the meandering course creates Argive patterns in the city, Varro can showcase the originary Etruscan, Sabine, and quasi-Roman struggle from a new but familiarly conflict-driven perspective highlighting issues of trust and shifting allegiances.⁷¹ Beginning from Rome's tumultuous early days, Varro produces a notable Tuscan leader (Caeles, the form that Varro prefers to Caelius, Vibenna), who weighed in on Romulus' side in the war against the Sabines; the Caelian hill, site of the first of the shrines, took its (thereby Etruscan) name from him (*Ling.* 5.46).

With Caeles' death, Varro recounts, his followers began to seem less like a positive addition to Rome's strength and more like a live threat, occupying a dangerously strategic position (*Ling.* 5.46). They came under suspicion specifically for the impressive way they had fortified their Caelian stronghold and were said to have therefore been relocated to the plain below ("*quod nimis munita loca tenerent neque sine suspicione essent, deducti dicuntur in planum*"). Hence, Varro guides readers to a landmark still significant in his own day, the Vicus Tuscus. Others from Caeles' band, somehow free from the suspicion ("*a suspicione liber essent*," *Ling.* 5.46) that clouded their fellow settlers, were instead brought to the place called Caeliolum—they got to keep a diminutive degree of elevation for their community but with a less iconically central location.⁷²

This story makes the Vicus Tuscus simultaneously an Other space and an iconic centerpiece, physically cradled between Capitoline and Palatine ("*ideo ibi Vortumnum stare, quod is deus Etruriae princeps*"—it's where Vertumnus stands, because he is the chief god of Etruria). It is significant that in this gloss Varro recalls readers to the semi-foreignness of Vertumnus as he oversees and indeed landmarks the principal route linking the Forum Romanum, the Forum Boarium, Wherry-Velabrum, and the ex-lagoon Circus Maximus (which will be key sites for Varro's final Roman itinerary).

The vividness of the story is presumably heightened by the compression point in the real route as readers imagined it or recalled their daily perambulations as it squeezed between the Temple of Castor and the Basilica Julia.⁷³ Rome's Vicus Tuscus was not just a residual ghetto; it was part of a densely urban *uicus*, a route used for display and pageantry and a zone of conspicuous consumption. Mediating the patterns of movement that linked Rome's key political, commercial, and spectacular nodes, it routed traffic between Tiber and Forum.⁷⁴ It was also, of course, overlooked by the iconic emplacements of Capitoline and Palatine and contained within the intensely Roman civic space of the Forum itself.⁷⁵

Unlike their untrustworthy but centrally settled compatriots, the "good" or "trustworthy" Etruscans, presumably remaining happy on the Caeliolum, fade out of narrative view. Perhaps, unlike the ambitious Etruscan Tarquins, helpful and collaborative Etruscans, happy to assist and then to fade away, superficially appear to have little narrative value.

From Caeles' Caelian, readers arrive at the Carinae (*Ling.* 5.47).⁷⁶ There were already ceremonial qualities in the narrative air (via the ceremonial Vicus Tuscus, one parade route), making an infrastructural link to Varro's development of the Carinae; water (the Carinae, or "keels") might make for another. As Varro tells it, kinship with *caerimonia* is made available because what characterizes the conjunction of Caelian to Carinae is, *inter eas* (between them), the Caeriolensis (*cael—caer—car*). This delivers the fourth shrine of region 1, as Varro puts it (quoting the records: "near the Minervium, on the route up the Caelian, in a booth," *Ling.* 5.47). The Carinae itself, he says, has "caeremonial" roots, marking the origin of the Via Sacra, which extends, rising, eventually famous ("*huius Sacrae Viae pars haec sola uolgo nota*"), from the Forum to the Arx and here recalled in its augural, festal role.⁷⁷

On the etymology of Subura itself, we met Varro's preferred etymology earlier (linking the name to a *pagus Succusanus*.)⁷⁸ This *Succusan* district, which runs up to ("*succurrit*") the Carinae, connects back to the Forum and the civic heart of the city by way of its textual link to the Via Sacra. Varro also outlines but dismisses the neat explanation (attributed to Junius) that it was "*sub antique urbe*" (*Ling.* 5.48). This latter etymology would have defined it as a zone, we might suppose, under the city's gaze and protection or at least influence; somewhere that a semi-outsider tribe might likely set themselves up. The real-life Subura of Varro's day was probably the valley bounded by the Viminal and Esquiline, but what Varro is alluding to (and dismissing) seems to be a much more fluid notion of a delimited encounter zone given shape by the testimony (*testimonium*) of an archaic urban earth wall and taking in the Caelian slopes (at least) in some fashion.⁷⁹

The Sacra Via (proceeding *from* the Carinae, "*quod hinc oritur caput Sacrae Viae*") is the start of organized, processional civic behavior, toward which the archaic Succusa, in becoming the regularized contemporary Subura, hastens.⁸⁰ The reality of Succusa lingers (*nunc*), according to Varro, as the origin of term in the persisting topographic abbreviation: SVC: "<*quod in nota etiam> nunc scribitur <SVC> tertia littera C, non B*" (<because still, in abbreviation,> it's now written <SVC>, with the third letter as C, not B).⁸¹ This neat rebuttal (however much an invented rationale) shows readers how, rather than taking Junius' easy-to-follow topographic explanation at face value, they need to learn how to identify the etiologies lurking in seemingly unpromising or even unknowable (linguistic) anomalies.

Although Varro's layering phrase *etiam nunc* is absent here, its baseline qualities for book 5 are still apparent as the tour continues.⁸² The next stop is another liminal site: the Esquiline (*Ling.* 5.49). There are those, Varro reports, who have recorded the derivation as being from the watchposts of the king ("*ab excubiis regis dictas*") and others who make the link the oaks (*aesculi*) planted by King Tullius. Again, Varro guides readers to a preferred explanation, the second, which by topographic contiguity takes in the Beech Grove, the sanctuary of the Oak-Grove Lares, and an ambiguous reference to a sanctuary of some sort (perhaps two separate ones, either *lacus*, lake, or the preferred *lucus*, grove)[83] sacred to Mefitis (warding off the kinds of noxious gases common in swampy and volcanic regions) and to Juno Lucina (in her role, therefore, as patron of childbirth).

The *aedes* of Juno Lucina was a venerable foundation (notionally dating to 375), soon to be restored again (by Q. Pedius, in 41), and Varro returns to Juno Lucina herself at some length (as a persona of Diana) when he tackles divine etymologies.[84] When Ovid later deals with Juno Lucina in the *Fasti*, all sorts of reasons are given to him (supposedly by Mars) to explain why she has bagged such a prime spot in the calendar.[85] Drawn into Ovid's picture is a series of explanations: the role of the Sabine women in brokering peace between their Roman husbands and their warring Sabine kin, the conception of Romulus and Remus, and the violent struggle and sacrifice that accompany childbirth. This, too, is a time of rebirth and regeneration in the cosmic sense, so Varro's perhaps ironic comment—apparently qualifying a statement about this Juno's "*angusti fines*"—that greed now rules instead ("*non mirum*") suggests an acerbic swipe. As Varro asserts when he returns to Juno Lucina later in book 5, this is Juno as patron of childbirth, and she is feeling the pinch: Juno's light is the enabler of (the right kind of) sex, and from sex and the confines of birth spring new beginnings, but achieving such growth appropriately is not without struggle.[86]

Varro's Juno Lucina becomes one element in his exploration of instability (and scope for developing and undermining authority) in the semantics of religion, and her later conflation with Diana might remind readers of the contingency in these divine names and originary attributes. There may also be an Italian dimension to be explored: at *Ling* 5.69, Juno Lucina is made distinctively Latin, and Cicero would recall that she had been part of the peace deal when Rome incorporated Tusculum into citizenship (381).[87] This version of Juno Lucina signals a peaceful accord between Republican Rome and its former local enemy—Rome's first really large-scale incorporation of another people set a precedent of reciprocal concessions and no hard feelings. However, on feeding *auaritia* (*Ling*. 5.49) back in, we gain a sense of problematic nuances developing over time ("*iam diu . . . late auaritia*"), alienating Rome from its generous and culturally open history, taking in a broad-brush myth of Etruscan decadence and luxuriousness, and hinting at the current state of ancient sites (such as the temple of Juno Lucina) that positively commemorated Rome's syncretic past.[88]

Zoning: Regions 2–4 and Onward

The cluster of urban groves in the trip through Esquiline region 2 (*Ling.* 5.49–50), like modern grassy lawns, shows how nature has been persuaded to accept the confines and restrictions of civilization and continues to thrive within safely defined limits. All citizens, readers might imagine, even those without extensive ancestral estates, rustic property, or the wherewithal for plantings in town, can participate in the benevolent strangeness and wild-woods symbolism of the sacred grove.[89]

The Esquiline is at once a high point, providing sightlines and thus itself also distinctive for Rome's skyline, and a site that instantiates the complexity of *colles* versus *montes* (especially if one compares the passages mapping *regiones* 2 and 3, *Ling.* 5.49–52). The Esquiline is "mountainous" twice over when examined in detail: "*Esquiliae duo montes habiti*," but it appears that these peaks—Cispian (Cespian) and Oppian (the latter added by Mueller, making sense of the quote ascribed to the *Rites of the Argei* that follows)—are *montes* by courtesy, "*quod . . . suo antiquo nomine etiam nunc in sacris appellatur*" (because [each] by the ancient name [*mons*], even now, in the rites it is thus called, *Ling.* 5.50). Varro's comment hints that the distinctive qualities persist primarily in sacrificial and antiquarian contexts—perhaps, as in twenty-first-century Rome, unrecognizable out of context—making the topographic authority of a Seven-heights festival and ritualized itinerary less lucid and inevitable than one might suppose.[90]

The indigestible written record that Varro calls *Rites of the Argei* gives substance to Varro's primary research and also features significantly when we reach the ostentatiously hilly (the *Collina* has *five* hills!) third region (*Ling.* 5.51–52). This zone's hills are named for eponymous sanctuaries of gods, but two are singled out for star billing ("*e quis nobiles duo*," *Ling.* 5.51). First, the Viminal, a steeply sloping hill forming a high promontory between the Cispian and the Quirinal. The name here is first explained through a gratuitously circular logic: Jupiter Viminius ("of the willows"), at a willow grove by which an altar to Jupiter was erected, spins off a name for god and hill alike. This derivation unites human sacral practice with cosmic forces and natural topography, but Varro backs readers away from the arcana of this etymology with a conclusive, banal, and tersely expressed natural alternative: there simply were willow groves there.

The second famous hill in region 3 is, unsurprisingly, the Quirinal. Unlike the steep, narrow, and for the most part residential (where developed) real-world

Viminal, the Quirinal is characteristically part of the story of Rome's expansion. This is the hill whose association with Quirinus (assimilated to Romulus) and/or the Sabines (Quirites, who came from Cures with Titus Tatius for the war and stayed for the peace) would devour and consign to oblivion nearby toponyms.[91] Through these associations, the Quirinal etymology mirrors Varro's contextual framing of the Caelian and co-locates it oppositionally during the legendary Sabine War. Like the Caelian, it was fortified by the migrant soldiers who set up camp there ("*quod ibi habuerint castra,*" *Ling.* 5.51), but, unlike the allies who held the Caelian and were ultimately treated with some suspicion, the enemies who grabbed (what would become—or perhaps already was, if we keep the flavor of Varro's *etiam nunc* patterning) the Quirinal eventually help to overwrite pre-Sabine Roman space.

Again, we see mythic religious traditions and scholarly research collide. If one consults the *Rites of the Argei*, as Varro's marked-up use of quotation strongly implies that he has done—"it is evident [*apparet*], based on the *Rites of the Argei* where it is recorded thus [*scriptum sic est*], that there were numerous other 'hills'" (*Ling.* 5.52)—one finds that the celebrated Quirinal is thanks to Varro redefined in the light of many "lesser" hills (each with its own eponymous altar and Argei shrine). These hills were until now, until recuperated by dint of Varro's excavatory endeavors, overwritten ("*nomina obliterauit*") by the stronger Quirinal brand (*Ling.* 5.52).[92]

Region 4 showcases the rumbling of the big mythological guns (*Ling.* 5.53). Here, we reach the Palatine and an etymology that Varro will return to again. The Pallantes, aka Palatines, accompanied Evander on his travels (thus echoing the pattern of the Argei with Hercules); in arriving (and staying), they made a name for the place. This first etymology makes the Palatine blank space before the arrival of the Greek migrants, and such an explanation implicitly counterbalances the localized migrant stories clustered around Romulus, while also offsetting the Italian and mercenary qualities of stories Varro has told about the other hills' settlement. Version 2 is entirely different. It offers a tribe of first peoples—people from (Varro's) Reatine territory, specifically, from Pallatium. This Sabine Palatine delicately marks up the city-forming role of Varro's sort of person. Other possibilities follow: maybe it was named for King Latinus' wife Palanto? Or (ending with a literary joke) why not follow Naevius' take on the etymology from *pecus* (a flock of sheep), whose own "language" gives the onomatopoeic Baaaalatine? We are here moving deeply into the city-founding story cycles, and Varro has brought us to the fifth and sixth Argei shrines perhaps particularly in order to develop the endgame for the procession in that direction.

At shrines 5 and 6 (still in region 4) Varro reaches the Cermalus (here, Germalus), with its *aedes* of Romulus, and then the Velia, with the Deified Penates (*Ling* 5.54). Having started in a pre- or proto-Roman landscape, this tour comes full circle in a world to be marked up via the Trojan cycle. Germalus gets its name from the *germani* (brothers) Romulus and Remus:

> quod ad ficum ruminalem, et ii ibi inuenti, quo aqua hiberna Tiberis eos detulerat in alueolo expositos. (Varro, *Ling.* 5.54)

> Because it is at the Suckling Fig, and they were discovered there, where the wintery flood of the Tiber had deposited them in the basket in which they had been exposed.

No "perhaps" or alternative explanation intrudes, and no explanation is offered for why they were exposed or how they were found. This is all we are going to get.

At the Velia (a much more distinctive hill than the Cermalus in Varro's day), the etymology starts with managed polyphony: "*Veliae unde essent plures accepi causas, in quis quod...*" (I have found a range of explanations for "Veliae," among which is that ..., *Ling.* 5.54).[93] Deploying a plural form (Veliae) but quoting a singular (Velia) in the *Rites of the Argei* might hint at the kinds of toponymic wiggle room in play. Varro's Veliae may be a plurality and enjoy a plethora of etymologies, but only one *causa* is delivered. We are again with Varro in a hilly, sheep-grazed landscape, as he tells how, before the invention of shearing, the Palatine shepherds resorted to plucking the wool in the place now called Velia (*Ling.* 5.54). This produces a bonus etymology: a fleece (*uellus*) is thus the civilized product of the primitive plucking (*uellere*) of sheep, and fleeces (or perhaps pelts and woolen cloth more generally) all recall an action associated with a rustic but decidedly nonspecific (in ethnographic terms) vision of the site destined to be Rome.[94] This segue, drawing a sightline between Paaaalatine and Velia, also pushes readers away from the specifics of Romulus and Remus and toward a more generically rural or even literary-pastoral scene. Nevertheless, it still nods to the tradition of shepherds built into the foundation story.

With this, Varro offers context by turning readers' minds (at *Ling.* 5.55–56) to what is specifically "field" land (*ager Romanus*). As with Rome's four regions, the primal three-way division of land types is presented without further debate, allowing Varro to draws the strands unproblematically together with the statement that it is from this "natural" division that the three first tribes gain their identity. Varro then produces Ennius (in annalistic mode) to authorize the etymologies for the tribal names, which follow Roman territory—etymologies with a strongly Etruscan flavor: "*sed omnia haec uocabula Tusca, ut Volnius, qui tragoedias Tuscas scripsit, dicebat*" (but all these words are Etruscan, as Volnius, who wrote tragedies in Etruscan, stated, *Ling.* 5.55), through which identification Varro connects Titus Tatius (Titienses), Romulus (Ramnes), and "Lucumo" (Luceres—probably here referring to Tarquinius Priscus).[95]

Taken together, this set of etymologies hooks Varro up with the publicly minded antiquarian urges of a Junius (cited as the authority for the Luceres), the gravitas of Ennius, and the hybrid Greco-Etruscan cadences of tragedy by the otherwise unknown Volnius. It also locates this antique, migrant, Hellenized world more broadly at the origins of the later four-part *urban* development of tribes named for the still current city regions: Suburan, Palatine, Esquiline, Colline, and the add-on (suburban) Romilian, somehow envisaged as nestling beneath Rome's walls. The other, country, tribes are summarily dismissed: after all, Varro reminds us, he has trodden this ground already in his earlier *Book of the Tribes* (*Ling.* 5.56), so there is no point in wasting space on unimportant detail here. With that, he draws this arc to a conclusion (and moves on to cosmic forces).

Ways and Means

I left Varro at the Jars in the first section of this chapter, but in that itinerary he next addresses byways and turns to the toponym Argiletum. "*Sunt qui scripserunt*" (some wrote), Varro says, that this got its name from "*argola seu [F]*, because he came to this place and was buried there" (*Ling.* 1.157).[96] If with Kent (1951) we read "*ab Argo La<ri>saeo*," we get a story concerning Evander and the "execution" and burial of his (treacherous) guest Argus, a tale subsequently told by Vergil and commented on by Servius (ap. *Aen.* 8.345–46).[97] In narrative terms, the availability of this story would also neatly counterpoint the burials represented by the previous sites (at the Gaulish Tombs; the Jars), but Varro's second etymology (one also noted by Servius) reports a very different explanation: the name Argiletum comes from *argilla*, or potters' clay (which is the type of soil there).[98] We have moved from a site of the punishment and death of foreigner(s) to a manufactory etymology, characterizing the earth as ideally suited to meaningful extraction and production. That story would represent the very reverse of burial.[99]

This Argiletum is as much a site as a route, but its real-world identity as a way into the Forum makes it the ideal bridge to Varro's next cluster of sites: routes starting with the Cliuus Publicius (*Ling.* 5.158).[100] By definition, a *cliuus* inclines, and this sloping street runs up and down the northern slope of the Aventine (already etymologized for through-readers). Varro characterizes it by its builders, the mid-third-century Plebeian Aediles L. and M. Publicius Malleolus.[101] Readers might have in their mind's eye the temple of Diana likely on the skyline, or they might be imagining themselves returning to Varro's recently defined Lauretum (*Ling.* 5.152) or Armilustrium (*Ling.* 5.153). Alternatively, the Cliuus itself has a very distinctive historical resonance—as the site of a memorable phase in the chaos surrounding Hannibal's near hit on Rome in 211—one that could well have colored readings of his account.

As Livy tells the tale, it sounds like one of those stories: everyone expected Hannibal to attack the city; Roman defensive energies were focused on two gates (the Porta Collina and the Porta Esquilina) and on the Arx and Capitol (Livy 26.10.5–7); at the same time a troop of about 1,200 Roman allies, Numidians, were quartered on the Aventine. When the consuls (Cn. Fulvius Centumalus and P. Sulpicius Galba) ordered this allied force to support the main defensive effort, they came marching down the Cliuus Publicius—to the consternation of many (not in the know) watching from the Arx and Capitoline, who mistook the Numidians' approach for a hostile advance.[102] A riot ensued, with Rome saved from disaster mostly because those within the walls were too scared to flee the city (and escape what seemed to be the enemy within) to what lay without: Hannibal.

"*Cliuos Public<i>us ab aedilibus plebei Publici<i>s qui eum publice aedificarunt*" (*Ling.* 5.158). If the text is accurate, Varro writes *publicus* for *publicius*. The joke of making the name of the historic Plebeian Aediles (Publicius) into a word (*publicus*) that has already signified Public (*Ling.* 5.80; in the sense "of the State" and repeated here in that sense) is too good to pass up. What could ensue runs thus: the Public[i]an Rise, built from the hearth "up" (*aedifico*) by the Public[i]ans, on Public authority. What else? *Public[i]us* might punningly recall other instances of *publice*, seen last at the Aequimaelium (*Ling.* 5.157) but also in the public-works demolition of Macellus' house, making way for the Macellum (*Ling.* 5.147).[103] This is a different kind of public work, and Ovid would later emphasize how the public-servant brothers transformed a wild and unproductive place (a steep crag) into a useful part of the urban network, in the process and in effect defining "*publica cura*" (*Fast.* 5.290).[104] That this major access route to and from the once ghettoized Aventine should have been constructed by plebeian aediles, Brothers Public[i]i, acting with public authority and building infrastructure for the public good, is important for Varro's positive gloss on Rome as a conglomeration of appropriately integrated and mediated heterogeneity.

When Varro draws two more Rises into the frame—the Pullius and the Cosconius ("*Simili de causa Pullius et Cosconius, quod ab his uiocuris dicuntur aedificati,*" *Ling.* 5.158)—he emphasizes the humane qualities of roads as sites that move people and produce, that are constructed and cared for by individuals, but that are designed for public use and community benefit. The Cliuus Pullius suggests itself as another almost-word-association (Pu[b]li[ci]us/Pullius). Varro's first readers would know this Rise to be right on the other side of town: it originated from the point where the Cliuus Suburanus divided at the Porticus Liuiae, with the more northerly branch feeding into the Argiletum and the southerly branch (the Pullius) crossing the Oppian slopes somewhere near the Fagutal and running down through the Velia to meet the Via Sacra.[105] The other Rise, the Cosconius, is connected aetiologically to this one (both were constructed by officials in charge of streets), and the two are linked to the more famous Publicius by one of Varro's hot terms: similarity.[106]

Varro's is the only recorded mention of the Cosconius Rise, although he does elsewhere reference a historical Cosconius, author of grammatical and legal treatises.[107] This Rise is the one that goes up and down close by the Temple of Flora, where a venerable shrine to Jupiter, Juno, and Minerva (older than the Capitoline complex) produces the toponym Capitolium Vetus (the Old Capitol).[108] The nudge to remember the depth of time and to recall the complexity of how overlays add nuance and richness to urban space is apposite. Varro's narrative association of Flora with the Cliuus Publicius might eventually echo through Ovid's deployment of Flora as narrator when he retells the story of the Cliuus Publicius a couple of generations later.[109]

Immediately after this, the text moves to the Esquiline (*Ling.* 5.159) and returns to the term *uicus*.[110] Three specific *uici* are brought into play, each with a telling story in drawing this phase of Varro's gazetteer to a conclusion. First is the African Quarter (*Vicus Africus*, where African hostages were kept, word has it, during the Punic War); next is the Good Quarter (*Vicus Cyprius*), named by the Sabines from the word *cyprum*, supposedly because it was formerly a Sabine neighborhood and they named it for the good omen of their achieving Roman citizenship (*cyprum*, Varro carefully explains, is the Sabine word for "good"; he makes no mention of Venus *Cypria*, or trees). Finally, we visit the nearby Accursed Quarter (*Vicus Sceleratus*). This got its name not from a people at a moment of conflict or a foreign-language import signaling integration and resolution but from an act of horror. Livy book 1 recounts how this site commemorates the spot where (King) Tarquinius Superbus' wife Tullia ordered her carriage to be driven over her father's corpse; her father was the man whose name, Cicero's family name too, readers saw attached to the Tullianum dungeon.[111]

Varro's tour of Rome's sites ends here, in a network of streets in the Carinae area (taking in the Oppian and Cispian slopes). The Accursed Quarter delves into a dark phase in Rome's history, but one that would eventually see the beginnings of the Republic and bring stability, albeit through personal and civic tragedy. The Tarquins themselves were Etruscans—another wave of migration embodied and eventually naturalized in the cityscape. Here, however, their presence highlights the persisting duality of Etruscan (flawed) and Sabine (good) integration for Roman self-fashioning.

Gates (Coming and Going)

I began the second section of this chapter with cityscapes rising out of an interrogation of the natural world (see first section), an account that moved from Varro's idea of place, through cosmic forces, ethnographic patterning, and water, on to the quality and measure of a world subdivided into agricultural territories (*Ling.* 5.13–40). Entering Rome via its iconic heights, as we did, highlights nature's generative role in this city's formation. Varro's logic makes paramount the zones of interface for the natural environment, the productive landscape, and urban form.[112]

With a ritualized progress around the shrines of the Argei, readers were implicitly encouraged to imagine more than the trite connection between high places, citadels, and religious sites. Instead, the Argei in Varro's context evoke what connects individuals in a group of travelers, forced from home on a divinely ordained mission, finding and constructing "sanctuary" in a fashion that draws out the natural elegance of a hill-defined cityscape. Once Varro has done with domestic etymologies (and after a textual lacuna), the significance of the edges of this city comes back into focus by way of an etymological tour around the Servian walls and the gates of Rome (*Ling.* 5.163–65).

The circuit starts in medias res, clearly at the eastern ramparts (since moving on also means moving south), with a pause at the sanctuary of Tutilina. This, readers learn, was the area where Ennius lived (according to Porcius).[113] Narrative logic dictates that this must be west of the Porta Capena (whose etymology is presumably lost in the gap) and somewhere near the Remoria/Murcus, because what follows is the Porta Naevia (*Ling.* 5.163). Ennius' ghostly presence, versifying somewhere on the Aventine slopes, suggests a delicate pun in Varro's choice of *colo* to characterize that poetic activity; it is not impossible that Varro is playing up, in antiquarian mode, some special Ennian affection for recondite Tutilina (who might have overlapped with the Camenae), while also invoking for his *locus* (or home) a site of *cultus*.[114]

Next, the Porta Naevia, which (Varro says) takes its name from the Naevian groves (*nemora*). It features, for example, in Livy: one of those historically redolent sites evoking stirring deeds from the earliest days of the Republic (Livy 2.11.8–9). Alert readers might also wonder whether there is unusual piquancy in the decision to associate these Naevian groves with a Naevian Gate specifically in the vicinity of Ennius—it seems too good a juxtaposition to miss. The next gate, the Porta Rauduscula, probably punctuated the Republican-era street known to have followed the depression between the Aventine peaks. Its disappearance (like that of the Porta Naevia) may hint at the combined venerable antiquity and insignificance of these gates as late first-century thoroughfares, yet still Varro chooses to recognize and refresh them in the collective memory.

Varro's explanation of the Porta Rauduscula offers a tantalizing glimpse back to a past when the gate (in Varro's mind's eye) was a magnificent site—copper-clad—"*quod aerata fuit.*" *Raudus* conjures up the world of primitive coinage and crude monetary systems that such an antique and off-the-beaten-track locale might invoke. The sense that these ancient gates are sites of interface between different worlds is not dispelled by the next gate, the Porta Lavernalis. Today the Via di Porta Lavernale commemorates the one-time mural gate at the south end of the Aventine. The gate itself, Varro asserts, gets its name from an altar to another low-profile deity, perhaps low-rent and low on morals (Laverna).[115]

From here Varro swings north and away from the Servian city limits to join Romulus' walls ("*Praeterea intra muros uideo portas,*" *Ling.* 5.164; the "walls within the walls," memory sites perhaps, rather than a dimensional intervention in the landscape). This brings the gazetteer to the deeply ancient (but very famous) Porta Mugonia.[116] The fame may be literally all in the telling since it seems unlikely (given that the Romulean walls were no longer standing) that there was any physical "gate" in situ. Nevertheless, its memory, especially its vivid presence at historical moments, may just about have guaranteed its persistence as a long-disembodied but still well-known landmark.[117] "*Mucionis a mugitu, quod ea pecus in buceta tum <ante> antiquum oppidum exigebant.*"[118] Through this gate, in Varro, ghostly herds of cows still process, sounding out the onomatopoeic etymology and recalling Varro's Forum "B/Mooarium" and "Baaaalatine."[119]

The next gate in the imagined inner circuit, the Porta Romanula (the "Little Roman"), connects New Street—presumably as it debouches into the Velabrum—with a sanctuary of the goddess Volupia (perhaps somewhere near the Scalae

Graecae).[120] On next reaching the Porta Ianualis, Varro becomes expansive (*Ling.* 5.165).

The Porta Ianualis (named for Janus) need not be read as a third gate in Romulus' walls in Varro's account but may be seen as the third in a sequence of meaningful portals memorialized within the Servian walls. It evokes the shrine of Janus Geminus (*Ling.* 5.156), and on the basis of the tangle of connecting accounts, it seems likely to represent an alternative way of thinking about the same site.[121] This is evident when naming this gate (or portal) elicits from Varro a story apparently recounted by Piso in his *Annales*, whereby after (Numa) Pompilius it was ruled ("*ius institutum*") that the gate (*porta*)

> sit aperta semper, nisi cum bellus sit nusquam. Traditum est memoriae Pompilio rege fuisse opertam et post Tito Manlio consule bello Carth*h*aginiensi primo confecto, et eodem anno apertam. (Varro, *Ling.* 5.165)

should always be open unless there was war nowhere. The traditional story has it that when [Numa] Pompilius was king, it was closed, and after when Titus Manlius [Torquatus] was consul at the end of the first war with Carthage, and then it was opened in that same year.

The traditional quality of the etiology and its similarity to stories about Janus Geminus are emphasized by Varro's signaling of constructed memory (*traditum*), yet at the same time this story clearly moves substantially from "tradition" to a grounded sense of historicity, and variants continue to be retold in landmark Latin texts. It hints at epochal moments inscribed on the city by way of its gates or archetypal doorways, the *habitus* they instantiate, and the duality of the examples (one, anomalously, a beloved king; the other, delivered by a consul, invoking a crucial, cathartic moment in the peninsular shift to Mediterranean empire).

With this, Varro's Roman gazetteers are complete. The mind, of course, is ever free to stroll through vanished or otherwise inaccessible cityscapes; this makes Varro's Roman *imaginaire* a powerful tool, one that enables readers to re-experience the new-old city from unexpected viewpoints (as Cicero explicitly recognized) and to access historical vistas overlaying familiar paths. Readers can still share in this (albeit from our varying twenty-first-century perspectives) by simply meandering through contemporary Roman locales, enjoying the perplexing commemorative markup of allusive street names, info boards, hoardings hiding who knows what delights to be excavated, all jostling with buildings and fiats of planning that reflect modern Italy's struggle to nationhood and reclamation of Rome as capital.

Locating the Divine

This chapter ends with a particularly interesting site of intersection between cultivatable and uncontrollable nature and its forces, one that connects urban and natural zones of habitation with the cosmos. In the context of the scheme investigated in the first section and the relationship between *numen* and the built environment discussed in the second through the fifth sections, Varro's exploration of a potential relationship between *templum* and *tescum*—the wildlands—is crucial. It is also an ideal example for considering the power of etymology to produce the unifying and consensus-building mode that gives *De Lingua Latina* its greatest significance.[122] Book 7 is Varro's book of verse ("*Dicam in hoc libro de uerbis quae a poetis sunt posita*"[123]), as we saw in chapter 3, but already in book 6 Plautus' "eternal 'temples' of the sky" have whetted readers' appetites.[124] It was in book 6, too, that readers learned (concerning augural pronouncements, *effata*) that it is formal, ritualized augural utterance that speaks *templa* into existence.[125] *Templa*, therefore, are already boundary crossing (prose to verse; human to divine; terrestrial to celestial; phenomenological to epistemological).

In the following material Varro homes in on a specific illustrative instance of *templum*: the ancient ceremonial form laid down for taking auspices on the Arx (*Ling.* 7.8–9). Here, *templum* refers to a separate place, in effect, a precinct bounded by defined verbal authority. The Latin is problematic, but the gist of the geospecific ceremonial formula presented by Varro implies that temples (*templa*) and wildlands (*tesca*) are intrinsically connected for ritual purposes; the formula pairs the two sites three times.[126] Varro's "temples" thus are intrinsically connected to the kind of sacro-idyllic landscaping and landscape art, and its framing, that was gaining rapidly in popularity in the late first century.[127] As if this visual intertext were not clear enough,

> In hoc templo faciundo arbores constitui fines apparet et intra eas regiones qua oculi conspiciant, id est tueamur, a quo templum dictum, et contemplare, ut apud Ennium in Medea. (Varro, *Ling.* 7.9)

> In making this "temple" it is evident that trees are constituted as boundaries, and between them are those zones which the eyes observe, so that "we gaze," from which was said "temple" [*templum*], and "contemplate" [*contemplare*], as in Ennius in *Medea*.

The frailty of trees as hardline boundaries should be evident to throughreaders, who will recall the presence of uncontrollable hidden roots. Here above ground, and still (*Ling.* 7.9) in the context of the Arx, trees moderate the *templum* in important ways. These trees interleave the idea of wild (the forest) and cultivated (woodland, orchards, groves, and gardens) nature. *Tesca*, Varro eventually concludes (7.11), are places where human and divine meet (the country estates, in effect, of some deities, as he almost puts it at *Ling.* 7.10) and, specifically, where humans connect with and gaze upon mysterious forces.[128] These *templa* thus enrich through-readers' understanding of the manifestations of god-haunted space in urban sacred groves.

In the quoted passage (*Ling.* 7.9), boundary trees emblematize a collaboration between nature and humankind; without them, the ritual gaze has no frame and civilization stalls. Varro's connection of *templum* to *tueor* is against the grain of typical contemporary use, and he works hard to strengthen the case. He insists we draw together ideas of control, curatorship, epistemology, and vision (notions embodied in "the Gaze") when contemplating such sites. This is underscored further when the augural formula for the creation ("*facit*") of a *templum* is "for viewing" ("*conspicione*"), within a boundaried or defined ("*finiat*") vista (*Ling.* 7.9); this ocular range ("*oculorum conspectum*") is set by the considered gaze of the augur himself. A quote from Ennius' *Medea* follows the passage just quoted (*Ling.* 7.9) and illustrates the nexus concisely: prima facie it shows that *contempla* and *conspicare* have similar meaning by connecting the imperatives *contempla* ("survey!") and *aspice* ("behold!) as the operators on the object, a *templum* of Ceres. But Varro takes readers further: some add, he says, that *conspicio* embraces the action of another verb, *cortumio*, whose only other appearance is in Varro's just earlier citation of the augural formulation unique to Rome's Arx. *Cortumio*, he proposes, "*dicitur a cordis uisu: cor enim cortumionis origo.*"[129] Varro's unique *cortumio*, presented here as if standard *parole*, could translate as "perception."

Readers might recall from book 6 that *cor* featured in another of Varro's significant public etymologies, that of *curia* (*cor urat*, what burns the heart; with the Curia Hostilia a stop on his second tour of Rome).[130] For *cor*, here at *Ling.* 7.9, alongside the more straightforward power of the heart as an organizational principle of human life, the resonances I find most compelling are both visceral and emotionally charged.[131] Varro's emphasis on the obscure *cortumio* (and reading in the resonances of *cor*) comes into focus when the next section brings us back to the Forum and the Curia.

> Quod addit templa ut si<n>t *tesca*, aiunt sancta esse qui glossas scripserunt. Id est falsum: nam Curia Hostilia templum est et sanctum non est;

sed hoc ut putarent aedem sacram esse templum <eo uidetur>¹³² esse factum quod in urbe Roma pleraeque aedes sacrae sunt templa, eadem sancta, et quod loca quaedam agrestia, qu*ae* alicuius dei sunt, dic*u*ntur tesca. (Varro, *Ling.* 7.10)

As far as adding that "temples" are "wildernesses," those who have written glossaries say that this is about inviolability. But this is incorrect: for the Curia Hostilia is a temple and is not inviolable. But that there should be those who think a temple to be a consecrated building seems to have come about because in the city of Rome, very many consecrated buildings are temples, and likewise inviolable, and because certain rustic places, which are the domain of some god, are called "wildernesses."

Leeching the wild places into the city allows Varro to demonstrate how ways of seeing effect ontological change. This leads to a series of quotes from Accius (*Philoctetes of Lemnos*) to show how wild, mysterious, deserted spots, haunted by *numen* in effect, are *tesca*, but this is not because they are *sancta* but because of their mysterious qualities, which cause men *attuentur* (to gaze at them) → *tuesca* → *tesca* (*Ling.* 7.11).¹³³ Verse enables the human gaze to make sense of *templum* and *tesca*—civilization and wilderness.

After working through *tueor* (*Ling.* 7.12), Varro quietly introduces the next linked theme: the passage of time.¹³⁴ Although time will be tackled in different contexts in chapters 7 and 8, Varro's thoughts on the moon are important to the present chapter's focus on world formation (*Ling.* 7.16). The moon (a changing feature, varying its path in elevation, latitude, and longitude) is echoed on earth at three-way crossroads statues of Diana Trivia.¹³⁵ Latona's children, Diana and Apollo, are together the Deliads, twin children of Delos (possibly a Varronian coinage). Delos is also the famously metapoetic and wandering island nymph of Callimachus' *Aetia*, and Varro ties together these literary, historical, liminal, and cult threads when he turns to the umbilicus.¹³⁶

I discussed this passage (*Ling.* 7.17) in chapter 3 when considering Varro's agenda for inspiring the production of Latin discourse; I return to it here to emphasize how this (relatively long) excursus is also an important example of how Varro reinforces the relationship between gods and the natural world and reframes that relationship as distinctively and inevitably contingent upon urban concerns. This is not about topographic centrality but about the invention of geopolitical centrality. Indeed, not only is Varro not buying the notion of a geographic "center" for the physical earth, he even says that if there is one, it is not Delphi's money-making "Center of the Earth" tourist attraction. The "treasury" containing the ὀμφαλός is hardly even at the center of Delphi, but it is what the Greeks call ὀμφαλός, and the tomb of Python.[137] With this in mind, a Latin *umbilicus* picks up on this collusion within which center is a metaphorically and sociopolitically determined concept, nods to the Roman interest in locating centrality specifically in the city,[138] and feeds in a literary-critical alert—*umbilicus* also signals the book scroll itself.[139]

Conclusion

The material explored in this chapter shows how Varro makes it possible to engage in reflection on what the Argei itinerary (and its annual progress through sites made iconic by their link to legendary Rome) means: to oneself as a reader or to the community of readers within which one locates oneself. How seriously or even deeply does anyone take the Herculean connection mapped out via this ceremony? And how does close attention to Varro's etymological nuggets supercharge the Argei as landmarks and waypoints? The urban geographer Kevin Lynch has suggested that spaces engage in a dialogue with those who move through them, generating unique "melodic" sequences.[140] In this Roman tour, and given the scarcity of more straightforward directional terminology, "gesture spaces," or signs to navigate between sites ("turn left at . . . , "a mile farther . . . ," "two blocks past the altar of . . . ," "take Via . . ."), the hills sinuously obtrude to sequencing the experience.[141] Reference to the *Rites of the Argei* economically emplots the relationship between shrines and urban infrastructure by way of the unspoken (in the context of this narrative arc) annual procession and the associated documentary record.

Varro's highpoints rear their heads in a fluid and primitive network (before Rome, there were always hills; there will always be hills, even if you sometimes need a storyboard to know that what you are on is/was a "hill" at all). They connect nodes while also instantiating dialogue between stasis and motion: hills connote up and down, movement and status; they draw the eye and empower the wide-ranging gaze; they make for visibility but also encourage emphasis on landmark sights; they imply fortifications, monumentality, and permanence; and they texture different kinds of movement, whether stair, ramp, short-of-breath climb or leisurely-to-headlong descent. By articulating the link from tribes to the authenticity of a world of Sabine, Etruscan, and newly Roman connections, Varro encourages perception of a user-oriented urban network reaching from now to then, and this will continue to reverberate through the second urban site visit.[142] Just as the Argei shrines showcase how older urban forms could assimilate and take strength from migrant legend, so the need for new explanation and exegesis of all these traditions emphasizes the lively possibility of rewriting tradition.

Readers, moving through a space colored by Varro's etymologies and reconfigured by the routes that he plots, continuously activate new cityscapes within which trip switches and tracked changes will continue to be available on every subsequent visit—imaginary or real—as encounters with edges and points of contact or transition (hills, walls, gates, markets, roads, the Tiber) become emboldened in this urban "armature."[143] By contrast, intramurally, "passage architecture" (the features that help orient movement between nodes and locales) is left for the most part to the creativity and imagination of the primed reader. Accompanied by Varro, readers have the toolkit with which to recuperate and renovate an integrated and humane city in control of its past but also to re-view how and why certain changes stick.

chapter 6

Powering Up the Community

ORDER IS A CORE PRINCIPLE FOR *De Lingua Latina*—up/down, in/out, right/wrong, similar/dissimilar—mapped within social, poetic, linguistic, and political frameworks. Previous chapters have explored this organizing principle in discourse and in sociocultural and spatial contexts. The times and political flashpoints from which Varro's understanding of order developed make his etymologies for politico-religious and military roles (discussed in the first three sections), including kingship (explored in the fourth), especially interesting. This chapter situates Varro's explanations as part of a unifying framework that aligns with the grammatology of the second hexad and sheds light on the available nuances for the value of these etymologies in operational currency.[1] Overall, this material shows how meaningful political analysis may emerge from a miscellaneous text and exemplifies the scientific potential of the etymological mode when adopted by appropriately engaged citizens.

Addressing Public Office

Varro's etymologies for the vocabulary of politico-religious power are embedded in one of *De Lingua Latina*'s longer arcs (*Ling.* 5.80–91), proceeding from a sequence that starts when he concludes on places and their associated terms (*Ling.* 5.57) and then moves on in orderly fashion to the things (immortal and mortal) that inhabit places.[2] This material brought out Latin's dependence on Greek with a force and clarity unusual in *De Lingua Latina*, sensitizing through-readers to the vivid presence of migratory words in Latin ("*uocabula peregrina*," *Ling.* 5.77) just as the text turns to the vocabulary for terrestrial creatures (*Ling.* 5.80).

> De animalibus in locis <u>terrestribus quae sunt hominum propria primum</u>, deinde de pecore, tertio <u>de feris</u> **scribam. Incipiam** <u>ab honore publico</u>. (Varro, *Ling.* 5.80)

About the living creatures that inhabit the terrestrial spots, it is first concerning vocabulary appropriate to humans, next, to domestic animals, and third to <u>wild beasts</u> that **I shall write. I shall begin** from <u>public office</u>.

The juxtaposition of *scribam* and *incipiam*—as I have discussed—makes programmatic a connection between wild beasts and public office and underscores the process of de- and refamiliarization that Varro's political role call of hierarchies of office will tease out. Naming and being named are what separate (the right sort of) men from wild beasts, and nowhere is this clearer than in Romespeaking humanity's top jobs:

<u>Consul</u> nominatus qui <u>consuleret</u> **populum et senatum**, <u>nisi</u> illinc **potius** unde Accius ait in Bruto: "qui recte <u>consulat</u>, <u>consul</u> ciat."[3] (Varro, *Ling.* 5.80)

The <u>consul</u> is named as one who should *consult* [take account of/care for] **the people and the senate**; well, that's **unless** the term instead derives from whence Accius has it in the *Brutus*: "Let him who correctly <u>counsels</u> be called <u>consul</u>."

At least here in Varro's book, the consul exists only insofar as there are a people and a senate, and he is by definition so "named" or "nominated" ("*nominatus*") only in order to undertake specific activity on behalf of others.[4] In his later discussion of conjunctions Varro wryly observes that they have no need to inflect because a man or a horse can be tied up with the same rope, and, similarly, what links "Tullius" and "Antonius" as consuls works as well for formulating any consular pairing (*Ling.* 8.10). Taking this together with Varro's etymology (in *Ling.* 5.80), we might initially see an emphasis on republican tradition—in echoing the formula *senatus populusque Romanus*—but with the crucial twist that the people rather than the senate come first; moreover, the adaptability of the organizing principle (reflecting how language might run to catch up with reality) rather than its individual elements is what make things work.[5] Contemporary context makes it unlikely that this is an unexamined or off-the-cuff reformulation, and Varro could easily have revised or edited the passage had it become uncomfortable after 44, given the work-in-progress practices common in his circle.[6]

If that were all, it would already be interesting, but the surprising bite of Varro's PSQR is underscored by the brisk destabilization of meaning that follows: "*nisi . . . potius*" (*Ling.* 5.80), in Varro's second use of the formula as the text stands. The formula is distinctive enough in terms of signaling an editorializing intervention that it might be expected to highlight a point of significance, especially since Varro's follow-up exploration of *consul* by way of Accius' *Brutus* would already be painfully funny if Suetonius (*Iul.* 80.3) is right in his account of a popular contemporary joke juxtaposing Brutus and Caesar—this becomes significant for Varro on *dictator*, as we will see. When introduced by *nisi... potius*, the ethical dimension (*recte*) underscores the contingencies. Not all conciliar acts are equal, and only a thoroughly correct, honorable **co**(u)**ns***u*ling truly empowers the **consul**tant as consul and by definition as the right man for the job.

When he next turns to *praetor*, Varro again develops the etymology through literary quotation:[7]

> Praetor dictus qui praeiret iure et exercitu; a quo id Lucilius:
>   **Ergo** praetorum est ante praeire.
> (Varro, *Ling.* 5.80)

> Praetor is so-called as the one who leads the way for law and army; whence this, from Lucilius:
>   **Therefore** being a praetor means to lead from the front.

Putting *praetor* second, as Varro does, makes no etymological sense, especially in the context of Cicero's exegesis in *De Legibus*, where the functions of praetors, judges, and consuls represent a key political trinity:[8]

> Regio imperio duo sunto, iique <a> praeeundo iudicando consulendo praetores iudices consules appellamino; militiae summum ius habento, nemini parento; ollis salus populi suprema lex esto. (Cic. *Leg.* 3.8.2)

> Let there be two men holding royal power of command, and from the acts of leading, judging, and advising, let them be called praetors [leaders], judges, consuls. Let them have supreme power in military matters and be subject to none. For them let the safety of the people be the highest ruling principle.

Cicero structures the proposal so that *praeeo* and *praetor* feature first in each trio and thereby articulate a balance between authoritative, military, judicial, and deliberative arms of government, albeit one that is introduced and given shape by the requirement for two almost-kings.[9] Regal power is modulated, for his Rome, by its refashioning in the context of three resonant skills and titles and two holders, not by any dialogic relationship with the people.

Varro's consul lacks his Ciceronian counterpart's royal gloss and distinctive autonomy; by contrast, Varro's praetor, summed up in punchy Lucilian argot, is the action hero: *of course* and by definition ("*ergo . . . praeire*") a praetor is out in front and in the lead, in terms of both the tenets of the state (*ius*) and the massed ranks of the army (*exercitus*). Varro's balancing act between these two, the only two regular magistracies to receive detailed etymological attention *and* literary enrichment, shows the nuances of power adjusted between different kinds of leadership—operational and executive; strategic, reactive, and proactive—and a requirement to serve, advise, and inspire. Other roles and titles are sketched for the most part briefly, although with some attention to the need for defenders of plebeian rights.[10] The military and plebeian tribunes, with inbuilt originary overtones of sociopolitical tension, immediately precede the reappearance of the consul when Varro reaches the position of dictator:

Dictator, quod a consule dicebatur, cui dicto audientes omnes essent. (Varro, *Ling.* 5.82)

Dictator? That's because he was dicted by the consul as the one to whose dictum everyone must pay attention).

If we try to step into the role of an early audience for Varro sometime during the months after the Ides of March in 44, we would have found the genesis of the dictator and his relationship to the traditional position of consul gripping.[11] Later that year, contemporary sensitivity could also put in play the events of the *Ludi Apollinares* (under the control of the absent urban praetor, Brutus) from which a production of the *Brutus* was pulled at short notice.[12] Well-known plots and revivals such as this had been around long enough to give audiences time to enrich them with new cultural and personal meaning. Suetonius recounts a graffito playing on *consul* and *rex* that appeared on the base of Caesar's statue after the Lupercalia of 44; it seems to offer a comparable and decidedly popular riff linking the consulship, Brutus, and Caesar.[13] The potential for collision between audience markups in allowing a performance of Accius' *Brutus* after Caesar's assassination is evident in the (acting urban praetor C. Antonius') decision to substitute a different play.

Later (*Ling.* 6.61) Varro would redefine the dictator as the one who "needs 'to be declared' [*debet dici*] by the consul." Taking these two explanations together makes for an interesting contrast with the political analysis Cicero ascribes to Scipio:[14]

Scipio: "in this way our people [*noster populus*], in peacetime and in domestic affairs, give orders and threaten, they raise objections, they harry, they challenge [*imperat ... minatur, recusat, appellat, prouocat*] the magistrates. Yet when at war, they treat them like kings [*sic paret ut regi*]—safety proves a stronger force than their arbitrary lusts [*salus quam libido*]. In the most serious wars, however, our folk have typically wanted to be under the total command of one individual, with no power-sharing, and his title indicates the nature of his power [*ipsum nomen uim suae potestatis indicat*]. For a *dictator* is so-called because diktats are his mode of operation, but in our books, Laelius, you see him called 'master of the people' [*Nam dictator quidem ab eo appellatur quia dicitur, sed in nostris libris uides eum Laeli magistrum populi appellari*]." (Cic. *Rep.* 1.63)

Cicero's interest in filtering dictatorship through the willfulness and timorousness of the people finds later echoes, notably in his Scipio's comments on the genesis of tyranny.[15] The exposition of a dictator as a kind of crisis king by popular demand, and for that reason perhaps by inference inherently problematic, is of course part of Scipio's attempt to explain the situation when the ideal king is an impossibility. It is also significant that Cicero gives Scipio the phrase "*sine collega omne imperium nostri penes singulos esse uoluerunt*" to gloss the power dynamics demanded by the people—they want, in effect, to hand themselves over to a paterfamilias, like a swarm of children, or a herd of women, or even a gang of slaves.[16]

For Varro (at *Ling.* 6.61), rather than balancing the role of pronouncement between the act of making the dictator and the definition of his activities (as he did earlier, *Ling.* 5.82), what counts is the assertion that "dictatorial" quality is embedded in the *process* of a dictator's creation *by the consul* as master *of the people*—not in his governmental function, his autocratic qualities, or the power of his speech.[17] Nor, conversely, is the dictator here implicated in a kind of popular wartime frenzy to abdicate responsibility.

Just as the vividness of Varro's treatment of the praetor overshadowed his consul, his dictator, whose word is law, seems nonetheless to be hustled out of the way by a military functionary, the *magister equitum*.

Magister equitum, quod summa potestas huius in equites et accensos, ut est summa populi dictator, a quo is quoque magister populi appellatus. (Varro, *Ling.* 5.82)

The master of horse, because supreme power is his, over the cavalry [equestrians] and auxiliaries, just as the dictator is supreme over the people, from which he is also called master of the people.

After that, all other functionaries are addenda: "*Reliqui, quod minores quam hi magistri, dicti magistratus, ut ab albo albatus*"—"as for the rest, because they are *inferior* to these *maestros*, they are termed *magistrates*, just as from 'white' is said 'whitened'" (*Ling.* 5.82). The *magister* (dictator, *magister equitum*) is a maestro through and through, whereas the *magistratus* simply holds magisterial attributes. The difference is subtle, but Varro's comparative explanation (*albus, albatus*) extends the semiotic field in suggestive ways. From *albatus* comes the idea of "a white x," or someone whitened, or white-clad; this enriches *albus*, a descriptor for the pallor of fear, for Alba Longa (precursor to Rome), for whiteness, colorlessness, lucidity, fairness, even old age, to name a few qualities in play.[18] Yet Varro's choice of the essentially adjectival *albus* as a comparator for nominal *magister* emphasizes the fragility of visual analogy for determining similarity. The political candidate (*candidatus*), of course, turns out in a gleaming white toga, so the visual frame of reference is nonetheless evident.[19]

Religious Roles and Structures

The ensuing etymologies shift focus, and Varro turns next to a different grouping within the pantheon of civic functionaries: priesthoods (*Ling.* 5.83–86), with the contextualizing and systemic opener "*Sacerdotes uniuersi a sacris dicti*" (Priests as a group get their name from sacred rites, *Ling.* 5.83).[20]

The visually associative transition from *magistratus* to *alb(at)us* to *sacerdotes* visually encourages readers toward something removed from the mundane world; for instance in the 30s, if later accounts of the story's currency are credible, a white chicken with a sprig of laurel dropped (safely by an eagle) into Livia's lap, sometime around the occasion of her marriage to Octavian.[21] That anecdote presupposes something special in the whiteness and in the notion of a subsequent genealogy attaching to it: while the dynasty lasts, the descendant chickens and laurels flourish.[22] As noted earlier, remarkable, distinguished, white things also recall the complementary legend of Alba Longa as proto-Rome, founded by the omen of the *sus alba*.[23] One further cluster of senses for *albus* adds extra value to Varro's transition: "propitious," "rare," or of distinguished parentage.[24]

The sacral and legendary resonances brought into play by *albus* continue when Varro underlines the following etymology with a personal aside:

Pontufices, ut Sc*a*euola Quintus pontufex maximus dicebat, a posse et facere, ut po<n>tifices.²⁵ **Ego** a ponte **arbitror**: nam ab his Sublicius est *factus* primum ut restitutus s*a*epe, cum ideo sacra et u*l*s et cis Tiberim non mediocri ritu fiant. Curiones dicti a curiis, qui fiunt ut in his sacra faciant. (Varro, *Ling.* 5.83)

Archpriests, as Quintus Scaevola the Pontifex Maximus put it, are those who can and do, as if they were can-doers. **But in my opinion** the name comes from bridge: it was by these people that the Piles [Bridge] was first constructed, and frequently restored, since that's the context for rites celebrated on far and near banks of the Tiber with no small ceremony. Curiones were named after Curiae, as the ones who exist in order to perform the rites in these [Curiae].

Q. Mucius Scaevola (Pontifex) is given the authoritative line on the eponymous qualities of the Pontifex Maximus. Scaevola's notoriety, however, is rather more likely to have been lodged in his contribution to the Lex Licinia-Mucia (in 95), his defeat (by Crassus) in the celebrity trial known as the Causa Curiana (in 92), and his Sullan sympathies (resulting in his death, in 82).²⁶ As a famous (and Sullan) casualty of civil war, Scaevola might here stand in for wrongheadedness and defeat (underscored by Varro's firm rebuttal of his etymology, "*ego arbitror*"). If so, it makes sense that the can-do quality of the famously unsuccessful Scaevola's explanation of *pontifices* is quickly superseded by Varro's derivation from something more consensus-focused than Scaevola managed to offer: the bridging term *pons*.²⁷ The significance of the Pons Sublicius for Varro's Rome is familiar to through-readers from its appearance earlier in book 5, and Varro's formulation emphasizes the physically connective quality of the structure.

Next follow *curiones* (and *curiae*). Curia was not just an early political unit; it was most concretely experienced in Rome's civic center as the term for "meeting house." The people associated with the Curiae might be priests, as proposed here, or senators, as two subsequent encounters draw out,²⁸ but leaving it there ignores the potential wordplay on *curia*, which draws in the discredited etymological authority of Scaevola with which Varro opened this section (*Ling.* 5.83). Scaevola's famous forensic defeat in the Causa Curiana continued to resonate as a piece of case law, as evidenced by the extensive attention paid by Cicero in his *De Oratore*. Indeed, it featured in exemplary fashion in both orators' arguments during the trial of Caecina and proved a significant touchstone in Cicero's forensic theory.²⁹ If one possible reading of *De Lingua Latina* makes it a long reply in an ongoing conversation with Cicero, this pun becomes razor sharp.

Varro makes only a brief foray into *flamines*, whose characteristic look—their covered, head-banded garb—is the explanation offered for their name and who are distinguished by their direct relationship with the various gods whose rites they perform (*Ling*. 5.84).³⁰ From there, Varro turns his attention to two particularly resonant sets of religious functionaries:

> Salii ab salitando, quod facere in comitiis in sacris quotannis et solent et debent. Luperci, quod Lupercalibus in Lupercali sacra fiunt. Fratres Aruales dicti qui sacra publica faciunt propterea ut fruges ferant arua: a ferendo et aruis Fratris Aruales dicti. Sunt qui a fratria dixerunt: fratria est Graecum uocabulum partis hominum, ut <Ne>apoli etiam nunc. Sodales Titii <ab auibus titiantibus>³¹ dicti, quas in auguriis certis obseruare solent. (Varro, *Ling*. 5.85)

> The Salii take their name from "dancing," which they are accustomed and indeed obliged to do in assembly-places as part of the annual rites. The Luperci, because at the Lupercalia, in the Lupercal, they enact the sacred rites. Arval "Brothers" are so called as the ones who perform the public rites so that arable land may bear fruits: from ferendo ["progressing a task"/"producing"] and "arable fields" comes the name Arval "Brothers" [*sc*. "bearers"]. There are those who have said that they were named from "brotherhood"; fratria is the Greek word for a part of the people as is even now the case in [Ne]apolis. The Twitish Comrades are named <from the twittering birds> which they are accustomed to observe in certain augural practices.

For the Salii, Varro chooses not to explore *why* (war-)"dancing" or to interrogate their origins. Perhaps he has already untangled the logic in one of his earlier works.³² Certainly the Salii very visibly performed elements of their backstory when they paraded the *ancilia* annually during the month of March and then again (associated with the Armilustrium), as part of the October cleansing of the *ancilia* in the Campus Martius).³³ Nevertheless, by using the blandest form of verbal-similarity-based etymology, "*salii ab salitando*," Varro ostentatiously avoids engaging the obvious intertext: "Salian" discourse (the *Carmen Saliare*) was by then a byword for the infamously obscure and unintelligible (readers will shortly meet his own intervention in the debate).³⁴

By contrast to the sprightly Salii, Varro's static Lupercalian etymology focuses on the Lupercal cave and the associated shrine where the wolf suckled Romulus and Remus, even though the Luperci really were famous for ranging around the city as part of their cult rites.³⁵ Romulus' sexy fertility ritual is in this way linked and subordinated (secondary and compressed in narrative and spatial terms) to the world of active citizenship embodied in the Salii. Depending on the date of composition and any possible revisions, Varro's Luperci are also standing well clear from the problematic events of the Lupercalia of 44. This was the year when Antony, lead runner of the new Luperci *Iuliani*, reportedly offered Caesar a diadem just at the moment when he was embedding himself in the festival's annual (re)foundation extravaganza.³⁶ In contrast to Cicero's volubility and his deeply glossy approach to retelling this event, Varro's Luperci leave it up to his reader(s) to problematize or pause over the etymology or eventually to recall or (re)consider the resonance of February 44.

The Salii and the Luperci combine to produce a landscape enlivened with fertility, dancing, music, and benevolent nature, and they prepare the way thematically for the laborious agricultural semiotics ascribed to the "Arable Brothers." Varro's sequencing of priesthoods and festivals in this passage makes for a progressively collaborative and organized worldview. Civilization rests on getting things done. His system also recognizes and explicitly includes the wider countryside. Varro directs readers from the sacred confines and spaces of the city to the worked territory without and, ultimately, to Greece (in particular, to the flavor of Greekness still flourishing in communities along the Italian peninsula).f³⁷ The Band of Tweeters, Varro's final group in this passage, might recall the prevalence of augury as a characteristic sign of Etruscan religious practice. In narrative terms, augurs' association with the *lituus*—the crook-ended staff legendarily first used in Rome by Romulus—gives coherence to the arc.³⁸ Augury, through an archaizing filter, can recall Numa and Romulus and returns readers full circle to the Salii and Luperci.³⁹

A Military Parade

Despite appearances, Varro did not entirely wrap up on politics with his exploration of *magister* and *magistratus*. The interlude on priesthoods is just that, and a longish piece on the Fetiales, Rome's priestly *corps diplomatique*, marks a thematic transition to a politically alert section on military roles.

Fetiales, quod fidei **publicae** inter populos praeerant: nam per hos fiebat ut iustum conciperetur bellum, et inde desitum, ut f<o>edere fides pacis constitueretur. Ex his mittebantur, ante quam conciperetur, qui **res** repeterent, et per hos etiam nunc fit foedus, quod fidus Ennius scribit dictum. (Varro, *Ling.* 5.86)

<u>Fetiales</u> are thus because they took the lead on matters of **official** <u>good faith</u> between peoples. For it was through them that the declaration of a just war could be made and from them that a cessation would be decreed, so that <u>by a treaty</u>, <u>good faith</u> in the peace might be established. Some of them were sent before a war should be declared, in order to seek **restitution**, and it is through them, even now, that a <u>treaty</u> (which Ennius writes was spoken as <u>troth-y</u>) is made.⁴⁰

Varro's etymology for the Fetiales is semantically unremarkable.⁴¹ What it highlights is the changing parameters of *fides* and *foedus* in late Republican semiotics, perhaps most memorably exemplified in Catullus 76.⁴² Clearly, one important quality of the State ("*qui res repeterent*," res publica) continues to be good faith, of which a concept of natural law or justice is the defining principle. Evidence for this good faith is manifest in select individual "mediators" (implicitly, as priests, they have a line of communication to the gods).

To add context, we can look to Servius' commentary on *Aeneid* 9.52:

First steps to war . . .
When they wanted to declare war [*bellum indicere*], the *pater patratus*, that is, the Chief of the Fetials, would set out for the border with the enemies [*ad hostium fines*]. Once there he would utter certain solemnities, saying in a clear voice that they were declaring war for specific reasons [*propter certas causas*], whether because the adversaries had injured Rome's allies [*socios*], or because they had not returned seized animals or captives. This is called the *clarigatio* [perhaps, "clarification" of reparations], from the clarity of his voice [or expression of the demand]. After this *clarigatio* a spear is thrown [*hasta . . . missa*] into their territorial limits, an indication that hostilities [*pugnae*] have commenced. The Fetials throw the spear after the thirty-three days from when they had demanded restitution from their enemies. . . . Varro in his *Calenus* says that "generals, when they were on the point of entering hostile land, for the purpose of an omen they used first to throw a spear into the field, so that they might thus seize a place for their camp."⁴³

This *Calenus* was one of Varro's *Logistorici*.⁴⁴ Q. Fufius Calenus (*cos.* 47) was Caesar's partisan and the very man who would eventually rescue Varro from the proscriptions that claimed Cicero's life. *Calenus* likely dates to sometime soon after 40 (the year of Calenus' death), at which point Calenus' legions smoothly joined Octavian's faction. It is tempting to think that Varro may have ornamented his slightly later work of political and personal gratitude with a vivid twist on the whole problem of how to ensure that right was on one's military side in the opening of hostilities: the "new" telling of the legend of the casting of the spear in order to mark a war as just and appropriate eclipses any prior claim of the Fetiales to a different and more authentic practice, back when treaties (as Ennius has it) pronounced good faith.[45]

The Fetiales explained and with good faith in imperial relationships raised as an issue, Varro returns to the praetor (*Ling.* 5.87), after whom etymologies come thick and fast. Next, the imperator (whose power flows from the people and who is their defender),[46] then legates (with loyalties separately to senate and to people), the army (*exercitus* develops its identity through frequent practice—*exercitando*), and the "selective" process—the levy—which creates the legion ("*legio, quod leguntur milites in delectu*").[47] Missing from this catalog is *dux*, a word whose military connotations overlap with *praetor* but from which Varro textually dissociates it.

Despite the physical complexities of intratextual reading practice without careful bookmarking of scrolls, the effort in skimming forward (and back) between this point and books 6 and 10 (where *dux* is treated) pays off, as of course does a second through-reading, when the later instances activate the full ramifications of the earlier passage(s). The first gloss (*Ling.* 6.62) shows that to be a leader (*dux*) means to have the qualities of an educator (in effect, one who is influential over the coming generation). Belatedly, therefore, Varro's first discussion of *dux* (*Ling.* 6.62), flowing from *dico* (*Ling.* 6.61), picks up and develops on book 5's exploration of militaria and performative power.

Duco develops from the didactic qualities of *dico*, Varro asserts, and so *dux*, the one who leads, is a special case of the complex and compelling potency of dictatorial speech acts. Given the structural significance of *dico*, Carruthers' exploration of *ducere* as a mode within whose symbolic frame of reference sits "the experience of artistic form as an ongoing, dynamic process" is especially apt.[48] But where the dictator, the master of the people, solidifies the link to book 5 by returning as a function of the consul, "*quod is a consule debet dici*" (because he must be named by the consul, *Ling.* 6.61), *dux* continues to sit outside that scheme. Following the trail to book 10 (*Ling.* 10.56–57) means re-encountering *dux* as a model word for the difficulty of inferring plurality from singulars: many leaders (*duces*), by a process of elimination (of the letter "e"), produce one singular *dux* without much difficulty. The reverse (Varro indicates) is harder to imagine, and it is difficult not to see in this a real-world thrust at a systemic political dilemma.[49]

Examples from across his works suggest that for Cicero, *dux* plays a significantly flexible role in articulating potentially awkward encounters with the truth or with figures for whom definition via formal and official power terminology might raise eyebrows or switch on overly complicated resonances.[50] For through-readers deep in book 5, of course, the delights of *dux* and the re-emergence of the consul and dictator are still to come. Returning to book 5, we rejoin Varro at *cohors* (*Ling.* 5.88); this is a term in which he shows a lingering interest:

> Cohors, quod ut in uilla ex pluribus tectis coniungitur ac quiddam fit **unum**, sic hic ex manipulis pluribus copulatur: cohors quae in uilla, quod circa eum locum pecus cooreretur, tametsi cohortem in uilla *Hy*psicrates dicit esse Graece χόρτον apud poetas dictam. Manipul*u*s exercitus minima manus quae **unum** sequitur signum. (Varro, *Ling.* 5.88)

> The cohort—because just as on an estate where from the joining of several buildings a kind of **unity** [i.e., the *cohors* farmyard] is manifest, thus a [military] cohort emerges from the linking of several maniples. The cohort on an estate is so named because in and around that place the flock musters, although Hypsicrates says that the cohort on an estate is the Greek "garden," as the poets have it. The maniple is the smallest troop in the army that follows its own **unique** standard.

There is a breathtaking simplicity to Varro's manipulation of the hackneyed citizen-farmer-soldier tropes of Roman identity. First, cohorts are a product of the villa—drawn from the complex engineered form of the multibuilding estate with its many "roofs." The villa's intellectual and leisurely qualities within Varro's milieu and its contemporary association with the display of wealth and power might at first seem slyly to hint at a political undertone. Villas place the reader in a world of privilege and even violently acquisitive rivalry, as Varro could at least later attest (depending on the exact sequence of composition and revision in the context of Antony's land grab from Varro at Casinum). The "unity" is ultimately only superficial, and, although the figurative use of "roof" to signify "building" is a common one, it signals here the difference between simultaneously literal and metaphorical realities. Hence, the bond linking maniples into cohorts is likely to be subject to scrutiny.

Maniples were the traditional military organizational unit below the level of legion. If Marius' changes to the military define the point where the cohort becomes the standard sublegionary unit, then the other factor that comes into play when hitching the cohort to the villa-estate is the question of veteran settlements and how to reward a "career" soldier effectively.[51] Varro's role on Caesar's Land Commission connects him to the military backstory underpinning the agrarian legislation of 59, and, read metaphorically, the story here suggests that solid, united cohorts depend on an acknowledged and at least superficially functioning link between the traditional military divisions (the maniples, recalling the first days of Roman military identity), the productive countryside divided up into properties (and properties available for parceling out to suit political needs), and the physical qualities of a cohort defined as a plurality of solid, persisting units.[52]

When Varro expands the etymology, the villa-estate is further politicized by a phrasal echo of the opening. The echo ("*cohors . . . in uilla*") transforms the figurative villa cohort that Varro started with from a static group of buildings locked into place ("*coniungitur*," "*copulatur*") into a mobile site where the flock gains its definitive identity ("*cooritur*")—a place of becoming. Hypsicrates' alternative explanation (in the passage quoted) expands the Latin *imaginaire* by drawing *cohors* out into the cultured experience of the Hellenized Mediterranean.[53] This may be the Hypsicrates who crops up in Josephus as a source for Strabo's account of Caesar's Alexandrian campaign; if so, it makes for another tiny, pleasing link to contemporary politics.[54]

The villa, evoking in the late Republic an elite space of philosophical strolls and political performance, is here at once the source of substantial military power (the new, larger "cohort" unit) and also a site looking toward the Hellenistic kingdoms (Hypsicrates' Pontus) and, eventually, to the power play that would persist in the wake of Caesar's unexpected death. *Villa* metaphorically produces a crop of soldiers, a striking image, while Varro's return to maniple at the end of this passage recenters readers in the verbal politics of military organization. "Cohort" draws on a world of literary allusion, Greek philosophical idyll—and the politics of military loyalty, structure, and the control of armed troops. Maniple, the handful of handpicked men, is the baseline unit to which Varro returns us.[55] Elsewhere, Varro typically uses *signum* (the standard that the maniple follows) to indicate constellations, but on two occasions it means statue; if read as a monumental or emblematic human figure, *signum* offers a glimpse of the unique close-knit band following something iconic, individuated, and connected to a body of corporeal power (*manus*).[56]

This is not the end of Varro's military parade. Three more "sections" (*Ling.* 5.89–91) work through the tribal qualities of *milites* and their archetypal weaponry, followed by the auxiliaries who augment the ranks ("*auxilium appellatum ab auctu, cum accesserant ei qui adiumento essent alienigenae*," *Ling.* 5.90—the others whose rationale was to provide assistance but who became part of the regular force) and then a gaggle of different military characters and tactics whose role is at once separate and integral.⁵⁷

> **Milites**, quod <u>trium</u> **milium** <u>primo</u> legio fiebat ac singulae <u>tribus</u> Titiensium, Ramnium, Lucerum <u>milia</u> **militum** mittebant. Hastati dicti qui <u>primi</u> hastis pugnabant, pilani qui pilis, **principes** qui a <u>principio</u> gladiis; ea post commutata re militari minus illustria sunt. Pilani **tria*r*ii** quoque dicti, quod in acie <u>tertio</u> ordine extremi **subsidio** deponebantur; quod hi **subsidebant** ab eo **subsidium** dictum, a quo Plautus:
> Agite nunc, **subsid*i*te** omnes quasi solent **triarii**
> (Varro, *Ling.* 5.89)

> **Soldiers**, because at <u>first three</u> "**thousands**" formed the legion, and the individual **tribes** of Titienses, Ramnes, and Luceres sent **soldiers** in <u>thousands</u>. The spearmen were named from those who fought, <u>first</u> row, with spears; the javelin-men were those who fought with javelins; the **first-men** those who fought from the <u>first</u> with swords. These terms would become less illustrative after military tactics had changed. The javelin-men are also called **third-men**, because in the line of battle they were set to the rear, in the <u>third</u> line, as **reserves**. Because these men used to **stand down**, from that, "**reserve force**" got its name. Whence Plautus says:
> Come now, all of you **stand down**, as **third-line men** do.

Soldiers are *milites*, Varro says, because legions were made up of three "thousands" (*milia*), which maps with apparent neatness onto the three tribes who sent a thousand men each: Titienses, Ramnes, and Luceres (*Ling.* 5.55–56, developed at 5.89).⁵⁸ Varro continues with his explanation of the types of warfare practiced by the men of each battle line, and the juxtaposition between this and the vanished early Roman world of archaic tribes suggests a primal quality to Rome's military disposition. From the first battle line to the "first-men" (*principes*), sword-fighters, two kinds of "first" are in play. The dual senses of primacy could mean that things are less straightforward than the story initially suggests and, as Varro observes immediately after this, that subsequent changes to military tactics (an explanation that helps to makes sense of the etymology as he tells it) broke the link between naming and role.⁵⁹ Perhaps as an example, we hear that the javelin-men, although listed second and notionally equally significant in the tribal legion, were at some stage to be defined as "in reserve," because they settled down to hold the rear ("*subsidebant*"); hence, the reserves (or, perhaps, settlers).⁶⁰ Being one of the first men (or first-men; the oddness of Varro's etymology for swordsmen must be deliberate) or a man of the military line carries no etymologically backed guarantee that one will not eventually end up off the (expansionary, imperializing) front page and *in subsidio*.

If we read this episode (*Ling.* 5.89) as something more than Varro flailing to impose etymological logic on fractious terminology, we find that just being called *princeps*, "first," does not mean one is part of a stable semiotic system that delivers *auctoritas* in perpetuity. Varro's contextualization of the excursus makes it clear that the *principes*, like their fellow militarists (the spear- and javelin-men), are echoes of a vanished order and an episteme readily available only to the antiquarian mindset. This is, in such a reading, about more than simple military definitions. These tribe names speak Etruscan into Latin, says Volnius the *Etruscan* tragedian ("*omnia haec uocabula Tusca*," *Ling.* 5.55). They conjure up a world in which such vanished voices spoke powerfully and eloquently to the development of Latin as both language and culture but whose effect as reifying devices within a primitive *imaginaire* has lost its force.⁶¹

The three antique Romulean tribes were also, of course, due to morph into something else: the four urban tribes, tribes whose role had for a long time held the pass against the prospect of new voting blocks, born of the growth in the urban plebs and freedmen.⁶² This makes for a particularly acute intratextual connection if we map *Ling.* 5.89 back onto Varro's Argei (*Ling.* 5.45). His Argive *principes*, settlers too, have become a kind of sacral reserve force for Rome's ongoing security and prosperity. Like these characters, Hercules' Argive companions settled (for) Rome. The to-and-fro interplay between terms, times, and jostling Roman identities partly masks but also perhaps highlights how hard (and worthwhile) it is to put distinctive names and schemes to things: even Varro's Sevenheights—site and festival—remains contestable ground.⁶³

Finally (*Ling.* 5.91), Varro rounds up with another tribal etymology, tackling *turma* (cavalry troop).

<u>Turma terima</u> (E in U abiit), quod <u>ter</u> deni equites <u>ex tribus tribubus</u> Titiensium, Ramnium, Lucerum fiebant. Itaque primi singularum <u>decuriarum decuriones</u> dicti, qui ab eo in singulis <u>turmis</u> sunt etiam nunc <u>terni</u>. Quos hi primo administros ipsi sibi <u>adoptabant</u>, <u>optiones</u> uocari coepti, quos nunc propter ambitionem <u>tribuni</u> faciunt. (Varro, *Ling.* 5.91)

"<u>Troop</u>" is from <u>terima</u> (E transformed into U), because they were made up of <u>three</u> sets of ten horsemen from the <u>three tribes</u> of Titienses, Ramnes, and Luceres. Therefore the first man in each individual *decade* was called <u>decurion</u> [leader of ten], of whom, based on this, there are even now <u>three</u> per <u>troop</u>. Those whom these [leaders] first themselves <u>chose</u> as their aides—<u>the chosen</u>, they were called from the start—those [chosen] are now "made" by the <u>tribunes</u>, in service of their ambition.

Turma becomes noteworthy when Varro delves into the ancestral word cloud and finds a link to the otherwise unattested *terima*. He finds his rationale in a "u"-for-"e" swap. A *turma* is, of course, a military unit, but, etymologically, Varro's threefold explanation seems designed to echo and reinforce the triadic, tribal quality of having three "ten-pack" equestrian units (and their three "tenth-man" leaders, *decuriones*) make up each troop.[64] Organizationally, equestrians operate in tens, so Varro's scheme showcases two jostling species of numerologically glossed etymology: tribal threesomes, followed at a granular level by three-times-three decades whose individual leaders (decurions) are subordinate to the tribal structure by virtue of their title (they are about the tens, not the threes). The triadic tribal backstory recalls the interplay between twins (Romulus and Remus) and triplets (adding in Titus Tatius; dealing with the absent Remus; processing persisting Etruscan otherness via the Luceres) in Rome's origins.[65]

Once, Varro goes on to say, the Leaders of Ten (decurions) had adjutants known as "the chosen," but now ambition (political maneuvering) has taken them from these deeply *tribal* structures to a new mode of appointment associated with military power (the *Tribune*).[66] As earlier, Varro homes in on numerical roots, but what were his alternatives? If it were not for this elegant concoction, Varro's *termen* (and, with particular aptness, *termina*) might have opened up a rich seam for exploration of boundaries, even—or perhaps especially—without any bona fide etymological connection.[67] One explanation might be that connecting *termen* with questions of limits (and the potential political, military, imperial, ethical, and personal tangle they might evoke) could be a prickly addition to Latin's militarized zone. *Termen* without restrictive limits, in this way, remains part of an intelligible, finite, Greco-Italic, rustic world; it questions the nature of territory (*territorium*), evokes Greeks and wanderings round the Mediterranean, before stopping to walk readers along the Italian and specifically Latinized bounds instead.[68]

Missing *Rex*

But what about Varro on *rex*, a term with genuinely frictive potential in the context of Caesar's maneuvering in the mid-40s? Chasing contemporary etymologies for *rex* might send modern readers first to Sallust and Cicero, whence Augustine later extracted "*annua imperia binosque imperatores sibi fecerunt, qui consules appellati sunt a consulendo, non reges aut domini a regnando atque dominando.*"[69] Monarchy here presupposes the idea of an already operative but unindividuated regal power: the term "king" derives from the act or process of "ruling." The *rex* (civic or religious) in this sense is a manifestation of a more diffuse ur-power, perhaps even of the balancing act necessary to maintain good relations with and between natural forces. This *rex* would embody a wider organizational principle ensuring harmony between citizens and universe.[70]

No etymology for *rex* features in book 5's exploration of priestly and political titles; nevertheless, *rex* does appear in the extant *De Lingua Latina*. The most interesting example is in book 10, but to get there, through-readers will already have built up a pattern of associations that repays attention. Early in book 5, *rex* marks up *Latinus* and *Romulus*.[71]

> Non enim uidebatur consentaneum qua<e>re<re> me in eo uerbo quod **finxisset** Ennius causam, neglegere quod ante rex Latinus **finxisset**, cum poeticis multis uerbis magis delecter quam utar, antiquis magis utar quam delecter. An non potius mea uerba illa quae hereditate a Romulo rege uenerunt quam quae a poeta Liuio relicta? (Varro, *Ling.* 5.9)

> For it did not seem appropriate that I should hunt the source for a word that Ennius had **formed** and neglect what King Latinus had earlier **formed** just because I derive more pleasure than utility from a multitude of poetic words and more utility than pleasure from the ancient ones. Indeed, are those not my words that have arrived though inheritance from King Romulus, rather than those relics from the poet Livius?

The first significance is in the semiotics of the two names and the company they keep. Varro sets King Latinus alongside Ennius as an original wordsmith, implicitly downgrading the agency of the more extravagantly foundational figure of King Romulus (or reliquary claims made on "the poet" Livius Andronicus' behalf).[72] In this version, King **Latin**us shaped ("*finxisset*") Latin, whereas it merely passes by hereditary transmission from King **Rom(e)**ulus. From a programmatic and political perspective, what is most significant is that *rex* is emphatically included.

The significance of *rex* develops when Varro explains:

> Sunt qui Tiberim priscum nomen Latinum Albulam uocitatum litteris tradiderint, posterius propter Tiberinum regem Latinorum mutatum, quod ibi interierit: nam hoc eius ut tradunt sepulcrum. (Varro, *Ling.* 5.30)

There are those who have handed down, in their writings, the story that the Tiber was dubbed Albula as its early Latin name, later changed on account of Tiberinus, <u>king</u> of the Latins, because he died there—this was, as they tell it, his burial place.

This means that the first three deployments of *rex* after the restart of *De Lingua Latina* in book 5 are all associated with complexly Romano-Latin figures. These characters exemplify heterogeneity in Rome's self-fashioning, while at the same time pointing up some delicately autochthonic angles on how discourse is rooted in place (river, tomb) and how place gets its defining meaning from storytelling ("*uocitatum litteris tradiderint*," "*tradunt*"). The Albulan river in this way becomes heir to the Latin King Tibe*r*inus and, in flowing as the Tiber, continues (*Ling.* 5.32) to "tell" that fluid, palimpsestic story of monarchy and death; their territory, or field-land (*ager*),[73] plugs a people into the big stories of what would become Latium and then Rome, but local town foundations jostle for authority while pre-Roman and pre-Latin cities persist.[74]

Varro next bundles *rex* with Aventine etymologies ("*alii ab rege Auentino Albano*," others draw it from King Aventinus, the Alban, *Ling.* 5.43). Scrolling on to *Ling.* 5.46, we see Romulus being assisted by Tuscan *dux* Caeles Vibenna against King Tatius—unlike the allied leader, Caeles ("Caelian") Vibenna, royal Tatius will fail to gain an eponymous monument in Rome's urban fabric,[75] although through Ennius comes the information that he brought polyphonously syncretistic altars to Rome:

> e<t> ar*a*e Sabinum linguam olent, quae Tati regis uoto sunt Romae dedicatae ... e quis nonnulla nomina in utraque lingua habent radices, ut arbores quae in confinio natae in utroque agro serp*u*nt. (Varro, *Ling.* 5.74)

The altars too are redolent of Sabine speech, which by the vow of King Tatius were dedicated at Rome ... several of these names have roots in both languages, like trees which, born in the borderlands, creep into both territories.

At the end of the tour of the Argive city, discussed in chapter 5, *rex* transfers to the world of the gods, first by way of a tag from Ennius (Jupiter: of gods and mankind, father and king, *Ling.* 5.65) and then through Varro's emphasis on the indigenous, potent, and uncontrollable qualities of language as a force of nature. *Rex* will, however, return when Varro gazes back to the time of King Tullius and his monumental subterranean Tullianum, etymologizing the Carcer.[76]

Unsurprisingly, *rex* is peppered most generously through books 5 and 6, the books in which excavation of political history is to the fore. Without working exhaustively through all the examples in book 6, it is still piquant to discover that the next royal rendezvous discovers *rex* reinvented primarily as a priestly one-off, no explanation on offer.[77] The "king" sacrifices a ram in the Regia on the *dies Agonales*.

> Dies Agonales per quos rex in Regia arietem immolat, dicti ab "agon," eo quod interrogat <minister sacrificii "agone?">: nisi si a Graeca lingua, ubi ἄγων princeps, ab eo quod immolat>ur a principe ciuitatis et princeps gregis immolatur.[78] (Varro, *Ling.* 6.12)

> The dies Agonales, during which the rex sacrifices a ram in the Regia, are so-called from agon, because he asks <[that is] the assistant at the sacrifice asks "shall I complete the task?"; that's unless it is from the Greek language, where ἄγων means "leader," from the fact that the sacrifice is undertaken> by the chief of the state, and the chief of the flock is sacrificed.

This passage, fragmentary though it is, leads almost immediately to the Luperci and the Salii (discussed in the second section of this chapter, "Religious Roles and Structures"), which it contextualizes.[79] A Sabine gloss is provided when the *rex* announces the festival on the Nones, using its alternate title, *februatus* (*Ling.* 6.13). With hindsight, *rex* thus becomes part of the context for Varro's Lupercalia. The nexus is completed at *Ling.* 6.14 (on the Liberalia) when Varro connects the sacred *rex* to the Salii via the Salian Books by way of the tag "Agonensis" (in the process highlighting a connexion with his earlier comments on the Agonia, *Ling.* 6.12). It is also possible that this material has come adrift through a copyist's error from Varro's earlier discussion of the *rex* at the *dies Agonales*, which it seems to complement. If so, instead of glossing the Liberalia, it adds weight to an etymology through *agon* in dialogue with *princeps*.[80] Taken together, something novel emerges when Varro connects the Luperci and the Salii to the terms *rex* and *agon* and binds the four via the arcana of the Salian tomes and the venerable antiquity of augury as a vital pre-Roman practice. As a quartet, these terms and practices embed a quality of inevitability (the iterative nature of festivals and the persistence of even unintelligible formulae within ritual) in the revolutionary processes of history.

Aside from the four noted examples, in every other instance until the ambiguities of its sole appearance in book 10, *rex* is used to signify political kingship. If we pursue the occurrences, we see that shortly after the legendarily wealthy and (eastern) foreigner King Attalus sends Magna Mater to Rome (*Ling.* 6.15), another *rex*, Servius Tullius, becomes a namegiver (an etymologist's original source) when he creates a name-day by dedicating a sanctuary to Fors Fortuna (*Ling.* 6.17). The temple of Fors Fortuna to which Varro alludes is the Roman site of Fortuna with the most antique origin story—so it might seem well suited to a "just so" etymology. Once founded, it simply gives rise in Varro's scheme to the naming of a day for Fors Fortuna—because it recalls the day of the sanctuary's dedication.[81] Chapter 8 returns to the festival in detail, but the point here is that Fors Fortuna emphasizes how "other" qualities can cluster around the *rex*.

When Titus Tatius was *rex*, he brought to Rome the Curenses, who would there become Quirites ("*Quirites a Curensibus*"). Onomatopoeic etymologies are on Varro's mind.[82] The background noise is murmuring, roaring, groaning, shouting, rattling.[83] Two verse quotes then ramp up the tension: "Arms resound, a roar builds," and "nothing from your provocation rattles me"; finally, Varro tells how a raucous urban soundscape is deeply associated with Titus Tatius' removal of men from Cures (who will become Quirites) to Rome.[84]

> Vicina horum **quiritare**, iubilare. **Quiritare** dicitur is qui **Quiritum** fidem clamans inplorat. **Quirites** a **Curensibus**; ab his cum Tatio rege in societatem uenerunt ciuitatis. Ut **quiritare** urbanorum, sic iubilare rusticorum: itaque hos imitans Aprissius ait: "Io bucco!—Quis me iubilat?—Vicinus tuus antiquus." Sic triumphare appellatum, quod cum imperatore milites redeuntes clamitant per Urbem in Capitolium eunti "<I>o triumphe"; id a θριάμβῳ ac Graeco Liberi cognomento potest dictum. (Varro, *Ling.* 6.68)

Close to these are "**to cry aloud**" and "to whoop with joy." He is said "**to cry aloud**" who shouting loudly invokes the guaranty of the **Quirites**. **Quirites** derives from **Curenses**, that is, from those who came with King Tatius to join the fellowship of the state. Just as "**to cry aloud**" is city-speak, so rustics "whoop with joy"; in this way, imitating them, Aprissius says, "Hey, flabby-chops!—Who's whooping at me?—Your long-time neighbour!" Thus, "to triumph" is what it's called when soldiers, returning with the general through the city and as he makes his way en route to the Capitolium, shout out, "Hey! Triumph!" This terminology could be traced from θρίαμβος,[85] in its sense as a Greek cognomen of Liber.

Soldiers, the one-time alter egos of farmers in the conservative imagination and already metaphorically villa-born in their cohorts (*Ling.* 5.88), are here related "thus" [*sic*]—at their most triumphant and visible urban moment—not just to kings but also to jolly, knockabout comedy rustics, themselves redolent of Samnite Atelliana.[86] The repeated *uicinus* marks up the connection between city/country semantics and stock-character verbal roughhousing, instantiating a semiotic link between the cut and thrust of rural and also of military discourse. The triumphing cries of soldiers are akin to the free speech and friendly insults between countrymen: unlike the urbane *quirito*, *iubilo* will receive no etymology. Rustic cries and their military echoes might thus be imagined to be authentic in ways that a citified expression of emotion cannot match. Yet lurking silently in the background is another relevant etymological link—that *curis* and *Curitis* tie Sabine Cures, Quirinal, and Romulus together by translation. *Curis*, as Ovid later proposes, was the long-ago Sabine word for spear (*hasta*), and Juno Spear-bearer in this way might feed into a developing civic-military frame of reference indicating the composite and engineered quality of Roman citizenship at its deepest level.[87] Quirites are Sabine freebooters; they are urbanites and rustics; they are Italians, Romans; and, as the excursus concludes, they are also part of a greater Hellenic community.

Crying out (*quirito*) emphasizes a fracture between Romulus' urban Romans (testing the implications of reinvention as Quirites) and the simultaneously rustic and explicitly regal and Sabine domain of *King* Tatius and the men of Cures. Yet, in joining the *ciuitas*, it is these subject-folk from Cures who generate the urbane, even literary Latin verb *quirito* (and the descriptor Quirites) in Varro's scheme. By contrast, this vision of king-free Rome is alive with triumphing soldiers whooping and hollering in procession (*iubilo*) just like jolly (or boorish?) countrymen.[88] Against such a backdrop, Liber the Dionysiac god of wine sits comfortably. The roughhouse world of Atellan stage shows is invoked neatly by the slapstick humor of the quoted line from Aprissius, but there is potentially more to the scene than this. This line's theatrical origins nod to the god's role in dramatic festivals, and its juxtaposition with the ritualized and by association rustic shout "*Io triumphe!*" allows the politically sensitive Greek cult to interrogate Roman postmonarchical political performance and military success.[89] Ultimately, I suggest, this passage delivers a thought experiment ("*potest dictum*") whereby heterogeneous Greco-Italian origins and the mysterious, politically edgy world of Bacchic cult (with its intimations of autocracy and despotism) sit behind every instance of a Roman general's ultimate military success and his relationship with his troops.[90] The occasion, therefore, is not one of the simple pleasure of imagining happy Italian peasants and hearty soldiery.

Elsewhere in the text, *rex* reappears in Varro's formal discussion of the Nones ("the people of the fields used to assemble in the city, before the *rex*. Traces of these practices are apparent in the rites celebrated on the Nones at the Arx, because that's when the *rex* announces [the month's holiday] to the people the first of the monthly holidays") and Ides ("named because the Etruscans say Itus, or, rather, because the Sabines say Idus").[91] Kalends, Nones, and Ides were unaffected by Caesar's new calendar, and Varro's attention spotlights this recent stability. His excavation flags up a deep-rooted connection between 1 January and the New Year, one that belies the alignment of consular and calendrical chronologies in 153.[92]

Here, we see the focal, community-forming role of a *rex* with respect to long-ago rustic citizens. The day when country dwellers would coalesce in the city draws Roman, Etruscan, and Sabine together through discourse (Nones relate numerically to Ides), the cosmos (new moon; change, revolution, permanence), and semantics (Ides evokes Rome's two cultural touchstone precursors and frenemies). Specifying the Nones of February, Varro had earlier noted (*Ling.* 6.13), the *rex* names the Lupercalia *februatus* because *februm* meant "purification" in Sabine, giving the Lupercalia a purificatory impetus—"*ut in Antiquitatum libris demonstraui.*"[93] As context for the *rex* at the Nones, this information evokes Romulus by association for both role and title.

Two last passages add interest. Book 7 adds more context to the relationship between the *rex* and the military, using literary markup:

In Cornicula:
    Qui regi <u>latrocinatus</u> decem annos Demetrio.
<u>Latrones</u> dicti ab <u>latere</u>, qui circum <u>latera</u> erant regi atque ad <u>latera</u> habebant ferrum, quos postea a stipatione stipatores appellarunt, et quid conducebantur: ea enim merces Graece dicitur λάτρον. Ab eo ueteres poetae nonnunquam milites appellant <u>latrones</u>. <At nunc uiarum obsessores dicuntur latrones,> quod item ut milites <sunt> cum ferro, aut quod <u>latent</u> ad insidias faciendas.
    Apud N*a*euium:
    Risi egomet mecum cassabundum ire ebrium.
Cassabundum a cadendo. Idem:
    D*i*abathra in pedibus habebat, erat amictus ep*i*croco.
Utrumque uocabulum Graecum.[94] (Varro, *Ling.* 7.52–53)

In *The Tiny Crow* we have:
    That ten-year <u>sell-sword</u>, a man for King Demetrius.
<u>Latrones</u> [sell-swords] get their name from <u>latus</u> [side]: the men clustering at the <u>sides</u>, round and about, of the king, and bearing a sword at their own <u>sides</u>. They are the ones who afterward, from the term "bodyguarding," were called "bodyguards" and who worked for hire: this kind of salary is called in Greek λάτρον. From this, the old poets occasionally called

soldiers <u>sell-swords</u>. <But now "sell-swords" is what highwaymen are called> because just like soldiers they have swords or because <u>they lie</u> in hiding to make their ambuscades.
 In Naevius:
  Me, myself, and I had a good laugh at a drunk tottering along.
Cassabundus [tottering] from *cadere* [to fall]. The same author has:
  Pantofles on his feet, he used to have; he was mantled in a gauzy
   gown.
Both these words are Greek.

Varro's paired citation of these two passages problematizes the orderly and normative role of the *rex* by contextualizing him first in terms of the notionally violent politics of the Hellenistic kingdoms and their growing friction with Rome ("Demetrius" might stand in for a number of different kings, including Demetrius Poliorketes); next, with the idea of personal armies and salaryman soldiers, a topos that blends the mercenary with the brigand; and finally, in relation to the ridiculous spectacle of the man who can't hold his drink. The continuum ranges from military professionalism (tainted by association with eastern monarchy) through to inappropriate violence (armed men lying in wait for the unwary to ambush them) and conspicuous, excessive consumption (the drunkard, and the pantofle-wearing sybarite, in turn characterized by the kind of garb that Cicero enjoyed ascribing to Verres but that might also invoke Caesar's reported adoption of "monarchical" attire or even Cicero's Mark Antony).[95] It is Varro who puts the pantofles adjacent to the king, and he leaves his readers to draw their own conclusions, but the quote from Naevius (with its implication of self-scrutiny, "*egomet mecum*") implies that we should be looking at, analyzing, and processing the spectacle.

Finally:

Quadruplices deiunctae in casibus sunt uocabulorum, ut rex regi, <lex legi>,[96] coniunctae sunt triplices in uerborum tribus temporibus, ut legebam. (Varro, *Ling.* 10.47)

[Regularities] in the cases of nouns are fourfold and disjoined, as in *rex* [king] and *regi* [to/for the king], <law, to/for the law>; they are conjoined and threefold in the three tenses of verbs, as in "I was reading."

Kings, as this short passage deconstructs them, embody a (word) family's complex regularity. There is diversity of descent, and the (semantic) context changes the appearance and sense of each individual (morphological) iteration of "king," yet despite the dangers of excess and chaotic singularity that monarchy might signal, the "king" still always plays by the rules. This figure is maintained successfully (and exemplarily) within the semiotic system, if one has the skill to "read" (Varro's text) and the power and knowledge to select him right.

Conclusion

The appearance of *latrones* in Varro's final book on etymology—figures who are at once parasitic on and servants of organized civic communities of various flavors—helps weave together a skein of allusions that this chapter's explorations have unraveled. In a detailed discussion Thomas Grünewald outlines some of the crucial ways in which the discourse of banditry and brigandage took on an acerbic political note during the first century.[97] The archetypal bandit is one who programmatically seizes that which is not his own and who dispossesses others on a scale that has culture-shifting implications: where bandits roam or bodyguards (the other spoke in the wheel) operate, the behavior of a community, its self-fashioning and perceived integrity and inviolability, are altered. Bandits and mercenaries change the terrain and spaces that they (are perceived to) occupy. This doubly territorial quality is interesting for reading Varro because it chimes with a culture of what Cicero assiduously portrayed as thugs for hire in Rome.[98] It dovetails with the brutal rhetoric subsequently deployed by Cicero against Antony, whom one might read as the superbandit, carousing, violating, pillaging and despoiling real citizen property and the metapoetic goods of Roman citizenship.[99]

That the figure of the king can signify order *and* dysfunction recalls the complexities of Varro's agenda. His interrogation of Latin polices boundaries—epistemological, cultural, semantic—and, in doing so, highlights the plurality of what a polysemic approach to historical linguistics offers. This is not just about canonization or recuperation. Nativization, in particular a perception that Roman Latin "borrows" from older, more authentic Italian Latin(s), might suggest one-way colonial annexation, yet the authority of Italian Romans such as Varro to recharge the resultant discourse of power and order though a process of reclamation and restructuring highlights the influence of ostentatious hybridity. In effect, by outlining a flexible system of hierarchies whose roles are understood deeply enough to allow them some plasticity of meaning, Varro indicates how an organization can be refashioned organically in response to cultural forces. Chapter 7 picks up on this principle, with the familial quality of Varro's Romespeak as its focus.

chapter 7

A Family Affair

"*Quare quod quattuor genera prima rerum, totidem uerborum*":[1] *De Lingua Latina* makes manifest a vivid and powerful relationship between the stuff of ontological reality and the structures of language. This develops the texture of Varro's deployment of quotation, opens a deeper channel into the psyche of Romespeak than the system of civic, religious, and military etymologies discussed in chapter 6, and gets to the heart of his linguistic model. Through an archaeology of grammar Varro ranges across persisting tropes, from the grand and legendary (the mythic journey from Troy to Italy) to the quotidian (pigs, slaves, family ties). He also explores the affective and formative relationships that plug Latin *langue* into Roman *parole*, the discourse world this produces, and the universe that Romespeakers inhabit.[2]

To get a sense of the significance of grammar for generating Roman community at a basic structural level, through discourse, this chapter's first section is a quick excursus into Varro's technical terminology for declensions. This is the stemma, one might say, for Varro's Romespeaking family album.[3] The second section illustrates the intricate grammatical connections between paternity, generation, and family, concluding with Rome's Trojan ancestry. When a people has territory and a genealogy, a practical eye might turn to the wider context and seek out a worldview; in the third section the focus shifts in that direction, examining the relationships that link the names, identities, and relationships that collect around the gods. In the fourth section I discuss the phenomenological underpinning to nongrammatical time-words, the context within which human organization becomes possible. The final section offers a case study showing that unexpected pairings ("wolf" and "hare" and how they connect to "father-in-law") demonstrate what becomes possible when practitioners of Latin can command outré, hidden links in order to create an integrative episteme.

<A Case of Diversion>

Grammar is what makes everything intelligible. Without structure and systematization there is no communication and no "Rome." Ancient grammatical terminology does not neatly prefigure contemporary schematization, but the question of how Varro designates the notional headwords for his grammatology of nouns is important if the connotations of doing grammar in the mid-40s are to be meaningful. This foray into Varro on similarity and the clannishness of case takes us through the terminology of declension (family ties) in a way that helps elucidate how and why Romespeak needs *De Lingua Latina*.

Grammar, this section argues, is Varro's primary community-fashioning tool—the consensus he reaches on the relationship between analogy and anomaly in stemmatizing grammatical relationships symbolizes and perhaps prefigures a political resolution for Rome's factionalism that would ultimately fully develop only in Varro's extreme old age. For this reason, Varro's discursive introduction to the pitfalls awaiting the unwary when trying to identify and work with "likeness" as an organizational principle is especially striking. This is no straightforward task, he makes clear. Careful attention must be paid if one is not to slide into error and misrecognize superficial similarity as equivalence or, worse, not recognize that two separate things are in play. Varro's example is the feckless unfortunate (*indiligens*) who mixes his stitching and his swine ("*Quid enim similius potest uidere . . . quam . . . suis et suis*").[4]

Indiligens is uncommon in this era, as represented by surviving texts. In contrast to its relatively high-frequency comedic appearance in Plautus and Terence, it crops up only occasionally in Caesar's commentaries; while Cicero, in his study of composition, gives its adverbial form a literary-critical gloss.[5] For Varro, specifically in this context (stitching and swine), I suggest that it calls to mind a negation of Cato's buzzword, *diligens*.[6] There is a charming, homely quality to the homonym disaster (*suis*) that exemplifies Varro's *indiligens*; pigs are important for Cato and, as becomes apparent later, for Varro, too. Being *indiligens* with *langue* and *parole* makes one an anti-(Elder) Cato, perhaps? *Diligens* certainly evokes an old-world value system that was deeply interesting to the public figures of the late Republic. This down-to-earth mood is evoked again when Varro concludes his introductory discussion:

> Sed ne **astutius** uidear posuisse duo genera esse similitudinum sola, cum utriusque inferiores species sint plures, si de his reticuero, ut mihi relinquam **latebras**, repetam ab origine similitudinum quae in conferendis uerbis et inclinandis **sequendae** aut **uitandae** sint. (Varro, *Ling.* 10.13)

But I don't want to seem to be **pulling a fast one** in having proposed that there are only two classes of similarity, when in both there are many subforms. If I keep quiet about these it would be as if I were leaving myself a **bolt-hole**. So I start again, from the origin of the similarities that (in the comparison of words and their inflections) must be **pursued** or **evaded**.

The terminology evokes the chase but also the canniness (*astutia*) often associated with figures from comedy—the grammatologist as wily slave who alone understands and commands the processes of inflection![7] Varro's invocation of native cunning and ordinary pastimes makes his intellectual remit lushly expansive, shifting his textual *imaginaire* from the frame of urbane pursuits. The quotidian world intervenes to support and enrich the complex arcana of grammatology and recalls his audience to the real-world significance of doing Latin right. A Latin grammar might seem to be an esoteric project in the 40s, of interest primarily to conservative intellectuals and schoolmasters, but when Varro redraws *parole* (swimming in the pool of language: "*in consuetudine uehementer natat*," *Ling.* 10.16) and when custom tries to twin *Roma/Romanus* and *Capua/Capuanus*, Varro's attentive audience will know better.[8] The swimming pool of *parole* is then recast vividly in Varro's next metaphor, taking readers from the pool (or the sea) to the arena:

> [on parts of speech] Etiam illud accedit ut in articulis habere analogias ostendere sit difficile, quod singula sint uerba, hic contra facile, quod magna sit copia similium nominatuum. Quare non tam hanc partem ab illa diuidendum quam illud uidendum, ut satis sit uerecundi<ae> etiam illam in eandem **arenam** uocare **pugnatum**. (Varro, *Ling.* 10.19)

Add to this also that it is difficult to show that there are Regularities within articles, because they are each individual to themselves. By contrast here [in nouns] it is easy, because there is a great abundance of similar nominals. Therefore it is not so much about a need to divide this part from that as it is about needing to see clearly the shame attached to calling that other part into the same **arena** to **do battle**.[9]

Analogia, says Varro, is best evidenced in nouns as part of a spoken and morphologically consistent system, a family. The practice and custom of saying something in particular ways (*habitus*) is more powerful a driver than any model requiring contiguity between signified entities.[10] This material is part of a wider discussion of Regularity in articles and nouns and introduces Varro's diagrammatic, checkerboard model for understanding cases.[11] Spectacle and violence are as embedded in Varro's grammatology as in the discourse-rich political contests that confronted Varro's audience on a daily basis. In grammar as in life, gamesmanship counts:

> Ad hunc quadruplicem fontem ordines deriguntur bini, uni transuersi, alteri derecti, ut in **tabula** solet in qua **latrunculis ludunt**. (Varro, *Ling.* 10.22)

> To this quadruple source, two sets of lines are set in place, one set transversely, the others straight up, just as is typical on a **board** on which people **game with "pawns."**

Like the checkerboard, the arena (*ludo*) frames and structures combative behavior, but "gaming" can have deceitful, mocking, or even orchestrating senses. Combine this with the unusual *latrunculus* (from the semantic field of *latro*, a pawn, and a mercenary, but one whose loyalties and morals are apt to turn vicious) and the grammatologist's world suddenly looks violent and manipulative.[12]

I began this section with Varro's interest in similarities, specifically, declinables. Grammatical terminology labels nouns as *nomen* and *uocabulum*.[13] *Nomen*, with its clannish implications, evokes family ties. For the nominative case, *nominatiuus* is the first in what Varro clearly intended to be a distinctive intervention, unpacking the terminology of case from something of a grammarians' grab bag.[14] The distinctiveness that he brought to this task is illustrated in the accusative case, which he bundles with the genitive at *Ling.* 8.66–67 when proposing (in line with book 8's agenda) that *analogia* cannot exist because some cases have acceptable variants within individual declensions.[15]

> Item quod in **patrico** casu hoc genus dispariliter dicuntur **ciuitatum parentum** et **ciuitatium parentium**, in accusandi hos <u>montes fontes</u> et hos <u>montis fontis</u>. (Varro, *Ling.* 8.66)

> Likewise, [Regularity does not exist] because in the **genitive** case there is disparity in this class of words, which are said in the forms "**of states**," "**of parents**," and *ciuitatium* and *parentium*, and in the accusative, these give "<u>mountains</u>," "<u>springs</u>," and *montis, fontis*.

The genitive is going to feature significantly later (in the next section); here I want to pause on the accusative as illustrative of Varro's originality in putting grammar center stage within his milieu. Varro is the first attested source for *accusatiuus*. Earlier in book 8 (*Ling.* 8.16) he made a Herculean task of outlining Latin's system of cases as a story shared with Greek, despite Greek's missing ablative. Samantha Schad raises but does not chase down a possibility that (especially in the etymological and antiquarian mindset) Varro may even have originated the odd *accusatiuus*, rooted perhaps, though not necessarily, in a mis-calque (on his part) from the Greek αἰτιατική.[16] The possibility of this kind of error is there, but a more interesting gloss is that the sudden appearance here of "accusative" is traceable back to the on/off rivalry between Varro and Cicero. Let me explain.

De Lingua Latina 8 is all about the (devil's argument) case against Regularity. The quoted passage concerning disparities in what we would call third-declension genitives and accusatives can, in fact, dovetail with the accusative case as the Aristotelian "effect" case. Civic Rome as a generative principle and Rome's embodiment in the figure of the parent are not monolithic or monovalent; the two aspects can embrace superficial anomalies in form (plus or minus "i") while continuing to sustain an intelligible unity.

The paternal "genitive" (*patricus*) situates fatherhood and generation of networks at the heart of grammar; here grammatology links genitive and the ensuing (reading teleologically) accusative forms to effect a distinctive and iconically Roman landscape. If one can get one's head around how reading the catalog as a designed scheme makes the accusative the effect produced *by the genitive*, it is thematically satisfactory that the next examples develop the terminology of Rome's most iconic prehistoric topography (hills and water). Being able to work with such eruptions of anomaly implies a generosity in discourse and interpretation. By way of Varro's gen(er)itive examples and the (accusative) effect of the complementary landscape that follows, a very concise history of Rome emerges in which anomaly plays a key role. Read in this way, annexing *accuso* and turning it to grammar becomes especially meaningful when Cicero is the reader. As a "calling to account" term, *accuso* was a verb much in demand by Cicero: again and again his forensic oratory makes a case for accountability, and, in its ownership of the rhetoric of *j'accuse*, Cicero's presence in this grammatical coinage (if that's what it is, on Varro's part) is solidified.[17]

Not all Varro's treatments of case remain; it is likely that his explanation of the terminology of the dative is lost to the lacuna after *Ling.* 10.23. Nevertheless, in what remains there is a personal quality to his examples of male and female names that display an underlying genitive and dative congruity: Terentius, Plaut[i]us, and Marc[i]us—two comedians (Terence, Plautus) jostle with (M. Terentius) Varro and (M. Tullius) Cicero.[18] The apparent distinctions between a plurality of *Terentiei* and *Terentiae* scions dissolve when they are assimilated to discourse (and brought into the sociopolitical frame) via the dative as *Terentieis*.[19] The dative filter shows how tightly Latin can knit the citizen body together—this is the case that adds complexity to the directness of accusative effect, drawing in the notion of affect, of persona, of intent, and of reciprocity. This is where complex societies develop.

As with the dative, Varro's definition of the vocative (*uocandi*) is absent, but the case does feature in book 8's severe castigation of the woeful logic of the pro-Regularity "faction" ("Since they are ignorant of how 'likeness' ought to be grappled with, they are incapable of speaking about Regularity"): these are, we learn, people who cannot even spot a likeness between Menaechmi twins without waiting to see if their children too are similar (for goodness' sake!).[20] On the ablative case, Varro will later squeeze out some juicy properties and associations. Grounding one's exploration in the inherent and natural qualities that pattern Regularity in inflection is to be recommended, readers will learn (*Ling.* 10.61), but if one wants to focus on singular forms, one should take one's cue from the sixth case (the as yet unnamed ablative), the one that is all Latin's own ("*qui est proprius Latinus*," *Ling.* 10.62).[21]

The ablative is the case that gives voice to Hercules (through-readers, reaching book 10, should recall *Ling.* 8.16), and the ensuing list of examples presents the five ablative vowel endings:[22]

> Sin ab singulari quis potius proficisci uolet, ini*ti*um facere oportebit ab sexto casu, qui est proprius Latinus: nam eius casuis litterarum discriminibus facilius reliquorum uarietate<m> discernere poterit, quod ei habent exitus aut in A, ut hac terra, aut in E, ut hac lance, aut in I, ut hac <c>l*a*ui, aut in O, ut hoc caelo, aut in U, ut hoc uersu. (Varro, *Ling.* 10.62)

> If [rather than starting to explore Regularity by way of the nominative plural form, as recommended] one should rather prefer to go from the singular, one should make a start from the sixth case, which is Latin's own. It is from the differences in the letters of this case that one can more easily discern the variation in the others, because its forms have an ending either in A, as in "earth," or in E, as in "platter," or in I, as in "key," or in O, as in "sky," or in U, as in "verse."

This ablative cluster takes in land (*terra*), serving plate (*lance*), key (*<c>laui*),[23] sky (*caelo*), and verse (*uersu*). The first thing to note is that the polyvalent *terra* (land, country, earth) is matched in the concluding term "verse." *Versus* is a line of poetry *and* a field-land term for measuring or (repetitively) marking up the land.[24] The literary-critical undertones are also present in *lanx*, if we accept a connection between Varro's Menippean poetics and a dishy salmagundi of spicy titbits.[25] *Caelum* was not just a buzzword in Varro's semiotic universe; it was philosophically implicated in the Epicurean zeitgeist, exemplified in Lucretius.[26] In this small example, grammar's habitual familiarity can be spun out into cosmic force.

Engendering Romespeak

In the context of grammatology, one family member is crucial: the father, indelibly lodged in the genitive case. Moreover, even though Rome might easily have been rebranded Romulus & Sons, the motif of founding fathers (the gen[er]itive patricians) never lost its authority. Anthony Corbeill's detailed analysis of the world-fashioning potential of grammatical gender (and, indeed, the discourse of its study) has exposed a distinctively Roman (and Latin) interest in manifestations of gender flux in language.[27] Varro's interest in the nuances of how "father" maps onto *familia*(*s*) is part of this story and exemplifies what Corbeill calls "a deeper motivation than simply the urge to have students and readers learn proper modes of speaking."[28] Paternity is especially lacking in book 5's etymologizing of humanocentric vocabulary as systems of power ("I shall begin from public office," *Ling.* 5.80), and its grammatical implications make it an important part of the discussion for this chapter.

Fathers are of great significance in the divine, cosmic sphere (*Ling.* 5.57–74), and this is context worth exploring before we consider divine family ties more expansively in the next section. One tiny etymological sidestep takes Varro from Ennius' Jupiter to a touchdown on paternity:

Quod hi<nc> omnes et sub hoc, eundem, appellans dicit:
　　Diuumque hominumque pater rex.
Pater, quod patefacit semen: nam tum esse conceptum <pat>et, inde cum exit quod oritur. (Varro, *Ling.* 5.65)

Because all are from and beneath him [Iu-p*a*ter], addressing him [Ennius] speaks thus:
　　Of gods and humankind, O father, king.

"<u>Father</u>" because he "<u>fathers</u>" the seed: for that's the moment when conception is <<u>manifest</u>>—whence emerges that which is born.

Keeping Mueller's emendation (*patet*), as Kent does, allows for a delicious gender pun on the masculinity of laying things bare at the moment of creation, but the etymology is already interesting. Turning to Cicero:

> After the death of Tatius total dominion had relapsed to [Romulus], although he had, along with Tatius, appointed <u>leading citizens</u> [*principes*] to a royal council [*in regium consilium*] (they were the ones who, because of affection [*caritatem*], were called <u>Fathers</u> [*patres*]). He had also distributed the populace, grouped under his own name, under that of Tatius, and that of Lucumo (an ally of Romulus killed during the Sabine war), into three tribes and thirty *curiae* (which *curiae* he named from those of the captured Sabine girls who had afterward been advocates of peace and alliance). Although indeed this was all organized during Tatius' lifetime, nevertheless after he had been killed, Romulus **ruled** all the more by way of the **authority** and **counsel** of the <u>Fathers</u> [*patrum auctoritate consilioque regnauit*]. (Cic. *Rep.* 2.14)

Here, the leading men (*principes*) are *patres*, conjuring up the nexus of filial affection, esteem, and high regard embodied in *caritas*.[29] In Cicero's work on friendship, affection (*caritas*) between children and parents ("*inter natos et parentes*") is the primary humane example (Cic. *Amic.* 8.27), while Cicero's "*Iuppiter, id est iuuans pater*" ("Jupiter, the father who keeps on helping," Cic. *Nat. D.* 2.64) further glosses the juxtaposition of Jupiter *pater* and *rex* in Ennius (*Ling.* 5.65): "*Diuumque hominumque*" (of gods and humans he is father and king).[30] *Pater* continues to reverberate as Varro continues with Jupiter, moving from an etymology for "dayfather" into Greek and Sabine landscapes of paternalism and then to the Dayfather's guise as alpha and omega when embodied as Orcus (*Ling.* 5.66).

Overall, this material shows how fathers are both of (by way of Jupiter and his curatorial role for humankind) and somehow outside (because only treated as a facet of Jupiter) Varro's systematization of human power dynamics in book 5. Rather than guide readers into the sociocultural domesticity of *pater* and *familia*, "father" will drift on into a series of powerful and disturbing associations, for example, invoking the implacable forces of restitution,[31] and the dark days of monarchy that populate Rome's legendary history.[32] These uncontrollable semiotic systems (divine forces, abandoned political models, mythic tropes) alienate *pater* from a straightforward, organized, and mature operating system, but Varro shows how to rethink this position, transforming and civilizing the violent, sexually dominant Iu-*pater* when he draws fatherhood into generative grammar.

Knowing something of the culturally constructive possibilities of Varro's grammatology is important for getting the most from Varro's *patricus* (genitive).[33] For a start, book 8 (arguing against Regularity) offers *pater* and *patres* (nominative singular and plural); "father" and "fathers" or, intuitively, "senators" (*Ling.* 8.48). The two are clearly of a family but at the same time are emblematic of how declension can be a process of orderly divergence, keeping alive a replicable relationship with a word's inflected clan. Yet jump just a little further ahead (*Ling.* 8.73) and one finds Varro unhappy with the inconsistent application of Regularity even by its staunch supporters, confronting the possessive family values of *pater familias* (in the light of what ought to be the regular declension scheme for a *familia*-type noun):[34]

> Cum dicatur da pat**ri** famili**as**, si analogias sequi uellent, non debuerunt dicere hic pat**er** famili**as**, quod est ut Atini**ae** Catini**ae** famili**ae**, sic una Atini**a** Catini**a** famili**a**. Item plures pat**res** famili**as** dicere non debuerunt, sed, ut Sisenna scribet, pat**res** famili**arum**. (Varro, *Ling.* 8.73)

> While "give to the father of the household" [dative] is said, if people really wished to follow Regularities they ought not to say *pater familias* [nominative plus genitive, both singular], because just as it is with "of Atinia," "of Catinia," so it should be *familiae* [genitive -ae], thus similarly with Atinia and Catinia [nominative singular], so *familia*. Likewise, they ought not to say the plural "fathers of a household" [nominative plural plus genitive singular], but as Sisenna writes: "fathers of households."

This passage shows how unpacking *pater familias* (this [nominative] head <of> family) demonstrates the role of *parole* in making sense of divergence from the norms of *langue*. Read in this way, it is therefore crucial to the whole Varronian program. Manifest in this passage is how *familias* emerges as a persisting archaic genitive form evoking the Greek genitive (singular, feminine), while the "correct" *familiae* gets the cold shoulder. Through this anomalous familial genitive in -*as*, the compound formula points to a strangely reassuring persistence across Greco-Latin. It is a *longue durée* stability not matched by the shifting (if orderly, by-the-book) inflection of *pater*.

A curious reader might wonder at Varro's decision to illustrate the nonargument with the family names Atinia and Catinia. Sorting the one from the other, the *gens* Atinia was an old (for the most part) undistinguished plebeian one. Cicero mentions a branch from Aricia, and we might imagine the name conjures up an unshowy world of quotidian service to the res publica.[35] *Catiniae*, the matching second example of a supposedly regular family genitive, must be even more modest, since the name fails to survive. There is nothing especially interesting, it seems, in Atinia or Catinia, but to hammer out the result of (tongue-in-cheek?) support for *patres familiarum*, Varro makes L. Cornelius Sisenna (the opponent of Cicero in his breakthrough performance against Verres) his contemporary authority.[36] To follow Sisenna's argument, Varro hammers home, readers must (clumsily) imagine the form to embody many fathers representing an orderly plurality of diverse households or "families."

Themes linking Varro's *pater* and the gen(er)itive principle are part of a broader system of productive classification, and this is exemplified in *genus*. A fragment of Varro outlines the significance for the Romespeaker: "*potestatis nostrae est illis rebus dare genera, quae ex natura genus non habent*" (it is in our power to give gender [/identity/form/family/species] to those things that by nature have no gender [/identity/form/family/species]).[37] Corbeill cites this fragment as part of a sophisticated discussion by way of which he identifies *genus* as Varro's go-to grammatical *gender* term.[38] Aspects of De Lingua Latina do support that reading, for example, "*tria genera*" presented as masculine, feminine, and neuter (*Ling*. 9.57), or the tri-columnar grammar grid with each *genus* gendered (*Ling*. 10.22).[39] But, as *Ling*. 9.57 also demonstrates, Varro's *genus* seems to be about more than just gender; it provides the means to undertake high-level and epistemologically complex triage for verbs as well as nouns and adjectives.[40]

Words do, in Varro, participate in "a biology of sexual reproduction,"[41] but, as book 9 shows, the scheme has more overarching significance and wider interest than an etymological pun (*genus*, the gendering generator) might suggest. *Genus is* grammar, and its formalizing qualities in Varro operate biological kinship across every kind of word, even where grammatical gender itself is not the primary quality at issue.[42] The kinship and familial qualities of Varro's *genus* imply an essential biological quality that implicates and embraces gender but does not always emphasize or depend upon it so much as it does the power to engender.[43] *Genus* (signaling "parent" or "begetter" slightly ahead of "father"), although a male-flavored common noun, still allows both sexes to participate in fashioning the Romespeaking clan, even if paternal efforts and creativity are expected to be the most potent.

By the time Varro gets to book 10, through-readers should be sensitive to paternity's potential resonances. The *pater* of book 10 is as much a grammatical marker as the representative of the relationship between language, family and identity:

Nam nunnunquam alterum ex altero uidetur, ut Chrysippus scribit, quemadmodum pater ex filio et filius ex patre, neque minus in fornicibus propter sinistram dextra stat quam propter dextra*m* sinistra. (Varro, *Ling.* 10.59)[44]

For it's not out of the question that the one [form] can be recognized from the other, as Chrysippus writes, just as the father from the son and the son from the father; and no less in arches does the right side stand firm on account of the left than the left on account of the right.

Lest we take this too seriously, there's a vein of humor. Fathers and sons, elements in a self-sustaining generative system, meld with an iconic Roman architectural form, the *fornix*. It takes two (sides), Varro memorably observes, to maintain the erection (*sto*). The smuttiness is not only concretized in the proud curves of the *fornix* but also embodied in the popular association between prostitution and the arcades, or underground vaults.[45] Analogy makes this happen because, as Varro has told us, when we see one element of a (semiotic) couple, we may see a whole different thing. A son's ability to refract and reflect his father is particularly piquant in the context of Cicero's professional insistence on the significance of the father-son relationship (explored with gusto by James May) in his often bawdy and viciously funny speech in defense of M. Caelius Rufus, a decade or so earlier.[46] If the joke works, Varro's scenario also emphasizes how family relationships are not always without their kinks and that each generation has something to offer to the other.[47]

A relationship between father and son is obvious, but what about Rome's national family tree, a construct very much in the air in the mid-first century? *De Lingua Latina* 5, for instance, recounts Rome's Trojan origins as a follow-up to an account of Latium's Etruscan city foundation rituals, in the process creating a Latio-Etruscan environment for Rome, a city whose *pomerium* traces its roots to Etruscan practice.[48] The stemma emphasizes the place of Latin civilization in enabling Rome's descent:

Oppidum quod <u>primum conditum</u> in <u>Latio stirpis Romanae</u>, Lauinium: nam **ibi** dii Penates nostri. **Hoc** a <u>Latini</u> filia, quae coniuncta Aeneae,

Lavinia, appellat*u*<m>.⁴⁹ **Hinc** post triginta annos oppidum alterum <u>conditur</u>, Alba; **id** ab sue alba nominatum. **Haec** e naui Aeneae cum fu<g>isset Lauinium, triginta parit porcos; ex **hoc** prodigio post Lauinium <u>conditum</u> annis triginta **haec** <u>urbs facta</u>, propter colorem suis et loci naturam Alba Longa <u>dicta</u>. **Hinc** mater <u>Romuli</u> Rhea, ex **hac** Romulus, **hinc** <u>Roma</u>. (Varro, *Ling.* 5.144)

The town which was <u>first founded</u> of the <u>Roman genealogy</u>, in <u>Latium</u>, was Lavinium: for **there** are our Penates. **This** was named from the daughter of <u>Latinus</u> who was wedded to Aeneas: Lavinia. **From this**, after thirty years, another town <u>was founded</u>: Alba. It was named from the white sow. **This one**, when she had escaped from Aeneas' ship to Lavinium, gave birth to thirty piglets. It was from **this** prodigy, thirty years after the foundation of Lavinium, that **the other** <u>city was established</u>—on account of the color of the sow and the nature of the place <u>it was called</u> Alba Longa.⁵⁰ **From here**, the mother of <u>Romulus</u>, Rhea; **from her**, Romulus, **from him**, <u>Rome</u>.

Varro's emphatic use of demonstratives hammers out a deep sense of connectivity in the story, very different from any straightforward relationship between father and son. He starts by saying that, in the first place, this is all about a town in Latium. Latium is the first site of a foundation that can be called distinctively Roman in retrospect, a land from which a Roman genealogy can be traced.⁵¹ Latium is steeped in family, not political, organizational tropes: it delivers (father) Latinus, a daughter, a son-in-law, and their shared "family" (the matronymic Lavinium stands in here for an offspring, paralleling the prodigious white sow whose babies determine when the next generation—Alba Longa—will emerge and what it will recall). Rhea, Romulus, and Rome all follow swiftly (*hinc, hac, hinc*).⁵²

The distinctively grammatical significance of family, as Rome developed a literate and more obviously contemporary identity, comes through clearly if we turn to *Ling.* 6.69. Here, Varro draws a connection between the impersonal notion of promising (*spondere*) and the individuated, first-person conjugated form ("*Spondere est dicere spondeo, a sponte*") and ties it to *uoluntas*—making promises is a manifestation of one's own inclination.⁵³ This calls two quotations to Varro's mind (*itaque*). The first, ascribed to Lucilius, paraphrases a supposedly sexy interlude where a "Cretan woman" (read "nymphet")⁵⁴ willingly accompanies "the author" home for some bedroom action; he is on a promise, she is flinging off all her clothes ("*ut tunicam et cetera*"): all of course her own idea. Varro's second instance quotes from Terence: better "by one's own inclination to do right than out of fear of another."[55] The two allusions more or rather less amusingly and economically illustrate the grainy quality of desire, inclination, "face," and social norms.

Taking Lucilius' grubby anecdote first:

Itaque Lucilius scribit de Cretaea, cum ad se cubitum uenerit sua uoluntate, sponte ipsam suapte adductam, ut tunicam et cetera reiceret. (Varro, *Ling.* 6.69)

That's why Lucilius writes of the Cretan "nymphet" that when she had come home with him willingly for bedroom action, by that same inclination she was led on to throw off her tunic, and all the rest.

The comedy eagerness in the telling is hammed up by the alliterative quality of the paraphrase's "*cum ad se cubitum uenerit sua uoluntate*," the echoing third-person pronouns, and the punning charge of *uenio*—a wordplay in the air, as noted more seriously by Cicero.[56] But, by hinting that this is a "good-time gal," the citation undermines the synonymous solemnity of Varro's own "*a sponte*" and "*a uoluntate*," conjured up at the beginning of the segment. As scripted, "she" is neither capable of serious, informed free will nor a suitable candidate for socially binding promises; in thrall instead to *uoluntas*, connoting sexual willfulness, she's coming because she really wants to.

The quotation from Terence's *Adelphoe* alludes to a different kind of fundamental relationship: that between generations, specifically regarding the role of nature versus nurture. Micio is speaking, an indulgent "father" and man about town whose upbringing of his nephew Aeschinus emphasizes openness and freedom of behavior as socially enhancing traits.

Eandem uoluntatem Terentius significat, cum ait satius esse:
 Sua sponte recte facere quam alieno metu.
(Varro, *Ling.* 6.69)

That same "desire" is what Terence means when he says that it is better:
 By inclination to do right, than from fear of another.

The face-off here is between keeping true to oneself (oneself as an individual and one's shared self within a community) ("*sua sponte*") and acting in response to fear of the "other" (*alienus*). In the *Adelphoe*, famously premiered in 106 at the funeral games of one of Rome's great heroes, L. Aemilius Paullus Macedonicus, Terence was parading a kind of systemic breakdown in family ethics for the entertainment and scrutiny of a diverse crowd, all set to recognize an exceptional paterfamilias, to applaud his sons' pietas, and (in effect) to acclaim the successful transmission of auctoritas and public service from one generation to the next.[57] As argued by Matthew Leigh, there is a particular piquancy to this juxtaposition of Greek plot and Roman "history" in the making, set against adoptive sons and (in oblique ways) zealous fathers. Moreover, Terence was an author extensively quoted by Cicero.[58]

With that in mind, when Varro puts these two poetic quotations back to back, he allows the sexy Cretan woman, who openly and artlessly (or so it seems) indulges her desires and sheds her clothes, to reverberate against the plot of Terence's comedy. The punchline for the *Adelphoe* is the discombobulation of Micio (the "father" who sets the scene in prologue fashion, *Adel.* 38–80, and who works the educative line that openness in everything leads to ingenuousness and personal integrity) by the apparent triumph of Demea. Demea closes the play with his ostentatious parade of hard living and tough love, thereby capturing the hearts from overly easygoing, generous Micio (*Adel.* 985–95). Yet this valedictorian is at heart a sophist. Aeschinus, the drifter-son who might have seemed naturally suited to the mores of Lucilius' escapade and thus Varro's context, eventually drifts back to the virtuous rigor paraded by his natural father, Demea. But it is Demea's skillful understanding of self-fashioning in verse, rather than any real moral substance, that delivers the triumph for his authoritarian model.[59]

Leigh's conclusions highlight an interplay between the roles of the general and that of the father in Terence's drama and add significantly to Varro's potential frame of reference.[60] For a start, Varro's quoted tagline is the payoff for Micio's first assertion of what makes a great father; the line after Varro's selection continues: "*hoc pater et dominus interest. Hoc qui nequit | fateatur nescire imperare liberis*" (this is what separates a father from a lord and master. The man who can't do this | should admit that he doesn't know how to rule [/govern] children, *Adel.* 76–77). A little earlier, the topos was initiated when Demea commented that "he's way wide of the mark, in my book, who believes that power [*imperium*] grounded in force is weightier and more stable than that which is annexed [*adiungo*] through ties of friendship" (*Adel.* 65–67).

The parental slave driver, closing down free will, is a vivid figure in Roman culture, but this is not what transforms Varro's bundle of inferences into a coherent whole.[61] The killer moment must be when the well-schooled reader (like Aemilius Paullus' famously well-educated sons, or Cicero) realizes that

Varro has for some time been working around to a new way of looking at a *triumphator*'s authority, since, in fact, the bundle of etymologies that immediately precedes this cluster and that sets the scene somatically for the clamor of battle and the roar of the parade—this is a sequence (*Ling.* 6.67–68), digging into the interplay between ethos and ethnicity in language, that has surfaced repeatedly in my study.

Summing up on Varro's two quotations and their implications, the theme of family connections is crucial, and it is in verse that this is most powerfully expressed and reified. It straddles those bonds that are fixed (by birth) and voluntary (desire, inclination, marriage, and, perhaps via the performance context for *Adelphoe*, adoption) and encompasses parental responsibility as well as filial and legal social networks. As the text continues, whereas the quote from Terence hinted at a father's role in fashioning his sons—through education, example, and natural or legal filiation—the next example explicitly addresses the role of daughters in adding texture to the sociolinguistic fabric. We saw "girls" feature as sexual adventurers or scenery for Lucilius and Terence (*Ling.* 6.69); Varro's next segue introduces the promise of a bride but also the money that goes with her.

Despite requiring (minor) emendation through sections 69–72, Varro's subject matter (girls, marriage, and the attendant social contracts) effectively bridges the domains of domesticity and civic life and uses verse to bring the explanations to life. First, when he illustrates the financial package involved in a betrothal, he bounces off a Naevian allusion about mutual promissory arrangements ("*consponsi*") bundling daughters and dowries. "Were money or a daughter 'promised' [*spondebatur*] on account of a marriage," he observes, "both the money and the girl who had been 'pledged' [*desponsa erat*] were called 'pledged' [*sponsa*]; the money that had been demanded as mutual surety against breach of promise was called a guaranteeing-deposit [*sponsio*]"; the man to whom the pledge was made was called "betrothed" (*sponsus*), while the day on which the promise was made was the "betrothal day" (*sponsalis*).[62]

Next, a tag from comedy gives a perhaps plaintive, fragmentary demand (or threat) illustrating the familial, emotional shifts that the betrothal of a daughter incurs: "do you promise your daughter to my son as a wife?"[63] What follows suggests that the matter is bound up in a psychodrama offstage: Varro hints at broken promises and equates "selling" one's soul with the betrothal of a daughter ("*Sic despondisse animum quoque dicitur, ut despondisse filiam*") because both acts mark the limits of voluntary autarky ("*quod suae spontis statuerat finem*").[64] Building new family ties requires dialogue and reciprocity. "To respond" (*respondeo*), Varro states, is to engage in a positive dialogue; one cannot

A Family Affair   199

"respond" by saying "no" (that would simply be a negation, not a response), so any real response is a positive entanglement, and means you're done (as an individual).[65] On one level this material riffs further on the formulas that bind individuals and families in marriage, but it is also about ethos and intentionality. If said as a joke ("*si iocandi*"), *respondeo* has no legal force, and this filters into the seriocomedy of drama with a quote echoing in counterpoint the previous comedic tag about matrimony ("don't you remember that you promised your daughter to me?").[66]

Familiarizing the Divine

In the previous section of this chapter I explored (humanocentric) genealogical matters, initially crossing Varro's interest in the discourse-enriching possibilities of verse quotation with his enthusiasm for how grammar intersects with mythography. In this section, the "family" theme returns, but with specific reference to the webs of relativity linking Varro's gods. Varro maps a primordial cosmography onto an extended family of creator-gods,[67] who reinforce the world-forming and totalizing qualities of grammar and syntax. Gods are everywhere (because generation/inflection is) in Varro's verbal universe, so my discussion could never be an exhaustive treatment. Instead, this section focuses on one run of etymologies, starting at *Ling.* 5.57 and ending with a syncretic roundup at 5.74.[68]

First, consider the gradual deconstruction of primal forces into acculturated characters. This is a scheme that Varro commences with Venus (a product of heavenly fire and earthly water; recall how the political resonances of this Venus featured in chapter 2) and follows up with Saturn.[69] Whereas Venus represented a literal combination of the primal elements and their personae, a new way of beginning, Saturn (once, Latium's king) is instead by definition and association more pragmatic in his associations.

Quare quod caelum principium, ab <u>satu</u> est dictus <u>Saturnus</u>, et quod ignis, <u>Saturnalibus</u> cerei superioribus mittuntur. Terra <u>Ops</u>, quod hic omne <u>opus</u> et hac <u>opus</u> ad uiuendum, et ideo dicitur <u>Ops</u> mater, quod terra mater. Haec enim
      Terris gentis omnis peperit et resumit denuo,
quae
      Dat cibaria,
ut ait Ennius, quae
      Quod <u>gerit</u> fruges, <u>Ceres</u>;
antiquis enim quod nunc G C.[70] (Varro, *Ling.* 5.64)

From whence, because the sky is the first principle, it's from <u>sowing</u> that <u>Saturn</u> was named; and because it's also fire, thus at <u>Saturnalia</u> wax-lights are proffered to those higher up. The earth is Ops, because here is every "<u>work</u>," and this place is the <u>prerequisite</u> for living; and therefore <u>Ops</u> is termed "mother," because of mother earth. For she is the one who
    In lands and peoples all has produced and receives them back again, she who
    Doles out the rations,
as Ennius says, who is,
    Because she <u>bears</u> the fruit, <u>Ceres</u>;
For in the language of long ago, what is now "G" was "C."

Saturn is the agent of generation, rather than simply a passive (falling, unstoppable) force, as Venus was in her origins. His sexy masculinity—like that of "seedy" Jupiter (*Ling.* 5.65)—is all about "sowing," designed to fulfill Earth's need. In Saturn's gang, sexual reproduction is part of the vigor that civilization requires. It is his illuminating power, marking the dark-days festival Saturnalia and associating it with a new domesticated fire, that allows civilization to make it through the winter. Being human also means being terrestrial, and the labor embodied in Saturn and his relationship with Earth is neatly characterized in the play on Ops and *opus*. The motif of Saturn producing new life by burying seed in the earth meshes with the Ennian quotations in which burying is crucial to the end as well as the beginning of life, literally and metaphorically.[71]

The morphological slippage behind the punningly named (*Ger-*) Ceres underlines the difficulty in unpicking the various shifting identities in play for these primal deities. One might expect something rather more canon-forming from Varro, but, rather than wanting these passages to stand in for the authority of something like his *Antiquitates Rerum Diuinarum*, readers can enjoy the tangled complexity that he offers as a species of find-the-word game. That Varro sees the disjunction between naming, scientific enquiry, and ideation is one way of reading his decision to confront readers next with Sky and Earth. As he goes on to say, they have yet more guises to model: they are Jupiter and Juno. "Jupiter is," according to Ennius, "the one whom the Greeks call Air: he's the wind and the clouds and the following rain, and out of the rain he returns as cold, wind, then back to air."[72]

Introducing Ennius (*Ling.* 5.66) extends Rome's claim over the semiotic range of *Iupiter* (in fact, Juno does not feature in the Ennian evidence presented at this point; her "proof" must wait until Varro has fully fixed Jupiter's network). Varro has previously ascribed an authenticity to Ennian usage that suggests some sympathy with the religio-scientific mashup quoted, but the convergence of the two worldviews is uneasy. Connecting *pater* etymologically to *patefacio* (Varro's next gambit; we touched on this in the previous section) introduces what seems to be an acknowledgment, perhaps a wry one, of the dissonance between the scientific perspective and Ennius' down-home Jupiter, who assists rustics and urbanites alike: "*Hoc idem magis ostendit antiquius Iouis nomen*" (this shows the same thing, only more so: the ancient name of Jupiter).[73] With this, Varro proposes a cosmic connection available to the etymologically skilled, one that can smooth over the epistemological gaps: long ago ("*nam olim*"), he says, Jupiter was called *Diouis* and *Diespater* (that is, *Dies Pater* or Father Day). This shows readers that old-school Romans too understood that personification was a mode of understanding rather than reality itself. From this old equation between day and production, Varro continues, *dei* and *dius* and *diuum* (deities, god, sky: the whole thing!) get their names.

Dius Fidius (Good Faith) exists as a spinoff from Father Day/Jupiter via this minicatalog; this *diuum*, which is the *caelum* (sky), needs open air where invoked, even if by the cheat of having a temple with holes for making the sky visible from within (*Ling.* 5.66). Varro deploys Aelius to emphasize the strength of the relationship between this deity and Jupiter and to re-engage with the wider issue of religious syncretism. It is on Aelius' authority that Romans can understand this god to be son of Diouis in the same manner as the Greeks name Castor "Zeus-son," yet in Sabine, Dius Fidius maps onto Sancus; in Greek, to Hercules. Finally, it is a small hop for Varro to draw a line to *Dispater* (playing around with Dis, Pluto) and thus to return the story to where all things return—the earth as a consuming force and finisher of life's beginnings (*ortus*), thus (by oppositional association) Orcus.[74]

Recognizing and appropriately naming a deity or an aspect of a deity is crucial, and the complex outlined here shows Varro gently acknowledging how different words, from different languages and sociopolitical contexts, often fail to map precisely back and forth from discourse to cosmos. The world really does look different, has a different flavor of reality, depending on one's cultural roots. As Cicero puts it:

> Come now: do we hold that the gods are named in these very words [*uocabulis*] by which they are named by us [*a nobis nominatur*]? First, as many as there are languages [*linguae*] among humans, so many are the names [*nomina*] of the gods; for it is not as it is with yourself—"Velleius" wherever you are—that Vulcan in Italy is thus the same in Africa and in Spain. (Cic. *Nat. D.* 1.83–84)

A Roman and a Latin speaker is always himself (it would seem), but comprehensively mapping names and entities metalinguistically is a challenge that Cicero's interlocutors do acknowledge.[75] Varro's underlying cosmological principles must, in this sense, be exploring the blurring and value-deadening potential of unreflective syncretism. If it were simply the case that x = y deity, for example, then the power of command over one coherent semiotic system would be significantly diminished. Difference would no longer be intrinsically of interest, and the role of the scholar and intellectual would become merely of curiosity value, if even that.

So (returning briefly to one of Varro's earlier comments) when Harpocrates gestures for silence, there is a real urgency to judging the extent to which Varro can or might choose to develop these cross-cultural analogies.[76] If it is the case that "gods' names are subject to the processes of coinage and borrowing and the vagaries of usage that [Varro] so meticulously documents regarding everyday words," as Clifford Ando suggests, then "the semantic problem rests with the naming of gods in the first place, and with the epistemic foundation upon which practices of naming must rely."[77] Perhaps if one has Varro as a guide, the "problem" becomes a point of interest and ultimately part of the solution.

To draw this set of strands together, Varro has made clear that "Jupiter" is one way of signaling the entity similarly referenced as Saturn (like sky, a "beginning"), Sky, Father Day, and Serapis, but his *haecitas* as "Jupiter" is solidly Roman and pragmatic; he is a "helping" god (as represented in Ennius, cited earlier) and, because Juno is his consort, she becomes a particularly nuanced Earth (as well as answering to Isis). Family matters.

Varro's discussion of Juno (*Ling.* 5.57, 67) has a circularity. She is Juno *and* Earth, because Jupiter is her husband and also Sky, but she is *named* Juno because together with Jupiter "she helps" (*iuuat*), and she is queen because all earthly things are hers—*rex* was not, however, offered as an option for her consort (*Ling.* 5.67). From Juno, Varro turns briskly to Sun and Moon.

By way of a *uel . . . uel* construction, Varro's *Sol* is either a Sabine migrant or (as the "solitary" god) a Latinate coinage (*Ling.* 5.68). In narrative terms, Sol develops and particularizes the theme of daylight (after Father Day), while Moon points up the different kinds of skyey luminance nature proffers.[78] Moon is, however, the only night-shiner mentioned in this context ("*uel quod sola lucet noctu*"). Stars do not feature, and the logic might be related to Varro's decision to develop the etymology in a particular direction:

Itaque ea dicta <u>Noctiluca</u> in Palatio: nam ibi <u>noctu lucet</u> templum. (Varro, *Ling.* 5.68)

Therefore [Moon] is called <u>Shines-by-Night</u> on the Palatine: for there, <u>by night</u>, her "temple" <u>shines</u>.

The focused gaze skyward that a *templum* conjures up means that what falls within its confines, the signs to which it might relate, are distinctively codified. Stars do not exist for the purpose of this *templum*, and by transference the permanent physical space on the Palatine to which Varro seems to refer becomes a kind of beacon in its own right.[79] This Romano-Sabine moon has a compatriot in the guise of Diana, but, whereas Diana can be paired with Apollo, Varro emphasizes that "Apollo" is a Greek word while "Diana" is Latin. Here, the term "Latin" helps elide the Roma-Latium dissonance, and in breaking the familial pairing by ethnicity Varro excludes Apollo emphatically.

Diana Trivia (at *Ling.* 7.16) offers multifarious possibilities; in the coinage *Diuiana* (for Moon) Varro seems to be switching on some of the same ideas that will be reconceptualized in a cosmic sense in this triad's final book. The Moon's range is high and wide,[80] setting the scene for the later crossroads association. This ability to face different ways is shaded by an Ennian observation: the moon has an existence below ground, where she is Proserpina, the creeping serpent (supported by a line from Plautus), following a convoluted but ultimately regular trajectory. Absent, however, is any allusion to Greek Persephone.

Readers might well wonder where Varro is heading. The answer makes structural sense: under- and overground Proserpina-Moon has another guide, Juno (*Ling.* 5.69). Thus, Varro cleverly ends this set of etymologies by leading his audience back to the place it was before Sun and Moon (*Ling.* 5.67), drawing the two sets of deities together. Juno Lucina, an ethnically Latin way of signaling the Moon, seems to be rooted in one of two possible explanations: either the fact that for Latins (and, he suggests, natural scientists, *physici*) Moon is a facet of Earth (thus, Juno) and she shines (*lucet*) or because her changing shape and transit map time, and (specifically) make time a reproductive quality. From conception to birth, lunar time, not solar, is crucial; measuring the months (and phases of the moon) from conception to emergence into the metaphorical (or literal) light of another moon locates this form of origin story within an intelligible and predictable taxonomy. So, like Juno, the Moon is a "helping" deity (rooted in *iuuo*) and an illuminating one (*lux*), and thus *of course* the two are connected.

The etymology is a nice one, but its intense focus on wordplay and Latin originality might give pause. Especially when we reach the final lunar phase:

> Hoc uidisse antiquas apparet, quod mulieres potissimum supercilia sua attribuerunt ei deae. Hic enim debuit maxime collocari Iuno <u>Lucina</u>, ubi ab diis <u>lux</u> datur oculis. (Varro, *Ling.* 5.69.)

Evidently, old-time women spotted this, because wives in particular have made over their eyebrows to that goddess. For in this respect Juno Lucina ought especially to be lodged where light is given by the gods to the eyes.

The quirky yet intelligible and homespun quality of this story of family life jars with the more straightforwardly academic tone of what precedes, and the hint of the dressing table and the vanity set is made all the stronger by the overtones of offended virtue lurking in *supercilium*.[81] The gods grant light, but the eyebrows, accredited to Juno, provide the comfort (and perhaps seclusion) of shade and keep the all-important eyes out of the clarity of full light.

A different sort of gift of light comes next: fire (*Ling.* 5.70). "Light" and especially the idea of (blazing) light as a divine gift might raise expectations of Prometheus, but this etymology is about the physical quality of fire as a burning, violent life force. The Sun (or Apollo) lurks in the notion of fire as the animating principle, without which, darkness and death; Varro instead signposts the fierce uncontrollability of fire: from *uis ac uiolentia* Vulcan was named. Vulcan recurs in Varro's list of altars that are redolent of Sabine language[82] and that trace their foundation to King Tatius (*Ling.* 5.74)—we return to this shortly—and he also crops up when (along with some more obscure deities) he helps distinguish one group of *flamines* from another (*Ling.* 5.84); at *Ling.* 6.20 the Volcanalia makes for a fiery test of the biddability of animals (driven over a fire); finally at *Ling.* 7.11 his hilltop *templa* help mark up the wildness theme for "temple."

Blazing Vulcan develops Varro's overarching theme (that is, the primordial gods and their linguistic ontology) by mapping an attribute of Jupiter (thunderbolt-wielding god) onto the good old *local* boy: from what a blaze does (*fulget*), he assimilates *fulgor* (lightning flash) and *fulmen* (thunderbolt) and the flash of one zapped by a thunderbolt (*fulgur*).[83] This convergence between Vulcan (as a personification of fire's violence) and Jupiter's iconic thunderbolt (part of the remit of Sky, albeit not included by Varro) leads oppositionally to *Lymphae* (water nymphs) and in particular to one: Juturna (*Ling.* 5.71). Varro's occlusion of νύμφη, by swapping an "L" for an "N," allows him to proffer a sympathetic derivation based on water's "slippery sliding."

This situates the etymology associatively in the territory of the wide-ranging, wayfaring moon and the wriggling serpent, and both of course were tropes associated with a "helping" deity. So when Varro turns to one particular "lymph" Juturna (*Iuturna*), it barely causes a ripple that her name is from her "helping" function ("*quae iuuaret*"; like Juno) rather than from her waters. Her spring (and there is no reason to assume that her spring and shrine in the Forum are not what Varro has in mind) is a place of pilgrimage for the sick who seek help. From here, etymologies proceed for named water sources and their flow, and from these, directly, gods are named. Varro's examples are Tiberinus, Velinia (from a Sabine lake), and the *Commotiles* or "Restless" nymphs of the Cutilian Lake near Varro's own Reate, which has its own floating island.

Water sources are related neatly to <u>Ne</u>ptune ("because the sea 'veils' [ob<u>nub</u>it] the lands as clouds [*nubes*] do the sky," *Ling.* 5.72), and Varro tacks on some associatively maritime deities. Next, Bellona, then Mars is wheeled out either as the leader of men (*mares*) in war or because (*aut quod*) in Sabine speech he is Mamers (*Ling.* 5.73)—a new way of considering Mars' generative role for Rome. Varro has no need explicitly to discount *mares*: the Sabines favor Ma(me)rs, and the next juxtaposition ("*Quirinus a Quiritibus*"), added to the inclusion of a gaggle of honorable manly qualities associated with leadership, masculinity, and public service, frames this material in terms of service and duty and Italic roots. The burdensome nature of honor reverberates through the quoted line, perhaps proverbial, "onerous is the honor which maintains the state."[84] From here it will be a short textual jump to Varro's helpful siblings, Castor and Pollux: Castor simply is a Greek name (readers are now given to understand), while the form Pollux has migrated and successfully transformed. Once upon a time, Latin orthography had Polluces, like Pollideuces, not Pollux. This kind of harmonious (fraternal, between *paroles*) alliance is of course embodied in Concordia (from "a heart in harmony"), to which Varro turns before shifting back to Sabine affairs.

A catalog of deities and altars redolent of Sabine language and foundation by Tatius (as noted earlier in this section) keeps the focus Italian; Tatius' dedication keeps resonating, ensuring that the tang of otherness persists, but particularly significant is how Varro closes out this discussion:

> E quis nonnulla nomina in utraque lingua habent radices, ut arbores quae in confinio natae in utroque agro serpunt: potest enim Saturnus hic de alia causa esse dictus atque in Sabinis, et sic Diana, de quibus supra dictum est. (Varro, *Ling.* 5.74)

From these [the list of Tatius' Sabine-scented deities], some names have roots in either language, just as trees that are born on the boundary creep between the fields: for he can be termed Saturn here, but for another reason altogether among the Sabines, and thus Diana; about these two, the discussion is above.

This passage's tricky roots, working away to a subterranean arboreal agenda, recall readers to an underlying authenticity that Romespeak develops. Varro's ongoing interest in highlighting the need to dig for meaning in order to develop a joined-up community able to speak to its own and others' pasts is vividly evoked here. This is not an argument for boundary-blind multiculturalism, I suggest, rather an example of testing a distinctive position: points of distinction and difference need not undermine community.

Beginning Chronology

Chapter 4 considered the contextual richness of Varro's explanation of time as a grammatical principle of organization, and time connects grammar, syntax, and lived experience for even the simplest community. The human consequences of developing hierarchies (and thus "sequence") occupied much of chapter 6. Very early in book 6, Varro signals how he connects time, language, and ontology:

> In hoc dicam de uocabulis temporum et earum rerum quae in agendo fiunt aut dicuntur cum tempore aliquo. . . . Dicemus primo de temporibus, *t*um quae per ea fiunt, sed ita ut ante de **natura** eorum: ea enim **dux** fuit ad uocabula imponenda homini. . . . Id **diuisum** in partes aliquot **maxime ab** solis et lunae **cursu**. Itaque **ab eorum** <u>tenore temperato tempus</u> dictum, unde **tempestiua**; et a <u>mot*u*</u> eorum qui toto caelo coniunctus <u>mundus</u>. (Varro, *Ling.* 6.1, 3)

> In this [book] I shall speak about the vocabulary of times, and of those matters that come about through being put into action or are verbalized with some time factor [i.e., verbs; which have tenses]. . . . We shall talk first about times, then about those things that come about through them, but in such a way as first to speak about their <u>essential qualities</u>: for that was the **commanding officer** for humankind in the imposition of vocabulary. . . . [Time] is **divided** into several parts, **notably by the course** of the sun and the moon. Therefore from their **tempered tenor time** is named; whence **timely things**. And from their <u>motion</u>, that which is bound together with the whole sky: the <u>world</u>.

Varro's military metaphor is nuanced by civic imperatives that connect human understanding of a life's course with the passage of celestial time—the course (*cursus*) of sun and moon.[85] This *cursus* might reimagine ambitious families jostling phenomenologically for place in Roman politics; the emphatic alliteration highlights how this *cursus* has the power to parcel up the world.[86]

In an almost throwaway inclusion, *mundus* (from *motus*) emphasizes Rome's paradigmatic potential.[87] In the process, the semiotics of *mundus* sweep readers from dressing-table glamour ("*mundus . . . a munditia*," *Ling.* 5.129) to the new book's cosmic concerns.[88]

Day (*Ling.* 6.4), Jupiter's business in book 5, in this case is a measurable product of human calibration and a positive instance of technocracy. The *techne* behind sundials exemplifies the measurement of time as a feature of complex civilization, and Varro's sundial shows what is shared but also (by way of ancient morphological divergence) what is uniquely acculturated in this process. The ancient type of sundial remains sufficient for Praeneste,[89] whereas Rome innovates (as Varro tells it), as is evident in the famous water clock set up by "Cornelius" as a feature at the Basilica of Aemilius and Fulvius almost 150 years before. A Roman solution, in this model, is also indicative of the significance of bundled family names not just to articulate depth of historicity but also as a marker for continuity allied to change. A long-gone Cornelius archetype sponsored a civic monument with the power to make irregular phenomena part of an intelligible system. Thus, a memorable and famous family name makes sun and water, in moderation guarantors of flourishing agriculture, tell civic time for a sophisticated polity, a process that also has implications for *langue* and *parole*.[90] The unusual verb of foundation, *inumbro* (to cast a shadow, to mark with shade, to darken), adumbrates how the once radically novel water clock puts the old-fashioned but still practical low-tech gnomon and (sun)dial in the shade.

Of course, there remain times when time cannot be told, as readers see from what follows. Luckily and self-evidently, morning and day's end ("*suprema summum diei*") are straightforward once one has the concept of measuring a day sorted out. Varro proceeds by way of dusk (indeterminable yet intelligible) to how moon and stars rule the impenetrability of night (*Ling.* 6.5–7). With the hybridity of daily time, its embodiment in the peoples of Latium, its potential for monumentalization, and its Roman taxonomy in place, Varro proposes a change in perspective. This will mean examining the implacable and *Regular* natural forces that, like *analogia* for language formation, deliver coherent annalistic historicity: the annual solar cycle, whence from *anuli*, to *ani*—little to big "rings"—Varro arrives at the annual circuit, *annus* (*Ling.* 6.8) before narrowing focus again to the seasons and their characteristics (*Ling.* 6.9). In this version, readers gradually come to see that the vocabulary of the year has many of its roots in Rome, Latium, and Latin. The exceptions offered are Spring, where Varro recounts bushes (*uirgulta*) starting to turn green (*uirere*; unless *uiuere*, to live) as the year turns (*uertere*), unless (*nisi quod*, offering a less picturesque explanation) the Ionians' *uir* word is behind it; and second, Summer (*aestas*), from heat (*aestus*), whence summer pasture (*aestiuum*) is needed; unless (*nisi forte*) the much less positive "scorching," from Greek (αἴθεσθαι), is the source (*Ling.* 6.9).

The month's lunar story is ostentatiously different in taking readers immediately to Greece before offering the Latin as a transliteration: "*Luna quod Graece olim dicta μήνη, unde illorum μῆνες, ab eo nostri*" ("Moon," because in Greek it was *at one time* called μήνη, whence their "months," from this comes ours, *Ling.* 6.10). The problem of counting months and days in correct alignment with the seasons was only recently and partly resolved by Caesar. Varro's complex account hints at the need to acknowledge external, creative solutions to a problem not uniquely Roman. Perhaps for this reason Varro characterizes the Athenian approach to parsing lunar time as well-thought out (*diligentius*), a system of between-month days straddling the old and new moons, and ordering—while also acknowledging—the in-between quality of some times.

It is clear that the phenomenology of time involves thinking across cultures and languages and accepting a commonality in identifying which elements best signal and give structure to its passage. The humane factor is developed further in the artificial measure that follows: the *lustrum* (*Ling.* 6.11), bridging the gap between natural (or universal) and humane (political, variously flavored) chronologies. Varro comes up with a deeply civic account of the etymology in which it is all about the purging, releasing, or dissolving (*luo, soluo*) of accumulating taxes and tributes (*uectigalia, tributa*), as organized every five years by the censors.[91] Humanocentric too is *seclum*, the name attached to a hundred-year period that marked the longest an old man (*senex*) might be expected to live. Zooming out to a cosmic focus, eternity (*aeuum*) recalls readers to what links Romans directly to Greeks within a world in which (as one illustrative quote puts it) "not all of time is sufficient for deep learning"; the joke here is that Varro is quoting his frequent friend Plautus (*Truculentus, The Savage*) and has left out a crucial word that completes (or undermines) the sense: "*amanti*" ("for a lover")—in Plautus, the sense of "time" is as much (a lover's) "lifespan" as it is a gesture to eternity.

Wolves, Hares, and Fathers-in-Law

Despite the signposted division between books 5–7 and 8–10, the extant text represents a unity when read in the context of Varro's authorial agency and the narrative strands he uses to weave a thematic and structural series of patterns. In the preceding section of this chapter I explored ways in which Varro's etymologization of chronological vocabulary intersects subtly with his construction of good discourse as the product of a marriage between formal and vernacular modes. We can see this exemplified in a different way by reading his grammatology of family relations against two seemingly unrelated treatments where family nonetheless becomes thematically significant. To begin from an unusual association, I propose the three occasions in the extant *De Lingua Latina* where "wolf" and "hare" are paired.[92]

Varro's etymology for "hare" starts by taking *lepus* from a Sicilian (and Aeolian) Greek form, λέπορις (*Ling.* 5.101).[93] The suggestion looks like one of his more straightforward offerings, an instance of Latin transliterating Greek, but it triggers a substantial proposition concerning a historical relationship between peoples. Consultating the ancient annals, Varro observes, tells Romans that the Sicilians were from Rome, too ("*a Roma quod orti Siculi*"), and so maybe (*fortasse*) what looks like an evidently Greek root for "hare" disguises its potential to signify a formerly shared language in which Rome's site retains the ordinary position.

Hares, however, are rarely serious or civic in literature; at best, symbolization of erotic control is a likelier association.[94] So what difference might the hookup with the wolf make? The two animals, hare and wolf, are recurring characters in fable, a form that delights in creating a parallel world, one that holds up a playful and sometimes satirical didactic mirror. Aesopian fable typically delivers a punchline, but this kind of certitude is not how Varronian etymology works. Animals in fables do, however, enable a subtle exploration of different registers—take, for example, the talking creatures in Horatian satire—while also embracing their literary possibilities for interrogating the problematic or complex intellectual, political, even emotional cruxes of the urban animal.[95] Fabulous thinking at the points of intersection between ethics, identity, and behavior and between sense-speaking human and nonspeaking being makes sense in a context where plain speaking or Romespeaking is compromised.[96]

The heterogeneity of fable relates closely to satire, another of Varro's favored genres, but his hare-and-wolf team are initially an innocuous duo. Nevertheless, because of the unusualness of the pairing, readers might momentarily misread or expect the more obvious motif of a hare pursued by a dog. Ovid vividly embroiders this potentiality when he has Calliope recount her terror as she hid from Alpheus:

"perhaps it's as the <u>lamb</u> feels,
when it hears the **wolves** howling around the high folds,
or the **<u>hare</u>**, who hiding in the briars discerns the hostile
muzzles of the **dogs** and dares no movement of its body?"
Ovid, *Met.* 5.626–29

Ovid's formulation makes curiously iconic an odd kind of kinship between the terrified hare and the fearsome wolf because the encircling duo of lamb and dog make for an obvious practical farmer's pair.[97] The quartet is also interesting because the dog is both guardian of domestic animals and an animal of the chase, as Varro observed in his later work *De Re Rustica*. The dog wants to be off after the hare, but the hare too is of course a prized domestic resource. The sheepdog, in fact, is a natural opponent of his wild alter ego, the wolf, which in turn has no legendary animosity toward the hare.[98] Varro was later to make the "warren" (*leporarium*, apparently by then a retro poverty-chic name for an easy-pickings, managed game preserve, complete with deer and boar) a star turn for one of the interlocutors (Blackbird) in his countryside handbook.[99]

Varro's first pairing of "hare" and "wolf" illustrates the book 8 argument proposed by his anti-Regularity persona: "wolf" and "hare" make plain that from similar nominative forms, unlike the ideal model displayed in "good" and "bad,"[100] can appear dissimilarities in inflection (*Ling.* 8.34). Family ties do not necessarily make sense of reality. Completing the group, Priam and Paris are just dissimilar in every way, while the apparently unconnected "Jupiter" and "sheep" turn out to have a deeply dative (*dandi*) relationship. The same basic point is rehashed focusing on *surus* (stake), *lupus*, and *lepus* and their dative and ablative divergence; the odd inclusion here is *surus*, which seems to be unnecessary, unless included for the joke on Hannibal's famous elephant, Surus (*Ling.* 8.68).[101]

Finally (at *Ling.* 9.91), Varro's pro-Regularity persona bundles the Greek names Melicertes and Philomedes with "wolf" and "hare" but adds in "father-in-law" and "lean."[102] Book 9 presents a position that appears to be more appealing to Varro than the case he ostentatiously argued in book 8, and his treatment of the "vocative" dissimilarities on revisiting the point here is more personally nuanced than the equivalent passage in book 8.[103] How we form relationship-building speech can create coherence from what looks superficially like dissonance. For the two Greek names and for *lupus* and *lepus*, the vocative is still the case at issue; in the last pair, a tri- versus a bisyllabic genitive joins the mix. *Socer* (father-in-law) is a term that often crops up in Cicero's densely networked textual world.[104] It is not an uncommon term in itself, of course, but, given Catullan usage (where without any gloss his audience is expected to "get" that "*socer generque*" means Caesar and Pompey), readers in the know might find that the resonance continues to reverberate.[105]

It is, however, Quintilian, discussing reason, tradition, authority, and usage in language (and how Regularity fits in), who cements the significance of "hare" and "wolf" as a pair in Varro's *imaginaire*. The comments are a prelude to having some fun with Varronian "enthusiasm" (Quint. *Inst.* 1.6.32–38), but, in the context of taking a sardonic swipe at Varro's likely failure in convincing Cicero of his wilder flights of fancy, he observes:

> But we must remember that the model of Regularity [*analogiae*] cannot be applied across the board, since in many instances it contradicts itself. Without a doubt, certain among the erudite have tried to mount a defense. For example, when it is noted that "hare" and "wolf" are similar in form [in the nominative], yet in the other cases and the plural differ significantly, such people reply that they are not true parallel forms because "hare" is an epicene, while "wolf" is masculine. This, even though Varro, in the book in which he describes the beginnings of Rome, says "wolf" is feminine, in line with Ennius and Fabius Pictor. But those same scholars, when they were asked why "boar" and "father" make such different genitive forms, vigorously maintained that the one was a fixed, the latter a relative noun. What is more, since both were brought over from Greek, they resorted to the logic that πατρός makes for "*patris,*" and κάπρου, "*apri.*" (Quint. *Inst.* 1.6.12–13)

Reading Varro's "hare" and "wolf" only in this obvious context would encourage the kind of face-value literalism that Varro is at pains to dissuade. From Quintilian's perspective Varro's assiduity (and Quintillian here seems to ignore the set-piece quality of the arguments in *Ling.* 8 and 9) has simply led him down a one-way street into absurdity. With Ovid's creative example in the mix and in the context of fabulous thinking, it is Quintilian's by-the-book reading of Varro that emerges as formulaic and superficial (or, perhaps, vastly tongue in cheek).

In fact, Varro himself notes that the basic argument he is making can stand some extra weight and proceeds as follows:

> similia non solum a facie dici, sed etiam ab aliqua coniuncta ui et potestate, quae et oculis et auribus latere soleant. (Varro, *Ling.* 9.92)

> the likenesses in utterances are not only in form but also in some associated strength and power, which is usually hidden from eyes and ears.

These are not superficial connections, he says, or easy to ascertain: they speak to implicit power networks, nevertheless with real currency ("*ui et potestate*"). This assertion—in effect, that power lies in the capability to read and also to construe between the lines—is a bravura gesture in the context of the increasingly metapolitical nature of power in the 40s. When Varro associates this argument with the wolf-and-hare pair—predator and prey, but not of each other; both variously associated with the rescue of Romulus and Remus, thus also similar *and* dissimilar, like twins—he emphasizes the wider interest of strengthening what connects this twosome; this becomes apparent if we follow the father-in-law into book 10.[106]

Varro's concluding deployment of *socer* (the new factor in the argument from book 9) sits in book 10 (*Ling.* 10.28).[107] Context is everything:

> Ut actor stolam muliebrem sic Perpenna et Caecinna et <S>purinna figura muliebra dicuntur habere nomina, non mulierum.
>
> Flexurae quoque similitudo uidenda ideo quod alia uerba quam ui<a>m habeant ex ipsis uerbis, unde declinantur, apparet, ut quemadmodum oportet ut*i* praetor consul, praetori consuli; alia ex transitu intelleguntur, ut socer macer, quod alterum fit socerum, alterum macrum, quorum utrumque in reliquis a transitu suam uiam sequitur et in singularibus et in multitudinis declinationibus. Hoc fit ideo quod naturarum genera sunt duo quae inter se conferri possunt, unum quod per se uideri potest, ut homo et equus, alterum sine assumpta aliqua re extrinsecus perspici non possit, ut eques et equiso uterque enim dicitur ab equo. (Varro, *Ling.* 10.27–28)

As an actor in a woman's stola, so Perpenna, Caecinna, and Spurinna are said to have names that are womanly in form, not women's names.

The similarity of the inflexion needs also to be watched because some words hold to a path [reading *uiam*, not *uim*, force] that is evident in the very words themselves (that is from whence they decline)—as the way in which it is appropriate to use *praetor* and *consul* [nominative], (and then dative) *praetori*, *consuli*. Others are intelligible only through the process of transformation, such as in *socer* (father-in-law) and *macer* (lean) [nominative], where one becomes *socerum* and the other *macrum* (accusative); after the transition, each then follows its own path for the remaining forms, in singular and in plural inflections. It plays out thus for this reason, because there are two classes of natures that are comparable with each other: one that is self-evidently visible, such as in "man" and "horse," the other of which is imperceptible without bringing in something external [to the word(s)], such as in "horseman" and "stableboy," for both are spoken forms from "horse."

If through-readers look back to *Ling.* 8.81,[108] these figures have already taken on nominal comic force. In the wake of a girly-*looking* masculine Perpenn*a*, L. Aelia and Q. Mucia rub shoulders with various Greek island names, whose party trick, like that of the city of Athens, is conjuring up adjectival forms divorced from sociopolitical reality (Athenaeus the rhetorician *is not Athenian*!). Instead, what Varro makes possible is the switching on of a much more nebulous, allusive frame of reference.

Conclusion

This chapter picked up on the political hierarchies addressed in chapter 6 by reimagining the community at its most basic level, a family. If grammar is peculiarly "in the family," family itself is also best understood as possessing an odd kind of grammar. Family also has structural implications for the text: it recalls to our attention, as we meander through the etymological books (5–7), that a grammatical agenda is informing Varro's authorial decisions throughout. Declension and conjugation are not organizationally or thematically in opposition to etymology; instead, they are two complementary ways of thinking about teleology and derivation when marking Rome up. The patterns of inflection in which Varro is interested give him scope to represent language as a system of consensus formation that has its own ancestral values, its own *loci et imagines*, and its own closeted skeletons. We need to keep in mind that idea of trajectory, an optimistic process linking Romespeakers to their deepest roots but also locating them on the cutting edge of making the future possible. Varro returns repeatedly to the cycle of life for his examples, his figurative domain, and his exegesis of syntax. Varro's approach therefore showcases one version of the multidirectional outcomes resultant upon selecting, categorizing, and accommodating language(s) at a point of convergence.[109] Shaping what happens next, ensuring that what emerges really is Romespeak and that it retains and reenergizes a newly dynamic and rooted form, is where the didactic impulse in writing *De Lingua Latina* emerges.

chapter 8

Varro's *Fasti*

VARRO'S CALENDRICAL ETYMOLOGIES embroider the Roman year with culture-specific stories.[1] In the process of exploring Varro's *fasti* (and *nefasti*), this chapter shows in detail how Varro's year, complete with *lacunae* and intriguing omissions, can immerse readers in an episteme that was vividly, raucously omnipresent in the experience of everyday life.[2] Scholarship on Roman religion has tackled the factual quality of Varro's festivals with enthusiasm. This chapter instead re-injects some of the widest contextual possibilities, structuring a reading that explicitly divides Varro's festivals and distinctive days by calendar months. Denis Feeney's eloquent exploration of *Caesar's Calendar* has proved especially important to my throughreading, but I have also drawn substantially on the sine qua non, R. E. A. Palmer.[3]

Varro's interest in the functionalist and narrative qualities of marking time is evident in the contrasting types of festal etymologies that he selects and in his organization of the material (from fixed festivals to floating festivals and then day and month designators).[4] To reflect these sequences meaningfully and in the spirit of Varro's scholarly encyclopedism, I first present Varro's year in sequence through his cycle of fixed religious festivals. In the second section, I examine floating festivals, and in the third I turn to humanocentric calendrical vocabulary. A brief discussion of Varro's names for the months, presented in the fourth section, leads to some conclusions.

Initially striking in Varro's calendar are its apparent separation of civic from religious time and his decision to set the gods first, reversing his strategy in the *Antiquitates*, where (according to Augustine) Varro says that "just as there is a painter before there is any painting, a builder before a building, so city states exist before their civic institutions." For that Varro, matters (*res*) divine fell under "civic institutions" and thus had to be considered after human affairs.[5] *De*

Lingua Latina's deconstruction and reimagination of the two-pronged approach taken in his landmark *Antiquitates* (the work Cicero suggested had "led us home," *Acad.* 1.9) makes no concessions to an audience unsure of how and why the civic and religio-natural years might be storyboarded differently. What it does, in echoing and reversing Varro's own earlier scheme, is emphasize a dialogue between human and divine in the maintenance of order and balance and in the substance of life and community.

For Feeney, Varro has no "instinctive reflex to conceive of the civil operations and the natural operations as a duet . . . [and] the opportunity to make a meaningful connection between the state's calendar and the operations of the natural cycle of the year is not taken up."[6] Yet in the *Antiquitates* Varro had already made clear that the two, in Rome at least, are inextricably linked: a Roman manifestation of gods and divine affairs will inevitably be a Roman construct, telling on every aspect of the Roman experience and mind-set.

When Varro returns to the topic in *De Lingua Latina* and makes an organizational reversal, Cicero and others will surely have been alert to the implied contingency. He expects a reader who knows that whichever way one orders the treatments, both elements are clearly required for the whole to exist. This is especially true because Varro's model reader (Cicero) is already attuned to the necessary links between place, people, and environment that generate civic institutions and is to be further sensitized to the dialogic implications by means of the reversal of precedence in the conversation, as one text (the *Antiquitates*, so admired by Cicero) refreshes the next.[7]

Divine Days

Varro makes a programmatic beginning: "*dicam prius*" (I shall speak first, *Ling.* 6.12). Civic (*ciuilia*) temporal vocabulary will introduce and explain the festal days instituted for gods and then mankind. Drawing on the authoritative power of *dico*, explored across chapters 2 and 3, this deceptively straightforward structural assertion is all the explanation Varro offers, eliding the eventual need for clarification (*Ling* 6.25), evident when we discover that this first calendar sequence is specifically concerned with fixed-day festivals. Floating festivals make a separate cycle, and the gods, because their dedicated days feature first, shape the civic year (*Ling.* 6.12–26). Citizen time (say, making days *nefasti*, or Ides) will only fill out the system subsequently (*Ling.* 6.27–32) before the gods return to center stage (when etymologizing the months' names, *Ling.* 6.33–34) and close the narrative arc. For ease of navigation I have emboldened the festival names and provided standard dates to emphasize relational thinking for Varro's presentation of these events.

January

First, the **Dies Agonales** (*Ling.* 6.12) take readers to 9 January. This sequence of days (with the text quoted in full) cropped up in the context of *rex* in chapter 6. The *new* New Year joins the Priest King in Rome, at the "Palace," and witnesses a performance that recurs annually in January, March, May, and December (*De Lingua Latina* does not mention the recurrence).[8] Ovid's treatment will emphasize performance and struggle (*Fast.* 1.317–36); for Varro, this is all about the politics of how human systems shape the natural world. Thus, the leader of the herd is sacrificed by the leader of the state ("*a principe ciuitatis et princeps gregis immolatur*").[9]

In keeping with the sequence of fixed festivals, Varro moves next to Carmentis' days (**Carmentalia**—11, 15 January). The intervening Compitalia will not appear until the "floating" festivals (*Ling.* 6.25):[10]

> Carmentalia **nominantur** quod sacra tum et feriae Carmentis.
> Lupercalia **dicta**, quod in Lupercali Luperci sacra **faciunt**. Rex cum ferias menstruas Nonis Februariis **edicit**, hunc diem februatum **appellat**. (Varro, *Ling.* 6.12–13)

> The Carmentalia: **named** because that is when there are sacrifices and festivals of Carmentis.
> The Lupercalia: so **called** because in the Lupercal the Luperci **make** sacrifices. When the King **announces** the monthly festivals on the Nones of February, this day he **calls** *februatus*.

Varro's narrative hustles readers along with a colorless etymology, taking readers briskly to a more complex approach to the Lupercalia immediately after.

Almost Missing February

Varro's direct juxtaposition of Carmentis and the **Lupercalia** (15 February) elides the days of the Parentalia, which provided an occasion to revisit private grief and family history in a shared, communal context.[11] The dead eventually feature in Varro's February, but not until the later Feralia, in which they are restricted to their tombs as hosts for their descendants.

Like the Carmentalia, the Lupercalia opens blandly in Varro but becomes by contrast more complex in an extended contextualizing explanation.[12] Instead of a straightforward etymology or a legendary *causa*, this is a tale of biculturalism. When the Priest King pronounces the monthly festivals on the Nones of February, he terms this day *februatus*. Why? Varro's answer is that "*Februm*

Sabini purgamentum" (*februm* for the Sabines is "purification," *Ling.* 6.13), so Lupercalia and Februatio are two names for the same event. Varro reminds readers that he has demonstrated this already: "*ut in antiquitatum libris demonstraui*" (*Ling.* 6.13); antiquarian and scholarly, this makes no room for the sexy shenanigans and hard-to-ignore carnivalesque legends clustering around Romulus and Remus.[13]

Quirinalia (17 February) is "*Quirinalia a Quirino*"; it gets its name from Quirinus because it is a festival of Quirinus. Written by Varro, this frustrating etymology might call to mind the Quirina tribe, a network connecting him to Reate, Romulus, and Quirinus,[14] but, rather than magnify allusions for this day's foundational significance, Varro adds down-home bathos and also underscores this calendar's interest in inclusivity. It transpires that Quirinus must share the date with the bakers who do not get a day off on their own **Furnacalia** holiday.

> Et eorum hominum, qui **Fur**nacalibus suis non **fuer**unt **fer**iati. **Fer**alia ab *inferis* et *ferendo*, quod **fer**unt tum epulas ad sepulcrum quibus ius ibi parentare. Terminalia, quod is dies anni extremus constitutus: duodecimus enim mensis fuit Februarius et cum intercalatur **inferiores** quinque dies duodecimo demuntur mense. **Ecurria** ab **equorum** cursu: eo die enim ludis currunt in Martio Campo. (Varro, *Ling.* 6.13)

> And also of those men who, on their own **Furnacalia**, were not on **holiday**. Feralia [21 February] comes from "**the infernal ones**" and from "**bearing**," because that is when they "**bear**" banquets to the tomb as just desserts for those to whom ancestral rites are due there.[15] The Terminalia [23 February], because this was set as the last day of the year: for the twelfth month was once February and when there's an intercalation, the five "**inferior**" days are subtracted from the twelfth month. The **Ecurria** [27 February, 24 March] from the running of **horses**: for on that day they run races in the games on the Campus Martius.

Bakers cannot be on holiday for Oven-Lady Day (Fornax) and therefore need an alternative holiday. More subtly, these characters help Varro to make a point about monolithic etymologies. Fornacalia (more usual than Furnacalia) was a "movable" feast in the sense that one's proper day depended on one's curia (if one had one and knew it and its role);[16] so it is another partial anomaly in this section. If challenged, Varro could justify its inclusion here with his focus on the final day's fixed overlap with Quirinalia, rounding up all those for whom identifying with a traditional curia is impossible and for whom Quirinus becomes the focus. Palmer centers Rome's sacral framework around *Curiae*, and this proposition makes particularly good sense when reading Varro: thus, to a Roman, *Curiae* represent an atavastic mainline to authentic historical consciousness, recalling the tensions, productively overcome, at the point of becoming a people.[17]

In this light, Varro's seemingly heterogeneous festal bundle in this passage emphasizes a complex shared quality to the sequence, and in the joint celebration represented by Quirinalia he recognizes that there was a significant body of citizens ineligible for participation in the traditional curial festival. These people needed a day linking what should have been "their own" Fornacalia—had they had a specific curia—with the inclusive Quirinalia. "Sabine" Quirinus acknowledges and embraces the population shifts and the changing sociocultural realities that the curiae structurally ignore.[18]

The potential interest in this festival is clear from Ovid's folksy version, sending up the curial rank and file: the first "bakers" were the clueless farmers who managed to work out how to bake grain by trial and error and deified *fornax* (oven, furnace) to try to get an edge on baking technology.[19] As Ovid has it, they are too stupid to check the Forum notices indicating which date the festival should fall for each Curia; hence, for some it drifts to the last available date (that is, creating an overlap with the Quirinalia).

Next in sequence, **Feralia** (21 February), before a race into March. The Feralia at last introduces the dead, albeit confined to their tombs; by contrast, in Ovid's verses, this marks a time when the dead roam.[20] Varro's dead are aggressively jealous of their rites and privileges (*fero* [connotatively, *ferus*]; *ius*), and fulfill a significant narrative role in heralding the (old) year's end. They signal the importance of paying respects to the past, in its place, and visiting the *inferi* highlights the power of endings to influence beginnings, sitting as the festival does just before **Terminalia** and the old year's end. But of course this is no longer the annual countdown to New Year; hence, approaching March in this way also highlights human power to shape the religious calendar to suit contemporary needs.[21] In the same vein, the **Ecurria** can do double duty, straddling February and March (linking old old year and old new year) and pointing up the calendrical time shift that Caesar's reform had effected—for months that gained extra days, anything requiring relative "dating" after the Ides required recalibration.[22] Varro's direct reference to the only recently unnecessary intercalation hints at the problems of calendar shifts for scholarship but also acknowledges the immutable natural forces that underpin the phenomena of temporal cycles.

March

Varro's account (as quoted in the previous section) emphasizes topographic circumscription by pinning Mars' **Equirria** (Ecurria, in Varro) to the Campus. By contrast the **Liberalia** (17 March) pops up all over the city:

Liberalia dicta, quod **per totum oppidum** eo die **sedent** <ut> sacerdotes Liberi anus hedera coronatae cum libis et foculo pro emptore sacrificantes. In libris **Saliorum** quorum cognomen Agonensium, forsitan hic dies ideo appellatur potius Agonia. (Varro, *Ling.* 6.14)

The Liberalia is named because **through the whole town**, on that day, are **sitting** as priests of Liber old women crowned with ivy, with honeyed cakes and a brazier, and if there's someone to pay, making the sacrifice. In the books of the **Salii** tagged the Agonenses, perhaps on that account this day is instead called the Agonia.

Kent argues that the development of the Liberalia into another iteration of the Agonia (as discussed in chapter 6) is evidence of scribal miscopying;[23] if so, the mix-up entered the canon early, as it was present (via Macrobius) in the early fifth century CE.[24] Leaving the sentence as it stands draws the *Martial* Salii persuasively into the picture. Liber gains community-forming associations from the Salian Books and invokes the implicit political topography of the Salian dance (March was full of Salian processions); at the same time, against the backdrop of the Liberalia, the March processions of the Argei were (implicitly, here) taking place.[25]

Because of the calendrical complexity of March, it is worth teasing out the associative possibilities in some depth. Book 7's revised account (Liberalia, Argei, and so on) reimagines the scene after a quote from Ennius evoking the legendarily sexy chitchat (*suauis*) between Numa and Egeria (*Ling* 7.42). Readers learn by way of a second quote that:

> Libaque, fictores, Argeos et tutulatos.
> Liba, quod libandi causa fiunt. Fictores dicti a fingendis libis. Argei ab Argis; Argei fiunt e scirpeis, simulacra hominum XXVII; ea quotannis de Ponte Sublicio a sacerdotibus publice d*e*ici solent in Tiberim. Tutulati dicti hi, qui in sacris in capitibus habere solent ut metam; id tutulus appellatus ab eo quod matres familias crines conuolutos ad uerticem capitis quos habent ui*t*<ta> uelatos dicebantur tutuli, siue ab eo quod id tuendi causa capilli fiebat, siue ab eo quod altissimum in urbe quod est, Arcs, tutissimum uocatur. (Varro, *Ling.* 7.43–44)

> Honey cakes, and their craftsmen, Argei, and topknot-wearers. Honey cakes, because their purpose is sacrificial. Craftsmen, so called because they "craft" the honey cakes. Argei from Argos; the Argei are made from rushes, human images, twenty-seven of them. These, annually, from

the Pons Sublicius [Bridge-on-Piles] are typically thrown by the Priests for the public into the Tiber. These are termed *tutulati*, because at the sacrifices they are accustomed to have on their heads a kind of *meta* [the conical turning-post at the circus]. This is called *tutulus* from the fact that the complex up-do favored by matrons, high on their heads, wrapped with a chaste fillet, used to be called a *tutulus*—whether from the fact that this was a creation designed to "secure" the hair or because the highest thing in the city, that is, the citadel, is called "the most secure."

To sum up: first *Ling.* 6.14 associates the Liberalia (characterized by tableaux: seated old women) with the Agonia (Liber and Mars, lively processions, war). Next, on later reaching *Ling.* 7.43–44, readers accrue a connection from the Liberalia to the Argei (perhaps evoking *Ling.* 5.45–54, the Argei as a structuring motif and connection to Hercules' arrival at the beginnings of Roman community). As a triad, Liberalia, January's Agonia, and the Argei might invoke the December Septimontium (recalling *Ling.* 5.41) and the final Agonia of the "new" calendar (in December).[26] A March Agonia, tied to Liber, nods to the role of March as "old" new beginning for the calendar, while the month as a whole is kicked off and interspersed with Salian processions (providing continuity).

By using his Ecurria to bridge the February–March gap, Varro takes readers from the raucous landscape of flying hooves on Mars' Field to the static old women manifesting civic Liber, but in the process he elides not only some of February but also festivals in March: for instance, the Matronalia, the bona fide dancing procession of the Salii (1 March), not to mention the feast day of Anna Perenna (what would become the tricky Ides, 15 March).

March as a whole, as Rome recovered from Caesar's assassination, might have seemed a month to edit carefully were the text already circulating. If *De Lingua Latina* was still being reworked or refined in 44, whether for Cicero or for wider publication, some judicious rationale must have been brought to bear on how March would play out. One meta-reading for an overarching story might look like this: starting from February, after the Lupercalia, things become complicated. Leader-cum-god Romulus-Quirinus shares his day with some festally dispossessed tradesmen (the bakers), who lack integration into Rome's early basic units (*curiae*).[27] There might be some reverberation from the lavish food offerings due to the Roman dead (whose missing Parentalia contemporary readers should have noticed). The dead, "down below," are still liable to rise up (symbolically, at least). Dead ends highlight the frangibility of chronology: even the god of endings could not keep hold of his year-closing significance, and Rome's racetrack (*cursus*) mentality (from the display on the Campus to the politics of the magistracies and sponsored entertainment) might evoke the competitive autocratic impulse ratcheting up the political temperature.

Hitting March running, the Liberalia could thus presage happy days and Roman triumphs (compare the role of Liber at *Ling.* 6.68), but this is also a day marking an annual rite of passage—when boys adopt the *toga uirilis*—and although wine is signaled by the ivy wreathing their heads, Varro's old women seem to cast a pall over any intimations of fertility (especially in the month of the former but no longer new year).[28] The sober, mercantile quality at the fore in this explanation tells the audience that for now at least, the new beginnings and fertility emblematized in the absent Matronalia and feast of Anna Perenna are on hold.

What succeeds the Liberalia (at *Ling.* 6.14) is an antiquarian discussion of regional diversity in days named for their numerical position in the calendar: the **Qui*n*quatrus** and (taking us explicitly past the Ides, Varro says)[29] the Tusculan **Sexatrus** (six days post-Ides) and **Septimatrus** (another Tusculum/Rome crossover).

> Quinquatrus: his dies unus ab nominis errore obseruatur proinde ut sint quinque; dictus, ut ab **Tusculanis** post diem sextum **Idus** similiter uocatur Sexatrus et post diem septimum Septimatrus, sic hic, quod erat post diem quintum **Idus**, Quinquatrus. (Varro, *Ling.* 6.14)

> Quinquatrus: this is one day but from an error in translating is observed as if it were five; the appellation is just as when **Tusculans** similarly call the sixth day after the **Ides** Sexatrus and the seventh day after, Septimatrus; thus here it was that the fifth day after the **Ides** was Quinquatrus.

March had traditionally been a long (thirty-one-day) month, so in theory one might continue to count down happily to the Kalends of April once past the fifteenth. Varro's odd, antiquarian gloss on these March dates fixes them instead to the Etrusco-Sabine Ides (see *Ling.* 6.28) and highlights this crafting of the year as a technical entity and the ripples it might effect.[30] Varro's comments, I suggest, show how Caesar's new calendar might make space for new-old versions of days and rites to regain prominence if Romans are appropriately in tune with their past and able to grasp the opportunity for such subtle modes of self-fashioning. For unchanged March, counting down to the Kalends in fact retained its old form because only the traditionally "short" months were glitchy; nevertheless, moving past the Ides might well evoke a frisson for Varro's early audience. Of course, the resonance of these numerical festal vicissitudes, depending on where one stands, take on much more significance if the text was still subject to revision in the summer of 44 or after. In that case, the very recent renaming of *Quintilis* as the new *July*, noted with not a small dose of irony by Cicero the day after the Nones,[31] makes the *five*-six-seven naming in Varro's calendar all the more piquant; more on this in July.

Varro sees out March with the **Tubulustrium** (festal purification of the sacrificial trumpets in the Cobblers Hall), which stands in without fanfare for what seem in fact to have been two festivals (23 March and May).[32]

April

Varro's audience might have expected him next to explain the Veneralia, on the Kalends of April, a day also linked to Fortuna Virilis.[33] With summer 44 hindsight, unpacking associations with Venus might be just as dangerous a task as tackling the Ides of March; Varro's omission, or excision, of Venus, read that way, conceals intriguing possibilities.

Venus Verticordia was the Venus of the Kalends of April. She had a recent temple (sixty or seventy years old when Varro was at work), probably in the Vallis Murcia area. This foundation for Venus Verticordia was the result of the discovery and punishment of unchaste Vestal Virgins; their chastity was necessary for Rome's success, and the dedication sought to neutralize and guard against further sexual impropriety.[34] Other politically significant and memorable sites of Venus, from a contemporary perspective, include the temples founded by Pompey (Venus Victrix) and Caesar (Venus Genetrix). Pompey's temple (dedicated in 55, completed in 52) was a famously tiny appendage to his massive theater complex on the Campus Martius. For Pompey, there was perhaps a repurposing of Sulla's winning Greek brand, Aphrodite, not to mention muscling in on increasingly determined Julian claims to be Venus' heirs[35] and the bonus of a divine gloss on his military success as endorsed by Rome's always-a-winner first mother.[36] Caesar's Venus reifies and instantiates a potent Julian genealogy, and Ancestral Venus must have been an obvious icon for the focal point of his (still unfinished on his death) Forum. The planning had been under way in some sense since 54 (as evidenced in Cicero's gleeful epistolary comments to Atticus on his own part in the project), and the temple was eventually dedicated in 46 (in the still incomplete new Forum) on the concluding day of Caesar's triumph.[37]

Varro's April mood is instead decidedly foreign (eastern) and rustic Italian. It is also all about mothers, making Venus' absence more pointed. The **Megale[n]sia** (4 April) opens Varro's month.[38] Varro presents the name as intrinsically Greek ("*Megalesia dicta a Graecis*," *Ling.* 6.15), despite, as he continues, the Great Mother's arrival in Rome from King Attalus of Pergamum at the direction of the Sibylline books.[39] Varro laconically conjures up the goddess swapping her temple near the city wall of Pergamum for a Roman advent, an occasion that takes readers back to 204. Her Palatine temple, completed and dedicated by M. Junius Brutus in 191, was the focus for what became a popular and lavishly celebrated festival. Varro omits this Brutus and keeps quiet too about the excesses associated with the festival although they were such that (according to Gellius) a senatorial decree restricting expenditure was considered appropriate in 161.[40] The narrative flow implies that, rather than shoring up a Greek etymology by way of μεγάλη θεός, Megalesia takes its name from the Pergamene temple, the Megalesion, perhaps best described as meta-Greek.

Readers might have expected some allusion to the dramatic performances associated with the Megalensia; instead, Varro turns to the **Fordicidia** (15 April), to which he allocates equal space (twenty-five words). Varro's first maternal figure for April's sequence was the eastern, potent Cybele, almost an alternative Venus. Fordicidia is a very different beast[41] and leads straight to the **Palilia** (Parilia, 21 April), which briefly and perhaps for narrative reasons displaces the **Cerialia** (19 April).[42] The text runs:

> Fordicidia a fordis bubus; bos forda quae fert in uentre; quod eo die publice immolantur boues praegnantes in curiis complures, a fordis caedendis Fordicidia dicta. Palilia dicta a Pale, quod ei feriae, ut Cerialia a Cerere. (Varro, *Ling.* 6.15)

> Fordicidia, from cows with calf; a cow "with calf" is one who is still carrying. Because on that day several pregnant cows are sacrificed in public, in curial assembly, it was from the cows with calf that were to be slaughtered that the Fordicidia got its name. The Palilia got its name from Pales, because it's a festival for her, as with Cerialia from Ceres.

Fordicidia is a practice-based term: it describes a key element of the festival, but Varro, unlike Ovid, gives no rationale for the sacrifice itself. This public act of slaughter—repeated annually, generative of new vocabulary—is divorced from (what Ovid offers as) the context. In Ovid, Rome was struggling to ensure the agricultural harvest and was saved when Numa solved a riddle told to him by Faunus in a dream: slaughter cows to Tellus, but each cow must deliver two lives.

For Varro, a linguistic Sabinism lurking in the name Fordicidia, meshing with Numa's role as its engineer, might well have prompted him to spotlight this unglamorous festival.[43] From the one cow, two lives were delivered for sacrifice, ensuring Rome's agricultural fertility. From Romulus and Remus, equal until the moment when suddenly they were not, one life sacrificed ensured the genesis of Rome, not just as a "psychical entity" but as a laboriously worked landscape of human graft and habitation.[44] One more context that might have encouraged Varro to emphasize the homely beasts of Fordicidia over Parilia was the events of 45: the arrival in Rome of the news of Caesar's victory at Munda and the attendant flummery (crowns, games honoring Caesar) bulked up the festival to commemorate his achievement.[45] Moreover, literary evidence suggests that a web of nuances was already developing around the festival and its association with Rome's birthday.[46]

Commenting on Ovid's later treatment of the Parilia, in terms that highlight why Varro might have been sensitive to its difficulty for a consensus position, Feeney observes that "the power of the passage [in the *Fasti*] comes from the attempt to harmonize its Roman totalizing impetus (all explanations lead to Rome) with the fragmented and contradictory atmosphere created by the competition of frameworks."[47] The Parilia marks the beginning of the shepherds' year and of Rome year zero; by contrast, Fordicidia implicitly generates Rome in a way that avoids any civil war nuances that Parilia's presence might provoke, yet nonetheless emphasizes Varro's leitmotiv: strength and unity through diversity. Two come from one and become one in their sacrificial value.[48]

Such delicate connections are supported in the wider associative context if recalled (as Cicero and others among Varro's original readers surely might have). The ashes of the unborn calves sacrificed at Fordicidia and preserved by the Vestals were part of the Chief Vestal's mix for the *suffimen*. In combination with the blood of the October Horse, this made a sprinkle for the Parilia's purificatory bonfires.[49] The Vestals—publicly, professionally chaste women, *pace* Venus Verticordia—guaranteed the transition from the ending of the old year (Mars, the October Horse; agricultural and traditionally military undertones) to the first hints of the community's new cycle of activity in Spring (Tellus, spring births, Mars' children, a new city). That Varro mentions the February Ecurria but not Mars' opening of March or the closing of the productive year (October) is striking, and, like his occlusion of Venus (the Veneralia), it hints at tactical silences and the possibilities of strategic realignment of the contents.

Varro's Cerialia (tacitly, agriculture) is made to slot neatly after the Parilia (tacitly, shepherding), in the wake of the bovine Fordicidia story. Cerialia also eases the way to the next event, the **Vinalia** (23 April, 19 August), refining the agricultural focus from cereal crops to grapes and their end product before turning to blight with a briefer write-up for **Robigalia** (25 April).

Vinalia a <u>uino</u>; his dies Iouis, non Veneris. Huius rei cura non leuis in Latio: nam aliquot locis <u>uindemiae</u> primum ab sacerdotibus publice fiebant, **ut Romae etiam nunc**: nam flamen Dialis auspicatur <u>uindemiam</u> et ut iussit <u>uinum</u> legere, agna Ioui facit, inter cuius exta caesa et porrecta flamen pr<im>us <u>uinum</u> legit. In **Tusculanis** portis est scriptum:

<u>Vinum</u> nouum ne uehatur in urbem ante quam <u>Vinalia</u> *k*alentur. <u>Robigalia</u> dicta ab <u>Robigo</u>; secundum segetes huic deo sacrificatur, ne robigo occupet segetes. (Varro, *Ling.* 6.16)

<u>Vinalia</u>, from "<u>vino</u>"; this is Jupiter's day, not Venus.' No slight care attaches to this event in Latium: for in some places the <u>vintages</u> were first prepared by the priests on behalf of the populace, as **at Rome even now**. The Flamen Dialis [Jupiter's priest] makes the <u>vintage</u>'s beginning auspicious and when he has ordered the grapes to be gathered [selected/identified], he commits a lamb to Jupiter, between the excision of whose vital organs and their offering the priest selects [identifies] the first <u>grapes</u>. On the **Tusculan** Gates is written:

The new <u>wine</u> shall not be carried into the city until the <u>Vinalia</u> has been proclaimed [/convoked].

<u>Robigalia</u> gets its name from <u>Robigus</u>: all along the cornfields sacrifice is made to this deity, lest mildew invade the crops.

The April Vinalia was another Janus-faced festival, looking back to authorize the previous year's vintage but also marking out prospectively the coming year's crop. Its story here rescripts civic Jupiter as a mediator between country (vines, harvest, weather) and city (Jupiter as the biggest noise in the urban pantheon) and looks forward to the fertility of the coming season (the sacrificial lamb).[50] Varro's emphasis on the Latinity and Joviality of the festival is striking.[51] Here, April prefigures the celebration and classification of a year's successful vintage and the annual struggle to avert the blight that might befall crops—Robigalia. One year ends; another, full of the catastrophes that nature can visit on a farmer, begins. As this calendar economically demonstrates, there are many different ways of, and times for, beginning a new year.

[May]

The Robigalia took readers into the fields to walk the crops. Varro's turn to June's Vestalia will abruptly send readers back to the hearth and home fires.[52] The disappearance of May's fixed festivals might result from some hitch in textual transmission, but, if intentional, as many of Varro's silences clearly are, the omission repays careful consideration.

Ovid's roll call for May (*Fasti* 5), something like fifty years later, gives a literary sense of the kinds of etymological quests that Varro likely had access to. It is not a month of big-name, weighty holidays, yet it does represent yet another new beginning of sorts: the Lemuria.[53] The *lemures* feature as distinctively Roman ancestral dead (by allusion, in Nonus) in Varro's *De Vita Populi Romani* but are not (by this name) a familiar item in the literature of the era.[54] Ovid's festal etiology links the term to the murder of Remus under the broader etymological banner of *Maius* as the month of the *maiores*.[55]

The Lemuria might be characterized as a very old-school festival ("*ritus erit ueteris*," *priscus mos*, "*ueteris ritus*"), rooted as it was in the Roman cultivation of the dead.[56] In a gory, vivid nocturnal apparition, Ovid's Remus will ask their foster parents to have Romulus formalize the honor done at his funeral. Romulus complies, instigating the **R**emuria, yet,

> **R**ough [*aspera*] was changed to **l**enient [*lenem*] through long [*longo*] ages
> of this letter [*littera*], which stood first in the name;
> and soon **l**emures was also how the spirits of the silent [*silentium*] were termed:
> here is the meaning of the word, that is the power of its expression.
> (Ov. *Fast.* 5.481–84)

This centrality of Latin language to Roman foundation, coupled with the phonetic shift between then and "now," makes Varronian sense of Ovid's recurring deployment of Mercury (Arcadia, Evander) and Remus as keynotes for May.[57] As Ovid puts it, the Lemuria is ripe for etymologizing: "Whence the day was called, what marks the origin of the name, | escapes me: that's a discovery for some god to make."[58] By implication, this suggests that an etymology for Lemuria was a problem unsolved by Varro.

May is also the month of the second procession of the Argei. Ovid's 14 May verses present the Argei, Hercules and Cacus, and Evander; taken in tandem with Dionysius of Halicarnassus' contemporary account, we get a taste of how Varro might have concocted a May Argei etymology.[59] What makes this absence potentially meaningful rather than simply unfortunate is Varro's excision of the Argei from March (too), despite his obvious interest in their procession and their landmark urban status. In Ovid's version, rush images of ancient men are thrown into the Tiber from the "Oak" bridge by a virgin (by implication, "by the Vestal Virgins," with Dionysius to hand), recalling the time ("*fama uetus*," *Fast.* 5.625) when Rome was Saturnia and Jupiter prophetically told the prehistoric clans to sacrifice two bodies in the Tuscan River in honor of Saturn (the old man with the sickle). Hercules changed the live sacrifice to a drowning of rush men, and thus Roman practice now follows Hercules' lead. With a neat play on words and semiotic range, Ovid also offers a brutal alternative political story: a way of understanding how the Saepta's voting "bridges" enshrined a vicious generational conflict—young men hurled the old off "bridges" to ensure they could grasp the balance of voting power. It remains to Tiber himself, appealed to by Ovid's narrator, to present what he expects will be the truth.

As also evident in Varro's story (*Ling.* 5.45), Hercules' Argive companions saw a new home in the landscape:

> On these hills [*montibus*] they sited their hope and their home [*spemque laremque*].
> Yet often by the sweet love [*dulci . . . amore*] of their homeland [*patria*] were they moved.
> (Ov. *Fast.* 5.652–53)

One such melancholy Argive asked for his remains to be thrown into the Tiber so that in death he might wash up again in his native country. His squeamish heir decided to bury him in "Ausonian" soil, with a rush image making the watery journey to Greece in his stead. Basic concinnity suggests at least that Ovid was working with comparable paradigms.

Missing May *and* omitting the April Floralia makes Varro's transition to June feel lacunose, whether or not May etymologies were ever explicitly in place. In Varro's later countryside handbook, Robigus and Flora snuggle up neatly.[60] Through-readers of the text as it stands might recall how *Ling.* 5 saw Flora feature in Varro's Roman topopoesie; there, Flora's Cliuus directed readers to a Quirinal chapel of Jupiter, Juno, and Minerva, one older than the Capitoline temple and known as the Capitolium Vetus.[61] For anyone accustomed to strolling Rome's streets, Flora might well thus connote the legendary whiff of Sabinism ("*Sabinum linguam olent*," *Ling.* 5.74) attending Tatius' ancient foundation of an altar.

As things stand, it is impossible to know why May would have fallen neatly out of the textual transmission. The narrative thrust achieved in *Fasti* 5 shows what one might do with these festivals and demonstrates a colorful etymological palette. If Ovid is echoing elements of a lost Varronian calendar segment, Varro's explorations were evidently as rich and complex as one would expect. June at least will open with a featured festival that exemplifies Varro's willingness to confound narrative expectations.

June

"*Dies Vestalia ut uirgines Vestales a Vesta*" (*Ling.* 6.17)—the **Vestalia** (centered on 9 June), like the Vestal Virgins, derives from Vesta. Through-readers know well that Varro found Vesta thematically interesting, and this terse treatment depends for its significance on readers knowing or recalling the previously highlighted archaic, Sabine quality of Vesta, evoked every time her name is uttered.[62] Varro's "just so" etymological calendar headline in book 6 shows how, in embracing and normalizing Vesta, Latin's brand of heterogeneity continues to embed Sabine speech in Roman experience.

Starting June with Vesta also means skipping various picturesque festivals that we know from Ovid's verses on the month but that may or may not have had particular currency—for example, Ovid's Carna, controller of the Kalends and (Ovid claims) previously lost in the mists of time, or Mind, evoking the dark days of the Punic Wars and Rome's appeal to *Mens*.[63] No Matralia either (11 June); instead Varro's next event is the **Lesser Quinquatrus** (13 June):

Quinquatrus minusculae dictae Iuniae Idus ab similitudine maiorum, quod tibicines *tum* feriati **uagantur** per urbem et **conueniunt** ad Aedem Mineruae. (Varro, *Ling.* 6.17)

Lesser Quinquatrus is what the Ides of June are called, from a similarity with the Greater, because the holidaying pipers **roam** the whole city before **convening** at the Temple of Minerva.

Readers might recall (*Ling.* 6.14) that Varro gave little to go on for the events of the main Quinquatrus, where his focus was on the cultural politics of dating schemes. By contrast, this lively scene conjures up roving bands of musicians permeating every part of the city, seemingly in chaos ("*uagantur*") but in fact with a topographic and religious goal ("*conueniunt*"). The scant time spent on Sabine Vesta's day seems even more noteworthy because it is followed directly by this noisy, urban romp toward Minerva, but we should be wary of always assuming that Sabinism is Varro's overwhelming enthusiasm; Minerva has contemporary interest that a Cicero might read in.

Pipers bridge the worlds of religious cult and the profane world of parties, musical entertainments, and drama; Minerva, possibly the recent recipient of a small foundation on the Campus funded by Pompey's military successes, gives their seriocomic entertainment role a different character.[64] Pipers flourish in the world of Plautus, adding literary-dramatic flavor supported by Varro's scholarly enthusiasms, but Ovid's etiology for the festival adds a different spin.[65] "Why does the wandering piper march throughout the city?" asks Ovid's interlocutor; once (Minerva answers), such music was held in high esteem, but times changed and the musicians emigrated to Tibur. By a trick, the drunken gang of pipers was lured back to Rome: this celebration evokes these long-ago events. Varro here alludes to Minerva's Aventine temple, but the reverberations from his one-time support for Pompey (shared with Cicero) might well call Pompey's still fairly recent construction project to mind.[66] One aspect of Minerva's Aventine temple was likely to have been especially meaningful for Varro: its role (recalled by Festus) as a focus for authors from around the long-ago time when Rome was beginning to develop a broad literary culture.[67]

Relatively speaking, Varro treats the June Quinquatrus expansively, even if without much etymological heft. **Fors Fortuna** (24 June) follows and, by juxtaposition with the Quinquatrus, exemplifies another way in which saying not very much might associatively signify more.[68]

Dies Fortis Fortunae appellatus ab Seruio Tullio rege, quod is fanum Fortis Fortunae secundum Tiberim extra urbem Romam dedicauit Iunio mense. (Varro, *Ling.* 6.17)

The Day of Fors Fortuna was named by King Servius Tullius, because he dedicated a sanctuary to Fors Fortuna alongside the Tiber, outside the city, Rome, in the month of June.

The predicative nuances of double naming (Fors Fortuna) drive a deity's potential for intervening in mortal affairs along selected channels, and Varro's attention to "the Goddess who Brings" signals economically how a wider political and civic frame of reference might come into play.[69]

The formulation is rare but is to be found in Terence (a focus of scholarly attention for Cicero and Caesar too) and subsequently in Columella's countryside poem. Cicero and Caesar, riffing on Terence, rate him highly;[70] Varro, if we read a Menippean fragment right, makes Terence master of ethos (or, perhaps, character), "*in quibus partibus in argumentis Caecilius poscit palmam, | in ethesin Terentius, in sermonibus Plautus.*"[71] Columella's example, by contrast, would make a clear connection between hard work, canny practice, and the success that leads to financial reward; it also emphasizes a link between Fors

Fortuna (here, "Bountiful Lady") and a subsistence world, away from politics, mega-farms, industrial-scale business, or military glory (10.315–17).

Varro makes no attempt to unpack either *fors* or *fortuna*, even though (or is it precisely because?) these words were heavily freighted in this era; especially the case if we recall Cicero's association of Fortuna with Pompey and Caesar's subsequent relationship with her.[72] We met this material in my discussion of *rex* (chapter 6), and Fortuna's pervasive significance encourages a closer look at Varro's account.[73] Readers encounter Fors Fortuna at her royally instituted home snug up against the Tiber (*secundum Tiberim*). This instantiation of Fortuna had, through riverine association, strong associations with travel and trade. What is more, her "architect" in this case, Servius Tullius, was storied as the child of a captured foreign slave woman in the household of Tarquinius Priscus.[74] The legend therefore bundles two different kinds of Roman foundation (practical and storybook), both of which hint at complex multiethnicity and a different kind of political worldview. It also explicitly situates this dedication *outside* the city; an outsider (Servius Tullius) takes regal power and honors an outsider's deity, with an eye to the main chance.

Varro's circular argument for Lady Bountiful Day makes her name and Tiber-side sanctuary a function of the regal period. Servius Tullius, second in the Etruscan line of kings, was known as the king who acceded by popular acclaim, the one who monetarized the economy, extended the Roman franchise, created a distinctive urban icon (the walls), and had an enslaved noblewoman as his mother. That he also might or might not have had a divine father adds piquancy. His career neatly combines luck and graft, and his understanding of the give and take that Fors Fortuna embodies is addressed in the specifics of Varro's emphasis (it is *"secundum Tiberim extra urbem Romam"*). This signals the interconnectedness of Rome and its local neighbors (source of Tiber and Servius himself) but also the quality of openness to the Other necessary for Rome to keep up the deal with Lady Bountiful (Servius makes the walls that reframe Rome but, by making this an extra-urban foundation, shows their limitations).

Five/July

Although Varro later iterates *Quin*tilis as month five—the first of the enumerative mensal countdown to *December* (*Ling.* 6.34)—he has already experienced the seismic shift in measuring time instantiated from January 45.[75] Here, Varro reaches **Runaway People Day** (5 July):

Dies Poplifugia uidetur nominatus, quod eo die tumultu repente fugerit populus: non multo enim post hic dies quam decessus Gallorum ex Urbe, et qui tum sub Urbe populi, ut **Fic**uleates ac Fidenates et finitimi alii, contra nos coniurarunt. Aliquot huius d<i>ei uestigia <u>fugae</u> in sacris apparent, de quibus rebus Antiquitatum Libri plura referunt. Nonae <u>Caprotinae</u>, quod eo die in Latio **Iunoni** <u>Caprotinae</u> mulieres sacrifi**c**ant et sub *caprifico fac*iunt; e *caprifico* adhibent uirgam. Cur hoc, toga praetexta data eis Apollinaribus Ludis docuit populum. (Varro, *Ling.* 6.18)

<u>Runaway People</u> day seems to have been so named because back on that tumultuous day, <u>the people</u> suddenly <u>ran for it</u>: this came not long after the retreat of the Gauls from the city, when the peoples who were near to the city—such as the **Fic**uleans and Fidenians and others on our borders—banded together against us. Several traces of this day's <u>run-for-it</u> appear in the sacrifices, about which the *Books of the Antiquities* deliver more information. *Caprotine* [Goaty] Nones [7 July], because on that day in Latium the women make sacrifice to **Juno** <u>Caprotina</u>, and they **make** it beneath a <u>goatfig</u> tree. They use a switch from the <u>goatfig</u>. Why this? The bordered toga given to them at the Games of Apollo showed the people just why.

The intensity of the wordplay in this passage suggests that Varro lingered over it. What might this cluster of holiday memories evoke? The Poplifugia is remarkable in the fixed festal calendar for its reference to what looks like a specific historic event: part of the story of Rome's survival after the Gallic sack. Varro's pile-up of associations explores the interconnectedness of times and memories around these days (drawing in the **Caprotine Nones**, for helpful Juno, then the **Ludi Apollinares**).

Names, as the final festival in this group indicates, need not retain popular memory of their original connotations to remain potent. This means that while Varro starts with the lurking disaster of defeat and the abandonment of Rome, the implied landscape of chaos is transformed (by juxtaposition with Juno Caprotina's Nones) into a civilized festival honoring Apollo (emblematic of controlled syncretism).[76] Nevertheless, the civic security and order of Apollo's games, albeit safely contained in the Circus, are enriched by Lupercalian undertones (the goatfig switch) and nuanced by the powerful non-Roman, and female, qualities of Juno and her worshippers.

Varro's interest in the tag "Goatfig Tree" for Juno (*Ling.* 6.18) brings the Ficus Ruminalis into the picture (encountered at *Ling.* 5.54) but also ties in the Fig-folk (Ficuleans); the sappy switch (*uirga*) evokes the goatskins of the Luperci, the sacrificial goats, and the rawhide thongs of the postsacrificial carnival through the streets. This avatar of Juno has had to give way, however, to Apollo—only through the vestigial memories instantiated in the Circus (and their reflux through Varro) is her input kept alive.[77]

Varro's version of the "flight" was not the only one available. Dionysius of Halicarnassus, for instance, links the Poplifugia to the popular alarm following Romulus' disappearance.[78] This story proposes a legend of flight in the wake of the removal of a popular and charismatic leader from the city and might have been in the frame by way of Varro's "goatfig" follow-up. Depending on its currency in the mid-40s and how much and how late Varro continued to (re)craft the text, this vanishing-act etymology must by summer 44 have offered a distinctly acerbic contextual twist. When read against Dionysius' account, we can see Varro's version anew: an us-and-them story, with different flavors of otherness tested against Rome's citizen body and ending with Latium reintegrated forcibly into core Roman identity. Rather than telling his audience about how the two events (flight and sacrifices) are connected, he makes it a story about the role of the antiquarian in shaping available modes of self-fashioning.

Without hardware (*uestigia* in the Books of Antiquities, the toga ceremony) no one might recall the story of the goatfig tree and why Juno is associated with it.[79] Even in Varro, no one remembers the daring sally made by the Romans' slave women who, having got the temporarily triumphant Fidenians and friends drunk, signaled to Rome's men to launch a counterattack and retake their city. Indeed, Varro's story casts Juno's role into oblivion, recalled only emblematically through the toga ceremony at Apollo's games. These games, held in the Circus Maximus, dated to the turmoil of the Punic Wars, when Rome was under direct threat from Hannibal (hooking in the Gallic sack and subsequent flight).[80]

From Apollo and the circus, Varro turns to Neptune, then the **Furrinalia** [25 July].

> Neptunalia a Neptuno: euis enim dei feriae. Furrinalia <a> Furrina, quod ei deae feriae public*ae* dies is; cuius deae honos apud antiquos: nam ei sacra instituta annua et flamen attributus; **nunc uix nomen notum** paucis. (Varro, *Ling.* 6.19)

> Neptunalia from Neptune: it's the feast day of that god. Furrinalia from Furrina, because it's for that goddess that the day is a public feast day. This goddess was honored among the ancients: for an annual sacrifice was instituted and a Flamen assigned; yet **now** her **name** is scarcely **known**.

Varro's terse **Neptunalia** (23 July) packs a punch only if one sees it as prefiguring the Consualia a month later (21 August) and in particular the bride-nap *in Circo* that Consus' festival made possible. Through-readers might expect a link with Consus, but on the first read-through, only Varro's earlier etymology of Neptune (touched on in chapter 7) provides direct context:

> Neptunus, quod mare terras ob<u>nubit</u> ut <u>nubes</u> caelum, ab <u>nuptu</u>, id est opertione, ut antiqui, a quo <u>nuptiae</u>, <u>nuptus</u> dictus. (Varro, *Ling.* 5.72)

> <u>Neptune</u> (because the sea <u>veils</u> the lands as the <u>clouds</u> the sky), is from <u>veiling</u>, that is, from a covering, as per the old-timers, from which <u>nuptials</u> and <u>wedlock's veil</u> are said.

Relentless verbal repetition drives this earlier, book 5 etymology, reflecting a cosmic marriage of land and sea, clouds and sky in mortal practice. Book 6 (*Ling.* 6.19) almost elides Neptune in favor of one of Varro's "forgotten" figures: Furrina, still honored (although now no one knows why) with a state holiday. Readers have, of course, met Furrina before with Varro, when tackling the shared etymological obscurity of the priests of Diovis (read him as Jove if he is to make his mark),[81] Furrina, and Falacer.[82]

When citing this trio in book 5, Varro observed that "*horum singuli cognomina habent ab eo deo cui sacra faciunt; sed partim sunt aperta, partim obscura.*"[83] The comment might have become more pointed if recalled in the autumn of 44, going by Cicero's bitter assertion that Caesar already had his own Flamen, like Mars, like Jove, in Antony.[84] Furrina's resonant oblivion when she reappears in book 6, taken in the context of her connection to an etymological discussion (taking in the Flamen Dialis) of how one maps priesthoods to gods and rites, is intriguing. Furrina closes out July.

August

August opens late, at the **Portunalia** (17 August). Portunus, exposing Rome to trade from within and without the peninsula, continues Varro's ongoing interest in boundaries but also elbows out festivals that might have proved equally liminal openers. Take the Nemoralia (13 August)—Diana of Woody and distinctly Latin Nemi connected Rome annually (through the commemoration of her Aventine temple, legendarily founded by Servius Tullius) to the early power politics of the Latin League (Nemi HQ).[85] Varro's interest in the Latin qualities of Aventine Diana featured when he described Rome in book 5, but here the opportunity to evoke the Etruscan temple and its Aventine satellite is passed over.[86] Instead, time flows directly to Rome's Tiber port (and Portunus), then on out to the country proper and the "rustic" **Vinalia** (19 August).

This second Vinalia recalls harvest, cultivation, and fertility by way of the generative role of Venus, patroness of (market-)gardens. It can only be a sly wordplay here ("*Vinalia rustica dicuntur... quod tum Veneri dedicata aedes*," it was called the Rustic *Vinalia*... because it was then that a temple was dedicated to *Venus*, *Ling*. 6.20) that encourages the exclusion of what is really happening (as Varro's estate-owning readers would know)—picking the grapes.[87]

August is a busy month: having confronted Venus in (re)productive mode Varro shifts focus. Rustic pragmatics gives way to the state festival of Consus (**Consualia**, 21 August) and the **Volcanalia**:

> et in Circo ad aram eius ab sacerdotibus ludi illi, quibus uirgines Sabinae raptae. Volcanalia a Volcano, quod ei tum feriae et quod eo die populus pro se in ignem animalia mittit. (Varro, *Ling*. 6.20)

> and in the Circus at his altar those games were celebrated by the priests, at which the unmarried Sabine girls were snatched. The Volcanalia (23 August) is from Volcan because that was his festival and because on that day the people on their own behalf drive animals into a fire.

Varro makes no attempt to link Consus etymologically to *consilium* in this context (as Ovid does).[88] If readers want extant parallels, Livy (perhaps writing up his early historical material in the late 30s) would link the festival to Romulus and Neptune, making a kind of sense of its combined subterranean and horsey qualities.[89] Consus' festival, with its connection to fertility during the hot days leading to harvest, generated a viable community (Sabine women joined with Roman men). Community forming is also at stake for the Volcanalia; according to Dionysius, the fiery cult of Vulcan was focused on a site somehow above but close to the Forum and formed the early locus of public business for the young city.[90] The payoff is that the festival calls for the people as a whole, with an act of boundary marking involving fire in the Forum. In the mid to late 40s, this cluster of associations will reverberate against the events surrounding Clodius' pyre and its consumption of the Curia (in 52), with potential bite from Caesar's recent funeral (for Varro's early audience).[91] The connotations of a ritual action at a site close to the *memoria* enshrined in the current Ficus Ruminalis, in conjunction with the Consualia, produce a rich array of afterimages.[92]

Reaching the **Opeconsiva** (25 August, *Ling*. 6.21) adds weight to an imagined Forum vista. If Caesar's pyre is on readers' minds after Volcanalia, how apt that Varro turns now to a shrine in the Regia. Ops, a goddess of "plenty," associated with sowing and harvest through the epithet Consiva (Ops "who sows," connecting etymologically, albeit here tacitly, to *consero*), might also be imagined to have links with Consus—although Varro makes no such suggestion.[93] Ops' shrine in the Regia is, Varro states, restricted to the veiled priest and Vestals. There is a striking collision of profligate plenty (after the somatic connotations of the popular mass sacrifice that Varro ascribes to Volcanalia) with the restricted personnel and tightly managed sexuality of Opeconsiva participants.[94] Readers recalling Varro on *oppidum* ("*Et oppidum ab opi dictum, quod munitur opis causa ubi sint et quod opus est ad uitam gerendam ubi habeant tuto,*" Ling. 5.141) will recall too the lively etymological pile-up he deployed to connect "*op-*" forms to the basic town-foundation imperative.[95]

The **Volturnalia**, Volturnus' day (assigned to 27 August), is "just so" in this context—and hard to pin down from other sources. Through-readers, perhaps knowing Lucretius' throwaway on roaring, booming Volturnus and even recalling a fragment from Ennius ("quoted" by Varro), may feel they have met this enigmatic character already.[96]

> Tiberis quod caput extra Latium, si inde nomen quoque exfluit in linguam nostram, nihil <ad> ἐτυμολόγον Latinum, ut, quod oritur ex Samnio, Volturnus nihil ad Latinam linguam: a*t* quod proximum oppidum ab eo secundum mare Volturnum, ad nos, iam Latinum uocabulum, ut Tiberinus no<me>n. Et colonia enim nostra Volturnum et deus Tiberinus. (Varro, *Ling.* 5.29)

> The Tiber, because its headwaters are outside Latium, were it only thence that the name also floods into our language it would be of no account to the Latin etymologist; by the same argument, because it rises from Samnium, Volturnus is as nothing for the Latin language. Yet because the closest town to it following the seacoast is Volturnum, it comes to us and is now a Latin word, just like the name Tiberinus. For we have both a colony Volturnum and a god Tiberinus.[97]

Varro's logic is tenuous, but nonetheless pumps up the fluid connections for a festival that defies etymological endeavor; perhaps it is the very fragility of the rationale and resistance to etymological expertise that gets Volturnus and his festival onto Varro's list.[98]

[September]

(no place here for the Ludi Romani—an unusual lacuna, but hardly suggesting a gripping etymology)[99]

October

The next event is the **Meditrinalia** (11 October).[100] Varro flags the change of month explicitly:

Octobri mense Meditrinalia dies dictus a medendo, quod Flaccus flamen Martialis dicebat hoc die solitum uinum <nouum> et uetus libari et degustari medicamenti causa; quod facere solent etiam nunc multi cum dicunt:
Nouum uetus uinum bibo: nouo ueteri morbo medeor. (Varro, *Ling.* 6.21)

In the month of **October** the Meditrinalia day is named from healing: Flaccus, Mars' priest, used to say that on this day was wont to be libated wine new and old and to be tasted for medicinal purposes. Even now, many make a habit of this when they say:
New and old wine I drink: from new and old illnesses I'm relieved.

The casually unspecified "Flaccus" and the lack of explanation for why Mars' priest might be an authority on the subject suggest that Varro is nodding graciously to an older contemporary, L. Valerius Flaccus (*cos.* 100) rather than asserting an authoritative role for Mars (or his priest) in the scholarly recuperation of lost tradition.[101] This Flaccus' negotiation of the political tensions in the early first century might make his pronouncements on "healing" from war and resolution between "old" and "new" (whether in terms of politics or grape-must) particularly acute.

Fons and **Fontinalia** (13 October) mark the next stop.[102] Fons (as *fons*) previously featured as the refreshing outpouring from water's originary smooth, level surface.[103] With Fons, Varro's Rome seems renewed: because of upsurging water, (religious) life is possible, marked by the garlands strewn into springs and the garlanded well-heads.[104] With the **Armilustrium** (19 October) Varro perversely bypasses the October Horse sacrifice to Mars on the Campus and arrives at the Aventine for a different kind of Martial event, one likely to have (military-)year ending implications.[105]

One of Varro's apparently innocuous suggestions takes prime position: **armed** men perform the rites at the **Armi**lustrium; "*nisi locus potius dictus ab his*" (unless the place is, rather, named from this) is the brisk qualification. Instead of an autochthonic commingling of space/place tagging human activity, the etymologist can dig deeper. "To play" (*ludere*) and "purification" (*lustrum*) are both swept into the mix, zoning the games as military but also bathing the event in the measured fluidity of a danced lustration. As Varro puts it, "*id est quod circumibant ludentes ancilibus armati*" (that is, because they trod the circuit in ludic time, armed with the sacred shields).[106]

[November]

November's quiet is reflected in its absence.

December

With 17 December comes **Saturnalia**, Saturn's day, followed (counting three on, Roman style) by Ops' festival, **Opalia** (19 December). If readers have in mind the August Opeconsiva festival and attendant links to Janus and Saturn, they will be unsurprised that Varro finds the minor December festival a useful narrative coda to Saturnalia. An echo of harvest's Plenty at a time of year when produce was in short supply might anyway have guaranteed the Opalia's place in this calendar, but Ops' connections to Saturn solidify a rationale for inclusion. Whatever Varro's ultimate goal, from Opalia develops a colorfully presented and complex sequence concluding this phase in the calendar. The text is compromised in part, but I present it here in Kent's version, with significant corrigenda:

> Angeronalia ab Angerona, cui sacrificium fit in Curia Acculeia et cuius feriae publicae is dies. Larentinae, quem diem quidam in scribendo Larentalia appellant, ab **Acca Larent**ia nominatus, cui sacerdotes nostri publice parentant e sexto die,[107] qui a*b* ea [*atra*] dicitur dies [*diem*] Parent<ali>um [tarentum] Accas Larentinas [tarentinas].
>
> Hoc sacrificium fit in Velabro, qua in Nouam Viam exitur, ut aiunt quidam ad sepulcrum Accae, ut quod ibi prope faciunt diis Manibus seruilibus sacerdotes; qui uterque locus extra urbem antiquam fuit non longe a Porta Romanula, de qua in priore libro dixi. Dies Septimontium nominatus ab his septem montibus, in quis sita Urbs est; Feriae non populi, sed montanorum modo, ut Paganalibus, qui sunt alicuius pagi.
>
> De statutis diebus dixi. (Varro, *Ling.* 6.23–25)

> Angeronalia [21 December] derives from Angerona, to whom sacrifice is made in the Acculeian Curia and whose public festival is on this day. The Larentine [23 December], which day by some write as Larentalia, is named from Acca Larentia, to whom our priests publicly offer sacrifice [as an ancestor] on the sixth [seventh] day, which from her is called the day of the Parentalia of Acca Larentia.

This sacrifice is made in the Velabrum where it debouches into New Street, at the tomb of <u>Acca</u> as some tell it, since hard by there the priests attend to the divine spirits of dead slaves. Both these places were outside the ancient city, not far from the Porta Romanula [Little Roman Gate], about which I spoke in an earlier book. <u>Sevenheights</u> Day [11 December] was named from these <u>seven heights</u>, on which the city is sited. It's not a universal holiday, just for the <u>hill-folk</u>; as with the <u>Paganalia</u> [early January], for those from the <u>countryside</u>.

What there is to say about the fixed days, I've said it.

Angerona and Acca Larentia are in dialogue with Saturn and Ops through this juxtaposition. The idea of a foundational mystery for Rome thereby weaves through the mythos for the latter couple. Angerona, a female deity represented indicating her closed, sealed mouth, signals secrecy and the power of hidden knowledge: Rome's preceptor, icon, and guardian.[108] Yet while Varro appears to have started a hare running on some actual revelation by one "Valerius Soranus," Francis Cairns is surely right to suggest that Varro's Angerona must, like Pliny's, be emblematic of a perceived power of language and the need to police it at the point where Rome's primal, originary potential lies.[109] She is an admonitory figure ensuring Roman discretion, not a potent protector in her own right. Her rites' celebration in the Curia *Accu*leia blurs the lines with *Acc*a Larentia, and recalls readers to the historically modelled exclusivity and individuating qualities of each *curia*. The Curia looks after its own; Acca, readers might come to think, looks out for the excluded.[110]

This associative tapestry has richly topopoetic qualities.[111] Varro's evocative description of Acca's place in the city curates a display of two unusual female deities at sites relating to ideas of interiority, boundaries, infrastructure, sense of community, and the lively diversity of early Rome.[112] Angerona might (by her December position) be read as initiating change and be associated with the mysterious quality of how to understand a community's first crystallization. Indeed, Varro's emphasis on the civic force of her celebration hints at the wider significance. Varro's Acca Larentia opens a conduit to Rome's ancestral figures, but she is also marked out as a focus for scholarly debate, even some uncertainty ("*quidam in scribendo . . . appellant . . . ut aiunt quidam*"). This is especially interesting since she appears here to take on an instantiating role for the civic importance of formally acknowledging slaves in the beginnings of the new city, its urban armature, and its ultimate success. When Varro juxtaposes Angerona with Acca Larentia, an insider-outsider figure associated variously with Romulus and Remus, Rome's Lares, and Hercules, and also modeled as in some way a benefactor of Rome, he also makes for a more interesting reading of a set of urban features.

Varro's "Tomb of Acca" offers an important focus for slaves, otherwise lost to mass graves. Its location in the once watery Velabrum (significant in book 5), together with Varro's contrasting emphasis on the interiority of the Porta Romanula (again in book 5), a site that etymologically fashions a Rome in microcosm from a gate,[113] suggests that excluded voices and foundation stories could become louder in this reading. When Varro follows up with a backward glance to Sevenheights day (11 December) while looking forward to Paganalia (which sneaks in here to make the pair,[114] even though it is not one of the fixed festivals), that notion of dialectic, binary vitality, and an overarching heterogeneity marks the crucial end point for this phase in the *fasti*: "what there is to say about the fixed days," he concludes, "I've said it."

Floating Signifiers

De statutis diebus dixi; de annalibus nec d<i>e statutis dicam. (Varro, *Ling.* 6.25)

Concerning the fixed days, I have spoken; concerning the annual festivals not fixed to a day, I shall now speak.

Annual events without a fixed day form a more compact set. First announced ("*dicam*"—Varro's first-person singular neatly ventriloquizes the pronouncing magistrate) is **Compitalia**. This is where the Lares oversee Roman networking, and so where roads meet ("*competunt*") makes for a crossroads ("*competa*") sacrifice.[115] Compitalia involves *uici*, so the Servian *regiones* and neighborhoods, discussed by Dionysius of Halicarnassus, help flesh out what Varro's early audiences might have adduced.[116]

Dionysius' antiquarian filter shows how this festival's explanation mainlines the world of the legendary kings, whereby royal decree (from Servius) gave local protectors—standing, statuesque, marking clusters of houses—annual offerings from each family in gratitude. Slaves (loved by the Lares) were to be honored participants in this festival, a practice that persisted to his own day, Dionysius suggests, because the annual removal of marks of servitude tightens the bonds of humanity between masters and slaves for the whole community.[117] Dionysius' account is no doubt colored by the Augustan reorganization of the city, but its emphasis on "neighborhood religion and the rites associated with the neighborhood holiday of Compitalia" suggests strong links to Varro's slightly different crossroads emphasis.[118]

Lares protect the household, and, as Varro emphasized back in book 5, the hearth—tended by the slaves—is synecdochically the home.[119] Compitalia emblematizes why the monarchy ended: its suppression by Tarquinius Superbus, "along with other holidays that allowed people to gather together and possibly plot insurrection," was indicative of losses of freedom of expression that were restored only when L. Junius Brutus, first tyrannicide and founding consul, restored the festival and founded the Republic.[120] The complexly associative quality of Compitalia as reflected in later authors' writings hints at what a late republican audience might have called to mind. Livy, no doubt drawing on earlier scholarship, makes Servius' mother a prisoner of war, a slave in the household of Tarquinius Priscus;[121] Pliny's account produces a stickier connection with the Lares, making this mother a Cinderella figure, a slave woman impregnated by a disembodied phallus.[122] Lares are the ideal figures with which to develop Acca Larentia's thematic impact on this time of year.

The annual iterative cycle of these days is significant: "*Quotannis is dies concipitur*" (every year, this day is reconceived), but, as recently as 64, a senatorial decree had abolished at least some of the *collegia Compitalicia* and temporarily put a stop to the entertainments associated with the public ritual.[123] For Cicero and their coterie, the politics of the festival's fix in 58 must have recalled Cicero's speech *In Pisonem*.[124] The *collegia* were local associations, rooted in the interests of the *uici*—religious but also mercantile, and increasingly political. Moreover, even more so than Saturnalia, Compitalia seems to have been a "popular" festival, focused on the world and the interests of the *plebs urbana*.[125] Like the Septimontium and Paganalia, its emphasis is on Rome as a collective of microcosms.[126]

It was the potential for this localism to support increasing levels of political violence and systemic disruption that saw through the ban in 64. It is also possible that the kinds of dramatic variety performance that the festival may have featured were ideal for developing the political agenda of theater audiences, giving rise to spectacular grassroots activism (or leading to brutal demagoguery, depending on one's point of view).[127]

Compitalia therefore has the potential to signal the religio-civic flux of recent decades and to highlight the dangers of allowing societal divisions to coalesce along political fractures; it also emphasizes the ongoing vitality of what were believed to be truly archaic eruptions of civic unruliness, positive opportunities for letting off steam when effectively managed. In juxtaposition with the **Latin Festival**, casting Rome's gaze out to the Alban Hills, the in/out dynamic and Compitalia's roots at the intersection of slave, king, and god in legendary history make the shared Latin sacrificial meal (Varro's emphasis) fit especially well.

The Latin Festival is straightforwardly interesting for its significance at the imagined authentic March start to the old new year. Its (typically April) date was announced annually by the consuls when they took office. This made sense when March was the beginning of the consular year too.

The Latin Festival was

> dictus a <u>Latinis</u> populis, quibus ex **Albano** Monte ex sacris carnem petere fuit ius cum **Romanis**, a quibus <u>Latinis Latinae</u> dictae. (Varro, *Ling.* 6.25)

> Named from the <u>Latin</u> peoples, for whom there was a right, along with the **Romans**, to partake in the meat from the sacrifices on the **Alban** Mount. From these <u>Latins</u> it was named <u>Latin</u>.

I have followed the emendation from *carmen* ("song") to *carnem*,[128] but whether the shared foundational experience is in carving meat or meter, in Varro's version, the overall point stands: the festival is named for the inclusion of Latins alongside Romans, in a rite to which they gave their name. What gives it power is that while the Latins partake "*cum Romanis*," Romans ultimately cede some control over the sign (a Roman day in Varro's catalog, but with a Latin name) to create a new unity; the potency of Alba as a *lieu de mémoire* in the broadest sense is also a Varronian motif.[129] Moreover, Varro's structural juxtaposition of "Alban" and "Roman" within a "Latin" embrace economically tells a story of foundation whereby speaking Latin, even to assert Roman control, makes discourse simultaneously "ours" and "theirs."

Territorial politics are again at stake when Varro returns readers to the agricultural countryside with the **Seeding Festival** (Sementiuae) and the country districts festival, **Paganicae** (just previously termed Paganalia).[130] In calendar terms, this marks a shift back a few months to January when the Pontiffs set the Seeding Festival date. Its name signals its purpose: *sementis* (seeding) because it's there to mark the time for sowing (*satio*). When introducing the Paganicae, Varro repeats the phrasing "*causa susceptae*" ("undertaken for the sake of") from the Sementiuae, and the festival supports "*eiusdem agriculturae*" (that same agriculture). The Paganicae enabled the Pagus ("country" district) to celebrate en masse in its own fields ("*ut haberent in agris*," *Ling.* 6.26), and *ager* was at once a defining programmatic indicator (along with the Vinalia and Curia Calabra) for the etymologist's endeavor (*Ling.* 5.13) and the basic unit of fieldland (*Ling.* 5.34) whose productivity was foundational to community formation (*Ling.* 5.37).[131] This reading finds delicate encouragement for an optimistic contiguity between an array of ostensibly disparate Roman groups, and recalls

Varro's dynamic set-up for *forum* (where people came to exchange goods and ideas) as a site that realizes the countryside in the cityscape but also transforms countryfolk into people with a dependency on the city as well as vice versa.[132]

The text appends a short coda to the movable feasts—nonannual festivals with no fixed place in the calendar and those with no formal name of their own. Varro's example is the apotropaic **Novendialis**, a nine-day response to some ghastly prodigy or a ninth-day memorial ceremony for the dead.[133] In narrative terms, this festival is a structurally satisfying example of closure. What is more, its edible overtones keep readers in the agricultural produce zone, and it also looks back silently to the (February) Feralia's food offerings to the dead.[134] With this, Varro moves on to the days organized for mortal purposes.[135]

Manmade Time

Day-names take Varro from *habitus* to what he calls the "obvious"—how names attach to months.[136] First up are **Kalends**, from their distinctive activity. This is the day on which the monthly **Nones** (derived from "ninth," or "new") are announced ("*calantur*"), identifying whether the date will fall on the fifth or the seventh and proclaimed "*a pontificibus . . . in Capitolio in Curia Calabra*" (by the pontiffs, on the Capitoline, in the Proclamation Hall). Varro conjured up this venue early in book 5 as one of his two examples of what he terms "*societas uerborum*," the fellowship that bonds vocabulary of place and attendant activity, a locus that is realized (*aperio*) only through a monthly combination of words and action.[137]

Varro is unusually blunt in his conclusion on the **Ides**: some days have simply been translated apparently intact from the peoples of Latium, plugging the monthly proclamations into a culturally polyphonous ontological framework.[138] Of course thinking about the monthly line-up, Varro recalls that the Etrusco-Sabine Ides ultimately determine the position of Roman Nones, the moment for conference and stocktaking. Kalends kickstart each cycle, but each of the three fixed monthly points acts as a goal toward which the three sequences of days progress by name. After the Ides, Varro and his readers will be counting down to Kalends.[139] The **"dark days"** (*dies atri*) that follow each fixed point indicate that rushing into new undertakings immediately after one of the signposts is unwise, and especially so after the Ides in the long months immediately following Caesar's reforms.

The historiographical quality of these "dark days" is absent from Varro's account, but he holds over one of the most significantly persistent dark days, the **Day of the Allia** disaster (back in 390), to the very end of this sequence (after **Dung-Cleaning Day**, at Vesta's temple):

Dies <u>Alliensis</u> ab <u>Allia</u> fluuio dictus: nam ibi exercitu nostro fugato Galli obsederunt Romam. (Varro, *Ling.* 6.32)

The Day of the <u>Allia</u> is called after the River <u>Allia</u>; for it was from there, when our army was put to flight, that the Gauls laid siege to Rome.

Livy makes this event the source for all *dies atri*, commemorating a tribune's catastrophic failure to make the appropriate sacrifices on the day after the Ides of Quintilis, thereby exposing the army to divine disfavor when it confronted the Gauls two days later.[140] Varro moves briskly from unspecified dark days, however, to refocus on a topos familiar from the beginning of the civic days: speech.

Dies fasti, per quos praetoribus omnia uerba sine piaculo licet fari; comitiales dicti, quod tum ut <in Comitio> esset populus constitutum est ad suffragium ferundum, nisi si quae feriae conceptae essent, propter quas non liceret, <ut> Compitalia et Latinae.
    Contrarii horum uocantur dies nefasti, per quos dies nefas fari praetorem "do," "dico," "addico"; itaque non potest agi: necesse est aliquo <eorum> uti uerbo, cum lege qui<d> peragitur. Quod si tum imprudens id uerbum emisit ac quem manumisit, ille nihilo minus est liber, sed uitio, ut magistratus uitio creatus nihilo setius magistratus. (Varro, *Ling.* 6.30)

Good-speech days: those during which it is permitted to the praetors to speak all words without guilt. **Comitiales** are called because then is when it is established that the people should cast their votes in the Comitium, unless some festival had been declared on account of which it is not permissible, such as Compitalia or Latinae.
    The opposite of these are called **forbidden-speech days**, on which days the praetor is forbidden to speak out the forms "I give," "I pronounce," "I assign." Therefore it is not possible to take action, since using some from these words is necessary in order to conduct business according to the law. But if, at such a time, he [the praetor] has inadvertently uttered such a word and manumitted someone, that man is nonetheless free, but with a mark of misfortune [flaw, blemish], just as a magistrate elected under a similar cloud is nonetheless a magistrate.

At the heart of this passage is the enormous significance of speech and its power to color and disrupt as well as to regulate civic life.[141] We see the contextual power associated with particular formulae and how their utterance meshes with the business of the community and its self-regulation through discourse and as a function of chronology. Days of free speech and popular politics are juxtaposed with days when a praetor must negotiate the semiotic shoals with some care. As Varro goes on to say, a praetor can expiate a legal glitch occasioned by careless speech if he makes a sacrifice, but this works only if the mistake was genuine. For the unfortunate freedman (for example), no expiation is offered to allow him to lose the unfortunate gloss to his manumission.

Before he wraps up on hemerology with the Day of the Allia, Varro works through the oddities, starting with **divided days**, where forbidden-speech status makes morning and evening useless for conducting business but allows a divide to open up between the two, making civic business possible.[142] A variant, the day termed "**when the chief-priest [*rex*] has entered the Comitia: Good-speech**," gives a moment of political unity (the pronouncement by the chief priest of the appropriate sacrificial formulae to the assembly, after which legal action is permitted: "*itaque post id tempus lege actum saepe*").[143]

Month Names (At Last)

When Denis Feeney noted Varro's failure to explore how natural and civil times intertwine, he was also highlighting a key aspect of Varro's methodology: using detailed taxonomical triage to separate out key elements leading to interesting cases of delayed gratification in meaning.[144] Months, presented right at the end of the narrative arc, encourage readers to reconsider the systems already outlined and to frame the fixed festivals anew. "I have now pronounced on what pertains to the vocabulary of specific days," Varro observes, and, since a rationale for names of months is plain to see ("*aperta*"), he zips briskly through them.[145] If one counts from Mars' March, following ancestral ways ("*si a Martio, ut antiqui constituerunt, numeres*," *Ling.* 6.33), one comes to Venus inasmuch as she is Aphrodite, according to scholarly authority (Fulvius and Junius).[146] But although Varro's deployment of citation might have shored up an April-Aphrodite link, he quickly disses his sources with an indicative first-person assertion "I think," uncommon in *De Lingua Latina*:[147]

> Cuius nomen **ego** antiquis litteris quod nusquam **inueni**, magis **puto** dictum, quod uer omnia <u>aperit</u>, <u>Aprilem</u>. (Varro, *Ling.* 6.33)

> But **I** have never **found** her name in ancient writings, so **I think** it more likely that it was named <u>April</u> because spring <u>opens</u> all.

The reverberative direct juxtaposition of verb and noun strengthens the sense of inevitability for this linguistic explanation, especially as a wordplay coming hard on the heels of Varro's comment on the "apparent" or in-plain-sight quality of months' names. Scholarly research in this instance bows the knee to stating the obvious. To which Varro, moving on, adds for good measure that *Maius* recalls the *maiores*, while *Iunius* evokes the younger (or more recent) generation (*Ling.* 6.33).[148]

All of this associative density might remind readers that although Varro exhorted his audience to "count" from March (*numero*), there is no clear opportunity to put this in action until month five: Quintilis and from there up to December—it's numbers all the way.[149]

Whether or not one imagines Varro putting on a spurt of productivity and completing *De Lingua Latina* in late 45 or early 44, the fact remains that Quintilis became Iulius well within a plausible time frame for a postcirculation period of revision.[150] That firm assertion of Quintilis as number five belies the wholly scrutinized cognitive friction in commencing the festal year with January. Quintilis was already really month seven, not five, even before its rescripting as Iulius in 44 (not yet a year after Cicero's plaint that Varro seems not to be making progress with finishing *De Lingua Latina*) and the brouhaha surrounding the name/date for the Ludi Apollinares of July of the same year. The renaming was well enough bruited about at least by late June 44 to feature as a source of infuriation for Cicero and Brutus; although perhaps Cicero is more sharply amused, in his response, than angry.[151] Early July's two colorful epistolary sallies show how the shift was perceived: deeply political as well as foregrounding the calendar's increasingly explicit ideological flexibility.

Itane? "Nones <u>Iuliis</u>?" Di hercule istis! Sed **stomachari** totum diem licet. Quicquamne **turpius** quam **Bruto** "<u>Iulius</u>?" Nihil uidi. (Cic. *Att.* 16.1 [8 July 44])

Ibi **Brutus**. Quam ille **doluit** de "Nonis <u>Iulius</u>!" Mirifice **est conturbatus**. Itaque sese scripturum aiebat ut uenationem eam quae postridie ludis Apollinaris futura est proscriberent in "II Id. <u>Quint.</u>" (Cic. *Att.* 16.4 [10 July 44])

WHAT!? "Nones of <u>July</u>"? By Hercules is it indeed! But one can be **sick to the stomach** all day long. Could anything be **worse** than "<u>July</u>" for **Brutus**? Nothing that I've seen.

Brutus was there [at Nesis]. How he was **suffering** about the "Nones of July"! He was extraordinarily upset. So he said he would write to them that the Hunt that is to take place the day after the Games of Apollo, they should publicize as for "14th of Fifth Month."

Adding insult to injury, Brutus might have added, was that Octavian's games for Caesar (20 July) would then trump Brutus' primacy in the celebration of the Ludi Apollinares, diminish the profile that his sponsorship offered him, and complete what was effectively a rescripting of July for Caesar's memory and for his heir. This matters, for an etymologist, and Varro's choice and its lack of subsequent revision seems especially deliberate.[152]

When Varro reaches month ten he does the add-ons. First of these, from (Janus) the first-placed of the gods, comes the one called January (Ianuarius); the other, with a nod to scholarly authority, was called *February*, but the effort needed to make this rationale work ("*ab diis inferis*") is unconvincing to him, he says; "myself, I reckon 'February' from *dies februatus*—purification day—when the *populus* is purified," and this relocates the text to the world of the naked Luperci and their ritual encirclement of the ancient Palatine town, girdled with flocks of folk.[153] This represents a pastoral, low-key reading of a festival especially notorious for its celebration in 44 and to become even more so when Cicero launched into Philippic vitriol against Antony seven months later.[154] With that,

> quod ad temporum uocabula Latina attinet, hactenus sit satis dictum.
> (Varro, *Ling.* 6.35)

as regards what attaches to Latin vocabulary of time, let what has been said so far be enough.

Conclusion

This chapter's exploration of festivals from across Varro's year has traced some of the hows and whys for rethinking Varro's calendar as a data source or even as an attempt to record what Mary Beard (1987) has termed "a complex of times." On the face of it, readers might conclude that Varro lost an opportunity to articulate a barnstorming position on the politics of calendars and their dialogue with the natural order, but through-readers may find consistency in this chapter's case studies with a bigger scheme for Varro's project *De Lingua Latina*. This is not a teleological information handbook or a linear exegesis of how things connect. Instead, it is more like a matrix—a series of contexts for understanding and working Latin discourse. For the user, this model poses significant intellectual challenges but also offers rewards; it underscores the significance of Varro's project in enriching how time and place (natural and civic, religious and human) confront each other and how the right readers can be trained to draw (out) conclusions.

The "handbook" or manual that sets out to define and systematize a foreign language in use offers challenges of nuance and translation that a native speaker might alternately find awkward, funny, and ridiculous. But this is a handbook about Latin, in Latin, and for one audience already acknowledged as a master of the language (i.e., Cicero). If one responds to Varro's manual, whether by assimilation or resistance, one accepts that the interrogation of positionality and the occasional acceptance of absurdity engender a richer and more authoritative command of the language. One becomes, perhaps, the compleat communicator, a translator-cum-mediator, equipped to reel off appropriate, grandstanding rationales for how and why a fluid, intelligent command of Latin itself—being alert to the totalizing potential of Latin—is a controlling factor in politics. The ability to describe and explain Latin terminology in Latin and also the ability to combine these skills in order to convey the nature of Latin semiotics are complementary endeavors.

Varro interests himself and assumes "our" interest in language as an artificial *and* social construct—intensely personal and at the same time constitutive of a community subject to shared environmental and cosmic forces. To be sure, the civic and religious are examined as separable entities, but the reversal of what makes for a correct order of investigation (from *Antiquitates* to *De Lingua Latina*) and delicate indications of epistemological overflow between the two worlds highlight the fragility of the separation. In every meaningful sense, civic and religious worlds are entwined in their dependence on nature. When Varro articulates (in the *Antiquitates*) and reverses (in *De Lingua Latina*) a separation between the civic and religious frameworks, he tacitly manifests an underlying unity between natural and social orders—whichever way one looks at it, the Romespeaker of the Year not only can have it both ways but must.

Conclusion

Ending Up with Varro

"THE GREAT THING ABOUT HUMAN LANGUAGE," as once remarked by the poet, etymologist, and physician Lewis Thomas, "is that it prevents us from sticking to the matter at hand."[1] This has been a substantial study of a short(ened) book, once itself much bigger. Here, in *Language and Authority in "De Lingua Latina,"* I have sought to join in and amplify a latter-day conversation about Latin with Varro (he was barely dead before he became a focus for imaginative recuperation along these lines, as Vitruvius makes clear).[2] Its search for Varro's Romespeak has tunneled its way into the deceptive neutrality with which *De Lingua Latina* appears happy to provide data ready for snippet-style exploitation and found that stories and narrative emerge for cultivation, much like Varro's roots and branches of language. What is more, the ostensibly different concerns of the two (mostly) surviving triads, read together, deliver a powerful intervention that shores up consensus politics and articulates a remarkably optimistic vision of what Rome, expertly equipped with sufficient Romespeakers, could achieve. This version of the message might have been unpalatable to some of Varro's early audiences, but he was as much a provocateur as he was a scholar.[3]

"Texts resist readers by yielding their communicative cargo with less richness than they were freighted by their authors."[4] Writing in 1969, Michel Foucault (now famously) followed up on Roland Barthes' 1967 exploration of the "death" of the author with a nod to Samuel Beckett's observation "What matter who's speaking."[5] Yet for classicists and others working on cultures at once deeply familiar and perturbingly alien, opening a channel of communication to authors of surviving texts has been an importantly imperfect key to a disciplinary dilemma: how can classical antiquity continue to speak to "us," and vice versa? Varro's variant on this problem (identifying and enlisting the right legendary and historical figures to fight his corner on the matter of whose language was and is Latin and how to set "now" and "then" in dialogue) sharpens a sense that his concerns might still resonate directly with contemporary scholarship. The scholarly Varro might well seem an obvious analogue for the modern researcher seeking a personal relationship with the past, but Varro would likely urge caution: all scholarship on past cultures (even "ours") faces a challenge: how to negotiate the relationship between perceived content (perceived in the now) and the siren call of essentialism (a yearning to find authentic meaning, transmitted more or less intact from author to audience).[6]

Chapter 1 made a case for reading the author into the centrifugal paratext on the grounds that it matters why (and when) an author speaks—and who readers think the author is—every bit as much as what a text says. It mattered first and foremost to ancient authors, primed by and working within particular horizons of expectation; in every audience's tussle with a literary text, this impetus, the desire to know more, remains part of the baggage. Thus, in Umberto Eco's sense, my approach has been tactically expanding on (i.e., Eco's "blowing up") *De Lingua Latina*.[7] This has meant acknowledging that *De Lingua Latina* is a handbook about Latin, in Latin, by the foremost scholar and *littérateur* of his generation; a handbook designed for an audience already acknowledged as a master of the language, that is, Cicero, and more broadly, that circle. Varro's early readers were educated to grandstand oratorically in the Forum, courts, and senate; his intervention shows how description and exegesis in Latin of Latin terminology, and the ability to bundle these skills in order to convey the nature of things via Latin prose discourse, became complementary endeavors with political force.[8] This authorial Varro interests himself and assumes readers' interest in the intersection between what really needs to be articulated, the perceptual and associative spinoffs from such an authentic reality, and the equally powerful impetus of language as an artificial and social construct.[9] Some of what I have proposed should with hindsight appear obvious; that is the point. Indeed, Varro's complex and nuanced approach to consensus found so ready an audience that what survived was its powerful message rather than the text itself.

In the new world that was already emerging in Varro's extreme old age, the different kinds of appeal to traditional values that fired a Cicero (or a Caesar) to power were mutating rapidly, in the process becoming fit for the very different politics and epistemology of the Principate. The creation of "Augustus" would shape a world in which Varro's model was the inevitable model and inevitably assimilated. Varro's Romespeak, I have been arguing, was already beginning to show what a new kind of consensus could offer—his etymologies nudge readers into a receptive frame of mind, but it is in his (surviving) grammatical triad that Romespeak is most clearly systematized. With this outcome in mind, two summary reviews of the implications of Varro's second triad draw this conclusion to a close.

Disputare in Utramque Parte: Reviewing Books 8–10

This section's title returns us to my big-picture conclusions on Varro's combination of dialectic and grammatology. My goal throughout this study has been twofold—to illuminate the delights of Varro's unique literarity but also to reinforce the political and wider socionormative implications of key Varronian interests. These interests are the operation of language within discourse (and the relationship between *langue* and *parole*) and how singular opinions expressed separately by individuals—often exemplified in Varro's omnivorous use of verse quotation—or through non-Latin media can produce plurality and dialectic. Through dialectic, such individual interventions in Latin are systematized (*ratio*) and can deliver unity and cohesion (*consuetudo*). The ideological undertones of this reading are lodged in the trio of Cicero, Caesar, and Varro. All three interested themselves in modes of expression and style, all three wrote on the subject, and Caesar and Varro both dedicated books on Latin to Cicero.[10] Cicero's *consuetudo* is an elitist model—it situates power ostensibly with the community writ large but deprives the *populus* of access to knowledge (after all, why would they need it if *consuetudo* rules?) that nevertheless will persist among the right people. Caesar's *ratio* is by contrast a democratizing force, for those who know they need to—and can afford to—learn.[11]

Cicero's *Brutus*, triangulating the characters "Atticus," "Brutus," and "Cicero," adds context. "Atticus" starts by suggesting that Caesar needs to be included in the conspectus of the top orators, especially because his eloquence was hard won through enthusiastic attention to his studies. After some flowery discussion of Caesar's compliments to Cicero's eloquence[12] and Cicero's assertion of why art matters more than military glory or civic endeavors despite what the man on the street might think (*Brut.* 256–57), they return to Caesar. "Cicero" sums up, saying that even when something is rightly popular because necessary, it is still important to weight the balance in favor of quality rather than of quantity (*Brut.* 257). Things that are necessary should not be supported merely for that reason alone, which implies but does not insist that popularity ought in effect to be discounted.

> [Atticus:] Caesar, however, in his application of theory [*rationem*] to flawed, corrupt, habitual use, amends with sound and uncorrupted usage [*consuetudinem uitiosam et corruptam pura et incorrupta consuetudine emendat*]. And so to these choice [*elegantiam*] Latin words—whether

orator or not, equally necessary for every free-born Roman citizen—he has added those ornaments of oratorical eloquence [*oratoria ornamenta dicendi*] such that he seems to display a well-painted work of art [*tabulas bene pictas*] in an ideal light. Since he holds this particular distinction, over and above what is commonplace [*in communibus*], I can conceive of no one to whom he ought to yield the prize [*debeat cedere*]. (Cic. *Brut.* 261)

This lengthy passage, excerpted here, sketches Caesar as a Latin guru—almost a combination of Svengali and charlatan.[13] It also presents readers with a vignette in which "Cicero" and his companions (that is to say, Cicero and his other "selves") worry away at the relationship between terminology, novelty, and national dignity bound up in the process of "cultivating" speech and expanding the significance of Latin (especially at the expense of militarism).[14] Tacitly, it responds to and develops a "conversation" with Caesar that was formally initiated by Cicero in *De Oratore* and which Caesar would continue in *De Analogia*.[15] The metaphor of the painting and the light in which it is displayed is a curious one, with the role of the "light" distinctly ambivalent, but the underlying message is clear: by the time of writing, Caesar's mastery is smothering all competition.[16]

Speaking Latin should be easy and natural, for the right sort of people (Romans, citizens), so the thorny question that Cicero skirts is: how to evaluate and characterize the kind of studiously, ostentatiously "correct" Latin that Caesar (who tells Cicero that strange and unusual words are reefs upon which one may founder)[17] has made his shtick?[18] How much does politics add nuance to a technical evaluation of Caesar's speech?[19] We might suspect that between the mid-50s and the mid-40s Cicero has had some time to retrench, but, despite the changes in circumstance over the decade, Cicero seems still to envisage the possibility of reimagining *analogia* as something separate from common use in the widest sense and thus altogether distinct from "popularity." By making Caesar's "correctness" a stalking horse for *anomalia*, then, Cicero is continuing to worry away at the nuances of positionality that Caesar was making available. Yet, perhaps just as Cicero is recognizing more of a need for an accommodation with Caesar, Caesar is making that compromise position harder for a Cicero to reach.

Fronto's memorable vision of Caesar writing an excellently well-judged (*scrupulossimus*) work *De Analogia* while simultaneously trouncing the Gauls has the General pinning down declensions as the missiles fly, and modeling paradigms while the bugles and trumpets sound.[20] It shows what a long reach Caesar's treatise had, not just (perhaps not even primarily) a monument to the detail of his learning but a sign of the elegance with which controlling Gaul and mapping the minutiae of Latin could converge—a sign, thus, of a symbiosis between linguistic and territorial *imperium*. And, as David Wray sums up, persona games shoring up personal *auctoritas* might also be in play: "By [claiming to write] his grammatical treatise on analogy with Gallic missiles whizzing past his head . . . Caesar personates, in a single gesture, both Hellenistic high cultural excellence and 'Roman' heroic fearlessness in the face of death."[21] With this politicization of linguistic scholarship in mind, I return to Varro.

Given the role that Varro allots to *consuetudo* (produced and employed by the collective), there ought to be some significance in the relationship that he finds between singulars and plurals. Tackling plurals and (in various senses) plurality, Varro addresses the difference between a collective and unspecific plural and a particularizing plural, in a way that might also have invoked Caesar's paradigms.[22] Book 8 tests the potential for *consuetudo* to normalize discourse and correct glitches (*Ling.* 8.27–38), but it is also clear, by the time readers reach book 10, that the rational world of inflectional morphology is required for a balanced system. Varro thus sketches an entente between a *communis opinio* position (Cicero) and the individual imposition of logic (Caesar) even as he pokes fun at both by taking them to extremes.[23]

The examples he selects repeat from book 8 to 9, replicating a basic pattern, with book 9 echoing and riffing on book 8, and supporting a concluding assertion of singularity as an end-stopping linguistic form in itself, requiring no corresponding plural (*Ling.* 9.63–65).[24] Some collective "entities," Varro asserts, simply cannot exist (or, perhaps, be conceptualized) as individual elements. Earlier, in book 8, Varro had set up *cicer* alongside the arcane *siser* (English, skirret; apparently, a type of water parsnip) as two nouns that are always singularities.[25] There are lots of these ("*singularia solum sunt multa*"), yet still he selects one that plays on his dedicatee's name and another for which his use here is the first recorded example. Not an obvious example for proving a commonplace, and perhaps highlighting the subtle humor of the one and only "chickpea."[26]

This means that when through-readers revisit this topic with Varro (*Ling.* 9.63), the paradigm becomes a little more emphatic. Varro observes in book 9 that those who find fault with (*reprehendo*) the concept of Regularity use the singularity of *cicer* (and the plurality of *scalae*) as a rationale for denying what should be self-evident; what's their problem? "*Analogiae fundamentum esse obliuiscuntur naturam et usu<m>. Singulare est quod natura unum significat*" (the bottom line, for Regularity, is what they have forgotten: nature *and* usage work together). In effect, there is by nature nothing in a *cicer* that is twofold or that has the potential to express any kind of variety in essence. A *cicer* expresses its fundamental qualities consistently and as a unity (not like Varro's example of a singular collective, "*unae biga*," a two-horse team).

Varro continues to get mileage out of the singular qualities of the chickpea, returning to the potential joke in the final (extant) book: whatever grammatical position we start from, he states, it's in our power ("*in nostro dominatu*") to set words to entities, but we in turn have to admit ourselves subject to nature once we attempt to move from words to discourse.[27] "Our" *cicer* (singular) is the product of human volition, fixing one "word" (rather than any other) on an entity; yet still this "anomaly" declines in orderly fashion.[28] In a passage shortly after, Varro expands: when one is making a point ("*in demonstrando*"), one needs to be aware that a word's plural form is a better sign of its essential nature and lineage than its singular; singular forms are closest to *anomalia*, to the whims of human language formation ("*ab lubidine hominum*"), whereas the "collective" plural can guide one back to the etymological foundations.[29] He then wraps up this phase by arguing that:

> Principium id potissimum sequi debemus, ut in eo fundamentum sit natura, quod in declinationibus ibi facilior ratio. Facile est enim animaduertere, peccatum magis cadere posse in impositiones eas quae fiunt plerumque in rectis casibus singularibus, quod homines imperiti et dispersi uocabula rebus imponunt, quocumque eos libido inuitauit: natura incorrupta plerumque est suapte sponte, nisi qui eam usu inscio deprauabit. (Varro, *Ling.* 10.60)

> The principle [with declensions] that we ought to follow to the utmost is that nature is fundamental in this, because in inflection, it is there that the easier [more cooperative] system resides. For it is easy to observe that error can slip in especially through those impositions [associated with *uoluntas*] that are mostly made in the nominative singular, because mankind, unskilled and scattered, set names to things in accord with whatever way inclination invited. Nature, however, is for the most part in its own right uncorrupted, unless someone perverts it by ignorant use.

As long as appropriately knowledgeable people are able to keep track of anomalies as they occur and monitor the fickle preferences of the "singular" individuals that make up the Latin collective, the paradigms that deliver a mostly self-regulating system will maintain the natural order: "*a natura libido humana corrigetur, non a libidine natura, quod qui impositionem sequi uoluerint facient contra*" (human waywardness will be corrected by nature, not vice versa, because those who had wished to volunteer for an individual's right to "imposition" will end up in the other camp, *Ling.* 10.61).

The intensely civic qualities of Varro's connection between words, inflection, and discourse come to a head, I suggest, about halfway through book 10 (a little earlier than the passage just discussed). Varro starts to unpack the terminology by advising his readers that what Latin conceptualizes as a system of proportional relationships ("*ratio pro portione*") is what the Greeks would term ἀνὰ λόγον, and it is from this concept, shared by Greek and Latin speakers, that Latin's *analogia* derives (*Ling.* 10.37); it constitutes a regular and reciprocal relationship between two entities—each of which might be separately termed an analogue—but that tells equally on both (Greek and Latin speakers alike). Varro's first example makes this abundantly clear and bundles in an aside to Plautus for good measure: in a set of twins (let's call them "Menaechmi," *Ling.* 10.38),[30] when we describe one as being like the other, we are in fact making one twin only the object of our comment; when we say that taken as a pair, a similarity is present in which both of them partake, we are making *analogia*—a proportional and intelligible relationship of similarity (or, perhaps, communality) between two entities, generating something new and even interesting. With that comment, I suggest, my proposal that Varro's interest in singulars and plurals is significant comes back into focus.

The significance of Regularity for developing and cementing Latinate social networking is also inherent in this passage's exposition of *ratio* (*Ling.* 10.37) and it bounces around concepts considered by Davide Del Bello (2007) as much as it implicates the methods of network theory.[31] *Ratio* signals the proportionality in orderly relationships that underpins the (*from the Greek*) term *analogia*. That the literary brothers are twins allows Varro to exploit twins' unifying quality of "likeness," a quality that is distinct from any individuating characteristics either twin might be said to have. Varro's second example is about coinage, unified as a social unit of exchange, whatever its base material.[32] Once done with currency (and currency materials), Varro then turns to other more conceptual community-forming matters; here, sociability is explicitly foregrounded:

> Ut sodalis et sodalitas, ciuis et ciuitas non est idem, sed utrumque ab eodem ac coniunctum, sic ἀνάλογον et ἀναλογία idem non est, sed item est congeneratum. Quare si homines sustuleris, sodalis sustuleris; si sodalis, sodalitatem: sic item si sustuleris λόγον, sustuleris ἀνάλογον; si id, ἀναλογίαν. (Varro, *Ling.* 10.39)

> Just as "comrade" and "comradeship," "citizen" and "citizenship" are not identical, but both derive from the same thing and are connected, so analogue and analogy are not the same but are similarly related. Therefore if

you do away with men, you do away with the "comrade"; if the comrade's made away with, there goes "comradeship." Thus, in the same way, if you do away with the reasoned relationship, you do away with the proportionality in relationships; with this gone, thus goes the whole system of complex agreement (*analogia*).

I have taken some liberties with the translation here, to drive the point of this reading home more explicitly. What does not come out in translation, however, is the complex process of mediation between modes of speech, of discourse, and of language that Varro's dips into Greek terminology occasion. The normalizing deployment of Greek terms here reminds an audience that this is about the accommodation of alterity, which (increasingly) empire and the models of available citizenship require.[33] Sharing a fundamental organizational vocabulary with Greek speakers emphasizes that civilized peoples share a deeply embedded frame of reference (as Varro noted earlier, the process of modeling derivation and norms is something that Greeks and Latins alike have already produced books about).[34] The development of this point is emphasized in the next sentence: the sample terms chosen by Varro are all cognate (that is—it's a family affair, and family means those with whom we share a communicative mode), so to get real value from *De Lingua Latina* one needs to be *listening* actively (not mindlessly hanging on Varro's every word), feeding in learned and remembered data, and therefore developing and networking one's own new work-in-progress paradigms in response.[35]

What the passage makes abundantly clear is that there is a deep connection, akin to blood ties, between terms that hammer out a notion of productive equivalency within particular social contexts and that define the individual and collective qualities of citizen life as springing from a shared origin, an essential source "logos" that underpins them. Telling, also, is Varro's decision to lead his audience from his first examples—prioritizing the family unit and (next) the material currency of financial transactions—to more conceptual and also more complex terms that ultimately deliver a community and a shared set of values in dialogue with those individual beginnings.[36] *Analogia* matters on an individual and nitty-gritty level, but, in the end, without the sustaining principle, something rather larger is destroyed.

In addition to prepping his audience for the full weight of his synthetic proposal on *analogia* (one half of a blueprint for integrated living), the passage sets up a first-person address to the reader. It delivers clear marching orders: "since there is such a close kinship between these," Varro explains, "you yourself must listen, paying minute attention rather than waiting to be told; that is, when I have said something about either of the two [elements in the family unit], it will hold for both in common. You shouldn't wait until I rehash it in writing somewhere down the line; rather, you should yourself keep up the pursuit of the train of thought."[37] This is a significant statement of empowerment of the reader, emphasizing that Varro is providing the toolkit that we ourselves need to polish and hone and apply critically to the text as we read it through. It makes it clear that the role of the reader is very closely aligned to the role that Varro has identified for himself: the skilled hunter and tracker—albeit with the maestro always ahead of us in the pursuit. Finally, it embeds the communality and family values that underpin Latin within a Greco-Latin frame, demonstrating individual responsibility for the creation and emplotment of the social and semantic relationships that keep discourse on the move.

Ending Up

Book 10's importance, narratologically, is that this is where Varro spells out the case for compromise between the two competing positions; having allocated the first spot to those who decry Regularity (which we might sense is his least favored position),[38] book 9 performs a spirited argument for Regularity across the board. Usage, he states firmly, consists of regular and irregular words and their families, just as humanity resides in a union of body and spirit.[39] Varro now promises to rebut the arguments of book 8 one by one and to go even further (leaving book 8 as the Cinderella argument, *Ling.* 9.7). Finally, at the commencement of book 10, Varro's own sense of identification with his project and its significance is fully illuminated.[40] Readers already know that crimes against language should be avoided because they are deeply associated with crimes against the community (*Ling.* 9.114), and, as Varro re-emphasizes (alluding to *Ling.* 9.5), the people as a whole (*populus*) need a paradigm that delivers a unifying practice, but when broken down to an individual level there remains a need for (appropriate) diversity. On a cultural level, this shows up especially clearly at the end of book 9: the right (or perhaps responsibility, *ius*) of the poet to deviate from normal idiom is far more than that of the orator (*Ling.* 9.115). And since (Varro makes the claim) no one has previously set out what *anomalia* and *analogia* really signify, "*ipse eius rei formam exponam*" (I shall, myself, set an outline to the subject).[41] Explicitly, the whole point of Varro's project is to deliver a new or newly complete understanding of unity in diversity, the parts and the whole.

He returns to both these issues later and in more complex form. Regularity, the mode and idiom of a community, does not simply exist as a static concept, "*cum nisi in his uerbis quae declinantur non possit esse analogia*" (since only in declined words can Regularity be present, *Ling.* 10.14). Only choice and active participation deliver community of understanding and therefore identity, a reading encouraged by the fact that this passage leads into the discussion of the derivation of *Roma* itself (*Ling.* 10.15) discussed in chapter 1. The foundation of *analogia* is a concept of similarity that underpins all matters (*res*) and spoken words (*uoces*).[42] Logical Regularity (the Regularity one hopes to find; perhaps, also, the communal ideal), in order to become part of the logic of shared idiom and thus to generate active meaning, needs to be grounded in patterns of use— not all the clothes that can be made are equally wearable (*Ling.* 10.72). So what we need to take into consideration is, first, ancient usage; second, contemporary usage; and, third, models that do not fall into either category—the domain of poets (*Ling.* 10.73). Regularity in the paradigms needs to remain in dialogue with Regularity delivered by everyday use, one part of which operates as poetic range.[43]

Although books 8–10 are the first half of a new triadic pair and clearly mark a content shift from the etymologies of books 5–7, my study has traced more and less well-marked connecting paths from book 5 to book 10. Varro's enthusiasm for picking through the storehouse of Latin, a Latin that generously embraces not just Italic but also Mediterranean languages, delivers family history in books 5–7 and family trees in books 8–10. I began *Language and Authority in "De Lingua Latina"* by suggesting that miscellany is one mode to consider when attempting to categorize Varro's working practice, but miscellany, in Varro, is far from anarchic. Cataloging also featured as a comparative model for Varro's modus operandi in my introduction, but Varro avoids that mode's tendency to fetishize paradoxography (whereby exceptions and oddities become ways of telling on broader cultural and ontological paradigms in an imperial system).[44] Cataloging can seem to exhibit an author (or editor) at his or her most ostentatiously transparent and flamboyant, seemingly presenting a set of interconnected facts within a soaring, overarching structure that speaks of panoptic mastery.[45] Yet even where the "catalog" form might seem to deliver transparency, there are pitfalls as well as opportunities to shine.

In his difficult and often opaque study *Les mots et les choses*, Michel Foucault makes an argument worth restating in this context. He proposes that preservation generates taxonomy, and so every catalog or list (that is, every act of conscious preservation, here, of language and its systems) is ideologically flavored and produces its own rhetoric.[46] Conversely, without active preservation and curation, that is without a "Varro," persisting antiquarian traces are just that: devoid of the power to participate in culture formation in a meaningful way.[47] Varro's project might thus be to reinvent Latin as an episteme for synchronous and diachronous citizen self-fashioning (in other words, Romespeak). What

Foucault later calls "resemblance," "repetition," and "propagation" are all features of a systematization that suits Varro's project down to the ground: they enable an author (or reader) to discover something that apparently was always already there (which is, after all, what filling in the gaps represents), a background process that ensures the stability of the operating system.[48]

Words in use, as Wittgenstein puts it, deliver "a complicated network of similarities overlapping and criss-crossing: 'family resemblances'... build, features, color of eyes, gait, temperament, and so on."[49] Discourse, in this sense, cultivates a permeable family tree, accessible to those who know it root and branch. Competing forces are in play throughout: tradition, the desire for novelty, the flexibility of speech in use, and the kinds of sociopolitical drivers for change, stasis, and policing within language that shimmer through all six extant books. And this is even before one factors in the intensely personal quality of every speech act, flavored by accent, intonation, pacing, and mood, not to mention the hindsight with which one might judge (and later, in tranquility, rewrite) one's own and others' public pronouncements.

The *autho*ritative principle, in Foucault, defies clear definition; nevertheless, the idea of a "spirit" with which readers can establish "a community of meanings, symbolic links, and an interplay of resemblance and reflection" between phenomena and that can allow "the sovereignty of collective consciousness to emerge as the principle of unity and explanation" is seductive and fruitful.[50] Looking at Varro on "Project Varro," chapters 2–4 explored issues of the relationship between authorship and voice that are germane in this context here and resonate with the methodologies of cultural memory formulated by Jan Assmann.[51]

Varro's brand of etymology is not simply a manifestation of intellectual endeavor, research, or historical consciousness; instead, it represents a characteristic, totalizing mode of thinking and an organizing principle for *De Lingua Latina* and Romespeak.[52] His evident enthusiasm for identifying and demolishing assumed correlations between morphology and ontology by way of deep antiquarian research is matched by his interest in constructing new knowledge from old.[53] The identification of a coherent scheme in which like and less-like terms, etymologized, deliver a satisfying narrative unity is hugely important when attempting to model a through-reading agenda.

Etymology's figurative dynamics mean that its mastery depends substantially on a coherent concept of how associative connections work. Similarity and similarity-based structure continue to underpin aspects of Varro's Romespeak when he turns from an explicitly etymological opening hexad (books 2–7) to the matter of derivation and development in language and semiotics (books 8–10). In book 10, Varro articulates a clear position of similarity and dissimilarity that sheds light on the overarching structural and familial force of an etymological turn of mind (*Ling.* 10.3, 13) and encourages rereading of *everything* that has gone before. The work of the etymologist, in Varro's book, is therefore not altogether dissimilar to that of a genealogist. Hence, a deep understanding of the correlation between shared understanding of the roots and branches of meaning and the paths of derivation that ensue is what constitutes a meaningful cultural and linguistic syntax. When Varro makes it possible to ferret out and find meaning in similarity and dissimilarity (of etymologies; between etymologies and common use; in terminology between peoples or eras; in grammatical declination) he is also approaching the question of what Rome represents and what it will become.

The Varro dilemma, if we want to conceive it in that way, would be that his fame is largely predicated on the enormity of his oeuvre (as Augustine summed up, this was a man who read so much that we might doubt his time left to write but who confounds that expectation by having written more than anyone might think possible),[54] yet for his posterity, no textual habeas corpus or full autopsy is possible. In this way, identifying the historical Varro too closely with his absent back catalog, making "Varro" a function of that loss and reading what survives as fragmentary in that sense, is to admit defeat in advance. Petrarch already understood this implicitly: he wrote his own "lost" Varro into being, but as a shadow of what might have been had a man who combined scholarship with military success and statesmanship not been lost to more degenerate eras.[55] If Varro (man and work) is to shine again, some imaginative gap-filling and generosity of spirit will be required, and, across the associative readings that I have proposed, my aim is to cultivate new territories and wider-spreading root systems for Varro's trees.[56]

Voltaire once wrote:

Ses antiques fatras ne sont point inutiles,
Il faut des passe-temps de toutes les façons,
Et l'on peut quelquefois supporter les Varrons,
Quoiqu'on adore les Virgiles.[57]
                    (Voltaire, *Épigramme à M. de Cideville sur
                    les livres de Dom Calmet* [1754])

Varro gets deep under the skin of Latin, and Voltaire's mockery of Dom Calmet uncovers a serious point. The forces that cause paradigms to shift and empires to fall are often unseen and frequently relentless. Varro worms his way through the semantic field, and he produces irritating, funny, obvious, and bizarre etymologies and fans the flames of a grammatical dispute that might not otherwise have ignited; yet in the process he teaches Romans to speak a generously spirited Latin, and he recalls Cicero and Caesar to the negotiating table. If Caesar and Cicero had lived, Varro's, not Vergil's, palimpsestic Rome, a city always attuned to its migrant, transitory roots and enthusiastic in its embrace of polyphony, might have become the city most visited. Had Octavian not successfully delivered the novel consensus politics of the Augustan Principate, the narrative force and novel message of *De Lingua Latina* might well have ensured its complete survival, an example of what might have been.

Notes

Abbreviations

Abbreviations of ancient authors and texts follow the conventions of the *Oxford Classical Dictionary*.

ACIV = 1976. *Atti Congresso Internazionale di Studi Varroniani, Rieti Settembre 1974*, 2 vols. Rieti: Centro di Studi Varroniani.

ANRW = Temporini, H., and W. Haas, eds. 1972 onward. *Aufstieg und Niedergang der römischen Welt*. Berlin: Walter de Gruyter.

Augustinus = Augustinus, A., ed. 1554. *Editio Vulgata*. Rome: Vinc. Luchinus.

BNP = Cancik, H., and H. Schneider, eds. [Antiquity], and M. Landfester, ed. [Classical Tradition]. *Brill's New Pauly Online*. http://referenceworks.brillonline.com/browse/brill-s-new-pauly.

Bücheler = Bücheler, F., ed. (1882) 1963. *Petronii Satirae et Liber Priapeorum: Adiectae sunt Varronis et Senecae Saturae Similesque Reliquiae*. Berlin: Weidmann.

CAH = *Cambridge Ancient History*, 19 vols. Cambridge: Cambridge University Press.

CIL = 1863-. Königlich Preussische Akademie des Wissenschaften zu Berlin. *Corpus Inscriptionum Latinarum*. Berlin: Georgium Reimerum.

FGrH = Jacoby, F., ed. 1954–64. *Die Fragmente der griechischen Historiker*. Leiden: Brill.

FRH = Beck, H., and W. Walter, eds. 2001, 2004. *Die frühen römischen Historiker*, 2 vols. Darmstadt: Wissenschaftliche Buchgesellschaft.

Funaioli = Funaioli, H., ed. 1907. *Grammaticae Romanae fragmenta*. Leipzig: Teubner.

Groth = Groth, A. 1880. *De M. Terenti Varronis de Lingua Latina librorum Codice Florentino*. Argentorati/Strasbourg: Truebner.

GS = Goetz, G., and F. Schoell, eds. 1910. *M. Terenti Varronis de Lingua Latina quae supersunt*. Leipzig: Teubner.

ILLRP = Degrassi, A. 1963–65. *Inscriptiones Latinae Liberae Rei Publicae*, 2 vols. 2nd ed. Florence: La Nuova Italia.

Kent = Kent, R. G., ed. and trans. 1951. *Varro: On the Latin Language*, 2 vols. Rev. ed. Cambridge, MA: Harvard University Press.

Laetus = Pomponius Laetus, ed. 1471. *Varro, de Lingua Latina* [*Editio princeps*]. Rome: Georgius Lauer.

LTUR = Steinby, E. M., ed. 1993–2000. *Lexicon Topographicum Urbis Romae*, 6 vols. Rome: Edizioni Quasar.
Maltby = Maltby, R. 1991. *A Lexicon of Ancient Latin Etymologies*. ARCA 25. Leeds: Francis Cairns.
Mueller = Mueller, K. O., ed. 1833. *M. Terenti Varronis de Lingua Latina librorum quae supersunt*. Leipzig: Weidmann.
OLD = Glare, P. G. W., ed. 1968–82. *Oxford Latin Dictionary*. Oxford: Clarendon Press.
PHI = PHI *Latin Texts: Classical Latin Texts, a resource prepared by The Packhard Humanities Institute*. http://latin.packhum.org/.
RE = Pauly, A., G. Wissowa, W. Kroll, et al., eds. 1894–1980. *Realencyclopädie der Classischen Altertumswissenschaft*. Stuttgart: Metzler.
ROL = Warmington, E. H., ed. and trans. 1935, rev. 1956. *Remains of Old Latin*, 4 vols. Cambridge, MA: Harvard University Press.
Scaliger = Scaliger, J. 1565. *J. Scaligeri coniectanea in M. Terentium Varronem de Lingua Latina*. Paris: R. Stephanus.
Scioppius = Scioppius, G., ed. 1602. *M. Terentii Varronis De Lingua Latina ex recensione Gasp. Sciopii*. Ingolstad: A. Sartorius.
Servius = Thilo, G., ed. 1881. *Maurus Servius Honoratus. In Vergilii carmina comentarii. Servii Grammatici qui feruntur in Vergilii carmina commentarii; recensuerunt Georgius Thilo et Hermannus Hagen*. Leipzig: Teubner.
TLL = *Thesaurus Linguae Latinae*. 2009 (online). Berlin: De Gruyter.
Vahl. = Vahlen, I., ed. 1903. *Ennianae Poesis Reliquiae*. Leipzig: Teubner.

A Roadmap for a Ruinous Text

1. Ax 1995, 147–49, sums up on structure, with an invaluable textual map at 148.

2. See Kent 1951, xii–xvii, for an overview of the manuscript tradition, and xxvii–xxxiii on the editions.

3. Kent 1951, xlix, provides details and some examples.

4. Although following the numbering in Kent, my reading slightly prefers the flow of sense across 10.42–50 as reorganized by Taylor 1996 (explained at 136–39), whereby chapters 43–44 are moved to between chapters 50 and 51.

5. The examples listed for similar words inflecting in *dis*similar (<*dis*>*similiter*) ways and similar inflections from dissimilars, as followed by Kent, is better explained by Taylor 1996 as a follow-up to 10.42.

6. Following *F* and reading *leui* rather than *claui* as accepted by Kent.

7. Following Taylor 1996 and finding a short (because the material should be self-evident) lacuna replacing what might have been said about the first kind of Regularity.

8. Following the spirit of Kent's text but sticking more closely to Taylor 1996.

9. Following Taylor 1996.

Introduction

1. Ady, ably dismissing the "why bother with it?" argument (which James Joyce's *Finnegans Wake* still ignites), in 1986.

2. The standard catalog is cobbled together from Jerome and other citations (see *BNP* s.v. Varro [2] Terentius, M. [Reatinus]). The estimate of seventy-four individually titled works, running to some 620 books, seems plausible. Reference in the catalog to an epitome of *De Lingua Latina* suggests that Varro may have condensed his twenty-five-book work into a more compact nine scrolls.

3. Varro, "*Der bedeutendste röm. Universalschriftsteller*," Klaus Sallmann, in *BNP* s.v. Varro (2) Terentius, M. (Reatinus).

4. Following *F*, at this point Varro refines his task as being to focus on the application of words to things in poetic usage ("*et ea quae sunt in consuetudine apud poetas*"). Since Varro is clearly not focusing solely on poetic practice and is evidently interested in popular parlance (e.g., *Ling.* 5.6), the emendation proposed by Spengel (1885) is attractive: the insertion before "*poetas*" of "*populum et ea quae inueniuntur apud*." Dangel 2001 provides a useful conspectus for Varro's poetic citations; on colloquialism as a topos, see Ferri and Probert 2010.

5. Two occurrences of *opinor* in *Ling.* 6.64 (interesting because it qualifies the etymology for *sermo*; and see Quint. *Inst.* 1.6.1), 7.70.

6. This version of the etymological project responds to an agonistic reading of the role of etymology in Plato's *Cratylus*. See especially Baxter 1992, Mackenzie 1986, Sedley 1998 and 2003, where Platonic etymology marks the successful analysis of words "as if they were time capsules—encoded packages of information left for us by our distant ancestors about the objects they designate" (2003, 7). This trend is summed up by Riley 2005, 6–7, while Ademollo 2011, 11–14, takes the argument in a differently profitable direction, that separating and scrutinizing how entities and names interact can open up important questions about denotative and connotative values when one is exploring what makes a perfect language and its relationship to the forces of historical change.

7. Taylor 1996a, 4, observes: "We can safely conclude that Varro, unlike ancient historians for example, never bothered to add the literary polish to his works that we might otherwise expect." "Polish," however, is only the most superficial facet of what constitutes literariness most meaningfully.

8. Rust 2009, 31, refines the term "miscellany" to deliver instead the tag "knowledge collection" for Gellius *NA*, and her view of a deeply structural (as she puts it, "radical") disorder (a kind of entropy, one might suggest) continues to be important here.

9. Keulen 2009 developed this kind of large-scale creatively imaginative reading for a similarly (although differently) challenging author, Gellius.

10. On making "antiquarianism" signify a refusal to propose robustly synthetic interpretive strategies, see Momigliano 1950 (cf. the more complex position outlined in Momigliano 1961). On Momigliano's antiquarianism, Phillips 1996, and its influence: Haskell 1993, 159–200, who devotes a chapter to Gibbon in similar terms.

11. Cic. *Nat. D.* 3.62.

12. Bloomer 1997a, 50; see also Sluiter 2015 passim. Relevant work on etymology in Vergil, Propertius, and Ovid (e.g. Michalopoulos 1998, 2001; J. F. Miller 1992; O'Hara 1996, 2001) evidences the reach of this mode within the decades after Varro, and its

backward glance (see also Pieroni 2011, for the tradition). Throughout this book I have found network theory to be a useful conceptual framework for approaching etymology (see, e.g., Ferrer i Cancho 2008 for a clear introduction, but also scene-setting in Taylor 2002).

13. Paraphrasing Gunderson 2009, 6, on Gellius.

14. Gell. *NA* 13.31. See Gunderson 2009, 176–78.

15. Della Corte 1954; Bezzola and Ramat 1957, 46 (*Trionfo della Fama* 3.38). By contrast, e.g., Boissier 1861, 1–26, manages to make Varro, as an individual, worthy but stodgy.

16. Piras 2000 traces the manuscript tradition in enormous detail; Reynolds 1983, 430–31, remains an excellent overview.

17. On Varro, *Ling.*, we have about four pages in Rawson 1985, 125–29. Bloomer 1997a takes a refreshing and imaginative approach, while Levene 2005 is both a precursor to Wiseman 2009 and an alternative model for why Varro matters.

18. Baier 1997, 15–27, presents a sober study of the parallelism.

19. All dates are BCE unless otherwise specified. Attempting encyclopedism on Varroniana, Philipp Brandenburg's bibliographical resource is extensive and well organized.

20. In particular, see D. J. Taylor 1974, 1988, 1996a, 1996b; for a sample of the outstanding groundwork I have benefited from, including editions and studies, see, e.g., GS 1910; Dahlmann 1932, 1940; Collart 1954a, 1954b, 1978; Della Corte 1954; Traglia 1956, 1963, 1993; Della Casa 1969; *ACIV* 1976; Riposati 1976b; Riganti 1978; Cavazza 1981; Pfaffel 1981; Flobert 1985, 2001; Ax 1995, 1996; Baier 1997, 1999, 2001; Piras 1998, 2015; Coleman 2001; Maltby 2001 (now joined by De Vaan 2008); Salvadore 2001; Hinds 2006; Blank 2008; Zehnacker 2008.

21. "Legendo autem et scribendo uitam procudito," Varro, *Sat. Men.* 555.1 (Non. 156 M).

22. "Risi [uisi] multum lusi modice," Varro, *Sat. Men.* 548 ("Tithonus") (Non. 343 M). Cf. Hor. *Epist.* 1.14.36.

23. Greenblatt 1980; Dugan 2005. Cf. Foucault (1969) 1977, (1984) 1988.

24. Hölkeskamp (2004) 2010, 108–9, poses the wider questions.

25. McClaverty 1991, although not specifically tackling the problem of fragmentary texts, makes some illuminating comments about what signals "the author's . . . attitude to identity"; even the choice of (in)visibility makes a minimally self-conscious author intrude. As Eco 1994, 3, recalls, a text is a "lazy machine" requiring collaboration to complete the product. Henderson 2010 makes for an interesting parallel of what this kind of hindsight/insight project might look like, but, as a whole, Stray 2010 does not excavate the kinds of issue that face Varro and his readers.

26. For a quick overview of the interrelationships, see Kumaniecki 1962; Leach 1999.

27. Aug. *De civ. D.* 6.2. See Nora's work, e.g. 2001.

28. On ethnoscapes, see A. D. Smith 1999, 150–52, and drawing in syntax, Goddard 2002. Spencer 2010, 33, 36–38, 44–46, sums up relevant context on landscape and cites recent critical discussion.

29. Casey 2001 gives us "placial memory," discussing Bourdieu 1977's formulation *habitus*.

30. E.g., Cic. *Leg.* 1.3, 2.4, 2.5 (telling stories makes spaces meaningful; on the duality of what one calls "home"), *Nat. D.* 2.152, and *Acad.* 2.127 (human intervention or scrutiny makes for a new natural order); Livy 5.51.1–54.7 (Camillus' speech). Vasaly 1993, 12, 15–20 (on another story from Livy: the topicality of the trial of Manlius Capitolinus) and passim, proposes key aspects of this with a focus on Cicero, a hugely influential and detailed analysis. See Foucault (1969) 2002, 120.

31. This analysis draws substantially on the exegesis of the development of *Latinitas*, with reference to Cicero, in Clackson and Horrocks 2007; although they separate grammar from rhetorical technique, their comment that "the definition of *Latinitas* became increasingly bound up with a program of promoting linguistic and cultural ideals through literary activity" is crucial (2007, 187, cf. 202, 206). On the dangers of getting oratory wrong, see e.g., Wisse 2013.

32. Cf. Tac. *Dial.* 21, Aper on Cicero and Caesar as poets (among other things), and at §23 (cuttingly) on Varro as a stylist (as per Quint. *Inst.* 10.1.95). Reworking Sedley 2003, 1, one might see in this kind of conversation the structure of thought itself. Garcea 2012 is especially compelling on the politico-cultural tangle that grammar might represent (summed up by Fronto in the famous comment on Caesar's composition of *De Analogia*: "*inter tela uolantia de nominibus declinandis, de uerborum aspirationibus et rationibus inter classica et tubas*" (*De Bello Parthico* 9). Hock and Joseph 2009, 215–18, entertainingly set up the friction between the fascination for "fuzzy" semantics on the part of nonlinguists and the order and precision of syntax, beloved by linguists.

33. I discuss this passage elsewhere, extensively: Spencer 2011b, 2011c, 2015a, 2015b. Cf. *Ling.* 5.4.

34. Spencer 2011b, n. 22, discusses the difficulty of conclusively identifying "Mucius" and "Brutus." Questions raised by this passage might include the extent to which Varro is circling the issue of "archaic neologism"; for background on which, see, e.g., Lebek 1970 (see also Nicolas 2000).

35. Despite the metaphorical flight of fancy (and as Lakoff and Johnson 2003 make clear, metaphors are serious business), Varro's point remains potent and chimes with Eco's reading model: do we test only as many "paths" through the wood as get us to our goal? Or do we "walk so as to discover what the wood is like and find out why some paths are accessible and others are not" (Eco 1994, 27; see also Del Bello 2007); for a detailed contemporary summary of all the factors, see Hock and Joseph 2009, 1–20.

36. Cic. *Brut.* 258.

37. Cf. Mangen 2008, whose hypertext reading-strategies analysis hints at a more resonant connection between scroll and digital media than between either format and the codex. This topic also refers to cultures of reading tackled by Small 1997, 141–55 (regarding research techniques), 156–77 (on compositional techniques), 193–96 (on using quotations); on quotation (in Festus), see North 2007. Useful here: e.g., Johnson 2000, Starr 2001, and Rust 2009, 8–9 (introducing Gellius) and 188–98 (on Seneca and Gellius).

38. Kritzman 1981 edited a theoretically rich collection of approaches that help to clarify the congruence of accidental and designed fragmentation (e.g., Rosand 1981). Within Classics, see especially Dionisotti 1997 (in the excellent Most 1997) and, e.g.,

Manuwald 2001, Cornell 2013, 4–20 (with J. W. Rich and J. Briscoe). On Plutarch, König 2007 ties together issues relevant to Varro (where fragmentation may be structural as well as lossy). On the methodological value of Ennius in this context, see Gildenhard 2003 (focusing on genre) and Elliott 2013, 1–17 (interrogating the interplay between transmission and editorialization); on Cato, see Briscoe 2010.

39. Eco 1984, 80.

40. Henderson 2007, 210; cf. 2007, 22, on the issue of "completeness" for Isid. *Orig.* For more on these issues, see, e.g., Gunderson 2009, 46 (and passim); Keulen 2009, 17–23 (and projecting "texts and authors that matter" and "rewards and punishments," at 21, 23), 87–94 (on the schoolteacher's mere list); Rust 2009, 51–59 (on inclusion and exclusion).

41. The problem of the technical handbook and literariness, and the relatively recent genesis of interest in the mode/genre, is interestingly addressed by van Mal-Maeder 2007, and in Glinister, Woods, North, and Crawford 2007. See Carey 2003 (Pliny); Anderson 2004 (Gellius); Murphy 2004 (Pliny); Gunderson 2009 (Gellius); Keulen 2009 (Gellius); Rust 2009 (Gellius); Doody 2010 (Pliny).

42. Rust 2009, 30–31: "miscellaneous," "1. The contents . . . relate to many disciplines. 2. The chapters are written in several formats, including first-person narratives, dialogues, short notes, and short treatises. 3. These chapters are randomly arrayed throughout the work, so that different topics and styles follow one another without connection." Cf. Eco 1984, 79.

43. Blank 2008 is very much of this opinion with regard to Varro's historian's-eye-view approach to etymology. Cf. Cavazza 1981, 72–73, who observes on Varro's antiquarian vein but is less convinced of the structural logic; nevertheless, he observes acutely that etymology is a mode of thinking characteristic of Varro: "L'etimologia è una <<forma di pensiero>>, un veicolo di studio, riveste una funzione eziologica, diviene chiave per l'antichità romana, un cammino non sempre sicuro ma talora valido per l'antiquario e lo storico delle origini di Roma" (73).

44. Varro, *Ling.* 5.25 (three times); 5.38, 5.80, 5.166, 6.4, 6.22, 7.21 (PHI online database).

45. The extravagant wordplay in this lengthy passage (*Ling.* 5.25) takes in *pote* (can be), *puteus* (well, cistern, pit), *nisi . . . potius* (unless, rather), *potus* (a drink), *Puteoli* (a town on the Bay of Naples renowned for its volcanic springs), *putor* (stench), *putidus* (fetid), *puticuli* (grave pits), and *putesco* (to putrify).

46. Gunderson 2009, 5.

47. One might wonder whether the comprehensiveness of Varro's study and his fame as a scholar (as witnessed by Cicero, Quintilian, Gellius, and others) may in part have led to his cannibalization by subsequent citation and allusion rather than the production of full copies.

48. Foucault (1969) 2002, 24.

49. One might take as an example Robert Maltby's outstanding contribution to the organization of ancient Latin etymologies (Maltby 1991). Many an entry finds its exegesis only in Varro, so when one consults in order to explore the roots of Varro's more obscure explanations, one finds oneself returned to the starting point.

50. That Caesar's *De Analogia* was (probably) written while he was in Cisalpine Gaul will be further grist for the mill when we focus on *oratio*. See Hendrickson 1906, Dahlmann 1935, Horsfall 1972 to sample the problems in pinning down a date for Caesar's text. The introduction to Garcea 2012 is admirable on the ramifications.

51. On Varro's cases, see Calboli 2001a, 2001b.

52. Cf. Varro, *Ling.* 8.28—having noted a disparity in the genitive of Hercules, *Herculi-is* (8.26), Varro meanders on through the book's required argument against Regularity, observing on the different designs of clothing that do the same basic job, separately, for men and women (a toga is just as useful, even though it's most unlike a tunic . . .). Here, the dissimilarity is key to the utility. At 8.75–78 the irregularity in comparatives is his anti-Regularity argument's focus, e.g., the personally descriptive quality of kinship as imagined through naming (cf. 9.60–61). See also *Ling.* 9.71–72 (on distinctive trisyllabic name forms, so, e.g., Scipiones).

53. "*Quas si quis seruet analogias, pro insano sit reprehendus,*" *Ling.* 8.33. Blank 2005, on this persona, argues that Varro is drawing for detail on Epicurean scholarship, but it remains the case that Varro often seems reluctant to map the history of scholarship in the way modern readers have hoped.

54. "*Quod in pluribus est dissimilitudo, ut non sit in sermone sequenda analogia,*" *Ling.* 8.37.

55. E.g., *Ling.* 9.48, where the comparison is again to gendered dress (returned to at 10.28), or the discongruity in naming between the polyphonous children of Jupiter and the paradigmatic children of a Terentius (*Ling.* 9.55).

56. "Like in the motions of the heavens," *Ling.* 9.34. The lousy sense of *lens* may have appeared later than Varro, although, in tandem with the shaggy wolf, the itch would seem to be scratched.

57. "*Ut ab Romulo Romuli Romulum et ab dico dicebam dixeram,*" *Ling.* 9.34.

58. Cf. Cic. *Nat. D.* 3.62–64: criticizing etymology as a backstop for mythology. By contrast, Cic. *Top.* 35–37 shows verbal symbolism to have real-world force (see also, e.g., Cic. *De or.* 2.256–57). Cicero draws out issues raised by Aristotle, e.g., Arist. *Rh.* 1400b17–25; *Top.* 112a32–38; on the Platonic position, see Silverman 1992.

59. Although Varro rarely uses the Greek forms (we find them again only at *Ling.* 10.38, 39), the emendation from Latin to Greek here makes orthographic sense based on F and the context, and it also delivers a neat twist when Varro shifts to the Latin forms after the emphatic "*ut ego arbitror.*"

60. Zehnacker 2008, 422, sums up economically, but for a detailed exposition of the Hellenistic afterlife of this approach, Long and Sedley 1987 make an invaluable contribution (especially on Epicurean developments and how Stilo fits in).

61. Cf. Varro, *Ling.* 10.37, 43–50, where a granular understanding of the rational mathematical underpinning of "Analogy" is on display. Schironi 2007 is illuminating here.

62. The anti-Analogist relies on there being nouns with shared case forms (e.g., where a second declension noun is the same in dative and ablative singular) but not all nouns having the same number of shared case forms; hence the argument that there is no Regularity in cases (*Ling.* 8.63–65, 68). Where—e.g., with Greek letters—only one case form exists at all, Varro's anti-Analogist says that simply being wholly foreign (even

"*penitus barbara*") is no answer to the question of why such "anomalies" exist. After all, Greeks can articulate a full, logically derived set of cases for Latin words, for Persian words, and the whole rest of the pack designated by Greeks as "barbarous."

63. Strabo made extensive use of Artemidorus' geography, so it was clearly *au courant* by the time he was writing. Although this is a sandy foundation, I am encouraged to include the joke because Artemidorus also wrote an Ἰωνικὰ Ὑπομνήματα, which would—if in the mix—play on the imagined slave called "Ion" from "Ionia," completing the alt.Artemidorus (*FGrH* 438). Artemidorus of Tarsus, (perhaps) a collector of bucolic poetry in the early first century, could also be a reverberation (although Cilicia drags one much farther east).

64. I discuss this passage, with *Ling.* 5.12, in Spencer 2015a, 100–101. Writing in the 1970s, Lefebvre ([1974] 1991, 3–4) commented polemically on the problems of Foucaultian "space" as set out in the 1969 work *L'Archéologie du savoir* and highlighted its dis-ease with the intersection between epistemology and lived experience (e.g., Foucault [1969] 2002, 170, 201). On language as movement, see, e.g., Fruyt 2012, 107. The chariot metaphor takes readers back to Plato's *Phaedrus*, but, especially relevant for Varro, the likely take-up (horses) in Lucil. Frag. 1280–86 [Porph. *in Hor. Carm.* 1.27.1]. Cf. Lucr. 6.46–47; Hor. *Sat.* 1.1.114–16; Verg. *Georg.* 1.512–14 (and Henderson 1995, 108).

65. Farrell 2001, 36–39; cf. Cic. *Nat. D.* 1.8, *Fin.* 1.10, *Arch.* 23. One might also consult his *Brutus* and *De Oratore*.

66. Lucr. 3.258–60. cf. Varro, *Ling.* 5.13. Atherton 2005 offers helpful context here.

67. Waquet 1998 coined the phrase. Benveniste (1966–74) 1971 (especially, note 43–48, 223–30), and Benveniste et al. 1966, 7–14, influentially located identity in language, focusing on the power of the speaker to determine the story in ways that seem to echo some of Varro's concerns; cf. Lotman 1990, 124–25, who in the 1980s coined the term "semiosphere" to conjure up a totalizing system boundaried by acts of translation. Brisset 2004 (on translation and identity) is a useful comparator.

68. The river emblematizes problems confronting a community's cultural memory. Without a guide, each experience of how the *riuus* relates to the *fons* and what the course of the *riuus* represents is inaccessible. On the links to Lucretius and Callimachus, see Brown 1982, 80–82. Origins for rivers, especially the Nile, were already objects of fascination; Williams 2008, 230 (discussing Sen. *NQ* 4a.2.3–16) sums up conceptually relevant epistemological issues.

69. Syme 1939, 249; my emphasis.

70. There is no evidence that Varro's work was conceived as dinner-party performance material, but it could certainly be used to generate material for educated conversation and evaluative, discriminatory participation in convivial entertainment (compare, e.g., Cic. *Brut.* 183–88, on evaluating oratory); compare, e.g., the material produced and recorded by the Elder Seneca or Valerius Maximus' memorable nuggets. M. B. Roller 2006, 9, sums up relevant scholarship on Roman dining and equates convivial and courtroom performance. Varro's poetry *might* have been performed as after-dinner entertainment; concretely, the relentless use of verse-snippet quotation to illustrate analyses and prove conclusions in *De Lingua Latina* provides a comparable exemplar.

71. Bloomer 2011, 137.
72. See Collart 1954b, xiv, xxv–xxvi, xlv, on "*télégraphique*" style.

Chapter 1. Networking Varro

1. Naevius' so-called epitaph (*ROL* 2, 154–55).
2. Ver. Fl. ap. Fest. 434 L.
3. Symmachus, *Ep.* 1.2; contra, August. *De civ. D.* 4.1 has Varro: "*Romae natus et educatus.*"
4. Pease 1995 outlines this (potential for) trouble with authors. Cf. Della Corte 1954 and Riposati 1976a, trying to get a feel for Varro the man of letters.
5. Bloomer 1997b.
6. Butler 2002, 4–5. Epstein 1991a is a landmark collection for exploring a new role for biographical criticism; particularly useful, e.g., Epstein 1991b, Ross 1991, Walker 1991. Cf. Foucault (1969) 1977.
7. E.g., Cic. *Leg.* 2.5 for the clearest iteration. On the ethical resonances of playing off origins/Romanness in Cicero, Salmon 1972; Vasaly 1993, 30–33. Farney 2007, 5–26, provides useful detail; Spencer 2010, 36–41, sums up for the ethos of landscape and place. On Rome, C. J. Smith 2006, 187–88, 194, 201, is invaluable. See also Kretschmer 1920 (terminology), Collart 1954b, 232–33, Riposati 1976b, and, more generally, Poucet 1967, Briquel 1996.
8. Varro ap. Dion. Hal. *Ant. Rom.* 2.48. See Capdeville 1996 on Modius Fabidius as a kind of Romulus; there are clearly also elements of *pius* Aeneas in play here too. Wiseman 2009, 97–98, discusses the Romulus/Quirinus connection with reference to Varro and Reate, but more generally see Palmer 1970, 160–72. On genealogical power play in the late Republic, see Wiseman 1974.
9. Dion. Hal. 1.13–15 provides context (n.b. 1.14 for emphasis on how Reatine Varro had a role in creating this episteme), and see 2.49 on Sabines; Rawson 1969, 100–106, sets out the background judiciously. See also Farney 2007, 97–104 (an expansive but detailed discussion), who rightly notes that Briquel 1996 underplays Cato's "*Spartanisme.*" Collart 1954b, 229–43, is both thoughtful and helpful here; see also Collart 1954b, 211–18, on "Arcadianism" in Varro and 1954b, 246, on the mashup of Sabine and Etruscan in Varro, and Musti 1985 (comparing a range of ancient literary perspectives). Farney 2007, 105–11, articulates much of the debate concerning multiethnicity, while Gruen 2011, 243–49, presents a rich analysis of the competing foundation legends with an emphasis on the idea of the story and the role of "nativism."
10. Rawson 1969, 81–106; Dench 1995, 56–61. See, e.g., Ov. *Fast.* 1.260; Dion. Hal. 2.49.4; Plut. *Vit. Rom.* 16.1, *Vit. Num.* 1. Dench 1998, 139, suggests, in effect, that the Elder Cato fabricated the Spartan Sabine tradition in its most developed form. If so, this generated an off-the-peg package, pulling together the moral mystique of Cato and the notion of an alternative, austere Hellenic ancestry ready for Romans of Sabine origin to try on. For Sabine cheerleading in Varro, see Collart 1954b, 241–43 (as Collart puts it at 243, Varro does seem to push for a Sabine monopoly on "*l'histoire primitive*"), and Riposati 1976b, but I agree with Burman 2018 that this is not to the detriment of Varro's broader embrace of Italian identities as part of an optimistic pluralism.

11. Rawson 1969, 82–83, 99–106, traces Roman Spartanism.

12. Farney 2007, 101 (in detail, note 75), on Cato ap. Serv. auct. ad Verg. *Aen.* 8.638 = *FRH* 3 F2.22. Dench 1996 succinctly introduces the role of austerity in Italian identity. On Cato in this context, Gotter 2003, Cornell 2009, and (in depth, with full bibliography) Sciarrino 2011 (see especially 3–4 and comments at 16) are invaluable. Ferriss-Hill 2011, 279–81, draws relevant conclusions on how Verg. *Aen.* 7 illuminates a role for Sabellic languages in nation formation.

13. C. J. Smith 2006, 201.

14. Wallace-Hadrill 2008, 26, and, more expansively, 2008, 73–143. I find G. Anderson 2004 (on Gellius as a storyteller) compelling in this context. For storytelling motifs more generally, see Hansen 2002. B. Anderson 2006's modeling of nationalism in dialogue with creativity and ethnology is particularly helpful.

15. Swain 2002 makes a carefully argued case for how Greek weaves in and out of Cicero's network. He is particularly good on how "unmarked" choices and "violation" of language codes and norms are important for understanding the effects Cicero (and Varro) might have sought. Recent relevant and concise treatments of ideology and codes in language: Rochette 2010, 2011, Clackson 2011c, and Mullen 2011.

16. See Farney 2007, 90–91, 95–96, 102–3. Spartan mark-up for Roman sites of meaning is clearly a topos with enduring significance, even if Aeneas and Troy would subsequently triumph in the Augustan era as legendary "founders." See further Wiseman 1974.

17. On one Sabinus: "*etsi modestus eius uultus sermoque constans habere quiddam a Curibus uidebatur*"—there's a rightness to his looks and conversation that fits with what's expected of someone from Cures (Cic. *Fam.* 15.20.1).

18. C. Terentius Varro, cos. 216; see Arkenberg 1993, 327–38, 335–37. Citing Cato (*Orig.* Fr 50 =) Dion. Hal. *Ant. Rom.* 2.49.2–3 makes Reate an early center point for what would become Sabine ascendency across the region.

19. Dench 1995, 68. Isaac 2004, 406–10, neatly sums up on the Greco-Roman stereotype of "mountainy men."

20. Antiochus embodied the philosophical tensions of the era. The idea that there was a knowable truth was at the ethical heart of Stoicism, yet Antiochus was also an Academician (see Cic. *Acad.* 2.69). Reconciling Academic skepticism (the dialectic method emphasizing the exploration of a question rather than the delivery of an answer) with Stoic ontology and emphasis on the cognitive processing of sensory perception (Cic. *Acad.* 2.33, 35–36, cf. 2.18, on Philo) was a difficult balancing act. On Antiochus, see Barnes 1989, and factoring in (Plutarch's) Cicero as part of the mix, Tatum 2001.

21. Cic. *Acad.* 1.12.

22. Baier 1997, 17–27, makes a usefully close comparison between the two men and their trajectories. Bloomer 1997a, 53–55, is particularly interested in the dedication-game. Kumaniecki 1962 and Ward 1970 (especially 123–24) substantiate the networks involved.

23. Kronenberg 2009, 108–9.

24. Bloomer 1997b suggests how control of *personae* might have been built in as a necessary skill from an early age.

25. One of the particularly original aspects of *De Lingua Latina* is its expression of Varro's interest in dialectology (see Collart 1954b, 111). Clackson and Horrocks 2007, 183–228, provide a clear and concise overview of elite Latin usage in this era, but see also Murphy 1998, whose important article cites the well-known plaudit from Caesar to Cicero on the triumph of language-as-power (Pliny *HN* 7.117).

26. Plato, *Crat*. 388c–89a, presents the case for the *nomothete*, the skilled operator who fashions the system of words with respect to nature and use (one angle explored by Varro, *Ling*. 8–10). For key issues regarding naming and etymology in the *Cratylus*, see Ademollo 2011, 3–13. Barney 2001, 69–72, is invaluable on etymology in the formation of language, but see also 2001, 81–110, on the role of the expert in problematizing etymology (cf. Varro, *Ling*. 7.1–4, also cited by Barney 2001, 85; Ferrante 1962 represents an interesting example of how to draw Varro and Plato together).

27. Rust 2009, 64, neatly formulates "citation as genealogy," a significant narrative mode for public intellectual interaction in the late Republic's increasingly no-holds-barred style of competition.

28. For the *triumuir capitalis* post, see Gell. *NA* 13.12.5–6. This sketch of Varro's career is very much indebted to Della Corte 1954 and suggests a coherent biography that is rather more definitive than the nature of the evidence necessarily encourages. Nevertheless, it continues the thought experiment of a knowable, flesh-and-blood Varro.

29. App. *B Civ*. 4.47; Varro, *Rust*. 2.10.8–9 (dramatic date, 67). It's also possible that Varro was quaestor to L. Cinna in 85 (see App. *B Civ*. 1.77). For his time in Spain, see Varro, *Rust*. 3.12.7 (dramatic date, 50).

30. Gell. *NA* 14.7.1–3.

31. Gell. *NA* 13.12.6.

32. E.g., the sequence of allusions in Plin. *HN* 3.101, 7.115, 16.7, 18.307; consider, too, the nuances of Varro's *Logistoricus Pius aut de pace*. Weinstock 1971, 268–69, argues strongly that Metellus Scipio (*cos*. 52) was a key character for understanding how Varro might have brought antiquarianism into the political limelight on Caesar's behalf (cf. Caes. *BCiv*. 3.57.4, Gell. *NA* 17.18, on this Metellus' status as a game-changer). However, Horsfall 1972, 122–24, makes a good case for problematizing this identification of "Pius" as the consul of 52 (the Metellus who persuaded the senate to take a hard line against Caesar in 49) because of the oddness in an implied Varro/Caesar relationship. Identifying this "Pius" as the consul of 80 does not solve all the problems of internal logic, however. Much depends on what kind of relationship we imagine between Varro and Caesar. As context for Naevius' relationship with the Metelli within Varro's citation practices, see Gruen 1990, 96–106.

33. Cic. *Fam*. 7.3.2 gives a taste of Cicero's unhappiness with matters when he reached Pompey's camp in Dyrrachium. Cic. *Phil*. 2.37 denies that there was inappropriate behavior on his part. Dugan 2001, 65–66, argues incisively that *in Pisonem* illustrates the quandary faced by Cicero, confronted by the apparent unity of the triumvirs. Dugan 2001, 66 n. 108, pulls together key evidence. The renewal of the pact at Luca in 56 must indeed have made Cicero's position particularly difficult (see, e.g., Cic. *Att*. 9.2a).

34. Varro, *Rust*. 2 *praef*. 6 and passim. Cf. the Elder Pliny n. 36.

35. Like Taylor 1974, 7 n. 10, I find no conclusive solution to the question of dating the text. Indeed, the process of condensing the work into an epitome, if this was Varro's own later endeavor, might have encouraged him to revisit aspects of the full-length version (Bryant 2002 is interesting on the process of editing and revision with reference to texts and the screen). Bloomer 1997a, 251–53 n. 14, explores how dedication illuminates the timeline. On the complex processes involved in producing a "finished" work, see Habinek 1998, 103–21, Murphy 1998, Gurd 2007 (especially Gurd 2007, 51); on the sociology of reading, see Johnson 2000 and now (relevant although with a later chronological focus) 2010, 3–16, and (on Gellius) 98–136. As Murphy 1998 makes clear, there was an assumption that works were in progress and subject to (even radical) intervention for much longer than might be imagined. Even works that had reached the point of formal copying could be altered—as when Cicero asks Atticus to swap out the erroneously recycled (from *Academica* 3) preface to his *De Gloria* and glue in the new one he is sending, to fill the gap (Cic. *Att.* 16.6.4; cf. *Att.* 16.2.3)—see Murphy 1998, 499–500. One might also cite, e.g., Cic. *QFr.* 3.5.1–2, *Att.* 6.1.8, 6.2.3 (on Cic. *Rep.*); for the discussion of feedback and revision concerning points of topography and linguistics, see Gurd 2007, 55–57, including the suggestion that Varro might have been part of the critics' circle. Cic. *Acad.* 1.2–3 is discussed in chapter 2. Although her focus is on how texts shape reading strategies, Rust 2009, 192–98 (discussing explicit excerption), considers the artificially but also ostentatiously incomplete text as an authorial device. Chapter 8 and my concluding chapter return to this topic.

36. Plin. *HN* 6.51; Varro, *Ling.* 7.109. Neither reference is particularly clear or detailed regarding specific involvement on Varro's part.

37. App, *B Civ.* 2.9 (cf. the work of the same title, on a Sparta-Athens-Thebes coalition, by the fourth-century rhetorician and historian Anaximenes of Lampsacus). The Τρικάρανος is lost, and opinions about its form and content vary widely. See Astbury 1967, 407, for a detailed assertion of the popular "negative" reading; Baier 1997, 21–23, provides useful general summings up and plumps for a polito-philosophical tract. Wiseman 2009, 117, finds Fantham 2003, 111 ("a political comment . . . but hardly a hostile one"), persuasive but also sums up carefully (cf. Zucchelli 1976; Bloomer 1997a, 256 n. 33). We should be wary of taking Appian's date as definitive; nevertheless, some time in the 50s makes good sense. See also Pelling 2011, 334–35.

38. Varro, *De Vita Populi Romani* (post 47, dedicated to Atticus, see Rawson 1985, 102; possibly dating to the aftermath of Caesar's assassination; for more of Atticus, see Perlwitz 1992), Riposati 1939 fr. 121 = Nonius 802L. Cf. Horsfall 1972, 124–25, on Varro's *De Gente Populi Romani*, and (in detail) Taylor 1934.

39. See Brown and Levinson 1987, still hugely influential; more recently, see, e.g., Watts 2003.

40. Laughton 1978 focuses on humor, while Fantham 2004, 186–208, offers excellent Ciceronian context for the role of wit as a weapon. See also Henderson 1998, 31 (and cf. 101). Plass 1988, 1–25, is still useful, albeit focused on Tacitus and imperial historiography.

41. Instituted by the Lex Iulia Agraria. Following up on his invitation to replace Cosconius on the Board of Twenty, Cicero commented to Atticus in 49: "*sunt enim illi*

apud bonos inuidiosi, ego apud improbos" (there is no love lost for them among honorable men, or for me among the ne'er-do-wells, Cic. *Att.* 2.19.4; 59), cf. 9.2a.1. Vell. Pat. 2.45.2. One might compare Cicero's later (46) letter to Varro for a gloss on the "three-headedness" of the new gang—here (Cic. *Fam.* 9.7.1) he makes himself and Varro an Iliadic two-header (cf. Hom. *Iliad* 10.224).

42. Caes. *BCiv.* 2.17–20; see also 2.19.4–20.8 (affairs at Corduba, Sept. 49).

43. Wiseman 2009, 123–25, spins a satisfying story, citing the evidence judiciously. Astbury 1967, 405–7, is useful here on the detail. See also Baier 1997, 15–18; Dahlmann 1976, 163; Della Corte 1954, 115–26; Kumaniecki 1962, 224–28. As Caesar's account continues (*BCiv.* 2.17.4–21.3), we see how military reality overtook Varro, forcing his hand. On Caesar, see Damon 1993, 191–94, although I do not find Caesar's treatment here to be straightforwardly negative about Varro.

44. Cic. *Att.* 2.25.1. See Eurip. *Andr.* 448 (where the line continues "nothing wholesome, everything underhand") and *Phoen.* 393 (the line runs: "we must put up with the follies of the powerful"). For the sequence: Cic. *Att.* 2.20.1, 2.21.6, 2.22.4, probably running through from July 59 to the end of the year. Cf. Cic. *Att.* 3.15.1, 3, where the exiled Cicero confirms receipt of news from Varro via Atticus: Pompey's good will (*uoluntas*) and the hope of something positive (*expectatio*) from Caesar. Cicero seems both to value this two-pronged "attack" and also to disbelieve Varro's commitment to the cause ("*atque utinam ipse Varro incumbat in causam!*").

45. Cic. *Att.* 2.22.4.

46. See Weinstock 1971, 112–27.

47. Cic. *Att.* 3.18.1. Cf., e.g., *Att.* 4.2.5 (October 57), alluding in passing to the shared friendship; *Att.* 4.14.1 has Cicero ask Atticus to allow him to use his library at Rome, singling out Varro's works as key materials (May 54).

48. Cic. *Att.* 3.15.3, from Thessaloniki (58).

49. "I know that you always shared my distress, in seeing, as we did—a great disaster [*ingens malum*]—the annihilation of one of the two armies and its leader, but recognizing that the very worst of all evils [*extremum malorum omnium*] is victory in a civil war. So that I shuddered at the outcome even if it should fall to those we had joined. Cruel accusations against the disengaged [*otiosi*] were bandied around, dragging in your inclinations and my speech alike. Right now, if our friends [*nostri*] had taken power, there would have been excesses; they were enraged [*intemperantes*] with us, as if we had determined to save our own skins, and not advised them likewise," Cic. *Fam.* 9.6.3. Cf. Cic. *Att.* 11.6.2 (in 48) and Cato's comments to Cicero, as presented by Plutarch (Plut. *Vit. Cic.* 38).

50. Cic. *Div.* 1.68. Cic. *Att.* 11.12.2 suggests how Cicero in 47 viewed his own subsequent role in whitewashing his brother to prime a reconciliation with Caesar.

51. Writing in 49: Cic. *Att.* 8.16.2, 10.4.8; cf. *Lig.* 13–16, 29–30.

52. I have found Jehne 2006, 235–37, on memory and epistemology in Caesar's Gallic War commentary, useful in taking a position on how and why Varro's skill set (and the dedication) might have been particularly appealing to Caesar, but see also Raaflaub 2010.

53. *BNP* s.v. Terentius, M. (Reatinus) [2], IV "Encyclopaedia and specialist treatises" (d); cited as a possible source for Plin. *HN* 33.136; cf. 7.95–99. Nothing is known about what tone or form this might have taken. See Horsfall 1972, 123 n. 34, on dating the work.

54. Cic. *Fam.* 9.2.2 (to Varro, late April, 46); cf. *Fam.* 9.5.2 (to Varro, late May, 46).

55. Cic. *Fam.* 9.2.3–4 explains why for Cicero, even a chance meeting on the road out of town might topple his reputation for steadiness; by contrast, perhaps with a cutting undertone, Varro's "escape" seems by contrast to be unproblematic for both.

56. Cf. Cic. *Fam.* 9.3.

57. Yates 1966, 32–41, started the ball rolling. See also, e.g., Blum 1969, Farrell 1997, Small 1997, Narducci 2003, Romano 2003, Walter 2004, Gowing 2005, Stein-Hölkeskamp and Hölkeskamp 2006, M. B. Roller 2010, Spencer 2011c. Brockmeier 2002 succinctly discusses the wider dimensions of this kind of analysis (following Assmann 1995; see also King 2000, Niebisch 2008), while Burgin 1996 offers a more "visual" focus. Neisser 1989, Olick 2003, Ricoeur (2000) 2004, and A. D. Smith 1999, in different ways, open a range of complementary approaches.

58. Cic. *Acad.* 1.9.

59. *OLD* s.v. *quaero*, senses 6, 8, and 9 in particular, for this reading; and, of course, cf. Varro, *Ling.* 6.79.

60. Cicero's excursus on the art of memory (*De or.* 2.351–60, M. Antonius speaking, dramatic date 91; text complete by 55) contextualizes this reading. We might also note that Varro's exploration of *facio* sits at *Ling.* 6.78 (just before his treatment of *quaero*); sometimes one who speaks is said to "make words," and, by Varro's explanation, this custom has commodified and concretized vocabulary (see chapter 3 for Varro's *facio*).

61. "Varro—of whom you write to me—shall be placed if I can just find a place for him . . . ; so I'm pondering how to contrive some way to squeeze a name-check in, without it seeming forced. That's what you'd like?"—Cic. *Att.* 4.16.2, in 54. In a lengthy study, Hall 2009 makes clear the challenges in reading "tone" in Cicero's correspondence, but reading through the Varro sequences produces a solid range of conversational moments for comparison.

62. This assessment rests on the minute extant portion of his corpus but does also draw on extensive Ciceronian allusions—and, of course, on Varro's survival skills. See Wiseman 2009, 127.

63. Suet. *Iul.* 44.2. On Varro's "celebrity," see Cic. *Att.* 13.19.3 (perhaps to be read in a snide tone). On the bibliophilic rapprochement, see Horsfall 1972, 122. Dix and Houston 2006 trace the ongoing role of libraries in Rome; Nicholls 2018 offers a clear overview building on recent work.

64. Properties that we know he lost include Casinum (site of his aviary, the subject of a lengthy description in Varro, *Rust.* 3.5.9–17; the famously graphic account of Antony's land grab is Cic. *Phil.* 2.103–5, refuting what seems to be a justification that Antony had purchased it from Caesar, who acquired it, perhaps by confiscation, after the defeat of Pompey), as well as the property at Cumae (Cic. *Acad.* 1.1) and by Vesuvius (Varro, *Rust.* 1.15). Whether he got any of these back is debatable. Casinum features vividly in Varro *Rust.* 3, but the conversation is set sometime in the late 50s (see Linderski 1985). Horsfall 1972 wonders whether Varro's comments would have been tinged with melancholy if the

property had been lost at the time of writing, while Taylor 1966, 135 n. 58, makes the unlikely suggestion that "in the writing of his dialogues Varro was less careful than Cicero."

65. Fufius features (to his detriment) in Cicero's *Philippics*; on his rescue of Varro: App. *B Civ.* 4.47. The flip side is that Cicero, who seems to have maintained good relations with his apparently unsatisfactory son-in-law and Caesarian P. Cornelius Dolabella, even after the divorce from his beloved Tullia (J. W. Crawford 1984, 225–27, is useful on the unpublished speech *Pro P. Cornelio Dolabella*; see Gildenhard 2011, 123–24, briefly, on Dolabella in *Phil.* 11.8–9; cf. *Phil.* 11.28; van der Blom 2010, 123–24, again briefly, on *Fam.* 9.14.6–8; cf. *Att.* 16.11.3), broke with him once he declared for Antony's cause (e.g., Cic. *Att.* 16.15.1). See also Della Corte 1954, 227–29.

66. Plin. *HN* 7.115, 35.10–11; cf. Ovid, *Trist.* 3.1.71–72; Isid. *Etym.* 6.5. See Bloomer 1997a, 255 n. 29. On the joke one might make about nomenclature and the Atrium Libertatis, see Spencer 2011b, 79.

67. Cic. *Off.* 1.48. For a socioeconomic reading of these "exchanges," see White 2010.

68. Stroup 2010, 96–97, tackles this literary to-ing and fro-ing, with a slightly different focus.

69. Stroup 2010, 66–110, is expansive on this topic, but see specifically at 193–94. Cf. Cic. *Att.* 13.12.2, where Cicero praises Atticus' marketing skills (for the speech *Pro Ligario*) and says he'll leave all future publicity in his hands. Stroup's important discussion is wide-ranging and carefully argued.

70. Cic. *Att.* 13.12.3.

71. Suet. *Tib.* 38, claiming proverbiality for the witticism.

72. Cf. Cic. *Att.* 9.7.1, where the nickname *celeripes* features.

73. Cf. Cic. *Att.* 13.25.3 (quoted in this section), for a differently filtered sense of what's at stake.

74. Cf. Cic. *Brut.* 17–19.

75. Cic. *Att.* 13.15.3.

76. *OLD* s.v. *promitto*, senses 6, 7 (although rare in the sense of "forebode"); s.v. *exspectatio*, sense 1.

77. Varro, *Ling.* 5.141, 179; *OLD* s.v. *munus*, senses 1, 2, 5c, and (regarding a dedication) 6a; for senses with largesse to the fore, *OLD* s.v. *munus*, 1a, 4a, 7, where the semantic range is pragmatic and draws in the obligation to the donor. Maltby 1991, 397, sets Varro at the head of the etymological tradition here. Stroup 2010, 88–89 (on the public qualities), 90–92 (on the textual qualities) examines *munus* in Cicero. See also *OLD* s.v. *flagito*.

78. Kronenberg 2009, 89, reads Cic. *Fam.* 9.1–8 as a series of "subtle jabs at Varro" (and I agree: the tone is more barbed, I think, than Leach 1999 reads it), and she quotes extensively from *Fam.* 9.2.5 in this context.

79. Hom. *Il.* 11.654; here, Cicero being Patroclus, describing (Varro-as-)Achilles.

80. Leach 1999, 139.

81. Leach 1999, 140.

82. Baier 1997, 27, "*Dies ist sicher nicht nur Koketterie.*" The comments Cicero ascribes to Varro at *Acad.* 1.4 may be part of a delicate process of negotiating difference between

the two men. That there is some ambivalence in how Varro is represented here might be indicated by the fact that although Cicero's Varro states that the translation of Greek philosophy into Latin is pointless (it can be of no assistance to the "unlearned" [*indocti*] and is pointless for the "learned" [*docti*], *Acad.* 1.4–5), the Varro character engages enthusiastically in philosophical debate in Latin (albeit as notionally textualized by Cicero), and in real life Varro had of course also written *De Philosophia*. Atticus rather unkindly (perhaps) suggests to Cicero that the three speaking parts in the *Academica* should be himself, C. Aurelius Cotta, and Varro, cutting Cicero out; Cicero tartly says that he has no intention of making himself the "dummy" (Cic. *Att.* 13.19.3).

83. For Varro's *dux* (*Ling.* 6.62; 10.56–57), see chapter 6.
84. Cic. *Acad.* 1.1 (cf. *Fam.* 9.8).
85. E.g., Cic. *Att.* 13.14.1.
86. Wiseman 2009, 109. Cf. Dugan 2005, 251–52.

87. Playing with the model in Beard 2002, I suggest a metanarrative developing along the lines of these key letters: Cic. *Att.* 13.12.3 (Varro is remarkably slow in writing something for *me*, so I'm turning the tables on him); 13.13.1 (how does Atticus know Varro wants the books?); 13.14.1 (is it really a good idea to send the books to Varro?); 13.16.1–2 (should I *really* address anything, and this in particular, to Varro?); 13.18 (how does Atticus *really* know about Varro's desire for a piece of Cicero?); 13.19.3, 5 (I'm not just a fanboy or trophy hunter [φιλένδοξος], plus, my version of the ideas is better than any "original"... but I'm still not sure the dedication should go ahead—let's talk); 13.21a.1 (I can't wait for Varro to have what I've written); 13.22.1 (best not to put one's concerns in writing); 13.23.2 (I'm proofreading; I'll blame you if the gift goes badly); 13.24.1 (*you* need to take charge of managing the presentation to Varro); 13.25.3 (why are you now saying that you're worried about taking responsibility? My letter of dedication is spot-on); 13.33a (speak of the devil and he'll appear); 13.35.2 (will he like the gift? It's your problem to manage it well [*tuo periculo fiet*], but brief me ASAP); 13.44 (have you actually given it to him? I've heard nothing); 13.21.3 (your suggested emendation spoiled my text; tell Varro to change the word back!).

88. Varro is tagged by Cicero in almost throwaway fashion in a few subsequent letters (the following year, after Caesar's assassination): *Att.* 15.5.3 (political chitchat); 15.27.5 (tell Varro I'm sorry to be slow in writing); 15.13.3 (so, you fancy the prospect of a Heracleidean dialogue from Varro? I'm not sure it'll outdo my efforts!); 15.13a.2 (I'm working on a magnificent treatment of *Duties* for my son Marcus; Varro is apparently going to turn up shortly here, so I'm off to Pompeii); 16.9 (I fear Antony's strength; Varro doesn't rate young Octavian's scheme; I see war looming); 16.11.3 (*you* like Varro's coffee-table book; still no sign of his Heracleidean piece); 16.12 (what a piquant business about Varro's coffee-table book! funniest thing I've heard in ages).

89. Nep. *Att.* 16.3 remarks on the correspondence as available for consultation in Atticus' house. As noted in n. 35, key studies are Murphy 1998 and Gurd 2007; unsurprisingly this topic weaves through Stroup 2010, e.g., 93–97, 111–12 (citing Cic. *Att.* 13.12.2–3), 193–94; for a cautious view of the evidence for the letters' availability and reception, see Nicholson 1998.

90. See Murphy 1998 and, more generally, Starr 1987; Habinek 1998, 103–21. Atticus may not have had Varro's enthusiasm for the formulaic *populusque*, but he too survived the proscriptions, dying (still, and remarkably, on good terms with both Antony *and* Octavian) in 32. His daughter Caecilia Attica was married to Octavian's CEO Marcus Agrippa, and *their* daughter (Vipsania) went on to marry the princeps' adoptive son (and eventual heir) Tiberius.

91. The full passage is Cic. *Phil.* 2.103–5.

92. *OLD* s.v. *fortuna*, sense 4 (see also senses 2, 6). Cf. Cic. *Off.* 2.71 ("fortune's favorites").

93. Cic. *Off.* 1.105, 126, 129, offer useful context for Antony here. Cf. Cic. *Off.* 1.139 for the motif of past versus present householders.

94. Stroup 2010, 131–40. Wiseman 2009, 117–20, suggests that in Cic. *Rep.*, *gubernator*—the metaphor of the ship's pilot as a stand-in for the wise ruler (e.g., *Rep.* 2.51)—is particularly pertinent. Wisemen's range of uses suggests at least that Cicero was testing the limits and effect of such a reframing for the *populus*. Stroup 2010, 49–51, convincingly argues that *De Lege Agraria* 2.4.9, 2.102, shows Cicero already exploring some of these ideas regarding the symbiosis between the *populus* and a good leader.

95. Morstein-Marx 2013, 45. On *populus*: Cic. *Off.* 1.53 (evocative of Varro and his milieu; cf. 1.69), 1.61 (greatness of spirit; context suggests probably not of the "masses"), 2.22 (what causes submission to an authority; contrast 3.84), 2.26, 29 (rapid degradation of the *ciuitas*), 2.41–42 (a good king is the bulwark of the masses; cf. 2.70), 2.55, 58 (the dilemma of popular largesse), 2.78 (greed posing as benevolence to the people—*popularis*), 3.15 (indiscriminate masses—*uulgus*; cf. 3.79), 3.19 (the people approve a tyrannicide), 3.109, 114 (people and senate; "*populi senatusque*" and vice versa). Cf. Cic. *Fam.* 12.24.2, written early in 43.

96. "There was no one whose well-being was of concern to so many," Cic. *Phil.* 2.104. Cf. Cic. *Acad.* 1.9 for significant context.

97. *OLD* s.v. *sanctus*, senses 3c, d (implications of mortality and old age, bundling scrupulousness and chastity with a sense of passivity; inviolability, too, implies disengagement); *OLD* s.v. *integer*, senses 1, 2, and 6b (being untouched or unstarted, undecided or open-minded, and unaffected by war or loss). Wiseman 2009, 119 n. 66, notes Cic. *Div.* 2.3 and *Leg.* 3.37 in a relevant context, but Cic. *Rep.* and *Off.* offer the obvious examples.

98. Wiseman 2009, 87, citing Dion. Hal. *Ant. Rom.* 2.7–29.

99. Varro, *Rust.* 3.2.1; 2 *praef.* 6, 2.8.3, cf. 3.2.3, 3.2.5, 3.2.9, 3.2.12.

100. Cicero, from Arpinum, was enrolled in the Cornelia tribe. The tribal assemblies (Concilium Plebis and Comitia Tributa; Plebs and Populus) had less kudos than the centuriate assembly but still carried significant historical weight and counted each vote equally. By the late Republic, they had also become the vehicle for the growing power of the tribunes and, more generally, evidenced the shifting nuances of how the factions manipulated legislative power. See, lucidly, Taylor 1966, 59–61, and more recently, e.g., Bispham 2007 (wide-ranging on municipalization), Dench 2005, 176–78 (focusing on identities), Sherwin-White 1973, 61–62 (on legal detail) and, more generally, 190–98. Cic. *Off.* 1.111 sketches another angle on Cicero's interest in language qua identity at around this time.

101. "*Nunc stipati seruis publicis non modo prendi non possunt sed etiam ultro submouent populum,*" Varro, *Antiquitates humanae* fr. 21.3 Mirsch 1882 = Gell. *NA* 13.13.4 (citing Varro as the authority ne plus ultra). Cf. Varro, *Ling.* 5.80, discussed in chapter 6.

102. The examples gathered by Wiseman 2009, 115 n. 44, may seem slender, but given the fragmentary nature of the surviving Varro one might in fact find them to be surprisingly compelling; see especially "*senatum populi Romani*," Varro fr. 58 Funaioli 1907 = Gell. *NA* 17.21.48; "*de diis . . . populi Romani publicis,*" Varro, *Antiquitates Diuinae* fr. 228 Cardauns 1976 = August. *De civ. D.* 7.17.

103. Wiseman 2009, 115 n. 44's collection of Ciceronian correspondences for Varro's "popular" enthusiasm: Cic. *Verr.* 2.1.156–57, 2.3.93, 2.4.25, 2.4.42 (cf. Cic. *Verr.* 2.5.175).

104. E.g., Cic. *Att.* 1.16.11, 2.1.8; *QFr.* 2.5.3. *OLD* s.v. *faex* showcases the intensely physical qualities of revulsion and disdain for "scum" or "dregs" of this kind.

105. See Varro, *Ling.* 5.7–8—the *populus* is the bottom line for doing etymology, and the higher levels work with and upon this foundation, moving through old-time grammar to philosophy and finally achieving a kind of holy of holies to whose *scientia* Varro says he has not yet arrived. Pfaffel 1981 is the extensive study of linguistics of this graduated scheme of Varro's. Bloomer 1997a, 60, is, I think, moving in a similar direction to this, but more explicitly at n. 42 (258). *Populus* itself is not an extant etymology in Varro, *Ling.*, nor does it feature etymologically in other authors of the era (see Maltby 1991, 485). The closest we get here is the compromised *populus* of the *Poplifugia* (People's Flight Day), *Ling.* 6.18 (discussed in chapter 8), a commemoration and reification of reactive popular chaos ("*tumultu repente fugerit*") following the Gallic departure ("*decessus,*" the spin here is interestingly delivered) from Rome (back in 390).

106. Bloomer 1997a, 44.

107. Varro, *Ling.* 8.6, 9.5–6, 9.18 (cf. 9.114, 10.74), 10.16. Cf. Cairns 1996.

108. This friction gets another rub-down at *Ling.* 9.59—like slaves, the gods too are subject to the authority of free Latins to impose names.

109. Varro, *Ling.* 9.1–5.

110. I am thinking here of Stroup 2010, 221's formulation "the poematic voice" to get at the idea of the poem as the embodiment of its author's social function. Cf. Stroup 2010, 86, 233; Habinek 1998, 109. On the crossover between oratory and poetry, see Stroup 2010, 140, 141–67.

111. Bloomer 1997a, 66–67.

112. Varro, *Ling.* 9.4; *OLD* s.v. *copula*, senses 1–3; cf. Isid. *Etym.* 19.19.6 (and, e.g., Plaut. *Epid.* 617).

113. The substitution of "s" ("*nos*") for "n" ("*non*") seems to avoid awkwardness and echo the pattern of the argument and is followed by Kent 1951.

114. Varro, *Ling.* 9.18.

115. When Varro tackles the naming of public slaves manumitted by towns, a hint of the tensions in the gaps dividing city, political system, and language emerges. Such freedmen, he says, would typically take the town name as their own (e.g., Fauentius and Reatinus), but now at Rome they take the name of the magistrate who presided over their manumission (*Ling.* 8.80, 8.83, cf. 8.54).

116. Chapter 4 revisits Varro, *Ling.* 8.80, in the context of *Ling.* 8.18–19 and 9.34.

117. *"proportione non est quod debuit esse"* (a lacuna is posited here; Kent 1951, 434 §80 3), Varro, *Ling.* 8.80.

118. The two emendations are from *ouilla* and *bouilla*; neither per se affects the argument here, but see the discussion of *bouilla*.

119. This phase is peppered with the "they say" formulation; Kent 1951, 474 §50 and passim animadverts a sequence of intra- and intertextual references, but Varro is also perfectly at home with the direct citation for this kind of proposition (e.g., *Ling.* 8.64, Crates); reading a more generalizing quality here is therefore acceptable and productive.

120. Cf. *Ling.* 5.144, discussed in chapter 7.

121. Cf. Maltby 1991 s.v. *ouile, Ouilia, ouilla*. The Ovile was also connected to the census. Taylor 1966, 47–58, 78–113, fleshes out detail. Cicero's interest in the project is set out at, e.g., *Att.* 4.17.7.

122. On punning with Bovillae in Cicero, MacLaren 1966, 197–202. Cicero's perhaps comparable injection of irony into *De Republica* is the focus of Fox 2000.

123. On Caesar and Bovillae, see Weinstock 1971, 5–12. We might note that Varro and Hyginus both produced studies of Rome's notionally Trojan families (Weinstock 1971, 4 n. 6, gives the references).

124. Suet. *Aug.* 100; see Badian 2009, 14–15 (a cautious analysis). For the late second-century Julian "dedication," see *ILLRP* 270.

125. Cic. *Att.* 5.13.1; cf. *Mil.* 14, 27–29, 53–55; useful too is Asconius' riff on the speech (citing Clark 1907, 31–32 C, 34–35 C, 44 C). Lintott 1974 presents a thorough exegesis of the speech, with May 2001 as a good example of recent analysis. That Caesar's assassination is also near a religious site with complex personal connotations (Pompey's Temple of Venus) makes for a neat bookend. The text encourages this reading: sacrificial Bovillae, with connotations of typically white animals and a propitious beginning, follows in the text after dark days and men ("black" generating "the man in black," or "the mourner"). Cf. Albius and Atrius, the two names derived from substantives, just before further comments on deriving Roma from Romulus (Varro, *Ling.* 8.80).

126. E.g., starting from *Ling.* 5.29, 68, 78; for the Latin people, see, e.g., 5.30, 43, 69, 6.25, 7.28.

127. Varro, *Ling.* 10.15.

128. See additionally Varro, *Ling.* 10.60–61, 72, 74, 78.

129. Cf. Baier 1997, 185, summarizing what we might term Varro's acutely tuned sensibility. On the "struggle" central to consensus and its performative negotiation, and the negotiation of exclusivity as a key factor in community, see Hölkeskamp 2013.

130. Horsfall 1982, 286.

131. Cf. Pease 1995.

132. Bloomer 1997a, 47.

Chapter 2. Romespeaking

1. Cic. *Brut.* 140.

2. See Stroup 2010, 130, on Cicero's new model audience in the *Brutus*. See Sluiter 2015, 20–21, on Plat. *Crat.* 405a–406a.

3. Many elements of this chapter are indebted to and build on work undertaken as part of the Cambridge Craven Seminar on Varro (May 2011) and from which Spencer 2015b derives.

4. Barker and Galasiński 2001, 21; on the processes of acculturation, see Short 2007; Sluiter 1990, 2015.

5. Varro, *Ling.* 8.51, accepting the emendations gathered up by Kent 1951 (cf. *Ling.* 7.57, acknowledging the role of labels for explaining paintings). Mackenzie 1986 makes a fine case for an underpinning aporia to Plato's *Cratylus*, a case that Varro might seem to be addressing by rebooting the concerns of *Cratylus* with Roman pragmatics to the fore.

6. Varro returns to Myrmecides at 9.108, where similar forms (examples, first-person singulars *dolo* and *colo*) can generate different forms in the perfect tense; one must add in additional things (Varro suggests the second-person-singular forms) to perceive the distinctions effectively. The appropriate way to view Myrmecides' tiny ivories is the point of comparison offered. Barney 2001, 57–70, 94–106, is especially useful when thinking this through in relation to Plato's *Cratylus*. Jokes about "natural" language and naming (e.g., Forum Boarium) flicker throughout; this issue resurfaces as we proceed.

7. On Varro's "tracks" and paths, see Spencer 2011c, 68–70.

8. On Quintilian's grammatology and its historical context, see Ax 2011.

9. Wendling 1893 sets up some basic premises. Etymology underpins Cicero's discussions across a range of works, e.g., *Top.*, *Nat. D.*, *De or.*, *Leg.*

10. See Costa 2000, 146 n. 45, on if-clauses.

11. Here, I have not followed Kent's approved emendation, "*Dico VI hunc dicare <circum metulas>*" (*Ling.* 6.61); it seems to me unnecessary. This interest in what Saussure (1916) 1983, 28–32 (using the standard pagination), does with the "*image acoustique*" flicks on and off through the text.

12. The context: when he has accepted the power, "*accepta potestate*," *Ling.* 6.61.

13. As Keith 1992, 105, observes, we can see this nexus in an Ovidian wordplay half a century or so later (Ov. *Met.* 2.706).

14. F reads "*hinc illa indicit illum*"; this does not make satisfactory sense in context and has been emended, logically, to "*indicit bellum*" (Turnebus 1565), which Kent 1951 follows.

15. Through-readers should also recall and compare Varro's early, theatrically glossed definition of the office of consul (see chapter 6).

16. Depending on when Varro finalized (or stopped revising), Caesar's funeral could well be the elephant in the room; factoring in Cicero's personal history, the funeral of Clodius is a lively subtext.

17. Carruthers 1992, 104, 105. Pfaffel 1987 argues for empiricism as Varro's most "modern" quality as an etymologist, but this strips away too much of the literary quality of what my argument discovers in the text, read through.

18. See Corbeill 1996 (especially 174–217).

19. *Magister* as a comparative derivation suggests that the dictator remains (semiotically speaking) relative to the people; he gains existence as a function of the people as a whole.

20. Varro, *Ling.* 6.62. *Dux* is in Varro's mix at this point, discussed in chapter 6, where it fits better thematically.

21. The term "*translaticio*" makes sense as an emendation from *translatio*, which would be an easy miscopying. The tie-in with *disputatio* comes via the inclusion of *putator* ("pruner") in the earlier etymological field.

22. Through-readers will have encountered it earlier (*Ling.* 6.36, in a discussion of inflection) and will revisit it briefly later (*Ling.* 8.11, 9.32). Chapter 4 explores Varro's conjunction of *lego* with *scribo*.

23. *Sors, consortes, sortilegi*, Varro, *Ling.* 6.65. *Sors* might connote in this context a sense of public collective equality (here come the *consortes*, colleagues), a sense whereby all citizens alike are enmeshed in the power of chance or destiny. *OLD* s.v. *sors* 4, 5, 8 (with usage that becomes current by the 30s/20s), and 9. Cf. Cic. *Planc.* 67; *Dom.* 64; *Pis.* 50.

24. This blending of conceptual and pragmatic in etymology chimes with what Short 2008, 106–7, terms a "vocabulary of spatial motion" associated with vocabulary and phraseology relating to mental activity. Cf. Cic. *Nat. D.* 2.140, 142–43, a visceral description.

25. Through-readers will have been sensitized by *Ling.* 6.41, discussed with reference to *ago* (where Greek fails to feature).

26. "Therefore in the same way 'legates,' because they are chosen that they may be dispatched on behalf of the State."

27. *Legulus* is a relatively unusual word; Varro includes it in his emblematic list of employments (*Ling.* 5.94). For other (prior) usage (based on a *PHI* search): only Cato, *Agr.* 64, 144, 146.

28. Varro, *Rust.* 1.23.2, 1.32.2. Cf. Caes. *BCiv.* 3.47.6.

29. The dramatic date for Cic. *Nat. D.* is difficult to pin down: Cicero offers extremely (and unusually so) minimal "color" and scenography. Some time in the 70s is conjectured (see, e.g., Levine 1957, 12–13).

30. Borrowing terminology from Carruthers 1992, 106.

31. Carruthers 1992, 107, with quote from 108.

32. Varro, *Ling.* 7.2 (the text is problematic and full of editorial intervention, but the basic sense is as proposed); see Spencer 2015b, 80–82. Chapter 3 takes Varro and verse as a focus.

33. Sluiter 2015.

34. Cf. Cato's famous comment in the preface to his treatise on agriculture (when discussing the community of citizen identity) that "our" ancestors (*maiores*) citizens thought the best praise of a *bonus* was to call him a worthy cultivator and farmer (see Reay 2005 on this kind of self-fashioning). Chapter 3 returns to Varro, *Ling.* 7.4, and Cato.

35. Corn and cornfields crop up at many key moments; see, e.g., Varro, *Ling.* 6.45, 7.109. For discussion of this passage from a slightly different angle (focusing on the interdependence between urban space and rustic endeavor), see Spencer 2011b.

36. Spencer 2011b and 2011c discuss these passages extensively. "Memory" underpins much of what follows in this chapter.

37. Carruthers 1992, 107 (discussing Gregory the Great).

38. Difficult words, Varro notes, are those that themselves in their root form typically have no link (*"societas"*) to the Greek language and those whose origins are perhaps the more complex because Latin (*"uernacula"*) memory (*"memoria . . . nostra"*) sees a genesis for them, yet cannot lay claim to them. These are words whose roots are immigrant, yet that have become part of Latin discourse; cf. Varro's assertion of his parameters at *Ling.* 5.10. The text has some problems here (*Ling.* 6.40), but I think this is the basic sense.

39. Varro, *Ling.* 6.51–67 in total; this chapter concentrates on 6.51–60. See further chapter 4.

40. "Narration, by which we get to know about an event." The abrupt transition from *Ling.* 6.50–51 runs *"sic cum se habent, laeta. Narro, cum alterum facio narum"* (when this is how things are, the word is "happy." "I narrate" is when I make someone else "knowledgeable."). The form *narus* (accepting the emendation from *narrus*, from Victorius' notes on *B*, via Augustinus 1554) is a variant on *gnarus, a, um*; see Cic. *Orat.* 15, 36. *Narro* has the same relationship with the *gn-* form, but whereas *gnarus* is more common than *narus*, *gnarigo* is extremely rare (*OLD* and *TLL* s.v. *gnarigo* give Livius Andronicus as the only attestation).

41. Varro returns to Fauns at *Ling.* 7.36, discussed in the section "Glossing and Enriching" in this chapter.

42. Cf. Varro, *Ling.* 6.56 (talking requires understanding), and compare Lucr. 5.222–24 (cf. 5.335–37 [the poet's primacy]; 1029–32 [the drive to communicate]). On speech and authority in similar contexts, see Bettini 2006, 2008. Short 2007, 24–25, outlines the deeper context for speech and its oversight by watchful deities.

43. Stroup 2010, 251–64, unpacks the cultural capital of the associated term *eloquentia*, significant as a backdrop to this discussion; see Varro, *Ling.* 6.56–57, the section "The End Result: Speaking Well" in this chapter, and, more broadly, chapter 4.

44. One of Varro's popular suggestions: it filters into what's known as Varro ap. Isid. *Etym.* 8.7.3 (cf. 7.12.15 without the attribution to Varro).

45. It's worth noting that when Varro first looks at these days he formulates as *dies fasti*; here, to emphasize the "speech" rather than the time, the formula is emphatically reversed (i.e., with the "speech" term leading): *fasti* and *nefasti* precede *dies*.

46. *Ling.* 6.42, discussed in the section "Action" in this chapter.

47. "Pronouncements," "they have pronounced," "to be pronounced," "are pronounced"—variations on *effari*. Recall *fines* at Varro, *Ling.* 5.13, discussed in the section "Romespeak and Etymology" in this chapter. This cluster approaches qualities associated with the "performative utterances" of Austin 1962; see also J. H. Miller 2001.

48. Verg. *Aen.* 1.279; cf. Ovid, *Fast.* 2.639–84 (on the Terminalia), which takes a similar trajectory from individual to public reification of "boundaries" through speech (especially, 2.679–84).

49. Varro, *Ling.* 6.55; potentially resonating against Arist. *Pol.* 1253a8. De Melo 2011 gives a sense of the language world this might evoke.

50. *Famosi* is later matched in the positive with *famigerabile*. The ideas expressed here sit well with the role of this text as a riposte/returned favor to Cic. *Acad.*; cf. Cic. *Acad.* 2.83.

51. "By speaking one misleads, and then does the opposite of what one has said," Varro, *Ling.* 6.55.

52. The incident (*ROL* 1.148–49), commented on by Festus, happened during the Istrian War (178–77 BCE); King Epulo was apparently scoping out the Roman position.

53. Compare Cic. *Leg.* 2.31 on the absolute authority of the augur to determine political process and public business; Cicero's oblique comments about the Bibulus affair, in 59, color *Att.* 8.3.3, in 49 (see Suet. *Iul.* 20.1, and, e.g., Cic. *Att.* 2.16). J. Smith 1992 summarizes some key issues of interplay between religious, aesthetic, and epistemic agenda.

54. "*Speculator, quem mittimus ante, ut respiciat quae uolumus*," Varro, *Ling.* 6.82, perhaps nodding to the line from Ennius about King Epulo.

55. Cf. Varro, *Ling.* 8.44, 9.102. *Ling.* 10.31, 33 develop the "verbal"/action-based nexus. *Scribo* recurs as a key example (in book 8) when Varro discusses the kinds of words that generate new words and forms by inflection, a discussion that leads into a wider exploration of nouns and verbs; see *Ling.* 8.12; cf. 9.102, 10.33.

56. On *uates*, see especially Newman 1967, passim, with Hinds 2006 making the leap to Varro. The stimulating and challenging analysis of song/speech proposed by Habinek 2005, 59–74, is especially useful here and contextualizes my reading of Varro's *loquor* in defining Romespeak in the sections "Action" and "The End Result: Speaking Well" in this chapter and in chapter 4.

57. Through-readers will recall *Ling.* 6.52–55 on *fari-fatur* in the context of storytelling (*narro*).

58. For more on this passage, see Hinds 2006, and Spencer 2015b, 79–80. We might recall that victory wreaths could be either laurel or myrtle, signaling Apollo or Venus, depending on the context. One of Caesar's senate-granted privileges, as recorded by Suetonius (*Iul.* 45), was to wear a laurel wreath in everyday life. On wreaths, see Val. Max. 3.6.5 (discussing Papirius Maso). See, e.g., M. H. Crawford 1974, catalog numbers 314/1a–c (coinage of L. Aurelius Cotta, Trib. Pl. 103), for a good example of how this iconography operated fluidly.

59. *Glos<s>emata, Ling.* 7.34. The passage makes sense if one takes the emendation proposed by Mueller 1883, as Kent does, and reads "*Camilla<m> qui glos<s>emata interpretati dixerunt administram.*" The Greek term γλώσσημα is rare. For *glossema*, see also Varro, *Ling.* 7.107. Quint. *Inst.* 1.8.15 gives another instance of this very unusual word; see also *glossemata*, Asin. ap. Suet. *Gram. et rhet.* 22.

60. Aesch. Fr. 152.

61. The other examples: Varro, *Ling.* 5.22, 7.17, 7.95 (*interpres*); 7.2 (*interpretatio*). See McElduff and Sciarrino 2011 for the kinds of issue in play more generally, and now Rener 1989, 328–29, and McElduff 2009. I am thinking here of Isidore's later formulation: "*Interpres, quod inter partes medius sit duarum linguarum, dum transferet*" (*Etym.* 10.123): "Interpreter"—because between the parts, in the middle (one is situated) of two languages, that's what happens when one translates.

62. Vergil's Camilla: e.g., *Aen.* 7.803, 11.535. Hardwick 1990 remains a useful survey. For more detail, see Arrigoni 1982 (trying out the "traditional" nature of the character) versus Horsfall 1988 and Capdeville 1992 (both arguing for Vergilian *inuentio*).

63. The text at *Ling.* 7.34 is particularly subject to emendation; the tweaks necessary to deliver the "male" *camillus/casmilus* work in context, but one would not want to press them too hard. Camillus, of course, resonates strongly in Roman history: think especially of M. Furius Camillus, conqueror of Veii in 396 and then defender of Rome from Gallic annihilation (see, e.g., Verg. *Aen.* 6.825; Livy 5.46; Hor. *Carm.* 1.12.42). For detailed discussion, see Maltby 1991, 99–100 s.v. *camillus*.

64. O'Hara 2001 usefully unpacks Callimachus as a pattern for Vergilian word games. This interplay participates in the *"image acoustique"*; see Saussure (1916) 1983, 28–32.

65. Verg. *Aen.* 11.778–93.

66. E.g., Verg. *Aen.* 7.803–7, 11.508–9, 535–38.

67. Verg. *Aen.* 11.542–43, recounts how Casmilla produces Camilla: a spelling change from mother to daughter. Servius' comment (ascribing the Pacuvius quote, here elided, to Medea): "from the name Casmilla, Statius Tullianus in book 1, *On the Names of Things*, cites Callimachus as having said that among the Etruscans, Camillus was what Mercury was called, by which name signifying an attendant of the gods. Hence Virgil rightly said that Metabus called his daughter Camilla, on the basis that she was an attendant of Diana . . . the Romans also used to call noble prepubescent boys and girls 'camillus' and 'camilla,' who served as attendants upon the *flaminicae* and *flamines*." This matches the contemporary Macrobius, *Sat.* 3.8.6. C. J. Smith 2006, 351–52, situates this in the Roman socioreligious context.

68. On Vergil's Camilla in context, see Boyd 1992.

69. Ov. *Met.* 3.1–4.603. On Cadmus and the myth, see Vian 1963 (in some detail); for this episode in Ovid, see Hardie 1990 (Janan 2009 presents a tour de force Lacanian analysis of Ovid's Thebes, but it's not quite what's required for my purpose here), in Statius, see Braund 2006.

70. E.g., Hdt. 5.58.

71. Hdt. 5.58–61. "Cadmus" is a complex figure with a huge bibliography, probably reflecting at least two bundles of myths and many reorientations of plot. Berman 2004 unpacks some of this very usefully.

72. Vian 1963, 216–25. NB Verg. *Aen.* 12.514–15 draws Onites, fighting on the Rutulian side, into the battle; he is immediately dispatched by Aeneas. Onites (according to Vergil) is the son of one of the five surviving Spartoi (Echion, the "Snake-Man")—added Etrusco-Spartan gloss to the developing picture; Saunders 1940, 539, 541, ties Onites instead to the Argonautica cycle (see Val. Fl. 4.734) and Dionysiac cult. Erskine 2001, 131–56, is excellent on wandering Greek heroes founding Italian towns.

73. Ov. *Met.* 4.563–603.

74. "*Hinc Casmilus nominatur Samothrece<s> mysteri<i>s dius quidam amminister diis magnis,*" Varro, *Ling.* 7.34. Taking Kent 1951's text, "from this, Casmilus is named in the Samothracian mysteries: a certain divinity who attends on the Great Gods."

75. An alternative formulation might have been *opinor*, which has a less forceful sense of certainty, or *credo*, which again offers less background substantiation. Chapter 3 briefly revisits *arbitror* in Varro, *Ling*.

76. In Cicero's writings to Atticus, *arbitror* is also a favorite. A corpus search of Latin literature (*PHI*) delivers Cicero as by far and away the most frequent exemplar. The

quantity of Ciceronian material available is one factor, but genre, voice, and agenda are clearly significant.

77. *Arbitror* in this usage: *Ling.* 5.83, 6.34, 6.97, 7.34, 7.40, 7.73, 8.23, 9.95, 10.11, 10.75 (by contrast, the entire three-book *De Re Rustica* offers only eight instances). Cf. two instances for *opinor*, two for *credo*, in the extant Varro, *Ling.*

78. PHI search for "*arbitror*": Plautus, forty-five instances; Terence, thirty-one.

79. Varro, *Ling.* 5.58; world-building is a focus for chapter 7's discussion of cosmic forces and language. Hdt. 2.51 talks of the Cabiri's special care for sailors, which association probably explains how they came to be identified with the Dioscuri. Varro's very recent quotation from Accius' *Philoctetes* (at *Ling.* 7.11) is also likely to reverberate. Beard 1994 and L. E. Roller 1999 offer useful context here.

80. See also Macrob. *Sat.* 3.4.7–9.

81. Verg. *Aen.* 7.206–10.

82. "*Et hi quos Augurum Libri scriptos habent sic . . .*" (and these are those whom the Books of the Augurs include/indicate/contain in writing to be . . .), Varro, *Ling.* 5.58; i.e., Varro does not use *dico* (for example) but chooses instead the more complex *habeo* to describe how the books transmit information. For Varro's other direct references to this *opus*, see *Ling.* 5.21, 6.64, 7.8, and specifically as authoritative, *Ling.* 5.33, 6.76, 7.51. Linderski 1986, 2241–56, is especially helpful on the complexities of the augural *corpus*, with Corbeill 2010 and Beard 2012 drawing out the rich semiology of Ciceronian redeployment (Cic. *Har. Resp.*); Beard 2012, 13–14, is acute on the ostentatious self-referentiality of the interpretive logic underpinning the augural process; see also the ideas in Rüpke 2004a regarding action and "script." For fragments of the "books," see Regell 1878 (unpub. diss., which I have not managed to consult), 1882.

83. "*Apud En<n>i<u>m*" is an emendation (replacing "*Apud enim*") in Pomponius Laetus' *Editio princeps* (1471).

84. Varro and Ennius are the only two exemplars for *subulo* in first-century literary Latin; Livy 43.17 namechecks P. Decius Subulo, Tr. Pl. 120, Pr. 115 (Farney 2007, 131, 148, picks up briefly on Subulo, a supporter of the Gracchi mentioned as "Decius" at, e.g., Cic. *De or.* 2.132–36, *Orat.* 128).

85. Varro, *Ling.* 7.36; Ennius' lines are preserved at Cic. *Brut.* 71 (*ROL* 1.82–83).

86. The text has, as I have reflected, had significant emendation here. Kent 1951 follows the suggested replacement of "*antiquos*" with "*antiqui*." This alters the sense a little; my translation is looser than usual to attempt to reflect both versions. Similarly, Kent's presentation of the double insertion "*futura, a*" embeds a prophetic quality that one might want to experiment with eliding. Hence, I attempted a translation that allows the insertion to be cut out if preferred.

87. Thomas 2004 sums up the "problem" of Saturn elegantly.

88. Varro, *Ling.* 5.62 (introduced in the section "Glossing and Enriching" in this chapter); *uieo* may also feature at *Ling.* 5.140 (the "woven" body of a wagon), but the text needs emendation to deliver that.

89. Varro on memory, *Ling.* 6.43–44.

90. This partakes implicitly in what was explicit for *Ling.* 6.61, discussed in the section "Romespeak" in this chapter, in the context of Saussure's "*image acoustique*" ([1916]

1983, 28–32). See, e.g., de Jonge 2008, 60–65 on the Greek/Latin dialogue and its implications (in Dionysius). To transliterate or not is part of the endemic textual problem of what Varro (or his amanuensis) actually wrote or conceptualized for representing "Greek" words. Varro's contemporaries swapped between the two, e.g., Cic. *Att.* 9.13.4 vs, *Off.* 3.19 (dealing with *turannos*). On Cicero, see Boldrer 2003. Wallace 2011 provides invaluable background; Gibson 2011 discusses the danger of making assertions based on manuscript evidence. Biville 1989, 2000, Myers-Scotton 1988, and Mullen 2011 propose especially helpful frameworks for thinking about how orthography relates to identity. The diverse cultural models explored in Jaffe et al. 2012 offer striking evidence of the politicization of orthography.

91. Spencer 2015b, 75–78, 84–88.

92. E.g., Cic. *Off.* 1.17, 19, 83, 101, 111, 141–42, 145–49, 153; 2.3.

93. On etymology as performative exegesis, see, e.g., Ford 1999.

94. Chariot races, battle, the passage of time, triumphs military and intellectual; in chapter 7, examining *Ling.* 6.1, 3, *curro* (*Ling.* 5.153), the frame of reference available from Plato's *Cratylus* is particularly worth noting. Making the connection work with Virgil's *Georgics*, see, e.g., Gale 2000, 143–95, 262 n. 104; more generally, see Nelis 2008. Connecting to Greek tragic drama: on the Greek quality of triumphs, see Varro, *Ling.* 6.68; cf. Sumi 2002 on Sulla. On the visual and "dramatic" in Triumphs, see e.g., Beard 2007, 147–52, 159–86; Hölscher (1987) 2004, 38–45. Focusing more on the politics are Sumi 2005, 25–35 (games, and triumphs), 215–17; Itgenshorst 2005 (making a tension between various sociopolitical groups a developing feature of the Republican triumph), 2006; and Östenberg 2009, 15–16, 62–71. Cic. *Lucull.* 68 is interesting in this context: an example of the charioteer as *agitator callidus*, reining himself in before any mad dash causes problems.

95. See Spencer 2015a, 105.

96. E.g., Hor. *Carm.* 1.9.22, 2.6.14 (on which, Rimell 2015, 82–101); Prop. 4.9.65.

97. As noted in Spencer 2015b, 86–88, we can see relevant, comparable use at Cic. *Brut.* 196–99 (and on *Latinitas* in this, see Dugan 2005, 179–82); Sall. *Cat.* 20.7; Hor. *Sat.* 1.6.17–18, *Carm.* 3.1.1.

98. My argument here is indebted to Corbeill 2010.

99. Rasmussen 2003, 160, and 2003, 164–68, on the case of M. Calpurnius Bibulus (in 59). See also Rüpke 2004b, 182, and, more generally, e.g., Rosenberger 2007.

100. Cic. *Nat. D.* 2.7–12 (NB *Nat. D.* 2.7, where Lucilius observes that "because of the neglectfulness of the nobility the discipline of augury has been lost, the reality of auspices is treated with contempt; nothing more than outward show is retained." Cf. Cic. *Div.* 1.25–33, 2.70–83 (pros and cons for auspices and augury). Krostenko 2000 explores Cic. *Div.* as a symbolic, figurative primer for normalizing Roman religious practice. Cf. Varro, *Rust.* 1.40.5, for a (perhaps ironic) maneuver distancing those who pay attention to haruspices from the speaker (Stolo, "Mr. Sucker") and his audience. Linderski 1982, 37–38, memorably sums up the tensions in Cic. *Div.*: "When Cicero could not control the augur Antonius or the haruspex Spurinna, when the gods started talking the language of Caesar, he preferred not to believe in their enunciation." Cf. Rawson 1978.

Beard 2012 suggests why saying "Haruspices" to Cicero might prove unexpectedly edgy (Varro, *Ling.* sticks with "Augurs"; Haruspices also appear at Varro, *Sat. Men.* 558.2 = ap. Non. 410 M). Green 2009 teases out some of the dynamic resonances of augury as Rome moved into the Principate. For overviews of the political contexts, see Santangelo 2012 (focusing on law), 2013a.

101. At *Ling.* 6.95 Varro explores the relative significance of consul versus augur when he tackles the *exercitus* (*Ling* 6.95), but the augurs maintain core areas of dominance, carving up the sky to deliver arcane knowledge (*Ling.* 6.53; cf. 5.85, 7.8). Elsewhere, augural practice instantiates communication in the broadest sense, e.g., *Ling.* 6.64, 76. Chapter 3 returns to this topic.

102. See Spencer 2015b, 88–92, for the detail.

103. On which, see Spencer 2018.

104. Depending on whether one accepts the Goetz and Schoell 1910 solution (swapping *axitiosae* for *ac sitiose*; deriving from *Editio Aldina*, Aldus Minutius, Venice 1513; amended 1527). The cs-/x- slippage seems possible, but there is also the possibility of an interplay (or confusion) with *ascisco* (taking something or someone to oneself). For *ascitae*, see Maltby s.v. *Ascitae* (2), with the term eventually plugging heretics back into ἄσκος.

105. "Claudius writes that women making common cause in entreaties are clearly shown to be unionised." Taking Varro's "Claudius" to be one and the same as the character in Cic. *Fam.* 9.16.4 (cf. *Att.* 1.20.7), a grammarian and Plautine scholar and son-in-law of Aelius Stilo (with whom Varro and Cicero studied and whose intellectual heir Cicero makes Varro): "'*quam scientiam Varro noster acceptam ab illo auctamque per sese, uir ingenio praestans omnique doctrina, pluribus et inlustrioribus litteris explicauit*'" (which branch of knowledge our friend Varro received from him, and further enhanced in his own right: a man of outstanding intellect and the greatest erudition, adding depth by means of many and distinguished writings, Cic. *Brut.* 205). See Rawson 1985, 76, 273 (proposing the possibility of equating Claudius with Ser. Clodius), 278.

106. Following arguments developed in Edwards 1993 and Richlin 1993. See, e.g., Cic. *Cat.* 2.22, *Verr.* 2.5.81; Sen. *Controv.* 2.1.6.

107. Varro, *Ling.* 6.58–68. Recall *Ling.* 7.66, discussed in the section "*Narro*: Telling Tales and Making Speech" in this chapter.

108. "*Pro idem ualet quod ante*," *Ling.* 6.58. Kent has accepted some emendation for §58, which I am following.

109. Whether we are dealing with lurking homonyms between Greek and Italo-Latin here or something more distinctly a result of hybridization is impossible to know.

110. Varro's *loquor* reappears in the section "The End Result: Speaking Well" in this chapter and in chapter 4.

111. "*Quod a uerbo Graeco potest declinatum*," Varro, *Ling.* 6.58.

112. "*Loqui ab loco dictum*," "'to talk' is said from 'place'" (*Ling.* 6.56). At *Ling.* 5.14–15 Varro explains how placiality operates through an etymology connecting speech and *locus*. See chapter 5 for discussion, Casey 1993 introducing the theory, and Short 2008, 120–22, on the placiality of ideas and metaphors.

113. Chrysippus (of Soli, 280–07), who led the Stoic school at Athens after Cleanthes. Through-readers met Chrysippus before (*Ling.* 6.2); still in book 6, he also features at 6.11; he recurs at *Ling.* 9.1 (see chapter 4) and then (finally) at 10.59.

114. Habinek 2005, 70–74. The relationship between speech and song is a focus for chapter 3, but the argument commenced here responds to ideas raised by Habinek 2005, 104–9.

115. *Proloquor* is not especially common; it appears to crop up most vividly for our purposes in drama, e.g., Enn. ap. Non. 232.24 (Sc. 337 Vahl.), ap. Cic. *Tusc.* 3.26.63 (Sc. 257 Vahl.), Ter. *Phorm.* 2.1.53, *An.* 1.5.21; Plaut. *Amph.* 1.1.248, prol. 50, *Capt.* prol. 6, *Epid.* 3.4.32, id. *Aul.* 2.1.19; but cf. Cic. *Orat.* 147; and (later) Prop. 3.13.59.

116. "*In fanis Sabinis, e cella dei qui loquuntur*" (*loquuntur*, for *eloquuntur*, with Kent). For more on *fana*, see Varro, *Ling.* 6.54. Sanctuaries are places of reciprocity and dialogue; the dedication of offerings and sacrifices is to the fore at 6.54 but also earlier at 5.112. At *Sat. Men.* 115 (ap. Non. 544 M), the humor of gods creeping about sanctuaries in search of a drink is another angle.

117. The precise character of what these women are doing when they approach a fellow woman to talk to her is either (as Kent agrees; with manuscript G and Augustinus) *consolandi* (in order to console) or (following F) *consulendi* (in order to consult). The former makes sense of the gender difference (from *colloquium*) and gets at the notion of *adlocutio* as a form of address rather than conversation.

118. Swapping out "*condeant*" for "*concinant*" (Mueller 1833) is probably the only logical solution here.

119. Varro, *Ling.* 8.5.

120. Varro, *Ling.* 8.6.

121. Callim. *Aet.* 1.2; *Hymn* 2.111–12, with an afterlife, e.g., Lightfoot 1999 on fr. 32; cf. Catull. 65, and 68b.57–62 (a *riuus* trickles refreshingly down a mountain, inspiring the poet back to literary life); Hor. *Carm.* 3.13—the famous *fons Bandusiae*. See Brown 1982 on the motif in development from Callimachus to Lucretius.

122. Hes. *Theog.* 1–34.

123. Hor. *Carm.* 3.30; recalling now Varro, *Ling.* 6.49, *monumentum*. See Jaeger 1997, 15–26.

Chapter 3. Inspiring Latin

1. Quint. *Inst.* 1.8.11. See Kaster 2005, 6–7, regarding the problems of understanding how emotion nuances lexical authority; the volume is a richly rewarding study; for Varro's verse quotation, see Piras 2015 (Garbarino 1978 looks more broadly at poetic word usage in Latin prose, offering wider context).

2. Book 7 is missing its opening page in the primary ms (F). My reading is very much in tune with Baier's (1997) analysis of Varro as a plugged-in operator (although Baier 1997 is not concerned with narratology or with *De Lingua Latina* per se).

3. Compare Virg. *Aen.* 9.602, where Numanus Remulus riffs on Turnus when exhorting the Latins: there's no tale-telling Ulysses ("*fandi factor Ulixes*") here.

4. *OLD* s.v. *fingo*—with sense 9, to "fabricate," an interesting, fictive, undertone.

5. Varro, *Ling.* 6.41–42.

6. *Quaestor*—accepting Kent's emendation from "*conquestor*" to "*tum quaestor.*"

7. See, e.g., Piras 1998, who has undertaken impressive cataloging of relevant examples.

8. Passages that do not feature here but that could flesh out this topic include a poetically militaristic farmyard (*Ling.* 5.88), onomatopoeia (e.g., *Ling.* 6.67), the power of the poets (e.g., *Ling.* 5.1, 5.7, 5.9, 9.17, 9.115; 10.35), and a scatter-gun array of approaches to Ennius (see especially *Ling.* 6.80–83) and, widely, to Pacuvius (in passing—consult Kent's index and Piras 1998).

9. On the *Carmen Saliare* as quintessentially "old" but still semiotically important, see e.g., Varro, *Ling.* 6.49 (and in the context of book 7, 7.2, 3). Cf. 5.85, marking up *salii* as from *salto*; the popular, archaic *locus classicus* for verse in Latin is itself derived early in Varro's scheme from a richly performative act. For Varro's etymology of *carmen*, see the second section of this chapter, "Varro on Song."

10. With Kent, following the emendation Aelii for Helii.

11. Jauss 1970.

12. E.g., Cic. *Tusc* 5.108, the citation is unascribed, but Cic. *De or.* 1.246 makes the identification and proverbiality likely; cf. Hor. *Carm.* 1.7.

13. One might argue that the text's lossy quality here makes meaningful analysis impossible, but despite textual frailty, one can make the best of it and find a path (much as Varro's modus operandi advises). Epimenides' slumber fails to feature as a highlight in Latin; struggling to find examples, cf. Pliny *HN* 7.175.

14. Epimenides: Diog. Laert. 1.109–15, Plut. *Vit. Sol.* 12; Paus 1.14.4. Dodds 1951, 141–43, collects up the evidence.

15. E.g., "Teucer" distilled in Verg. *Aen.*

16. Habinek 2005, 80–81, but with no consideration of Varro's (attempted) revival of the debate.

17. In book 5, exemplifying the second "stage" of etymology, Varro gives readers two interlocking areas of expertise connected to mastery of *grammatica antiqua*: "how the poet has fashioned each word that he has devised and derived" (*Ling.* 5.7). The third "stage," to which Varro modestly aspires, is a deeper, philosophical understanding of words' roots.

18. Kent 1951 inserts *quae*.

19. Habinek 2005, 61.

20. Habinek 2005, 61–62.

21. Habinek 2005, 67. Compare the formulas at Cat. *Agr.* 140, where the whole point might always have been that the speaker was not in control of the utterances, a point toward which Habinek 2005, 74–76, is moving.

22. Recall Servius on *cano*, the *Aeneid*'s first verb: "*polysemus sermo est.*"

23. Maltby s.v. *osculum, i*; Schad 2007 s.v. *diminutiuus*.

24. Cicero was additionally connected to Caecina through the defense speech he had delivered on Caecina's father's behalf, back in 69 (*Caecin.*).

25. The letter also gives Cicero the opportunity adroitly to remodel the role of Pompey's defeat in his own personal history (Cic. *Fam.* 6.6.4–6, 10).

26. Cic. *Fam.* 6.6.8–9 (not in the passage quoted).

27. Varro, *Ling.* 6.77; discussed in chapter 2, "Action," and in the first section of this chapter, "Poets, Artfulness, and Textuality."

28. Another example of this kind of object-to-action derivation, leaning on Ennius, concerns *fossa* (ditch), which generates Ennius' "excavatory" terminology ("*fodiendo*," *Ling.* 7.100).

29. Sluiter 2015.

30. "'*Iam dudum ab ludis animus atque aures auent, / Auide expectantes nuntium.' Propter hanc aurium auiditatem theatra replentur*," Varro, *Ling.* 6.83.

31. This reading supports Habinek (2005, 106–9) on the seriousness of *ludi* as a species of appropriation of capital (see also Flower 1995). Varro's extant text lacks an etymology for *theatrum*. At *Ling.* 6.83, "eager ears" keep theaters full, and at 9.58 Varro observes that a theater can be "deaf" ("*sic surdum theatrum*"), presumably referring to both space and audience; Varro, *Sat. Men.* 218 (ap. Non. 325 M) riffs on theaters, but the place where Varro seems to indicate interest in the politics of theaters, especially Pompey's, comes to us through Gellius. Gellius cites Varro as having intervened in a debate on how to record order of election versus number of elections to a magistracy, specifically regarding how Pompey should write *tertio* (third in a sequence) or *tertium* (three times) to record his consulships (*NA* 10.1.6–8). Gellius makes clear that Cicero was deeply involved, according to Tiro, in Pompey's attempt to get this inscription on the temple of Venus Victrix just right but not keen to undermine Varro's authoritative intervention on the side of *consul tertium* (Varro, Gellius notes, called Pompey *timidus* for fence-sitting, with "*tert*" as the final version in the inscription).

32. Varro, *Ling.* 7.26–29, 32, developed at 7.35–36. The sequence here is part of Varro on "beginnings," to which the fourth section of this chapter, "In the Beginning, Starting from Scratch, or Ending Up?," returns.

33. "'*Musas quas memorant nosce<s> nos esse <Camenas>*'" (those whom they tell of as the Muses, know them to be us Camenae, *Ling.* 7.26)—reading "*musas*" rather than "*curuamus ac*" (which, as Kent suggests, seems to be the product of a backward-glancing run-on from §25) means accepting Scaliger's emendation.

34. "*Ut in Carmine Saliorum sunt haec*" (as here in the Salian Hymn), Varro, *Ling.* 7.26. Note that what follows at *Ling.* 7.27 has been substantially emended and appears to start more abruptly than might be expected. Without the full quote from the (already problematic) *Carmen Saliare* (if further lines form at least part of what's missing), it is difficult to know how §27 originally commenced. Nevertheless, in *F*, the section does commence neatly at the beginning of a line, suggesting at least that the scribe considered this to be a natural point to recommence. For this reason I am tempted by Kent 1951, 295 n. i: what was omitted was more of the *Carmen Saliare* (assuming we take Varro's quotation practice at face value). For ancient audiences, this may just have been too much strange old unintelligible stuff for the copyist to engage with.

35. Varro, *Ling.* 7.34, discussed extensively in chapter 2, in the fourth section of this chapter, "Glossing and Enriching."

36. I am indebted to Massimo Platini, who, on hearing about this material, replied with an Italian joke (similarly taking in word games and the need to know something

about antiquity): "*Cosa fa Bruto senza Cassio? Non pissia*" (How goes Brutus without Cassius? No pissing!). *Pissia*, a made-up word, plays on the correct form *piscia* (*pisciare*, to piss) and the similarity between *Cassio* and *cazzo* (cock). The sibilant alliteration (-ssi) adds to the pun.

37. Livy 1.7.8 also gives the form "Carmenta" (associating her with *fatiloquia*), which suggests that it was probably also in play when Varro was composing. Habinek 2005, 222–30, explores Carmentis' significance for understanding "song"; what the actual process of etymologization might have looked like (2005, 228–29) clearly embraces the associative reading for which I argue in Varro and that supports Habinek's broad conclusions on Carmentis' cross-cultural polyvalence.

38. Verg. *Aen.* 8.339–41. See also, e.g., Ov. *Fast.* 1.461–636. Varro's etymology of Carmenta (or Carmentis), if there was one, does not survive (cf. Varro ap. Gell. 16.16, flagging up Carmentis as a kind of bifold, Janus type, whose gaze encompasses what's past and what's ahead). He does, however, make a brief stop at Carmentis' Carmentalia (*Ling.* 6.12), as noted in chapter 8.

39. Varro, *Ling.* 7.27.

40. Varro, *Ling.* 7.28. "Manilius" suggests the well-known and influential Manilii, but there is nothing to indicate whether the author is a prominent member of the clan or even a freedman; similarly, an identity for "Papinius" is unclear; other suggestions are Pomponius (via Priscian) and Pompilius. Picking one is not especially important; the point is that the quotation delivers the right jokey etymological effect.

41. "*quae usque radices in Oscam linguam egit*," Varro, *Ling.* 7.28.

42. Reading "*genuere*" instead of the emendation "*tenuere*" in the Ennius quote, although either works equally well.

43. The Papinius epigram needed emendation to deliver something pithy as the genders did not add up to the concluding joke; the gist is clear, however.

44. "*nostri etiam nunc Forum Vetus appellant*," Varro, *Ling.* 7.29. Varro on *forum*, *Ling.* 5.145–46, 148, discussed in chapter 5; see also Spencer 2011b, 76–77; 2015a, 105–7; and 2018, 57–58, 59, 61–62.

45. The earlier assertion adds weight to Kent 1951's decision to emend *ostii* to read *Osci* (*Ling.* 7.29).

46. Cooley 2002 illustrates the persistence of Oscan as an overlap with Latin in Pompeii after Sulla. Varro's comments show a sophisticated understanding of how *langue* and *parole* contribute to multilayering in linguistic development.

47. This form "*ambagio*" is not attested elsewhere in Classical Latin; *adagio*, too, is unusual but not unheard of. One might wonder, given the sense that Varro is pushing, whether there's an extra joke—to get *ambagio* one also needs to change a letter (*ambago*—albeit unusual—is the obvious solution) or two (*ambages*, the word Varro has only just finished with at §30, is even more odd an elision).

48. Varro, *Ling.* 7.32. On forms relating to *ambit-*, Spencer 2011b, 64–66; Tatum 2013. Proverbs clearly have a role in fixing culture orally, and mnemonically and in parading one's command of compendia of knowledge; see, e.g., Ong 2002, 34, 44, and, in relation to Rome, O'Neill 2003.

49. The revelatory quality of Varro's dogs situates them in the same frame as Habinek's birds, but through the detail of etymology and allusion Varro makes much plainer what can be inferred from Habinek's examples (2005, 82–85).

50. Varro, *Ling.* 7.2, 7.4; cf. 5.1. For Varro's "meanders," see Linderski 1986, 2264.

51. Varro, *Ling.* 7.65.

52. This is one of the text's more anarchic moments. The reconstruction also leans on Mueller 1833 for *strittabillae*, while the final word, *tantulae*, is given as *sordidae* in Gellius 3.3.6, and Nonius 169.9 M.

53. Following Spengel, L. 1826 in reading "*siccam significat*" for the unsatisfactory "*sic assignificat*."

54. Q. Aurelius Opillus, who went into exile with P. Rutilius Rufus in 92 (we might recall that L. Aelius Stilo accompanied Q. Caecilius Metellus Numidicus into exile in 100 and may have aided his propaganda for recall, successful in 99). Rawson 1985, 4, 67, plausibly argues that the exile may have been a "stance" designed to elide Opillus' declining prestige at Rome and seen through by Rutilius Rufus.

55. Cic. *De or.* 3.171, *Brut.* 274 (discussing M. Calidius, orator, and praetor in 53; remarking on the pliancy and flexibility of his rhetoric), *Orat.* 149 (duplicating *De or.* 3.171). In this era, *uermiculus* also crops up in Lucretius (2.899, 3.728), and Varro uses it at *Rust.* 3.16.17.

56. *OLD* s.v. *frons, -ndis, -ntis*.

57. Valerius is possibly Q. Valerius Soranus; cf. Enn. ap. Fest. 258 M; Pac. ap. Non 336 M (and, a couple of decades later, Verg. *Aen.* 6.238).

58. See Rüpke 2012, 57–58. Liv. 22.51.9 makes gruesome capital of Tydeus gobbling Melanippus' brains (the story must have been a popular shocker; e.g., Ov. *Ibis* 515, Apollod. 3.6.5; cf. Hom. *Il.* 4.376–98, Aesch. *Sept.* 407–14).

59. Programmatic introduction at *Ling.* 7.5.

60. Baldi 1999, Calboli 2009, and Clackson and Horrocks 2007 offer important context for the readings in this section. For *templum* as a spatial construct, see, in chapter 5, the section "Locating the Divine."

61. Introduced in chapter 2.

62. Enn. *Var.* 11 (*ROL* i.450); cf. Ov. *Met.* 14.814; *Fast.* 2.487 (without *templa*, but indicative of the familiarity of the material). The Naevius quote is unidentified.

63. Varro, *Ling.* 7.6, quoting Enn. *Ann.* 65–66 (*ROL* i.22–23); the popularity of the quote is evidenced by its later use by Ovid (although omitting *templa*), cf. Ov. *Met.* 14.814; *Fast.* 2.487.

64. Cf. Cic. *Leg.* 1.3; *Rep.* 1.25, 2.20; and, with a nod to Ennius, Cic. *Tusc.* 1.28.

65. Cic. *Div.* 1.40–41. Cicero's Quintus (see Beard 1986, 44–45) describes the dream sequence as a poet's potent fiction (*Div.* 1.42).

66. Linderski 1986, 2263–64, asks how Varro could logically have adduced Pacuvius' quote as a sane example of a terrestrial *templum* in the strictest augural sense; he answers his own question thus: "clarity of composition was not among Varro's many literary virtues" (at 2264)!

67. Linderski 1986, 2264.

68. This translation accepts Scioppius' version, reading *intueor*: "*Quaqua in<tu>iti era<n>t oculi, a tuendo primo templum dictum: quocirca caelum qua attuimur dictum templum*," Varro, *Ling.* 7.7.
69. Enn. *Ann.* 541 ROL i.450–51.
70. E.g., Thuc.1.18.1, 6.5.3; Pind. *Ol.* 13.80; Polyb. 34.1.3; Hdt. 1.91, 3.80; Pl. *Cra.* 426c.
71. Maltby highlights the possible connection with *orior*. For ὄρνυμι relevantly, e.g., Hes. *Theog.* 190; Hom. *Il.* 3.10. The association of *origines* and forms of *condo/conditor* in Livy's first book, the book policing the gap between pre- and post-foundation for the site and people of Rome, points up the political quality of starting a project; see, e.g., Liv. 1.7, 15; 3.24.
72. Varro, *Ling.* 6.96.
73. Varro, *Ling.* 6.90–95.
74. How Cato-centric is the terminology? A *PHI* search for Catonian *origin-es* makes Cic. *Brut.* 66, 89, 294 the only text in play; for *origin-ibus*, Cic. *De or.* 1.227; *Brut.* 75, *Tusc.* 1.3.11, 4.3.15; *Sen.* 75; *origin-um*, Cic. *Planc.* 66.12; *Sen.* 38; *origin-em*, Cic. *Rep.* 2.3. Forms in *origin-* not referring to Cato: e.g., Catull. 4.15; Gavius Bassus [titular, *Commentarii de Origine Vocabulorum*]; Cic. *Brut.* 253; *Fin.* 4.17; *Nat. D.* 1.36; *Tim.* 9; Lucret. 3.331, 3.686, 3.771, 5.301, 5.548, 5.678; Sall. *Iug.* 19.1.
75. E.g., when Varro introduces Plautus' *Friuolaria* (*Ling.* 7.58) and cites Cato as the explicator for the quoted term "*accensi*" (cf. *Ling.* 9.107, bundling Cato and Ennius). *Origo* (variously declined) features thirteen times in book 5, eleven times in book 6, seventeen times in book 7; usage then drops off rapidly: it features once in book 8, once in book 9, and twice in book 10 (as extant). Cato is name-checked sixteen times in Varro, *Rust.* (primarily in book 1).
76. As Sciarrino 2004, 324 n. 2, sums up in detail, Cato's *Origines* has tended to be characterized as the first prose "history" of Italy in Latin (Sciarrino 2011 makes a concerted attempt to reconceptualize a compositional context for Cato; Gotter 2003 is still useful in this context).
77. This reflects issues raised by Bispham 2007, which could be dragged back to Cato's pioneering work on "origins" without doing violence to the evidentiary frame. Cf. Torelli 1999, who explores the possibility of pushing the *tota Italia* tag (deployed, e.g., by Augustus, *Mon. Anc.* 25.2) back into the second century. Cf. Ando 2002, 126–27 (focus on the politics of "Italy"); Dench 1995, 19 (try-out for making this text as a new kind of document of culture).
78. Cato, *Orig.* 1.6 (ap. Serv. *A.* 1.6 [= *FRH* 3 F1.6]).
79. The pithy phrase is from Sciarrino 2004, 343.
80. Sciarrino 2004, 346–47 (at 347). Cf. The well-known passage at Cic. *Tusc.* 4.3, drawing in Sciarrino 2004, 338 on Livy 7.2.4–7.
81. In this context, note Varro's vivid metaphor at 7.2: *amminicula*, "tools," the kind of elucidatory devices one might deploy to open up meaning in language.
82. For Cato's *Origines* in this sense, see Sciarrino 2004, 353.
83. See McElduff 2009 (and more briefly, McElduff 2004—the "translation" and originality problem); this issue (what is "translation"?) is also central to Spencer 2011a.

84. E.g., Hom. *Il.* 4.525, 13.568, *Od.* 1.50 (as midpoint); Hdt. 7.60.2; Strabo 9.3.6 (Delphi).

85. Varro, *Ling.* 7.17. On Pythagoreanism in the Republic, e.g., Mastrocinque 2007, 381–84 (for the longer story, Ferrero 1955).

86. I have in mind the passage cited at Cic. *Brut.* 252, but cf. Gell. *NA* 19.8.6.

87. But see Cic. *Orat.* 155: irregular speech is licensed through use.

88. It also sits well with the programmatic force of *incipiam* in book 7.

89. *OLD* s.v. *pertineo* 1 gives placiality; s.v. *pono* 1 (military overtones starting to develop; placiality already in the frame) and 3 (foundational connotations).

90. Foucault (1969) 2002, 25. On Martial *inter alia* and this topic, see Roman 2001, 126–29, 133–38.

91. On the trio of "action" terms (introduced in chapter 2), see Spencer 2011b and 2015c, 86–88.

92. Cf. Cic. *Or.* 153–160 (adding and subtracting letters): "speech should delight the ears" (*Or.* 159). For Cicero's Greek loan words, Oksala 1953 collects data; on plurality more broadly, see Oniga 2003.

93. Discussing Cic. *Tusc.* 1.3, Sciarrino 2004, 333, observes: "What stands out in Cicero's account is that the beginning of poetry in Rome is associated with the acceptance of a specific category of people which Cicero names by adopting the Greek term *poeta*. Furthermore, by using a Greek term Cicero alludes to (but does not dwell on) the fact that in the second century BCE 'poetry' stood for performances carried out by elite 'others' based on scripts and therefore distinct from those that used to inform ancestral banquets. Cato, on the other hand, articulates in more detail the link between poetry and non-elite individuals in the *carmen de moribus*. . . . Not only does Cato evaluate poetry by asserting that no prestige is reaped from the activities that revolve around it but he also confirms that poetry is a profession, a *techne*, by using the Latin equivalent, *ars*. Moreover, he legitimizes his judgment by invoking the opinion of the ancestors and associates the *poetae* with the ancestral *grassatores*. Through this link, Cato reinforces the subordinate position of the poets and substantiates the exclusive character of convivial occasions."

94. Lucret. 5.1442–43.

95. Varro, *Ling.* 7.4. Cf. Cic. *Or.* 123: "I'm not looking for a pupil."

96. Varro, *Ling.* 7.5.

97. What Habinek 1998, 34–68, 88–102, terms "culture wars."

98. E.g., Cic. *Tusc.* 1.3.

99. The text is problematic at *Ling.* 7.107–8, but a stable sequence runs from an epic-heroic world (sword tips, victory songs), to stagey goats (signaling a genre shift to drama), to knowing (too much), unity of time and place, blandishments and promises of different sorts, slaves, young boys, plots, brilliant illumination, and the oddly crisscrossing link between elucidating and making opaque (in various senses) where oppositionality signals family ties.

100. Foucault (1969) 2002, 26.

101. Varro, *Ling.* 7.109.

Chapter 4. *Oratio* and the Read/Write Experience

1. Wittgenstein (1953) 2009, §49.

2. On this nascent era in rhetoric and its theoretical development down to Aristotle, see Kennedy 1994, 11–63.

3. Again, I find myself returning to Kennedy 1994, 102–58 (on developments at Rome), but Stroup 2007 provides an excellently nuanced contextualizing analysis. Habinek 1998, 88–102, remains essential for unpacking Rome's late Republican "culture wars."

4. McElduff 2013, passim, opens the complexity of what it meant to "translate" from Greek in this era, in all sorts of ways.

5. Dugan 2007 gives an excellent overview of trends in scholarship on Roman rhetoric, while Powell 2011 makes sense of Latin rhetorical discourse. Gaines 2007 economically sketches the development of handbooks for rhetoric at Rome. On Cicero as a rhetorician, May 2007 is exemplary. Setting this in context: Sinclair 1994, Willi 2010; extensively: Dugan 2005. All in various ways explore the politics of language and word choice in driving political agenda. Garcea 2012 shows one way of getting Caesar center-stage.

6. Cic. *De or.* 1.12. Powell 2011 tackles the broad issues at stake for decoupling language from rhetorical discourse systems, while Ferri and Probert 2010 provide an overview of what constitutes "colloquialism."

7. Wittgenstein (1953) 2009, §241–42.

8. Varro, *Ling.* 10.42–43. Recall the linguist as hunter, e.g., *Ling.* 5.5 (featuring initially in my introduction but significant throughout) or 7.2 (discussed in chapter 3) and etymologies as underground roots, e.g., *Ling.* 5.13, 7.4 (first discussed in chapter 2 but important throughout).

9. Varro, *Ling.* 5.1, 5.2, and, e.g., 6.40, 7.52–53. A comparable question, which in the extant text Varro does not raise, is the matter of the difference between being called Greek or a Hellene.

10. Stroh 2006, 186–88, captures and develops this tension beyond Varro.

11. See Spencer 2011c; the verb appears to gain currency only during the Second Sophistic, with various senses of "speaking as a Roman" as well as "speaking Latin" (see, e.g., App. *Hann.* 41, *Mith.* 10, *B Civ.* 1.41, 2.91; Dio Chrys. *Or.* 37.40; Cass. Dio 50.6.4).

12. Cic. *Fam.* 7.5.3, 7.16.3, 7.18.3 (cf. Quint. *Inst. Or.* 6.2.8). By contrast, Ov. *Pont.* 1.2.67 delivers the idiom *lingua Romana*, and Pliny (*HN* 31.8) preserves an epigram on Cicero (ascribed to one of his freedmen, M. Tullius Laurea, see Hollis 2007 §194) with the same formulation, also, e.g., Gell. *NA* 1.18.1 (cf. Apul. *Flor.* 18; *De Mundo* 11). Cf. Plin. *Ep.* 2.10.2. What is noteworthy is that it does not appear to be in use at or before the time when Varro was likely to have been writing *De Lingua Latina*.

13. Varro, *Ling.* 6.40.

14. Recall, e.g., Varro's *ago* (*Ling.* 6.41), discussed in chapter 2. In general, see Bhatia and Ritchie 2005 on the theory; in more detail, see Kroll and Dussias 2005. There is an extensive bibliography on bilingualism and identity; see, e.g., Adams 2003a, 2003b; Dunkel 2000; cf. Ingold 1993.

15. Nora 2001. Recall, e.g., *Ling.* 6.56 on locational loquacity.

16. Varro, *Ling.* 6.58; see chapter 2.

17. The issue of centrality, shortcuts, and their "novelty" in Rome must be part of the friction in the persistence of "new" in naming; see Newsome 2011 for some of the contexts, and a methodological discussion focussing on the infrastructure.

18. Varro, *Ling.* 6.61, is especially hard to fix, textually. For δεικνύω we can thank L. Spengel 1826; one might also adopt δείκνυμαι (see Mueller 1833), or Scaliger's δείκω. For the fragment of Ennius we should thank Festus 153 a 15–21 M. *Ling.* 6.61 and *dico* featured in chapter 2's set-up of Romespeak; the contrast between what is spoken and what is set down is featured in chapter 3.

19. For further grist, see *Ling.* 6.78.

20. Ov. *Met.* 2.706 offers a comparable wordplay, juxtaposing *dicitur* and *index* for etymological punning effect—a rustic, Battus, is an indiscreet speaker whose speech is inevitably indiscreet. See Ernout and Meillet 1959, 172.

21. Habinek 2005, 66.

22. See Varro, *Ling.* 9.3; cf. *Ling.* 10.31, where *dico* features (among others) in the set of key verb forms.

23. Varro, *Ling.* 8.45.

24. "*Ut nonnunquam ab homine locus, ab eo loco homo, ut ab Romulo Roma, ab Roma Romanus.*" Cf. *Ling.* 8.80, where the proposition is used to disprove the existence of Regularity. Cf. *Ling.* 9.50, 10.15.

25. Cavazza 2004, discussing Gellius, adds substantially to the discussion here.

26. Speculatively, Syrian might have seemed like a usefully foreign wild-card language; recently annexed by Pompey and newly a Roman province (64), Syria drew the negotiation between Rome and the east into the frame (Antiochid claims to Syria in the late 70s ripple through Cicero's prosecution of Verres, e.g., *Verr.* 2.4.61, 67–68), but might also recall an inglorious instance in Clodius' career when he stirred up trouble in Antioch (recounted by Dio 36.17.3). Syria was latterly in the contextual mix for Cicero's governorship of Cilicia (51–50), but, more interesting, was a focus for his barnstorming speech in 56, *On the Consular Provinces* (3, 9–10).

27. Brisset 2004 unpacks these issues with emphasis on how the idea of a "native language" makes a difference to groups' understanding of shared and divergent discourse. Clackson 2011b provides a thorough survey of Latin inflectional morphology, for which, of course, Varro's thinking is a key factor; Matthews 1972, 1991 remain useful background.

28. In this I differ from the position of consensus through exclusivity outlined by Hölkeskamp 2013, with whose conclusions my reading of Varro otherwise sits well.

29. This phrase has benefited, from the point of view of sense, from emendation: Kent has stuck with Spengel 1885, moving "*analogias uerborum exprimendas*" forward from its position after "*simili*" in F.

30. Stroup 2010, 165–66. Cf. 2010, 198–99, on the beginnings of this in Cic. *De or.* (and in Cic. *Brut.*).

31. For *os*, bone, and the death ritual, see Varro, *Ling.* 5.23 (we met *os*, mouth, in chapter 3, *Ling.* 6.76). Cf. other "mouth" terms: e.g., *dens* (*Ling.* 8.67 and, by transference in agriculture, 5.135), *facies* (*Ling.* 6.78—see again chapter 3; and by transference in linguistics, *Ling.* 9.92, cited earlier in this chapter).

32. Caes. *BGall.* 1.1.1–2 ("*hi omnes lingua, institutis, legibus inter se differunt*"). Caesar, of course, was the celebrity proponent of *analogia*.

33. Cic. *Brut.* 309–11 makes the case implicitly but plainly. Cf. Cic. *Att.* 2.20 commenting (in 59) on the popular copying and promulgation of Bibulus' edicts and acts.

34. Varro goes on to quote Ennius to illustrate that when the case being made was particularly significant, "learnedness" (again, a divergence from everyday parole) became a sine qua non: "*legebantur potissimum qui causam commodiss<im>e orare poterant. Itaque Ennius ait: 'Oratores doctiloqui,'*" *Ling.* 7.41.

35. Cic. *De or.* 3.139–140.

36. Cic. *De or.* 1.35–44 ("Scaevola"), 1.45–73 ("Crassus"), 1.76–81 ("Antonius" chips in; the problem of ideal vs. reality).

37. The matter recurs at *Ling.* 9.48, in the book outlining the pro-Regularity case.

38. Varro, *Ling.* 8.26.

39. Varro, *Ling.* 8.27.

40. Varro, *Ling.* 8.28–31.

41. Kroon 2011 is a useful conspectus for particles and Latin discourse.

42. The text has some oddities here, for which Kent 1951 suggests a set of plausible solutions. The argument presented has avoided leaning on these proposed emendations.

43. E.g., Hom. *Il.* 1.247–84.

44. Roisman 2005, 28, 36, 38.

45. Dining-room furniture recurs in a metaphor at *Ling.* 9.47.

46. Examples that work for considering Varro's metaphor include Cicero's famous diatribe against Verres' excessive dinners (*Verr.* 2.3.68, 2.5.33), to be contrasted with *De or.* 1.27, and *Att.* 5.1.3–4; a little later, see Hor. *Sat.* 2.4, 2.8. Wilkins 2003 usefully sums up on Roman dining as a Mediterranean practice. Gowers 1993 is the go-to study for food and satire, which one might imagine simmering away here (given the tone of what follows, but also Varro's devil's-advocate argument on the pleasures of diversity in furniture whereby not all couches in a house are identical, *Ling.* 8.32; countered at 9.47—a dining set should be just that). On dining and excess, see Edwards 1993, 186–88. On reclining, see M. B. Roller 2003, 380–93 (male dining), 393–404 (female dining).

47. Varro, *Ling.* 9.10–11. Cf. 9.29–30, where the model "body" is an argument for Regularity in speech.

48. Varro, *Ling.* 9.10–16.

49. The emendation to *rationem* makes sense; the ms (*F*) has "*orationem*," perhaps a slip from "*orationis*" in the next clause.

50. A looser than usual translation for this passage. I take *subucula* (undertunic; tackled by Varro at *Ling.* 5.131; part of female dress) plus *uxor* together to deliver something like "slip," "camisole," or other respectable female underwear; this is mindful that there is a slight tension between each wife having her own inevitably boring array of identical underwear and a hint that all wives end up in the same identikit underwear.

51. Varro, *Ling.* 6.63, 6.64, 8.3, 8.25, 8.30, 8.37, 9.1, 9.19, 9.33, 9.107.

52. Here I keep to the emendation from *ratio* to *oratio* but note that the sense works equally well (albeit differently) without it.

53. *OLD* s.v. *comprehendo*, 1, 5, 6, 7, 9, 10, 11. See, e.g., Cic. *Att.* 12.21.1, *Brut.* 19.

54. *OLD homo* s.v. 2 (for constraints/fallibility in the frame of reference).

55. Willi 2010, 233–34, sums up.

56. Varro, *Ling.* 10.59, developing a metaphor of family likenesses; *Ling.* 6.56 (semblance of speech). Cf. *Ling.* 6.11.

57. Bathing and the public versus private bath(s) is part of a discussion of singular/plural challenges raised by those who decry Regularity (*Ling.* 9.68). Varro has an answer rooted in the development of a Roman architectural norm from a Greek blow-in design.

58. Varro, *Ling.* 9.33. Recall the second section of this chapter.

59. For *uerbum*, see especially Varro, *Ling.* 10.77. Occasionally (e.g., 8.12, 8.53), *uerbum* takes on the specialized sense "verb." For "noun," Varro typically uses *uocabulum* (e.g., *Ling.* 5.116, 5.170, 5.175, 5.178, 6.5, 6.59, 7.26, 7.53, 7.86, 8.40, 8.58, 8.71, 9.41, 9.54, 9.66, 10.20, 10.35, 10.54, 10.81; *Rust.* 1.48.2; *Ant. Rerum Div.* 89.5).

60. Introducing *ludo* might call *ludus* to mind, and if one wanted to develop a more distinctively politicized reading, then the Games could form part of the scenery. Spencer 2011c, 61–63, discusses some possible implications for "running" in *De Lingua Latina*.

61. The emendation from *lego* to *lege*—which certainly makes sense—draws on two other mss (*V*, *b*).

62. Although not in the extant text, the pragmatics of the call to the census are recorded at *Ling.* 6.86 (Astin 1988b, 15, sets the detail out). Livy 1.141.3–8 explains the origins, showing how this was still of significant interest; the import of the 169/168 censorship in Livy (43.15.6, 43.15.16; 44.16.8; 45.15) is unpacked by Astin 1988a (cf., e.g., Cic. *Leg.* 3.7). On a decline of the censorship's weightiness, exploring Sulla's role, Ryan 1996; cf. Astin 1985.

63. The other example for *lecte* is Ov. *Met.* 13.640. For the superlative form, see Stat. *Silv.* 5.1.247.

64. Cosconius is, presumably, Q. Cosconius (*fl.* 100).

65. Varro, *Ling.* 6.36–39.

66. Varro, *Ling.* 6.39.

67. E.g., Plaut. *Pseud.* 414; Catull. 64.4; Cic. *Cat.* 3.5.11. Cf. Cic. *Rep.* 1.8.1, *Fam.* 1.9.25, *De or.* 2.85.

68. E.g., Plaut. *Amph.* 241; Cic. *Phil.* 9.4; cf. Cic. *Cat.* 2.3.5, *Phil.* 7.21 (hanging around, in different ways).

69. See, e.g., Cic. *Brut.* 161; *Mil.* 79; *Clu.* 103. Recall *lego*, *curro*, *ludo* (*Ling.* 6.37)—a similar bell curve of physical exertion and relaxation.

70. E.g., Cic. *Sest.* 15.33; Plaut. *Pseud.* 800, Varro, *Rust.* 2 *praef.*

71. Again, I am using "read" as a catch-all representative translation, but the other senses of *lego* need to be kept in mind, as becomes clear later.

72. Varro, *Ling.* 6.38.

73. "*principia uerborum postulet mille*," Varro, *Ling.* 6.39.

74. This is a whistle-stop summary to give a sense of narrative momentum. It elides the various derivations that Varro adduces and outlines. Aspects were discussed earlier (see also chapters 2 and 3).

75. "*Sermo, opinor, est a serie, unde sertum . . . sermo enim non potest in uno hominem esse solo, sed ubi <o>ratio cum altero coniuncta*" (*Ling.* 6.64).

76. "to join hand-to-hand combat" (*conserere manu<m>*); "'lot' [*sors*] from which 'colleagues' [*consortes*], and 'lots' [*sortes*] because in them are joined [*iuncta*] temporal with human affairs. From these, 'lot-pickers'; whence money lent at interest is the 'principal' [*sors*] because it joins one outlay to another" (*Ling.* 6.65).

77. Cf. Lee 1978 on sight/sound in Epicurus.

78. "*Neque quae didicissemus, ex his, quae inter se rerum cognatio esset, appareret*" (and nor, from these that we should have learned, would it be clear what the essential kinship between them would be), *Ling.* 8.3. This takes *cognatio rerum* to be alluding to what the "reality" or "deep meaning" of the relationships would be.

79. Varro, *Ling.* 8.57. The other similar examples are *amator* and *salutator*. The first is a commonplace, whereas *salutator* gains frequency of use only in the mid-first century CE. *Cantator* and *fertor* have failed to descend from their respective verbs, Varro continues, but here usage rather than insistence on the paradigms is what should be followed.

80. Gurd 2012, 49–76, sums up the nuances of textuality (the work-in-progress) and its implications for what we might think of as the monumental text, for Cicero; Varronian practice is hinting its collaboration as part of this world.

81. *Ling.* 8.58 is where Varro's anti-Regularity persona famously says that there should be a past participle but is not. He returns to participles at *Ling.* 10.34 (although the actual discussion is lost to a lacuna), proposing (10.48) that completed action terms and incomplete action terms form distinct families (this builds on the pre-Regularity position proposed in book 9); see Serbat 1976, 314–15.

82. The point is that each of the tenses is internally consistent (*amatus sum* is followed by *amatus est*) and also reflects the broader clan paradigms (the perfect passive form, for this kind of verb, behaves in this way).

83. "Thus in this [verbs] the source is in the form indicating the person who is speaking and the present tense, such as 'I write,' 'I read.'" For how this continues to play out in book 10: *Ling.* 10.25 (where *lego* sits—at the end of the queue—with sewing, running, and teaching), 10.31 (where Varro starts on verbs), then 10.33 (on complete/incomplete forms, bundled with buying, eating, writing—with which *lego* is specifically paired, and spinning off into the ongoing states *scriptito/lectito*—then burning, anointing, praising, and blaming), and finally at 10.47–48 (discussed in the following paragraphs).

84. As Kent's 1951 text stands, *lex* is delivered via an insertion proposed by Mueller 1833 ("*Quadruplices deiunctae in casibus sunt uocabulorum, ut rex regi, <lex legi>*"). There is no etymology of *rex* or *lex* in the extant text, but since Varro moves on to *lego* next, the creation of this pair does make sense intellectually.

85. Varro turns to music and medicine for an additional gloss: the cithara's seven strings are called "eight," because strings one and four are proportionally relational in the same way as strings four and seven (i.e., string four "counts" twice). Similarly, doctors observe illness across a seven-day period and similarly find a proportional relationship between days one and four and between days four and seven, with day four predicting the situation on day seven (*Ling.* 10.46).

86. In a fragment ascribed to book 8 and presented by Gellius (*NA* 2.25, Varro Fr. 5) in an introduction to *analogia* and *anomalia*, *pundo* and *tundo* hook up with *paro*, *lauo*, and *pingo*, making for a very different semiotic range.

87. Varro comments: "*quarum rerum quod nec fundamenta, ut deb<u>it, posita ab ullo neque ordo ac natura, ut res postulat, explicita, ipse eius rei formam exponam*" (And since the foundations of these things have not, as should have been done, been laid by anyone, nor have their order and nature, as the matter requires, been set down, I myself shall outline the shape of the subject, *Ling.* 10.1).

88. Compare, e.g., Varro, *Ling.* 5.5, 6.2. See, e.g., Moatti 2003 on the late Republic's hunger for cultural guidance.

89. Following up here on reading strategies and models of community formation developed by Stroup 2010. One might also feed in, e.g., the epistoliterarity of, e.g., Cic. *Off.* Halla-aho 2011, 430–38, sets out key debates on tone, colloquialism, "natural" language, and literarity in epistolary Latin.

90. Stroup 2010, 167 (my emphasis).

91. *Oratio* also features in the word cloud attending on *oro* (*Ling.* 6.76, discussed in chapter 3).

92. Forsyth 2011, 5–6, quoted. Cf. Varro, *Ling.* 8.4, for "family" traits.

Chapter 5. As Old as the Hills

1. Mumford (1938) 1970, 256.

2. I am thinking about something like Ida Östenberg's coinage, "power walk" (2015). Elements of this chapter rework ideas from and develop other aspects of Varro's Roman itineraries, complementing those explored in Spencer 2015a (the result of two enormously productive workshops on *The Moving City* [Rome, 2011, 2012], supported by the Swedish and Norwegian Institutes); Spencer 2011b and 2018 complete these studies of Varro's Rome building. Cancik 1985–86 vividly works through the relationship between systems, symbols, and spaces in Varro's Rome, with useful illustrations. On movement, working with models developed by Lefebvre (1974) 1991, see O'Sullivan 2011, 2015; Laurence and Newsome 2011. On Varro's Rome more generally, see Zehnacker 2008.

3. Rutledge 2012, 167.

4. Mumford (1938) 1970, 4.

5. The integration of temporality into studies of experience and procession through space, especially the "rhythmanalysis" developed in Lefebvre and Régulier-Lefebvre 1985, is important here; as developed across Spencer 2111a, 2015a, 2018, de Certeau's "walking rhetorics" and "pedestrian speech acts" ([1974] 1984, 97–102, xxii) also add significant value.

6. Talbert 2004, on Murphy 2004—Rome is always one end of the itinerary, "the touchstone to which themes or foreign items are invariably related, or against which they are measured." See now Vout 2012, 11–14 and passim. Murphy 2004, 131–33 (responding to Purcell 1990), reflects on the different forms an itinerary (broadly conceived) might take and (e.g.) explores the view from above and the infrastructural role of nature (2004, 137–63).

7. Boyer 1994, 192.

8. In Eco 1984's sense of the sign as the product of an interpreter, who recognizes, determines, and formulates the possibility of a relationship between an event, an antecedent, and a consequent (1984, 31–32, 46). Recall Cic. *Acad.* 1.9 (first cited in chapter 1).

Golledge 1999 collects a range of "wayfinding" approaches useful for this chapter, but see also Ingold 2000, 219–42.

9. Recent studies focusing relevantly (for this urban context) on Roman space and memory: e.g., Wiseman 1987; Edwards 1996, 27–43; Gotter 2003; Walter 2004 (e.g., at 155–79); Gowing 2005; Hölscher 2006, 100–13; Stein-Hölkeskamp 2006; Larmour and Spencer 2007a; Wallace-Hadrill 2008, 259–312 (where "knowing" makes for a productive angle on how knowledge develops); M. B. Roller 2010; Spencer 2011c. Brockmeier 2002 helpfully characterizes the narrative qualities of memory. Walter 2004 sets out in great depth recent debate on the production of memory in the late republic and in one weighty chapter (7) scrutinizes in impressive detail the literary production of memory (or, to put it another way, the literariness of memory) in the Republic; Rodriguez Mayorgas 2010 is an excellent case study on the role of Romulus/Aeneas in this era; Farrell 1997 is invaluable on the technical qualities of how memory is banked in classical thinking.

10. Baudrillard (1981) 1983, 12.

11. Garden 2006, 399. Outlined for Varro at Spencer 2015a. Here, I recall Varro, *Ling.* 5.3, 5. On Cicero's negotiation of how history meets antiquarianism, see Rawson 1972, while Rawson 1985, 243–47, 312–16, surveys Varronian antiquarianism; on feeding in nostalgia and Cic. *Rep.*, see Asmis 2005.

12. See Short 2008, 120–22; locations can "stand for" opinions.

13. Varro, *Ling.* 5.13, as discussed in chapter 2. Eco 1984, 64–68's critiques of figurative (philosophical) "trees," in particular his Figures 2.7 and 2.8, get at the embedded cognitive and conceptual ramifications productively.

14. Soja 1996, 11. Varro seeing: *uideo* (6.80), *cerno* (6.81), *spectare* (6.82), *tueor* (7.9, 12), *conspico* (7.9). Seeing, like remembering, is at the heart of what it means to be Roman. When one sees or looks, one is also undertaking complex cognitive processes to which Varro gives textual form. Seeing connects to strength (*uis*), while *cerno* adds "to create" to the frame; Varro's inclusion of *tueor* as a verb of sight enhances a cultural agenda. *Tueor* involves "seeing" in processes of guarding, tending, and maintaining (*OLD* s.v. *tueor*, senses 2–7). This draws on issues of (over)sight raised by Lucr. 2.1–13 (on which, see Fowler 2002 ad loc.). Varro here prefigures developments in Augustan culture explored by Alden Smith 2005 with reference to Merleau-Ponty, but the idea of a "poetics of space" as developed in Bachelard (1958) 1994 is particularly useful for its focus on object-oriented spatial perception.

15. Benjamin 1999a, N1,9 (458). Jenks 1995 is useful here, but see also Baudelaire (1863) 1965, and Benjamin (1935–39) 1997, 66, 128 (on Baudelaire); cf. Benjamin's model of the *flâneur*: one who must make narrative sense of apparently random or incongruous objects and sites, piece by piece (or fragmentarily), developing the notion of the constellation as epistemological model—Benjamin 1999a, N2a,3 (462), H°,16 (845). On Varro and *flâneur* practice, see Spencer 2018.

16. Itinerary 1, *Ling.* 5.41–56 (including the Argei shrines); itinerary 2, *Ling.* 5.141–65.

17. Varro, *Ling.* 5.16. Varro, *Ling.* 5.17, backstops the all-encompassing qualitative division of heaven and earth with a programmatic quote from Lucilius (corrected from Lucretius). The contextual significance of "what the world looks like" is central to Ingold 2000, 209–18.

18. Varro expands and concludes that explanation by suggesting that night reveals the starry sky from the dazzling cloak of daylight (*Ling.* 5.18); this draws on his previous suggestion of a binary meaning for *caelum*: an all-encompassing "ether" (quoting Pacuvius, "'*Hoc uide circum supraque quod complexu continet / Terram*'") and also the location of the stars ("'*Id quod nostri caelum memorant*,'" *Ling.* 5.17).

19. Varro, *Ling.* 5.19–20. Crucially, the heavenly vault is given color through quotation, with the stars ornamenting the passage of a chariot across the heavens, the sky as a shield, and (in a named quote from Ennius), the sky as a giant arched space ("'*Caeli ingentes fornices*'").

20. Vitruvius' *cau-a-edium* is interesting here as a domestic scheme that connects Italy to Greece ("Tuscan," "Corinthian" style).

21. "Thus the beginnings of 'sky'—formed from 'chaos,' then 'hollow'; whence everything, in Hesiod's book." We could note that *cauerna* does duty for ships' holds at Cic. *De or.* 3.180 (cf. Lucr. 2.553 [ship], 4.171, 391, 6.252, 597, 683 [sky]).

22. Varro, *Ling.* 5.22–40, follows the compressed story of Arcadian exile, Evander, down the roads, into the corporeal soil, through the waters, to geopolitical taxonomy, peninsular Italy, and agricultural landscapes, until we reach Rome.

23. Rome's plains (*campi*) and hills (*colles*) featured at *Ling.* 5.36: a *campus* is the plain from which one takes (*capere*) agricultural produce; a *collis* is named for the act of cultivation (*colere*) it (perhaps) requires. That would seem to be one implication (another might be that hilly terrain requires respectful collaboration between humans and environment). Maltby 1991, 101, 140, makes Varro the etymological authority. For the hills as enduring objects and generators of the Gaze, Vout 2007.

24. Fraschetti 1996 is the obvious point of reference; see also Palmer 1970, 122–32 (concise and thorough).

25. Strabo 5.3.7 fails to add the "seven" but identifies a slew of hills, which happen to be Capitoline, Palatine, Quirinal, Caelian, Aventine (ὄρος characterizes these two), Esquiline, Viminal.

26. Stevenson 2004, 119, 120, emphasizes the significance of antiquarianism in this era and, in particular, Varro's landmark status as a point of reference. As noted by Eco 1984, 130, "Etymologies, however, do not necessarily tell the truth" in terms of structural semantics. Again, recall Cic. *Acad.* 1.9.

27. Gelsomino 1975, at length, then 1976a, 1976b. As Palombi 2006 has recently summed up, the motif quickly becomes integral to Augustan Romescapes. Harris 1997, in an unfortunately absurdist reading of Varro's etymologies, notes his originality as a theorist. Vout 2012 is interesting on the delights of Varro's seven-hill model, within a detailed evaluation of Varro's contribution (2012, 67–75).

28. Writing to Atticus on 26 June 50, Cicero uses "ἐξ ἄστεως ἑπταλόφου" (*Att.* 6.5.2), making Rome (in Greek) the city of seven hills (and likely recalling the legendarily Seven-Gated Thebes). Gelsomino 1976a firmly rebuts all suggestions that Cicero could have come up with the formulation independently. For Varronian heptomania, Gellius (*NA* 3.10) famously observed "that there has been noted in the number seven a certain force and capability in many natural phenomena, on which M. Varro expounds at length in his *Hebdomades*." Adams 2003a, 329–30, addresses the code-switching here,

suggesting it is about information hygiene. Collart 1954a, xv–xix, discusses the numbers games that Varro makes available, with three, four, and nine all playing structural roles and (Collart argues) evidencing a *tendresse* for Pythagoreanism with echoes in Sabine culture. Cf. *Ling.* 5.11, 5.13.

29. Prop. 3.11.57.

30. On Rome's Seven Hills, geographically and geologically, see Heiken, Funiciello, and De Rita 2005, a memorable study emphasizing the deep import of the "hills" on the development of the city and its people. For a culturally and reception-focused approach, see Vout 2012. See Holland 1953 on the terminology of S(a)eptimontium and teasing out Verrius Flaccus and Festus.

31. *OLD* s.v. *compr(eh)endo*, sense 7, is the obvious meaning, but other senses linger metaphorically at least; I suggest embracing sense 11 (a taxonomic embrace, commanding the episteme), senses 5 and 6 (to seize upon and find), sense 2 (to take root) and sense 4 (to hold together, or unite disparate things).

32. Vout 2012, 74.

33. Vout 2012, 61–62, sums up on "sevenliness" as she puts it—seven being one of those numbers Varro tries out as an organizational principle, as in his well-known (Ausonius, *Mosella* 306–7) 700-fold *Hebdomades*.

34. Varro's *pagi* resurface when he turns to festivals (see chapter 8) and lend nuance to his exploration of *curiae* and inclusivity versus diversity in Rome's origins and development (see chapter 6). Wallace-Hadrill 2008, 261, also notices Varro's connection between Sevenheights and the Paganalia.

35. Drawing on Suet. *Iul.* 46.

36. Zehnacker 2008, 426, comes close to arguing this but does not explore the role of a handbook such as Varro's in actualizing a new identity for the sites discussed. I have in mind Gaze theory, as outlined in Merleau-Ponty (1964) 1968 (e.g., 1968, 131–32).

37. Soja 1996, 116. Although the cases are, necessarily, different in so many ways, there is also value in reading in recent work on Los Angeles, a city in which migrant contribution continues to be a flashpoint despite a historically immigrant- and "encounter-" based foundation story (see, e.g., Scott and Soja 1996).

38. Lacan (1966) 2006, 419, 421–24 [#503, 504–7]. Pompey's severed head might well flicker into a late Republican frame of reference, much as M. B. Roller 1997 outlines for Cicero (cf. Malamud 2003). Edwards 1996, 82–85, influentially draws together the heady issues for the Capitoline. On the Capitoline head more generally, see Vout 2007, 301–3, 309, 313–20 (including significant bibliography on the magisterial gaze). Reusser 1993 and Tagliamonte 1993 provide helpful surveys of the Capitol as a site.

39. Here, incorporating the Gaze of Lacan's later essays, e.g., Lacan (1964) 2004, #96, and more generally in "Anamorphosis," e.g., 83–85 [#1498–1526]. As argued at Lacan (1964) 2004, 88–89, 92 [#1597–1608, 1653–1990] (referring to Hans Holbein's *The Ambassadors*), the thing that viewers are attempting to encompass and to organize meaningfully as a constituent part of their episteme will typically require a kind of (cognitive) squint to make it work. Thus, each viewer's mental shuffle combines preexisting reality paradigms while framing a new or differently conceptualized entity. See Žižek 2006, especially the

chapter "Lacan as Viewer of *Alien*." On the meaning of "cultural revelations" for Lacan, see Feldstein 1996.

40. Drawing on Vout 2007, 321. For the Capitoline as a symbol of empire, see, e.g., Liv. 1.55 (at point of foundation), 5.54 (Camillus' speech). Lactantius (*de Opificio Dei* 5.6) records Varro identifying a source quality for the *caput*.

41. This is the only instance in the extant text where the formulation "*dicitur inuentum*" occurs. Reading through Lacan (1964) 2004, 103 [#1863], there is a sense in which the desire to plug into a lost authenticity draws together issues of the performance of masculinity and *auctoritas* familiar from late Republican cultural production.

42. Hölscher 2006 imaginatively collects up the complex nuances of the Capitol as a site of, and in, reception.

43. See Livy 1.55 (on the Capitoline works), 1.56 (on the ensuing urban works).

44. Freud (1930) 1991, 257–58.

45. Welch 2005, 17 and passim, is the place to start for Tarpeia. Ovid (*Fast*. 4.807–62) reverberates with the Vestals' connection to the nearby Pons Sublicius. Linking the Parilia and Tarpeia's treachery seems to have been Propertius' innovation (4.4)—chapter 8 returns to the festival.

46. OLD s.v. *fundamentum*; *fodio*. Based on a *PHI* search, the only other instance of this pairing of the two words is at Vitr. 5.12.5, where it is utterly prosaic. The alternative senses are switched on by the context (e.g., violent death, regime change, buried body parts).

47. "*Saturniam terram, ut etiam Ennius appellat*" (*Ling*. 5.42), picked up at Ov. *Fast*. 5.625; memorably, Saturnian land (*tellus*) will feature at Verg. *Aen*. 8.329.

48. Leaning here on the terminology of space syntax, for the development of which, see Hillier 2003a, 2003b; Hillier and Hanson 1984; on its use for ancient Rome, see, e.g., Spencer 2010, 47–56.

49. For Junius, recall "Mucius and Brutus," Varro, *Ling*. 5.5, discussed in chapter 2; on the two characters, see Spencer 2011b, n. 22, and, more generally, Spencer 2015c, 76–77. Varro's Roman gates (and walls) are the subject of the seventh section of this chapter, "Gates (Coming and Going)."

50. For the location of the Porta Pandana above (or perhaps confusingly close to) the Porta Carmentalis, compare Polyaenus, *Strat*. 8.25.1, with Dion. Hal. *Ant. Rom*. 10.14.2 (the latter may, if we follow this line, be conflating the two gates because of their contiguity; cf. Solin. 1.13).

51. Fest. 246 L, 496 L; Polyaenus, *Strat*. 8.25.1. Polyaenus was of course addressing L. Verus and M. Aurelius.

52. "*Ab auibus, quod eo se ab Tiberi aues*," *Ling*. 5.43. Readers should recall Varro's Thebris, when he recounts its stories to explore whether the Tiber is even a suitable subject for an ἐτυμολόγος *Latinus* (*Ling*. 5.30).

53. I am also thinking here of the temple's role as an asylum, its connection to Servius Tullius, and its monumental (and still in situ in Varro's day) bronze pillar recording the mid-fifth-century Lex Icilia by which Aventine land was distributed to plebeians (Dion. Hal. *Ant. Rom*. 4.26, 10.32.1–5; Livy 1.45.2–3, 3.31.1).

54. Varro goes on to define *uelabrum* etymologically at *Ling.* 5.44. I've chosen "wherry" rather than "ferry" as an English approximation because it conveys the sense of a very light craft, designed for portage; this I think chimes better with a landscape of rafts traversing swampy pools than the ponderous "ferry."

55. The disruptive power of the Tiber continued to be felt in Rome well into the twentieth century, and Aldrete 2007 evokes the danger posed by the Tiber flood. On the wateriness of Roman identity, see Purcell 1996 and Larmour and Spencer 2007a, 18–19 (with references summed up at 19 n. 51); Spencer 2007, 64–65, 86–87 and passim. We should note that as late as 363 BCE the Circus Maximus area was subject to flooding (Liv. 7.3.1–2). The Aqua Appia's emergence near the Porta Trigemina puts it in the mix for considering the historical significance of control of water manifest in this area.

56. Coarelli 1993a, 203. For Varro's etymology of *forum*, see Spencer 2015a, 105–6.

57. "*Aequimaelium, quod a<e>quata Maeli domus publice, quod regnum occupare uoluit is*" ("Aequimaelium," since the house of Maelius leveled by the state was there, [leveled] because he wanted to take the state as his kingdom, *Ling.* 5.157). Livy 4.13–14 tells the story, which is part of the Cincinnatus cycle. On the story, see Lowrie 2010. Kent has produced a text that fits convincingly with Livy's version.

58. There is so far no final word on exactly where these sites lay. Richardson 1992, 60, and Haselberger et al. 2002, 253, develop a case for the Forum Boarium, perhaps between the Pons Sublicius and the Vicus Iugarius, and associated (via the Doliola) with where the Cloaca Maxima debouches. Returning to issues remaining from his 1988 overview, Coarelli 1993a, 1995a, tackles the difficulties for ad Busta Gallica and the Doliola and reads Varro's grammar as keeping ad Busta Gallica and Doliola with the Aequimaelium, inside the Servian walls, but with a different conclusion, namely that ad Busta Gallica is situated on the Capitoline slope facing the Forum Romanum and Doliola, where the Cloaca Maxima makes its entrance into the Velabrum (1995a, 21).

59. Cf. Plut. *Vit. Marc.* 3: in the context of renewed conflict with the Gauls after the first Punic War, the Sibylline books insisted that the only way to avoid renewed Gallic disaster was to perform an act of human sacrifice and bury two Greeks and two Gauls alive, hence ad Busta Gallica. The Lacus Curtius is another clear point of congruity for this topos; see Spencer 2007 passim. On memory and phenomenology, Casey 2000 introduces the theory clearly; Cifani 2018 sets out some of the complexities of "hidden" versus "forgotten" memories for topographic encounters.

60. "*Cum Argeorum sacraria septem et uigenti in <quattuor> partis urbi<s> sunt disposita*"; the text needs some sort of emendation to deliver this sense, but it is sense that chimes with the message of the conclusion the section, *Ling.* 5.45. Wallace-Hadrill 2008, 260–69, is especially useful for this phase in the narrative and fruitfully draws in (and develops on) Fraschetti 1990, 132–203.

61. *Ling.* 5.45 (The Argei, they think, were named for the chiefs who with Argive Hercules had come to Rome and settled in Saturnia).

62. Palmer 1970, 84–97, is invaluable for the Argei. Collart 1954a is also significantly useful for probing the kind of story Varro tells.

63. As told by Ov. *Fast.* 5.621–22; 603; cf. 3.791. Compare Livy 1.21.5. The Pons Sublicius was unusually heavily freighted with patriotic significance and quirky construction

features. Livy (1.33.6) and Dion. Hal. *Ant. Rom.* (3.45.2) tell the story of its construction by Ancus Marcius (cf. Plut. *Vit. Numa* 9.2–3); add in Dion. Hal. *Ant. Rom.* 9. 68.2, Plin. *HN* 36.100, and Serv. *ad Aen.* 8.646, and one has the oddness of its construction without the use of metal.

64. Consulting Maltby 1991 s.v. *Argei* delivers Varro as the Republican authority, but looking back an entry, we see that *Argea* (1991, 49) adds a sepulchral and distinctively topographic nuance: "*Argea loca Romae appellantur, quod in his sepulti essent quidam Argiuorum inlustres uiri*" (there are places in Rome called Argea, because in them were buried certain famous men of Argos, Fest. 19 L). Festus' deployment of Verrius Flaccus situates this version at least within a generation of Varro.

65. Palmer 1970, 89–90, argues persuasively for how old thatched bundles from Rome's surviving archaic huts became, by linguistic slippage, rush dolls, then "old men" (*senes*).

66. Livy 1.33.1–2; Strabo 5.3.7 (Ancus Marcius embraced the Caelian and the Aventine); Dion. Hal. *Ant. Rom.* 1.79.12 notes the connection with Romulus' and Remus' late adolescence (cf. 1.84.3; at 1.32.2 he notes a link between Evander and the Aventine; at 10.32.2–4 he outlines the Lex Ilicia); at 3.43.1–2 he details Ancus Marcius' enclosure of the Aventine.

67. These stories had currency: see, e.g., Livy 2.10.2–11; Dion. Hal. *Ant. Rom.* 5.23.2–24.3; Val. Max. 3.2.1.

68. Servius was another figure associated with integrating Rome's sites and peoples, and he gave his name to the earliest walls. Cf. Gellius *NA* 13.14.1–4, 7, regarding the Pomerium and Servius Tullius. For Servius Tullius' Diana on the Aventine, see Livy 1.45; Dion. Hal. *Ant. Rom.* 4.25.3–4.26.5. See now Mignone 2016, 43–47.

69. Beness and Hillard 2001, building on Wiseman 1998, with detailed references. For possible nuances of Gracchus, see, e.g., Cic. *Har. resp.* 41, 43; compare *Brut.* 124–26. In both texts Cicero speaks *in propria persona*. I am reminded of Cicero's comments introducing Clodius' gerrymandering of sacred space: "*Verum tamen antiqua negligimus: etiamne ea negligemus, quae fiunt cum maxime, quae uidemus?*" (But in truth, we neglect antiquity, yet shall we also neglect that which now more than ever we see with our own eyes? Cic. *Har. resp.* 32). This seems to be much more a story of political self-fashioning than one focused primarily on purification (for which reading, see Ziolkowski 1998–99).

70. On the Forum Boarium, see Haselberger et al. 2002, 131–33, cf. Coarelli 1995b (and Hercules/temples); Ziolkowski 1988. Varro, *Ling.* 6.54, returns to Hercules, emphasizing his rights and citizens' obligations toward him.

71. See Poe 1978, a detailed argument, but one that assumes a more denotative and cartographic instinct in Varro than the text supports. Welch 1999, focusing on the tribal qualities of Varro's account, catches the textuality of Varro's style better.

72. This diminutive of the Caelian seems to indicate a known area, see Cic. *Har. resp.* 32 ("*sanctissimum Dianae sacellum in Caeliculo*," the venerable shrine of Diana, on the Little Caelian). The slopes of this hill were relatively gentle, and Cicero suggests that it was already built up, at least around the small shrine of Diana (itself destroyed by L. Calpurnius Piso in 58, as Cicero recounts; Palmer 1970, 125–26, suggests an agenda for Piso's actions).

73. Livy 27.37.15; Dion. Hal. *Ant. Rom.* 5.36.4; Cic. *Verr.* 2.1.154.

74. Cic. *Verr.* 2.1.154; Hor. *Sat.* 2.3.228.

75. Purcell 1995 remains a good introduction to the complexity of the Republican Forum.

76. On which site, see Ziolkowski 1996; see more recently Haselberger et al. 2002, 81–82.

77. Accepting the emendation to *caerimonia* from *cerionia* (*Ling.* 5.47), as presented, Kent 1951.1 ad loc. Nothing else makes sense in the context of the Via Sacra and ritual processions. See Maltby 1991, 93 s.v. *Caerimonia*. *Caeriolensis* here is also morphologically fragile—*ceroliensis*, *cerulensis*, and *ceroniensem* are all present—and may even echo or impute an ancient slippage between the Carinae/Caelian association. Varro's interest in the "keel" as an analogy for skeleton or backbone is part of a juxtaposition of *carinae* and *caput* (a fragmentary allusion from Lactantius, *De Officio Dei* 5.6).

78. "*Sed <ego a> pago potius Succusano dictam puto Succusam*" (but I rather reckon that <from> the Succusan district it was called Succusa, Varro, *Ling.* 5.48). See this chapter's second section, "Sevenheights: Ups and Downs."

79. Introducing ambiguity, Varro makes the framing device for this district (i.e., the height that gives it shape) the place "*qui terreus murus uocatur*" (which is called [the] Earth Wall), and this might undercut the evidentiary quality of *testimonium*. On defining the topography, see Welch 1999, 380–81. Varro's etymological investigation became canonical (irrespective, perhaps, of reality in the ground); see Maltby 1991, 590. The Subura was a noisy, bustling, crowded, intensely urban zone (on which, Malmberg 2009), with significant political texture: according to Suetonius (*Iul.* 46), Caesar had a property there. Its high-density occupation brought the variety of Roman urban life and habitation sharply into focus, while the Argiletum drew in the public and civic world of the Forum, at the Lacus Curtius. Cf. Livy 3.13.2.

80. Varro, *Ling.* 5.47, "because from here rises the head of the Sacra Via." The noisy hurly-burly of Varro's contemporary Subura would, in this way, form a prequel for the systematized razzamatazz or ritual of the Via Sacra—when it was doing duty as a sacred or processional route.

81. Varro, *Ling.* 5.48. *SVC* is an insertion that fills a three-letter "gap" in *F* in a way that meshes with what seems to be same story in Quint. *Inst.* 1.7.29. Without the inserted (and plausible) reference to an abbreviation *SVC* (or evidence that Succusa was in use as an alternative name), Subura and Succusa are more difficult to connect, making Varro's assertion harder to swallow. Nevertheless, a toponym alluding tacitly to real memories of a former name Succusa (and not necessarily hanging on the abbreviation or commonplace) could still work.

82. *Etiam nunc* as a phrasal unit occurs four times in this first "tour" of Rome (*Ling.* 5.41, 42, 44, 50), then recurs at 5.85, 86, 91, 106, 117, 118, 121, 122, 123, 126, 130, 146, 154, 162, 166, 177, 182, 183; in book 6, it crops up only five times, then three times in book 7 and once in book 9. Even allowing for the occasionally fragmentary state of the text, there is a clear emphasis on this topos of past-in-present. Cf. Zehnacker 2008, 426.

83. Laetus (*non uid.*); as followed by Kent 1951.1.

84. Varro, *Ling.* 5.69 (discussed in chapter 7), and see Ando 2005 for the semantics of divine naming. For the restoration of this *aedes*, see *CIL* VI.358.

85. C. J. Smith 2000, 142–50, discusses the complexities of Juno, Fortuna, and Mater Matuta, connecting the Matronalia, on "old" New Year's Day (1 March), and exploring how Ov. *Fast.* 3.167–258 feeds in.

86. The narrow confines (or "defile") suggest the kind of military associations one might perhaps recall from the conjunction of *angustus* and *finis* at Caes. *BGall.* 1.11; on Caesar's rhetoric of topographic modeling in this text, see Krebs 2006. The phrasing is not a common one. This Juno seems to be squeezed by greed (it is tempting, too, to see in this a calendar allusion—months, made *this* Juno's domain at *Ling.* 5.69, are also getting their boundaries changed), but the brief allusion also hints at how such a conflict between public-spirited procreation and selfishness can be disentangled if it can be recognized—"*non mirum,*" perhaps this is an etymology readers are expected to see for themselves.

87. Building on Orlin 2010, 41–42 (cf. 2010, 37–41, on the Etruscan goddess Uni and Juno Regina).

88. Bittarello 2009 sums up the issues for Othering Etruscans at Rome.

89. On the democracy of lawns, see Weinstein 1996, 26. Caesar's public park across the Tiber was still to come, and porticus gardens have a different vibe.

90. As Wallace-Hadrill 2008, 261, notes. Cf. Varro, *Ling.* 5.41 and 6.24.

91. "*Sunt qui . . . sunt qui,*" Varro, *Ling.* 5.51. Cf. Ov. *Fast.* 2.477. The cannibalizing Quirinal: *Quod uocabulum coniunctarum regionum nomina obliuerit*" (this word has overwritten the names of adjacent zones, *Ling.* 5.52).

92. Gods: Salus names the Collis Salutaris; Dius Fidius is presented without editorializing for the connection to Collis Mucialis, a relationship that might well have tickled Varro's contemporaries had he recounted it—perhaps it was too obvious to need the narratorial push (according to Martial, e.g., 8.30, a staging of the Mucius "Scaevola" episode was a popular feature in imperial spectacular entertainments). If a then-and-now link with the Mucii Lefties (Scaevola) draws in a legendary, failed but at least right-minded attempt by a Mucius to assassinate the Etruscan invader Porsenna, ultimately leading to a treaty with Rome (Livy 2.12.1–13.5, which puts us back in the legendary aftermath of Horatius' defense of the Pons Sublicius), the Collis Latiaris embeds a different sort of modeling of Roman-Italian relations—Cicero (*Mil.* 85; on which, Vasaly 1993, 23–24, emphasizes the role of ethos of place) notes Jupiter Latiaris as patron of the Latin federation. "*Horum deorum arae, a quibus cognomina habent, in eius regionis partibus sunt*" (*Ling.* 5.52). These mythohistorical deities and associates tales have become bundled with the Argei legend and its contemporary practice, but topographically muted—at least according to Varro.

93. The toponyms Velia (s.) and Veliae (pl.) appear to have been in use simultaneously (Varro's quotation of the *Rites of the Argei* has "*in Veliam,*" *Ling.* 5.54), cf. Livy 2.7.11–12. The Velia, for the most part now impossible to get a sense of in the wake of the cutting of the Via dell'Impero (/ dei Fori Imperiali), overlooked the Via Sacra and nudged up against the Carinae and the Oppian. For the topography, see Haselberger et al. 2002, 254.

94. Spencer 2018, 52–61, examines the widest frame for reading agribusiness and rural commerce into the frame for this itinerary.

95. Maltby 1991, s.v. *Luceres, Ramnes, Titienses*. Cic. *Rep.* 2.14 is the comparable contemporary instance for this etymology, but presented as data rather than as part of a literary and semantic project, as here. Cf. Dion. Hal. *Ant. Rom.* 3.48.2.

96. "*Quod is huc uenerit ibique sit sepultus*," Varro, *Ling.* 5.157.

97. M. B. Roller 2010, 117–19, elegantly teases out the different stories and implications.

98. "*Alii ab argilla, quod ibi id genus terrae sit*," Varro, *Ling.* 5.157 (cf. Cato, *Agr.* 40.2). Varro does enjoy inhum(or)ation; see, e.g., *Ling.* 5.24–25, on which, see Hinds 2006, 45–46.

99. On different kinds of "underground" in Varro's Roman itineraries, including the Lauretum and the Lautumiae/Carcer, see Spencer 2018, 62–63.

100. On Varro's terminology of roads, with a material cultural focus, see Kaiser 2011, and for a quirkily personal journey, see Kaster 2012. On movement as a structural force in *De Lingua Latina*, see Spencer 2011b, 2015a, 2018.

101. Haselberger et al. 2002, 90, summarizes.

102. "*Quos cum ex arce Capitolioque cliuo Publicio in equis decurrentes quidam uidissent, captum Auentinum conclamauerunt*" (When some from the Arx and Capitoline had seen them riding down the Cliuus Publicius, they shouted that the Aventine had been captured, Livy 26.10).

103. Hinds 2006, 43–45, is convinced.

104. Ovid's fleshed-out story (*Fast.* 5.287–94) is set on 2 May, the Floralia, which becomes significant shortly. Ovid makes this a story about encroachment on common-land grazing rights by the powerful, brought to justice by the Publicii, and with the resulting fine instituting games for Flora and the eponymous Cliuus.

105. Taking the line produced by Haselberger et al. 2002, 90–91.

106. See Varro, *Ling.* 8.23–25 and books 8–10 passim. NB "*dissimilia finguntur, sed etiam ab isdem uocabulis dissimilia neque a dissimilibus similia, sed etiam eadem*" (dissimilars are created [sc. from similar], but also from the same words come dissimilars, and there's also the derivation of similar words from dissimilar ones, and even creating identical words from dissimilars, *Ling.* 8.35).

107. Varro, *Ling.* 6.36, 89. *BNP* sc. "Cosconius" I.5 identifies this grammarian with the Q. Cosconius name-checked in Suetonius *Ter.* 5 (i.e., *fl.* 159). If this is the family responsible for the Cliuus, one might draw in, e.g., *BNP* "Cosconius" I.3 (tr. pl. 59, aedile 57). The Plebeian name Cosconius is attested to the third century, so fits in that sense with a link to the brothers Publicius.

108. Haselberger et al. 2002, 80, sums up the debate on location and proposes the northwest part of the Quirinal.

109. Ov. *Fast.* 5.287–294, and n. 103 above.

110. On Varro's *uicus* (*Ling.* 5.8, 46, 145, 159, 160), see Spencer 2011b, 70; 2015a, 103–4, 104–5; and compare Wallace-Hadrill 2008, 269–75. I translate *uicus* as "Quarter" to emphasize the "neighborhood" qualities that Varro draws on. This remains a complex district to imagine, as Palombi 1997 shows.

111. See Livy 1.48.7. Poor Cicero, too, had a daughter Tullia, who predeceased him and from whose loss he perhaps never fully recovered. On Varro's Tullianum, see Spencer 2018, 62–63. Frank 1924 contextualizes the Tullianum against Sallust's Catiline, another literary construct.

112. An "edge-city"—Garreau 1991. Zukin 1991 makes a lucid argument (with bearing for Rome in transition) regarding the relationship between the means of production, its landscapes, and inhabitants.

113. "*Cum de Ennio scribens dicit eum coluisse Tutilinae loca*" (when writing about Ennius [Porcius] says that he dwelt in [/cultivated] the locality of Tutilina, *Ling.* 5.163).

114. Badian 1972, 165–67, argues for an overlap between the Camenae (high-profile and suitably "literary" objects of esteem for an author) and Tutulina (obscure, at best); he runs with the idea that Varro means "Porta Capena" when he says "Tutulina," giving another quirky, antiquarian take on how names change radically. Cic. *Acad. Pr.* 2.51 reports Ennius living somewhere near Servius Sulpicius Galba later in his life, and the family (Badian notes) did have Aventine property, but to the west. This variant might put Ennius near Minerva's Aventine "citadel" (Ov. *Fast.* 6.728).

115. Varro, *Ling.* 5.163. See, e.g., Plaut. *Aul.* 445–46; Hor. *Ep.* 1.16.57–62.

116. See Livy 1.12.3; Ov. *Tr.* 3.1.29–32; Dion. Hal. *Ant. Rom.* 2.50.3.

117. Drawing on Haselberger et al. 2002, 196.

118. "Of Mucio, from mooing, because it was where they drove out the herds to the pastures which were at that time in front of the ancient town," Varro, *Ling.* 5.164.

119. See Spencer 2018, 58–59.

120. Richardson 1992, 433, details one possible hypothesis. See Haselberger et al. 2002, 185, for more context.

121. See Livy 1.19.2 (who also recounts the closure in 30, after Actium), Plin. *HN* 34.33 on Numa's foundation of Janus Geminus; Serv. *ap Aen.* 1.291 on foundation by Romulus and Titus Tatius; Verg. *Aen.* 7.607, Plut. *Num.* 20.1 on the twin-door aspect; Liv. 1.19.2, Ov. *Fast.* 1.257–8 on location by the Argiletum. The hot water associated with the Porta features at Ov. *Fast.* 1.263–76, Serv. *ap Aen.* 1.291, 8.361, Macrob. *Sat.*1.9.17–18.

122. Varro, *Ling.* 7.6–9, 7.10–11.

123. "I shall speak in this book about the words set down by the poets," Varro, *Ling.* 7.5.

124. Varro, *Ling.* 6.11.

125. "*Hinc effari templa dicuntur*," Varro, *Ling.* 6.54. Cf. Varro, *Ling.* 7.8.

126. Subject to the emendations accepted by Kent. *Templum* in Cicero buzzes especially loudly around *Verr.*, *Dom.*, *Sest.*

127. Note the connection with Vitr. *De arch.* 7.5.2 and the drama of landscape-frescoed corridors. See Short 2008, 122–26, on Varro's contribution to the notion of the augural rite as the creation of what he terms a mental map layered onto real-world topography.

128. As Varro puts it at *Ling.* 7.11, Accius was not wrong when he made *tesca* places "*ubi mysteria fiunt attuentur*" (where mysteries are made real subject to the gaze). Cf. 7.10 (discussed below): "[why do people think a temple is a consecrated building?]

Because in the city of Rome, very many consecrated buildings are *templa*, and likewise inviolable, [*sancta*], and because certain rustic places, which are the domain of some god, are called *tesca*."

129. "This form is spoken from the vision of the heart: for the heart is the origin of 'perception,'" Varro, *Ling.* 7.9.

130. Varro, *Ling.* 6.46; see Spencer 2015b, 90–91.

131. See, e.g., Cic. *Div.* 1.119—recalling how a heartless sacrificial ox confronted Caesar when Caesar was offering sacrifices, this coinciding with his first appearance on a golden throne in purple robe, and the foreshadowing of his death this presaged; cf. Lucr. 1.923.

132. Although the emendation (GS, via Kent) is new cloth, it does emphasize the personalization of the argument here and fits elegantly with the theme of seeing/perceiving. Cf. Varro, *Ling.* 7.12, where *curo* and *uideo* are equated.

133. Varro's quoted lines from Accius refer to the Cabiri, the mysterious Samothracian Great Gods, recall Varro, *Ling.* 5.58, discussed in chapter 2. Royo and Gruet 2008 outline some of the strangeness in literary Rome's relationship with the countryside.

134. Varro, *Ling.* 7.14–16. Relevant here is Pavone 2001, on *Ling.* 7.12 and 7.50.

135. For more on Varro's Diana (*Ling.* 5.68–69), see chapter 7.

136. Drawing here on the detailed analysis of the wandering component to Callimachus' Delos recently undertaken by Klooster 2012. Cf. A. M. Miller 1986, 31–45 (rhetorical geography, Apollo and Delos as birthplace); Montiglio 2005, 14–15 (wandering Delos); Montiglio 2005, 99 (Apollo as wanderer, by contrast to the seeming fixity with which he enters Varro's vignette here).

137. Cf. Cic. *Div.* 2.115.

138. Consider, e.g., the idea of *Roma Quadrata*, the (soon to be established) Golden Milestone, and the sketchily attested *mundus* feature; see Coarelli 1996, 1999.

139. See Catull. 22.7. Cf. the contextually relevant term *mundus*, whose adjectival connotations of elegance take in the notion of appropriate cultivation *and* literary critical discourse, Hor. *Ep.* 1.20.1–2 (see Williams 1992, 180). As Varro warned readers early on (*Ling.* 5.2), signified and signifier are not always operating within the same frame of reference.

140. Lynch 1960, 107.

141. See Haviland 2000 on the connections between gestures and cognitive mapping, and Hillier 2003a on vision, movement, and cognition.

142. Ingold 2000, on comprehension of and dwelling within ecological space, has introduced and shaped ideas that inspired these conclusions.

143. MacDonald 1986, 3, 18–19. Cf. Kaiser 2011, 199.

Chapter 6. Powering Up the Community

1. Varro, *Ling.* 5.80–91, cf. 10.47.

2. Gods: *Ling.* 5.57–74; mortal creatures, air, water, and land: *Ling.* 5.75–76; amphibians: *Ling.* 5.78–79.

3. Here, following Goetz and Schoell 1910, "*consul ciat*," rather than Kent 1951. Cf. Cic. *De or.* 2.165, *Leg.* 3.8.2, *Pis.* 23; Varro, *De Vita Populi Romani* fr. 68 (ap. Non. 16 M).

4. Maltby 1991, 152, provides extensive comparative instances; note especially Cic. *Leg* 3.8, *De or.* 2.165, *Pis.* 23, *Rep.* 2.31. Dyck 2004, 457, observes what seems to be Varro's unique role in explicitly drawing together the people and the senate in his *De Vita Populi Romani*, by connecting consul (who consults the senate) and praetor (who guides the people); see Riposati 1939 fr. 68 = Non. 24 M. As Purcell 2003, 345, notes, it makes a difference *when* we think Varro wrote his account of the life of the Roman people—was he, as Baier 1997, 17, has it, riding post for what would become the Augustan era? Or is this still a work of Caesar's world or of either set of Triumvirs? If it postdates Pharsalus, it suggests that Varro was gradually radicalizing his position toward something like a *commonwealth of equals; if it is contemporaneous with or postdates *De Lingua Latina*, this might suggest that Varro was positioning himself at the van of something more akin to the Augustan experiment.

5. Ebel 1991 draws together earlier instances of formal use of the reverse version of the tag; Gareth Sears kindly pointed me to evidence via the Clauss-Slaby inscriptional database, which makes abundantly clear that SPQR is the typical formulation of record. Useful literary comparisons include Cicero's formal communiqué from his province to the magistrates and senate (Cic. *Fam.* 15.2.4, 5; September 51). Here, as a result of a directive from Rome ("*uestra auctoritas*"), he contacted King Ariobarzanes, whose well-being was of great concern to the people and senate ("*salutem eius regis populo senatuique magnae curae esse*"). Ariobarzanes' response reverses the formula, restabilizing it (in Cicero's account) in addressing the *senatus populusque*. Cf. Cic. *Planc.* 90, *Philipp.* 6.4.

6. Pina Polo 2011 surveys the early phase of the adoption of the consulship as supreme magistracy (after ca. 367, enacted as the leges Liciniae Sextiae); on the praetorship, Brennan 2000 highlights the ambiguity of the relationship between the magistracies excellently. For an interestingly provocative approach to the magistracies' literary and historical genealogies, see Billows 1989. More concisely, see e.g., Cornell 1995, 218–30, and Forsythe 2005, 150–55 (building on Stewart 1998), both of whom differently emphasize the possible belatedness of consul as the defining title for the supreme magistracy and the ambiguity of praetor (which looks as if it should be the top job, perhaps supported by Livy 7.3.5, but becomes a subordinate role at least in the fourth century).

7. Lucil. 1160M. See Stewart 1998, 113–15. For a similar version, from Varro's biography of the Roman people, *De Vita Populi Romani* fr. 68 (ap Non. 23 M). At *Ling* 5.87, discussed later, Varro returns to *praetor*.

8. Dyck 2004, 455–59, teases out the implications of Cicero's treatment here, arguing for an overarching reading that goes beyond the technical detail to present a glimpse of the more transcendent magisterial ethos at the heart of Cicero's vision of ideal leadership. Cf. Cic. *Rep.* 2.31. Dating Cic. *Leg.* to the 50s, Dyck 2004, 5–7, is judicious in setting out the various issues; 2004, 15–20, on political contexts. That the dialogue also represents a homage to his roots in Arpinum is particularly apt.

9. Varro, *Ling.* 6.88, presents *iudex* as a name invoking *consul* by another, older route. Dyck 2004, 455–59 unpacks the implications of the Ciceronian passage. In many ways, Cic. *Leg.* is a morality tale, adumbrating Clodius' life and death and Cicero's exile and return as "a moral tale of crime punished and virtue rewarded," Dyck 2004, 17. The position ascribed to "Marcus" Cicero himself is typically one of moderation and support

for the kind of concord deliverable through a balanced constitution; (right knowledge of) the law should be one part in ensuring the stability of such a system, and that's what Cicero delivers in *De Legibus*.

10. Varro, *Ling.* 5.81, gives censor, aedile, quaestors (and quaesitores), tribunes of the soldiers and of the plebs. Praetor and tribune come back into focus later in this chapter.

11. See Dyck 2004, 462, on the difficulty of getting to the root of the term "dictator." In book 7 (a historical vignette about debt and debt slavery), Varro reintroduces the dictator: "*Hoc C. Poetelio <Li>bone Visolo dictatore sublatum ne fieret, et omnes qui Bonam Copiam iurarunt, ne essent nexi dissoluti*" (When Gaius Poetelius Libo Visulus was dictator this [bondslavery] was no longer tolerated, and all those who swore an oath before Lady Bountiful were released from their restraints, *Ling.* 7.105).

12. Cic. *Att.* 16.2.3, 16.5.1; cf. *Phil.* 1.36. See Erasmo 2004, 99–101. Accius was, apparently, on good terms with another Brutus (D. Iunius Brutus Callaicus), making piquant the composition of a *Brutus* (for usefully different readings of Accius' relationship with Brutus: Baldarelli 2004, 15–22; Manuwald 2001, 119–21, 223–24); Cic. *Sest.* 117–23 makes clear that revivals of Accius' *Brutus* happened, e.g., in games given in 57 by the consul P. Cornelius Lentulus Spinther.

13. "*Brutus, quia reges eiecit, consul primus factus est: / hic, quia consules eiecit, rex postremo factus est*" (Brutus, because he ejected the kings, became the first consul; this one [Caesar], because he ejected the consuls, was finally made king, Suet. *Iul.* 80.3). The uncertainty in dating *De Lingua Latina* makes it difficult to press this very hard, although it tantalizes. Chapter 8 revisits the Ludi in the context of the festal calendar and naming months.

14. Cic. *Rep.* 1.63 (dramatic date, 129; date of composition, the late 50s). Stevenson 2005 tackles Cicero on Scipio's "dictatorship" in depth. Cf. the oddly backhanded encomium, Hor. *Carm.* 4.9.34–44.

15. Cic. *Rep.* 1.68.

16. *OLD* s.v. *penes* 1, 2, with implications of "in the household of," "in the power of." Asmis 2005 is particularly useful here, while Richardson 1991 broadly sums up key issues for how *imperium* is qualified in discourse. Joining *omnis* to *imperium* is tantalizing—more obviously one might have expected *summum* or *maximum*. On Roman "constitutionality" more generally, see Lintott 1999.

17. Also in play for Varro, *Ling.* 6.61, is the dramatic quality of Cic. *Rep.*—Cicero ventriloquizes Scipio by wearing him like a mask (see Spencer 2011a, 102–3); Varro speaks *qua* "Varro."

18. *Albus, -a, -um* has already established itself as a Varronian leitmotif, and compare *Ling.* 5.30—helping to explain the Tiber (chapters 1 [naming towns, people], 4 [on discourse formation and naming], and 5 [the Latinity of the Aventine], have already discussed its multiple appearances; it will crop up again in chapters 7 and 8).

19. Relevantly, see Varro, *Ling.* 5.28, 8.17 (by contrast, 8.38, 77).

20. Beard 1990 offers a clear survey with regard to priesthoods.

21. See, e.g., Plin. *HN* 15.136–137; Suet. *Galb.* 1; Dio Cass. 48.52.3-4.

22. Cf. Juv. 13.141. See Flory 1989 on the omen and Augustus.

23. Verg. *Aen* 8.42–49, 81–83 (cf. *Aen*. 3.389–93). The intensity of Varro's interest in *sus* can be seen expansively a little later in the text (*Ling* 5.109–10), but also at *Rust*. 2.4.4. Horsfall 1974 details the complexities of marrying Vergil's chronology to earlier iterations. See Spencer 2018, 59–61, on pigs and consumer culture in Varro.

24. *OLD*, s.v. *albus*, senses 7 (see, e.g., Cic. *Fam*. 7.28.2, with implications of rarity; Hor. *Ep*. 2.2.189, where *albus* is in a binary good/bad relationship with *ater*), and 8 (Hor. *Ep*. 2.1.196—rare *white* elephants).

25. For *pontifices*, I have followed Goetz and Schoell 1910, cf. Varro, *Ling*. 5.4 (as also observed by Kent 1951, 80).

26. On the Causa Curiana, see in detail Vaughn 1985.

27. It's just about possible that Caesar might be in play here, especially when one later meets Varro's Flamen Dialis. As Taylor 1941, 116, notes (discussing Caesar's nomination as Flamen Dialis), "both because Caesar did not meet the requirements of the priesthood and because of opposition to Cinna, Scaevola would not have inaugurated Caesar. Cinna met his death in the year of Caesar's marriage with Cornelia, and Scaevola was slain by order of the younger Marius on the eve of Sulla's victory. But *Scaevola's death came too late* for the Marians to secure the election of a new *pontifex maximus* who might have inaugurated Caesar" (my emphasis). Caesar would eventually be elected to the position of Pontifex Maximus in 63 and then to the praetorship in 62. Tatum 2008, 35, and, more generally, 61–79. These were years of note for Cicero, and therefore memorable, with the Bona Dea scandal (which implicated Caesar) and Cicero's nemesis Clodius making headlines.

28. Varro, *Ling*. 5.155; and in the context of the verb *curare*, 6.46.

29. Cic. *Caecin*. 67 (and, in toto, 67–70); dating the speech is not straightforward, but tradition locates it to 69 (see Marinone 2004, 19, and, expansively, Frier 1983); cf. (jumping forward to the year 55) *De or*. 1.39.180, 1.57.242–45, 2.6.24, 2.32.140–45, 2.54.220–23. Also in the mix, see e.g., *Brut*. 145, 194–99; *Top*. 10.44. Q. Mucius Scaevola (Augur) might also be imagined in the background, featuring as he does as a character in Cic. *Rep*., *De or*., and *Laelius*. To be a Scaevola would become proverbial for jurisprudential excellence (e.g., Cic. *Orat*. 1.180, 2.144; Hor. *Ep*. 2.2.89)!

30. Caesar's youthful nomination to the office of Flamen Dialis in the mid-80s may not have resulted in his investiture, but if he had made a career in that role, Varro's Rome would have been a very different place. Famously, this Flamen was prohibited from taking oaths, spending more than a night or so away from Rome, seeing a corpse or the army arrayed for war, or mounting a horse (Gell. 10.15). Whether or not Caesar was formally inaugurated as Flamen Dialis is unclear; see Taylor 1941, 113–15.

31. Goetz and Schoell 1910 do not suggest any insertion where I have followed Kent 1951 in including <*ab auibus titiantibus*>, but the logic calls for something along these lines.

32. Varro hints (at least) at limited prior treatment of the (associated) Lupercalia, commenting at *Ling*. 6.13.

33. There were two *collegia* of Salii, one located on the Palatine (consecrated to Mars but also associated with Romulus' *lituus* or "crook," Cic. *Div*. 1.17); the other, the Collini (or Agonales/Agonenses, see, e.g., Livy 1.20; Dion. Hal. *Ant. Rom*. 2.70, 3.32), on the

Quirinal and associated with Quirinus and a foundation by Tullus Hostilius fulfilling a vow following his victory over the Sabines (Livy 5.52; Dion. Hal. *Ant. Rom.* 2.70). On their (traditional) institution by Numa, to honor Mars and guard the sacred shields (the *ancilia*; Numa's shield and replicas designed to distract from the original), see, e.g., Cic. *Rep.* 2.14, 2.26; Livy 1.20; Ov. *Fast.* 3.377–78; Dion. Hal. *Ant. Rom.* 2.70; Plut. *Vit. Num.* 13. The connection of the Salii Collini to the term *agon* meshes with the alternative tradition of a Greek origin (see Plut. *Vit. Num.* 13; Serv. *Ad Aen.* 2.325, 8.285). This also ties them to Varro's expansion of *rex* and the *dies Agonalia* (discussed in the fourth section, "Missing *Rex*," in connection with *Ling.* 6.14). See BNP s.v. *Salii*, 2. Beard, North, and Price 1998, 43, discuss the nuances, and provide key bibliography.

34. Varro, *Ling.* 5.110; cf. 7.2–3 (where a skeptical aside downgrades Numa's role); 7.26, 27 (old forms in the verses plug contemporary Romespeakers into the semiotics of ancient discourse; and cf. 9.61). Gordon 1990 teases out the role of unintelligibility lucidly; see now Habinek 2005, 1–7, 8–28 (persuasively detailed case study exploring the Salian rite as a complexly palimpsestic and multidimensional "talisman of sovereignty" [at 2005, 53]).

35. The Lupercalia, on 15 February, had carnival aspects (see Tert. *De spect.* 5.3; Cic. *Cael.* 26; Livy 1.5.2) and could be read as a fertility ritual (Ov. *Fast.* 2.425–52). It delivered citizens into a (safe) pre-Roman wilderness on the cusp of becoming Rome (Livy 1.5; Dion. Hal. *Ant. Rom.* 1.79.8–80.4; cf. Ov. *Fast.* 2.283–358), an ideal overlay for the resonant Forum and Palatine landscape through which the seminaked Luperci ran (slapping bystanders, especially female, with sacrificial-goatskin straps as they went; Varro, *Ling.* 6.13). See further the careful search for meaning in the Lupercalia via association with Faunus and its civic resonance at Wiseman 1995a, 77–88, and throughout; on the symbolic potential, with extensive bibliography, Koptev 2005, passim. I am persuaded by North and McLynn 2008's conclusions, especially on the problem of historicity and the flexing in the various associated stories. My reading of Varro's Lupercalia, in line with my interpretation of his interest in the Argei, makes the vignettes about much more than purification ritual (contra Ziolkowski 1998–99).

36. Key here, for reading Varro's silence, is the contemporary spin developed by Cic. *Phil.* 2.84–86 (cf. *Phil.* 13.31); Dio's account (45.30) placing Antony specifically among the new *Julian* team of Luperci, as their leader, is also relevant. I am very much in sympathy with the carnivalesque analysis developed by Binder 1997, and draw here too on North 2008, 155–59, especially in the conclusion that "Caesar's central purpose of the day was to associate himself and his *gens* with the foundation myths of Rome . . . [plugging into] a community and its transition through time past, present and future linked in the performance of inherited rituals" (159).

37. On Rome as a site supersaturated with numinosity, factor in Camillus' comments as presented at Livy 5.51. The emendation "*Neapoli*" (for *apoli*) seems plausible but even if omitted still sends us toward communities organized in Greek terms.

38. See de Grummond 2013 for an overview of the processes. Aulus Caecina (see Cic. *Fam.* 6.5–9), Nigidius Figulus, and Tarquitius Priscus all interested themselves in the unique qualities of Etruscan religious practice during this era. See Beard, North, and

Price 1998, 152–54. On birds and Etruscan religion, see de Grummond 2006b, 42. On the ritual staff known as the *lituus*, see Cic. *Div.* 1.30, 2.80; Livy 1.18.7; Verg. *Aen.* 7.187.

39. At Varro, *Ling.* 6.13, Lupercalia and Quirinalia are connected, again entangling Luperci and Salii. We might compare *Ling.* 7.104, where examples of hard-to-etymologize twittering and cheeping words cross over into theatrical use (for an audience), and later: Varro, *Rust.* 3.5.13 on the bird theater.

40. I have coined "troth-y" as a match for "treaty" to get at the promissory wordplay that Varro creates through his citation of Ennius.

41. Cf. Cic. *Off.* 1.36. Varro's version is implicit in Cic. *Leg.* 2.21, and Maltby 1991, 231, allocates source status on Fetialis to this passage in Varro. Maltby 1991, 237, uses Varro on Fetiales to trace *foedus* back to Ennian *fidus*, while (in a complex entry) a Ciceronian connection between *foedus* and *fides* is traceable through, e.g., Servius *ad Aen.* 8.641. Zollschan 2011 adds weight to the argument for the persistent currency of the Fetials in the late Republic.

42. Cf. Catull. 29—draining honor and bona fides from traditional political terminology; on new *fides*: Catull. 109. See also, e.g., Cic. *Rep.* 1.2; and on Pompey's virtues: *Leg. Man.* 13.36–16.46. On *fides* among the "virtues," see Fears 1981, 841–69.

43. For Varro specifically, the Latin runs: "*Varro in Caleno ita ait 'duces cum primum hostilem agrum introituri erant, ominis causa prius hastam in eum agrum mittebant, ut castris locum caperent'*" (Serv. Dan.). Note Varro's quoted use of *dux* in Servius' account to define the spear-thrower. *Dux* was not a typical term for part of the military chain of command in this era, so the conjunction with Fetialis in *Ling.* may indicate a use of juxtaposition to encourage scrutiny of the shifting vocabulary of military power.

44. On the *Logistorici*, exemplary studies with a philosophical angle, focused on individual Romans and probably a product of the 50s/40s, see Dahlmann and Heisterhagen 1957.

45. For Octavian as Fetialis, *Mon. Anc.* 4.7. Wiedemann 1986, 482–83, is hugely convincing, since there is likely to be such a short timespan separating Varro's study of Latin from his *Calenus*. Supporting Wiedemann's argument for an Octavianic context, a *PHI* database search delivers fifty-one hits for *fetial-*, of which (focusing on the chronologically relevant authors) five are from Cicero, one (this one) from Varro, thirty-eight from Livy (cf. fourteen instances in Servius, the next higher user), one from Augustus, two from Valerius Maximus, one from Velleius Paterculus, with four from Pliny the Elder. Cf. Varro, *De Vita Populi Romani* 2 (ap. Non. 529M), quoted in the otherwise unattested form *faetiales*. Ando 2008, 115–16, contextualizes briefly.

46. "*Imperator, ab imperio populi qui eos, qui id attemptasse<n>t, oppressi<t> hosti*" (the Imperator, armed with popular imprimatur, launches attacks as a form of defense of the people, *Ling.* 5.87).

47. Varro, *Ling.* 5.87.

48. Carruthers 2010, 190.

49. *Trabs* is the other example Varro cites (*Ling.* 10.56–57); "tree-trunk," "timber," or "beam," but with the sense "wood" (or "shaft") as a sexy in-joke (when paired with the manly *dux*). For Varro's Rome, the problem of too many leaders and the unlikelihood of one successful leader allowing power to leak or flow down meaningfully through the

system was all too real. The underlying cause (the competitive and powerful aristocracy, leading to intense oligarchic rivalry) might also be spun as productive, as Livy would do a couple of decades or so later in a less turbulent context (Livy 9.16–19).

50. For Cicero's *dux* as an off-kilter Roman military/leadership figure, a keyword (nominative-singular) search of *PHI* delivers, e.g., Cic. *Att.* 7.7.6 (*auctoritas* and *audacia* make for Caesar, *dux*), 7.13.1 (civil war as end result of one thoroughly abandoned citizen's recklessness; *dux* as ἀστρατήγητος), 7.21.1 (the other sort of disastrous leadership "*noster dux nusquam sit, nihil agat, nec nomina dant*," the *dux* in flight from his own people); *Leg.* 3.23 (the tribune of the people as a kind of safety net *dux*); *Nat. D.* 1.40 (Chrysippus makes Jupiter a kind of natural law personified: "*quasi dux uitae et magistra officiorum sit*"); *Rep.* 1.68 (*dux* as tyrant) and 6.17 (*dux* as Sol: *princeps et moderator* of the universe); *Dom.* 101 (Cicero as ironic counterfactual: *auctor et dux* of the Catilinarian conspiracy); *Fam.* 2.6.4 ("*dux nobis et auctor opus est*," laying on the compliments to C. Scribonius Curio); *Har. resp.* 57 ("*his dux est atque princeps*": Clodius); *Phil.* 2.37 (lost leaders), 3.31 (the Myrmillo-General, L. Antonius), 11.33 (Deiotarus *dux*), and 14.27 ("*princeps latronum duxque*," Antony, failed despoiler of Rome—temples, liberty, people); *Marcell.* 11 (Caesar: "*dux es et comes*") and 24 (looking back to the bouleversement in military ethics during civil war); *Mil.* 67 (sardonically, to Pompey); *Mur.* 50 (glossing Catiline); *Sull.* 33 (defining Lentulus but again glossing Catiline); *Sest.* 38 (Cicero as world savior of Rome). Cf. Cic. *De or.* 1.203, *Mil.* 39, *Sest.* 20, 61. Wiedemann 1986, 483, sums up on the *dux* as an irregular.

51. Drawing on the clear analyses of the early and middle phases in military organization in Rawlings 2007, 55–58; Hoyos 2007, 68–70. Cagniart 2007 usefully explores the connection between organizational and sociopolitical change in the purpose and composition of the army in Varro's time.

52. On the politics linking land and soldiery, Broadhead 2007 is illuminating. My reading of the topos of farmed landscape is developed at Spencer 2010, 31–46. The agribusiness of *manipulus* is evident at, e.g., Cato, *Agr.* 115.1, 156.2 (cf. Varro, *Rust.* 1.49.1).

53. Emended from *ipsicrates*. Hypsicrates, a Greek (from Amisus, Pontus, according to [Lucian] *Macr.* 22) historian and grammarian, was active in the late first century; for the connection with Varro, see, e.g., Gell. *NA* 16.12.6–7. Summed up via *FGrH* 190, "Hypsikrates von Amisos."

54. Joseph. *AJ* 14.137–39.

55. Cf. Varro, *Ling.* 6.85, where "*coniungit plures manus, manipulus.*" Note that when talking about soldiers and their interaction with leaders when in camp, Varro uses *manipulus* (*Ling.* 6.61). Isid. *Etym.* contributes: "*manipulum dicimus fascem faeni: et dictum manipulum quod manum inpleat*" (17.9.107), "*Sub Romulo autem fasciculos feni pro uexillis milites habuerunt: hinc et manipuli appellantur; manipulos enim dicimus fasces feni quod manum inpleant*" (18.3.5). Exemplifying slippage (*OLD* s.v. *manipulus*) e.g., Cato, *Agr.* 115.1; Varro, *Rust.* 1.49, 50; Columella, *Rust.* 2.18.2; Plin. *HN* 18.364; Servius *Ad Aen.* 11.870.

56. Statue: Varro, *Ling.* 9.78, 10.74.

57. Here, the *praesidium* sits in place outside the camp to make the region a safer place ("*quo tutior regio esset*"). The *prae-* prefix delivers military action; the *obsidium*, by

contrast, is a blocking entity, curtailing military activity on the enemy's part. Where *ob-* represents a negative, *in-* delivers the ambuscade, another kind of active-passive mashup and one echoing the formulation for the previous etymology "*quo minus hostis*," with "*facilius diminuerent hostis*" (that they might more easily diminish the enemy). Juxtaposing this terminological trio with *auxilium* (the first to be tackled after *milites*) and *duplicarii* (the final members of the group) bookends them with the unexpected bonus of foreign troops that stay to take Rome's side and the kinds of brave soldiers whose valor earns them double rations. The discussion in Palmer 1970, 5–14, on "threes" and "thirties" (cf. 29–34; 152–56 adds substantially to understanding Varro's angle(s).

58. On the tribes in this antiquarian context, see Palmer 1970, 152–56.

59. Rawson 1985, 240–41, tackles the inconcinnity in this etymology but finds it rooted in a methodological problem on Varro's part.

60. On *subsidium*, Maltby 1991, 590, makes this likely to be Varro's etymological coinage. Similarly, the militaristic gloss for *principes* appears to be Varro's; see Maltby 1991, 495. *Ling.* 5.45 benefits from a reread in the light of *subsido* in this context.

61. As Varro also observes (*Ling.* 5.55), the explanation for the naming derives mostly from Ennius—Titienses from Tatius, Ramnenses from Romulus—but with Luceres coming from Lucumo, according to "Junius."

62. The Lex Manilia of 67 shifted some of this restriction by (perhaps) recognizing the disconnect between where one lived and one's voting tribe and allowing freedmen to gain admittance to the rural voting tribes.

63. For the festival, see Varro, *Ling.* 6.24 (chapter 5).

64. Varro's version emphasizes what seem to be three equally authoritative decurions (i.e., highlights the triadic element), unlike (e.g.) Polyb. 6.25.1–2. Wiseman 2009, 87–89, sets out the higher-level numbering implications, proposing that Romulus' legendary three cavalry *centuriae* would work as follows via Varro: "10 × (3 × 10), ten *turmae* each consisting of a *decuria* from each *tribus*" (2009, 89).

65. Varro has already tackled tribes at *Ling.* 5.55–56 (see chapter 5), where he reminded us that he covered all this in his *Book of the Tribes*. On the Luceres, whose name (Varro has told us) is Etruscan, like Titienses and Ramnes: Cic. *Rep.* 2.14; Livy 1.13.8; Plut. *Vit. Rom.* 20.1. A less integrative view of the cavalry crops up at *Ling.* 7.56–57: auxiliaries (*ascriptiui*) is the term used for gap fillers in the ranks, but this was also how Varro described the label for *ferentarii* (*ascripti*) in paintings on show in the old Temple of Aesculapius (so called because they brought something useful or could wield only throwing weapons).

66. On *ambitio*, see Spencer 2011b, 64–66; "*Tribuni militum, quod terni tribus tribubus Ramnium, Lucerum, Titium olim ad exercitum mittebantur*" (the "Tribunes" of the soldiers, because *three* each from the *three* tribes of the Ramnes, Luceres, and Tities, were sent at one time to the army, *Ling.* 5.81). This passage featured briefly earlier in this chapter: each of the three (Etruscan; recall *Ling.* 5.55; cf. 5.91) tribes sent a representative to the army, and from this military beginning also developed the political office of tribune of the plebs; they reappear at *Ling.* 5.181, 6.87, 6.91. When readers reach *Ling.* 7.34 (discussed in chapter 2), they see the female equivalent modeled as *camilla* (a figure who also has a masculine guise).

67. For Varro's *termini* (*Ling.* 5.21), Spencer 2015a, 104. Another reverberation echoes from *tero* (part of the process of establishing *termini*, *Ling.* 5.21), whose senses "to burnish" or even "to *trivialize*" (by overuse) might add a playful lit. crit. wink (*OLD* s.v. *tero* 1, 6). These readings-in are (I suggest) fuzzy accretions to the semantic field, caught in what Gaisser 2002, 387, calls the "sticky" quality of texts.

68. Recalling Varro, *Ling.* 5.21, *ter-* also puts augury into the mix. On the books of the augurs (cited by Varro at *Ling.* 5.21 in this context), see Linderski 1986, 2244–52.

69. August. *De civ. D.* 5.12 (citing and glossing Sall. *Cat.* 7 and Cic. *Rep.* 1.26, 42): "they made annual the power to govern and shared between two governors called 'consuls' deriving from their advisory nature, rather than 'kings' or 'lords,' deriving from ruling or lordly qualities."

70. In this context (how kingship fits into the Roman *imaginaire*), Cornell 1995, 151–72 (NB 165–67), usefully sets out the imagined role of Etruscanism for the formation of Rome—as other chapters in the current book note, Etruscan *and* Sabine roles in Latin's development are important for Varro; Beard, North, and Price 1998, 54–61, tease out many implications for reading a transition from monarchy to republic via religious practice and its textualization. Evident in Lucretius, see also Livy 1.36.2-6 (on which see Beard 1989, exploring the range of civic and sociocultural operations within which qualitatively different power dynamics can lurk). Beard 1986, 36–41, and 1991, in addition to Feeney 1998, explores the textual qualities of religious representation as (invented) discourse. Recent developments in cognitive science approaches to religion (see, e.g., Lisdorf 2007, who [at 190–223] calls for a focus on identifying and reading the vocabulary) are helpfully summed up by Barrett 2011.

71. Contextualizing Varro, *Ling.* 5.9, see Spencer 2011c, 52–54.

72. Manuwald 2011, 30–40, sets the scene invaluably. Goldberg 1989 is very useful on Ennius and the friction between poetry and history, but see also Goldberg 2005, 23–27, and Manuwald 2011, 204–9; on Livius, see Goldberg 2005, 16–18 (in brief), Manuwald 2011, 188–93. Cf. Varro, *Ling.*, e.g., 7.3, on the association between poetics, (regal) antiquity, and Latino-Roman.

73. On *ager* and the developing power dynamics of the land, see 5.32, 34, 36–37, 55; on which, see Spencer 2011b, 58–60, 72.

74. Varro, *Ling.* 5.32, recounts how **Latinus'** kingdom delivers universal **Latian** territory, a world that identifies collectively via **Latianity** but maintains resonant local identities (Praeneste and Aricia). This passage makes Italic peoples paradigmatic for understanding pan-European naming and national identity. According to Varro, the Sabini and the Lucani are peoples and by straight transference, also nations; Apulia and Latium deliver names derived (*declinatus*) from people; Etruria and Tusci<a> are derivations but by transference make for people *and* nation. The legendary origins of Etruria are deeply murky—de Grummond 2006a, 201–8, sets out key issues as part of her in-depth study—but Wiseman 2004 passim weaves a set of analyses into something that nicely exemplifies the complex unknowability (probably even to Varro) and interconnectedness of much of the wider body of material.

75. Compare Varro, *Ling.* 5.49—King Tullius and sacral space in the city.

76. Varro, *Ling.* 5.151, Tullius and the Tullianum. Other instances of Rome's kingly monuments and sites: e.g., *Ling.* 5.152, 155, 157.

77. This instance is also distinguished by having no individuating name, emphasizing functionary qualities. Cf. Livy 2.2.1; *OLD* s.v. *rex*, sense 7a. More priestly kings: Varro, *Ling.* 6.13, 6.28, 6.31 (all nameless functionaries). At 6.15 boundaries are blurred slightly when *Pergamene* King Attalus is implicated in one of Rome's most significant religious festivals, the Megalensia (4 April): the Sibylline Books required Cybele (Magna Mater) to travel from Pergamum to Rome.

78. The insertion here is clunky, but I have presented it, with a translation, to allow for the possibility of missing Varronian unpacking as accepted by Kent 1951. One could run the text without it: "*eo quod interrogatur a principe*" (since that's what is asked by the leader of the state), allowing a simple reading-in of the interrogative *-ne* formulation and expecting readers to keep up with the code switching via Greco-Roman semantic slippage.

79. Varro, *Ling.* 6.13, 14.

80. Factoring in "*a principe ciuitatis et princeps gregis immolatur*," Varro, *Ling.* 6.12. North 1990 helpfully unpacks the primacy of ritual action for the various priesthoods, a complex of ideas within which Varro's agonistic gloss works well (see also Beard 1986, exploring divinatory discourse via Cicero). Santangelo 2013b, 244–45, outlines the need to be attuned to the multiplicity of nuances for *auctoritas* in ways that complement my reading. For Varro's *grex*, see *Ling.* 5.76.

81. On the primitive nature of this foundation, cf. Dion. Hal. *Ant. Rom.* 4.27, Ov. *Fast.* 6.783, Plut. *Quaest. Rom.* 281, and Richardson 1992, 154–55—a story that satisfied Romans, clearly, and entered the system (Fears 1981, 848, e.g., is not sanguine about the veracity of the story, but veracity is I think beside the point).

82. "*a similitudine sonitus dictus*," so called from the similarity to the sound (*Ling.* 6.67).

83. *Murmurari, fremere, gemere, clamare, crepare*, Varro, *Ling.* 6.67.

84. Compare *Ling.* 5.51 (the Quirinal shrine) and "*Quirinus a Quiritibus*" (*Ling.* 5.73). Maltby 1991 (s.v. *Quirinalis collis, Quirinus, Quirites, Quiritis, quirito*) is comprehensive. Relevant (reasonably contemporary) comparisons can be made with, e.g., Livy 1.13.5 (from Cures); Ov. *Fast.* 2.479 (*Quirites*); 511 (hill), showing how Cures (place) and Quirites (people) generate an ethnoplacial nexus. Note Verg. *G.* 3.27, where Quirinus glosses Augustus, and cf. Cic. *Rep.* 2.20.

85. The Greek form here is an emendation from *triambo* (introduced in the *Editio Aldina*, 1513).

86. Slotted in *BNP* into the category *Atellana fabula*, Aprissius (s.v.) is not elsewhere attested. The Atellan angle does, however, direct the gaze south of Rome, to Samnium, and toward Magna Graecia. Worth keeping in mind is that Bovillae, home of the Iulii but also significant for Cicero's Clodian fracas, is Samnite—cf. *Ling.* 7.29 (discussed in chapter 3). See Robinson 2003, 615, on the ideological pliability of the festivals clustering round the Quirinalia.

87. Looking for contemporary use, the closest example is Ov. *Am.* 3.13, which sets the rustic-civic Juno Curitis model going. See Littlewood 2006, lv–lvi and (on *Fast.* 6.49–50)

19–20. This is significant because it tackles Juno colluding in the subordination of Titus Tatius to Romulus; as Littlewood notes, Ovid's self-presentation with his wife, as participant in the rites of Juno Curitis at her hometown of Falerii (topographically, a link between Sabines and Etruscans), suggests an interest in exploring the available interplay between Sabine, Etruscan, and Roman qualities of identity at stake (Adams 2007, 182–87, draws important conclusions on the status quo for dialects in the Republic). See also chapter 5 on the nation-forming aspect of this integration.

88. Adams 2007, 155–56, unpacks usage of *quirito* and *iubilo* and evidences Varro's literary city-versus-rustic-country distinction. Cic. *De or*. 3.227 has Crassus make shouting, raising one's voice from the start of an utterance, *agreste*.

89. On Latin Liber, Maltby 1991, 337, marks out the full web of explanations (Rousselle 1987 has also been useful here). Dion. Hal. *Ant. Rom.* 6.17.3. Green 2002, 77–80, explores Varro's tangling of Ceres and Liber. Cf. Cic. *Nat. D.* 2.62, where "Balbus" (discussing deification of worthy mortals) says there are two contenders for identification as "Liber," but the key figure in this context is (Greek) Semele's son only, not the (Latin) Liber whom "our ancestors" worshiped as part of a family triad.

90. Pagán 2005, 50–67, is thoroughly helpful on the literary and cultural afterlife of the *S. C. de Bacchanalibus* (186). The substantial discussion of Liber and Republican ideology at Wiseman 2008, 84–139, makes a strong case, arguing that Roman attempts to map the role of Liber in the process of nation formation were crucial to the development of a historical sensibility. Nevertheless, while a sensibility that pushes the claims of Italic culture's clout in shaping Roman identity makes Varro's *Antiquitates Rerum Diuinarum* (dedicated to Caesar) appear straightforwardly conservative, the catholic quality of the project and its focus on the structural qualities of religion as a conservational framework for *habitus* might indicate that Varro's steer was more ambitious in its use of the gods than Wiseman thinks likely (cf. Momigliano 1984, who remarks on the oddness of trying to reconcile Varro's caustic sensibility with a fuddy-duddy survey of long-since irrelevant deities and cult; see also Van Nuffelen 2010). Appearing not long before *De Lingua Latina*, Varro's generation of deep roots for Roman religion at the very least provides a foundation for exploring what happens when language meets divine ritual.

91. Varro, *Ling.* 6.28 (partly reframing 6.13). The text for this whole section in the discussion is significantly fragile (5.27–32). On Juno and the cryptic formula of proclamation, see Riganti 1978, 128–29; Flobert 1985, 102–3, adds detail but cannot progress much further.

92. Feeney 2007, 170–72, is exceptionally lucid on this tricky issue; as he observes, "the consuls *were* the particular year" (2007, 171), but we must not confuse this with the separate question of a fixed date decontextualized from the consular sequence. Varro's *fasti* is the subject of chapter 8.

93. "*As I have shown in the Books of Antiquities*," Varro, *Ling.* 6.13; this is part of Varro's empire.

94. The *Cornicula* contextualizes the Armilustrium (Varro, *Ling.* 5.153). I do not follow the title emendation (*Cornicula<ria>*). In connection with brigandish mercenaries,

Cornicula (or *The Tiny Crow*) seems especially apt—a diminutive scavenger with a very loud and raucous caw. The phrasal addition is Kent's proposal, drawing on Festus 118.6 M; it is unnecessary for the basic point, but I retain it in this instance. On the play, see Ehrman 1993.

95. Cicero's Verres—the celebrity case and the source of his early success—would surely surface in Varro's dedicatee's mind (e.g., Cic. *Verr.* 2.5.86). For the background to Caesar and monarchical trappings, see Rawson 1975. Bell 1997, 10–16, outlines how Cicero might be read as bouncing off the issue of personal spectacle and decorum; see also Farney 2007, 20–22. Depending on the date of completion and/or any further revisions, the Antony who emerges from Cic. *Philipp.* 2 might also come into focus.

96. Addition proposed by Mueller and adopted by Kent.

97. Grünewald (1999) 2004, 73–80.

98. Lintott 1968, 74–88, provides abundant examples.

99. Grünewald (1999) 2004, 75, goes so far as to propose "tyrant" as the primary meaning for the rapacity embodied in *latro*, citing the frequency of the association in the *Philippics* as evidence. This misses a trick. Surely, the force of Cicero's point is in the mundane mercenary realities of brigandry, of soldiery-for-hire, crashing into the political street violence and its organizational counterpart in the machinery of politics, all rammed repeatedly down Antony's throat. Cf. Kaster 2006, 113, who draws on the convincing analysis of Habinek 1998, 69–87. Riggsby 2002 provides a coherent overview of the character and tone of Cicero's rhetoric after his return from exile, tracking the complexity of his refinement and repurposing of political vocabulary.

Chapter 7. A Family Affair

1. "Therefore because the primal classes of things are four, so many are those of words" (*Ling.* 5.13).

2. Danvers 2009, on awareness as a mode within ecological interdependence, has been a useful provocation for ideas in this chapter.

3. I am thinking here of Bourdieu (1980) 1990 and the concepts of misrecognition and masking introduced in that study. Hanks 2005, 75–79, is particularly useful on this aspect of Bourdieu's work and its development in linguistics. On the terminology in Greek, Dickey 2007, 219–65 is invaluable; see also Luhtala 2002.

4. "*Itaque quod diligenter uidendum est in uerbis . . . is locus maxime lubricus est*," Varro, *Ling.* 10.7.

5. In various forms: Caes. *BGall.* 2.33.2, 7.17.3, 7.71.3; *BCiv.* 3.8.3; Cic. *Inv. rhet.* 2.11, referring to what he has not incautiously achieved in book 1 ("*in libro primo non indiligenter expositum est*"). Elsewhere, Plaut. *Asin.* 273, *Bacch.* 201, *Mil.* 28, *Mostell.* 105, 110, *Persa* 557; Ter. *Phorm.* 788, *Ad.* 684; and cf. Cic. *Att.* 16.3.2, *QFr.* 1.2.7, 3.2.3; Varro, *Rust.* 1.18.2 (context: Cato).

6. Cato, *Agr.* 5.1, 5.6, 32.2, 45.1, 52.1, 61.2, 66.1, 67.2, 133.2, 142.1, 143.8. Compare use in Caesar's commentaries, where *diligen-* forms are deeply embedded, creating (especially in the Gallic books 3, 6, and 7, e.g., *BGall.* 3.16.6, 18.1, 20, 21, 25; 6.12, 13, 14, 34, 36; 7.4, 17, 29, 32, 60, 65, 71) a motif that tells subtly on the general's self-fashioning. Cicero's forensic oratory (especially his prosecution of Verres) is dripping with this form of scrupulous

care, but, e.g., Cic. *Fin.*, *Inv.*, *Brut.*, *De or.*, and *Tusc.* also deliver significant hits for variations on the term. Based on a *PHI* search for *diligen-*.

7. A *PHI* search indicates that before the first century, *astutus* and related forms were overwhelmingly part of the comedic literary mode: nineteen appearances in Plautus, nine in Terence. Twenty-first-century equivalence might be found in the Hiberno-English "cute hoor" or the Italian *furba*. Swiggers and Wouters 1996b, 1996c make the translation of grammatology a particular focus, although my reading of Varro here has a more literary agenda (see also Malmkjær 2005).

8. Cf. Varro, *Ling.* 8.56, and how *Parma* is not at all the same as *Roma*.

9. A slightly loose translation here is intended to get across what I believe to be Varro's main point. The emendation to *uerecundiae* is Kent's.

10. "In nomin<at>ibus magis expressa ac plus etiam in uocibus ac <syllabarum> similitudinibus quam in rebus suam optinet rationem," Varro, *Ling.* 10.19.

11. Varro, *Ling.* 10.22–23. There is a lacuna here in *F*, covering one whole page and two partial pages (indicated by a marginal note in F^2); the text picks up in midthought at 10.24.

12. Significant comparisons ripple through Varro, *Ling.* 10.68–72 (riffing on Regularity, the "good" and "goods" [*boni*], "us" vs. Greeks—good honest trades contrasted with epic heroes); cf. Cic. *Att.* 7.7. Recall the *latrones* of Varro, *Ling.* 7.52–53, discussed in chapter 6.

13. In general, Varro's *nomen* can indicate the label attached to a thing (e.g., 7.109) or one subset, "noun" (e.g., 9.89, in contrast to *uerbum*, when discussing homonyms), a usage that drifts interestingly into something more like proper noun (e.g., 8.45, in contrast to *uocabulum*).

14. "*Casuum uocabula alius alio modo appellauit; nos dicemus, qui nominandi causa dicitur, nominandi uel nominatiuum*" (the vocabulary of cases is already willy-nilly on call; *we* shall say that the one spoken for the purpose of naming is the "naming" or "nominative" [and a lacuna intervenes], Varro, *Ling.* 10.23). Tracking down the references to the full panoply of Latin grammatical terminology is a delight facilitated admirably by the magisterial Schad 2007.

15. The full set of exemplary words that behave unexpectedly in-case runs: *oui, oue, aui, aue* (variant ablatives); *puppis, puppes, restis, restes* (variant nominative plurals); *ciuitatum, ciuitatium, parentum, parentium* (genitive plurals); *montes, montis, fontes, fontis* (accusative plurals); next, *gens, mens, dens* have divergence in the genitive and accusative plural, with *gentium, gentis*, then *mentium, mentes*, finally, *dentum, dentes* (Varro's omission of the form in "i" for *dens* seems to be anomalous).

16. Drawing here on Schad 2007, 11 (s.v. *accustaiuus*). Schad raps Varro on the knuckles for failing to join the dots back to an Aristotelian αἰτιατόν as the semantic frame.

17. Sampling usage of *accuso* (first-person present indicative form), via *PHI*, delivers thirty-seven matches of which eight are from Cicero's forensic oratory and seven from his letters (six instances writing to Atticus, one to Quintus)—i.e., just over a fifth of the usage is Cicero's.

18. Varro, *Ling.* 8.36 (cf. 8.4, 25). Here and elsewhere (*Ling.* 10.21, 10.66), we see *dandi* as the technical term, a case of designation, duty, permission, and conferral. The frisson

from Terentius (cf. *Ling.* 8.7, 8.14, 9.38; in the last, *terra*, *Terentius*, and *faba*, root Varro in down-home rusticity) is evident; Plautus' plays were a major object of Varronian enthusiasm, meriting two works of influential scholarship and featuring heavily in the poetic elements of *De Lingua Latina*; Marcus, Varro's own praenomen (cf. *Ling.* 10.51—Marcus and Quintus, two Chickpeas, perhaps, hang out; "Marcus" is titular, and apostrophized, in a few of Varro's Menippean Satires; see Wiseman 2009, 144–47), is also of course also Cicero's; a more direct poke is given via the power of conjunctivity (*et*), alluded to in "Tullius and Antonius were Consuls" (*Ling.* 8.10).

19. The text follows the old forms in *-ei*.

20. Varro, *Ling.* 8.42–43, at 43. The issue is flagged up for later discussion; see, e.g., 10.7 and book 10 *passim*. The vocative also crops up at *Ling.* 8.68, 9.43, 9.91, 10.30.

21. Cf. Varro, *Ling.* 10.55–56.

22. I am reminded here of Vitr. *De arch.* 5.8.2 on theater design, resonance, and the management of sound. As Varro goes on to emphasize (*Ling.* 10.63–64), sound patterns, spoken words, are a significant part of what's at stake.

23. Groth's emendation from *leui* to *claui*—followed by Kent—makes sense of this as a sample fourth-declension ablative; *leui*, perhaps as a substantive use for a third-declension adjective, could also work but is less obviously logical in this group. The phrasing is "*ut hac <c>laui*": the "c" might have fallen victim to elision via copying.

24. Taking the measure, see Varro, *Rust.* 1.10.1. For the turn-by-turn furrows of ploughing, Columella, *Rust.* 2.2.25; Plin *HN* 18.19, 177. *OLD* s.v. *uersus, us* 4, 5 unpacks the separate literary nuances.

25. Coffey 1976, 11–18, sets out the pieces; Van Rooy 1966, 1–29, offers a usefully thorough survey-discussion of the evidence (with a particularly bullish approach to Diomedes' "channeling" of Varro on the origin story but also interesting on *lanx*, the pick-and-mix platter offered to the gods). Wiseman 2009, 143, makes satire Varro's own personal "bread and circuses." *Lanx* connects to *satura* via the scholia on Hor. *Sat.* 1.1.

26. A *PHI* search "[Lucr:DRN] *cael*" delivers 163 matches.

27. Corbeill 2008, 85–88.

28. Corbeill 2008, 90.

29. Cf. Sall. *Cat.* 6.6; Livy, 1.8.7; Isid. *Etym.* 9.4.10. For more on *caritas* and family values: e.g., Livy 1.34.5; Quint. *Inst.* 11.1.72. For a more political *pater* in Varro, *Ling.*, e.g., 6.91, where an antiquarian legal text draws *patres* (read in, senators) into the mix of magistrates and public figures. See Palmer 1970, 5–8 and (on Dion. Hal. *Ant. Rom.* 3.48.2; 2.37.2) 137–38, 144.

30. Compare Cic. *Nat. D.* 2.66, 123, 165. Cf. *Ling.* 7.51 (and the line ascribed by Varro to Naevius—"*patrem suum supremum optumum appellat*," she calls upon her own father, the highest and best—retrofitting Roman values to the Greco-Roman pantheon).

31. E.g., Varro, *Ling.* 7.12, cites Ennius for a line invoking father and kinsman as ethics police.

32. E.g., Varro, *Ling.* 5.159, recalls Tullia's desecration of her father's corpse.

33. See especially Varro, *Ling.* 8.67. Cf. *Ling.* 9.76, 85.

34. Varro, *Ling.* 8.74, follows up by unpacking cattle and Jupiter.

35. Cic. *Phil.* 3.16. A (second-century) Lex Atinia pushed for the acceptance of the tribunes of the people in the senate (Gell. *NA* 14.8.2). Aricia played a crucial role in the action when Clodius met his end, as Cicero knew (*Mil.* 51), and of course Octavian's mother, Atia, was from Aricia—apparently a source of mockery (as a *municipium*, a backwater) for Antony (*Philipp.* 3.15–17). Aricia is later called "bosky" by Martial (*Ep.* 13.19), while his "Laelia," who lives in Patrician Row ("*in uico . . . Patricio*"), has a dour father from Aricia (*Ep.* 68).

36. Sisenna was involved in the defense of Verres (Cic. *Verr.* 2.4.43); Cicero makes his scholarly (methodological) credentials a little suspect (Cic. *Leg.* 1.7; cf. *Brut.* 228), but his pro-Sullan (Sall. *Iug.* 95.2) history was nevertheless influential, despite Cicero's grumbles. Gell. *NA* 16.9.5 puts him in Varro's *logistoricus* on historiography. Rawson 1979, 328–29, argues plausibly that the Cornelii Sisennae may have had an Etruscan background, albeit sometime in the past.

37. Varro fr. 245 Funaioli.

38. Corbeill 2008, 76. For gender *tout court*, Varro deploys *sexus* in book 8 (*Ling.* 8.46); cf. Cic. *Inv. rhet.* 1.24. The semantic sexuality of nouns is, in Varro's book, deeply acculturated and evidence of changing customs (e.g., because of the domestication of doves and their resulting different uses, a new masculine form, *columbus*, developed, *Ling.* 9.56, and the discussion continues through sections 58–62).

39. See also *Ling.* 9.95, commenting on verb clans (*genera*).

40. Following Kent 1951: "*Natura cum tria genera transit et id est in usu discriminatu<m>, tum denique apparet, ut est in doctus et docta et doctum: doctrina enim per tria haec transire potest et usus docuit discriminare doctam rem ab hominibus et in his marem ac feminam. In mare et femina et neutro neque natura maris transit neque feminae neque neutra, et ideo non dicitur feminus femina feminum, sic reliqua: itaque singularibus ac secretis uocabulis appellati sunt.*" (When the natural order traverses three "types" and this distinction is formalized in use, then at last it is fully apparent—thus, "learned man," and "learned woman," and "learned entity." For learning can cross between these three, and use teaches how to distinguish a "learned matter" [f.] from humankind, and among the latter, the male and the female. In "male," "female," and "neither," the basic principles of male, female, and neither do not boundary-jump, and hence there's no natural grammatical speech pattern: "*she*male," "*fe*male," "*andro*gyne"; thus, across the board, each is called by unique and separate words.) See also *Ling.* 9.95, on verb clans (*genera*).

41. Corbeill 2008, 76.

42. See, e.g., Varro, *Ling.* 5.4, 5.13 (essentialism of *genus*); 5.33 (field-land participates in *genus* discourse; cf. 5.146, 9.27, 9.34, "produce" is part of the episteme; 6.64, gardening usage plays on generative nuances; 7.109, draws together *genus*, etymology, farming); 5.94 (skill sets as *genera*); 5.131 (kinds of dress); 6.1, 6.36, 8.9, 8.11–12, 8.20, 8.21, 8.39, 9.67, 9.95–96, 9.102–3, 10.48, 10.52 (nouns and verbs); 8.58–59, 9.110 (participles and gender); 5.79, 9.28, 9.113 (kinds of animal; cf. 9.29, human families and *genus* (cf. 9.40, gender-bending); 9.79 (anomalous or spurious typologies, from Alexander the Great to Roman dress; 10.8, species and [word-]form); 8.24, 8.51, 8.52–53, 9.10, 10.9–11, 16 (grammatology); 8.75, 8.78–79, 9.72 (comparatives as family); 10.14 (disambiguation problems—[in]declinables); 10.18 (pronouns); 10.30 (five declensions of "articles"); 10.35 (*ratio*

underpins *genus*); 10.42 (*genus* implicated in the poetics of simile; cf. 10.45); 9.57, 10.65 (*genus* speaks to a deep-level identification—the semantic field depends on the words being nouns/names and gendered); 9.90, 10.66 (*genus* can include made up families in which ancestral relationships are spurious if imagined; cf. 8.55, 9.102-3, the latter is a notable personal voice intervention by Varro); 10.70 (vernacular, migrant, and first-generation native models of Regularity—"*cuius genera sunt tria*"). The list is by no means exhaustive.

43. E.g., Varro, *Ling.* 10.21 (cf. 10.32, 33), where *genus* and *species* are set up as different parts of the grammatical toolkit. This model leans on *species* to signal discrete, formal, and morphological unities.

44. Cf. Varro, *Ling.* 10.41.

45. Adams 1982, 252, references Martial for *sto* in this sense (glossing Adams 1982, 57–59); cf. *OLD* s.v. *sto* sense 5a, and feed in sense 1c (e.g., Cic. *Verr.* 1.151); on erections, e.g., Adams 1982, 46, corrals a group of examples that sexualize the imagery of standing (as the converse to lying inert) in Varro's era. Wallace-Hadrill 1990 shows a deliberate terminological shift from *fornix* to *arcus* in the Principate, exactly because of the semiotic drift that Varro's nudge-nudge joke would make available. McGinn 2004, 250, is compelling on the evidence for architectural adoption of *arcus* as a real-world zoning model.

46. May 1995, on Cic. *Cael.* See, e.g., Cic. *Cael.* 48 (young men in brothels? It's practically *de rigueur*); cf. the well-known story circulating (later, at least) about the Elder Cato: he advised young men to visit brothels, but not excessively ("*cum uidisset hominem honestum e fornice exeuntem, laudauit*," Porphyrio and ps.-Acro on Hor. *Ser.* 1.2.31–32; context, Plaut. *Curc.* 33–38).

47. Unsurprisingly, this does not cross gender boundaries: noteworthy relationships map mothers to daughters as well as fathers to sons, developing the motif through mid(day) and mid(night) (*Ling.* 10.41) and on to an emotional "family" joining (inflected forms of) love and sorrow (*Ling.* 10.42).

48. Varro, *Ling.* 5.143 (context), 144 (founding Rome).

49. If one sticks with the unemended text, one has *appellata*, which describes Lavinia. The shift in attachment of the participle doesn't substantially alter the sense.

50. As Livy (1.3) suggests, "Longa" because the city extended along the ridge line of the Alban Mount.

51. See, for instance, Varro, *Ling.* 8.4, 7–8, 14—tracing a syn- and diachronicity in sociolinguistic genealogies.

52. Other places where one might imagine a Trojan backstory to be quietly in play, e.g., Varro, *Ling.* 8.3-4, 8.80-84, 9.44.

53. "*Nam id <idem> ualet et a uoluntate*," Varro, *Ling.* 6.69.

54. Reading *Cretaea* for *Gretea* is logical; note that the masculine form, *Cretaeus*, might stand in for Epimenides at Prop. 2.34.29 (although the text is massively debated). Melfi 2008 explores the Attic significance of Cretan nymphs.

55. Ter. *Ad.* 75.

56. "*Quae autem dea ad res omnes ueniret Venerem nostri nominauerunt*," Cic. *Nat. D.* 2.69; "*Venus quia uenit ad omnia*," Cic. *Nat. D.* 3.62. On Venus = sexual intercourse and the connections with *uenio*, see Adams 1982, 144, 176, 189.

57. The real-life sons are P. Cornelius Scipio Aemilianus Africanus Minor and Q. Fabius Maximus Aemilianus, both parceled out for strategic adoptions. It is worth noting some context: 161 saw the enactment of the sumptuary Lex Fannia, i.e., excess and the discourse of behavioral control were in the air.

58. Leigh 2004, 159–60. On Cicero's Terence, see Manuwald 2014, 181 and passim.

59. [Demea] "*quod te isti facilem / et festiuom putant, / id non fieri ex uera / uita neque adeo ex / aequo et bono, / sed ex adsentando / indulgendo et largiendo, / Micio.*" Ter. Ad. 985–88.

60. Leigh 2004, 190, cf. 177–78.

61. Leigh 2004, 178–89, economically sums up the wallpaper on generalship and models of *auctoritas* in the relevant context.

62. Varro, *Ling.* 6.70.

63. Accepted in Kent's version: "*Sponde<n> tuam gnatam filio uxorem meo?*" Varro, *Ling.* 6.71.

64. Varro, *Ling.* 6.71. Cf. the femininity of *spes*, 6.73, discussed in chapter 3.

65. Varro, *Ling.* 6.72.

66. Following Kent's text.

67. Varro, *Ling.* 5.57; cf. *Ling.* 5.60 (united with the cosmic forces, sky and earth generated everything).

68. The related matter of how Roman priesthoods got their names (*Ling.* 5.83–86) was tackled in chapter 6. Lurking behind all this is Cic. *Nat. D.* 3.62.

69. Varro, *Ling.* 5.61–63 (Venus), 5.64 (Saturn) and onward.

70. An emendation to flag up wordplay was required; making "*et*" read "*G C*" is the solution adopted by Kent, which I follow.

71. Enn. *Varia* 48, 49–50 (*ROL* i.412).

72. Varro, *Ling.* 5.65, quoting Enn. *Varia* 54–58 (*ROL* i.414). This argument is very much influenced by the line taken by Ando 2005.

73. Varro, *Ling.* 5.66.

74. The text has been substantially emended around the *ortus*/Orcus joke, but other examples of wordplay (as noted in earlier chapters; also, e.g., Varro, *Ling.* 8.74, 9.55) suggest that a beginnings/ends pun is likely.

75. See the preceding (much-quoted) comments on Epicureanism, voiced by C. Aurelius Cotta, Cic. *Nat. D.* 1.82. No doubt Velleius is also occasionally Οὐελλειος!

76. Varro, *Ling.* 5.57. See Ando 2005, 47–49.

77. Ando 2005, 48.

78. Cf. *Ling.* 5.74, where Sun and Moon are both among the immigrant deities sponsored by Titus Tatius (along with Diana and indeed Saturn, but not Apollo).

79. Andreussi 1996 (Luna); Aronen 1996 (Noctiluca). Cic. *Nat. D.* 2.69 talks about moonlight so bright as to mimic day, and the ability of Moon to change the experience of night into something equivalent to day suggests that Varro is interested here in the imperializing quality of light.

80. Varro might be playing on *diuido* (to separate, divide) and something like *de-ui(a)-are* (although this verb is found only in late Latin).

81. Quint. *Inst.* 11.3.79; cf. Cic. *Pis.* 9.20, and, for a different spin, Catull. 67.46.

82. Varro's mashup of auditory and olfactory senses is at *Ling.* 6.83.

83. Here I have not followed Kent in accepting the emendation from *fulgor* to *fulgur*, because if one keeps the former, then, without needing to emend *fulgur* to *fulgitum* (the last in the list of natural special effects), one switches on the flash and the zap of the bolt.

84. "*Onus est onos qui sustinet rem publicam*," Varro, *Ling.* 5.73.

85. *OLD* s.v. *diuido*, especially 3, 6, 7. Cf. *Ling* 7.60: "*Diuidia ab diuidendo dicta, quod diuisio distractio est doloris*" (dissension is said to emerge from "to divide," because from division comes the discord caused by pain). Measuring activity, understanding change: both require separators and skills in discrimination; the choice of verb might evoke Varro's odd throwaway on Diana as *Diuiana* (*Ling.* 5.68).

86. No Varronian etymology for *cursus* remains. The closest we get is *cursor*, at *Ling.* 8.15, but consider e.g., *curro*, to run, make haste (*Ling.* 5.153, 155), and associated with festivals, *Ling.* 6.13. Varro does not invoke the "chariot" motif for Sun or Moon, but the referent was clearly available (cf. Cic. *Nat. D.* 3.76; Tibull. 1.8.21; Hor. *Carm.* 1.22.21–22; Prop. 2.31.11; Ov. *Met.* 7.207–8; Man. 1.174–76, 1.198–200). Michels 1967, Samuel 1972, Rüpke (2001) 2007, 2007, and Feeney 2007 all inform my discussion.

87. For the Latinity of *mundus* (versus κόσμος), see Varro, *Sat. Men.* 420 (similarly, Plin. *HN* 2.8); cf. Varro, *Logistorici* 38.5, 39.4. Isid. *Etym.* 3.9 offers a similar angle ("*mundus... quia semper in motu est*"). Summer and winter (i.e., seasonal temporality) underpin the trope of fiery sky and moist earth, developing Jupiter's *pater*nal qualities (*Ling.* 5.65). *Mundus* topographically centers the course of time and its world-shaping qualities on the Forum; the explanation ascribed to Cato (Festus 144L) tallies with this. Plutarch's *mundus* (*Vit. Rom.* 11) is hard to reconcile with the model ascribed to Cato, but the plurality of representations suggests that it might have had synecdochic qualities as space, topographic feature, and structure or monument—compare *templum* (discussed in chapter 5).

88. Cf. Varro, *Men.* 420.

89. For Praeneste as the home of uncouth speech, see Adams 2003b, 192; 2007, 119–21. On Praeneste and dialect matters, see Coleman 1990.

90. The Cornelius in question: P. Cornelius Scipio Nasica Corculum, censor (with M. Popilius Laenas) in 159. Pliny, *HN* 7.215 tells the story. Varro omits to mention that this was Rome's first such clock (which it was), nor does the text connect the construction to Cornelius' role as censor. It was a well-known sight, so Varro might have expected readers to recall the data from memory.

91. See Maltby 1991 s.v. *lustrum* (1).

92. Varro, *Ling.* 8.34, 8.68, 9.91 (cf. Varro, *Rust* 3.12). A *PHI* search (#lep ~ #lup http://latin.packhum.org/search?q=%23lep+%7E+%23lup) offers interesting results.

93. Kent accepts the emendation (to include *Aeolis*) proposed by GS, which does mesh with Varro's second bite at the hare (*Rust.* 3.12.6). On the Aeolians (as one of the three flavors of Greeks), see Cic. *Flacc.* 64. Cf. Lucr. 1.721; Verg. *Aen.* 6.164, 8.416.

94. Thinking here of the joke in Ov. *Ars* 3.662 where the hare stands in for the object of desire and of course becomes a focus for erotic control (cf. Callim. *Anth. Pal.* 12.102 [= 31 Pf]; and exemplifying the contemporaneity for Varro, see Hor. *Sat.* 1.2.105–8). Gideon

Nisbet reminds me that a play on *lepus* (hare but also, by implication, λέπορις) and *lepos* (charm) might also be in play.

95. Hor. *Sat.* 2.8. See also, e.g., Catull. 2, 3 (the sparrow poems), Ov. *Am.* 2.6 (the parrot poem), Stat. *Silv.* 2.4, 2.5 (parrot; lion), Martial 1.6, 1.14, 1.22, 1.48, 1.51, 1.60, 1.104 (lion and hare); and, in prose, Babrius 98, Phaed. 4.1. Varro enjoys telling animal tales, too, in his country handbook (e.g., *Rust.* 3.16.7, bees).

96. See Henderson 2001, 157–60, exploring the fable/free-speech divide, and in general on powerful words, Graf 2004. Cf. Cic. (being Scipio) *Rep.* 4.12 (ap August. *De civ. D.* 2.9); Hor. *Sat.* 2.1.

97. See, e.g., Cato, *Agr.* 124; Varro, *Rust.* 2.9.2, 2.9.5, 2.9.15; Columella, *Rust.* 7.11.1–2.

98. The hare recurs at Ov. *Met.* 10.537–41; Orpheus' song of the story of Venus and Adonis has Venus cheer on the chase for safe prey (hares, stags, and hinds) and warn against the pursuit of such heroic prey as wild boar, wolves, bears, and lions. It is unsubtle: some wild things are less wild than others. Compare the quartet's outing in Ovid's later work: "Often in pursuit of a lamb the wolf was halted by his voice, / often in fleeing the ravening wolf, the lamb halted, / often dogs and hares lay down together in one covert" (as Ovid continues: a deer shares a scene with a lioness, a crow with an owl, a dove with a hawk), Ov. *Fast.* 2.85–87.

99. Varro, *Rust.* 3.3, 3.12–13.

100. "*A bono et malo bonum malum*," *Ling.* 8.34.

101. Varro's Plautine enthusiasm makes this pun too good to overlook (see Plaut. *Pseud.* 1218–21, cf. Plin. *HN* 8.5.11).

102. For Melicertes (who becomes Palaemon after drowning with his mother, Ino, and of course features in Verg. *G.* 1.437 and Ov. *Met.* 4.522, *Fast.* 6.494; cf. Pers. 5.103), see BNP. Philomedes does not have any obvious manifestation in Latin literature. Cf. their appearance at the same point in the argument with "wolf" and "hare," *Ling.* 8.68.

103. The discussion extends to *Ling.* 9.92, with two first-person singular verbs (*dixi, adiciam*).

104. The statistics for use of *socer* in the *PHI* corpus show that until Ovid (with a plethora of uses in the *Heroides* and *Metamorphoses*) beats his statistical count—and its weight—Cicero is the author with the highest surviving use (http://latin.packhum.org/stats?q=socer). The form *socrus* is much less common, although it does crop up in Varro, see n. 107.

105. Catull. 29.24.

106. For the hare as part of an iconographic dynamic (Faustulus the trapper who snares hare and babies; the wolf as hunter who adopts the babies/ought to prey on the weak), see, e.g., the third/second-century Italian engraved gem in the British Museum collection, "Sard gem engraved with Faustulus finding the she-wolf and Romulus and Remus beneath a tree; a hare hangs from one of the boughs," quoting the online catalog (record 1865,0712.162). The association between (deer and) hares and the Floralia, and thereby fertility and (contained) flourishing sexuality, would make for a nice addition. At the Floralia, according to Ovid (*Fast.* 5.174, 372) deer and *hares* were released in the Circus Maximus as honorific icons of Flora as protector of gardens and fields (*cultivated* wild nature), excluding the more dangerous wild woods and wild animals (Ken Dowden

kindly drew my attention to the "wild" symbolism of hares; see Keller 1909: 215–16); according to Persius (5.177–79), chickpeas were also thrown in the Circus (delighting the mob). Raaflaub 2006 looks at the wolf motif as part of Rome's memory landscape.

107. Varro's final *socer* is paired with the less common form *socrus* (which can cross over as mother-in-law) to illustrate one instance of where Regularity should not be expected (*Ling.* 10.82).

108. Cf. Varro, *Ling.* 8.41, 9.41.

109. Hock and Joseph 2009, 370–74, outline the issues.

Chapter 8. Varro's *Fasti*

1. Alongside Bourdieu (1980) 1990, I draw here on Gumperz 1992 ("contextualization cues") and 1996 (the rift between linguistic pedagogy and inferential processes); key to the Roman context and supported by a heavily etymological twist is the disjunction between possible or encouraged readings where technical learning is the ideal or expected outcome. Fruyt 2000 introduces the lexicographic niceties economically.

2. Varro, *Ling.* 6.29, 53. To understand Varro's distinctive approach, see Herbert-Brown 1994, 85, 88–91, exploring one direct instance of rivalry between Ovid and previous calendar etymologists Varro and L. Cincius on the etymology of April. We might assume that Varro's *Antiquitates* set down some substantial markers with which *De Lingua Latina* is in dialogue. Green 2002 and Robinson 2003 read Ovid very much in tune with my overview of Varro in this context.

3. Feeney 2007; Palmer 1970, especially 97–122.

4. Varro, *Ling.* 6.12–24, 25–26, 27–32, 33–34.

5. Aug. *De civ. D.* 6.4.

6. Feeney 2007, 200. Varro is sparing with month names in the festal catalog: February is named and etymologized (in the context of the priestly publicity for the Lupercalia and its antique position as month twelve of the "old" year, explaining Terminalia). "June" qualifies the Ides known as Lesser Quinquatrus; the Rustic Vinalia counts down to the Kalends of "September"; "October" is context for the obscure Meditrinalia. Months take center stage at *Ling.* 6.33–34.

7. Cic. *Acad.* 1.9. Worth factoring in, too, is that the "divine" books of the *Antiquitates* were dedicated to Caesar, and Caesar's role as Pontifex Maximus (elected 63) must ripple behind decisions about how to prioritize divine and human schema for the annual cycle. Walter 2006 succinctly scopes the relationship between calendars and the organization of Roman memory.

8. Ken Dowden jogged my elbow on some of the issues involved. The festival was for Janus, the door opener and new-/old-year invoker (cf. Ov. *Fast.* 5.721, where scrolling back is required); other Dies Agonales: 17 March, 21 May, 11 December; on Ovid's Agonalia, see J. F. Miller 1991, 14–22; on the links to Fasti Praenestini, see Wallace-Hadrill 1987, 225–26, 229; and for the nuances of Callimacheanism, see Frazel 2002. Consult especially *RE* s.v. *Agonalia* (571–72), including a clear discussion of the Liberalia overlap presented by Varro (*Ling.* 6.14).

9. Something like "[sacrificed] by the chief of state, and the chief of the flock is sacrificed." *Grex* works either straightforwardly as flock or herd of animals or as a crowd,

society, or (the common) herd of people (as in, e.g., Hor. *Carm.* 1.37.9). Varro, *Ling.* 5.76, connects *grex* to *greguli* (jackdaws) but allows shepherding in via comparison with Greek terminology (this strikes me as the kind of etymology perfect for some republican-era after-dinner game of Twenty Questions). Ziolkowski 1998–1999, 209, finds this most persuasive as a flotsam-and-jetsam signal, but the hook to a prehistoric Arcadian Palatine is too good to pass over. Ovid's calendrical vision in his *Fasti* is very different to Varro's, despite shared elements; Pasco-Pranger 1999–2000 and 2006 have been enormously helpful in underlining this for me.

10. Palmer 1970, 115–18, ties Carmentis persuasively to Acca (Larentia)—see "December," later in this chapter—and emphasizes her in/out (the Porta Carmentalis) qualities (on which, see, e.g., Livy 2.49.8, Ov. *Fast.* 2.201). He is not persuaded of a connection between Carmentis and Cermalus.

11. On the Parentalia (which commenced with a public sacrifice on 13 February and is a big-ticket omission in Varro), see what he might have done via Ov. *Fast.* 2.37–64; and with a hookup to the Lemuria (*Fast.* 5.25–26).

12. For the Lupercalia at *Ling.* 5.85, see chapter 6; cf. *Ling.* 6.35 (people and flock in a consubstantive relationship).

13. See North 2008, 147–49. Even if Varro made an end to his book before 44, Caesar's changes to the Lupercalia were already in play. Cic. *Cael.* 26 seems to suggest that the Lupercalia is a hangover (in its riotous sense) from a distinctly uncivilized era, lacking in formal laws and institutions. If this is in play, Varro's recuperation of Lupercalia for purification (and for or from Cicero) is especially interesting.

14. Quirina excludes Cornelian Cicero (see chapter 1).

15. Translating *ius* as "just desserts" is an attempt to catch the possible play on *ius* "sauce" or "broth" and *ius* "justice" or "right," see *OLD* s.v. *ius*^{2} 7. At Varro, *Ling.* 5.109, discussed in Spencer 2018, 59–60, cooking the meat in its own *ius* is heartily recommended.

16. Ov. *Fast.* 2.527–32.

17. Palmer 1970, 132–75.

18. See Palmer 1970, 161–62 (and on the background to Quirites/Quirinalia, at length, 162–72). Barchiesi 1997, 112–19, and Robinson 2003 have been especially influential on my reading, as has Curti 2000 on the rebooting of Quirinal as a hill of power (late fourth/early third centuries). The readings in Turfa 2006 scrutinizing the extent to which continuity is visible across archaeological and literary evidence have been invaluable.

19. Ov. *Fast.* 2.525–32; cf. Festus 304 L, 418 L.

20. Recent usefully detailed treatments of this time in Ovid (especially Ov. *Fast.* 2.551–54): Littlewood 2001, McDonough 2004.

21. Next might have followed the Regifugium (24 February)—any argument that its omission is down to its lack of divine aspect falls short when we confront the Poplifugia (*Ling.* 6.18). Ovid's treatment is extensive (*Fast.* 2.685–852). Whether or not it had its roots in the expulsion of the Tarquins, it could be (and was) represented that way. The politics of 45/44 may have made this agenda too tense.

22. Feeney 2007, 280 n. 106, is magisterial on the problem of retaining relative versus fixed days and dates in the newly lengthened months. Macr. *Sat.* 1.14.11 would (albeit later) suggest that maintaining relativity to the Ides was crucial.

23. Kent, 186–87, s.v. c.

24. Macr. *Sat.* 1.4.15.

25. *RE* 1.572–76 s.v. *agonenses* (especially 574–76 on the aspects most likely to evoke January-through-March associative links with reference to Varro's Dies Agonales and Ecurria). *RE* 2.689–700 s.v. *Argei* (especially, 693–97 on the network of connotations proposed here). Ov. *Fast.* 3.791 alludes to the March Argei; Nagy 1985 discusses their obscurity. An Argei procession took place across 16–17 March (see Palmer 1970, 84–97, on the minimal evidence, the curule significance, and plotting the shrines). See Forsythe 2012, 41–43, on the inevitability of Salii/Argei intersections in March.

26. Palmer 1970, 123; see Varro, *Ling.* 6.24. Taking 11 December for Septimontium and Agonalia.

27. Varro, *Ling.* 5.83 (connecting to the Argei rites), 5.51 (either there was a deity Quirinus, whose sanctuary gave name to the Quirinal hill, or the Quirites were from Cures, followers of Titus Tatius, and set up camp on the hill. Both versions manifest a citizen body and city-state strengthened by inclusivity and progressive transformation). *Ling.* 5.73 makes Quirinus' name derive from the *Quirites*. Palmer 1970, 172, observes of Varro's method "Scratch a Roman and find a Sabine," but it's a more nuanced project than that implies. Varro does not connect Romulus and Quirinus, but the mashup was clearly making the rounds fairly soon. Later, one can cite, e.g., Livy 1.16.6; Plut. *Vit. Rom.* 27.6, but cf. Cic. *Rep.* 2.20 (with a nod to Ennius). See Porte 1981, 305–14, and *RE* s.v. *Quirinus* cols. 1306–12.

28. For the rite of passage, see Cic. *Att.* 6.1.12. If we accept something of the rites that Augustine (*De civ. D.* 7.21) suggests that Varro recounts in honor of Liber outside Rome, then the tameness of the story in *De Lingua Latina* is extraordinary. Augustine, presumably summarizing, in horror, from *Ant. Div.*, presents this Liber as a phallic crossroads god, all about fertility, and inspiring dissolution when paraded iconically from country to town during his festival; the wreathing of the symbolic phallus by a respectable married woman is, here, the culmination.

29. "*Sic hic, quod erat post diem quintum Idus, Quinquatrus*" (thus here, since the fifth day after the Ides was the Quinquatrus, *Ling.* 6.14). Perhaps eventually reminding Cicero of his comments to Atticus, concerning the date, "*me Idus Martiae non delectant, Ille enim numquam reuertisset*," Cic. *Att.* 15.4.3.

30. Feeney 2007, 152–55, makes plain that something had to give, and it was calendrical notation. What Caesar did was "leave the festivals on the same 'day,' the same number of days after the Ides, even though this meant changing their 'date,' the notation that marked their position relative to the following Kalends" (2007, 154).

31. Cic. *Att.* 16.4. See the section "Month Names (At Last)."

32. See also Ov. *Fast.* 3.849–50, 5.725–26. The location of this Atrium is unknown.

33. Staples 1998, 103–12, analyzes the cult and ritual of Venus Verticordia persuasively, arguing that Fortuna Virilis represents one aspect of this Venus. Floratos 1960 is generally useful on the Veneralia. Fantham 1998, 115–16, teases out Ovid's position.

34. See Ov. *Fast.* 4.157–60.

35. Sulla Felix, Epaphroditos, "Aphrodite's chosen Roman," in the Greek East at least; see Balsdon 1951 (at 10).

36. See Temelini 2006 on the concrete nature of the iconography and its implications. Coin issues from 45/44 suggest the potency of this version of Venus, combining the goddess with a *nike*, globe, scepter, and star (e.g., M. H. Crawford 1974 type 480/4).

37. Cic. *Att.* 4.16–17. Dedication, 26 September (Dio Cass. 43.22.2); cf. Ov. *Fast.* 4.19–60, 6.375–76 (on Venus' family ties to Rome).

38. Varro, *Ling.* 6.15; April continues through to the end of 6.16.

39. Reasonably contemporary, Livy 29.14, 36.36 shows what Varro's audience might have "known."

40. Gell. *NA* 2.24, 18.2. Cybele's Vergilian fame: *Aen.* 2.788, 6.784–87, 7.139–40, 9.82, 10.252. Wilhelm 1988 is comprehensive on the background to an Augustan iteration.

41. See Ov. *Fast.* 4.641–66; "With the death of two cows, o king, Tellus will be reconciled to you: | let one heifer yield two lives in sacrifice," Ov. *Fast.* 4.665–66.

42. For the form Palilia (as against Parilia), Maltby 1991, s.v. *Palilia, Parilicius*.

43. On the Sabinism, see Whatmough 1921, and now Burman 2018 with extensive bibliography.

44. Quoting Freud (1930) 1991, 257–58. Linking Parilia with Romulus and Remus, see Varro, *Rust.* 2.1.9; cf. Tib. 2.5.87–90.

45. See Weinstock 1971, 184–86. On the games included in the festival in Julius Caesar's honor, see Beard, North, and Price 1998, 176. P. A. Miller 2004, 194, perceptively highlights the impact of Octavian's announcement of Caesar's deification on the Parilia for Propertius' choice of the Parilia for Tarpeia's treachery.

46. For the Parilia as Rome's birthday in this context, see Cic. *Div.* 2.98, Varro, *Rust.* 2.1.9 (cf. cf. Dion. Hal. *Ant. Rom.* 1.88.3); Rodriguez-Mayorgas 2010, 97–98.

47. Feeney 1998, 131; cf. Beard 1987 on the ambiguities of the Parilia. See also Livy 1.7.1–3.

48. For Parilia and Rome's birth from diverse origins, see Prop. 4.4.73–75; Ov. *Fast.* 4.721–862. Beard 1987 disentangles how and why the semiotics shifted in the Augustan era.

49. Fantham 1998, 230 (with references), on Ov. *Fast.* 4.733.

50. See Beard, North, and Price 1998, 15 (on ambiguities and role shifts), 45 (on the Vinalia). Feeney 2007, 199, takes Varro to task for ignoring the matter of seasonality by dropping "harvest" matters (how can one harvest grapes in April?) into the wrong (first, April) Vinalia. If readers recall this usage on reaching *Ling.* 6.36–37 (e.g.) it is evident that "gather" (i.e., physically harvest) does not have to be what's going on.

51. Venus instead figures at the "rustic" Vinalia (19 August). As we'll see, the 3 October feast of Meditrinalia combines both vintages, tacitly uniting Mars (via his priest's comments) with Jupiter and Venus.

52. Vestalia: 9 June. Only seven words.

53. Lemuria: 9, 11, 13 May (in this era).

54. Varro, *De Vita Populi Romani* 19.1 (ap. Non. 135 M); Hor. *Ep.* 2.2.208–9.

55. Ov. *Fast.* 5.4 (May as a crossroads month, challenging the wit of the etymologist), 5.71–78 (venerable age as a political force recognized by Romulus and mapped against family model—*patres*—with the newly empowered "elders" imprinting themselves on May while the younger generation follow in June—*Iunius*, for the "juniors").

56. Ov. *Fast.* 5.421, 5.428, 5.431. Ov. *Fast.* 5.419–44 (the customs associated with the festival), 445–92 (the etymology).

57. E.g., Mercury, Neptune, and Jupiter go traveling (*Fast.* 5.494–96), Mercury as a senatorially honored deity (15 May, Mercury's day and commemoration of his Circus-facing temple, *Fast.* 5.663–72; emphasizing his role as networker, go-between, and bridger of semiotic gaps), Mercury as purifier of businessmen in need of absolution, and patron of a spring by the Porta Capena (*Fast.* 5.673–92).

58. Ov. *Fast.* 5.445–46.

59. Ov. *Fast.* 5.621–62; cf. *Fas.* 3.791, and Dion. Halicar. *Ant. Rom.* 1.38.3 (complementary on the May procession).

60. Varro, *Rust.* 1.1.6.

61. Varro, *Ling.* 5.74 (Tatius, Flora et al., and Sabinism), 5.158 (the Old Capitol and the two Inclines); cf. 7.45 (reinforcing the connection between Flora and Sabine contributions; organizationally, succeeding the Argei narrative). One might have expected a telling of Remus and the Aventine somewhere in Varro's narrative, cf. Cic. *Div* 1.107.10 (*Remora* as *Roma*). Subsequently, Ov. *Fast.* 5.479 marks up the Aventine with the Remuria, cf. Dion. Hal. *Ant. Rom.* 1.85.6 (locating the site outside Rome), 1.86.2 (atop the Aventine); Plut. *Vit. Rom* 9.4, 11.1 (connecting Aventine burial augury and burial).

62. Recall *Ling.* 5.74: it is a small step, Varro says, from Sabine to Latin for anyone invoking Vesta, Salus, Fortuna, Fons, and Fides.

63. Ov. *Fast.* 6.101–82; 6.235–40 at 239; 6.241–48. At Varr. *Ling.* 6.27, where he might have drawn out Carna's story, the etymology is all about *calo*. On Carna and language, drawing in Carmentis, Habinek 2005, 251–53. Ovid's Vestalia is a tour de force taking in (among other things) the Trojan War, Palladium, prehistoric Rome, cosmic order, Priapus' attempted rape of Vesta during a really good party on Mt. Ida, and Vesta's role in saving the Capitol from the Gallic sack (*Fast.* 6.249–468).

64. Plin. *HN* 7.97 (on Pompey's Minerva); Palmer 1990 (on the foundation). Minerva was also associated with the inadvertent invention of the pipe (or flute).

65. Ov. *Fast.* 6.649–710. Other pipers/flutists in Varro, e.g., *Ling.* 6.75, 7.35 ("Tuscan"), 7.104 (drawing in Ennius), 8.61 (part of the anti-analogy argument); *Rust.* 1.2.17, 3.1.

66. Palmer 1990, 9–10, 13. The exact (and still uncertain) location is not significant for the allusion to work. Temelini 2006, 8, argues that Venus Victrix, the really showy divine relationship played up monumentally by Pompey, is also a snook cocked at Minerva, beaten both to the beauty queen prize *and* to the sexy Roman warrior (Pompey) by Venus.

67. Festus 446–48 L; cf. Val. Max. 3.7.11. On the *collegium*, see Horsfall 1976, and (judiciously) Gruen 1990, 88–91.

68. Champeaux's detailed study (1982) traces the position of Fortuna at Rome. That Fortuna could become entangled in political disputes (e.g., with Praeneste), 1982, 78–80; on Fortuna's non-Roman centers, 1982, 182–91.

69. On this kind of method, see, e.g., Lazarus 1985, 361.

70. Suetonius, making Caesar and Cicero a lit. crit. tag team for Terence: ap. Don. *Vita Ter.* 7.

71. Cicero and Caesar, Suet. *Vita Ter.* (ap. Don.); cf. Cic. *Att.* 3.7.10. Varro: "In making these distinctions, in plot it's Caecilius who takes the palm, | in characterization, Terence; in dialogue, Plautus" (Varro 399 ap. Non. 374 M). Goldberg 2005, 77, picks up on the discriminatory quality of canon formation this suggests but does not develop the Varronian context.

72. Maltby 1991 s.v. *fors, fortuna*. For *fortuna*, consider, e.g., Cic. *Leg. Man.* 47, cf. (specifically concerning the relationship between Pompey and the Roman people) 45, 49; cf. Cic. *Leg.* 2.11.28, *Balb.* 9; Caes. *BCiv.* 3.103.4. In general, see Erkell 1952, 120–28, 162–73 (addressing the issue of fickleness); for a conspectus of material in some detail, see Miano 2018, 137–47 (connecting Caesar, Fortuna, and Pompey), 152–53 (on temples).

73. Varro's fortune-telling skills were, of course, highlighted by Caesar (*BCiv.* 2.17); recall Cic. *Fam.* 9.8, and discussion in chapter 1.

74. E.g., Livy 1.39; Dion. Hal. *Ant. Rom.* 4.1. On Servius' tricksy accession, see Livy 1.41.

75. Plut. *Vit. Caes.* 59.3 proposes a Ciceronian riposte; cf. Ov. *Fast.* 1.310

76. See Orlin 2010, 36, 154–55.

77. Cf. Ov. *Fast.* 2.381–452, bundling Romulus and Remus, the Lupercal, the Circus, the Ficus Ruminalis, wolf and goats, fertility and societal meltdown, Juno, and the obscurity of childbirth/regeneration. The vision offered at *Ars am.* 1.101–34 is very differently nuanced. On divine goatiness, Wiseman 1995a.

78. Dion. Halicar. *Ant. Rom.* 2.56.5. Balsdon 1971 is still useful here; Woodard 2013, 38–49, sets Varro's account in context with Plutarch, where the association with Romulus that I find in Varro are explicitly present (via the Palus Caprae).

79. Palmer 1974 teases out Juno Caprotinae in detail.

80. First celebrated in 212. North 2000 underpins my reading: these Games were of clear antiquarian interest to a textual scholar. J. F. Miller 2009, 23–25, unpacks the associative nuances of Apollo for the early triumviral era. Back in 431 a Julian had founded Apollo's first major temple at Rome (Liv. 4.29.7), but Venus' genealogical possibilities must have seemed more promising to Caesar (and offered the chance to trump Pompey). In the wake of Caesar's death, Brutus grabbed Apollo as an icon, despite Antony's comparable attraction (both instantiated in coin issues, e.g., J. F. Miller 2009, 22 fig. 4, and summary at 2009, 30).

81. Cf. Ovid's inclusion of the Flamen Dialis as conduit to some version of Rome's prehistoric self, at the Lupercalia, *Fast.* 2.281–82. See further Holleman 1973a, 1973b.

82. Varro, *Ling.* 5.84, and cf. 7.45, a set encompassing "special priests" and their deities, including Furrina, dating to the reign of Numa.

83. "Individually each has an epithet from the god whose rites he performs; but some are obvious, others obscure," Varro, *Ling.* 5.84.

84. Cic. *Phil.* 2.110, 111.

85. One might also have hoped to hear Varro on Hercules at the Porta Trigemina, or on Castor and Pollux, or the Camenae. . . .

86. Varro, *Ling.* 5.43. Vitr. *De arch.* 4.8.4 recounts the Nemi temple's remarkability. Green 2000 is especially useful on the ramifications. It may be that in the 40s, the sanctuary's housing of the bones of Orestes was still awaiting an Augustan-era recuperation for Rome; Octavian, the new Orestes. See Champlin 2003, 309.

87. That Varro emphasized, back in April, that the first Vinalia was not Venus' day but Jupiter's helps to switch on this joke.

88. Ov. *Fast.* 3.212, 213; cf. Maltby 1991 s.v. *Consus* for this development, with detailed commentary by Riganti 1978, 116.

89. Liv. 1.9.6–16. Dion. Hal. *Ant. Rom.* 2.31.2–3 flags up the underground, hidden aspect of Consus' altar *in Circo*. Cf. Tac. *Ann.* 12.24.

90. Dion. Hal. *Ant. Rom.* 2.50.2 (cf. 6.67.2; 7.12.2, 11.39.1). Varro, *Ling.* 5.74 (like Dion. Hal. *Ant. Rom.* 2.50.3) associates Vulcan with Titus Tatius. Consensus appear to favor a location associated with (but above) the Comitium and the Temple of Concord (Livy 9.46.6). Compare Carafa 1998, 103–5, with Coarelli 1999's firm association with the Lapis Niger. Morstein-Marx 2004, 94–95, stitches together the associations with Romulus; Cornell 1995, 94, proposes that a cenotaph or heroon of Romulus is most likely as part of this nexus (see Pseud.-Acr. and Porphyry ad Hor. *Epod.* 16.13–14; cf. Festus 184 L; Dion. Hal. *Ant. Rom.* 1.87.2, 3.1.2).

91. Sumi 1997, 84–86, 98–99, vividly evokes events and reverberations surrounding Clodius' funeral; on echoes for Caesar's case, see App. *B. Civ.* 2.148 (Sumi 1997, 99, makes the connection clear).

92. On the Ficus, see Hunt 2012.

93. Recall Varro, *Ling.* 5.65, hooking up *terra* and Ops (as *Ops mater*). Maltby 1991 s.v. *Ops* teases out a parallel connection to Saturn; s.v. *Consivius*, an epithet of Janus as progenitor (Macrob. *Sat.* 1.9.15). Riganti 1978, 116–18, unpacks this material thoroughly.

94. See Takács 2008, 56–57.

95. "And '*town*' is named from '*strength*,' because it is fortified for '*strength*' in order that people may occupy it, and it's *necessary* to have safety in the place where life is spent." Cf. Varro, *Ling.* 5.64.

96. Kent switches Volturnus and Volturnalia for Vortunus and Vortunalia, which makes overall sense given *Ling.* 5.29. Lucr. 5.745, "*altitonans Volturnus*"; Varro, *Ling.* 7.45 delivers Ennius on the obscure (deriving from Numa's religious organization) Volturnal priest, attached to Volturnus.

97. Obviously if one reverts to the pre-emended "*ut Tiberinus* non," one gets something suggestive of a contrast between Volturnus (who gets linguistically assimilated) and Tiberinus (who does not), but the concluding sentence to the passage makes this unlikely.

98. In addition to the river, there was the mountain Voltur (in Samnium), but with Apulian impact (Lucr. 5.745; Hor. *Carm.* 3.4.9). See Palmer 1970, 102–3 (drawing out the augural potential, reading in Lucretius, and vultures).

99. The venerable Roman Games (including races and theatrical shows that sprawled way beyond the feast day itself, 13 September) celebrated the foundation of the Capitoline temple of Jupiter Optimus Maximus. Dion. Hal. *Ant. Rom.* 7.71.1–13 offers an extensive account, claiming authority for the description from Fabius Pictor rather than from personal observation. Dionysius uses the festival as an opportunity to underscore how Greek Roman practices are.

100. Riganti 1978, 118–19, is very doubtful regarding Varro's detail.

101. Building on *BNP*'s useful overview ("*Fasti*," Brill Online, accessed 11 November 2012, http://www.paulyonline.brill.nl/entries/brill-s-new-pauly/fasti-e410140), the Fasti Antiates Maiores, 60s (suggesting the traditional norms Varro was working with), include no other deities in the markup for the Meditrinalia. The Fasti Fratrum Arvalium (20s) and Amiterni (late Augustan/early Tiberian?) add a festival of Jupiter to the mix. For this Flaccus (whose father was also *flamen Martialis*, who was Marius' partner in the consulship, but later formalized Sulla as dictator), *BNP* s.v. V. Flaccus, L. [I.22].

102. Varro, *Ling.* 6.22.

103. Varro, *Ling.* 5.123 (water); cf. Cic. *Rep.* 6.27, *Tusc.* 1.53–54 (both linking *fons* with *origo*). Cic. *Leg.* 1.16 contextualizes a metaphorical usage (*fons* helps us access what lies beneath). Fons connects to Numa (Cic. *Leg.* 2.56) and (via C. Papirius Maso's dedication, funded by spoils) to imperial success in Corsica, back in 231 (Cic. *Nat. D.* 3.52). Maltby 1991 s.v. *Fontinalis porta* flags up a later connection between the gate and a sacred spring associated with the Fontanalia.

104. That Arn. *Adv. nat.* 3.29 much later makes Fons the son of Ianus and Iuturna, grandson of Volturnus, is a winsome addition.

105. See Palmer 1970, 231–32. The October Horse festival, linking agriculture and warfare at the place in Rome where the two are most evidently manifest (the Campus Martius), would seem to have been a perfect case for Varro's attention; indeed, Fordicidia (*Ling.* 6.15) appears to prefigure a treatment.

106. Varro, *Ling.* 6.22.

107. This material has sparked much debate; if one sticks with F ("*parent ante sexto die*") the dating sequence is still compromised (counting inclusively from Saturnalia). The Latin could with minor emendation deliver: they "offer an ancestral sacrifice on the seventh day which is called 'black.' They call it the Larentine Day of Acca Larentia." On Acca Larentia's origin stories, see Gell. *NA* 7; Macr. *Sat.* 1.10.7–17. Palmer 1970, 106–20's extensive, wide-ranging discussion (drawing in the sounds-alike January Carmentalia) is invaluable.

108. Rüpke (2001) 2007, 133–34 (in brief) and for detailed textual analysis of a tutelary name/deity nexus, see Cairns 2010. This all connects back to Varro *if* one reads in Serv. *Ad Aen.* 1.277. Flobert 1985, 95–96, provided a starting point for my reading.

109. Plin. *HN* 3.65 tells that this image of Angerona is iconic of the silence to be maintained where Rome's secret name is concerned (see Macrob. *Sat.* 3.9.2–5), but a tweak is provided from Macrobius' report that Verrius Flaccus rooted her name in the dispelling of mental cares and anguish (*angores*; Macrob. *Sat.* 1.10.7, who also cites Julius Modestus for a variant, 1.10.9). For a trenchant reanalysis, see Cairns 2010. I am persuaded, albeit on what Cairns admits to be slender evidence, of a connection between Ops and Roma feeding into this matrix (cf. Maltby 1991 s.v. *oppidum* [and recall *Ling.* 5.41], *ops*, discussed earlier with regard to Opeconsiva).

110. Palmer 1970, 75–79, interrogates the etymologies of the seven known *curiae*, Acculeia, Faucia, Foriensis, Rapta, Titia, Veliensis, Velitia; he adds two likely candidates, Tifata and Hersilia. It is likely that they emblematically represent early synoecism and thus a species of boundary-policing. Dion. Hal. *Ant. Rom.* 2.47.4 makes Varro the poster

boy for anyone interested in detaching the names of the *Curiae* from Rome's legendary Sabine women (by contrast to Varro, Cic. *Rep.* 2.14). Varro, *Ling.* 6.46 fashions a differently slanted etymology.

111. Richardson 1992, 101–2, reads the textual and narrative contiguity with Acca Larentia's tomb near the Porta Romanula to locate the Curia Acculeia somewhere in its vicinity. Factoring in Macrob. *Sat.* 1.10.7, which attaches a rite in Volupia's sacellum to Angerona's festival (on the basis that Volupia's altar featured a cult statue of Angerona with mouth bound and lips sealed), Richardson derives a cluster of connected cult sites in the Velabrum just outside the walls. By contrast, Coarelli 1983, 227–82, situates this Curia close to the Lacus Iuturnae, i.e., near where the Forum and Velabrum meet. Aronen 1993 concurs. Verzár-Bass 1998, 403, draws Acca Larentia's tomb into a wider discussion of who gets to remain dead in the city.

112. Palmer 1970, 106–15, presents a tour-de-force explanation; *BNP*, s.v. Acca Larentia sums up, but see Coarelli 2003, 50–53, on the specific issue of Acca as Mother of the Lares (his disagreement with Wiseman 1995b, on the Praenestine mirror, is not crucial for this reading). Varro, *Ling.* 9.60–61, identifies Mania as the mother of the Lares in a discussion of how men and women get their names from birth/family context (Mania from *mane*, morning-born). A connection between the dice game by means of which Acca is the victor's spoils for Hercules and Saturnalia textures the Janus motif coloring the decline of the year.

113. Varro's Porta Romanula: "*alteram Romanulam, ab Roma dictam*," *Ling.* 5.164.

114. Palmer 1970, 124, shows (implicitly) why Varro might have wanted to drag the *Pagi* into a scheme otherwise concluding the year focused on a *Curia*.

115. Varro, *Ling.* 6.25. See Stek 2009, 187–212, who brings the festival to life admirably.

116. Dion. Hal. *Ant. Rom.* 4.14.3–4. Lott 2004, 30–45, is invaluable for developing this reading.

117. Lott 2004, 38–51, explores ways in which the servile/popular associations resonated through the mid-late Republic.

118. Lott 2004, 33. Cf. Cato, *Agr.* 5.3, 57.1, which seems to bolster Varro's emphasis further. Lott 2004, 38, suggests that originally rural *uici* (founded in kinship, ethnicity, and geography) were reimagined in the urban *uici* as migrants remade the city in ways that echoed their roots.

119. On Lares, see Scheid 1990, 18–24, 587–98.

120. Lott 2004, 38; as Lott observes, one should add Macrob. *Sat.* 1.7.34–35 to Dion. Hal. *Ant. Rom.* 4.43.2 to get this full sweep, and this does mean confronting Macrobius' addition that human sacrifice was in part at issue for the festival's suppression. That said, the notion of a conflict between old and new ways is also clearly embedded in the pull between city and country celebrations, which Varro's emphasis on roads—arterial hook-ups—implicitly addresses.

121. Liv. 1.39.

122. Plin. *HN* 36.204.

123. For the abolition of the *ludi*, see Cic. *Pis.* 4, 27; first "reinstatement," in 58 (by L. Calpurnius Piso). Lott 2004, 51–59, teases out the confusion inasmuch as the evidence allows. Lott 2004, 62, notes Caesar's instatement of something like the *ludi Compitalicii*

but organized around the four urban regions instead (Suet. *Cae.* 39). The festival was restored in 7, under Augustus.

124. Cic. *Pis.* 4. Regarding fixing the Compitalia date, see Cic. *Att.* 7.7.

125. The servile agenda is also interesting, given the nearness to Acca Larentia and the sacrifice to the departed spirits of slaves, but cf. Cic. *Leg.* 2.29 for the gloss that *feriae* are intrinsically inclusive of slaves.

126. This is highlighted in Livy's account of how Compitalia saw *local* magistrates officially donning the *toga praetexta* (Livy 34.7.2), i.e., adopting the signifier of senior state magistracy. On the Paganalia, see Stek 2009, 173–80, 184–85.

127. Beacham 1999, 55–56. As Beacham observes, this kind of spectacular political space might have been used as a safety valve for public expression of opinion, but the line between facilitating lively displays of community opinion and creating a forum for fomenting discord and winding up the mob is a fine one, especially in elite perception.

128. Drawing on Habinek 2005, 251–53, and Carna/Carmentis as signs of primal sacrifice and renewal.

129. Simón 2011 activates my reading, emphasizing the significance of the journey en masse from Rome (and other towns) to what was once an Other foundational moment. Pina Polo 2011, 30–44, makes a substantial case for this festival as a prime outward-facing example of Roman civic power on parade, demonstrating its overarching role in modeling the authority and behavior of the consuls. Varro's key-term *albus/Alba*, e.g., *Ling.* 5.43, 5.144, 8.35, 8.38, 8.41, 8.80, 9.42, 9.55, 10.22, 10.24, 10.44, 10.73 (and superlatively: 8.52, 8.75). *Albula, Ling.* 5.30.

130. Varro, *Ling.* 6.24, and then here, 6.26.

131. Some say, Varro acknowledges, that it might simply be a verbal migrant from Greek (*Ling.* 5.34). But the attention lavished (by Varro) suggests otherwise (in narrative terms). At *Ling.* 5.35–36 Varro associatively links *sem-iter* (byway; he emphasizes the wordplay) to "*Ager cultus ab eo quod ibi cum terra semina coalescebant*" (Cultivated field-land, from this: the fact that there with the land the seeds united). Through-readers should recall here Varro's programmatic *semitae* (*Ling.* 5.5).

132. Recall Varro, *Ling.* 6.24, discussed in chapter 5, "Sevenheights: Ups and Downs." On Varro's Forum etymologies, see Spencer 2015a, 105–6; on agribusiness and the city/country mashup, see Spencer 2018, 52–61.

133. For the former, see, e.g., Cic. *QFr.* 3.5.1; Livy 1.31, 21.62, 23.31; for the latter, see, e.g., Hor. *Epod.* 17.48.

134. For Feralia, see *Ling.* 6.13.

135. "*Nunc iam, qui hominum causa constituti, uideamus*," Varro, *Ling.* 6.27.

136. "*Mensium nomina fere sunt aperta*," the names of months are, mostly, obvious. Varro, *Ling.* 6.33.

137. Varro, *Ling.* 5.13.

138. On the Etruscan whiff about the "Ides," see, e.g., Hor. *Carm.* 4.11.14–16.

139. Feeney 2007, 152–53, explains the detail of the rhythm.

140. Livy 6.1. Varro makes this follow on from a day known as "when the excrement has been carried away: good-speech"; this (he says) is the day when the temple of Vesta is cleansed of excrement, which is deposited at a specific place up the Capitoline Incline.

One might find in this contiguity (and Varro's decision to memorialize it) an echo of the Gaulish sack of the city, washing up, eventually unsuccessfully, against the Capitol. Cf. Ovid's rather different dynamic for the day, *Fast*. 6.713–14.

141. Cf. Varro, *Ling*. 6.51–53, which is contextually interesting: first, Varro deploys variants on "narrate" to create a sense of how a community of understanding develops through discourse, then he moves on to characterize speech as the sine qua non of humanity, after which he plugs speech into civic and territorial agenda through a discussion of *dies fasti* and *nefasti*. This connects to religious practice (*templa*) and the semiotic ontology of sacred space (*fana*, sanctuaries, are spoken into defined existence ["*pontifices in sacrando fati sint finem*"], *Ling*. 6.54).

142. Varro, *Ling*. 6.31.

143. "So, after that time, legal affairs are often conducted," Varro, *Ling*. 6.31.

144. Feeney 2007, 199–200.

145. Varro, *Ling*. 6.33; concluding at 6.34.

146. Fulvius—Servius Fulvius Flaccus, *cos*. 135; Junius—possibly M. Junius Brutus, cf. "Brutus" at Varro, *Ling*. 5.5. On the "Junius" of *Ling*. 5.42, see chapter 5, "Sevenheights: Ups and Downs"; chapter 6, "Addressing Public Office," explored the resonance of Accius' *Brutus* (*Ling*. 5.80).

147. E.g., Varro, *Ling*. 5.19, 5.15; when he etymologizes the Aventine (5.43); tackling the Suburra (with Junius' help) as a toponym grounded in morphological drift (5.48); explaining the cul-de-sac sausage and its Greek equivalent (5.111); situating the Muses firmly on *Mount* Olympus (7.20); a trope, curtailing his prolixity (7.109); on natural and imposed regularities of declension and their ethnoscapes—Rome and Tibur, two nouns, jostle with *dico* to ratify diversity as a meaningful part of the system(s) (9.34). Cf. *Arbitror*, discussed in chapter 2.

148. Ovid's preface to May in his *Fasti* would later give voice to Calliope for the opposition: *Maia*, most beautiful of the Pleiades and mother of Mercury, has a connection to Arcadian Evander that draws her into the prophesied foundation of Rome (*Fast*. 5.91–96). Cf. Ov. *Fast*. 5.599–602, where the Pleiades rising mark the turn of the seasons, ushering in Summer.

149. Varro, *Ling*. 6.34.

150. Recall chapter 1 on writing/editing circles of production. One might also cite, e.g., Varro's Curia Hostilia (no whispers of "Cornelia" or of the "Julia," completed by Augustus; no indication of an absence/building site where the Hostilia stood; see Coarelli 1993c) as an example of his interest in eliding contemporaneity (*Ling*. 5.155).

151. Ramsey and Licht 1997, 44–47, are invaluable, putting order to a wealth of detail mapping a clear trajectory for the festal tweaks taking place from Spring through to Summer 44. An additional argument for grabbing Quintilis for Caesar might well be the very one that Varro elides when cataloguing the months: it's the first month not otherwise marked by a divine, ritual, or civic tag.

152. Reading in Varro, *Ex Ephemeride* 230 (ap. Prisc. *GL*. 2.256 K), we get a succinct "quote" indicating Varro plugging the new name July into the system, and we know that Varro was interested in what the new Julian calendar could do (e.g., *Rust*. 1.27–28). There is no way to tell whether July was already named when he was first working on his

study of Latin. Rüpke (1995) 2011, 114–18, argues for real delicacy on Caesar's part in reframing the calendar (by vivid comparison with the French Revolutionary calendar reforms), but Feeney 2007, 184–89, better captures this as a shift from "the idealized corporatism of the Republic" (2007, 184) to the increasingly explicit personalization that Caesar's intervention made way for.

153. "*Id est Lupercis nudis lustratur antiquum oppidum Palatinum gregibus humanis cinctum*," *Ling.* 6.34. Cf. *Ling.* 6.13, discussed earlier in this chapter in the section "Almost Missing February."

154. Cic. *Phil.* 2.84–87.

Conclusion

1. Thomas 1974, 112.

2. "*Multi posterorum cum Varrone conferent sermonem de lingua latina*," Vitr. *De arch.* 9 Pr. 17.

3. E.g., when an "expert" (*artifex*) gets an area of expertise (*ars*) wrong, for instance the science of speech (*scientia orationis*), he is not disproving the system (*ratio*) but rather "laying bare his own lack of scientific knowledge" (*Ling.* 9.111, 112). See Henderson 2007, 5–9, 24, developing a comparable agenda developed around Isidore of Seville.

4. Shillingsburg 1997, 9.

5. Beckett 1967, 85.

6. On Varro's scholarly identity, see, e.g., Cic. *Brut.* 60; Quint. 10.1.95; Plin. *HN* 7.115; Gell. 4.9, 4.16, 14.7, 19.14; Aug. *De civ. D.* 6.2, 7.5, 19.22. Varro's enthusiasm for commandeering Latin's literary luminaries was tempered by a recognition of the fallibility of the "*opinor*" proof (recall Introduction, and chapters 2, 4); human perception is partial.

7. Eco 1984, 79, outlines some of the authoritative possibilities for "blowing up" (tactically expanding on) and "narcotizing" (controlled reticence) in the encyclopedic mode; cf. strategies outlined in Carey 2003, Murphy 2004, Henderson 2007, Gunderson 2009, Keulen 2009, Rust 2009.

8. One might compare this at least implicit agenda with Cicero's schematization of the beginnings and development of *ex tempore* oratory in Rome and the productive friction he envisages between a primary act (considered writing/composition) and a secondary process (speech/scripted performance) versus the unthinking world of the rhetorician for hire; e.g., Cic. *De or.* 1.202, 2.86 (cf. 1.83 versus 2.88—in effect, speaking one's mind works as a tactic for the young man); *Brut.* 226 (rabid speakers), 325 (rapid-fire oratory is un-Roman).

9. Here, see Ricoeur (1975) 1977.

10. Caesar's *De Analogia* was probably composed between 55 and 52 BCE. Gurd 2007, 56–68, is enormously useful for positioning Caesar within this analysis.

11. See Sinclair 1994.

12. Cic. *Brut.* 252–55. *Copia* (Cic. *Brut.* 253, 255) is particularly interesting, here, in conjunction with Cicero's emphasis on mapping the limits and rewards of military activity versus different species of linguistic endeavor.

13. Sinclair 1994 is excellent for contextualizing Caesar's role as language policeman (see also Rambaud 1979).

14. Lowrie 2009, 135–39, analyses this material compellingly.
15. See Cic. *De or.* 3.150.
16. Cf. Cic. *Brut.* 262.
17. Funaioli fr. 2.1, ap. Gell. 1.10.4. On Caesar the grammarian, see Willi 2010.
18. We might look back, here, to Gill's eloquently developed analysis of the classical "self," whereby reason, a key marker for humanity, is the vehicle for the delivery of a "good" (ethical) life. Human reason is a quality that is susceptible to representation and scrutiny in a public or collective context, and the act of undertaking such scrutiny is a significant feature of what makes the individual a microcosm of society and, at the same time, an active and self-aware participant in a process of identify formation that works both ways: Gill 1996, 11–12; 2006, 343; see also Kaster 2005, 132–40.
19. Hendrickson 1906 argued that the embellishment of speech ascribed here to Caesar is a comment on lavish "Asianism" in Latin eloquence, but he sees more contiguity between *De Oratore* and *Brutus* than I do.
20. Fronto 221 N.
21. Wray 2001, 208; cf. Wallace-Hadrill 2008, 69–70.
22. Gell. *N.A.* 19.8.7 (Funaioli fr. 3a.1) cites Caesar on "plurality," suggesting congruence with Caesar in Varro's position (but not his examples, as things stand).
23. For Cicero, see especially *De or.* 3.37–39, 48. This summary inevitably draws on Garcea 2012.
24. Ax 1995 is keen to see books 8–10 read in the context of 5–7 and argues that literariness is a key factor in understanding potential inconsistencies in the latter triad (in the context of reopening the vexed question of when the work as a whole was published).
25. Varro, *Ling.* 8.48. In a Menippean fragment (Bücheler 244.2, ap. Non. 204M) Varro links *cicer* to another homely food plant, *eruilia* (bitter vetch).
26. Plut. *Cic.* 1 gives us this joke on Cicero's name; we might, I think, reasonably assume that Plutarch's audience was not hearing the joke for the first time—he presents the pun as grounded in a nasally challenged ancestor, to whom the descriptive tag stuck, but has Cicero enhance it with a visual wordplay requesting an engraved chickpea as his icon. Varro's revised versions of the solitary chickpea: e.g. *Ling.* 9.63, 10.54.
27. Varro, *Ling.* 10.53.
28. Varro, *Ling.* 10.54.
29. Varro, *Ling.* 10.56. This passage has had significant emendation, so I have not leaned too heavily on the specific words in play. The final sentence (which stands securely) suggests that the emendations are delivering something pretty close to what was intended.
30. Varro could fairly expect readers to recall the early paradigmatic appearance of the Menaechmi in this triad of books (*Ling.* 8.42; the drama also featured at 7.54, 56).
31. Briskly introduced by Ferrer i Cancho 2008.
32. Coins, copper and silver, come in full and half sizes; hence, making this elemental, "*cum utrubique dicimus et in aere et in argento esse eandem rationem, tum dicimus de analogia*" (when we say that as in copper so in silver there is the same organizational principle, then we are talking about analogy, *Ling.* 10.38).
33. It remains important not to lean too heavily on orthography for the Greek terms; in *F*, a consistent case is difficult to articulate, and scribal choice is also a factor. As usual,

I am maintaining the text as presented by Kent 1951 (*F* is particularly faint at crucial points, here, too). Transliteration, if "original," can also deliver a message (see, e.g., Boldrer 2003), but a detailed argument is not sustainable here.

34. Varro, *Ling.* 8.23; cf. 8.64 on the problem of alphabets and naming. Cf. relevant examples dotted through Pl. *Cra.* 399c, 415cd, 419a, 437ab, on which Ademollo 2011 is invaluable.

35. As Varro puts it: "*debebis suptilius audire quam dici expectare . . . ut potius tu persequare animo*" (*Ling.* 10.40).

36. Cf. Xen. *Cyr.* 1.1, *Oec.* 9.14–15, 21.2.

37. "*Quae cum inter se tanta sint cognatione, debebis suptilius audire quam dici expectare, id est cum dixero quid de utroque et erit co<m>mune, <ne> expectes, dum ego in scribendo transferam in reliquum, sed ut potius tu persequare animo*," Varro, *Ling.* 10.40.

38. A nice example of how he makes the "anti-" case: *Ling.* 8.26–33, 37–43.

39. Varro, *Ling.* 9.3. Cf., e.g., Varro, *Ling.* 9.31–32, 45–46, 111–12.

40. We do need to keep in mind that we are missing the end of book 8 and the beginning of book 9, typically two key programmatic sites for Varro, as the relationship between the end of book 9 and opening of book 10, here, makes clear. See, e.g., *Ling.* 9.112–13. Cuzzolin and Haverling 2009 make a strong case, especially meaningful in this context, for finding genre trouble articulated in grammar, and, despite the missing programmatics, Varro's examples and analysis easily provoke alternative readings.

41. Varro, *Ling.* 10.1. At *Ling.* 10.75–76 Varro refines the statement—too much emphasis on the trees and not enough sense of the wood is what he's getting at, and grammarians such as Aristeas, Aristodemus, and Aristocles are not escaping censure; Varro does it better because Varro delivers a point-by-point exposition of the key terminology. A little later (*Ling.* 10.79–83) Varro is just beginning to discuss the instances where one should avoid seeking Regularity in discourse, namely indeclinables and others, but the book breaks off abruptly.

42. Varro, *Ling.* 10.72.

43. Not without some subtle self-congratulation, Varro explains all these terms and concepts at *Ling.* 10.77–78 (having demolished his own alt. persona's book 8 arguments explicitly at *Ling.* 9.111–12), saying that the poor professorial skills of authors writing on the subject of Regularity provide no sane argument for denying its existence—individuals who get it wrong expose their own inadequacy rather than affecting the underlying principle.

44. For this in the Elder Pliny, see, e.g., Carey 2003, Murphy 2004. More generally, Lisdorf 2004, developed at Lisdorf 2007, 206–23, when discussing the role of prodigies as both culture-fashioning and culturally conditioned, suggests that the plausible or minimally counterintuitive prodigy is more of an attention-grabber than the wholly bizarre or entirely intelligible (adapting his terminology). Kroll and Dusias 2005 set out the big issues on discourse and bilingualism succinctly, part of the comprehensive collection edited by Bhatia and Ritchie.

45. E.g., Doody 2010.

46. Foucault 1966, 86–91, 92–136 and passim.

47. Working here with the model Varro himself pushes—the uniqueness of his project and the linguist's expertise (e.g., *Ling.* 5.5). Varro does not (e.g.) cite his contemporary, P. Nigidius Figulus (Gellius' second-favorite scholar, Gell. 4.9.1) in the extant *De Lingua Latina*.

48. Foucault (1969) 2002, 23–24.

49. Wittgenstein (1953) 2009, §66, 67 (using the standard paragraph numbering). Ultimately, this returns the methodologies of network theory to the foreground.

50. Foucault (1969) 2002, 24.

51. For the theory, see Assmann 1995.

52. Cavazza 1981, 73, articulates the "*forma di pensiero*," albeit less convinced about the structural quality.

53. Dionysius of Halicarnassus' version of Latin claims to draw upon Varro for his account of Rome's origins, but only explicitly on his *Antiquitates*; see, e.g., de Jonge 2008, 64; Hill 1961. On the relationship between words and reality in antiquity more generally, see Calboli 1992, Manetti (1987) 1993, Sluiter 1990. On Dionysius, see de Jonge 2008, 53–59, noting that Dionysius "is always aware of the relationship between the form of words and their meaning, and he is concerned with the propriety (τὸ πρέπον) that should exist between the two: both the selection of words and the composition should be appropriate to the subject matter (τὸ ὑποκείμενον), the 'subject matter that underlies the words'" (54).

54. Aug. *De civ. D.* 6.2.

55. Petrarch, *Rerum Familiarium Libri* 24.6 (18.4 sees him thanking Boccaccio for a text of Varro).

56. See Foucault (1969) 2002, 25, 26–27.

57. "His ancient rubbish isn't entirely useless, / It serves to pass the time, anyway. / And one can for the most part bear the Grubs [les Varrons], / Even as one adores the Virgils."

Bibliography

Adams, J. N. 1982. *The Latin Sexual Vocabulary*. London: Duckworth.
———. 2003a. *Bilingualism and the Latin Language*. Cambridge: Cambridge University Press.
———. 2003b. "*Romanitas* and the Latin Language." *Classical Quarterly* 53, no. 1: 184–205.
———. 2007. *The Regional Diversification of Latin: 200 BC–AD 600*. Cambridge: Cambridge University Press.
Adams, J. N., M. Janse, and S. Swain, eds. 2002. *Bilingualism in Ancient Society: Language Contact and the Written Text*. Oxford: Oxford University Press.
Ademollo, F. 2011. *The Cratylus of Plato: A Commentary*. Cambridge: Cambridge University Press.
Ady, P. 1986. "Reading as a Communal Act of Discovery: *Finnegans Wake* in the Classroom." *Reader*, no. 16 (Fall): 50–62. http://www1.assumption.edu/users/ady/HHGateway/Etexts/adyfwrr.html.
Alden Smith, R. 2005. *The Primacy of Vision in Virgil's Aeneid*. Austin: University of Texas Press.
Aldrete, G. S. 2007. *Floods of the Tiber in Ancient Rome*. Baltimore, MD: Johns Hopkins University Press.
Anderson, B. 2006. *Imagined Communities: Reflections on the Origin and Spread of Nationalism*. 2nd rev. ed. London: Verso.
Anderson, G. 2004. "Aulus Gellius as a Storyteller." In L. Holford-Strevens and A. D. Vardi 2004, 105–17.
Ando, C. 2002. "Vergil's Italy: Ethnography and Politics in First-Century Rome." In *Clio and the Poets: Augustan Poetry and the Traditions of Ancient Historiography*, edited by D. S. Levene and D. P. Nelis, 123–42. Leiden: Brill.
———. 2005. "Interpretatio Romana." *Classical Philology* 100, no. 1: 41–51.
———. 2008. *The Matter of the Gods: Religion and the Roman Empire*. Berkeley: University of California Press.
Andreussi, M. 1996. "Luna, Aedes." In *LTUR* vol. III, 198.
Arkenberg, J. S. 1993. "Licinii Murenae, Terentii Varrones, and Varrones Murenae: I. A Prosopographical Study of Three Roman Families." *Historia* 42, no. 3: 326–51.

Aronen, J. 1993. "Curia Acculeia." In *LTUR* vol. I, 329–30.
———. 1996. "Noctiluca, Templum." In *LTUR* vol. III, 345.
Arrigoni, G. 1982. *Camilla, Amazzone e Sacerdotessa di Diana*. Milan: Cisalpino Goliardica.
Asmis, E. 2005. "A New Kind of Model: Cicero's Roman Constitution in *De republica*." *American Journal of Philology* 126, no. 3: 377–416.
Assmann, J. 1995. "Collective Memory and Cultural Identity." Translated by J. Czaplicka. *New German Critique* 65:125–33.
Astbury, R. 1967. "Varro and Pompey." *Classical Quarterly* n.s. 17, no. 2: 403–7.
Astin, A. E. 1985. "Cicero and the Censorship." *Classical Philology* 80, no. 3: 233–39.
———. 1988a. "Livy's Report of the *Lectio Senatus* and the *Recognitio Equitum* in the Censorship of 169-8 BC." *Historia* 37, no. 4: 487–90.
———. 1988b. "*Regimen Morum*." *Journal of Roman Studies* 78:14–34.
Atherton, C. 2005. "Lucretius on What Language Is Not." In D. Frede and B. Inwood 2005, 101–38.
Austin, J. L. 1962. *How to Do Things with Words*. Cambridge, MA: Harvard University Press.
Ax, W. 1995. "*Disputare in Utramque Partem*: Zum literarischen Plan und zur dialektischen Methode Varros in *De Lingua Latina* 8-10." *Rheinisches Museum* 138, no. 2: 146–77.
———. 1996. "Pragmatic Arguments in Morphology: Varro's Defence of Analogy in Book 9 of His *De Lingua Latina*." In P. Swiggers and A. Wouters 1996a, 105–19.
———. 2011. "Quintilian's 'Grammar' (*Inst.* 1.4-8) and Its Importance for the History of Roman Grammar." In S. Matthaios, F. Montanari, and A. Rengakos, eds. 2011, 331–46.
Bachelard, G. (1958) 1994. *The Poetics of Space*. Translated by M. Jolas. Boston, MA: Beacon Press.
Badian, E. 1972. "Ennius and His Friends." In *Ennius: Entretiens sur l'Antiquité Classique*, edited by O. Skutsch, 149–208. Entretiens de la Fondation Hardt 17. Geneva: Fondation Hardt.
———. 2009. "From the Iulii to Caesar." In Griffin 2009, 11–22.
Baier, T. 1997. *Werk und Wirkung Varros im Spiegel seiner Zeitgenossen: Von Cicero bis Ovid*. Hermes Einzelschriften 73. Stuttgart: Steiner.
———. 1999. "Myth and Politics in Varro's Historical Writings." *Échos du Monde Classique* n.s. 18, no. 3: 351–67.
———. 2001. "Varrone tra Analogia e Anomalia: Riflessioni sulla Teoria dell'Origine della Lingua e della Cultura in Varrone." In G. Calboli 2001, 1–19.
Baldarelli, B. 2004. *Accius und die vortrojanische Pelopidensage*. Paderborn: Schöningh.
Baldi, P. 1999. *The Foundations of Latin*. Rev. ed. 2002. Berlin: Mouton de Gruyter.
Baldi, P., and P. Cuzzolin, eds. 2009. *New Perspectives on Historical Latin Syntax 1: Syntax of the sentence*. Berlin: Mouton de Gruyter.
Balsdon, J. P. V. D. 1951. "Sulla Felix." *Journal of Roman Studies* 41:1–10.
———. 1971. "Dionysius on Romulus: A Political Pamphlet?" *Journal of Roman Studies* 61:18–27.
Barchiesi. A. 1997. *The Poet and the Prince*. Berkeley: University of California Press.

Barker, C., and D. Galasiński. 2001. *Cultural Studies and Discourse Analysis: A Dialogue on Language and Identity*. London: Sage.
Barnes, J. 1989. "Antiochus of Ascalon." In *Philosophia Togata: Essays on Philosophy and Roman Society*, edited by M. Griffin and J. Barnes, 51–96. Oxford: Clarendon Press.
Barney, R. 2001. *Names and Nature in Plato's Cratylus*. New York: Routledge.
Barrett, J. L. 2011. "Cognitive Science of Religion: Looking Back, Looking Forward." *Journal for the Scientific Study of Religion* 50, no. 2: 229–39.
Barthes, R. (1964) 1967. *Elements of Semiology*. Translated by A. Lavers and C. Smith. London: Jonathan Cape.
Baudelaire, C. (1863) 1965. "The Painter of Modern Life." In *The Painter of Modern Life, and Other Essays*, edited and translated by J. Mayne, 1–40. London: Phaidon.
Baudrillard, J. (1981) 1983. *Simulations*. Translated by P. Foss, P. Patton, and P. Beitchman. New York: Semiotext(e).
Baxter, T. M. S. 1992. *Cratylus: Plato's Critique of Naming*. Philosophia Antiqua 58. Leiden: Brill.
Beacham, R. C. 1999. *Spectacle Entertainments of Early Imperial Rome*. New Haven, CT: Yale University Press.
Beard, M. 1986. "Cicero and Divination: The Formation of a Latin Discourse." *Journal of Roman Studies* 76:33–46.
———. 1987. "A Complex of Times: No More Sheep on Romulus' Birthday." *Proceedings of the Cambridge Philological Society* 33:1–15.
———. 1989. "Acca Larentia Gains a Son: Myths and Priesthood at Rome." In *Images of Authority: Papers Presented to Joyce Reynolds on the Occasion of Her Seventieth Birthday*, edited by M. M. Mackenzie and C. Roueché, 41–61. Papers of the Cambridge Philological Society Suppl. 16. Cambridge: Cambridge Philological Society.
———. 1990. "Priesthood in the Roman Republic." In M. Beard and J. North 1990, 17–48.
———. 1994. "The Roman and the Foreign: The Cult of the 'Great Mother' in Imperial Rome." In *Shamanism, History, and the State*, edited by N. Thomas and C. Humphrey, 164–90. Ann Arbor: University of Michigan Press.
———. 2002. "Ciceronian Correspondences: Making a Book out of Letters." In *Classics in Progress: Essays on Ancient Greece and Rome*, edited by T. P. Wiseman, 103–44. London/Oxford: Oxford University Press.
———. 2007. *The Roman Triumph*. Cambridge, MA: Belknap/Harvard University Press.
———. 2012. "Cicero's 'Response of the *Haruspices*' and the Voice of the Gods." *Journal of Roman Studies* 102:20–39.
Beard, M., and J. North., eds. 1990. *Pagan Priests: Religion and Power in the Ancient World*. London: Duckworth.
Beard, M., J. North, and S. Price. 1998. *Religions of Rome*. Vol. 1, *A History*. Cambridge: Cambridge University Press.
Beck, H., A. Duplá, M. Jehne, and F. P. Polo, eds. 2011. *Consuls and Res Publica: Holding High Office in the Roman Republic*. Cambridge: Cambridge University Press.
Beckett, S. 1967. *Stories and Texts for Nothing*. New York: Grove Press.
Bell, A. J. E. 1997. "Cicero and the Spectacle of Power." *Journal of Roman Studies* 87:1–22.

Beness, J. L., and T. W. Hillard. 2001. "The Theatricality of the Deaths of C. Gracchus and Friends." *Classical Quarterly* 51, no. 1: 135–40.

Benjamin, W. (1927–40; 1982) 1999. *The Arcades Project*. Translated by H. Eiland and K. McLaughlin. Cambridge, MA: Harvard University Press.

——. (1935–39) 1997. *Charles Baudelaire: A Lyric Poet in the Era of High Capitalism*. Translated by H. Zohn. New York: Verso.

Benveniste, É. (1966–74) 1971. *Problems in General Linguistics*. Translated by M. E. Meek. Coral Gables, FL: University of Miami Press.

Benveniste, É., N. Chomsky, I. Fónagy, R. Jakobson, J. Kurylowicz, M. Leroy, A. Martinet, G. C. Paude, S. K. Šaumjan, A. Schaff, and A. Sommerfelt. 1966. *Problèmes du Langage*. Paris: Gallimard.

Berman, D. W. 2004. "The Double Foundation of Boiotian Thebes." *Transactions of the American Philological Association* 134, no. 1: 1–22.

Bettini, M. 2006. "Mythos/Fabula: Authoritative and Discredited Speech." *History of Religions* 45, no. 3: 195–212.

——. 2008. "Weighty Words, Suspect Speech: *Fari* in Roman Culture." *Arethusa* 41, no. 2: 313–75.

Bezzola, G., and R. Ramat, ed. and text. 1957. *Trionfi di Francesco Petrarca*. Milan: Rizzoli.

Bhatia, T. K., and W. C. Ritchie, eds. 2005. *The Handbook of Bilingualism*. Malden, MA: Blackwell.

Billows, R. 1989. "Legal Fiction and Political Reform at Rome in the Early Second Century BC." *Phoenix* 43, no. 2: 112–33.

Binder, G. 1997. "Kommunikative Elemente im römischen Staatskult am Ende der Republik: das Beispiel des Lupercalia des Jahres 44." In *Religiöse Kommunikation, Formen unde Praxis von der Neuzeit*, edited by G. Binder and K. Ehlich, 225–41.Trier: Wissenschaftlicher Verl. Trier.

Bispham, E. 2007. *From Asculum to Actium: The Municipalization of Italy from the Social War to Augustus*. Oxford: Clarendon Press.

Bispham, E., and C. J. Smith, eds. 2000. *Religion in Archaic and Republican Rome and Italy: Evidence and Experience*. Edinburgh: Edinburgh University Press.

Bittarello, M. B. 2009. "The Construction of Etruscan 'Otherness' in Latin Literature." *Greece and Rome* 56, no. 2: 211–33.

Biville, F. 1989. "Grec et Latin: Contacts Linguistiques et Création Lexicale. Pour une Typologie des Hellénismes Lexicaux du Latin." In *Actes du Ve Colloque de Linguistique Latine, Louvain-la-Neuve/Borzée, 31 Mars–4 Avril 1989*, edited by M. Lavency and D. Longrée, 29–40. CILL 15, nos. 1–4. Leuven: Peeters.

——. 2000. "Bilinguisme Gréco-Latin et Créations Éphémères de Discours." In M. Fruyt and C. Nicolas 2000, 91–107.

Blank, D. 2005. "Varro's Anti-Analogist." In D. Frede and B. Inwood 2005, 210–38.

——. 2008. "Varro and the Epistemological Status of Etymology." *Histoire Épistémologie Langage* 30:49–73.

Bloomer, W. M. 1997a. *Latinity and Literary Society at Rome*. Philadelphia: University of Pennsylvania Press.

———. 1997b. "Schooling in *Persona*: Imagination and Subordination in Roman Education." *Classical Antiquity* 16, no. 1: 57–78.

———. 2011. *The School of Rome: Latin Studies and the Origins of Liberal Education*. Berkeley: University of California Press.

Blum, H. 1969. *Die Antike Mnemotechnik*. Hildesheim: Georg Olms.

Boissier, G. 1861. *Étude sur la Vie et les Ouvrages de M. T. Varron*. Paris: Librairie de L. Hachette.

Boldrer, F. 2003. "Il Bilinguismo di Cicerone: *Scripta Graeca Latina* (*fam.* 15, 4)." In R. Oniga 2003, 131–50.

Bourdieu, P. 1977. *Outline of a Theory of Practice*. Translated by R. Nice. Cambridge: Cambridge University Press.

———. (1980) 1990. *The Logic of Practice*. Translated by R. Nice. Stanford, CA: Stanford University Press.

Boyd, B. W. 1992. "Virgil's Camilla and the Traditions of Catalogue and Ecphrasis (*Aeneid* 7.803–17)." *American Journal of Philology* 113, no. 2: 213–34.

Boyer, M. C. 1994. *The City of Collective Memory: Its Historical Imagery and Architectural Entertainments*. Cambridge, MA: MIT Press.

Brandenburg, P. n.d. http://www.varro-grammaticus.de/index.html.

Braund, D., and C. Gill, eds. 2003. *Myth, History, and Culture in Republican Rome: Studies in Honour of T. P. Wiseman*. Exeter: University of Exeter Press.

Braund, S. 2006. "A Tale of Two Cities: Statius, Thebes, and Rome." *Phoenix* 60, no. 3/4: 259–73.

Breed, B. W., C. Damon, and A. F. Rossi, eds. 2010. *Citizens of Discord: Rome and Its Civil Wars*. New York: Oxford University Press.

Brennan, T. C. 2000. *The Praetorship in the Roman Republic*. Vol. 1. New York: Oxford University Press.

Brenneis, D., and R. K. S. Macaulay, eds. 1996. *The Matrix of Language: Contemporary Linguistic Anthropology*. Boulder, CO: Westview Press.

Briquel, D. 1996. "La Tradizione Letteraria sull'Origine dei Sabini: Qualche Osservazione." In G. Maetzke and L. Tamagno Perna 1996, 29–40.

Briscoe, J. 2010. "The Fragments of Cato's *Origines*." In E. Dickey and A. Chahoud 2010, 154–60.

Brisset, A. 2004. "The Search for a Native Language: Translation and Cultural Identity." In *The Translation Studies Reader*, edited by L. Venuti, 337–68. 2nd ed. London: Routledge. [= Brisset, A. 1996. *A Sociocritique of Translation: Theatre and Alterity in Quebec, 1968–1988*. Translated by R. Gill and R. Gannon. Toronto: University of Toronto Press.]

Broadhead, W. 2007. "Colonization, Land Distribution, and Veteran Settlement." In P. Erdkamp 2007, 148–63.

Brockmeier, J. 2002. "Remembering and Forgetting: Narrative as Cultural Memory." *Culture & Psychology* 8, no. 1: 15–43.

Brown, P., and S. C. Levinson. 1987. *Politeness: Some Universals in Language Usage*. Cambridge: Cambridge University Press.

Brown, R. D. 1982. "Lucretius and Callimachus." *Illinois Classical Studies* 7, no. 1: 77–97.

Bryant, J. 2002. *The Fluid Text: A Theory of Revision and Editing for Book and Screen.* Ann Arbor: University of Michigan Press.

Burgin, V. 1996. *In/Different Spaces: Place and Memory in Visual Culture.* Berkeley: University of California Press.

Burman, A. C. 2018. "De Lingua Sabina: A Reappraisal of the Sabine Glosses." PhD diss. https://doi.org/10.17863/CAM.18502.

Butler, S. 2002. *The Hand of Cicero.* London: Routledge.

Cagniart, P. 2007. "The Late Republican Army (146–30 BC)." In P. Erdkamp 2007, 80–95.

Cairns, F. 1996. "Ancient 'Etymology' and Tibullus: On the Classification of 'Etymologies' and on 'Etymological Markers.'" *Proceedings of the Cambridge Philological Society* 42:24–59.

———. 2010. "*Roma* and Her Tutelary Deity: Names and Ancient Evidence." In *Ancient Historiography and Its Contexts: Studies in Honour of A. J. Woodman,* edited by C. S. Kraus, J. Marincola, and C. B. R. Pelling, 245–66. Oxford: Oxford University Press.

Calboli, G. 1992. "Bedeutung." In *Historisches Wörterbuch der Rhetorik,* edited by G. Ueding, 1372–99. Tübingen: Niemeyer.

———. 2001a. *Papers on Grammar VI.* Bologna: CLUEB.

———. 2001b. "Varrone e la Teoria dei Casi." In G. Calboli 2001a, 33–59.

———. 2009. "Latin Syntax and Greek." In P. Baldi and P. Cuzzolin 2009, 65–194.

Cancik, H. 1985–86. "Rome as Sacred Landscape: Varro and the End of Republican Religion in Rome." *Visible Religion* 4/5:250–65.

Capdeville, G. 1992. "La Jeunesse de Camille." *Mélanges de l'École Française de Rome. Antiquité* 104:303–38.

———. 1996. "Modius Fabidius: Una Versione sabina della Leggenda del Primo Re." In G. Maetzke and L. Tamagno Perna 1996, 49–85.

Carafa, P. 1998. *Il Comizio di Roma dalle Origini all'età di Augusto.* Bullettino della Commissione Archeologica Comunale di Roma Suppl. 5. Rome: L'Erma di Bretschneider.

Cardauns, B. 1976. *M. Terentius Varro Antiquitates Rerum Divinarum.* Wiesbaden: Steiner.

———. 2001. *Marcus Terentius Varro: Einführung in sein Werk.* Heidelberg: Universitätsverlag C. Winter.

Carey, S. 2003. *Pliny's Catalogue of Culture: Art and Empire in the Natural History.* Oxford: Oxford University Press.

Carruthers, M. 1992. "Inventional Mnemonics and the Ornaments of Style: The Case of Etymology." *Connotations* 2, no. 2: 103–14.

———. 2010. "The Concept of *Ductus,* Or Journeying through a Work of Art." In *Rhetoric Beyond Words,* edited by M. Carruthers, 190–213. Cambridge: Cambridge University Press.

Casey, E. S. 1993. *Getting Back into Place: Toward a Renewed Understanding of the Place-World.* Bloomington: Indiana University Press.

———. 2000. *Remembering: A Phenomenological Study.* 2nd ed. Bloomington: Indiana University Press.

———. 2001. "Between Geography and Philosophy: What Does It Mean to Be in the Place-World?" *Annals of the Association of American Geographers* 91, no. 4:683–93.

Cavazza, F. 1981. *Studio su Varrone Etimologo e Grammatico: La Lingua Latina come Modello di Struttura Linguistica.* Florence: La Nuova Italia.

———. 2004. "Gellius the Etymologist: Gellius' Etymologies and Modern Etymology." In L. Holford-Strevens and A. D. Vardi 2004, 65–104.

Champeaux, J. 1982. *Fortuna: Recherches sur le Culte de la Fortuna à Rome et dans le Monde Romaine des Origines à la Mort de César.* CEFR(A) 64. Rome: École Française de Rome.

Champlin, E. 2003. "Agamemnon at Rome: Roman Dynasts and Greek Heroes." In D. C. Braund and C. Gill 2003, 295–319.

Christol, A., and O. Spevak, eds. 2012. *Les Évolutions du Latin.* Paris: L'Harmattan.

Cifani, G. 2018. "Visibility Matters: Notes on Archaic Monuments and Collective Memory in Mid-Republican Rome." In *Omnium Annalium Monumenta: Historical Writing and Historical Evidence in Republican Rome*, edited by K. Sandberg and C. Smith, 390–403. Leiden: Brill.

Citroni, M., ed. 2003. *Memoria e Identità: La Cultura Romana Costruisce la Sua Immagine.* Florence: Università degli Studi di Firenze, Dipartamento di Scienze dell'Antichità.

Clackson, J., ed. 2011a. *A Companion to the Latin Language.* Chichester: Wiley-Blackwell.

———. 2011b. "The Forms of Latin: Inflectional Morphology." In J. Clackson 2011a, 105–17.

———. 2011c. "The Social Dialects of Latin." In J. Clackson 2011a, 505–26.

Clackson, J., and G. C. Horrocks. 2007. *The Blackwell History of the Latin Language.* Malden, MA: John Wiley and Sons.

Clark, A. C., ed. 1907. *Q. Asconii Pediani Orationum Ciceronis Quinque Enarratio.* Oxford: Clarendon Press.

Coarelli, F. 1983. *Il Foro Romano: Il Periodo Arcaico.* Rome: Quasar.

———. 1988. *Il Foro Boario dalle Origine alla Fine della Repubblica.* Rome: Quasar.

———. 1993a. "Ad Busta Gallica." In *LTUR* vol. I, 203–4.

———. 1993b. "Comitium." In *LTUR* vol. I, 309–14.

———. 1993c. "Curia Hostilia." In *LTUR* vol. I, 331–32.

———. 1995a. "Doliola." In *LTUR* vol. II, 20–21.

———. 1995b. "Forum Boarium." In *LTUR* vol. II, 295–97.

———. 1996. "Mundus." In *LTUR* vol. III, 288–89.

———. 1999. "Umbilicus Romae." In *LTUR* vol. V, 95–96.

———. 2003. "Remoria." In D. C. Braund and C. Gill 2003, 41–55.

Coffey, M. 1976. *Roman Satire.* London: Methuen.

Coleman, R. G. G. 1990. "Dialectal Variation in Republican Latin, with Special Reference to Praenestine." *Proceedings of the Cambridge Philological Society* n.s. 36:1–25.

———. 2001. "Varro as an Etymologist." *Journal of Latin Linguistics* 6, no. 1: 61–96.

Collart, J. 1954a. *Varron, De Lingua Latina, Livre V. Texte, Établi, Traduit et Annoté par J. Collart.* Paris: Les Belles Lettres.

———. 1954b. *Varron Grammairien Latin.* Publications de la Faculté des Lettres de l'Université de Strasbourg 121. Paris: Les Belles Lettres.

———, ed. 1978. *Varron, Grammaire Antique et Stylistique Latine.* Paris: Les Belles Lettres.

Cooley, A. E. "The Survival of Oscan in Roman Pompeii." In *Becoming Roman, Writing Latin? Literacy and Epigraphy in the Roman West*, edited by A. E. Cooley, 77–86.

Journal of Roman Archaeology Suppl. Series 48. Portsmouth, RI: Journal of Roman Archaeology.
Corbeill, A. 1996. *Controlling Laughter: Political Humor in the Late Roman Republic.* Princeton, NJ: Princeton University Press.
———. 2008. "*Genus quid est?* Roman Scholars on Grammatical Gender and Biological Sex." *Transactions of the American Philological Association* 138, no. 1: 75–105.
———. 2010. "The Function of a Divinely Inspired Text in Cicero's *De haruspicum responsis.*" In *Form and Function in Roman Oratory*, edited by D. H. Berry and A. Erskine, 139–54. Cambridge: Cambridge University Press.
Cornell, T. J. 1995. *The Beginnings of Rome: Italy and Rome from the Bronze Age to the Punic Wars (c. 1000–264 BC).* London: Routledge.
———. 2009. "Cato the Elder and the Origins of Roman Autobiography." In C. J. Smith and A. Powell 2009, 15–40.
———, ed. 2013. *The Fragments of the Roman Historians.* 4 vols. Oxford: Oxford University Press.
Costa, G. 2000. *Sulla Preistoria della Tradizione Poetica Italica.* Florence: Leo S. Olschki.
Crawford, J. W. 1984. *M. Tullius Cicero: The Lost and Unpublished Orations.* Göttingen: Vandenhoeck & Ruprecht.
Crawford, M. H. 1974. *Roman Republican Coinage.* 2 vols. Cambridge: Cambridge University Press.
Curti, E. 2000. "From Concordia to the Quirinal: Notes on Religion and Politics in Mid-Republican/Hellenistic Rome." In Bispham and Smith 2000, 77–91.
Cuzzolin, P., and G. Haverling. 2009. "Syntax, Sociolinguistics, and Literary Genres." In P. Baldi and P. Cuzzolin 2009, 19–64.
Dahlmann, H. 1932. *Varro und die Hellenistische Sprachtheorie.* Berlin: Weidmann.
———. 1935. "Caesars Schrift über die Analogie." *Rheinisches Museum* 84:258–75.
———. 1940. *Varro, De Lingua Latina Buch VIII.* Hermes Einzelschriften 7. Berlin: Weidmann.
———. 1976. "Zu Varros antiquarisch-historischen Werken, besonders den antiquitates rerum humanarum et divinarum." In *Atti Congresso Internazionale di Studi Varroniani I. Rieti Settembre 1974*, 163–76. Rieti: Centro di Studi Varroniani.
Dahlmann, H., and R. Heisterhagen. 1957. *Varronische Studien, i: Zu den Logistorici.* Wiesbaden: Steiner.
Damon, C. 1993. "Caesar's Practical Prose." *Classical Journal* 89, no. 2: 183–95.
Dangel, J. 2001. "Varron et les Citations Poétiques dans le *De Lingua Latina.*" In G. Calboli 2001, 97–122.
Danvers, J. 2009. "Being-in-the-World: The Ability to Think about the Self in Interconnection and Interdependence with the Surrounding World." In *Sustainability Literacy: Skills for a Changing World*, edited by A. Stibbe, 185–90. Dartington: Green Books.
De Certeau, M. (1974) 1984. *The Practice of Everyday Life.* Translated by S. Rendall. Berkeley: University of California Press.
De Grummond, N. T. 2006a. *Etruscan Myth, Sacred History, and Legend.* Philadelphia: University of Pennsylvania Museum of Archaeology and Anthropology.

———. 2006b. "Prophets and Priests." In *The Religion of the Etruscans*, edited by N. T. de Grummond and E. Simon, 22–44. Austin: University of Texas Press.

———. 2013. "Haruspicy and Augury: Sources and Procedures." In *The Etruscan World*, edited by J. Turfa, 539–56. Oxford: Oxford University Press.

De Jonge, C. C. 2008. *Between Grammar and Rhetoric: Dionysius of Halicarnassus on Language, Linguistics and Literature*. Mnemosyne Suppl. 301. Leiden: Brill.

Del Bello, D. 2007. *Forgotten Paths: Etymology and the Allegorical Mindset*. Washington, DC: Catholic University of America Press.

Della Casa, A. 1969. *Il Libro X del De Lingua Latina di Varrone*. Genoa: M. Bozzi.

Della Corte, F. 1954. *Varrone, il Terzo Gran Lume Romano*. Genoa: Istituto Universitario di Magistero.

De Melo, W. 2011. "The Language of Roman Comedy." In J. Clackson 2011a, 321–43.

Dench, E. 1995. *From Barbarians to New Men: Greek, Roman, and Modern Perceptions of Peoples of the Central Apennines*. Oxford: Oxford University Press.

———. 1996. "Images of Italian Austerity from Cato to Tacitus." In *Les Élites Municipales de l'Italie Péninsulaire des Gracques à Néron*, edited by M. Cébeillac-Gervasoni, 247–54. Naples: École Française de Rome.

———. 1998. "Austerity, Excess, Success, and Failure in Hellenistic and Early Imperial Italy." In *Parchments of Gender: Deciphering the Bodies of Antiquity*, edited by M. Wyke, 121–46. Oxford: Oxford University Press.

———. 2005. *Romulus' Asylum: Roman Identities from the Age of Alexander to the Age of Hadrian*. Oxford: Oxford University Press.

De Vaan, M. 2008. *Etymological Dictionary of Latin and the Other Italic Languages*. Leiden: Brill.

Dickey, E. 2007. *Ancient Greek Scholarship: A Guide to Finding, Reading, and Understanding Scholia, Commentaries, Lexica, and Grammatical Treatises, from Their Beginning to the Byzantine Period*. Oxford: Oxford University Press.

Dickey, E., and A. Chaoud, eds. 2010. *Colloquial and Literary Latin*. Cambridge: Cambridge University Press.

Dionisotti, A. C. 1997. "On Fragments in Classical Scholarship." In G. W. Most 1997, 1–33.

Dix, T. K., and G. W. Houston. 2006. "Public Libraries in the City of Rome: From the Augustan Age to the Time of Diocletian." *Mélanges de l'École Française de Rome. Antiquité* 118, no. 2: 671–717.

Dodds, E. R. 1951. *The Greeks and the Irrational*. Berkeley: University of California Press.

Dominik, W. J., and J. Hall, eds. 2007. *A Companion to Roman Rhetoric*. Malden, MA: Blackwell.

Doody, A. 2010. *Pliny's Encyclopedia: The Reception of the Natural History*. Cambridge: Cambridge University Press.

Dugan, J. 2001. "How to Make (and Break) a Cicero: *Epideixis*, Textuality, and Self-fashioning in the *Pro Archia* and *In Pisonem*." *Classical Antiquity* 20, no. 1: 35–77.

———. 2005. *Making a New Man: Ciceronian Self-Fashioning in the Rhetorical Works*. Oxford: Oxford University Press.

———. 2007. "Modern Critical Approaches to Roman Rhetoric." In W. J. Dominik and J. Hall 2007, 9–22.

Dunkel, G. E. 2000. "Remarks on Code-Switching in Cicero's Letters to Atticus." *Museum Helveticum* 57, no. 2: 122–29.

Dyck, A. R. 2004. *A Commentary on Cicero, De Legibus*. Ann Arbor: University of Michigan Press.

Ebel, C. 1991. "*Dum Populus Senatusque Romanus Vellet*." *Historia* 40, no. 4: 439–48.

Eco, U. 1984. *Semiotics and the Philosophy of Language*. Bloomington: Indiana University Press.

———. 1994. *Six Walks in the Fictional Woods*. Cambridge, MA: Harvard University Press.

Edwards, C. 1993. *The Politics of Immorality in Ancient Rome*. Cambridge: Cambridge University Press.

———. 1996. *Writing Rome: Textual Approaches to the City*. Cambridge: Cambridge University Press.

Ehrman, R. K. 1993. "The *Cornicula* Ascribed to Plautus." *Rheinisches Museum* 136, no. 3/4: 268–81.

Elliott, J. 2013. *Ennius and the Architecture of the Annales*. Cambridge: Cambridge University Press.

Epstein, W. H. 1991a. *Contesting the Subject: Essays in the Postmodern Theory and Practice of Biography and Biographical Criticism*. West Lafayette, IN: Purdue Research Foundation.

———. 1991b. "(Post)Modern Lives: Abducting the Biographical Subject." In W. H. Epstein 1991a, 217–36.

Erasmo, M. 2004. *Roman Tragedy: Theatre to Theatricality*. Austin: University of Texas Press.

Erdkamp, P., ed. 2007. *A Companion to the Roman Army*. Blackwell Companions to the Ancient World. Malden, MA: Blackwell.

Erkell, H. 1952. *Augustus, Felicitas, Fortuna. Lateinische Wortstudien*. Gothenburg: Elander.

Ernout, A., and Meillet, A. 1959. *Dictionnaire Étymologique de la Langue Latine: Histoire des Mots, I*. 4th ed. Paris: Klincksieck.

Erskine, A. 2001. *Troy between Greece and Rome: Local Tradition and Imperial Power*. Oxford: Oxford University Press.

Fantham, E. 1998. *Ovid: Fasti IV*. Cambridge: Cambridge University Press.

———. 2003. "Three Wise Men and the End of the Roman Republic." In *Caesar against Liberty? Perspectives on His Autocracy*, edited by F. Cairns and E. Fantham, 97–117. ARCA: Classical and Medieval Texts, Papers and Monographs 43. Cambridge: Francis Cairns.

———. 2004. *The Roman World of Cicero's De Oratore*. Oxford: Oxford University Press.

Farney, G. D. 2007. *Ethnic Identity and Aristocratic Competition in Republican Rome*. Cambridge: Cambridge University Press.

Farrell, J. 1997. "The Phenomenology of Memory in Roman Culture." *Classical Journal* 92, no. 4: 373–83.

———. 2001. *Latin Language and Latin Culture: From Ancient to Modern Times*. Cambridge: Cambridge University Press.

Feeney, D. 1998. *Literature and Religion at Rome: Cultures, Contexts, and Beliefs.* Cambridge: Cambridge University Press.

———. 2007. *Caesar's Calendar. Ancient Time and the Beginnings of History.* Berkeley: University of California Press.

Feldstein, R. 1996. "The Mirror of Manufactured Cultural Revelations." In *Reading Seminars I and II: Lacan's Return to Freud,* edited by R. Feldstein, B. Fink, and M. Jaanus, 130–72. Albany, NY: SUNY Press.

Ferrante, D. 1962. "Curiosità Etimologiche nel *Cratilo* di Platone e nel *De Lingua Latina* di Varrone." *Giornale Italiano di Filologia* 15:163–71.

Ferrer i Cancho, R. 2008. "Network Theory." In *The Cambridge Encyclopedia of the Language Sciences,* edited by P. C. Hogan, 555–57. Cambridge: Cambridge University Press.

Ferrero, L. 1955. *Storia del Pitagorismo nel Mondo Romano: Dalle Origini alla Fine della Repubblica.* Turin: Giappichelli.

Ferri, R., and P. Probert. 2010. "Roman Authors on Colloquial Language." In E. Dickey and A. Chaoud 2010, 12–41.

Ferriss-Hill, J. L. 2011. "Virgil's Program of Sabellic Etymologizing and the Construction of Italic Identity." *Transactions of the American Philological Association* 141, no. 2: 265–84.

Flobert, P. 1985. *La Langue Latine: Livre VI. Texte Établi, Traduit et Commenté par Pierre Flobert.* Paris: Les Belles Lettres.

———. 2001. "Varron et la Langue Poétique d'après le Livre VII du *De Lingua Latina*." In G. Calboli 2001, 123–33.

Floratos, C. 1960. "Veneralia." *Hermes* 88:197–216.

Flory, M. B. 1989. "Octavian and the Omen of the *Gallina Alba*." *Classical Journal* 84, no. 4: 343–56.

Flower, H. I. 1995. "*Fabulae Praetextae* in Context: When Were Plays on Contemporary Subjects Performed in Republican Rome?" *Classical Quarterly* 45, no. 1: 170–90.

———, ed. 2004. *The Cambridge Companion to the Roman Republic.* Cambridge: Cambridge University Press.

Ford A. 1999. "Performing Interpretation: Early Allegorical Exegesis of Homer." In *Epic Traditions in the Contemporary World: The Poetics of Community,* edited by M. Beissinger, J. Tylus, and S. L. Wofford, 33–53. Berkeley: University of California Press.

Forsythe, G. 2005. *A Critical History of Early Rome: From Prehistory to the First Punic War.* Berkeley: University of California Press.

———. 2012. *Time in Roman Religion: One Thousand Years of Religious History.* Routledge Studies in Ancient History 4. New York: Routledge.

Forsyth, M. 2011. *The Etymologicon: A Circular Stroll through the Hidden Connections of the English Language.* London: Icon Books.

Foucault, M. 1966. *Les Mots et les Choses: Une Archéologie des Sciences Humaines.* Paris: Gallimard.

———. (1969) 1977. "What Is an Author?" In *Language, Counter-Memory, Practice: Selected Essays and Interviews,* edited by D. F. Bouchard and translated by D. F. Bouchard and S. Simon. Ithaca, NY: Cornell University Press.

———. (1984) 1988. *The Care of the Self*. Vol. 3 of *The History of Sexuality*. Translated by R. Hurley. London: Allen Lane.

———. (1969) 2002. *The Archaeology of Knowledge*. Translated by A. M. Sheridan Smith. London: Routledge.

Fowler, D. 2002. *Lucretius on Atomic Motion: A Commentary on De Rerum Natura, Book Two, Lines 1–332*. Oxford: Oxford University Press.

Fox, M. 2000. "Dialogue and Irony in Cicero: Reading *De Republica*." In *Intratextuality: Greek and Roman Textual Relations*, edited by A. Sharrock and H. L. Morales, 263–86. Oxford: Oxford University Press.

Frank, T. 1924. "The Tullianum and Sallust's *Catiline*." *Classical Journal* 19, no. 8: 495–98.

Fraschetti, A. 1990. *Roma e il Principe*. Bari: Laterza.

———. 1996. "Montes." In *LTUR* vol. III, 282–87.

Frazel, T. D. 2002. "Ovid *Fasti* 1.325–26, and 'Lamb Festivals.'" *Classical Philology* 97, no. 1: 88–92.

Frede, D., and B. Inwood, eds. 2005. *Language and Learning: Philosophy of Language in the Hellenistic Age: Proceedings of the Ninth Symposium Hellenisticum*. Cambridge: Cambridge University Press.

Freud, S. (1930) 1991. *Civilization, Society and Religion: Group Psychology, Civilization and Its Discontents and Other Works*. Edited by A. Dickson. Translated by J. Strachey. Harmondsworth: Penguin.

Frier, B. W. 1983. "Urban Praetors and Rural Violence: The Legal Background of Cicero's *Pro Caecina*." *Transactions of the American Philological Association* 113:221–41.

Fruyt, M. 2000. "La Création Lexicale: Généralités Appliquées au Domaine Latin." In M. Fruyt and C. Nicolas 2000, 11–48.

———. 2012. "Évolution du Lexique et Groupements de Lexèmes en Latin." In A. Christol and O. Spevak 2012, 105–28.

Fruyt, M., and C. Nicolas, eds. 2000. *La Création Lexicale en Latin: Actes de la Table Ronde du IXe Colloque International de Linguistique Latine Organisée par Michèle Fruyt á Madrid le 16 Avril 1997*. Lingua Latina: Recherches Linguistiques du Centre Alfred Ernout 6. Paris: Presses de l'Université de Paris-Sorbonne.

Gaines, R. N. 2007. "Roman Rhetorical Handbooks." In W. J. Dominik and J. Hall 2007, 163–80.

Gaisser, J. H. 2002. "The Reception of Classical Texts in the Renaissance." In *The Italian Renaissance in the Twentieth Century: Acts of an International Conference, Florence, Villa I Tatti, June 9–11, 1999*, edited by A. J. Grieco, M. Rocke, and F. Gioffredi Superbi, 387–400. Florence: Leo S. Olschki.

Gale, M. R. 2000. *Virgil on the Nature of Things: The Georgics, Lucretius and the Didactic Tradition*. Cambridge: Cambridge University Press.

Garbarino, G. 1978. "Verba *Poetica* in Prosa Nella Teoria Retorica da Cicerone a Quintiliano." *Memorie Morali* series 5, *Classe di Scienze Morali* 2, 141–237. Turin: Academia delle Scienze di Torino.

Garcea, A. 2012. *Caesar's De Analogia: Edition, Translation, and Commentary*. Oxford: Oxford University Press.

Garden, M.-C. E. 2006. "The Heritagescape: Looking at Landscapes of the Past." *International Journal of Heritage Studies* 12, no. 5: 394–411.

Garreau, J. 1991. *Edge City: Life on the New Frontier*. New York: Doubleday.

Gelsomino, R. 1975. *Varrone e i Sette Colli di Roma*. Università degli Studi di Siena, Collana di Studi e Testi, 1. Rome: Herder.

———. 1976a. "Varrone e il Septimontium: Una Polemica." *Giornale Italiano di Filologia* n.s. 7, no. 28: 324–31.

———. 1976b. "Varrone e i Sette Colli di Roma, II." *ACIV* 2:379–88.

Gibson, B. 2011. "Latin Manuscripts and Textual Traditions." In J. Clackson 2011a, 40–58.

Gildenhard, I. 2003. "The 'Annalist' before the Annalists: Ennius and His *Annales*." In *Formen römischer Geschichtsschreibung von den Anfiscen bis Livius*, edited by U. Eigler et al., 93–114. Darmstadt: Wissenschaftliche Buchgesellschaft.

———. 2011. *Creative Eloquence: The Construction of Reality in Cicero's Speeches*. Oxford: Oxford University Press.

Gill, C. 1996. *Personality in Greek Epic, Tragedy, and Philosophy: The Self in Dialogue*. Oxford: Oxford University Press.

———. 2006. *The Structured Self in Hellenistic and Roman Thought*. Oxford: Oxford University Press.

Glinister, F., C. Woods, with J. A. North and M. H. Crawford, eds. 2007. *Verrius, Festus and Paul: Lexicography, Scholarship and Society*. Bulletin of the Institute of Classical Studies, Suppl. 93. London: Institute of Classical Studies, University of London.

Goddard, C. 2002. "Ethnosyntax, Ethnopragmatics, Sign-functions and Culture." In *Ethnosyntax: Explorations in Grammar and Culture*, edited by N. J. Enfield, 52–73. Oxford: Oxford University Press.

Goetz, G., and F. Schoell, eds. 1910. *M. Terenti Varronis De Lingua Latina Quae Supersunt*. Leipzig: Teubner.

Goldberg, S. M. 1989. "Poetry, Politics, and Ennius." *Transactions of the American Philological Association* 119:247–61.

———. 2005. *Constructing Literature in the Roman Republic: Poetry and its Reception*. New York: Cambridge University Press.

Golledge, R. G., ed. 1999. *Wayfinding Behavior: Cognitive Mapping and Other Spatial Processes*. Baltimore, MD: Johns Hopkins University Press.

Gordon, R. L. 1990. "From Republic to Principate: Priesthood, Religion and Theology." In *Pagan Priests: Religions and Power in the Ancient World*, edited by M. Beard and J. A. North, 177–98. Ithaca, NY: Cornell University Press.

Gotter, U. 2003. "Die Vergangenheit als Kampfplatz der Gegenwart: Catos (konter)revolutionäre Konstruktion des republikanischen Erinnerungsraums." In *Formen römischer Geschichtsscreibung von den Anfängen bis Livius: Gattungen—Autoren—Kontexte*, edited by U. Eigler et al., 115–34. Darmstadt: Wissenschaftliche Buchgesellschaft.

Gowers, E. 1993. *The Loaded Table: Representations of Food in Roman Literature*. Oxford: Oxford University Press.

Gowing, A. 2005. *Empire and Memory: The Representation of the Roman Republic in Imperial Culture*. Cambridge: Cambridge University Press.

Graf, F. 2004. "The Power of the Word in the Graeco-Roman World." In *La Potenza della Parola: Destinatari, Funzioni, Bersagli*, edited by S. Beta, 79–100. Siena: Università degli Studi and Edizioni Cadmo.

Green, C. M. C. 2000. "The Slayer and the King: *Rex Nemorensis* and the Sanctuary of Diana." *Arion* 7, no. 3: 24–63.

———. 2002. "Varro's Three Theologies and Their Influence on the *Fasti*." In *Ovid's Fasti: Historical Readings at Its Bimillenium*, edited by G. Herbert-Brown, 71–99. Oxford: Oxford University Press.

Green, S. J. 2009. "Malevolent Gods and Promethean Birds: Contesting Augury in Augustus' Rome." *Transactions of the American Philological Association* 139, no. 1: 147–67.

Greenblatt, S. 1980. *Renaissance Self-Fashioning: From More to Shakespeare*. Chicago: University of Chicago Press.

Griffin, M., ed. 2009. *A Companion to Julius Caesar*. Malden, MA: Wiley-Blackwell.

Gruen, E. S. 1990. *Studies in Greek Culture and Roman Policy*. Cincinnati Classical Studies, n.s. 17. Leiden: Brill.

———. 2011. *Rethinking the Other in Antiquity*. Princeton, NJ: Princeton University Press.

Grünewald, T. (1999) 2004. *Bandits in the Roman Empire: Myth and Reality*. Translated by J. F. Drinkwater. London: Routledge.

Gumperz, J. J. 1992. "Interviewing in Intercultural Settings." In *Talk at Work*, edited by P. Drew and J. Heritage, 302–30. Cambridge: Cambridge University Press.

———. 1996. "The Linguistic and Cultural Relativity of Inference." In *Rethinking Linguistic Relativity*, edited by J. J. Gumperz and S. C. Levinson, 374–406. Cambridge: Cambridge University Press.

Gunderson, E. 2009. *Nox Philologiae: Aulus Gellius and the Fantasy of the Roman Library*. Madison: University of Wisconsin Press.

Gurd, S. 2007. "Cicero and Editorial Revision." *Classical Antiquity* 26, no. 1: 49–80.

———. 2012. *Work in Progress: Literary Revision as Social Performance in Ancient Rome*. American Philological Association. American Classical Studies 57. Oxford: Oxford University Press.

Habinek, T. N. 1998. *The Politics of Latin Literature: Writing, Identity, and Empire in Ancient Rome*. Princeton, NJ: Princeton University Press.

———. 2005. *The World of Roman Song: From Ritualized Speech to Social Order*. Baltimore, MD: Johns Hopkins University Press.

Halla-aho, H. 2011. "Epistolary Latin." In J. Clackson 2011a, 426–44.

Hall, J. 2009. *Politeness and Politics in Cicero's Letters*. New York: Oxford University Press.

Hanks, W. F. 2005. "Pierre Bourdieu and the Practices of Language." *Annual Review of Anthropology* 34:67–83.

Hansen, W. 2002. *Ariadne's Thread: A Guide to International Tales Found in Classical Literature*. Ithaca, NY: Cornell University Press.

Hardie, P. 1990. "Ovid's Theban History: The First 'Anti-*Aeneid*'?" *Classical Quarterly* 40, no. 1: 224–35.

Hardwick, L. 1990. "Ancient Amazons—Heroes, Outsiders or Women?" *Greece and Rome* 37:14–35.
Harris, R. 1997. "Varro on Linguistic Regularity." In *Landmarks in Linguistic Thought I: The Western Tradition from Socrates to Saussure*, edited by R. Harris and T. J. Taylor, 47–59. 2nd ed. London: Routledge.
Harrison, S., ed. 2005. *A Companion to Latin Literature*. Malden, MA: Blackwell.
Haselberger, L., D. G. Romano, and E. A. Dumser, eds. 2002. *Mapping Augustan Rome*. Journal of Roman Archaeology Suppl. Series 50. Portsmouth, RI: Journal of Roman Archaeology.
Haskell, F. 1993. *History and Its Images: Art and the Interpretation of the Past*. New Haven, CT: Yale University Press.
Haviland, J. B. 2000. "Pointing, Gesture Spaces and Mental Maps." In *Language and Gesture*, edited by D. McNeill, 13–46. Cambridge: Cambridge University Press.
Heiken, G., R. Funiciello, and D. De Rita. 2005. *The Seven Hills of Rome: A Geological Tour of the Eternal City*. Princeton, NJ: Princeton University Press.
Henderson, J. 1995. "Pump Up the Volume: Juvenal *Satire* I 1–21." *Proceedings of the Cambridge Philological Society* 41:101–37.
———. 1998. *Fighting for Rome: Poets and Caesars, History and Civil War*. Cambridge: Cambridge University Press.
———, ed. and trans. 2001. *Telling Tales on Caesar: Roman Stories from Phaedrus*. Oxford: Oxford University Press.
———. 2007. *The Medieval World of Isidore of Seville: Truth from Words*. Cambridge: Cambridge University Press.
———. 2010. "A 1-ZYTHUM: DOMIMINA NUSTIO ILLUMEA, or out with the *OLD*." In C. Stray 2010, 139–76.
Hendrickson, G. L. 1906. "The *De Analogia* of Julius Caesar: Its Occasion, Nature and Date, with Additional Fragments." *Classical Philology* 1, no. 2: 97–120.
Herbert-Brown, G. 1994. *Ovid and the Fasti: An Historical Study*. Oxford: Clarendon Press.
Hill, H. 1961. "Dionysius of Halicarnassus and the Origins of Rome." *Journal of Roman Studies* 51:88–93.
Hillier, B. 2003a. "The Architectures of Seeing and Going: or, are Cities Shaped by Bodies or Minds? And Is There a Syntax of Spatial Cognition?" *Proceedings of the 4th International Space Syntax Symposium*. http://www.spacesyntax.net/SSS4.htm.
———. 2003b. "The Knowledge That Shapes the City: The Human City beneath the Social City." *Proceedings of the 4th International Space Syntax Symposium*. http://www.spacesyntax.net/SSS4.htm.
Hillier, B., and J. Hanson. 1984. *The Social Logic of Space*. Cambridge: Cambridge University Press.
Hinds, S. 2006. "Venus, Varro and the *Vates*: Toward the Limits of Etymologizing Interpretation." *Dictynna* 3:175–210. http://dictynna.revues.org/206.
Hock, H., and B. D. Joseph. 2009. *Language History, Language Change, and Language Relationship: An Introduction to Historical and Comparative Linguistics*. 2nd ed. Berlin: Mouton de Gruyter.

Holford-Strevens, L., and A. D. Vardi, eds. 2004. *The Worlds of Aulus Gellius*. Oxford: Oxford University Press.

Hölkeskamp, K.-J. (2004) 2010. *Reconstructing the Roman Republic: An Ancient Political Culture and Modern Research*. Rev. ed. Translated by H. Heitmann-Gordon. Princeton, NJ: Princeton University Press.

———. 2013. "Friends, Romans, Countrymen: Addressing the Roman People and the Rhetoric of Inclusion." In C. Steel and H. van der Blom 2013, 11–28.

Holland, L. A. 1953. "Septimontium or Saeptimontium?" *Transactions of the American Philological Association* 84:16–34.

Holleman, A. W. J. 1973a. "An Enigmatic Function of the Flamen Dialis (Ovid, *Fast.*, 2.282) and the Augustan Reform." *Numen* 20, no. 3: 222–28.

———. 1973b. "Ovid and the Lupercalia." *Historia* 22, no. 2: 260–68.

Hollis, A. S. 2007. *Fragments of Roman Poetry, c. 60 BC–AD 20*. Oxford: Oxford University Press.

Hölscher, F. 2006. "Das Capitol—das Haupt der Welt." In E. Stein-Hölkeskamp and K.-J. Hölkeskamp 2006, 75–99.

Hölscher, T. (1987) 2004. *The Language of Images in Roman Art*. Translated by A. M. Snodgrass and A. Künzl-Snodgrass. Cambridge: Cambridge University Press.

———. 2006. "Das Forum Romanum—die monumentale Geschichte Roms." In E. Stein-Hölkeskamp and K.-J. Hölkeskamp 2006, 100–22.

Horsfall, N. 1972. "Varro and Caesar: Three Chronological Problems." *Bulletin of the Institute of Classical Studies of the University of London* 19:120–28.

———. 1974. "Virgil's Roman Chronography." *Classical Quarterly* 24, no. 1: 111–15.

———. 1976. "The Collegium Poetarum." *Bulletin of the Institute of Classical Studies* 23:79–95.

———. 1982. "Prose and Mime." In *The Cambridge History of Classical Literature, vol.2: Latin Literature*, edited by E. J. Kenney and W. V. Clausen, 286–90. Cambridge: Cambridge University Press.

———. 1988. "Camilla o i Limiti dell'Invenzione." *Athenaeum* 66:31–51.

Hoyos, D. 2007. "The Age of Overseas Expansion (264–146 BC)." In P. Erdkamp 2007, 63–79.

Hunt, A. 2012. "Keeping the Memory Alive: The Physical Continuity of the *Ficus Ruminalis*." In *Memory and Urban Religion in the Ancient World*, edited by M. Bommas, J. Harrisson, P. Roy, and E. Theodorakopoulos, 111–28. London: Bloomsbury.

Ingold, T. 1993. "The Art of Translation in a Continuous World." In *Beyond Boundaries: Understanding, Translation and Anthropological Discourse*, edited by G. Palsson, 210–30. Oxford: Berg.

———. 2000. *The Perception of the Environment. Essays on Livelihood, Dwelling and Skill*. London: Routledge.

Isaac, B. 2004. *The Invention of Racism in Classical Antiquity*. Princeton, NJ: Princeton University Press.

Itgenshorst, T. 2005. *Tota Illa Pompa: Der Triumph in der Römischen Republik*. Hypomnemata, 161. Göttingen: Vandenhoeck & Ruprecht.

———. 2006. "Roman Commanders and Hellenistic Kings: On the 'Hellenization' of the Republican Triumph." *Ancient Society* 36:51–68.

Jaeger, M. K. 1997. *Livy's Written Rome*. Ann Arbor: University of Michigan Press.

Jaffe, A., J. Androutsopoulos, M. Sebba, and S. Johnson, eds. 2012. *Orthography as Social Action: Scripts, Spelling, Identity and Power*. Berlin: Walter de Gruyter.

Janan, M. 2009. *Reflections in a Serpent's Eye: Thebes in Ovid's Metamorphoses*. Oxford: Oxford University Press.

Jauss, H. R. 1970. "Literary History as a Challenge to Literary Theory." *New Literary History* 2, no. 1: 7–37.

Jehne, M. 2006. "Caesars *Gallischer Krieg*—Text und Tat." In E. Stein-Hölkeskamp and K.-J. Hölkeskamp 2006, 234–41.

Jenks, C. 1995. "Watching Your Step: The History and Practice of the Flâneur." In *Visual Culture*, edited by C. Jenks, 142–60. London: Routledge.

Johnson, W. A. 2000. "Towards a Sociology of Reading in Classical Antiquity." *American Journal of Philology* 121, no. 4: 593–627.

———. 2010. *Readers and Reading Culture in the High Roman Empire: A Study of Elite Communities*. New York: Oxford University Press.

Kaiser, A. 2011. *Roman Urban Street Networks*. Routledge Studies in Archaeology 2. Abingdon: Routledge.

Kaster, R. A. 2005. *Emotion, Restraint, and Community in Ancient Rome*. Oxford: Oxford University Press.

———. 2006. *Marcus Tullius Cicero: Speech on Behalf of Publius Sestius*. Oxford: Oxford University Press.

———. 2012. *The Appian Way: Ghost Road, Queen of Roads*. Chicago: University of Chicago Press.

Keith, A. M. 1992. *The Play of Fictions: Studies in Ovid's Metamorphoses Book 2*. Ann Arbor: University of Michigan Press.

Keller, O. 1909. *Die antike Tierwelt, Erster Band: Säugetiere*. Leipzig: Wilhelm Engelmann.

Kennedy, G. A. 1994. *A New History of Classical Rhetoric*. Princeton, NJ: Princeton University Press.

Kent, R. G. 1951. *Varro: On the Latin Language*. 2 vols. Rev. ed. Cambridge, MA: Harvard University Press.

Keulen, W. H. 2009. *Gellius the Satirist: Roman Cultural Authority in Attic Nights*. Mnemosyne Suppl. 297. Leiden: Brill.

King, N. A. 2000. *Memory, Narrative, Identity: Remembering the Self*. Edinburgh: Edinburgh University Press.

Klooster, J. 2012. "Visualizing the Impossible: The Wandering Landscape in the Delos Hymn of Callimachus." *Aitia* 2. http://aitia.revues.org/420.

König, J. 2007. "Fragmentation and Coherence in Plutarch's *Sympotic Questions*." In J. König and T. Whitmarsh 2007, 43–68.

König, J., and T. Whitmarsh, eds. 2007. *Ordering Knowledge in the Roman Empire*. Cambridge: Cambridge University Press.

Koptev, A. 2005. "'Three Brothers' at the Head of Archaic Rome: The King and His 'Consuls.'" *Historia* 54, no. 4: 382–423.

Krebs, C. B. 2006. "'Imaginary Geography' in Caesar's *Bellum Gallicum*." *American Journal of Philology* 127, no. 1: 111–36.

Kretschmer, P. 1920. "Lat. *Quirites* und *Quiritare*." *Glotta* 10:147–57.

Kritzman, L. D., ed. 1981. *Fragments: Incompletion and Discontinuity*. New York: New York Literary Forum.

Kroll, J. F., and P. E. Dussias. 2005. "The Comprehension of Words and Sentences in Two Languages." In T. K. Bhatia and W. C. Ritchie 2005, 216–43.

Kronenberg, L. 2009. *Allegories of Farming from Greece and Rome: Philosophical Satire in Xenophon, Varro, and Virgil*. Cambridge: Cambridge University Press.

Kroon, C. 2011. "Latin Particles and the Grammar of Discourse." In J. Clackson 2011a, 176–95.

Krostenko, B. A. 2000. "Beyond (Dis)belief: Rhetorical Form and Religious Symbol in Cicero's *De Divinatione*." *Transactions of the American Philological Association* 130:353–91.

Kumaniecki, K. 1962. "Cicerone e Varrone: Storia di una Conoscenza." *Athenaeum* 40:221–43.

Lacan, J. (1964) 2004. *The Seminar of Jacques Lacan, Book XI: The Four Fundamental Concepts of Psychoanalysis*. Edited by J.-A Miller. Translated by A. Sheridan. London: Karnac.

———. (1966) 2006. *Écrits: The First Complete Edition in English*. Translated by B. Fink. New York: W. W. Norton.

Lakoff, G., and M. Johnson. 2003. *Metaphors We Live By*. Rev. ed. Chicago: University of Chicago Press.

Larmour, D. H. J., and D. Spencer. 2007a. "'*Roma, Recepta*': A Topography of the Imagination." In D. H. J. Larmour and D. Spencer 2007b, 1–60.

———, eds. 2007b. *The Sites of Rome: Time, Space, Memory*. Oxford: Oxford University Press.

Laughton, E. 1978. "Humour in Varro." In J. Collart 1978, 105–11.

Laurence, R., and D. J. Newsome, eds. 2011. *Rome, Ostia, Pompeii: Movement and Space*. Oxford: Oxford University Press.

Lazarus, F. M. 1985. "On the Meaning of Fors Fortuna: A Hint from Terence." *American Journal of Philology* 106, no. 3: 359–67.

Leach, E. W. 1999. "Ciceronian 'Bi-Marcus': Correspondence with M. Terentius Varro and L. Papirius Paetus in 46 BCE." *Transactions of the American Philological Association* 129:139–79.

Lebek, W. D. 1970. *Verba Prisca: Die Anfänge des Archaisierens in der Lateinischen Beredsamkeit und Geschichtsschreibung*. Hypomnemata 25. Göttingen: Vandenhoeck & Ruprecht.

Lee, E. N. 1978. "The Sense of an Object: Epicurus on Seeing and Hearing." In *Studies in Perception: Interrelations in the History of Philosophy and Science*, edited by P. K. Machamer and R. G. Turnbull, 27–59. Columbus: Ohio State University Press.

Lefebvre, H. (1974) 1991. *The Production of Space*. Translated by D. Nicholson-Smith. Malden, MA: Blackwell.

Lefebvre, H., and C. Régulier-Lefebvre. 1985. "Le Projet Rhythmanalytique." *Communications* 41:191–99. [= 2003. "The Rhythmanalytical Project." *Henri Lefebvre: Key Writings*. Translated by E. Lebas. Edited by E. Kofman and S. Elden, 190–98. London: Continuum.]

Leigh, M. 2004. *Comedy and the Rise of Rome*. Oxford: Oxford University Press.

Levene, D. S. 2005. "The Late Republican/Triumviral Period: 90–40 BC." In S. Harrison 2005, 31–43.

Levine, P. 1957. "The Original Design and the Publication of the *De Natura Deorum*." *Harvard Studies in Classical Philology* 62:7–36.

Lightfoot, J. L. 1999. *Parthenius of Nicea: The Extant Works*. Edited and translated by Jane Lightfoot. Oxford: Clarendon Press.

Linderski, J. 1982. "Cicero and Roman Divination." *La Parola del Passato* 37:12–38.

———. 1985. "The Dramatic Date of Varro, *De Re Rustica*, Book III and the Elections in 54." *Historia* 34, no. 2: 248–54.

———. 1986. "The Augural Law." In *ANRW* 2.16.3:2146–312.

Lindsay, W. M., ed. 1904. *T. Macci Plauti Comoedia* 2. Oxford: Clarendon Press.

———, ed. 1913. *Sexti Pompei Festi di Verborum Significatu Quae Supersunt cum Pauli Epitome*. Leipzig: Teubner.

Lintott, A. 1968. *Violence in Republican Rome*. Oxford: Clarendon Press.

———. 1974. "Cicero and Milo." *Journal of Roman Studies* 64:62–78.

———. 1999. *The Constitution of the Roman Republic*. Oxford: Clarendon Press.

Lisdorf, A. 2004. "The Spread of Non-Natural Concepts: Evidence from the Roman Prodigy Lists." *Journal of Cognition and Culture* 4, no. 1: 151–73.

———. 2007. "The Dissemination of Divination in Roman Republican Times—A Cognitive Approach." PhD diss., University of Copenhagen. Archive for Religion & Cognition 21. http://www.csr-arc.com/view.php?arc=21.

Littlewood, R. J. 2001. "Ovid among the Family Dead: The Roman Founder Legend and Augustan Iconography in Ovid's *Feralia* and *Lemuria*." *Latomus* 60, no. 4: 916–35.

———. 2006. *A Commentary on Ovid's Fasti, Book 6*. Oxford: Oxford University Press.

Long, A. A., and Sedley, D. N. 1987. *The Hellenistic Philosophers*. 2 vols. Cambridge: Cambridge University Press.

Lotman, Y. 1990. *Universe of the Mind: A Semiotic Theory of Culture*. Translated by A. Shukman. Introduction by U. Eco. London: I. B. Tauris.

Lott, J. B. 2004. *The Neighborhoods of Augustan Rome*. New York: Cambridge University Press.

Lowrie, M. 2009. *Writing, Performance, and Authority in Augustan Rome*. Oxford: Oxford University Press.

———. 2010. "Spurius Maelius: Dictatorship and the *Homo Sacer*." In B. W. Breed, C. Damon, and A. F. Rossi 2010, 171–86.

Luhtala, A. 2002. "On Definitions in Ancient Grammar." In P. Swiggers and A. Wouters 2002, 257–85.

Lynch, K. 1960. *The Image of the City*. Cambridge, MA: MIT Press.

MacLaren, M. 1966. "Wordplays Involving *Bovillae* in Cicero's *Letters*." *American Journal of Philology* 87, no. 2: 192–202.

MacDonald, W. 1986. *The Architecture of the Roman Empire, vol. II: An Urban Appraisal.* New Haven, CT: Yale University Press.

Mackenzie, M. M. 1986. "Putting the *Cratylus* in Its Place." *Classical Quarterly* 36:124–50.

Maetzke, G., and L. Tamagno Perna, eds. 1996. *Identità e Civiltà dei Sabin: Atti del XVIII Convegno di Studi Etruschi ed Italici, Rieti-Magliano Sabina, 30 Maggio–3 Giugno 1993.* Florence: Olschki.

Malamud, M. 2003. "Pompey's Head and Cato's Snakes." *Classical Philology* 98, no. 1: 31–44.

Malmberg, S. 2009. "Finding Your Way in the Subura." In *TRAC 2008: Proceedings of the Eighteenth Annual Theoretical Roman Archaeology Conference, Amsterdam 2008,* edited by M. Driessen, S. Heeren, J. Hendriks, F. Kemmers, and R. Visser, 39–51. Oxford: Oxbow.

Malmkjær, K. 2005. *Linguistics and the Language of Translation.* Edinburgh: Edinburgh University Press.

Maltby, R. 1991. *A Lexicon of Ancient Latin Etymologies.* ARCA 25. Leeds: Francis Cairns.

———. 2001. "Greek in Varro." In G. Calboli 2001, 191–210.

Manetti, G. (1987) 1993. *Theories of the Sign in Classical Antiquity.* Translated by C. Richardson. Bloomington: Indiana University Press.

Mangen, A. 2008. "Hypertext Fiction Reading: Haptics and Immersion." *Journal of Research in Reading* 31, no. 4: 404–19.

Manuwald, G. 2001. *Fabulae praetextae: Spuren einer literarischen Gattung der Römer.* Zetemata 108. Munich: Beck.

———. 2011. *Roman Republican Theatre: A History.* Cambridge: Cambridge University Press.

———. 2014. "Cicero, an Interpreter of Terence." In *Terence and Interpretation,* edited by S. Papaioannou, 179–200. Cambridge: Cambridge Scholars Publishing.

Marinone, N. 2004. *Cronologia Ciceroniana.* 2nd ed. Bologna: Pàtron.

Mastrocinque, A. 2007. "Creating One's Own Religion: Intellectual Choices." In J. Rüpke 2007, 378–91.

Matthaios, S., F. Montanari, and A. Rengakos, eds. 2011. *Ancient Scholarship and Grammar: Archetypes, Concepts and Contexts.* Trends in Classics, Supplementary Vol. 8. Berlin: Walter de Gruyter.

Matthews, P. H. 1972. *Inflectional Morphology. A Theoretical Study Based on Aspects of Latin Verb Conjugation.* Cambridge: Cambridge University Press.

———. 1991. *Morphology.* 2nd ed. Cambridge: Cambridge University Press.

May, J. M. 1995. "Patron and Client, Father and Son in Cicero's *Pro Caelio*." *Classical Journal* 90, no. 4: 433–41.

———. 2001. "Cicero's *Pro Milone*: An Ideal Speech of an Ideal Orator." In *The Orator in Action and Theory in Greece and Rome,* edited by C. Wooten, 123–34. Leiden: Brill.

———. 2007. "Cicero as Rhetorician." In W. J. Dominik and J. Hall 2007, 250–63.

McClaverty, J. 1991. "Issues of Identity and Utterance: An Intentionalist Response to 'Textual Instability.'" In *Devils and Angels: Textual Editing and Literary Theory,* edited by P. Cohen, 134–51. Charlottesville: University Press of Virginia.

McDonough, C. M. 2004. "The Hag and the Household Gods: Silence, Speech, and the Family in Mid-February (Ovid *Fasti* 2.533–638)." *Classical Philology* 99, no. 4: 354–69.

McElduff, S. 2004. "More Than Menander's Acolyte: Terence on Translation." *Ramus* 33, no. 1–2: 120–29.

———. 2009. "Living at the Level of the Word: Cicero's Rejection of the Interpreter as Translator." *Translation Studies* 2, no. 2: 133–46.

———. 2013. *Surpassing the Source: Roman Theories of Translation*. London: Routledge.

McElduff, S., and E. Sciarrino, eds. 2011. *Complicating the History of Western Translation: The Ancient Mediterranean in Perspective*. Manchester: St. Jerome Publishing.

McGinn, T. A. J. 2004. *The Economy of Prostitution in the Roman World: A Study of Social History and the Brothel*. Ann Arbor: University of Michigan Press.

Melfi, M. 2008. "Cretan Nymphs: An Attic Hypothesis." In *Essays in Classical Archaeology for Eleni Hatzivassiliou, 1977–2007*, edited by D. Kurtz, 221–27. Oxford: The Beazley Archive/Archaeopress. (= BAR International 1796.)

Merleau-Ponty, M. (1964) 1968. *The Visible and the Invisible*. Translated by A. Lingis. Evanston, IL: Northwestern University Press.

Miano, D. 2018. *Fortuna: Deity and Concept in Archaic and Republican Italy*. Oxford: Oxford University Press.

Michalopoulos, A. 1998. "Some Cases of Propertian Etymologising." In *Papers of the Leeds International Latin Seminar 10, 1998: Greek Poetry, Drama, Prose, Roman Poetry*, edited by F. Cairns and M. Heath, 235–50. ARCA 38. Leeds: Francis Cairns.

———. 2001. *Ancient Etymologies in Ovid's Metamorphoses: A Commented Lexicon*. ARCA 40. Leeds: Francis Cairns.

Michels, A. K. 1967. *The Calendar of the Roman Republic*. Princeton, NJ: Princeton University Press.

Mignone, L. M. 2016. *The Republican Aventine and Rome's Social Order*. Ann Arbor: University of Michigan Press.

Miller, A. M. 1986. *From Delos to Delphi: A Literary Study of the Homeric Hymn to Apollo*. Mnemosyne Suppl. 93. Leiden: Brill.

Miller, J. F. 1991. *Ovid's Elegiac Festivals: Studies in the Fasti*. Frankfurt: Lang.

———. 1992. "The *Fasti* and Hellenistic Didactic: Ovid's Variant Aetiologies." *Arethusa* 25:11–32.

———. 2009. *Apollo, Augustus, and the Poets*. Cambridge: Cambridge University Press.

Miller, J. H. 2001. *Speech Acts in Literature*. Stanford, CA: Stanford University Press.

Miller, P. A. 2004. *Subjecting Verses: Latin Love Elegy and the Emergence of the Real*. Princeton, NJ: Princeton University Press.

Mirsch, P., ed. 1882. "De M. Terenti Varronis Antiquitatum rerum humanarum libris XXV." *Leipziger Studien zur Classischen Philologie* 5:1–144.

Moatti, C. 2003. "La Construction du Patrimoine Culturel à Rome aux 1er Siècle avant et 1er Siècle après J.-C." In M. Citroni 2003, 81–98.

Momigliano, A. 1950. "Ancient History and the Antiquarian." *Journal of the Warburg and Courtauld Institutes* 13:285–315.

———. 1961. "Historiography on Written Tradition and Historiography on Oral Tradition." *Atti della Accademia delle Scienze di Torini* 96:1–12.

———. 1984. "The Theological Efforts of the Roman Upper Classes in the First Century BC." *Classical Philology* 79, no. 3: 199–211.
Montiglio, S. 2005. *Wandering in Ancient Greek Culture*. Chicago: University of Chicago Press.
Morstein-Marx, R. 2004. *Mass Oratory and Political Power in the Late Roman Republic*. Cambridge: Cambridge University Press.
———. 2013. "'Cultural Hegemony' and the Communicative Power of the Roman Elite." In C. Steel and H. van der Blom 2013, 29–47.
Most, G. W., ed. 1997. *Collecting Fragments/Fragmente Sammeln*. Aporemata 1. Göttingen: Vandenhoeck and Ruprecht.
Mullen, A. 2011. "Latin and Other Languages: Societal and Individual Bilingualism." In J. Clackson 2011a, 527–48.
Mueller, K. O., ed. 1833. *M. Terenti Varronis De Lingua Latina librorum quae Supersunt*. Leipzig: Weidmann.
Mumford, L. (1938) 1970. *The Culture of Cities*. New York: Harcourt, Brace, Jovanovich.
Murphy, T. 1998. "Cicero's First Readers: Epistolary Evidence for the Dissemination of his Works." *Classical Quarterly* 48, no. 2: 492–505.
———. 2004. *Pliny the Elder's Natural History: The Empire in the Encyclopedia*. Oxford: Oxford University Press.
Musti, D. 1985. "I Due Volti della Sabina: Sulla Rappresentazione dei Sabini in Varrone, Dionigi, Strabone e Plutarco." In *Convegno di Studio Preistoria, Storia e Civiltà dei Sabini. Rieti, Ottobre 1982*, edited by B. Riposati, 75–98. Rieti: Centro di Studi Varroniani.
Myers-Scotton, C. 1988. "Differentiating Borrowing and Codeswitching." In *Linguistic Change and Contact: Proceedings of the Sixteenth Annual Conference on New Ways of Analyzing Variation*, edited by K. Ferrara, B. Brown, K. Walters, and J. Baugh, 318–25. Austin: Department of Linguistics, University of Texas.
Nagy, B. 1985. "The Argei Puzzle." *American Journal of Ancient History* 10:1–27.
Narducci, E. 2003. "La Memoria della Grecità nell'Imaginario delle Ville Ciceroniane." In M. Citroni 2003, 119–48.
Neisser, U. 1989. "Domains of Memory." In *Memory: Interdisciplinary Approaches*, edited by P. R. Solomon, G. R. Goethals, C. M. Kelly, and B. R. Stephens, 67–83. New York: Springer-Verlag.
Nelis, D. 2008. "Caesar, the Circus and the Charioteer in Vergil's *Georgics*." In J. Nelis-Clément and M. Roddaz 2008, 497–520.
Nelis-Clément, J., and M. Roddaz, eds. 2008. *Le Cirque Romain et Son Image*. Bordeaux: Ausonius.
Newman, J. K. 1967. *The Concept of Vates in Augustan Poetry*. Collection Latomus 89. Brussels: Latomus.
Newsome, D. J. 2011. "Movement and Fora in Rome (the Late Republic to the First Century CE)." In R. Laurence and D. J. Newsome 2011, 290–311.
Nicholls, M. 2018. "Libraries and Literary Culture in Rome." In *A Companion to the City of Rome*, edited by C. Holleran and A. Claridge, 343–61. Malden, MA: John Wiley & Sons.

Nicholson, J. 1998. "The Survival of Cicero's Letters." In *Studies in Latin Literature and Roman History 9*, edited by C. Deroux, 63–105. Collection Latomus 244. Brussels: Latomus.

Nicolas, C. 2000. "La Néologie Technique par Traduction chez Cicéron et la Notion de 'Verbumexverbalité.'" In M. Fruyt and C. Nicolas 2000, 109–46.

Niebisch, A. 2008. "Symbolic Space: Memory, Narrative, Writing." In *Symbolic Landscapes*, edited by G. Backhaus and J. Murungi, 323–37. Dordrecht: Springer.

Nora, P. 2001. "General Introduction." Translated by M. Trouille. In *Rethinking France: Les Lieux de Mémoire*, vol. 1, *The State*, edited by P. Nora and D. P. Jordan, translated by M. Trouille, vii–xxii. Chicago: University of Chicago Press.

North, J. A. 1990. "Diviners and Divination at Rome." In M. Beard and J. North 1990, 51–71.

———. 2000. "Prophet and Text in the Third Century BC." In Bispham and Smith 2000, 92–107.

———. 2007. "Why Does Festus Quote What He Quotes?" In F. Glinister, C. Woods, with J. A. North and M. H. Crawford 2007, 49–68.

———. 2008. "Caesar at the Lupercalia." *Journal of Roman Studies* 98:144–60.

North, J. A., and N. B. McLynn. 2008. "Postscript to the Lupercalia." *Journal of Roman Studies* 98:176–81.

O'Hara, J. J. 1996. *True Names: Vergil and the Alexandrian Tradition of Etymological Wordplay*. Ann Arbor: University of Michigan Press.

———. 2001. "Callimachean Influences on Vergilian Etymological Wordplay." *Classical Journal* 96, no. 4: 369–400.

Oksala, P. 1953. *Die griechischen Lehnwörter in der Prosaschriften Ciceros*. Helsinki: Suomalaisen Tiedeakatemia.

Olick, J. K. 2003. "Introduction." In *States of Memory: Continuities, Conflicts, and Transformations in National Retrospection*, edited by J. K. Olick, 1–16. Durham, NC: Duke University Press.

O'Neill, P. 2003. "Going Round in Circles: Popular Speech in Ancient Rome." *Classical Antiquity* 22, no. 1: 135–65.

Ong, W. J. 2002. *Orality and Literacy: The Technologizing of the Word*. 2nd ed. London: Routledge.

Oniga, R., ed. 2003. *Il Plurilinguismo nella Tradizione Letteraria Latina*. Rome: Il Calamo.

Orlin, E. M. 2010. *Foreign Cults in Rome: Creating a Roman Empire*. New York: Oxford University Press.

Östenberg, I. 2009. *Staging the World: Spoils, Captives, and Representations in the Roman Triumphal Procession*. Oxford: Oxford University Press.

———. 2015. "Power Walks: Aristocratic Escorted Movements in Republican Rome." In I. Östenberg, S. Malmberg, and J. Bjørnebye 2015, 13–22.

Östenberg, I., S. Malmberg, and J. Bjørnebye, eds. 2015. *The Moving City: Passages, Processions and Promenades in Ancient Rome*. London: Bloomsbury Academic.

O'Sullivan, T. M. 2011. *Walking in Roman Culture*. Cambridge: Cambridge University Press.

———. 2015. "Augustan Literary Tours: Walking and Reading the City." In I. Östenberg, S. Malmberg, and J. Bjørnebye 2015, 111–22.
Pagán, V. E. 2005. *Conspiracy Narratives in Roman History*. Austin: University of Texas Press.
Palmer, R. E. A. 1970. *The Archaic Community of the Romans*. Cambridge: Cambridge University Press.
Palombi, D. 1997. *Tra Palatino ed Esquilino: "Velia," "Carinae," "Fagutal," Storia Urbana di Tre Quartieri di Roman Antica*. Rome: Istituto Nazionale di Archeologia e Storia dell'Arte.
———. 2006. "Vecchie e Nuove Immagini per Roma Augustea: *Flavus Tiberis e Septem Colles*." In *Imaging Ancient Rome: Documentation, Visualization, Imagination: Proceedings of the Third Williams Symposium on Classical Architecture, Held at the American Academy in Rome, the British School at Rome, and the Deutsches Archäologisches Institut, Rome, on May 20–23, 2004*, edited by L. Haselberger and J. H. Humphrey 2006, 15–29. Portsmouth, RI: Journal of Roman Archaeology.
Pasco-Pranger, M. 1999–2000. "*Vates Operosus*: Vatic Poetics and Antiquarianism in Ovid's *Fasti*." *Classical World* 93, no. 3: 275–91.
———. 2006. *Founding the Year: Ovid's Fasti and the Poetics of the Roman Calendar*. Leiden: Brill.
Pavone, C. 2001. "La Tutela delle Fanciulle (Varrone *Ling*. VII 12) e la Stella della Sera (Varrone *Ling*. VII 50)." In G. Calboli 2001, 211–21.
Pease, D. E. 1995. "Author." In *Critical Terms for Literary Study*, edited by F. Lentricchia and T. McLaughlin, 105–17. 2nd ed. Chicago: University of Chicago Press.
Pelling, C. 2011. *Plutarch: Caesar*. Translated with introduction and commentary. Clarendon Ancient History Series. Oxford: Oxford University Press.
Pensabene, P. 1996. "Magna Mater, Aedes." In *LTUR* vol. III, 206–8.
Perlwitz, O. 1992. *Titus Pomponius Atticus: Untersuchungen zur Person eines einflussreichen Ritters in der ausgehenden Römischen Republik*. Stuttgart: Steiner.
Pfaffel, W. 1981. *Quartus Gradus Etymologiae: Untursuchungen zur Etymologie Varros in De Lingua Latina*. Beiträge zur klassischen Philologie, 131. Königstein: Hain.
———. 1987. "Wie modern war die varronische Etymologie?" In D. J. Taylor 1987, 207–28.
Phillips, M. S. 1996. "Reconsiderations on History and Antiquarianism: Arnaldo Momigliano and the Historiography of Eighteenth-Century Britain." *Journal of the History of Ideas* 57, no. 2: 297–316.
Pieroni, P. 2011. "Etymologien in den *Variae* Cassiodors." In *The Latin of Roman Lexicography*, edited by R. Ferri, 171–85. Ricerche sulle Lingue di Frammentaria Attestazione 7. Pisa: Fabrizio Serra Editore.
Pina Polo, F. 2011. *The Consul at Rome: The Civil Function of the Consuls in the Roman Republic*. Cambridge: Cambridge University Press.
Piras, G. 1998. *Varrone e i Poetica Verba: Studio sul Settimo Libro del De Lingua Latina*. Bologna: Pàtron.
———. 2000. "Per la Tradizione del *De Lingua Latina* di Varrone." In *Manuscripts and Tradition of Grammatical Texts from Antiquity to the Renaissance*, edited by M. De Nonno, P. De Paolis, and L. Holtz, 747–72. Cassino: Edizioni dell'Università.

———. 2015. "*Cum poeticis multis uerbis magis delecter quam utar*: Poetic Citations and Etymological Enquiry in Varro's *De Lingua Latina*." In *Varro Varius: The Polymath of the Roman World*, edited by D. J. Butterfield, 51–70. Cambridge Classical Journal Supplement 39. Cambridge: Cambridge Philological Society.

Plass, P. 1988. *Wit and the Writing of History: The Rhetoric of Historiography in Imperial Rome*. Madison: University of Wisconsin Press.

Poe, J. P. 1978. "The Septimontium and the Subura." *Transactions of the American Philological Association* 108:147–54.

Porte, D. 1981. "Romulus-Quirinus, Prince et Dieu, Dieu des Princes: Etude sur la Personnage de Quirinus et sur Son Évolution des Origines à Auguste." In *ANRW* 2.17.1:300–342.

Poucet, J. 1967. *Recherches sur la Légende Sabine des Origines de Rome*. Louvain: Université de Louvain.

Powell, J. G. F. 2011. "The Language of Roman Oratory and Rhetoric." In J. Clackson 2011a, 384–407.

Purcell, N. 1990. "The Creation of Provincial Landscape: The Roman Impact on Cisalpine Gaul." In *The Early Roman Empire in the West*, edited by T. Blagg and M. Millett, 7–29. Oxford: Oxbow.

———. 1995. "Forum Romanum [The Republican Period]." In *LTUR* vol. II, 325–36.

———. 1996. "Rome and the Management of Water: Environment, Culture and Power." In *Human Landscapes in Classical Antiquity: Environment and Culture*, edited by G. Shipley and J. Salmon, 180–212. London: Routledge.

———. 2003. "The Way We Used to Eat: Diet, Community, and History at Rome." *American Journal of Philology* 124, no. 3: 329–58.

Raaflaub, K. A. 2006. "Romulus und die Wölfin—Roms Anfänge zwischen Mythos und Geschichte." In E. Stein-Hölkeskamp and K. -J. Hölkeskamp 2006, 18–39.

———. 2010. "Creating a Grand Coalition of True Roman Citizens: On Caesar's Political Strategy in the Civil War." In B. W. Breed, C. Damon, and A. F. Rossi 2010, 159–70.

Rambaud, M. 1979. "César et la Rhétorique: A Propos de Cicéron." In *Colloque sur la Rhétorique: Calliope I*, edited by R. Chevallier, 19–39. Paris: Les Belles Lettres.

Ramsey, J. T., and A. L. Licht. 1997. *The Comet of 44 BC and Caesar's Funeral Games*. American Classical Studies 39. Atlanta, GA: Scholars Press.

Rasmussen, S. W. 2003. *Public Portents in Republican Rome*. Analecta Romana Instituti Danci Suppl. 34. Rome: L'Erma di Bretschneider.

Rawlings, L. 2007. "Army and Battle during the Conquest of Italy (350–264 BC)." In P. Erdkamp 2007, 45–62.

Rawson, E. 1969. *The Spartan Tradition in European Thought*. Oxford: Clarendon Press.

———. 1972. "Cicero the Historian and Cicero the Antiquarian." *Journal of Roman Studies* 62:33–45.

———. 1975. "Caesar's Heritage: Hellenistic Kings and Their Roman Equals." *Journal of Roman Studies* 65:148–59.

———. 1978. "Caesar, Etruria and the *Disciplina Etrusca*." *Journal of Roman Studies* 68:132–52.

———. 1979. "L. Cornelius Sisenna and the Early First Century BC." *Classical Quarterly* 29:327–46.

———. 1985. *Intellectual life in the Late Roman Republic*. London: Duckworth.

Rea, J. A. 2007. *Legendary Rome: Myth, Monuments, and Memory on the Palatine and Capitoline*. London: Duckworth.

Reay, B. 2005. "Agriculture, Writing and Cato's Aristocratic Self-Fashioning." *Classical Antiquity* 24, no. 2: 331–61.

Regell, P. 1878. "De augurum publicorum libris." PhD diss., Vratislaviae.

———. 1882. "Fragmenta Auguraliaa." *Programm, Königlichess Gymnasium zu Hirschberg* 164:3–19.

Rener, F. M. 1989. *Interpretatio: Language and Translation from Cicero to Tytler*. Amsterdam: Rodopi.

Reusser, C. 1993. "Capitolium (Republik und Kaiserzeit)." In *LTUR* vol. I, 232–33.

Reynolds, L. D., ed. 1983. *Texts and Transmission: A Survey of the Latin Classics*. Oxford: Clarendon Press.

Richardson, J. S. 1991. "*Imperium Romanum*: Empire and the Language of Power." *Journal of Roman Studies* 81:1–9.

Richardson, L. Jr. 1992. *A New Topographical Dictionary of Ancient Rome*. Baltimore, MD: Johns Hopkins University Press.

Richlin, A. 1993. "Not before Homosexuality: The Materiality of the *Cinaedus* and the Roman Law against Love between Men." *Journal of the History of Sexuality* 3, no. 4: 523–73.

Ricoeur, P. (1975) 1977. *The Rule of Metaphor: Multi-Disciplinary Studies in the Creation of Meaning in Language*. Translated by R. Czerny, with K. McLaughlin and J. Costello. Toronto: University of Toronto Press.

———. (2000) 2004. *Memory, History, Forgetting*. Translated by K. Blamey and D. Pellauer. Chicago: University of Chicago Press.

Riganti, E. 1978. *De Lingua Latina, Libro VI, Testo Critico, Traduzione e Commento a Cura di E. Riganti*. Bologna: Pàtron.

Riggsby, A. M. 2002. "The Post Reditum Speeches." In *Brill's Companion to Cicero: Oratory and Rhetoric*, edited by J. May, 159–95. Leiden: Brill.

Riley, M. W. 2005. *Plato's Cratylus: Argument, Form and Structure*. Amsterdam: Rodopi.

Rimell, V. 2015. *The Closure of Space in Roman Poetics: Empire's Inward Turn*. Cambridge: Cambridge University Press.

Riposati, B. 1939. *M. Terenti Varronis de Vita Populi Romani: Fonti, Esegesi, Edizione Critica dei Frammenti*. Pubblicazioni dell'Università Cattolica del S. Cuore 4, 33. Milan: Vita & Pensiero.

———. 1976a. "M. Terenzio Varrone: l'uomo e lo scrittore." In *ACIV* 1, 59–89.

———. 1976b. "Varrone e la Sua Terra Sabina." In *Rieti e il suo Territorio*, edited by P. Brezzi, C. Pietrangeli, A. Prandi, B. Riposati, and C. Verani, 215–36. Milan: Bestetti.

Robinson, M. 2003. "Festivals, Fools and the *Fasti*: The *Quirinalia* and the *Feriae Stultorum* (Ovid, *Fast.* II 475–532)." *Aevum Antiquum* n.s. 3:609–21.

Rochette, B. 2010. "Greek and Latin Bilingualism." In *A Companion to the Ancient Greek Language*, edited by E. J. Bakker, 281–93. Malden, MA: Wiley-Blackwell.

———. 2011. "Language Policies in the Roman Republic and Empire." In J. Clackson 2011a, 549–63.
Rodriguez Mayorgas, A. 2010. "Romulus, Aeneas and the Cultural Memory of the Roman Republic." *Athenaeum* 98, no. 1: 89–109.
Roisman, H. M. 2005. "Nestor the Good Counsellor." *Classical Quarterly* 55, no. 1: 17–38.
Roller, L. E. 1999. *In Search of God the Mother: The Cult of Anatolian Cybele*. Berkeley: University of California Press.
Roller, M. B. 1997. "Color-Blindness: Cicero's Death, Declamation, and the Production of History." *Classical Philology* 92, no. 2: 109–30.
———. 2003. "Horizontal Women: Posture and Sex in the Roman *Convivium*." *American Journal of Philology* 124, no. 3: 377–422.
———. 2006. *Dining Posture in Ancient Rome: Bodies, Values, and Status*. Princeton, NJ: Princeton University Press.
———. 2010. "Demolished Houses, Monumentality, and Memory in Roman Culture." *Classical Antiquity* 29:117–80.
Roman, L. 2001. "The Representation of Literary Materiality in Martial's *Epigrams*." *Journal of Roman Studies* 91:113–45.
Romano, E. 2003. "Il Concetto di Antico in Varrone." In M. Citroni 2003, 99–117.
Rosand, D. 1981. "Composition/Decomposition/ = Recomposition: Notes on the Fragmentary and Artistic Process." In L. D. Kritzman 1981, 17–30.
Rosenberger, V. 2007. "Republican *nobiles*: Controlling the *Res Publica*." In J. Rüpke 2007, 292–303.
Ross, V. 1991. "Too Close to Home: Repressing Biography, Instituting Authority." In W. H. Epstein 1991a, 135–65.
Rousselle, R. 1987. "Liber-Dionysus in Early Roman Drama." *Classical Journal* 82:193–98.
Royo, M., and B. Gruet. 2008. "Décrire Rome: Fragment et Totalité, la Ville Ancienne au Risque du Paysage." In *Roma Illustrata*, edited by P. Fleury and O. Desbordes, 377–92. Caen: Presses Universitaires de Caen.
Rüpke, J. (1995) 2011. *The Roman Calendar from Numa to Constantine: Time, History, and the Fasti*. Translated by D. M. B. Richardson. Malden, MA: Wiley-Blackwell.
———. (2001) 2007. *Religion of the Romans*. Translated and edited by R. L. Gordon. Cambridge: Polity Press.
———. 2004a. "*Acta aut agenda*: Relations of Script and Performance." In *Rituals in Ink: A Conference on Religion and Literary Production in Ancient Rome Held at Stanford University in February 2002*, edited by A. Barchiesi, J. Rüpke, and S. A. Stephens, 23–43. Stuttgart: Steiner.
———. 2004b. "Roman Religion." In H. Flower 2004, 179–95.
———, ed. 2007. *A Companion to Roman Religion*. Malden, MA: Blackwell.
———. 2012. *Religion in Republican Rome: Rationalization and Ritual Change*. Philadelphia: University of Pennsylvania Press.
Rust, E. M. 2009. "Ex angulis secretisque librorum: Reading, Writing, and Using Miscellaneous Knowledge in the Noctes Atticae." PhD diss., University of Southern California. http://digitallibrary.usc.edu/search/controller/view/usctheses-m2688.html?x=13 02799710564.

Rutledge, S. H. 2012. *Ancient Rome as a Museum: Power, Identity, and the Culture of Collecting*. Oxford: Oxford University Press.

Ryan, F. X. 1996. "The *Lectio Senatus* after Sulla." *Rheinisches Museum* 139, no. 2: 189–91.

Salmon, E. T. 1972. "*Cicero Romanus an Italicus anceps*." In *Cicero and Virgil: Studies in Honor of Harold Hunt*, edited by J. R. C. Martyn, 75–86. Amsterdam: Hakkert.

Salvadore, M. 2001. "Lettori di Varrone." In G. Calboli 2001, 247–60.

Samuel, A. E. 1972. *Greek and Roman Chronology: Calendars and Years in Classical Antiquity*. Munich: Beck.

Santangelo, F. 2012. "Law and Divination in the Late Roman Republic." In *Law and Religion in the Roman Republic*, edited by O. Tellegen-Couperus, 31–54. Leiden: Brill.

———. 2013a. *Divination, Prediction and the End of the Roman Republic*. Cambridge: Cambridge University Press.

———. 2013b. "Priestly *Auctoritas* in the Roman Republic." *Classical Quarterly* 63:743–63.

Saunders, C. 1940. "Sources of the Names of Trojans and Latins in Vergil's *Aeneid*." *Transactions of the American Philological Association* 71:537–55.

Saussure, F. de. (1916) 1983. *Course in General Linguistics*. Edited by C. Bally and A. Sechehaye, with A. Riedlinger. Translated by R. Harris. London: Duckworth.

Schad, S. 2007. *A Lexicon of Latin Grammatical Terminology*. Studia Erudita 6. Pisa: Serra.

Scheid, J. 1990. *Romulus et Ses Frères. Le Collège des Frères arvales: Modèle du Culte Public dans la Rome des Empereurs*. Bibliothèque des Écoles Françaises d'Athènes et de Rome 275. Rome: École Française de Rome.

Schironi, F. 2007. "Ἀναλογία, *analogia, proportio, ratio*: Loanwords, Calques, and Reinterpretations of a Greek Technical Word." In *Bilinguisme et Terminologie Grammaticale Gréco-Latine*, edited by L. Basset, F. Biville, B. Colombat, P. Swiggers, and A. Wouters, 321–38. Leuven: Peeters.

Sciarrino, E. 2004. "Putting Cato the Censor's *Origines* in its Place." *Classical Antiquity* 23, no. 2: 323–57.

———. 2011. *Cato the Censor and the Beginnings of Latin Prose: From Poetic Translation to Elite Transcription*. Columbus: Ohio State University Press.

Scott, A. J., and E. W. Soja, eds. 1996. *The City: Los Angeles and Urban Theory at the End of the Twentieth Century*. Los Angeles: University of California Press.

Serbat, G. 1976. "Les Temps du Verbe en latin. III: Le Parfait de l'Indicatif Actif." *Revue des Etudes Latines* 54:308–52.

Sedley, D. 1998. "The Etymologies in Plato's *Cratylus*." *Journal of Hellenic Studies* 118: 140–54.

———. 2003. *Plato's Cratylus*. Cambridge: Cambridge University Press.

Sherwin-White, A. N. 1973. *The Roman Citizenship*. 2nd ed. Oxford: Oxford University Press.

Shillingsburg, P. L. 1997. *Resisting Texts: Authority and Submission in Constructions of Meaning*. Ann Arbor: University of Michigan Press.

Short, W. M. 2007. "Sermo, Sanguis, Semen: An Anthropology of Language in Roman Culture." PhD diss., University of California, Berkeley.

———. 2008. "Thinking Places, Placing Thoughts: Spatial Metaphors of Mental Activity in Roman Culture." *I Quaderni del Ramo d'Oro* 1:106–29. http://www.qro.unisi.it/frontend/node/13.
Silverman, A. 1992. "Plato's *Cratylus*: The Naming of Nature and the Nature of Naming." *Oxford Studies in Ancient Philosophy* 10:25–71.
Simón, F. M. 2011. "The *Feriae Latinae* as Religious Legitimation of the Consuls' *imperium*." In H. Beck, A. Duplá, M. Jehne, and F. P. Polo 2011, 116–32.
Sinclair, P. 1994. "Political Declensions in Latin Grammar and Oratory, 55 BCE–CE 39." *Ramus* 23:92–109.
Sluiter, I. 1990. *Ancient Grammar in Context: Contributions to the Study of Ancient Linguistic Thought*. Amsterdam: VU University Press.
———. 2015. "Ancient Etymology: A Tool for Thinking." In *Brill's Companion to Ancient Greek Scholarship*, vol. 2, edited by F. Montanari, S. Matthaios, and A. Rengakos, 896–92. Leiden: Brill.
Small, J. P. 1997. *Wax Tablets of the Mind: Cognitive Studies of Memory and Literacy in Classical Antiquity*. London: Routledge.
Smith, A. D. 1999. *Myths and Memories of the Nation*. Oxford: Oxford University Press.
Smith, C. J. 2000. "Worshipping Mater Matuta: Ritual and Context." In E. Bispham and C. Smith 2000, 136–55.
———. 2006. *The Roman Clan: The Gens from Ancient Ideology to Modern Anthropology*. Cambridge: Cambridge University Press.
Smith, C. J., and A. Powell, eds. 2009. *The Lost Memoirs of Augustus and the Development of Roman Autobiography*. Swansea: Classical Press of Wales.
Smith, J. 1992. "The Slightly Different Thing That Is Said: Writing the Aesthetic Experience." In *Writing Worlds: Discourse, Text and Metaphor in the Representation of Landscape*, edited by T. J. Barnes and J. S. Duncan, 73–85. London: Routledge.
Soja, E. 1996. *Thirdspace: Journeys to Los Angeles and Other Real-and-Imagined Places*. Cambridge, MA: Blackwell.
Spencer, D. 2007. "Rome at a Gallop: Livy on *Not* Gazing, Jumping, or Toppling into the Void." In D. H. J. Larmour and D. Spencer 2007b, 61–101.
———. 2010. *Roman Landscape: Culture and Identity*. Greece & Rome New Surveys in the Classics 39. Cambridge: Cambridge University Press.
———. 2011a. "Horace and the Con/Straints of Translation." In S. McElduff and E. Sciarrino 2011, 101–16.
———. 2011b. "Movement and the Linguistic Turn: Reading Varro's *De Lingua Latina*." In R. Laurence and D. Newsome 2011, 57–80.
———. 2011c. "Ῥωμαΐζω . . . *ergo sum*: Becoming Roman in Varro's *De Lingua Latina*." In *Cultural Memory and Identity in Ancient Societies*, edited by M. Bommas, 43–60. London: Continuum.
———. 2015a. "Urban Flux: Varro's Rome in Progress." In I. Östenberg, S. Malmberg, and J. Bjørnebye 2015, 99–110.
———. 2015b. "Varro's Romespeak: *De Lingua Latina*." In *Varro Varius: The Polymath of the Roman World*, edited by D. J. Butterfield, 73–92. Cambridge Classical Journal Supplement 39. Cambridge: Cambridge Philological Society.

———. 2018. "Varro's Roman Way: Metastasis and Etymology." In *The Production of Space in Latin Literature*, edited by W. Fitzgerald and E. Spentzou, 45–68. Oxford: Oxford University Press.
Spengel, A., ed. 1885. *M. Terenti Varronis De Lingua Latina Libri*. Berlin: Weidmann.
Spengel, L., ed. 1826. *M. Terenti Varronis De Lingua Latina Libri Qui Supersunt*. Berlin: Duncker and Humbloth.
Staples, A. 1998. *From Good Goddess to Vestal Virgins: Sex and Category in Roman Religion*. London: Routledge.
Starr, R. J. 1987. "The Circulation of Literary Texts in the Roman World." *Classical Quarterly* 37:213–323.
———. 2001. "The Flexibility of Literary Meaning and the Role of the Reader in Roman Antiquity." *Latomus* 60, no. 2: 433–45.
Steel, C., and H. van der Blom, eds. 2013. *Community and Communication: Oratory and Politics in Republican Rome*. Oxford: Oxford University Press.
Steinby, E. M. 1993. "Basilica Aemilia." In *LTUR* vol. I (A–C), 167–68.
Stein-Hölkeskamp, E. 2006. "Das römische Haus—die *memoria* der Mauern." In Stein-Hölkeskamp and Hölkeskamp 2006, 300–20.
Stein-Hölkeskamp, E., and K.-J. Hölkeskamp, eds. 2006. *Erinnerungsorte der Antike: Die Römische Welt*. Munich: Beck.
Stek, T. D. 2009. *Cult Places and Cultural Change in Republican Italy: A Contextual Approach to Religious Aspects of Rural Society after the Roman Conquest*. Amsterdam: Amsterdam University Press.
Stevenson, A. J. 2004. "Gellius and the Roman Antiquarian Tradition." In L. Holford-Strevens and A. D. Vardi 2004, 118–55.
Stevenson, T. 2005. "Readings of Scipio's Dictatorship in Cicero's *De Re Publica* (6.12)." *Classical Quarterly* 55, no. 1: 140–52.
Stewart, R. 1998. *Public Office in Early Rome: Ritual Procedure and Political Practice*. Ann Arbor: University of Michigan Press.
Stray, C., ed. 2010. *Classical Dictionaries: Past, Present and Future*. London: Duckworth.
Stroh, W. 2006. "Latein als Weltsprache: Das Erbe der Größe." In Stein-Hölkeskamp and Hölkeskamp 2006, 185–201.
Stroup, S. C. 2007. "Greek Rhetoric Meets Rome: Expansion, Resistance, and Acculturation." In W. J. Dominik and J. Hall 2007, 23–37.
———. 2010. *Catullus, Cicero, and a Society of Patrons: The Generation of the Text*. Cambridge: Cambridge University Press.
Sumi, G. S. 1997. "Power and Ritual: The Crowd at Clodius' Funeral." *Historia* 46, no. 1: 80–102.
———. 2002. "Spectacles and Sulla's Public Image." *Historia* 51, no. 4: 414–32.
———. 2005. *Ceremony and Power. Performing Politics in Rome between Republic and Empire*. Ann Arbor: University of Michigan Press.
———. 2011. "Topography and Ideology: Caesar's Monument and the Aedes Divi Ivlii in Augustan Rome." *Classical Quarterly* 61, no. 1: 205–29.
Swain, S. C. R. 2002. "Bilingualism in Cicero? The Evidence of Code-Switching." In J. N. Adams, M. Janse, and S. C. R. Swain 2002, 128–67.

Swiggers, P., and A. Wouters, eds. 1996a. *Ancient Grammar: Content and Context*. Louvain: Peeters.
———. 1996b. "Content and Context in (Translating) Ancient Grammar." In P. Swiggers and A. Wouters 1996a, 123–61.
———. 1996c. "Translating Ancient Grammatical Texts." In *History of Linguistics 1996*, vol. 2, *From Classical to Contemporary Linguistics*, edited by D. Cram, A. R. Linn, and E. Nowak, 3–11. Amsterdam: John Benjamins Press, 1996.
———, eds. 2002. *Grammatical Theory and Philosophy of Language in Antiquity*. Orbis Suppl. 19. Leuven: Peeters.
———, eds. 2003. *Syntax in Antiquity*. Louvain: Peeters.
Syme, R. 1939. *The Roman Revolution*. Oxford: Clarendon Press.
Tagliamonte, G. 1993. "Capitolium (Fino alla Prima Età Repubblicana)." In *LTUR* vol. I, 226–31.
Takács, S. A. 2008. *Vestal Virgins, Sibyls, and Matrons: Women in Roman Religion*. Austin: University of Texas Press.
Talbert, R. 2004. "Review of Trevor Murphy. 2004. *Pliny the Elder's Natural Nistory: The Empire in the Encyclopdia*. Oxford: Oxford University Press." *Bryn Mawr Classical Review* 2004.12.23. http://bmcr.brynmawr.edu/2004/2004-12-23.
Tatum, W. J. 2001. "Plutarch on Antiochus of Ascalon: *Cicero* 4, 2." *Hermes* 129, no. 1: 139–42.
———. 2008. *Always I Am Caesar*. Malden, MA: Blackwell.
———. 2013. "Campaign Rhetoric." In C. Steel and H. van der Blom 2013, 133–50.
Taylor, D. J. 1974. *Declinatio: A Study of the Linguistic Theory of Marcus Terentius Varro*. Amsterdam: John Benjamins Press.
———. 1988. "Varro and the Origins of Latin Linguistic Theory." In *L'Héritage des Grammairiens Latins, de l'Antiquité aux Lumières: Actes du Colloque de Chantilly, 2–4 Septembre 1987*, edited by I. Rosier, 37–48. Paris: Société pour l'Information Grammaticale
———. 1996a. *De Lingua Latina X: A New Critical Text and English Translation with Prolegomena and Commentary*. Amsterdam: John Benjamins Press.
———. 1996b. "Style and Structure in Varro?" In P. Swiggers and A. Wouters 1996a, 91–103.
Taylor, L. R. 1934. "Varro's *De gente populi Romani*." *Classical Philology* 29, no. 3: 221–29.
———. 1941. "Caesar's Early Career." *Classical Philology* 36, no. 2: 113–32.
———. 1966. *Roman Voting Assemblies from the Hannibalic War to the Dictatorship of Caesar*. Ann Arbor: University of Michigan Press.
Taylor, M. C. 2002. *The Moment of Complexity: Emerging Network Culture*. Chicago: University of Chicago Press.
Temelini, M. A. 2006. "Pompey's Politics and the Presentation of his Theatre-Temple Complex, 61–52 BCE." *Studia Humaniora Tartuensia* 7:1–14.
Thomas, L. 1974. *The Lives of a Cell: Notes of a Biology Watcher*. New York: Viking Press.
Thomas, R. F. 2004. "Torn between Jupiter and Saturn: Ideology, Rhetoric and Culture in the *Aeneid*." *Classical Journal* 10, no. 2: 121–47.

Torelli, M. 1999. *Tota Italia: Essays in the Cultural Formation of Roman Italy*. Oxford: Clarendon Press.

Traglia, A. 1956. *De Lingua Latina Libro X, Introduzione, Testo, Traduzione, Commento*. Bari: Adriatica.

———. 1963. "Dottrine Etimologiche ed Etimologie Varroniane con Particolare Riguardo al Linguaggio Poetico." In *Varron: Six Exposés et Discussions*, edited by H. Dahlmann, A. Traglia, R. Schröter, J. Collart, F. della Corte, and C. O. Brink, 35–77. Entretiens sur l'Antiquité Classique 9. Vandoeuvres-Geneva: Fondation Hardt.

———. 1993. "Varrone Prosatore." In *Cultura e Lingue Classiche*, vol. 3, *3° Convegno di Aggiornamento e di Didattica, Palermo, 29 octobre–1 novembre 1989*, edited by B. Amata, 693–885. Rome: L'Erma di Bretschneider.

Turfa, J. MacIntosh. 2006. "Etruscan Religion at the Watershed: Before and after the Fourth Ccentury BCE." In *Religion in Republican Italy*, edited by C. E. Schultz and P. B. Harvey Jr., 62–89. Yale Classical Studies 33. Cambridge: Cambridge University Press.

Turnebus, A., ed. 1566. *Editio Turnebi*. Paris: A. Wechelus.

Van der Blom, H. 2010. *Cicero's Role Models: The Political Strategy of a Newcomer*. Oxford: Oxford University Press.

Van Mal-Maeder, D. 2007. *La Fiction des Déclamations*. Mnemosyne Suppl. 290. Leiden: Brill.

Van Nuffelen, P. 2010. "Varro's *Divine Antiquities*: Roman Religion as an Image of Truth." *Classical Philology* 105, no. 2: 162–88.

Van Rooy. C. A. 1966. *Studies in Classical Satire and Related Literary Theory*. Leiden: Brill.

Vasaly, A. 1993. *Representations: Images of the World in Ciceronian Oratory*. Berkeley: University of California Press.

Vaughn, J. W. 1985. "Law and Rhetoric in the Causa Curiana." *Classical Antiquity* 4:208–22.

Verzár-Bass, M. 1998. "A Proposito dei Mausolei Negli *Horti* e Nelle *Villae*." In *Horti Romani: Atti del Convegno Internazionale, Roma, 4–6 Maggio 1995*, edited by M. Cima and E. La Rocca, 401–24. Bullettino della Commissione Archeologica Comunale di Roma Suppl. 6. Rome: L'Erma di Bretschneider.

Vian, F. 1963. *Les Origines de Thèbes: Cadmos et les Spartes*. Paris: Klincksieck.

Vout, C. 2007. "Sizing Up Rome, or Theorizing the Overview." In D. H. J. Larmour and D. Spencer 2007b, 295–322.

———. 2012. *The Hills of Rome: Signature of an Eternal City*. Cambridge: Cambridge University Press.

Walker, C. 1991. "Persona Criticism and the Death of the Author." In W. H. Epstein 1991a, 109–121.

Wallace, R. 2011. "The Latin Alphabet and Orthography." In J. Clackson 2011a, 9–28.

Wallace-Hadrill, A. 1987. "Time for Augustus: Ovid, Augustus and the *Fasti*." In *Homo Viator: Classical Essays for John Bramble*, edited by M. Whitby, P. Hardie and M. Whitby, 221–30. Bristol: Bristol Classical Press.

———. 1990. "Roman Arches and Greek Honours: The Language of Power at Rome." *Proceedings of the Cambridge Philological Society* 36:143–81.

———. 2008. *Rome's Cultural Revolution*. Cambridge: Cambridge University Press.
Walter, U. 2004. *Memoria und Res Publica: Zur Geschichtskultur im Republikanischen Rom*. Frankfurt: Verlag Antike.
———. 2006. "Kalender, Fasten und Annalen—die Ordnung der Erinnerung." In E. Stein-Hölkeskamp and K.-J. Hölkeskamp 2006, 40–58.
Waquet, F. 1998. *Le Latin ou l'Empire d'un Signe*. Paris: Albin Michel.
Ward, A. M. 1970. "The Early Relationships between Cicero and Pompey until 80 BC." *Phoenix* 24:119–29.
Watts, R. J. 2003. *Politeness*. Cambridge: Cambridge University Press.
Weinstein, R. S. 1996. "The First American City." In A. J. Scott and E. W. Soja 1996, 22–46.
Weinstock, S. 1971. *Divus Julius*. Oxford: Clarendon Press.
Welch, K. 1999. "Subura." In *LTUR* vol. IV, 379–83.
Welch, T. S. 2005. *The Elegiac Cityscape: Propertius and the Meaning of Roman Monuments*. Columbus: Ohio State University Press.
Wendling, E. 1893. "Zu Posidonius und Varro." *Hermes* 28:335–53.
Whatmough, J. 1921. "*Fordus* and *Fordicidia*." *Classical Quarterly* 15, no. 2: 108–9.
White, P. 2010. *Cicero in Letters: Epistolary Relations of the Late Republic*. New York: Oxford University Press.
Wiedemann, T. E. J. 1986. "The Fetiales: A Reconsideration." *Classical Quarterly* 36: 478–90.
Wilhelm, R McK. 1988. "Cybele: The Great Mother of Augustan Order." *Vergilius* 34: 77–101.
Wilkins, J. 2003. "Land and Sea: Italy and the Mediterranean in the Roman Discourse of Dining." *American Journal of Philology* 124, no. 3: 359–75.
Willi, A. 2010. "Campaigning for *Utilitas*: Style, Grammar and Philosophy in C. Iulius Caesar." In E. Dickey and A. Chahoud 2010, 229–42.
Williams, G. D. 1992. "Representations of the Book-Roll in Latin Poetry: Ovid, *Tr.* 1,1,3–14 and Related Texts." *Mnemosyne* 45:178–89.
———. 2008. "Cold Dcience: Seneca on Hail and Snow in *Natural Questions* 4B." *Proceedings of the Cambridge Philological Society* 54:209–36.
Wiseman, T. P. 1974. "Legendary Genealogies in Late-Republican Rome." *Greece and Rome* 21:153–64.
———. 1987. "*Conspicui postes tectaque digna deo*: The Public Image of Aristocratic and Imperial Houses in the Late Republic and Early Empire." In *L'Urbs: Espace Urbaine et Histoire (Ier Siècle av. J.-C.–IIIe Siècle ap. J.-C.): Actes du Colloque International Organisé par la Centre National de la Recherche Scientifique et l'École Française de Rome. Rome, 8–12 Mai 1985*, 393–413. Collection de l'École Française de Rome 98. Rome: de Boccard.
———. 1995a. "The God of the Lupercal." *Journal of Roman Studies* 85:1–22.
———. 1995b. *Remus: A Roman Myth*. Cambridge: Cambridge University Press.
———. 1998. *Roman Drama and Roman History*. Exeter: University of Exeter Press.
———. 2004. *The Myths of Rome*. Exeter: University of Exeter Press.
———. 2008. *Unwritten Rome*. Exeter: University of Exeter Press.

———. 2009. *Remembering the Roman People: Essays on Late-Republican Politics and Literature*. Oxford: Oxford University Press.
Wisse, J. 2013. "The Bad Orator: Between Clumsy Delivery and Political Danger." In C. Steel and H. van der Blom 2013, 163–94.
Wittgenstein, L. (1953) 2009. *Philosophical Investigations*. Rev. 4th ed. Edited by P. M. S. Hacker and J. Schulte. Translated by G. E. M. Anscombe. Oxford: Blackwell.
Woodward, R. D. 2013. *Myth, Ritual, and the Warrior in Roman and Indo-European Antiquity*. Cambridge: Cambridge University Press.
Wray, D. 2001. *Catullus and the Poetics of Roman Manhood*. Cambridge: Cambridge University Press.
Yates, F. A. 1966. *The Art of Memory*. Chicago: University of Chicago Press.
Zehnacker, H. 2008. "La Description de Rome dans le Livre V du *De Lingua Latina* de Varron." In *Roma Illustrata: Représentations de la Ville, Actes du Colloque International de Caen, 6–8 octobre 2005*, edited by P. Fleury and O. Desbordes, 421–32. Caen: Presses Universitaires de Caen.
Ziolkowski, A. 1988. "Mummius' Temple of Hercules Victor and the Round Temple on the Tiber." *Phoenix* 42:309–33.
———. 1996. "Of Streets and Crossroads: The Location of the Carinae." *Memoirs of the American Academy in Rome* 41:121–51.
———. 1998–99. "Ritual Cleaning-Up of the City: From the Lupercalia to the Argei." *Ancient Society* 29:191–218.
Žižek, S. 2006. *How to Read Lacan*. London: Granta.
Zollschan, L. 2011. "The Longevity of the Fetial College." In *Law and Religion in the Roman Republic*, edited by O. Tellegen-Couperus, 119–44. Leiden: Brill.
Zucchelli, B. 1976. "L'Enigma del *Trikaranos*: Varrone di Fronte ai Triumviri." In *Atti Congresso Internazionale di Studi Varroniani II, Rieti Settembre 1974*, 609–25. Rieti: Centro di Studi Varroniani.
Zukin, S. 1991. *Landscapes of Power: From Detroit to Disney World*. Berkeley: University of California Press.

Index

Acca Larentia, 237–40, 331n10, 337n107, 338nn111–112, 339n125
Accius, 22, 83, 103–4, 157, 161–63, 285n79, 310n128, 311n133, 313n12, 340n146
Aeneas, 7, 56, 58, 79, 100, 195, 269n8, 270n16, 284n72, 301n9. *See also* Troy; Vergil
agriculture, 3, 21, 38–39, 46–50, 61, 65, 73, 95, 132–33, 147–48, 153, 171–72, 179–81, 184, 185, 190, 200, 205–6, 207, 210, 218, 223–25, 229–30, 233–35, 241–42, 246, 281n34, 289n8, 296n31, 317n52, 325n42, 337n105. *See also* foodstuffs and cooking
albus, -a, -um, 103, 104, 165, 313n18, 314n24, 339n129; Alba Fucens, 14; Alba Longa, 14, 39, 138, 165, 194–95, 241, 326n50, 339n129. *See also* Tiber, river: as Albula
analogia. *See* regularity
ancestors, ancestral practice, 8, 9, 17, 34–35, 42, 45–46, 54, 64–65, 71–72, 76, 82, 88–89, 96–97, 98, 99–100, 119, 146, 174–75, 184, 186, 197–98, 213, 217–18, 222–24, 226–27, 236, 237–39, 242, 244–45, 263n6, 269n10, 281n34, 294n93, 321n89, 325n38, 325–26n42, 334n56, 337n101, 337n107, 342n26. *See also* tradition
Angerona. *See* festivals: Angeronalia
animal husbandry. *See* agriculture; animals

animals, 48, 82–83, 132, 160–61, 169, 204, 209, 210, 234, 279n125, 325n42, 329n95, 330–31n9; birds, 53, 66, 74–76, 138, 167–68, 210, 292n49, 316n38; cows/oxen, 38, 153, 223–24, 310n118, 311n131, 333n41; dogs, 81, 209–10, 292n49, 329n98; goats, 231–32, 294n99, 315n35, 335n77; hares, 14, 184, 209–12, 328–29nn93–95, 329n98, 329n102, 329–30n106; horses, 39, 61, 93, 139, 161, 164–65, 174, 212, 217, 220, 224, 234, 236, 252, 268n64, 314n30, 337n105; pigs/boars, 184, 185, 194–95, 210, 211, 314n23, 329n98; sheep/lambs, 38–39, 48, 61, 147–48, 153, 171–72, 178, 209–10, 225, 329n98, 330–31n9; wolves, 14, 167–68, 184, 209–12, 329n98, 329n102, 330n106, 335n77
anomalia. *See* irregularity and anomaly
Antony, Marc, 20, 28, 168, 171, 315. *See also* Cicero: works of: *Philippics*
Apollo, 157, 203–4, 231, 232, 246, 283n58, 311n136, 335n80; in relation to Sol, 202–4, 327n78, 328n86
Argei, Argives, 174, 177, 227, 305nn–62, 306n64, 308n92, 315n35, 334n61; rites of, 130–31, 141–42, 146–48, 152, 158, 219–20, 226–27, 308n93, 332n25, 332n27; shrines of, 130, 139, 141–48, 158–59, 301n16, 305n61

379

astronomy and cosmology, 5, 54, 58, 60, 131–33, 199–203. *See also* augurs, augury, and auspicy

Atellan farce, 80, 180S

Atticus, correspondent of Cicero, 7, 10, 24–26, 27, 28, 29–34, 57, 105, 222, 250, 272n35, 273n44, 273n47, 275n69, 275–76n82, 276n87, 276–77nn89–90, 284n76, 302n28, 323n17, 332n29

augurs, augury, and auspicy, 52, 53–54, 58, 62–64, 74–76, 83–84, 132, 138, 144, 155–56, 167–68, 178, 225, 283n53, 285n82, 286–87n100, 288n101, 292n66, 310n127, 314n29, 319n68, 334n61, 336nn97–98. *See also* animals: birds; omens; religion: and priests; sight and vision; speech: prophetic

Bacchus. *See* Liber

bilingualism. *See* loan words and bilingualism

birds. *See* animals: birds

Bovillae, 39–40, 279n123

Cadmus. *See* Thebes

Caesar, Julius, and regularity, 8, 10, 89–90, 250–52, 265n32, 267n50, 297n32, 342n17, 342n22; as addressee and sparring partner, 7–10, 22–26, 34, 54, 107, 134, 169–72, 175, 181, 229, 260, 271n25, 271n32, 321n90, 330n7; assassination and funeral of, 28, 32, 40, 163, 220, 234, 245–46, 272n38, 279n125, 280n16, 336n91; calendrical reforms of, 181, 214, 220–22, 242, 331n13, 332n30, 338n123, 340–41n152; *Commentaries*, 16, 24–25, 273n43, 273n52, 308n86; as Greek-style intellectual, 8, 208, 250–52, 256; political career of, 22–23, 26, 39, 182, 218, 222, 224, 230, 273n44, 283n58, 311n131, 313n13, 314n27, 314n30, 315n36, 317n50, 322n95, 335n72, 335n80

calendar. *See* time

Callimachus and Callimachaeanism, 55, 57–59, 67, 78, 157–58, 268n68, 284n64, 284n67, 288n121, 330n8

Camenae, 19, 73–74, 77–79, 152, 290n33; as Muses, 57, 78, 340n147. *See also carmen* and song

Camilla, *camilla, -us,* 55–56, 58, 78, 284n63, 284n67, 318n66

carmen and song, 59, 72, 73–74, 75–76, 78–79, 81, 101, 241, 283n56, 291n37, 329n98. *See also* Camenae; Carmentis, Carmenta; music, musical instruments; Salii, cult and Hymn of the; speech: prophetic

Carmentis, Carmenta, 78–79, 216, 291nn37–38, 331n10, 334n63, 339n128. See also *carmen*; Rome: gates of; speech: prophetic

cases. *See* nouns

Cato, 92, 119, 294n93, 326n46; as agricultural writer, 49, 185–86, 281n27, 309n98, 317n52, 317n55, 322nn5–6, 329n97, 338n118; *Origines*, 20, 86–89, 93–94, 269nn9–10, 270n18, 293nn74–78, 293n82; as supporter of Pompey, 26

Catullus, 169, 210

childhood, children, and babies, 20, 51, 66, 117, 118, 145, 157, 164, 189, 191, 197, 224, 230, 267n55. *See also* family relationships; speech

Chrysippus, 66, 117–18

Cicero: as addressee and sparring partner, 4, 5–6, 8, 10, 13–14, 18, 21–22, 25–28, 30–33, 41, 43–44, 47–48, 57–58, 65–66, 75–76, 82–83, 85, 87, 90, 92–94, 105–6, 108–10, 127, 130, 133, 145, 151, 154, 171, 185, 188–89, 193, 197, 210–11, 215, 220, 222, 224, 228–29, 245, 247, 249–52, 260, 271n25, 272n35, 274n61, 276n87, 276n88, 323–24n18; and Clodius, 39–40, 76, 234, 280n16, 306n69, 312–13n9, 325n35; as Greek-style intellectual, 6, 17, 24, 32, 48, 96, 105–6, 256, 270n15, 294n93, 302–3n28, 341n8; and irregularity, 8, 251; in exile, 75–76; political career and views of, 20, 22–23, 24, 27, 35, 59, 182, 183, 193, 230, 233, 240, 245–46, 249–51, 169, 271n33, 272–73n41, 273n44, 273n49, 273n50, 274n55, 286–87n100, 289n25, 290n31, 296nn25–26, 312n5, 314n27, 316n41, 317n50

Cicero, works of: *Academica*, 30, 33–34, 40–41, 43, 57–58, 105–6, 215, 265n30, 275–76n82; *Brutus*, 108, 250–51; *De Amicitia*, 191; *De Diuinatione*, 26, 85, 286–87n100, 311n131; *De Legibus*, 162–63, 265n30, 269n7, 312–13n9; *De Natura Deorum*, 48, 105–6, 191, 201–2, 265n30, 267n58; *De Officiis*, 29, 61; *De Oratore*, 96, 108–9, 166, 251, 267n58; *De Republica*, 21, 28, 98, 163–64, 191, 277n94; *De Senectute*, 87; *In Pisonem*, 240; *Orator*, 92; *Philippics*, 22, 34, 57, 182–83, 246, 275n55, 322n99; *Pro Caelio*, 194; *Tusculan Disputations*, 92, 294n93. See also *De Lingua Latina*: dedication to Cicero

cogitatio, *cogito*, 34, 51, 62–63, 76. See also readers, as active participants and (s)electors

consuetudo. See usage, popular

Consus. See festivals: Consualia

cooking. See foodstuffs and cooking

Cures and the Curenses (Quirites), 20, 35, 147, 179–80, 205, 220, 270n17, 320n84, 331n18. See also Quirinus; Romulus

Curia and *curia / curiae*, 27, 156–57, 166, 191, 217–18, 220, 223, 234, 237–8, 241, 242, 303n34, 337–38n110, 340n150

custom. See ancestors, ancestral practice; habit, *habitus*

Cybele, 58, 179, 223, 320n77

day, 45, 100, 131, 202, 207–8, 214. See also festivals; Jupiter: as Diespater; time

declinatio. See inflection

De Lingua Latina: author's revision and epitomization of, 3, 23, 168, 171, 222, 245–46; date of composition of, 29, 168;

dedication to Cicero, 29–34, 57, 90, 252; as fragmentary text, 5, 10, 259; as literature, 3–4, 7–8, 13, 18, 51–52, 67–71, 81, 94, 102, 114–15, 117, 122, 134–36, 203, 213, 228, 233, 242, 248, 252, 257–59; as postmodern hypertext, 4, 10–12, 41, 86, 91, 94–95, 127–29, 246–47; as source for excerptors, 13, 41, 68, 249; structure of, xi–xii, xvi–xvii, xxiii, 3–4, 7–8, 12–15, 17, 66, 73, 86–87, 90, 208–9, 213, 250–52, 256–59; transmission of, xi, 10. See also Caesar, Julius, and regularity; Cicero: as addressee and sparring partner; irregularity; readers, as active participants and (s)electors; regularity; speech: as powerful communication; usage

Diana, 56, 138, 142, 145, 150, 157, 205, 233, 327n78, 328n85; as Luna (Moon), 202–4; as Trivia, 157, 203

dining, 111–12, 115, 268n70. See also foodstuffs and cooking

Dionysus. See Liber

discourse. See oratory, *oratio*; usage

drama and the stage, 45, 53, 57–58, 61–64, 69, 73–74, 75, 77, 82–83, 86, 88, 92, 100, 113, 163, 180, 185–86, 189, 198–99, 212–13, 223, 228, 240. See also Atellan farce; *carmen* and song; Ennius; Livius Andronicus; music, musical instruments; Pacuvius; Plautus; Terence

education, 12, 46, 49, 92–93, 98, 109, 111, 121, 170, 197–98, 249

Ennius, 44, 53, 55, 59–60, 72, 76–77, 79–81, 83–86, 102–4, 107–9, 132, 137, 149, 152, 153, 155–56, 168–69, 170, 176–77, 190–91, 199–202, 211, 219, 235, 265–66n38, 285n84, 289n8, 290n28, 297n34, 302n19, 310nn–114, 318n61, 334n65

entertainments and games, 120, 186–87, 220–21, 224, 231–35, 338–39n123

Etruscan language, people, and heritage, 20, 55, 58–59, 75–76, 142–43, 145–46,

Etruscan language, people, and heritage (*continued*)
    149, 152, 158, 168, 174–75, 181, 194, 221, 230, 233, 242, 269n9, 284n67, 308n88, 308n92, 315–16n38, 318n65, 319n70, 320–21n87, 325n36. *See also* kings and kingship
etymology: and cultural renewal, 3–5, 9–10, 129–30, 201, 205–6, 213; as performance of authority, 44–45, 62–63, 68, 71–73, 78, 81, 92, 110, 122, 131, 145, 154, 201–2, 209, 215; practice of, 9, 67; theory of, 258–59. *See also* loan words and bilingualism
eyes. *See* sight and vision

family relationships, 14, 15, 20, 38, 45, 54, 58, 72, 75, 78–79, 92, 104–5, 123, 138, 151, 165, 177, 184–89, 190–202, 209, 210, 211, 212–13, 217, 220, 222–23, 226, 230, 237, 240, 256–59, 284n67, 326n47. *See also* festivals: Parentalia; gender; tribes
farmers and farming. *See* agriculture
fauns. *See* speech: prophetic
festivals, 168, 179–80, 214–44; Agonia (Agonalia), 178, 216, 219–20, 314–15n33, 330n8, 332n25; Angeronalia, 237–38; Carmentalia, 216, 219n38, 337n107; Compitalia, 216, 239–40, 243; Consualia, 232–35; Ecurria (Equirria), 217–18, 220–21, 224, 332n25; Feralia, 217–18; Fordicidia, 223–24; Liberalia, 178, 218–21, 330n8; Lupercalia, 163, 167–68, 178, 181, 216–17, 220, 231, 314n32, 315n35, 316n39, 335n77; Meditrinalia, 236, 330n6, 333n51; Megalensia, 222–23, 320n77; Parentalia, 216, 220, 237–38, 331n11; Parilia (Palilia), 136, 223–24, 333n42, 333nn45–48; Saturnalia, 199–200, 237–38, 240, 338n112; Septimontium, 133–34, 146, 174, 220, 237–40, 303n34; Vestalia, 225, 228, 334n63; Vinalia, 224–25, 233–34, 333n50, 336n87; Volturnalia, 235, 336n96. *See also* Fortuna; gods; religion: and foundation of temples; ritual, rites
Flora, 151, 309n104, 329n106, 334n61
Fons and *fons* (springs), 17–18, 67, 72, 187, 204–5, 236, 266n45, 268n68, 334n57, 334n62, 337nn103–104. *See also* water
foodstuffs and cooking, 14, 47–48, 63, 80, 115, 190, 217–19, 220, 241, 252–53, 323–24n18, 331n15, 342nn25–26
Fors Fortuna. *See* Fortuna
Fortuna, 25, 34, 334n62, 335n72; as Fors Fortuna, 179, 229–30; as Virilis, 222, 332n33
Forum Boarium, 139–40, 142, 143, 153, 280n6
Forum Romanum, 27, 65, 99, 112–13, 139, 143–44, 149, 156, 205, 218, 234, 328n87, 339n132
freedmen. *See* slaves and freedmen
Furrina, 232–33

garlands and flowers, 46, 48, 115–16, 117, 236
Gellius, Aulus, 5, 10–12, 223, 290
gender, 78, 267n55, 288n117; and femininity, 20, 63–64, 66–67, 73, 79, 82–83, 112, 114–15, 117, 145, 164, 191, 195–96, 197, 198, 203–4, 212–13, 219–21, 230–31, 232, 234, 240, 288n117, 332n28; and grammar, 14, 38, 81, 190–99, 212, 325n38, 325–26n42; and masculinity, 190–94, 212–13. *See also* festivals; inflection; nouns; oratory, *oratio*: as performance of elite masculinity; Vestal Virgins
gods. *See* Acca Larentia; Apollo; Carmentis; Cybele; Diana; Flora; Fons; Fortuna; Furrina; Hercules; Janus; Juno; Jupiter; Lares; Liber; Mars; Mercury; Minerva; Neptune; Ops; Quirinus; Romulus; Saturn; Venus; Vulcan. *See also* festivals; religion; ritual, rites; *templum* and temple foundations
grammar. *See* gender: and grammar; inflection; nouns; speech; verbs

habit, *habitus*, 29, 30, 32, 42, 52, 54, 96–97, 104–5, 112–13, 154, 186–87, 190, 236, 242, 250–51, 264n29, 321n90. *See also* ancestors, ancestral practice; irregularity; regularity; tradition; usage
hearing, 68, 76–77, 86, 97, 105, 112–13, 119, 121, 211, 294n92
Hercules (Dius Fidius, Sancus), 14, 141, 142, 147, 174, 189, 201, 220, 226–27, 238–39, 306n70, 308n92, 338n112. *See also* Argei, Argives
hills. *See* Rome: hills of

inflection, 6, 14–17, 36, 38–40, 70–71, 76, 99, 101, 102–4, 107, 110–11, 112–13, 116–17, 120–21, 123–26, 161, 185–86, 189, 192, 199, 210, 212–13, 252–53, 256–57, 259, 262n5, 281n22, 283n55, 296n27, 319n74, 326n47. *See also* gender: and grammar; irregularity; nouns; regularity; time: periodization and measurement of; usage
inhabitation, 54, 69, 84, 98, 134, 155, 160–61, 181, 224, 307n79
irregularity and anomaly, 8–9, 11, 12–13, 16–17, 36–38, 40, 42–43, 85–86, 89–90, 98, 101–2, 109–12, 114–15, 117–19, 123, 124–26, 129, 135, 144, 185, 188, 192, 207, 210–11, 251–53, 256–57, 267n52, 294n87, 299n81, 299n86, 317n50. *See also* inflection; nouns; regularity; usage

Janus, 23, 154, 237, 246, 310n121, 330n8, 336n93
Juno, 151, 200, 227; as Caprotina, 231–32, 335n79; as Curitis, 180, 320–21n87; as Earth, 202; as Mother, 308n85, 335n77; Lucina, 70, 145–46, 203–4, 308n86; Regina, 308n87
Jupiter, 52, 86, 135, 151, 177, 190–91, 200, 201, 202, 204, 210, 225, 227, 317n50, 324n34, 328n87, 334n57, 336n87, 337n101; as Diespater, 201, 202, 207; as Diouis, 201; as Latiaris, 308n92; as Sky, 202, 204; as Viminius, 146

kings and kingship, 109, 126, 140, 143, 152, 163, 175–78, 180–82, 190–91, 216, 240, 244, 299n84, 313n13, 320n77, 331n21; Ancus Marcius, 141–42, 305–6n63, 306n66; Attalus, 179, 222–23; Aventinus, 138, 177; Latinus, 40, 58, 147, 176, 195, 319n74; Numa Pompilius, 72, 140, 154, 168, 219–20, 223–24, 310n121, 314–15nn33–34, 335n82, 336n96, 337n103; Servius Tullius, 142, 144–45, 151, 177, 179, 229–30, 233, 239–40, 304n53, 306n68, 319n75, 320n76; Tarquinius Priscus, 149, 230, 240; Tarquinius Superbus, 151–52, 240; Tiberinus, 176–77; Titus Tatius, 136, 147, 149, 175, 177, 179–80, 191, 204–5, 227, 310n121, 320–21n87, 327n78, 332n27, 336n90; Tullus Hostilius, 314–15n33. *See also* magistrates and political offices; militarism and its terminology; Quirinus; Rome; Romulus

Lares, 145, 238, 239–40, 338n112
Latin language: as dynamic system, 17–18, 37–40, 54, 65, 71–73, 77, 90, 93–94, 104–5, 111, 118, 121–2, 127, 183, 206, 213, 224; as embodied practice, 47, 54, 74–77, 83, 106–7, 116, 121, 214, 258; hybridity of, 4, 8, 20, 59, 64, 88, 99–105, 111, 125, 128, 135, 192, 208–9, 210, 228, 239, 256–57, 282; as language of Latium, 60, 79, 88, 98–99, 175–76, 183, 194–95, 207, 225, 232, 241, 319; and self-fashioning, 6–8, 11–12, 17, 22, 28, 41–42, 67, 70–71, 81, 88–89, 97, 112, 115, 192–93, 232, 247–48, 256. *See also* loan words and bilingualism
lego. *See* readers, as active participants and (s)electors
Liber, 179, 180, 218–21, 321n89, 321n90, 332n28; Bacchus, 84–85, 321n90. *See also* festivals: Agonia; festivals: Liberalia
Livius Andronicus, 71–72, 176
loan words and bilingualism, 44, 55, 57, 61, 86–89, 92–93, 94, 98–102, 105, 160,

loan words and bilingualism (*continued*) 179, 181–82, 211. *See also* Latin language: hybridity of; Varro: and Sabine identity
Luna. *See* Diana
Luperci and Lupercalia. *See* festivals: Lupercalia

magistrates and political offices, 8, 23, 32, 35, 44–46, 47, 64, 100–101, 102–3, 150, 154, 160–65, 170, 175–76, 181, 208, 212, 220–21, 241, 242–44, 278n115, 280n19, 287n101, 290n31, 298n62, 312n4, 312n6, 313nn10–11, 313n13, 319n69, 321n92, 324n29, 339n126, 339n129. *See also* militarism and its terminology; Rome
Magna Mater. *See* Cybele
marriage. *See* family relationships
Mars, 145, 205, 224, 233, 236, 244. *See also* festivals: Agonia; festivals: Ecurria (Equirria); festivals: Meditrinalia; militarism and its terminology
memory and mnemotechnics, 7, 27–28, 34, 45, 49–51, 59–60, 65, 67, 102, 127, 129–30, 135–36, 140, 153–54, 231–32, 234, 242, 258, 282n38, 305n59, 307n81
Mercury, 226, 284n67, 334n57, 340n148
militarism and its terminology, 32–33, 40, 44–45, 52, 63, 69, 93, 154, 162–65, 167–75, 179–82, 205, 206, 224, 236–37, 243, 250–52, 294n89, 308n86, 314–15n33, 316n43, 317n50, 317–18n57, 341n12. *See also* magistrates and political offices; Mars; Rome
Minerva, 151, 227, 228–29, 310n114, 334n64
moon, 157, 206, 208. *See also* Diana: as Luna
mos maiorum. *See* ancestors, ancestral practice
Muses. *See* Camenae
music, musical instruments, 59–60, 74, 168, 228–29, 285n84, 299n85. *See also carmen* and song

Naevius, 19, 85, 138, 147, 153, 198
Neptune, 205, 232–33, 234, 334n57

night, 71, 81, 131, 202–3, 207, 302n18, 326n47, 327n79. *See also* time
nouns, 36, 77, 99–100, 104, 110–11, 117, 124, 245, 252, 298n59, 283n55, 323n13; cases of, 14–15, 101, 103–4, 124, 126, 182–83, 185–90, 192–93, 210–11, 212, 267–68n62; proper, 14–15, 21, 29, 35–36, 38–40, 44, 48, 55–57, 65, 79, 94, 97–98, 99–100, 100–102, 105, 127, 129–30, 134–35, 137–38, 140, 142–43, 145–54, 161, 166–67, 173–74, 176–81, 188–89, 191–93, 195, 200–208, 210, 212–13, 252–53, 263n6. *See also* Aeneas; festivals; gender: and grammar; gods; inflection; irregularity; kings and kingship; magistrates and political offices; militarism and its terminology; regularity; Rome: bridges of; Rome: hills of; Romulus: and Rome's etymology; Tiber, river; time

omens, 151, 165, 169. *See also* augurs, augury, and auspicy; religion: and priests; speech: prophetic
Ops, 199–200, 234–35, 237–38, 336n93; as Opeconsiva, 234–35, 337n109; as Ops *mater*, with Terra, 199–200, 336n93
oratory, *oratio*, 7–8, 12, 35–36, 64, 68, 70, 87, 90, 96–97, 102–3, 106–15, 124–25, 127–28, 188, 256, 278n110, 341n3; as performance of elite masculinity, 27, 32, 44, 62, 72–75, 80, 88–89, 92, 96, 111–12, 249, 265n31, 268n70, 341n8. *See also* speech; usage
Oscan language, 79–80
Ovid: *Fasti*, 151, 180, 216, 218, 223–24, 226–29, 234, 309, 320–21, 329–31, 334–35; *Metamorphoses*, 56, 66, 129, 209–11, 280

Pacuvius, 55, 72, 85
pastoralism. *See* agriculture; animals
Plato: *Cratylus*, 12, 16, 22, 61, 263n6, 271n26, 280nn5–6
Plautus, 3, 58, 63–64, 73, 208, 229, 254, 287, 324, 335

poetry, poets, 11, 25, 35–37, 49, 54, 57, 60, 63–64, 68–69, 70–75, 81, 82–83, 85–86, 87–90, 92–94, 97, 102–4, 112–13, 124, 129, 152, 155, 157, 176, 181, 190, 197, 229, 256–57; meters of, 60, 82. See also *carmen* and song; drama and the stage; music and musical instruments; speech: prophetic

Pollio, Asinius, 28–29

Pompey the Great, 22–26, 33, 35, 54, 210, 222, 229–30, 290n31

priesthoods. *See* augurs, augury, and auspicy; kings and kingship; religion: and priests

processions. *See* festivals; ritual, rites

puns and wordplay, 11, 33, 39, 45, 47–48, 79–80, 93, 134, 150, 152, 166, 191, 193, 195–96, 200, 203–4, 213, 231, 234, 245–46, 252–53, 266n45, 279n122, 290–91n36, 296n20, 327n74, 342n26

Quirinus, 20, 205, 217–18, 314–15n33, 320n84, 332n27. *See also* festivals: Quirinalia; kings and kingship; Romulus: and Quirinus

Quirites. *See* Cures and the Curenses (Quirites)

ratio. See regularity

readers, as active participants and (s)electors, 3–4, 6–7, 9–13, 27–28, 41, 42–44, 45, 46–49, 54–59, 61–63, 67, 68–73, 75–78, 79–83, 85, 90–91, 93–95, 102, 110, 116–17, 119–28, 129–30, 133–36, 141–43, 152–53, 158–59, 165–66, 168, 170, 174–76, 183, 188–90, 193–94, 197–98, 200, 206–9, 210–13, 215, 220, 225, 227–28, 232–33, 235, 244–47, 248–50, 254–58. See also *cogitatio, cogito*; *De Lingua Latina*: as literature; writing as practice

Reate. *See* Varro: as Reatine

regularity, 8–9, 12–17, 36–40, 43, 89–90, 101–5, 109–19, 123–26, 144, 182–89, 192–95, 210–11, 252–59, 267n52, 296n24, 297n37, 297n47, 298n57, 299n81, 299n86, 325–26n42, 330n107, 340n147, 343n41, 343n43; and *ratio*, 3, 8, 13, 34, 37, 103, 131, 250, 253–54. *See also* Caesar, Julius, and regularity; habit, *habitus*; irregularity and anomaly; usage

religion, 4–5, 52, 55–58, 100, 108–9, 214–15, 179–80, 190–92, 199–207, 215, 315–16n38, 319n70, 321n90; and priests, 53–54, 165–70, 178, 216, 219–20, 225, 235–38, 241–44, 314n27, 320n77, 320n80, 330n6, 335n82. *See also* augurs, augury, and auspicy; festivals; gods; kings and kingship; ritual, rites; *templum* and temple foundations; time; Vestal Virgins

Remus. *See* Romulus: and Remus

ritual, rites, 11, 54, 56, 58, 66, 74, 101, 144, 155, 156, 165–68, 178, 180, 194, 198, 217–18, 221–23, 236, 238, 239, 240, 242, 246, 298n31, 307n77, 320n80; and processions, 48, 144, 167, 179–80, 198, 219, 220, 221, 222, 339n129. *See also* Argei, Argives; festivals; gods

Rome: bridges of, 141–42, 165–66, 219–20, 226–27, 304n45, 305n58, 305–6n63; gates of, 78–79, 137–38, 150, 152–54, 159, 237–39, 305n55, 310n114, 310n121, 334n57, 337n103, 338n111; hills of, 130, 133–39, 141–52, 158–59, 177, 179–80, 187–88, 227, 236–40, 246, 302n27, 306n72, 308n92, 331n18, 332n27; people of, 5, 34–38, 40, 45–46, 47, 74, 106, 108, 112–13, 161–65, 170, 180–81, 230–32, 234, 239–44, 246, 250, 256, 277nn94–95, 278n105, 312n5; Senate of, 108–9, 120, 142, 161–62, 277n95; streets of, 65, 99, 139, 143–44, 149–52, 153, 154, 158, 227, 231, 237–39, 305n58; tribes of, 35, 148–49, 158, 173–75, 191, 217–18, 277n100, 318n62, 318n64, 318n66, 339n140; walls of, 133, 134, 135, 142, 144, 149, 150, 152–54, 230, 305n58, 306n68. *See also* Curia and *curia / curiae*; festivals: Septimontium; Forum Boarium; Forum

Rome (*continued*)
 Romanum; magistrates and political offices; militarism and its terminology; Romulus; *templum* and temple foundations
Romulus, 234; apotheosis of, 85, 232, 336n90; and the foundation of Rome, 20–21, 60, 101–2, 136, 143, 147, 149, 153–54, 168, 176, 177, 180–81, 190–91, 195, 210; and Quirinus, 35, 146–47, 217, 220, 269n8, 332n27; and Remus, 85, 98, 102, 138, 145, 148, 167, 175, 212, 217, 224, 226, 238, 306n66, 329n106, 333n44, 334n61, 335n77; and Rome's etymology, 15, 38–40, 97–98, 101–2, 195, 279n125, 318n61, 320–21n87

Sabines. *See* Varro: and Sabine identity
Salii, cult and Hymn of the, 71–72, 77–79, 167–68, 178, 219–20, 289n9, 290n34, 314–15n33
Samnite language and heritage, 79, 180, 235, 320n86, 336nn97–98
satire, Menippean, 3, 23, 47–48, 190, 229, 323–24n18, 342n25
Saturn, Saturnia, and Saturnian, 54, 60, 137–38, 141, 199–200, 202, 205, 227, 304n47, 336n93. *See also* festivals: Saturnalia
sight and vision, 9, 43, 47, 49, 70–71, 72, 113–14, 121, 123, 124, 130–31, 135–37, 146, 148, 156–57, 158, 186, 194, 203–4, 211, 244, 301n14; and the gaze, 88, 156, 302n23, 303n36; and observation, 47, 53–54, 75–76, 119, 155, 158, 221. *See also* augurs, augury, and auspicy; readers, as active participants and (s)electors; speech: prophetic; *templum* and temple foundations
slaves and freedmen, 15–16, 17, 36, 120, 164, 174, 186, 230, 232, 237–40, 243–44, 268n63, 278n108, 278n115, 294n99, 313n111, 339n125
Sol. *See* Apollo: in relation to Sol

speech: as powerful communication, 16–17, 25–26, 27, 34, 36–38, 44–46, 48, 51–53, 64–67, 74–75, 81, 85, 94, 96–102, 105–6, 115–19, 122–23, 164, 170, 180, 186, 194, 210, 228, 243–44, 251, 258, 289n22; prophetic, 31, 51–54, 59–60, 75–77, 85, 227, 283n56, 340n148. *See also* augurs, augury, and auspicy, *carmen* and song; Carmentis, Carmenta; irregularity; oratory, *oratio*; regularity; usage
sun, 206–7. *See also* Apollo: in relation to Sol

templum and temple foundations, 44, 52, 56, 83–86, 135–38, 142–43, 148, 150–51, 179, 201, 203, 204; and *tesca*, 155–57. *See also* festivals; gods; religion; ritual, rites; Rome
Terence, 58, 185, 189, 196–98, 229, 288n115
terra, 48, 84, 140, 189–90, 199–200; and territory, 49–50, 132–33, 147, 149, 175, 177
Tiber, river, 138–39, 141–43, 148, 159, 166–67, 219–20, 226–27, 229–30, 233, 235; and Tiberinus, 176–77, 205, 235; and Volturnus, 336n97, 337n104; as Albula, 166–67. *See also* Argei, Argives
Tiberinus. *See* Tiber, river: and Tiberinus
time, 8–9, 85, 90, 92, 129, 131; calendrical and seasonal, 8, 52, 145, 178, 180–81, 203–4, 206–8, 214–47; periodization and measurement of, 72, 81, 88, 104–5, 106, 123, 134, 145, 151, 157, 177, 203–4, 206–8. *See also* Caesar: calendrical reforms of; day; festivals; inflection; moon; sun
tradition, 11, 28, 35, 39, 58, 60, 76, 80–81, 89–90, 93, 111–12, 137–38, 147–48, 154, 158–59, 161, 171–72, 221–22, 236, 249, 258. *See also* ancestors, ancestral practice; habit, *habitus*; regularity; usage
tribes. *See* Cures and the Curenses (Quirites); Curia and *curia* / *curiae*; Rome: tribes of

Trivia. *See* Diana
Troy, 58; and Trojan War, 14, 32, 38, 102–4, 110–11, 123–24, 148, 210, 334n63; and Aeneas as Roman and Julian origin, 7, 20, 56, 78–79, 100, 147, 184, 194–95, 222, 226, 279n123

uates. See carmen and song; speech: prophetic
usage, popular, 35–38, 40, 53, 76, 80–81, 100–102, 111–13, 115, 127–28, 202, 213, 250–51, 263n5, 270n17, 278n103; as control on linguistic theory, 8, 13–16, 36–37, 42, 66, 70, 92–94, 103–4, 106, 110, 112–13, 118–19, 186–87, 210–11, 250–52, 256–57, 263n4, 278n105, 299n79; and Saussure, *langue*, and *parole*, 8, 17, 35–36, 38, 89–90, 91, 94, 96–97, 119, 184–85, 192, 207, 250, 280n111, 285–86n90, 291n46. *See also* irregularity; regularity; Rome: people of; speech

Varro: and Casinum, 34, 79, 171, 274n64; as flesh-and-blood individual, 6–7, 13, 19–22, 28–29, 41, 171, 185, 245, 259; political career of, 21–26, 27–28, 32–33, 172; as political commentator, 4, 12–13, 18, 34–40, 45–46, 64, 68, 81–82, 89–90, 102, 128, 160–65, 182–83, 220–24, 229–30, 234, 236, 241–42, 245–49, 252–56, 312n4; as polymath and public intellectual, 3–4, 13, 21, 28–29, 34, 41, 58–59, 81–82, 94–95, 102, 127, 141, 247–49, 256–59, 266n47, 290n31; postclassical reception of, 5, 10, 259; as Reatine, 5, 19–20, 35, 59, 98, 147, 205, 217, 270n18; as Roman antiquarian, 4–6, 11–12, 22, 28, 44, 59, 77, 79, 83, 118, 129–30, 140, 142–46, 148–49, 152, 194–95, 209, 226, 229–33, 238, 257–58, 266n43; and Sabine identity, 19–21, 56, 59, 64, 66, 79–80, 135–36, 138, 142–43, 147, 151–52, 158, 177–81, 191, 201–5, 216–18, 221, 223, 227–28, 234, 242, 269n9, 319n70, 332n27. *See also* Cicero, as addressee and sparring partner; satire, Menippean
Varro, works of: *Antiquitates*, 26, 35, 200, 214–15, 247, 278n101, 321n90, 321n93, 330n2, 332n28, 344n53; *De Re Rustica*, 21–22, 48, 79, 210. *See also De Lingua Latina*
Venus, 39, 54, 60, 199–200, 225, 234, 244, 283n58, 326n56, 329n98, 335n80; as Cypria, 151; as Genetrix, 222; as Verticordia, 222–23, 224, 332n33; as Victrix, 222, 290n31, 334n66
verbs. *See* inflection; time
Vergil, 5, 52, 55–58, 74, 78–79, 129, 149, 169, 260
verse. *See carmen* and song; drama and the stage; music, musical instruments; speech: prophetic
Vesta. *See* festivals: Vestalia; Vestal Virgins
Vestal Virgins, 85, 135–36, 222, 224, 227. *See also* festivals: Vestalia
vision. *See* sight and vision
Volturnus. *See* festivals: Volturnalia; Tiber, river: and Volturnus
Vulcan, 201, 204, 234, 336n90

water, 67, 138–39, 144, 152, 187–88, 199, 204–5, 207, 227, 236, 238–39, 302n22, 305n55, 310n121, 311n2; and floods, marshes, swamps, wetness, 106, 139–41, 142, 145, 148, 235; lakes, 145, 205; rivers, 243, 268n68; seas, 59, 186, 205, 233. *See also* Fons and *fons*; Tiber, river
writing as practice, 3, 6, 22, 27, 54, 56, 57, 60, 68, 87, 90–91, 94–95, 110, 117, 121, 124–27, 160–61, 256, 299n83, 341n8. *See also* readers, as active participants and (s)electors

Wisconsin Studies in Classics

LAURA MCCLURE, MARK STANSBURY-O'DONNELL, AND
MATTHEW ROLLER, SERIES EDITORS

Romans and Barbarians: The Decline of the Western Empire
  E. A. THOMPSON

A History of Education in Antiquity
  H. I. MARROU Translated from the French by GEORGE LAMB

Accountability in Athenian Government
  JENNIFER TOLBERT ROBERTS

Festivals of Attica: An Archaeological Commentary
  ERIKA SIMON

Roman Cities: Les villes romaines
  PIERRE GRIMAL Edited and translated by G. MICHAEL WOLOCH

Ancient Greek Art and Iconography
  Edited by WARREN G. MOON

Greek Footwear and the Dating of Sculpture
  KATHERINE DOHAN MORROW

The Classical Epic Tradition
  JOHN KEVIN NEWMAN

Ancient Anatolia: Aspects of Change and Cultural Development
  Edited by JEANNY VORYS CANBY, EDITH PORADA, BRUNILDE SISMONDO RIDGWAY, and TAMARA STECH

Euripides and the Tragic Tradition
  ANN NORRIS MICHELINI

Wit and the Writing of History: The Rhetoric of Historiography in Imperial Rome
  PAUL PLASS

The Archaeology of the Olympics: The Olympics and Other Festivals in Antiquity
    Edited by WENDY J. RASCHKE

Tradition and Innovation in Late Antiquity
    Edited by F. M. CLOVER and R. S. HUMPHREYS

The Hellenistic Aesthetic
    BARBARA HUGHES FOWLER

Hellenistic Sculpture I: The Styles of ca. 331–200 B.C.
    BRUNILDE SISMONDO RIDGWAY

Hellenistic Poetry: An Anthology
    Selected and translated by BARBARA HUGHES FOWLER

Theocritus' Pastoral Analogies: The Formation of a Genre
    KATHRYN J. GUTZWILLER

Rome and India: The Ancient Sea Trade
    Edited by VIMALA BEGLEY and RICHARD DANIEL DE PUMA

Kallimachos: The Alexandrian Library and the Origins of Bibliography
    RUDOLF BLUM Translated by HANS H. WELLISCH

Myth, Ethos, and Actuality: Official Art in Fifth-Century B.C. Athens
    DAVID CASTRIOTA

Archaic Greek Poetry: An Anthology
    Selected and translated by BARBARA HUGHES FOWLER

Murlo and the Etruscans: Art and Society in Ancient Etruria
    Edited by RICHARD DANIEL DE PUMA and
    JOCELYN PENNY SMALL

The Wedding in Ancient Athens
    JOHN H. OAKLEY and REBECCA H. SINOS

The World of Roman Costume
    Edited by JUDITH LYNN SEBESTA and LARISSA BONFANTE

Greek Heroine Cults
    JENNIFER LARSON

Flinders Petrie: A Life in Archaeology
    MARGARET S. DROWER

Polykleitos, the Doryphoros, and Tradition
    Edited by WARREN G. MOON

The Game of Death in Ancient Rome: Arena Sport and Political Suicide
    PAUL PLASS
Polygnotos and Vase Painting in Classical Athens
    SUSAN B. MATHESON
Worshipping Athena: Panathenaia and Parthenon
    Edited by JENIFER NEILS
Hellenistic Architectural Sculpture: Figural Motifs in Western Anatolia and the Aegean Islands
    PAMELA A. WEBB
Fourth-Century Styles in Greek Sculpture
    BRUNILDE SISMONDO RIDGWAY
Ancient Goddesses: The Myths and the Evidence
    Edited by LUCY GOODISON and CHRISTINE MORRIS
Displaced Persons: The Literature of Exile from Cicero to Boethius
    JO-MARIE CLAASSEN
Hellenistic Sculpture II: The Styles of ca. 200–100 B.C.
    BRUNILDE SISMONDO RIDGWAY
Personal Styles in Early Cycladic Sculpture
    PAT GETZ-GENTLE
The Complete Poetry of Catullus
    CATULLUS Translated and with commentary by DAVID MULROY
Hellenistic Sculpture III: The Styles of ca. 100–31 B.C.
    BRUNILDE SISMONDO RIDGWAY
The Iconography of Sculptured Statue Bases in the Archaic and Classical Periods
    ANGELIKI KOSMOPOULOU
Discs of Splendor: The Relief Mirrors of the Etruscans
    ALEXANDRA A. CARPINO
Mail and Female: Epistolary Narrative and Desire in Ovid's "Heroides"
    SARA H. LINDHEIM
Modes of Viewing in Hellenistic Poetry and Art
    GRAHAM ZANKER
Religion in Ancient Etruria
    JEAN-RENÉ JANNOT Translated by JANE K. WHITEHEAD
Oedipus Rex
    SOPHOCLES A verse translation by DAVID MULROY, with introduction and notes

The Slave in Greece and Rome
>JOHN ANDREAU and RAYMOND DESCAT Translated by MARION LEOPOLD

Perfidy and Passion: Reintroducing the "Iliad"
>MARK BUCHAN

The Gift of Correspondence in Classical Rome: Friendship in Cicero's "Ad Familiares" and Seneca's "Moral Epistles"
>AMANDA WILCOX

Antigone
>SOPHOCLES A verse translation by DAVID MULROY, with introduction and notes

Aeschylus's "Suppliant Women": The Tragedy of Immigration
>GEOFFREY W. BAKEWELL

Couched in Death: "Klinai" and Identity in Anatolia and Beyond
>ELIZABETH P. BAUGHAN

Silence in Catullus
>BENJAMIN ELDON STEVENS

Odes
>HORACE Translated with commentary by DAVID R. SLAVITT

Shaping Ceremony: Monumental Steps and Greek Architecture
>MARY B. HOLLINSHEAD

Selected Epigrams
>MARTIAL Translated with notes by SUSAN MCLEAN

The Offense of Love: "Ars Amatoria," "Remedia Amoris," and "Tristia" 2
>OVID A verse translation by JULIA DYSON HEJDUK, with introduction and notes

Oedipus at Colonus
>SOPHOCLES A verse translation by DAVID MULROY, with introduction and notes

Women in Roman Republican Drama
>Edited by DOROTA DUTSCH, SHARON L. JAMES, and DAVID KONSTAN

Dream, Fantasy, and Visual Art in Roman Elegy
>EMMA SCIOLI

Agamemnon
>AESCHYLUS A verse translation by DAVID MULROY, with introduction and notes

Trojan Women, Helen, Hecuba: Three Plays about Women and the Trojan War
EURIPIDES Verse translations by FRANCIS BLESSINGTON, with introduction and notes

Echoing Hylas: A Study in Hellenistic and Roman Metapoetics
MARK HEERINK

Horace between Freedom and Slavery: The First Book of "Epistles"
STEPHANIE MCCARTER

The Play of Allusion in the "Historia Augusta"
DAVID ROHRBACHER

Repeat Performances: Ovidian Repetition and the "Metamorphoses"
Edited by LAUREL FULKERSON and TIM STOVER

Virgil and Joyce: Nationalism and Imperialism in the "Aeneid" and "Ulysses"
RANDALL J. POGORZELSKI

The Athenian Adonia in Context: The Adonis Festival as Cultural Practice
LAURIALAN REITZAMMER

Ctesias' "Persica" and Its Near Eastern Context
MATT WATERS

Silenced Voices: The Poetics of Speech in Ovid
BARTOLO A. NATOLI

Tragic Rites: Narrative and Ritual in Sophoclean Drama
ADRIANA BROOK

The Oresteia: "Agamemnon," "Libation Bearers," and "The Holy Goddesses"
AESCHYLUS A verse translation by DAVID MULROY, with introduction and notes

Athens, Etruria, and the Many Lives of Greek Figured Pottery
SHERAMY D. BUNDRICK

In the Flesh: Embodied Identities in Roman Elegy
ERIKA ZIMMERMANN DAMER

Language and Authority in "De Lingua Latina": Varro's Guide to Being Roman
DIANA SPENCER

Spear-Won Land: Sardis from the King's Peace to the Peace of Apamea
Edited by ANDREA M. BERLIN and PAUL KOSMIN

www.ingramcontent.com/pod-product-compliance
Lightning Source LLC
Chambersburg PA
CBHW070834160426
43192CB00012B/2190